Prose of the

Victorian Period

RIVERSIDE EDITIONS

RIVERSIDE EDITIONS

UNDER THE GENERAL EDITORSHIP OF

Gordon N. Ray

Prose of the
Victorian Period

SELECTED WITH AN INTRODUCTION AND NOTES BY

William E. Buckler

NEW YORK UNIVERSITY

HOUGHTON MIFFLIN COMPANY

BOSTON

PREFACE

It has been the abiding aim of the editor of this anthology to provide students with the largest possible selection of important non-fictional Victorian prose at the lowest possible price. Assuming that the most valuable commodity to the student of Victorian prose is the prose itself, he has in every way possible tried to save space for the selections themselves. Therefore, this volume does not contain elaborate introductions, supplementary appendices, or detailed bibliographies of the period or of individual authors. There is a general Introduction which invites a critical reading of Victorian prose; there is a bibliographical note which directs the student's attention to standard texts, biographies, and criticism, as well as to the principal bibliographical guides to the Victorian period; there is a select chronology for each author and a brief headnote at the beginning of each selection. The footnotes, too, have been kept minimal by the criterion of simple clarification. Therefore, if the context itself makes the significance of a reference clear or if the student can himself check the reference in so accessible a source as a standard college dictionary, no footnote has been given; even the authors' own footnotes have been omitted unless they retain real significance.

The texts included in the present volume are based on standard editions. The English spelling of the originals has been preserved throughout, though American spelling has, of course, been used in the editor's notes. Only quotation marks have been standardized throughout.

Acknowledgment of a debt is gratefully made to Professor William D. Templeman and the late Professor Charles Frederick Harrold, editors of *English Prose of the Victorian Era*, a comprehensive work which no editor of a volume of Victorian prose should ignore; to Professor Gordon N. Ray, of the University of Illinois, and Professor Walter Houghton, of Wellesley College, for helpful suggestions concerning the contents of this volume; and, most especially, to Miss Lois Fisher, Secretary to the Department of English of New York University, for assistance in the preparation of the manuscript.

W. E. B.

CONTENTS

JOHN HENRY NEWMAN (1801–1890)

JOHN STUART MILL (1806–1873)

JOHN RUSKIN (1819–1900)

MATTHEW ARNOLD (1822–1888)

THOMAS HENRY HUXLEY (1825–1895)

WALTER HORATIO PATER (1839–1894)

INTRODUCTION

by William E. Buckler

ONE OF THE GREAT FEATURES of the Victorian period, writes Oliver
Elton, was "the swift and splendid development of the art of prose." [1]
Between 1830 and 1880 English writers invented "a whole orchestra"
of new prose instruments, plain and sober, imaginative and ornate.
A new age had been born which demanded a "more expressive and
efficient language . . . to perform [its] intellectual tasks, and to express
[its] new troubles and visions. . . ."

> If the eighteenth century was the "age of reason and prose,"
> the nineteenth might be called the age of prose and imagination.
> Naturally there also [arose] new vices — a new brassiness,
> a new foppishness — of which prose had hardly seemed capable
> before; . . . and yet, seen from afar, they are but minor phenom-
> ena, like the rhetoric of Junius or Lyly's euphuism. And if we
> leave aside the distinction between pure and applied literature,
> and simply weigh the prose of the time against the verse, it
> would seem that while there is a great and noble body of
> achievement in verse, the achievement of prose, both in range
> and quality, is greater still.

More recently, another critic has asserted the claim of Victorian prose
upon our attention:

> Probably more prose from the half-century between the first
> Reform Act (1832) and the Queen's golden jubilee (1887) is
> still current than from any earlier half-century in our history;
> and, broadly speaking, it is read for its intrinsic satisfactions,
> that is, without historical allowance, which implies a tenacious
> literary achievement. [2]

These two critics, moreover, honestly commit themselves on just
what, in their judgments, the peculiar merits of Victorian prose are.
For Mr. Elton, they are "rapidity and amplitude of movement," qualities possessed also by Renaissance prose: "but then our Victorian

[1] *A Survey of English Literature 1830–1880* (London, 1920), I, 6–7, II,
366–371.

[2] Kenneth Allott, "Introduction," *Victorian Prose 1830–1880,* ed. Kenneth
and Miriam Allott (London, 1956), pp. xvii–xliii. This is Volume V of *The
Pelican Book of English Prose* published by Penguin.

prose, though it may not be, summit for summit, an absolutely greater performance, still has this advantage, that it is much more *formed* than our Renaissance prose. And it is more formed, because the classical age, with all its priceless lessons in the art of form — lessons in economy, precision, reasonableness, and ease — had come between." After the Victorians, English prose lost this rapidity and amplitude of movement because writers inclined "to concentrate on minute felicities of form, and to tessellate their style like a mosaic, or to carve it like ivory." This new inclination produced extraordinary effects in writers like Henry James and Robert Louis Stevenson, but it destroyed "rapidity and amplitude of movement": "The phrase: they are not happy till they have got the phrase! They save it up, and burnish it, and inlay it, till you cannot see the page for the phrase, and you have to read slowly, because these writers go slowly."

Mr. Allott, too, sees rapidity and amplitude of movement (he uses the words "vigorous, intricate and ample") as the dominant characteristics of Victorian prose:

> At the bread-and-butter level Victorian prose does not swashbuckle through phrase and figure with the Elizabethans, or distinguish itself by its propriety and pattern with the Augustans. On the other hand, it accommodates argument and exact narrative better than Elizabethan or Jacobean prose, and it spans imaginatively the moodier octaves of feeling which the Enlightenment was willing to leave unrecognized.

And Mr. Allott also sees the shift from Victorian to post-Victorian prose most clearly in the "slower tempo" of the latter, a tendency "to pause, reflect, and analyse more, even sometimes to meander and elaborate self-consciously . . . ."

In these two critics at least we have apparent agreement on Victorian prose: (1) it was a positive literary achievement; (2) its chief characteristic was energy; (3) it had more formal excellence than Elizabethan prose and more range than Augustan prose; and (4) a change in prose style came about toward the end of the Victorian period which was signalled principally by a change to a slower tempo, the aesthetic manifestation of the gradual recession of Victorian "self-assertion and an urgent 'will to survive.' " [3]

There is, of course, something of value here for students of Victorian literature; but it will not carry them far in their attempt to define the meaning and judge the truth of assertions about "the swift and splendid development of the art of [Victorian] prose." For this we want a suitable critical method.

[3] The phrase is Allott's, p. xviii.

Two Victorian scholars have recently made some tentative suggestions toward the formulation of such a critical method: Professor A. Dwight Culler, in "Method in the Study of Victorian Prose"[4]; and Professor Martin J. Svaglic, in "Method in the Study of Victorian Prose: Another View."[5] In his paper, Professor Culler does not deal specifically with method, though certainly if one accepts his assumptions about Victorian prose, one will find the rudiments of a method ready to hand. Professor Culler's real subject, however, is the "nature" of Victorian prose, and he defines this as a "mediatorial form" of literature which partakes of the nature of both poetry and the scientific treatise, existing as a "formal structure" and referring "to something which exists independently of that structure." That Victorian prose should have this character follows inevitably from the aim of the great Victorian critics: to bring "fact and value into some kind of meaningful relation." They did not, like the Romantics, concern themselves principally "with creating an inner world of value"; nor were they, like the Utilitarians, so "impressed by the degree to which man is conditioned by his environment" that they turned "to the objective world of nature" in an almost exclusive attempt, through science, "to understand and ultimately to control" that objective world. Had they been Romantics, they would characteristically have written poetry; had they been Utilitarians, they would have written scientific treatises. But they were Christian-humanists, and as such their characteristic mode of expression was "the mediatorial form of critical prose."

> The scientist, as C. S. Lewis has recently pointed out, does not properly believe: he knows. And the poet does not necessarily believe: he envisions. But the writer of critical prose stands in just that indirect and probable relation with his object which we call belief. Whether belief is a species of knowledge or a species of desire we do not know. It is an impassioned form of knowledge, and if in our criticism we would both feel the passion and gain the knowledge, we need to avoid both the bald paraphrase of doctrine, which was the older method of criticism, and also the empty analysis of form, which is the newer method. We need a broadly humanistic method which will involve, not that momentary suspension of disbelief which constitutes poetic faith, but that deliberate activation of real belief which constitutes a critical faith.

Professor Svaglic, on the other hand, does hazard a method of critical analysis for Victorian prose, though he does not pretend that

4 *The Victorian Newsletter*, Number 9 (Spring, 1956), pp. 1–4. Quotations by permission of the author.
5 *The Victorian Newsletter*, Number 11 (Spring, 1957), pp. 1–5. Quotations by permission of the author.

his method is "completely formed." Assuming that the works of the
Victorian prose critics — "Whatever their stylistic differences" — are
"in fact, works of argument which require initially the same kind of
analysis," he invites us to consider an author's statements of belief in
connection with "the rational structure of the argument which justifies
them." And he provides us with a specific formula for carrying this
consideration forward. We are (1) to seek out "the assumptions . . .
from which the argument starts out but which may be only implicit
in the essay to be analyzed"; (2) to "discover the places to which and
the order in which the argument moves"; (3) to know "the mode of
reasoning by which the essay gets from place to place"; and (4) to
remember "the specific purpose and problem of the essay in question,
as the writer conceives it." A student who fully explores this question
— "Into how many parts does the essay appear to fall — and why?" —
will be able to reconstruct the essay and "decide what value it still
has for his own life."

These two papers constitute brave excursions into a field which has,
above all others, been generally skirted by the critics; and therefore it
is not likely — the problem being so complex as it is and the signposts
so few — that the suggestions set forth in them will win unanimous
approval from students of Victorian prose. One may hesitate to affirm,
for example, that "bald paraphrase of doctrine" was in fact "the older
method of criticism," or that "empty analysis of form" is a just description of "the newer method." Further, it may not be clear to all that
even the most thoroughgoing analysis of an author's dialectic is com-
mensurate with literary criticism. And when style is relegated to a
parenthetical position, it is troublesome because, from one point of
view at least, style is the very thing we should be thinking about.

Mention of the word *style* brings us back to the Victorians themselves, for whom the subject had a never-ending fascination and on
which they made frequent pronouncements, both casual and formal.
For Macaulay, the "first law of writing, the law to which all other
laws are subordinate, is this, that the words employed shall be such
as convey to the reader the meaning of the writer." The written page,
says Newman, is "the lucid mirror" of its author's "mind and life";
and on it he tries "to give forth what he has within him; and from
his earnestness it comes to pass that, whatever be the splendour of his
diction or the harmony of his periods, he has with him the charm
of an incommunicable simplicity. Whatever be his subject, high or
low, he treats it suitably and for its own sake." Arnold is more abrupt:
"Have something to say, and say it as clearly as you can. That is
the only secret of style." The recurrent note here is the recurrent

note in most Victorian styles and theories of style — individualism; and this matter is sufficiently important to any critical approach to the art of Victorian prose to deserve considerable attention.

The most coherent and fully argued defense of stylistic individualism came from Walter Pater, himself a second-generation Victorian, whose essay on "Style" (1888 — see below, p. 553) it is still safe to call "on the whole, the best thing yet written on that much-written-about subject."[6] Several aspects of this essay, especially, underscore its importance to students of the "new prose" of the nineteenth century.

In the first place, Pater consciously separated himself from the neoclassic tradition which had had a vigorous following in the criticism of prose style for two hundred years, from Dryden, say, to George Saintsbury. These critics, Pater felt, had limited the art of prose *a priori* "by anticipations regarding the natural incapacity of the material with which this or that [prose] artist works. . . ." They were guilty, like Dryden, of the "arbitrary psychology" of the eighteenth century — "and with it the prejudice that there can be one only beauty of prose style. . . ." Matthew Arnold, for example, in "The Literary Influence of Academies" (see below, p. 441), would be guilty of such "anticipation" and "prejudice" for baldly assuming that "genius and imagination" are the "distinctive support of poetry," while "openness of mind and flexibility of intelligence" are the distinctive support of prose. And George Saintsbury, whom Pater acknowledged as a "lover" of "the tradition of that severer beauty" in English prose (see below, p. 557n), had posited a definition of style which Pater could not have considered more than fragmentary: "Style is the choice and arrangement of language with only a subordinate regard to the meaning to be conveyed. Its parts are the choice of the actual words to be used, the further selection and juxtaposition of these words, the structure of the clauses into which they are wrought, the arrangement of the clauses into sentences, and the composition of the sentences into paragraphs. Beyond the paragraph style can hardly be said to go, but within that limit it is supreme."[7]

Further, this school (again from Dryden to Saintsbury) had repeatedly insisted upon the distinction "between the laws and characteristic excellences of verse and prose composition." Pater, of course, admitted a distinction, but he warned against a critical limitation of "the proper functions of prose" so narrow as to exclude from criticism a consideration of "the poetry, the imaginative power" of prose. Dif-

[6] The judgment is George Saintsbury's, in *A History of Criticism* (New York, 1904), III, 548–549.

[7] "Modern English Prose [1876]," in *The Collected Essays and Papers of George Saintsbury* (London, 1923), III, 64.

ferent literary periods have "very different intellectual needs" and *therefore* want "great modifications in literary form." It was inevitable, certainly, that Dryden should insist upon the distinction between poetry and prose and to regard correctness (which to Pater was only a "humble merit of prose") as "the central literary excellence"; but it was inevitable, also, that "in the rotation of mind, the province of poetry in prose would find its assertor. . . ." Thus a century later, at the beginning of the nineteenth, Wordsworth came to regard "the true distinction between prose and poetry . . . as the almost technical or accidental one of the absence or presence of metrical beauty, or, say! metrical restraint . . ." and to turn his attention rather to the difference between "imaginative and unimaginative writing," as De Quincey, toward the middle of the nineteenth century, turned his mind to the difference between "the literature of power and the literature of knowledge."

In the Romantic-Victorian line of Wordsworth and De Quincey, therefore, but with slightly altered terms, Pater drew a distinction between "the literature of fact" and "the literature of the imaginative sense of fact"; and, admitting the difficulty of drawing a line between the two, he insisted upon the importance of drawing such a line if one is to discover the point at which fact ends and art begins. In science, "the functions of literature reduce themselves eventually to the transcribing of fact," and "the excellences of literary form in regard to science are reducible to various kinds of painstaking. . . ." But the conditions of art become operative in prose when the author begins, to any degree whatsoever, to "appeal to the reader to catch [his] spirit," to participate in "his peculiar intuition of a world, prospective, or discerned below the faulty conditions of the present, in either case changed somewhat from the actual world." (More recently, a major critic has said much the same thing: "Art is life at the remove of form. . . .") Whenever a writer becomes other than a transcriber, whenever his "sensibility" modifies the world "as it really is," he passes into the "domain of art proper." And in proportion as he achieves "the finer accommodation of speech to that vision within," he becomes a "fine" artist and serves literature's two-fold function: to instruct and to give pleasure ("to himself, of course, in the first instance").

In thus allowing for infinite variety in prose style (since "[d]ifferent classes of persons, at different times, make . . . very various demands upon literature"), Pater, as he himself recognized, seemed to invite a dangerous "relegation of style to the subjectivity, the mere caprice, of the individual, which must soon transform it into mannerism." Certainly there was such a danger, and some critics have let Pater stand self-indicted for the mere mention of it. But this is less than fair. Pater was writing his "Defence of Prose," as Oliver Elton has

said, "in the light of what the century had achieved." Looking back
on Scott and Wordsworth and De Quincey, on Newman and Matthew
Arnold, on Hugo, Stendhal, and Flaubert, Pater saw the prose of the
nineteenth century as "an instrument of many stops, meditative, observant, descriptive, eloquent, analytic, fervid"; and he saw, too, that
this was the inevitable result of (a) "the chaotic variety and complexity of [modern] interests" and (b) the "all-pervading naturalism," the
humble curiosity "about everything whatever as it really is," which
characterized the nineteenth-century intellectual and aesthetic temper.
For such an age, looking with almost equal intensity in upon itself
and out at the rapidly moving world around it, the basically "public"
prose of the Augustans was inadequate for any but limited men: the
Augustan prose formulary might enable Macaulay to tell his countrymen that England was "now the richest and most civilised spot in the
world"; but it would not much help Newman "mirror" his sense of
the "heart-piercing, reason-bewildering fact" of the world considered
"in its length and breadth." For this a more subjective, or "private,"
style was necessary; and it was to this private element in nineteenth-
century prose style that Pater gave long-overdue attention. Nor would
he concede validity to the charge of caprice: "Not so! since there is,
under the conditions supposed, for those elements of the man, for
every lineament of the vision within, the one word, recognisable by
the sensitive, by others 'who have intelligence' in the matter, as absolutely as ever anything can be in the evanescent and delicate region
of human language. The style, the manner, would be the man, not
in his unreasoned and really uncharacteristic caprices, involuntary or
affected, but in absolutely sincere apprehension of what is most real
to him." And how are we to determine, from the prose itself, if the
author is "absolutely sincere"? Pater tells us. A sincere author will
have within "a quickening motive" which will make him "jealous" of
anything which diverts the intelligence away from the subject he has
taken in hand. He will, therefore, if he is sincere, avoid "the flowers
in the garden" — from obvious personification lacking "rhetorical
motive" to the use of individual words without any real understanding
of their "physical elements or particles" — and will use ornament only
when it is "structural, or necessary." If an author uses any "uncharacteristic or tarnished or vulgar decoration," he is insincere. Arnold
— with whose Preface of 1853 (see below, p. 409) Pater's essay provides many interesting points of comparison and contrast — had told
the poet "to prefer his action to everything else. . . ." Pater told the
prose artist to prefer his "absolutely sincere apprehension of what is
most real to him" to everything else. In each case, the writer would
then be most likely to avoid "unreasoned and really uncharacteristic
caprices, involuntary or affected. . . ."

For Pater, imaginative prose was "the special and opportune art of the modern world," and he insisted that criticism of that prose — "In this late day certainly" — if it would be reasonable, be eclectic. The questions which such a criticism would ask concerning a particular piece of imaginative prose (besides the question of "sincerity") are implicit in Pater's essay and may be enumerated.

1. Has the author taken "a full, rich, complex matter to grapple with"?
(If not, his style will lack adequate motivation.)
2. Has he achieved, in his language, balance between propriety and originality?

(In this the writer must be a scholar: on the one hand, he must recognize the "abundant and often recondite laws" of his language and avoid both license ["neology," gipsy phrase"] and facility ["hackneyed illustration," "affectation of learning"]; and, on the other hand, he must, by assimilating new influences on his language and by purifying words in current but inexact use, generate "a vocabulary faithful to the colouring of his own spirit, and in the strictest sense original.")

3. Has he provided for the reader an intense *intellectual* challenge?

(Here Pater moves into the area of author-reader co-operation and sets up *intellectual* resistance as an attribute of good prose.)

4. Has he provided for the reader a worthwhile *formal* challenge?

(Again Pater is dealing with the author-reader relationship, but at this point he is concerned with the work's resistance as *art* rather than as *idea*. In prose considered as an art, "structure is all-important," and by structure Pater means "that architectural conception of a work, which foresees the end in the beginning, and never loses sight of it, and in every part is conscious of the rest, till the last sentence does but, with undiminished vigour, unfold and justify the first. . . ." Of course, finally, there can be no real separation between prose as *art* and prose as *idea* because structure itself becomes the essential test of the "original unity, the vital wholeness and identity, of the initiatory apprehension or view" because good writing, like logic, is simply the expression of the "unity . . . of the apprehending mind." Here, however, the reader's pleasure [often the fruit of a second reading] is more purely aesthetic. In the matter of structure, as in the matter of style generally, Pater is concerned lest the critic take too simple a view and warns that a sense of organic unity and completeness should not limit the richness and expressiveness of prose because the development of design in imaginative prose involves "many irregularities, surprises, and afterthoughts; the contingent as well as the necessary being subsumed under the unity of the whole" in "blithe, crisp" sentences; in sentences which are "long-contending, victoriously intricate"; in sentences in which there is "much contrivance, much adjustment, to bring a highly qualified matter into compass at one view.")

5. Has he given to his prose work his own (or its own) unique personality?

(This is what Pater calls "soul" in art, as opposed to the "mind" one discovers in formal structure. By soul Pater means a kind of all-pervasive atmosphere which is the result, not merely of the matter of the work, but of "matter as allied to, in 'electric affinity' with, peculiar form, and working in all cases by an immediate sympathetic contact. . . ." In the final analysis, this subtlest aspect of the prose [or literary] art is perceivable by intuition, can be appreciated, not strictly analyzed; but it is to be associated with the "one indispensable beauty" of literature — which is the author's truth "to some personal sense of fact, diverted somewhat from men's ordinary sense of it . . ." in a style which may be "reserved or opulent, terse, abundant, musical, stimulant, academic" so long as it enables the writer to expose his own "inward sense of things. . . .")

6. Has he devoted his art to "great ends"?

(Pater defines these "great ends" as (a) "the increase of men's happiness"; (b) "the redemption of the oppressed"; (c) "the enlargement of our sympathy with each other"; (d) "such presentment of new or old truth about ourselves and our relation to the world as may ennoble and fortify us in our sojourn here"; and (e) "the glory of God.")

There is little need here to make extravagant claims for Pater's essay, little need to go even so far as Saintsbury and call it "a great paper — a 'furthest' in certain directions." It is the statement of a Victorian critic that nineteenth-century English prose was, to a large extent, *sui generis* and therefore needed to be judged by a set of critical principles other than those which had been evolved, and were still generally current, to test the literary achievement of another age with different intellectual needs and different literary forms. A representation of the best prose of the middle years of the nineteenth century is given in the pages of this anthology, and the text of Pater's essay is printed at the end. The critic's work is therefore cut out for him: the prose in this anthology may be judged by Pater's principles, and, equally, Pater's principles may be tested by the prose in this anthology. And although it is the purpose of this introduction to pose a critical problem for the student, not to take it away from him, perhaps it would not be out of the way to suggest, in general, the critical direction in which he will be moving.

The prose styles of Mill and Huxley have been generally praised for the same reasons — for precise statement and simple clarity. And these are certainly qualities which they possess and for which their authors labored: Mill tells us that all of his books were written twice, and Huxley says that some of his essays were written half a dozen times before he could "get them into shape." Their styles are not, of course, identical: Mill's prose is that of mind speaking to mind and therefore does not depend upon color or energy to accomplish its author's purposes (Carlyle spoke of Mill's *Autobiography* as "the life of a logic-chopping engine, little more of human in it than if it had been done by a thing of mechanised iron"); in Huxley's style there is more liveliness, more spontaneity, a greater and more apposite richness of literary allusion — if not a fuller, then certainly a readier style. But Huxley and Mill, on Pater's terms at least, enter only a little way into the "domain of art proper." They were both scientific rationalists and as such devoted first of all to "the literature of fact," not to "the literature of the imaginative sense of fact." Their whole effort was to give the reader a picture of the world "as it really is," not their "peculiar intuition of a world, prospective, or discerned below the faulty conditions of the present, in either case changed somewhat from the actual world." It would be unfair, of course, to reduce their styles to "various kinds of painstaking." Mill had a fuller understanding of the complexity of the ethical and legislative problems of modern man than any other writer in the utilitarian tradition in which he worked; and Huxley frequently revealed a sense of life's mystery: "Sit down before fact as a little child, be prepared to give up every preconceived notion, follow humbly wherever and to whatever abysses nature leads, or you shall learn nothing. I have only begun to learn content and peace of mind since I have resolved at all risks to do this." But both were determined — perhaps, in part, because of their successful efforts to catch the popular ear — to leave the "willing intelligence" of the reader at all points satisfied as to their meaning and not to challenge him to strenuous and continuous effort to come by a "securer and more intimate grasp" of their imaginative sense of things. Thus their language was appropriate without being original; and their essays were clearly plotted, moved forward from point to point, but did not develop in a rich, cumulative design. So far as their prose styles go, therefore, Mill and Huxley were "journeymen" of a high order, but journeymen nonetheless.

Macaulay fares better, though, as Matthew Arnold said, "while the number of those who are delighted with rhetoric such as Macaulay's is always increasing, the number of those who are dissatisfied with it is always increasing too." Arnold, further, could read a typical sentence by Macaulay — for example, "It may safely be said that the literature now extant in the English language is of far greater value than all the literature which three hundred years ago was extant in all the languages of the world together," or, "It is pleasing to reflect that the public mind of England has softened while it has ripened, and that we have, in the course of ages, become not only a wiser, but also a kinder people" — and call it not only "exhilarating" and "profoundly true," but also "vulgar, and, besides being vulgar, retarding." What Arnold is saying here is no doubt right: that Macaulay's was a very powerful rhetoric devoted to very mean ends. And therefore, by Pater's test of greatness in art, Macaulay failed miserably. He was the sublimely confident, practical, materialistic, inflexible, quantitative, and effective spokesman *for* and *to* Philistines on the rise. Equipped with one of the most amazing memories on record, which he had early taken great pains to fill to overflowing, Macaulay spoke with an unequivocal authority and optimism that gave to the tens of thousands who read him a sense of intelligent participation and well-being. He rested, as Arnold says, in his "pre-eminence with perfect security" and appealed to the self-conceit of his generation.

This is to say, of course, that we do not much admire the "soul" of Macaulay's prose, which means, in turn, that the "soul" is surely there and that Macaulay's prose is an example of "the literature of the imaginative sense of fact." We must admit that Macaulay was stimulated by a "quickening motive" within, that he appeals to the reader to "catch" his spirit, and that his style is the expression of a "sincere apprehension of what [was] most real to him." His "soul" was, perhaps, not much refined as his mind was not subtle; but they were both energetic, and his style is characterized by an all-pervasive buoyancy and a bold, unmistakable architecture. He deals, not in mysteries, but in the plain "facts" of life with a firm hand in which "reach" and "grasp" are the same. Dramatic superlatives, unequivocal assertions, sharply outlined comparisons and contrasts, easy paradoxes, epigrams, antitheses, narratives rapid and vigorous, portraits strong and economical — these are the stylistic indices to the character of Macaulay, the man and the writer. Note, for example, what happens to the following sentence from the essay on Bacon when it is removed from the rectangle of the paragraph:

> It has lengthened life;
> it has mitigated pain;
> it has extingiushed diseases;
> it has increased the fertility of the soil;
> it has given new securities to the mariner;
> it has furnished new arms to the warrior;
> it has spanned great rivers and estuaries with bridges of form unknown to our fathers;

it has guided the thunderbolt innocuously from heaven to
earth;
it has lighted up the night with the splendour of day;
it has extended the range of the human vision;
it has multiplied the power of the human muscles;
it has accelerated motion;
it has annihilated distance. . . .

This is not very subtle form, but form it is; and by virtue of it Macaulay's prose belongs, in some degree, to the "domain of art proper."

And now we get into difficulties. Is Arnold a better prose stylist
than Carlyle, and, if so, *which* Arnold than *which* Carlyle? Is it the
Arnold who wrote the first of the two excerpts following that is
better than the Carlyle who wrote the second?

(1)   Beautiful city, — so venerable, so lovely, so unravaged
by the fierce intellectual life of our century, so serene!

There are our young barbarians, all at play!

And yet, steeped in sentiment as she lies, spreading her gardens
to the moonlight, and whispering from her towers the last enchantments of the Middle Age, who will deny that Oxford, by
her ineffable charm, keeps ever calling us nearer to the true goal
of all of us, to the ideal, to perfection, — to beauty, in a word,
which is only truth seen from another side? — nearer, perhaps,
than all the science of Tübingen. Adorable dreamer, whose
heart has been so romantic! who hast given thyself so prodigally,
given thyself to sides and to heroes not mine, only never to the
Philistines! home of lost causes, and forsaken beliefs, and unpopular names, and impossible loyalties! what example could
ever so inspire us to keep down the Philistine in ourselves, what
teacher could ever so save us from that bondage to which we are
all prone, that bondage which Goethe, in his incomparable lines
on the death of Schiller, makes it his friend's highest praise (and
nobly did Schiller deserve the praise) to have left miles out of
sight behind him; — the bondage of '*was uns alle bändigt, DAS
GEMEINE!*' Oxford will forgive me, even if I have unwittingly
drawn upon her a shot or two aimed at her unworthy son; for
she is generous, and the cause in which I fight is, after all, hers.
Apparations of a day, what is our puny warfare against the
Philistines, compared with the warfare which this queen of
romance has been waging against them for centuries, and will
wage after we are gone?

(2)   Inexpressibly delirious seems to me, at present in my
solitude, the puddle of Parliament and Public upon what it calls
the "Reform Measure"; that is to say, The calling in of new

supplies of blockheadism, gullibility, bribeability, amenability to beer and balderdash, by way of amending the woes we have had from our previous supplies of that bad article. The intellect of a man who believes in the possibility of "improvement" by such a method is to me a finished-off and shut-up intellect, with which I would not argue: mere waste of wind between us to exchange words on that class of topics.

Or is it the Arnold of the first of the two excerpts following that is better than the Carlyle of the second?

(1)   Englishmen are often heard complaining of the little gratitude foreign nations show them for their sympathy, their good-will. The reason is, that the foreigners think that an Englishman's good-will to a foreign cause, or dislike to it, is never grounded in a perception of its real merits and bearings, but in some chance circumstance. They say that the Englishman never, in these cases, really comprehends the situation, and so they can never feel him to be in living sympathy with them. I have got into much trouble for calling my countrymen Philistines, and all through these remarks I am determined never to use that word; but I wonder if there can be anything offensive in calling one's countryman a young man from the country. I hope not; and if not, I should say, for the benefit of those who have seen Mr. John Parry's amusing entertainment, that England and Englishmen, holding forth on some great crisis in a foreign country, — Poland, say, or Italy, — are apt to have on foreigners very much the effect of the young man from the country, who talks to the nursemaid after she has upset the perambulator. There is a terrible crisis, and the discourse of the young man from the country, excellent in itself, is felt not to touch the crisis vitally. Nevertheless, on he goes; the perambulator lies a wreck, the child screams, the nursemaid wrings her hands, the old gentleman storms, the policeman gesticulates, the crowd thickens; still, that astonishing young man talks on, serenely unconscious that he is not at the centre of the situation.

(2)   "Often also could I see the black Tempest marching in anger through the Distance: round some Schreckhorn, as yet grim-blue, would the eddying vapour gather, and there tumultuously eddy, and flow down like a mad witch's hair; till, after a space, it vanished, and, in the clear sunbeam, your Schreckhorn stood smiling grim-white, for the vapour had held snow. How thou fermentest and elaboratest, in thy great fermenting-vat and laboratory of an Atmosphere, of a World, O Nature! — Or what is Nature? Ha! why do I not name thee GOD? Art not thou the 'Living Garment of God'? O Heavens, is it, in very deed, HE, then, that ever speaks through thee; that lives and loves in thee, that lives and loves in me?

"Fore-shadows, call them rather fore-splendours, of that
Truth, and beginning of Truths, fell mysteriously over my soul.
Sweeter than Dayspring to the Shipwrecked in Nova Zembla;
ah, like the mother's voice to her little child that strays bewildered, weeping, in unknown tumults; like soft streamings of
celestial music to my too-exasperated heart, came that Evangel.
The Universe is not dead and demoniacal, a charnel-house with
spectres; but god-like, and my Father's!"

The lesson should be clear. When we reach a certain level of excellence in Victorian prose — the prose, say, of Ruskin and Pater,
Arnold and Carlyle — we cannot expect criticism to come to quick and
easy solutions. Each of these writers, living long in a complex and
exciting age, passed through several spiritual phases (Pater is a partial
exception), and in each therefore one will find differing stylistic manners — "reserved or opulent, terse, abundant, musical, stimulant, academic" — according to the strong spiritual pressures felt by the
author at the time of writing. The Carlyle of *Sartor Resartus* (under-
going acute personal struggle) is noticeably different from the Carlyle
(sick at heart "to look at the things now going on in England") of
Past and Present, who again differs from the author of *Shooting
Niagara* ("very fierce, exaggerative, ragged, unkempt, and defective").
It is an interesting exercise in this matter of style, for example, to take
Ruskin's essay "Of the Real Nature of Greatness of Style" (below,
p. 345), to compare it, stylistically, with "The Roots of Honour"
(below, p. 393), and then to consider possible reasons for the differences in the new direction which Ruskin's mind is seen to be
taking in "The Nature of Gothic" (below, p. 361). But this is not to
deny the truth of Pater's thesis, taken from Buffon, that "he style is
the man": the soul in crisis in Mill's *Autobiography* (below, p. 288) is
still a thing apart from that in Carlyle's *Sartor Resartus* (below, p. 85)
and Newman's *Apologia* (below, p. 225).

Each of these four authors has had his accuser among critics of
prose style. Ruskin has been called "a slave to his own thoughts and
fancies"; Arnold, it has been said, was possessed of a stylistic "mannerism" rather than a stylistic manner; Pater's style has been dismissed
as "wholly factitious and opaque" and Carlyle's as "gibberish," the
"unknown tongue" of fanaticism. But in our own day each would
find his able defender because each is, in his own way, a remarkably
fine prose stylist. One may perhaps question the absolute sincerity, in
Pater's sense, of Ruskin's early writing on art and the intellectual
resistance of his later social criticism; he may doubt that Pater himself
was devoted to "great ends" or that design in the prose of Carlyle and
Arnold is truly architectural. But one can hardly deny that Carlyle's
explosive rhetoric is the powerful product of a deeply felt anti-

mechanistic, anti-intellectual philosophy of life; or that, given Pater's temperament, his subject-matter, and his theory of style, his prose is the perfect accommodation of thought and feeling to language; or that Arnold's motives — (1) to "introduce a little order into this chaos by establishing in any quarter a single sound rule of criticism" and (2) to counteract the forces "of learning and ability applied to thicken the chaos," that is, to be a friend to the friends of light and to "chafe" its enemies — are discoverable in the manner as well as the matter of the prose.

That, among our authors, Newman would rank highest in point of style according to Pater's tests was inevitable: Pater called *The Idea of a University* "the perfect handling of a theory," and Newman's essay on "Literature" was obviously at the front of Pater's mind (perhaps even on his writing-table) as he was setting down his thoughts on style. Notice, for example, Newman's words on style and the man:

> And, while the many use language as they find it, the man of genius uses it indeed, but subjects it withal to his own purposes, and moulds it according to his own peculiarities. The throng and succession of ideas, thoughts, feelings, imaginations, aspirations, which pass within him, the abstractions, the juxtapositions, the comparisons, the discriminations, the conceptions, which are so original in him, his views of external things, his judgments upon life, manners, and history, the exercises of his wit, of his humour, of his depth, of his sagacity, all these innumerable and incessant creations, the very pulsation and throbbing of his intellect, does he image forth, to all does he give utterance, in a corresponding language, which is as multiform as this inward mental action itself and analogous to it, the faithful expression of his intense personality, attending on his own inward world of thought as its very shadow: so that we might as well say that one man's shadow is another's as that the style of a really gifted mind can belong to any but himself. It follows him about *as* a shadow. His thought and feeling are personal, and so his language is personal.

Newman, like Pater, understood the identity between thought and feeling and expression, and thus he parodied the product of their separation: "The man of thought comes to the man of words; and the man of words, duly instructed in the thought, dips the pen of desire into the ink of devotedness, and proceeds to spread it over the page of desolation. Then the nightingale of affection is heard to warble to the rose of loveliness, while the breeze of anxiety plays around the brow of expectation."

Newman wrote, he tells us, "for the most part out of the duties which lay upon him," and therefore his motive was always too vital to admit artificiality or pretension into his prose style. Moreover, Newman's sense of duty, personal or official, most often led him into fields unmarked by "the footprints, the paths, the landmarks, and the remains of former travellers"; he felt rather "like a navigator on a strange sea, who is out of sight of land, is surprised by night, and has to trust mainly to the rules and instruments of his science for reaching the port"; and therefore his writing is customarily filled with "the tension and suspense" of personal observation.

Had Newman been a less clear, less honest, less subtle thinker, these two conditions would not have co-operated to make him the greatest Victorian prose stylist. But while Newman was as critical of slipshod logic as Jeremy Bentham, he did not allow himself to be driven into Bentham's over-wary and limited understanding of human nature — its motives and its possibilities; while he was as humane as John Stuart Mill, he never deserted a premise in order to avoid a harsh and distasteful view; while he understood the value and importance of the Hellenic ideal as well as Arnold and Pater understood it, he knew that the difference between moral or religious and intellectual excellence was a difference, not of degree, but of kind: he recognized, as Browning recognized, that the cultured or educated man was not the infallible tribunal that some would make him; and since he knew what he believed more clearly than did Carlyle, Newman did not let personal disappointment drive him from his philosophical principles as it did Carlyle.

The "tension and suspense" of Newman's prose are the natural result of his clear, honest, subtle intelligence working with the materials which the duties of his life compelled him to consider in the circumstances in which he found himself. Always more or less in the middle of opposing forces — Christianity and liberalism, Protestantism and Catholicism, factions within the Establishment and contending groups within the Catholic Church — Newman wrote all his prose with the greatest attention to exact statement; always a gentleman intent upon maintaining what Arnold has called his "note of urbanity," he labored to avoid "direct collision with institutions or measures" and "disrespect towards those whose principles or whose policy" he disapproved; always an artist, he sought to persuade the reader to partake of *his* "peculiar intuition" of the world. Hence the clarity, the urbanity, the rich personal quality of Newman's prose.

Newman's art cost him heavily. "I write," he said, "I write again: I write a third time in the course of six months. Then I take the third: I literally fill the paper with corrections, so that another person could not read it. I then write it out fair for the printer. I put it by; I take it up; I begin to correct again: it will not do. Alterations multiply, pages are re-written, little lines sneak in and crawl about. The whole page is disfigured; I write again; I cannot count how many times this process is repeated." Nor was he compensated for his labor with the "keen and constant pleasure" which some writers claim: "It is one of my sayings, (so continually do I feel it) that the composition of a volume is like gestation and childbirth. I do not think that I ever thought out a question, or wrote my thoughts, without great pain, pain reaching to the body as well as to the mind. It has made me feel practically, that labour 'in sudore vultus sui,' is the lot of man, and that ignorance is truly one of his four wounds."

The fruit of so much labor and so little pleasure was a prose style which, in sincerity, in richness of thought and design, in strength of purpose, is the supreme achievement of a century of great prose writers.

A BIBLIOGRAPHICAL NOTE

1

Bibliographical Guides

Besides such standard general bibliographical works as the *Cambridge Bibliography of English Literature* (Volume III), important for identification of primary works, there is one major source of information concerning research and criticism in Victorian literature during the last twenty-five years: the annual Victorian Bibliography, first published in 1933 (covering the year 1932), in the May issues of *Modern Philology*. In 1958 (covering the year 1957) this annual bibliography will be moved to *Victorian Studies*. There are two collections of these bibliographies: *Bibliographies of Studies in Victorian Literature for the Thirteen Years 1932–1944*, ed. William D. Templeman (Urbana, 1945) and *Bibliographies of Studies in Victorian Literature for the Ten Years 1945–1954*, ed. Austin Wright (Urbana, 1956).

2

(a) *Standard editions*, (b) *standard biographies, and* (c) *a significant product of modern critical scholarship for each of the authors included in this anthology.*

MACAULAY

(a) *Works,* ed. Lady Trevelyan, 8 vols. (London, 1866).

(b) G. O. Trevelyan, *The Life and Letters of Lord Macaulay,* 2 vols. (London, 1876).

(c) R. C. Beatty, *Lord Macaulay, Victorian Liberal* (Norman, 1938).

CARLYLE

(a) *Works,* Centenary Edition, ed. H. D. Traill, 30 vols. (London, 1896–1899; New York, 1896–1901).

(b) James Anthony Froude, *Thomas Carlyle: A History of the First Forty Years of His Life,* 2 vols. (London, 1882) and *Thomas Carlyle: A History of His Life in London,* 2 vols. (London, 1884).

(c) Emery Neff, *Carlyle* (New York, 1932).

NEWMAN

(a) The collected works of Newman are published by Longmans, Green and Co., New York, in 41 volumes and at various dates. There is no single "standard edition."

(b) Wilfrid Ward, *The Life of Cardinal Newman,* 2 vols. (London, 1912).

(c) Charles F. Harrold, *John Henry Newman: An Expository and Critical Study of His Mind, Thought and Art* (New York, 1945).

MILL

(a) There is no single, complete "standard edition" of Mill's works. They have been published in various editions and at various dates. Henry Holt and Co., New York, has published a "Library Edition of the Miscellaneous Works": *Autobiography; Dissertations and Discussions,* 4 vols.; *Considerations on Representative Government; Examination of Sir William Hamilton's Philosophy,* 2 vols.; *On Liberty* and *The Subjection of Women; Comte's Positive Philosophy.*

(b) and (c) Michael St. John Packe, *The Life of John Stuart Mill* (New York, 1954).

RUSKIN

(a) *Works,* Library Edition, ed. E. T. Cook and Alexander Wedderburn, 39 vols. (London, 1903–1912).

(b) W. G. Collingwood, *The Life of John Ruskin* (Boston, 1902) and E. T. Cook, *The Life of Ruskin,* 2 vols. (London, 1911). However, Professor Helen Gill Viljoen is in the process of publishing what may prove to be the definitive biography of Ruskin. One volume, *Ruskin's Scottish Heritage,* has been published (1955) by the University of Illinois Press.

(c) R. H. Wilenski, *John Ruskin: An Introduction to Further Study of His Life and Work* (London, 1933).

ARNOLD

(a) *Works* (incomplete), 15 vols. (London, 1903–1904).

(b) There is no "standard biography" of Arnold, though at the turn of the century there were several essays in biography and criticism: George Saintsbury, *Matthew Arnold* (Edinburgh and New York, 1899); Herbert W. Paul, *Matthew Arnold* (London, 1902); George W. E. Russell, *Matthew Arnold* (New York, 1904).

(c) Lionel Trilling, *Matthew Arnold* (New York, 1939).

HUXLEY

(a) *Collected Essays*, 9 vols. (London and New York, 1893–1894):
I. *Methods and Results*. II. *Darwiniana*. III. *Science and Educa-
tion*. IV. *Science and Hebrew Tradition*. V. *Science and
Christian Tradition*. VI. *Hume, with Helps to the Study of
Berkeley*. VII. *Man's Place in Nature and Other Anthropological
Essays*. VIII. *Discourses, Biological and Geological*. IX. *Evolu-
tion and Ethics and Other Essays*.

(b) Leonard Huxley, *Life and Letters of Thomas Henry Huxley*, 2
vols. (New York, 1901).

(c) Huxley has received only the most incidental and fragmentary
notice from literary scholars during the past twenty-five years.

PATER

(a) *Works*, Library Edition, 10 vols. (London, 1910).

(b) Thomas Wright, *The Life of Walter Pater*, 2 vols. (London,
1907).

(c) Ruth C. Child, *The Aesthetic of Walter Pater* (New York, 1940).

Thomas Babington Macaulay

THOMAS BABINGTON MACAULAY

CHRONOLOGY

1800   Born October 25 at Rothley Temple, Leicestershire.

1818   Entered Trinity College, Cambridge.

1819, 1821   Received Chancellor's Medal for English Verse.

1824   Became a Fellow of Trinity.

1825   Contributed his first essay ("Milton") to the *Edinburgh Review*.

1826   Called to the bar.

1829   Became Commissioner of Bankruptcy; refused editorship of the *Edinburgh Review*.

1830   Entered Parliament.

1831   Gained high praise for a speech supporting the Reform Bill.

1834   Went to India as a member of the Supreme Council at £10,000 a year.

1839   Re-entered Parliament as Liberal member for Edinburgh; became Secretary-at-War.

1842   Published *Lays of Ancient Rome*.

1843   Published his *Collected Essays*, in three volumes.

1846   Became Paymaster-General.

1847   Lost his seat in Parliament.

1848   Published *History of England*, Vols. I–II.

1849   Became Lord Rector of the University of Glasgow.

1852   Re-entered Parliament for Edinburgh.

1855   Published *History of England*, Vols. III–IV.

1856   Resigned from Parliament.

1857   Raised to the peerage as Baron Macaulay of Rothley.

1859   Died December 28; buried in Westminster Abbey.

Milton

❰ This essay, which established Macaulay's literary fame with his contemporaries, was written as a review of Milton's newly discovered (1823) and published (1825) *Treatise on Christian Doctrine*. One indication of the importance of the essay is the fact that some students of the period have offered the date of its publication in the *Edinburgh Review* (August 1825) as the rightful beginning of Victorianism. However that may be, the essay provides an example of Macaulay's earliest prose style, certain propositions regarding poetry which deserve examination, and a historically significant comparison of Milton and Dante. Only that portion of the essay which deals with these matters is printed here. ❱

. . . It is by his poetry that Milton is best known; and it is of his poetry that we wish first to speak. By the general suffrage of the civilised world, his place has been assigned among the greatest masters of the art. His detractors, however, though outvoted, have not been silenced. There are many critics, and some of great name, who contrive in the same breath to extol the poems and to decry the poet. The works they acknowledge, considered in themselves, may be classed among the noblest productions of the human mind. But they will not allow the author to rank with those great men who, born in the infancy of civilisation, supplied, by their own powers, the want of instruction, and, though destitute of models themselves, bequeathed to posterity models which defy imitation. Milton, it is said, inherited what his predecessors created; he lived in an enlightened age; he received a finished education, and we must therefore, if we would form a just estimate of his powers, make large deductions in consideration of these advantages.

We venture to say, on the contrary, paradoxical as the remark may appear, that no poet has ever had to struggle with more unfavorable circumstances than Milton. He doubted, as he has himself owned, whether he had not been born "an age too late." For this notion Johnson has thought fit to make him the butt of much clumsy ridicule. The poet, we believe, understood the nature of his art better than the critic. He knew that his poetical genius derived no advantage from the civilisation which surrounded him, or from the learning which he had acquired; and he looked back with something like regret to the ruder age of simple words and vivid impressions.

We think that, as civilisation advances, poetry almost necessarily declines. Therefore, though we fervently admire those great works of the imagination which have appeared in dark ages, we do not admire them the more because they have appeared in dark ages. On the contrary, we hold that the most wonderful and splendid proof of genius is a great poem produced in a civilised age. We cannot understand why those who believe in that most orthodox article of literary faith, that the earliest poets are generally the best, should wonder at the rule as if it were the exception. Surely the uniformity of the phænomenon indicates a corresponding uniformity in the cause.

The fact is, that common observers reason from the progress of the experimental sciences to that of imitative arts. The improvement of the former is gradual and slow. Ages are spent in collecting materials, ages more in separating and combining them. Even when a system has been formed, there is still something to add, to alter, or to reject. Every generation enjoys the use of a vast hoard bequeathed to it by antiquity, and transmits that hoard, augmented by fresh acquisitions, to future ages. In these pursuits, therefore, the first speculators lie under great disadvantages, and, even when they fail, are entitled to praise. Their pupils, with far inferior intellectual powers, speedily surpass them in actual attainments. Every girl who has read Mrs. Marcet's [1] little dialogues on Political Economy could teach Montagu or Walpole many lessons in finance.[2] Any intelligent man may now, by resolutely applying himself for a few years to mathematics, learn more than the great Newton knew after half a century of study and meditation.

But it is not thus with music, with painting, or with sculpture. Still less is it thus with poetry. The progress of refinement rarely supplies these arts with better objects of imitation. It may indeed improve the instruments which are necessary to the mechanical operations of the musician, the sculptor, and the painter. But language, the machine of the poet, is best fitted for his purpose in its rudest state. Nations, like individuals, first perceive, and then abstract. They advance from particular images to general terms. Hence the vocabulary of an enlightened society is philosophical, that of a half-civilised people is poetical.

This change in the language of men is partly the cause and partly the effect of a corresponding change in the nature of their intellectual operations, of a change by which science gains and poetry loses. Generalisation is necessary to the advancement of knowledge; but particularity is indispensable to the creations of the imagination. In proportion as men know more and think more, they look less at individuals and more at classes. They therefore make better theories and worse poems. They give us vague phrases instead of images, and personified qualities instead of men. They may be better able to analyse human

1 Mrs. Jane Marcet (1769–1858), author of scientific textbooks in a popular vein.
2 Charles Montagu, Earl of Halifax (1661–1715) and Sir Robert Walpole (1676–1745), acute students of economics.

nature than their predecessors. But analysis is not the business of
the poet. His office is to portray, not to dissect. He may believe in
a moral sense, like Shaftesbury; he may refer all human actions to
self-interest, like Helvetius; or he may never think about the matter at
all. His creed on such subjects will no more influence his poetry, properly so called, than the notions which a painter may have conceived
respecting the lacrymal glands, or the circulation of the blood will
affect the tears of his Niobe, or the blushes of his Aurora. If Shakespeare had written a book on the motives of human actions, it is by
no means certain that it would have been a good one. It is extremely
improbable that it would have contained half so much able reasoning
on the subject as is to be found in the *Fable of the Bees*.[3] But could
Mandeville have created an Iago? Well as he knew how to resolve
characters into their elements, would he have been able to combine
those elements in such a manner as to make up a man, a real, living, individual man?

Perhaps no person can be a poet, or can even enjoy poetry, without
a certain unsoundness of mind, if anything which gives so much pleasure ought to be called unsoundness. By poetry we mean not all writing
in verse, nor even all good writing in verse. Our definition excludes
many metrical compositions which, on other grounds, deserve the
highest praise. By poetry we mean the art of employing words in
such a manner as to produce an illusion on the imagination, the art
of doing by means of words what the painter does by means of colours.
Thus the greatest of poets has described it, in lines universally admired for the vigour and felicity of their diction, and still more valuable on account of the just notion which they convey of the art in
which he excelled:

> "As the imagination bodies forth
> The forms of things unknown, the poet's pen
> Turns them to shapes, and gives to airy nothing
> A local habitation and a name."

These are the fruits of the "fine frenzy" which he ascribes to the
poet — a fine frenzy doubtless, but still a frenzy. Truth, indeed, is essential to poetry; but it is the truth of madness. The reasonings are
just; but the premises are false. After the first suppositions have
been made, everything ought to be consistent; but those first suppositions require a degree of credulity which almost amounts to a partial
and temporary derangement of the intellect. Hence of all people children are the most imaginative. They abandon themselves without
reserve to every illusion. Every image which is strongly presented to

---

[3] By Bernard de Mandeville (1670–1733), who maintained that private vice
may be a public benefit. He was opposed by Shaftesbury (1671–1713), author
of *Characteristics*, who stressed the individual's "moral sense."

their mental eye produces on them the effect of reality. No man, whatever his sensibility may be, is ever affected by *Hamlet* or *Lear*, as a little girl is affected by the story of poor Red Riding-hood. She knows that it is all false, that wolves cannot speak, that there are no wolves in England. Yet in spite of her knowledge she believes; she weeps; she trembles; she dares not go into a dark room lest she should feel the teeth of the monster at her throat. Such is the despotism of the imagination over uncultivated minds.

In a rude state of society men are children with a greater variety of ideas. It is therefore in such a state of society that we may expect to find the poetical temperament in its highest perfection. In an enlightened age there will be much intelligence, much science, much philosophy, abundance of just classification and subtle analysis, abundance of wit and eloquence, abundance of verses, and even of good ones; but little poetry. Men will judge and compare; but they will not create. They will talk about the old poets, and comment on them, and to a certain degree enjoy them. But they will scarcely be able to conceive the effect which poetry produced on their ruder ancestors, the agony, the ecstasy, the plenitude of belief. The Greek Rhapsodists, according to Plato, could scarce recite Homer without falling into convulsions. The Mohawk hardly feels the scalping knife while he shouts his death-song. The power which the ancient bards of Wales and Germany exercised over their auditors seems to modern readers almost miraculous. Such feelings are very rare in a civilised community, and most rare among those who participate most in its improvements. They linger longest amongst the peasantry.

Poetry produces an illusion on the eye of the mind, as a magic lantern produces an illusion on the eye of the body. And, as the magic lantern acts best in a dark room, poetry effects its purpose most completely in a dark age. As the light of knowledge breaks in upon its exhibitions, as the outlines of certainty become more and more definite, and the shades of probability more and more distinct, the hues and lineaments of the phantoms which the poet calls up grow fainter and fainter. We cannot unite the incompatible advantages of reality and deception, the clear discernment of truth and the exquisite enjoyment of fiction.

He who, in an enlightened and literary society, aspires to be a great poet must first become a little child, he must take to pieces the whole web of his mind. He must unlearn much of that knowledge which has perhaps constituted hitherto his chief title to superiority. His very talents will be a hindrance to him. His difficulties will be proportioned to his proficiency in the pursuits which are fashionable among his contemporaries; and that proficiency will in general be proportioned to the vigour and activity of his mind. And it is well if, after all his sacrifices and exertions, his works do not resemble a lisping man or a modern ruin. We have seen in our own time great talents, intense labour, and long meditation, employed in this struggle against the spirit of the age, and employed, we will not say absolutely in vain, but with dubious success and feeble applause.

If these reasonings be just, no poet has ever triumphed over greater difficulties than Milton. He received a learned education: he was a profound and elegant scholar: he had studied all the mysteries of Rabbinical literature: he was intimately acquainted with every language of modern Europe, from which either pleasure or information was then to be derived. He was perhaps the only great poet of later times who has been distinguished by the excellence of his Latin verse. The genius of Petrarch was scarcely of the first order; and his poems in the ancient language, though much praised by those who have never read them, are wretched compositions. Cowley, with all his admirable wit and ingenuity, had little imagination: nor indeed do we think his classical diction comparable to that of Milton. The authority of Johnson is against us on this point. But Johnson had studied the bad writers of the middle ages till he had become utterly insensible to the Augustan elegance and was as ill qualified to judge between two Latin styles as a habitual drunkard to set up for a wine-taster.

Versification in a dead language is an exotic, a far-fetched, costly, sickly, imitation of that which elsewhere may be found in healthful and spontaneous perfection. The soils on which this rarity flourishes are in general as ill suited to the production of vigorous native poetry as the flowerpots of a hot-house to the growth of oaks. That the author of the *Paradise Lost* should have written the *Epistle to Manso* [4] was truly wonderful. Never before were such marked originality and such exquisite mimicry found together. Indeed in all the Latin poems of Milton the artificial manner indispensable to such works is admirably preserved, while, at the same time, his genius gives to them a peculiar charm, an air of nobleness and freedom, which distinguishes them from all other writings of the same class. They remind us of the amusements of those angelic warriors who composed the cohort of Gabriel:

> "About him exercised heroic games
> The unarmed youth of heaven. But o'er their heads
> Celestial armoury, shields, helms, and spears
> Hung high, with diamond flaming, and with gold."

We cannot look upon the sportive exercises for which the genius of Milton ungirds itself, without catching a glimpse of the gorgeous and terrible panoply which it is accustomed to wear. The strength of his imagination triumphed over every obstacle. So intense and ardent was the fire of his mind, that it not only was not suffocated beneath

---

[4] A Latin epistle from Milton to Giovanni Battista Manso, Marquis of Villa, who had been kind to Milton on his visit to Italy.

the weight of fuel, but penetrated the whole superincumbent mass with its own heat and radiance.

It is not our intention to attempt anything like a complete examination of the poetry of Milton. The public has long been agreed as to the merit of the most remarkable passages, the incomparable harmony of the numbers, and the excellence of that style, which no rival has been able to equal, and no parodist to degrade, which displays in their highest perfection the idiomatic powers of the English tongue, and to which every ancient and every modern language has contributed something of grace, of energy, or of music. In the vast field of criticism on which we are entering, innumerable reapers have already put their sickles. Yet the harvest is so abundant that the negligent search of a straggling gleaner may be rewarded with a sheaf.

The most striking characteristic of the poetry of Milton is the extreme remoteness of the associations by means of which it acts on the reader. Its effect is produced, not so much by what it expresses, as by what it suggests; not so much by the ideas which it directly conveys, as by other ideas which are connected with them. He electrifies the mind through conductors. The most unimaginative man must understand the *Iliad*. Homer gives him no choice, and requires from him no exertion, but takes the whole upon himself, and sets the images in so clear a light, that it is impossible to be blind to them. The works of Milton cannot be comprehended or enjoyed, unless the mind of the reader co-operate with that of the writer. He does not paint a finished picture, or play for a mere passive listener. He sketches, and leaves others to fill up the outline. He strikes the keynote, and expects his hearer to make out the melody.

We often hear of the magical influence of poetry. The expression in general means nothing: but, applied to the writings of Milton, it is most appropriate. His poetry acts like an incantation. Its merit lies less in its obvious meaning than in its occult power. There would seem, at first sight, to be no more in his words than in other words. But they are words of enchantment. No sooner are they pronounced, than the past is present and the distant near. New forms of beauty start at once into existence, and all the burial-places of the memory give up their dead. Change the structure of the sentence, substitute one synonym for another, and the whole effect is destroyed. The spell loses its power: and he who should then hope to conjure with it would find himself as much mistaken as Cassim in the Arabian tale, when he stood crying, "Open Wheat," "Open Barley," to the door which obeyed no sound but "Open Sesame." The miserable failure of Dryden in his attempts to translate into his own diction some parts of the *Paradise Lost,* is a remarkable instance of this.[5]

In support of these observations we may remark, that scarcely any

5 Dryden, with Milton's permission, had turned *Paradise Lost* into an opera in rhymed couplets, *The State of Innocence and the Fall of Man* (1677).

passages in the poems of Milton are more generally known or more frequently repeated than those which are little more than muster-rolls of names. They are not always more appropriate or more melodious than other names. Every one of them is the first link in a long chain of associated ideas. Like the dwelling-place of our infancy revisited in manhood, like the song of our country heard in a strange land, they produce upon us an effect wholly independent of their intrinsic value. One transports us back to a remote period of history. Another places us among the novel scenes and manners of a distant region. A third evokes all the dear classical recollections of childhood, the schoolroom, the dog-eared Virgil, the holiday, and the prize. A fourth brings before us the splendid phantoms of chivalrous romance, the trophied lists, the embroidered housings, the quaint devices, the haunted forests, the enchanted gardens, the achievements of enamoured knights, and the smiles of rescued princesses.

In none of the works of Milton is his peculiar manner more happily displayed than in the *Allegro* and the *Penseroso*. It is impossible to conceive that the mechanism of language can be brought to a more exquisite degree of perfection. These poems differ from others, as attar of roses differs from ordinary rose water, the close packed essence from the thin diluted mixture. They are indeed not so much poems, as collections of hints, from each of which the reader is to make out a poem for himself. Every epithet is a text for a stanza.

The *Comus* and the *Samson Agonistes* are works which, though of very different merit, offer some marked points of resemblance. Both are lyric poems in the forms of plays. There are perhaps no two kinds of composition so essentially dissimilar as the drama and the ode. The business of the dramatist is to keep himself out of sight, and to let nothing appear but his characters. As soon as he attracts notice to his personal feelings, the illusion is broken. The effect is as unpleasant as that which is produced on the stage by the voice of a prompter or the entrance of a scene-shifter. Hence it was, that the tragedies of Byron were his least successful performances. They resemble those pasteboard pictures invented by the friend of children, Mr. Newbery,[6] in which a single moveable head goes round twenty different bodies, so that the same face looks out upon us successively, from the uniform of a hussar, the furs of a judge, and the rags of a beggar. In all the characters, patriots and tyrants, haters and lovers, the frown and sneer of Harold[7] were discernible in an instant. But this species of egotism, though fatal to the drama, is the inspiration of the ode. It is the part of the lyric poet to abandon himself, without reserve, to his own emotions.

Between these hostile elements many great men have endeavoured to effect an amalgamation, but never with complete success. The

6 John Newbery (1713–1767), originator of children's books.
7 Childe Harold, of Byron's poem.

Greek Drama, on the model of which the *Samson* was written, sprang from the Ode. The dialogue was ingrafted on the chorus, and naturally partook of its character. The genius of the greatest of the Athenian dramatists co-operated with the circumstances under which tragedy made its first appearance. Æschylus was, head and heart, a lyric poet. In his time, the Greeks had far more intercourse with the East than in the days of Homer; and they had not yet acquired that immense superiority in war, in science, and in the arts, which, in the following generation, led them to treat the Asiatics with contempt. From the narrative of Herodotus it should seem that they still looked up, with the veneration of disciples, to Egypt and Assyria. At this period, accordingly, it was natural that the literature of Greece should be tinctured with the Oriental style. And that style, we think, is discernible in the works of Pindar and Æschylus. The latter often reminds us of the Hebrew writers. The book of Job, indeed, in conduct and diction, bears a considerable resemblance to some of his dramas. Considered as plays, his works are absurd; considered as choruses, they are above all praise. If, for instance, we examine the address of Clytemnestra to Agamemnon on his return, or the description of the seven Argive chiefs, by the principles of dramatic writing, we shall instantly condemn them as monstrous. But if we forget the characters, and think only of the poetry, we shall admit that it has never been surpassed in energy and magnificence. Sophocles made the Greek Drama as dramatic as was consistent with its original form. His portraits of men have a sort of similarity; but it is the similarity not of a painting, but of a bas-relief. It suggests a resemblance; but it does not produce an illusion. Euripides attempted to carry the reform further. But it was a task far beyond his powers, perhaps beyond any powers. Instead of correcting what was bad, he destroyed what was excellent. He substituted crutches for stilts, bad sermons for good odes.

Milton, it is well known, admired Euripides highly, much more highly than, in our opinion, Euripides deserved. Indeed the caresses which this partiality leads our countryman to bestow on "sad Electra's poet," sometimes reminds us of the beautiful Queen of Fairy-land kissing the long ears of Bottom.[8] At all events, there can be no doubt that this veneration for the Athenian, whether just or not, was injurious to the *Samson Agonistes*. Had Milton taken Æschylus for his model, he would have given himself up to the lyric inspiration, and poured out profusely all the treasures of his mind, without bestowing a thought on those dramatic proprieties which the nature of the work rendered it impossible to preserve. In the attempt to reconcile things in their own nature inconsistent he has failed as everyone else must have failed. We cannot identify ourselves with the characters, as in a good play. We cannot identify ourselves with the poet, as in a good ode. The conflicting ingredients, like an acid and an alkali mixed,

8 In *A Midsummer-Night's Dream.*

neutralise each other. We are by no means insensible to the merits of this celebrated piece, to the severe dignity of the style, the graceful and pathetic solemnity of the opening speech, or the wild and barbaric melody which gives so striking an effect to the choral passages. But we think it, we confess, the least successful effort of the genius of Milton.

The *Comus* is framed on the model of the Italian Masque, as the *Samson* is framed on the model of the Greek Tragedy. It is certainly the noblest performance of the kind which exists in any language. It is as far superior to the *Faithful Shepherdess* as the *Faithful Shepherdess* is to the *Aminta*, or the *Aminta* to the *Pastor Fido*.[9] It was well for Milton that he had here no Euripides to mislead him. He understood and loved the literature of modern Italy. But he did not feel for it the same veneration which he entertained for the remains of Athenian and Roman poetry, consecrated by so many lofty and endearing recollections. The faults, moreover, of his Italian predecessors were of a kind to which his mind had a deadly antipathy. He could stoop to a plain style, sometimes even a bald style; but false brilliancy was his utter aversion. His muse had no objection to a russet attire; but she turned with disgust from the finery of Guarini, as tawdry and as paltry as the rags of a chimney-sweeper on May-day. Whatever ornaments she wears are of massive gold, not only dazzling to the sight, but capable of standing the severest test of the crucible.

Milton attended in the *Comus* to the distinction which he afterwards neglected in the *Samson*. He made his Masque what it ought to be, essentially lyrical, and dramatic only in semblance. He has not attempted a fruitless struggle against a defect inherent in the nature of that species of composition; and he has therefore succeeded, whereever success was not impossible. The speeches must be read as majestic soliloquies; and he who so reads them will be enraptured with their eloquence, their sublimity, and their music. The interruptions of the dialogue, however, impose a constraint upon the writer, and break the illusion of the reader. The finest passages are those which are lyric in form as well as in spirit. "I should much commend," says the excellent Sir Henry Wotton in a letter to Milton, "the tragical part if the lyrical did not ravish me with a certain Dorique delicacy in your songs and odes, whereunto, I must plainly confess to you, I have seen yet nóthing parallel in our language." The criticism was just. It is when Milton escapes from the shackles of the dialogue, when he is discharged from the labour of uniting two incongruous styles, when he is at liberty to indulge his choral raptures without reserve, that he rises even above himself. Then, like his own good Genius [10] bursting

9 Pastoral plays: *The Faithful Shepherdess* by John Fletcher; *Aminta* by Tasso; *Pastor Fido* by Guarini.
10 The attendant spirit in *Comus*.

from the earthly form and weeds of Thyrsis, he stands forth in celestial
freedom and beauty; he seems to cry exultingly,

> "Now my task is smoothly done,
> I can fly or I can run,"

to skim the earth, to soar above the clouds, to bathe in the Elysian
dew of the rainbow, and to inhale the balmy smells of nard and cassia,
which the musky winds of the zephyr scatter through the cedared
alleys of the Hesperides.

There are several of the minor poems of Milton on which we would
willingly make a few remarks. Still more willingly would we enter
into a detailed examination of that admirable poem, the *Paradise Regained*, which, strangely enough, is scarcely ever mentioned except as
an instance of the blindness of the parental affection which men of
letters bear towards the offspring of their intellects. That Milton was
mistaken in preferring this work, excellent as it is, to the *Paradise Lost*,
we readily admit. But we are sure that the superiority of the *Paradise
Lost* to the *Paradise Regained* is not more decided, than the superiority
of the *Paradise Regained* to every poem which has since made its appearance. Our limits, however, prevent us from discussing the point at
length. We hasten on to that extraordinary production which the
general suffrage of critics has placed in the highest class of human
compositions.

The only poem of modern times which can be compared with the
Paradise Lost is the *Divine Comedy*. The subject of Milton, in some
points, resembled that of Dante; but he has treated it in a widely
different manner. We cannot, we think, better illustrate our opinion
respecting our own great poet, than by contrasting him with the
father of Tuscan literature.

The poetry of Milton differs from that of Dante, as the hieroglyphics
of Egypt differed from the picture-writing of Mexico. The images
which Dante employs speak for themselves; they stand simply for
what they are. Those of Milton have a signification which is often
discernible only to the initiated. Their value depends less on what
they directly represent than on what they remotely suggest. However
strange, however grotesque, may be the appearance which Dante
undertakes to describe, he never shrinks from describing it. He gives
us the shape, the colour, the sound, the smell, the taste; he counts the
numbers; he measures the size. His similes are the illustrations of a
traveller. Unlike those of other poets, and especially of Milton, they
are introduced in a plain, business-like manner; not for the sake of any
beauty in the objects from which they are drawn; not for the sake
of any ornament which they may impart to the poem; but simply in
order to make the meaning of the writer as clear to the reader as it
is to himself. The ruins of the precipice which led from the sixth to

the seventh circle of hell were like those of the rock which fell into the
Adige on the south of Trent. The cataract of Phlegethon was like that
of Aqua Cheta at the monastery of St. Benedict. The place where the
heretics were confined in burning tombs resembled the vast cemetery
of Arles.

Now let us compare with the exact details of Dante the dim intimations of Milton. We will cite a few examples. The English poet
has never thought of taking the measure of Satan. He gives us merely
a vague idea of vast bulk. In one passage the fiend lies stretched out
huge in length, floating many a rood, equal in size to the earth-born
enemies of Jove, or to the sea-monster which the mariner mistakes
for an island. When he addresses himself to battle against the guardian angels, he stands like Teneriffe or Atlas: his stature reaches the
sky. Contrast with these descriptions the lines in which Dante has
described the gigantic spectre of Nimrod. "His face seemed to me as
long and as broad as the ball of St. Peter's at Rome; and his other
limbs were in proportion; so that the bank, which concealed him from
the waist downwards, nevertheless showed so much of him, that three
tall Germans would in vain have attempted to reach to his hair." We are
sensible that we do no justice to the admirable style of the Florentine
poet. But Mr. Cary's translation is not at hand; and our version, however rude, is sufficient to illustrate our meaning.

Once more, compare the lazar-house in the eleventh book of the
Paradise Lost with the last ward of Malebolge in Dante. Milton
avoids the loathsome details, and takes refuge in indistinct but solemn
and tremendous imagery. Despair hurrying from couch to couch to
mock the wretches with his attendance, Death shaking his dart over
them, but, in spite of supplications, delaying to strike. What says Dante?
"There was such a moan there as there would be if all the sick who, between July and September, are in the hospitals of Valdichiana, and
of the Tuscan swamps, and of Sardinia, were in one pit together; and
such a stench was issuing forth as is wont to issue from decayed limbs."

We will not take upon ourselves the invidious office of settling prece-
dency between two such writers. Each in his own department is incomparable; and each, we may remark, has wisely, or fortunately,
taken a subject adapted to exhibit his peculiar talent to the greatest
advantage. The *Divine Comedy* is a personal narrative. Dante is the
eye-witness and ear-witness of that which he relates. He is the very
man who has heard the tormented spirits crying out for the second
death, who has read the dusky characters on the portal within which
there is no hope, who has hidden his face from the terrors of the Gor-
gon, who has fled from the hooks and the seething pitch of Barbariccia
and Draghignazzo. His own hands have grasped the shaggy sides of
Lucifer. His own feet have climbed the mountain of expiation. His
own brow has been marked by the purifying angel. The reader would
throw aside such a tale in incredulous disgust, unless it were told

with the strongest air of veracity, with a sobriety even in its horrors, with the greatest precision and multiplicity in its details. The narrative of Milton in this respect differs from that of Dante, as the adventures of Amadis [11] differ from those of Gulliver. The author of Amadis would have made his book ridiculous if he had introduced those minute particulars which give such a charm to the work of Swift, the nautical observations, the affected delicacy about names, the official documents transcribed at full length, and all the unmeaning gossip and scandal of the court, springing out of nothing, and tending to nothing. We are not shocked at being told that a man who lived, nobody knows when, saw many very strange sights, and we can easily abandon ourselves to the illusion of the romance. But when Lemuel Gulliver, surgeon, resident at Rotherhithe, tells us of pygmies and giants, flying islands, and philosophising horses, nothing but such circumstantial touches could produce for a single moment a deception on the imagination.

Of all the poets who have introduced into their works the agency of supernatural beings, Milton has succeeded best. Here Dante decidedly yields to him: and as this is a point on which many rash and ill-considered judgments have been pronounced, we feel inclined to dwell on it a little longer. The most fatal error which a poet can possibly commit in the management of his machinery, is that of attempting to philosophise too much. Milton has been often censured for ascribing to spirits many functions of which spirits must be incapable. But these objections, though sanctioned by eminent names, originate, we venture to say, in profound ignorance of the art of poetry.

What is spirit? What are our own minds, the portion of spirit with which we are best acquainted? We observe certain phænomena. We cannot explain them into material causes. We therefore infer that there exists something which is not material. But of this something we have no idea. We can define it only by negatives. We can reason about it only by symbols. We use the word; but we have no image of the thing; and the business of poetry is with images, and not with words. The poet uses words indeed; but they are merely the instruments of his art, not its objects. They are the materials which he is to dispose in such a manner as to present a picture to the mental eye. And if they are not so disposed, they are no more entitled to be called poetry than a bale of canvas and a box of colours to be called a painting.

Logicians may reason about abstractions. But the great mass of men must have images. The strong tendency of the multitude in all ages and nations to idolatry can be explained on no other principle. The first inhabitants of Greece, there is reason to believe, worshipped one invisible Deity. But the necessity of having something more definite to adore produced, in a few centuries, the innumerable

[11] Amadis of Gaul, medieval knight-errant.

crowd of Gods and Goddesses. In like manner the ancient Persians thought it impious to exhibit the Creator under a human form. Yet even these transferred to the Sun the worship which, in speculation, they considered due only to the Supreme Mind. The history of the Jews is the record of a continued struggle between pure Theism, supported by the most terrible sanctions, and the strangely fascinating desire of having some visible and tangible object of adoration. Perhaps none of the secondary causes which Gibbon has assigned for the rapidity with which Christianity spread over the world, while Judaism scarcely ever acquired a proselyte, operated more powerfully than this feeling. God, the uncreated, the incomprehensible, the invisible, attracted few worshippers. A philosopher might admire so noble a conception; but the crowd turned away in disgust from words which presented no image to their minds. It was before Deity embodied in a human form, walking among men, partaking of their infirmities, leaning on their bosoms, weeping over their graves, slumbering in the manger, bleeding on the cross, that the prejudices of the Synagogue, and the doubts of the Academy, and the pride of the Portico, and the fasces of the Lictor,[12] and the swords of thirty legions, were humbled in the dust. Soon after Christianity had achieved its triumph, the principle which had assisted it began to corrupt it. It became a new Paganism. Patron saints assumed the offices of household gods. St. George took the place of Mars. St. Elmo [13] consoled the mariner for the loss of Castor and Pollux. The Virgin Mother and Cecilia succeeded to Venus and the Muses. The fascination of sex and loveliness was again joined to that of celestial dignity; and the homage of chivalry was blended with that of religion. Reformers have often made a stand against these feelings; but never with more than apparent and partial success. The men who demolished the images in cathedrals have not always been able to demolish those which were enshrined in their minds. It would not be difficult to show that in politics the same rule holds good. Doctrines, we are afraid, must generally be embodied before they can excite a strong public feeling. The multitude is more easily interested for the most unmeaning badge, or the most insignificant name, than for the most important principle.

From these considerations, we infer that no poet, who should affect that metaphysical accuracy for the want of which Milton has been blamed, would escape a disgraceful failure. Still, however, there was another extreme which, though far less dangerous, was also to be avoided. The imaginations of men are in a great measure under the control of their opinions. The most exquisite art of poetical colouring can produce no illusion, when it is employed to represent that which is at once perceived to be incongruous and absurd. Milton wrote in an age of philosophers and theologians. It was necessary, therefore,

[12] Emblems, therefore, of Roman dominion.
[13] Patron saint of sailors.

for him to abstain from giving such a shock to their understanding as
might break the charm which it was his object to throw over their
imaginations. This is the real explanation of the indistinctness and
inconsistency with which he has often been reproached. Dr. Johnson
acknowledges that it was absolutely necessary that the spirit should
be clothed with material forms. "But," says he, "the poet should have
secured the consistency of his system by keeping immateriality out
of sight, and seducing the reader to drop it from his thoughts." This
is easily said; but what if Milton could not seduce his readers to drop
immateriality from their thoughts? What if the contrary opinion had
taken so full a possession of the minds of men as to leave no room even
for the half belief which poetry requires? Such we suspect to have
been the case. It was impossible for the poet to adopt altogether the
material or the immaterial system. He therefore took his stand on the
debatable ground. He left the whole in ambiguity. He has doubtless,
by so doing, laid himself open to the charge of inconsistency. But,
though philosophically in the wrong, we cannot but believe that he
was poetically in the right. This task, which almost any other writer
would have found impracticable, was easy to him. The peculiar art
which he possessed of communicating his meaning circuitously through
a long succession of associated ideas, and of intimating more than he
expressed, enabled him to disguise those incongruities which he
could not avoid.

Poetry which relates to the beings of another world ought to be at
once mysterious and picturesque. That of Milton is so. That of
Dante is picturesque indeed beyond any that ever was written. Its
effect approaches to that produced by the pencil or the chisel. But it
is picturesque to the exclusion of all mystery. This is a fault on the
right side, a fault inseparable from the plan of Dante's poem, which,
as we have already observed, rendered the utmost accuracy of description necessary. Still it is a fault. The supernatural agents excite an
interest; but it is not the interest which is proper to supernatural
agents. We feel that we could talk to the ghosts and dæmons, without
any emotion of unearthly awe. We could, like Don Juan, ask them
to supper, and eat heartily in their company.[14] Dante's angels are
good men with wings. His devils are spiteful ugly executioners. His
dead men are merely living men in strange situations. The scene
which passes between the poet and Farinata is justly celebrated. Still,
Farinata in the burning tomb is exactly what Farinata would have been
at an *auto da fé*.[15] Nothing can be more touching than the first inter-
view of Dante and Beatrice. Yet what is it, but a lovely woman chid-
ing, with sweet austere composure, the lover for whose affection she is
grateful, but whose vices she reprobates? The feelings which give the

14 Don Juan was carried off to hell by the statue, animated by an evil spirit,
of a man he had murdered; he had invited the statue to dinner.
15 "Act of faith" — ceremony preceding execution by the Inquisition.

passage its charm would suit the streets of Florence as well as the summit of the Mount of Purgatory.

The spirits of Milton are unlike those of almost all other writers. His fiends, in particular, are wonderful creations. They are not metaphysical abstractions. They are not wicked men. They are not ugly beasts. They have no horns, no tails, none of the fee-faw-fum of Tasso and Klopstock. They have just enough in common with human nature to be intelligible to human beings. Their characters are, like their forms, marked by a certain dim resemblance to those of men, but exaggerated to gigantic dimensions, and veiled in mysterious gloom.

Perhaps the gods and dæmons of Æschylus may best bear a comparison with the angels and devils of Milton. The style of the Athenian had, as we have remarked, something of the Oriental character; and the same peculiarity may be traced in his mythology. It has nothing of the amenity and elegance which we generally find in the superstitions of Greece. All is rugged, barbaric, and colossal. The legends of Æschylus seem to harmonise less with the fragrant groves and graceful porticoes in which his countrymen paid their vows to the God of Light and Goddess of Desire,[16] than with those huge and grotesque labyrinths of eternal granite in which Egypt enshrined her mystic Osiris, or in which Hindustan still bows down to her seven-headed idols. His favourite gods are those of the elder generation, the sons of heaven and earth, compared with whom Jupiter himself was a stripling and an upstart, the gigantic Titans, and the inexorable Furies. Foremost among his creations of this class stands Prometheus, half fiend, half redeemer, the friend of man, the sullen and implacable enemy of Heaven. Prometheus bears undoubtedly a considerable resemblance to the Satan of Milton. In both we find the same impatience of control, the same ferocity, the same unconquerable pride. In both characters also are mingled, though in very different proportions, some kind and generous feelings. Prometheus, however, is hardly superhuman enough. He talks too much of his chains and his uneasy posture: he is rather too much depressed and agitated. His resolution seems to depend on the knowledge which he possesses that he holds the fate of his torturer in his hands, and that the hour of his release will surely come. But Satan is a creature of another sphere. The might of his intellectual nature is victorious over the extremity of pain. Amidst agonies which cannot be conceived without horror, he deliberates, resolves, and even exults. Against the sword of Michael, against the thunder of Jehovah, against the flaming lake, and the marl burning with solid fire, against the prospect of an eternity of unintermitted misery, his spirit bears up unbroken, resting on its own innate energies, requiring no support from anything external, nor even from hope itself.

To return for a moment to the parallel which we have been attempt-

16 Apollo and Aphrodite.

ing to draw between Milton and Dante, we would add that the poetry of these great men has in a considerable degree taken its character from their moral qualities. They are not egotists. They rarely obtrude their idiosyncrasies on their readers. They have nothing in common with those modern beggars for fame, who extort a pittance from the compassion of the inexperienced by exposing the nakedness and sores of their minds. Yet it would be difficult to name two writers whose works have been more completely, though undesignedly, coloured by their personal feelings.

The character of Milton was peculiarly distinguished by loftiness of spirit: that of Dante by intensity of feeling. In every line of the *Divine Comedy* we discern the asperity which is produced by pride struggling with misery. There is perhaps no work in the world so deeply and uniformly sorrowful. The melancholy of Dante was no fantastic caprice. It was not, as far as at this distance of time can be judged, the effect of external circumstances. It was from within. Neither love nor glory, neither the conflicts of earth nor the hope of heaven could dispel it. It turned every consolation and every pleasure into its own nature. It resembled that noxious Sardinian soil of which the intense bitterness is said to have been perceptible even in its honey. His mind was, in the noble language of the Hebrew poet, "a land of darkness, as darkness itself, and where the light was as darkness." The gloom of his character discolours all the passions of men, and all the face of nature, and tinges with its own livid hue the flowers of Paradise and the glories of the eternal throne. All the portraits of him are singularly characteristic. No person can look on the features, noble even to ruggedness, the dark furrows of the cheek, the haggard and woeful stare of the eye, the sullen and contemptuous curve of the lip, and doubt that they belong to a man too proud and too sensitive to be happy.

Milton was, like Dante, a statesman and a lover; and, like Dante, he had been unfortunate in ambition and in love. He had survived his health and his sight, the comforts of his home, and the prosperity of his party. Of the great men by whom he had been distinguished at his entrance into life, some had been taken away from the evil to come; some had carried into foreign climates their unconquerable hatred of oppression; some were pining in dungeons; and some had poured forth their blood on scaffolds. Venal and licentious scribblers, with just sufficient talent to clothe the thoughts of a pandar in the style of a bellman, were now the favourite writers of the Sovereign and of the public. It was a loathsome herd, which could be compared to nothing so fitly as to the rabble of Comus, grotesque monsters, half bestial, half human, dropping with wine, bloated with gluttony, and reeling in obscene dances. Amidst these that fair Muse was placed, like the chaste lady of the Masque, lofty, spotless, and serene, to be chattered at, and pointed at, and grinned at, by the whole rout of

Satyrs and Goblins. If ever despondency and asperity could be excused in any man, they might have been excused in Milton. But the strength of his mind overcame every calamity. Neither blindness, nor gout, nor age, nor penury, nor domestic afflictions, nor political disappointments, nor abuse, nor proscription, nor neglect, had power to disturb his sedate and majestic patience. His spirits do not seem to have been high, but they were singularly equable. His temper was serious, perhaps stern; but it was a temper which no sufferings could render sullen or fretful. Such as it was when, on the eve of great events, he returned from his travels, in the prime of health and manly beauty, loaded with literary distinctions, and glowing with patriotic hopes, such it continued to be when, after having experienced every calamity which is incident to our nature, old, poor, sightless and disgraced, he retired to his hovel to die.

Hence it was that, though he wrote the *Paradise Lost* at a time of life when images of beauty and tenderness are in general beginning to fade, even from those minds in which they have not been effaced by anxiety and disappointment, he adorned it with all that is most lovely and delightful in the physical and in the moral world. Neither Theocritus nor Ariosto had a finer or a more healthful sense of the pleasantness of external objects, or loved better to luxuriate amidst sunbeams and flowers, the songs of nightingales, the juice of summer fruits, and the coolness of shady fountains. His conception of love unites all the voluptuousness of the Oriental harem, and all the gallantry of the chivalric tournament, with all the pure and quiet affection of an English fireside. His poetry reminds us of the miracles of Alpine scenery. Nooks and dells, beautiful as fairyland, are embosomed in its most rugged and gigantic elevations. The roses and myrtles bloom unchilled on the verge of the avalanche.

Traces, indeed, of the peculiar character of Milton may be found in all his works; but it is most strongly displayed in the Sonnets. Those remarkable poems have been undervalued by critics who have not understood their nature. They have no epigrammatic point. There is none of the ingenuity of Filicaja [17] in the thought, none of the hard and brilliant enamel of Petrarch in the style. They are simple but majestic records of the feelings of the poet; as little tricked out for the public eye as his diary would have been. A victory, an unexpected attack upon the city, a momentary fit of depression or exultation, a jest thrown out against one of his books, a dream which for a short time restored to him that beautiful face over which the grave had closed for ever, led him to musings, which without effort shaped themselves into verse. The unity of sentiment and severity of style which characterise these little pieces remind us of the Greek Anthology,[18] or

---

[17] A Florentine versifier (1642–1707).
[18] A collection of some 4,500 poems, inscriptions, and so forth by several hundred writers of the 5th and 6th centuries B.C.

perhaps still more of the Collects of the English Liturgy. The noble poem on the Massacres of Piedmont [19] is strictly a collect in verse.

The sonnets are more or less striking, according as the occasions which gave birth to them are more or less interesting. But they are, almost without exception, dignified by a sobriety and greatness of mind to which we know not where to look for a parallel. It would, indeed, be scarcely safe to draw any decided inferences as to the character of a writer from passages directly egotistical. But the qualities which we have ascribed to Milton, though perhaps most strongly marked in those parts of his works which treat of his personal feelings, are distinguishable in every page, and impart to all his writings, prose and poetry, English, Latin, and Italian, a strong family likeness. . . .

Southey's Colloquies

❨ This essay, a review of Robert Southey's *Sir Thomas More: or, Colloquies on the Progress and Prospects of Society* (London, 1829), appeared in the *Edinburgh Review* for January 1830. Macaulay used the occasion to present a representative debate between the Romantic-Tory and the Practical-Whig traditions and to assert, for his own part, the optimistic, middle-class political point of view. The first part of the essay is omitted here. ❩

. . . The greater part of the two volumes before us is merely an amplification of these paragraphs. What does Mr. Southey mean by saying that religion is demonstrably the basis of civil government? He cannot surely mean that men have no motives except those derived from religion for establishing and supporting civil government, that no temporal advantage is derived from civil government, that men would experience no temporal inconvenience from living in a state of anarchy? If he allows, as we think he must allow, that it is for the good of mankind in this world to have civil government, and that the great majority of mankind have always thought it for their good in this world to have civil government, we then have a basis for government quite distinct from religion. It is true that the Christian religion sanctions government, as it sanctions everything which promotes the happiness and virtue of our species. But we are at a loss to conceive in what sense religion can be said to be the basis of government, in which religion is not also the basis of the practices of eating, drinking,

[19] Milton's sonnet beginning "Avenge, O Lord, thy slaughter'd saints."

and lighting fires in cold weather. Nothing in history is more certain than that government has existed, has received some obedience, and has given some protection, in times in which it derived no support from religion, in times in which there was no religion that influenced the hearts and lives of men. It was not from dread of Tartarus, or from belief in the Elysian fields, that an Athenian wished to have some institutions which might keep Orestes from filching his cloak, or Midias from breaking his head. "It is from religion," says Mr. Southey, "that power derives its authority, and laws their efficacy." From what religion does our power over the Hindoos derive its authority, or the law in virtue of which we hang Brahmins its efficacy? For thousands of years civil government has existed in almost every corner of the world, in ages of priestcraft, in ages of fanaticism, in ages of Epicurean indifference, in ages of enlightened piety. However pure or impure the faith of the people might be, whether they adored a beneficent or a malignant power, whether they thought the soul mortal or immortal, they have, as soon as they ceased to be absolute savages, found out their need of civil government, and instituted it accordingly. It is as universal as the practice of cookery. Yet, it is as certain, says Mr. Southey, as anything in abstract science, that government is founded on religion. We should like to know what notion Mr. Southey has of the demonstrations of abstract science. A very vague one, we suspect.

The proof proceeds. As religion is the basis of government, and as the State is secure in proportion as the people are attached to public institutions, it is therefore, says Mr. Southey, the first rule of policy, that the government should train the people in the way in which they should go; and it is plain that those who train them in any other way are undermining the State.

Now it does not appear to us to be the first object that people should always believe in the established religion and be attached to the established government. A religion may be false. A government may be oppressive. And whatever support government gives to false religions, or religion to oppressive governments, we consider as a clear evil.

The maxim, that governments ought to train the people in the way in which they should go, sounds well. But is there any reason for believing that a government is more likely to lead the people in the right way than the people to fall into the right way of themselves? Have there not been governments which were blind leaders of the blind? Are there not still such governments? Can it be laid down as a general rule that the movement of political and religious truth is rather downwards from the government to the people than upwards from the people to the government? These are questions which it is of importance to have clearly resolved. Mr. Southey declaims against public opinion, which is now, he tells us, usurping supreme power.

Formerly, according to him, the laws governed; now public opinion governs. What are laws but expressions of the opinion of some class which has power over the rest of the community? By what was the world ever governed but by the opinion of some person or persons? By what else can it ever be governed? What are all systems, religious, political, or scientific, but opinions resting on evidence more or less satisfactory? The question is not between human opinion and some higher and more certain mode of arriving at truth, but between opinion and opinion, between the opinions of one man and another, or of one class and another, or of one generation and another. Public opinion is not infallible; but can Mr. Southey construct any institutions which shall secure to us the guidance of an infallible opinion? Can Mr. Southey select any family, any profession, any class, in short, distinguished by any plain badge from the rest of the community, whose opinion is more likely to be just than this much abused public opinion? Would he choose the peers, for example? Or the two hundred tallest men in the country? Or the poor Knights of Windsor? Or children who are born with cauls? Or the seventh sons of seventh sons? We cannot suppose that he would recommend popular election; for that is merely an appeal to public opinion. And to say that society ought to be governed by the opinion of the wisest and best, though true, is useless. Whose opinion is to decide who are the wisest and best?

Mr. Southey and many other respectable people seem to think that, when they have once proved the moral and religious training of the people to be a most important object, it follows, of course, that it is an object which the government ought to pursue. They forget that we have to consider, not merely the goodness of the end, but also the fitness of the means. Neither in the natural nor in the political body have all members the same office. There is surely no contradiction in saying that a certain section of the community may be quite competent to protect the persons and property of the rest, yet quite unfit to direct our opinions, or to superintend our private habits.

So strong is the interest of a ruler to protect his subjects against all depredations and outrages except his own, so clear and simple are the means by which this end is to be effected, that men are probably better off under the worst governments in the world than they would be in a state of anarchy. Even when the appointment of magistrates has been left to chance, as in the Italian Republics, things have gone on far better than if there had been no magistrates at all, and if every man had done what seemed right in his own eyes. But we see no reason for thinking that the opinions of the magistrate on speculative questions are more likely to be right than those of any other man. None of the modes by which a magistrate is appointed, popular election, the accident of the lot, or the accident of birth, affords, as far as we can perceive, much security for his being wiser than any of his neighbours. The chance of his being wiser than all his neighbours together is still smaller. Now we cannot understand how it can be laid down that it is the duty and the right of one class to direct the opinions of another, unless it can be proved that the former class is more likely to form just opinions than the latter.

The duties of government would be, as Mr. Southey says that they are, paternal, if a government were necessarily as much superior in wisdom to a people as the most foolish father, for a time, is to the most intelligent child, and if a government loved a people as fathers generally love their children. But there is no reason to believe that a government will have either the paternal warmth of affection or the paternal superiority of intellect. Mr. Southey might as well say that the duties of the shoemaker are paternal, and that it is an usurpation in any man not of the craft to say that his shoes are bad and to insist on having better. The division of labour would be no blessing, if those by whom a thing is done were to pay no attention to the opinion of those for whom it is done. The shoemaker, in the *Relapse*, tells Lord Foppington that his Lordship is mistaken in supposing that his shoe pinches. "It does not pinch; it cannot pinch; I know my business; and I never made a better shoe." This is the way in which Mr. Southey would have a government treat a people who usurp the privilege of thinking. Nay, the shoemaker of Vanbrugh has the advantage in the comparison. He contented himself with regulating his customer's shoes, about which he had peculiar means of information, and did not presume to dictate about the coat and hat. But Mr. Southey would have the rulers of a country prescribe opinions to the people, not only about politics, but about matters concerning which a government has no peculiar sources of information, and concerning which any man in the streets may know as much and think as justly as the King, namely religion and morals.

Men are never so likely to settle a question rightly as when they discuss it freely. A government can interfere in discussion only by making it less free than it would otherwise be. Men are most likely to form just opinions when they have no other wish than to know the truth, and are exempt from all influence, either of hope or fear. Government, as government, can bring nothing but the influence of hopes and fears to support its doctrines. It carries on controversy, not with reasons, but with threats and bribes. If it employs reasons, it does so, not in virtue of any powers which belong to it as a government. Thus, instead of a contest between argument and argument, we have a contest between argument and force. Instead of a contest in which truth, from the natural constitution of the human mind, has a decided advantage over falsehood, we have a contest in which truth can be victorious only by accident.

And what, after all, is the security which this training gives to governments? Mr. Southey would scarcely propose that discussion should be more effectually shackled, that public opinion should be more strictly disciplined into conformity with established institutions, than in Spain and Italy. Yet we know that the restraints which exist in Spain and Italy have not prevented atheism from spreading among the educated classes, and especially among those whose office it is to minister at the altars of God. All our readers know how, at the time of the French Revolution, priest after priest came forward to declare that his doctrine, his ministry, his whole life, had been a lie, a mummery during which he could scarcely compose his countenance sufficiently to carry on the imposture. This was the case of a false, or at least of a grossly corrupted religion. Let us take then the case of all others most favourable to Mr. Southey's argument. Let us take that form of religion which he holds to be the purest, the system of the Arminian part of the Church of England. Let us take the form of government which he most admires and regrets, the government of England in the time of Charles the First. Would he wish to see a closer connection between Church and State than then existed? Would he wish for more powerful ecclesiastical tribunals? for a more zealous King? for a more active primate? Would he wish to see a more complete monopoly of public instruction given to the Established Church? Could any government do more to train the people in the way in which he would have them go? And in what did all this training end? The Report of the state of the Province of Canterbury, delivered by Laud to his master at the close of 1639, represents the Church of England as in the highest and most palmy state. So effectually had the Government pursued that policy which Mr. Southey wishes to see revived that there was scarcely the least appearance of dissent. Most of the bishops stated that all was well among their flocks. Seven or eight persons in the diocese of Peterborough had seemed refractory to the Church, but had made ample submission. In Norfolk and Suffolk all whom there had been reason to suspect had made profession of conformity, and appeared to observe it strictly. It is confessed that there was a little difficulty in bringing some of the vulgar in Suffolk to take the sacrament at the rails in the chancel. This was the only open instance of nonconformity which the vigilant eye of Laud could detect in all the dioceses of his twenty-one suffragans, on the very eve of a revolution in which primate, and Church, and monarch, and monarchy were to perish together.

At which time would Mr. Southey pronounce the constitution more secure: in 1639, when Laud presented this Report to Charles; or now, when thousands of meetings openly collect millions of dissenters, when designs against the tithes are openly avowed, when books attacking not only the Establishment, but the first principles of Christianity, are openly sold in the streets? The signs of discontent, he tells us, are stronger in England now than in France when the States-General met: and hence he would have us infer that a revolution like that of France may be at hand. Does he not know that the danger of states is to be estimated, not by what breaks out of the public mind, but by what stays in it? Can he conceive anything more terrible than the situation of a government which rules without apprehension over a people of hypocrites, which is flattered by the press and cursed in the inner chambers, which exults in the attachment and obedience of its subjects, and knows not that those subjects are leagued against it in a free-masonry of hatred, the sign of which is every day conveyed in the glance of ten thousand eyes, the pressure of ten thousand hands, and the tone of ten thousand voices? Profound and ingenious policy! Instead of curing the disease, to remove those symptoms by which alone its nature can be known! To leave the serpent his deadly sting, and deprive him only of his warning rattle!

When the people whom Charles had so assiduously trained in the good way had rewarded his paternal care by cutting off his head, a new kind of training came into fashion. Another government arose which, like the former, considered religion as its surest basis, and the religious discipline of the people as its first duty. Sanguinary laws were enacted against libertinism; profane pictures were burned; drapery was put on indecorous statues; the theatres were shut up; fast-days were numerous; and the Parliament resolved that no person should be admitted into any public employment, unless the House should be first satisfied of his vital godliness. We know what was the end of this training. We know that it ended in impiety, in filthy and heartless sensuality, in the dissolution of all ties of honour and morality. We know that at this very day scriptural phrases, scriptural names, perhaps some scriptural doctrines excite disgust and ridicule, solely because they are associated with the austerity of that period.

Thus has the experiment of training the people in established forms of religion been twice tried in England on a large scale, once by Charles and Laud, and once by the Puritans. The High Tories of our time still entertain many of the feelings and opinions of Charles and Laud, though in a mitigated form; nor is it difficult to see that the heirs of the Puritans are still amongst us. It would be desirable that each of these parties should remember how little advantage or honour it formerly derived from the closest alliance with power, that it fell by the support of rulers and rose by their opposition, that of the two systems that in which the people were at any time drilled was always at that time the unpopular system, that the training of the High Church ended in the reign of the Puritans, and that the training of the Puritans ended in the reign of the harlots.

This was quite natural. Nothing is so galling to a people not broken in from the birth as a paternal, or, in other words, a meddling government, a government which tells them what to read, and say, and eat, and drink, and wear. Our fathers could not bear it two hundred years ago; and we are not more patient than they. Mr. Southey thinks that the yoke of the Church is dropping off because it is loose. We feel convinced that it is borne only because it is easy, and that, in the instant in which an attempt is made to tighten it, it will be flung away. It will be neither the first nor the strongest yoke that has been broken asunder and trampled under foot in the day of the vengeance of England.

How far Mr. Southey would have the Government carry its measures for training the people in the doctrines of the Church, we are unable to discover. In one passage Sir Thomas More asks with great vehemence,

"Is it possible that your laws should suffer the unbelievers to exist as a party? Vetitum est adeo sceleris nihil?" [1]

Montesinos answers: "They avow themselves in defiance of the laws. The fashionable doctrine which the press at this time maintains is, that this is a matter in which the laws ought not to interfere, every man having a right, both to form what opinion he pleases upon religious subjects, and to promulgate that opinion."

It is clear, therefore, that Mr. Southey would not give full and perfect toleration to infidelity. In another passage, however, he observes with some truth, though too sweepingly, that "any degree of intolerance short of that full extent which the Papal Church exercises where it has the power, acts upon the opinions which it is intended to suppress, like pruning upon vigorous plants; they grow the stronger for it." These two passages, put together, would lead us to the conclusion that, in Mr. Southey's opinion, the utmost severity ever employed by the Roman Catholic Church in the days of its greatest power ought to be employed against unbelievers in England; in plain words, that Carlile and his shopmen ought to be burned in Smithfield, and that every person who, when called upon, should decline to make a solemn profession of Christianity ought to suffer the same fate. We do not, however, believe that Mr. Southey would recommend such a course, though his language would, according to all the rules of logic, justify us in supposing this to be his meaning. His opinions form no system at all. He never sees, at one glance, more of a question than will furnish matter for one flowing and well-turned sentence; so that it would be the height of unfairness to charge him personally with holding a doctrine merely because that doctrine is deducible, though by the closest and most accurate reasoning, from the premises which he has laid down. We are, therefore, left completely in the dark as to Mr. Southey's opinions about toleration. Immediately after censuring the Government for not punishing infidels, he proceeds to discuss the question of the Catholic disabilities, now, thank God, removed, and defends them on the ground that the Catholic doctrines tend to persecution, and that the Catholics persecuted when they had power.

"They must persecute," says he, "if they believe their own creed, for

---

1 "Is wrongdoing so wholly allowed?" Montesinos (whose answer follows) was a legendary Spanish hero.

conscience-sake; and if they do not believe it, they must persecute for policy; because it is only by intolerance that so corrupt and injurious a system can be upheld."

That unbelievers should not be persecuted is an instance of national depravity at which the glorified spirits stand aghast. Yet a sect of Christians is to be excluded from power, because those who formerly held the same opinions were guilty of persecution. We have said that we do not very well know what Mr. Southey's opinion about toleration is. But, on the whole, we take it to be this, that everybody is to tolerate him, and that he is to tolerate nobody.

We will not be deterred by any fear of misrepresentation from expressing our hearty approbation of the mild, wise, and eminently Christian manner in which the Church and the Government have lately acted with respect to blasphemous publications. We praise them for not having thought it necessary to encircle a religion pure, merciful, and philosophical, a religion to the evidence of which the highest intellects have yielded, with the defences of a false and bloody superstition. The ark of God was never taken till it was surrounded by the arms of earthly defenders. In captivity, its sanctity was sufficient to vindicate it from insult, and to lay the hostile fiend prostrate on the threshold of his own temple. The real security of Christianity is to be found in its benevolent morality, in its exquisite adaptation to the human heart, in the facility with which its scheme accommodates itself to the capacity of every human intellect, in the consolation which it bears to the house of mourning, in the light with which it brightens the great mystery of the grave. To such a system it can bring no addition of dignity or of strength, that it is part and parcel of the common law. It is not now for the first time left to rely on the force of its own evidences and the attractions of its own beauty. Its sublime theology confounded the Grecian schools in the fair conflict of reason with reason. The bravest and wisest of the Cæsars found their arms and their policy unavailing, when opposed to the weapons that were not carnal and the kingdom that was not of this world. The victory which Porphyry and Diocletian failed to gain [2] is not, to all appearance, reserved for any of those who have in this age, directed their attacks against the last restraint of the powerful and the last hope of the wretched. The whole history of Christianity shows, that she is in far greater danger of being corrupted by the alliance of power, than of being crushed by its opposition. Those who thrust temporal sovereignty upon her treat her as their prototypes treated her author. They bow the knee, and spit upon her; they cry "Hail!" and smite her on the cheek; they put a sceptre in her hand, but it is a fragile reed; they crown her, but it is with thorns; they cover with purple the wounds which their own hands have inflicted on her; and inscribe

[2] Porphyry, Neo-Platonic philosopher of the 3rd century critical of Christianity; Diocletian, Roman Emperor and notorious persecutor of Christians.

magnificent titles over the cross on which they have fixed her to perish in ignominy and pain.

The general view which Mr. Southey takes of the prospects of society is very gloomy; but we comfort ourselves with the consideration that Mr. Southey is no prophet. He foretold, we remember, on the very eve of the abolition of the Test and Corporation Acts,[3] that these hateful laws were immortal, and that pious minds would long be gratified by seeing the most solemn religious rite of the Church profaned for the purpose of upholding her political supremacy. In the book before us, he says that Catholics cannot possibly be admitted into Parliament until those whom Johnson called "the bottomless Whigs" come into power. While the book was in the press, the prophecy was falsified; and a Tory of the Tories, Mr. Southey's own favourite hero, won and wore that noblest wreath, "Ob cives servatos."[4]

The signs of the times, Mr. Southey tells us, are very threatening. His fears for the country would decidedly preponderate over his hopes, but for a firm reliance on the mercy of God. Now, as we know that God has once suffered the civilised world to be overrun by savages, and the Christian religion to be corrupted by doctrines which made it, for some ages, almost as bad as Paganism, we cannot think it inconsistent with his attributes that similar calamities should again befall mankind.

We look, however, on the state of the world, and of this kingdom in particular, with much greater satisfaction and with better hopes. Mr. Southey speaks with contempt of those who think the savage state happier than the social. On this subject, he says, Rousseau never imposed on him even in his youth. But he conceives that a community which has advanced a little way in civilisation is happier than one which has made greater progress. The Britons in the time of Cæsar were happier, he suspects, than the English of the nineteenth century. On the whole, he selects the generation which preceded the Reformation as that in which the people of this country were better off than at any time before or since.

This opinion rests on nothing, as far as we can see, except his own individual associations. He is a man of letters; and a life destitute of literary pleasures seems insipid to him. He abhors the spirit of the present generation, the severity of its studies, the boldness of its inquiries, and the disdain with which it regards some old prejudices by which his own mind is held in bondage. He dislikes an utterly unenlightened age; he dislikes an investigating and reforming age. The first twenty years of the sixteenth century would have exactly suited him. They furnished just the quantity of intellectual excitement which he

[3] Acts, repealed in 1828, prohibiting Dissenters from holding public office.
[4] "On account of the citizens delivered" — an allusion to the emancipation of the Catholics (1829) and the Duke of Wellington.

requires. The learned few read and wrote largely. A scholar was held
in high estimation. But the rabble did not presume to think; and even
the most inquiring and independent of the educated classes paid more
reverence to authority, and less to reason, than is usual in our time.
This is a state of things in which Mr. Southey would have found himself quite comfortable; and, accordingly, he pronounces it the happiest
state of things ever known in the world.

The savages were wretched, says Mr. Southey; but the people in
the time of Sir Thomas More were happier than either they or we.
Now we think it quite certain that we have the advantage over the
contemporaries of Sir Thomas More, in every point in which they had
any advantage over savages.

Mr. Southey does not even pretend to maintain that the people in
the sixteenth century were better lodged or clothed than at present.
He seems to admit that in these respects there has been some little improvement. It is indeed a matter about which scarcely any doubt can
exist in the most perverse mind that the improvements of machinery
have lowered the price of manufactured articles, and have brought
within the reach of the poorest some conveniences which Sir Thomas
More or his master could not have obtained at any price.

The labouring classes, however, were, according to Mr. Southey,
better fed three hundred years ago than at present. We believe that
he is completely in error on this point. The condition of servants in
noble and wealthy families, and of scholars at the Universities, must
surely have been better in those times than that of day-labourers;
and we are sure that it was not better than that of our workhouse
paupers. From the household book of the Northumberland family, we
find that in one of the greatest establishments of the kingdom the
servants lived very much as common sailors live now. In the reign of
Edward the Sixth the state of the students at Cambridge is described
to us, on the very best authority, as most wretched. Many of them
dined on pottage made of a farthing's worth of beef with a little salt
and oatmeal, and literally nothing else. This account we have from
a contemporary master of St. John's. Our parish poor now eat wheaten
bread. In the sixteenth century the labourer was glad to get barley,
and was often forced to content himself with poorer fare. In Harrison's introduction to Holinshed [5] we have an account of the state of
our working population in the "golden days," as Mr. Southey calls
them, "of good Queen Bess." "The gentilitie," says he, "commonly
provide themselves sufficiently of wheat for their own tables, whylest
their household and poore neighbours in some shires are inforced to
content themselves with rye or barleic; yea, and in time of dearth,
many with bread made eyther of beanes, peason, or otes, or of altogether, and some acornes among. I will not say that this extremity is

5 William Harrison (1534–1593), author of a "Description of England" published with Holinshed's *Chronicles* in 1577.

oft so well to be seen in time of plentie as of dearth; but if I should I could easily bring my trial: for albeit there be much more grounde eared nowe almost in everye place then hathe beene of late yeares, yet such a price of corne continueth in eache towne and markete, without any just cause, that the artificer and poore labouring man is not able to reach unto it, but is driven to content himself with horse-corne." We should like to see what the effect would be of putting any parish in England now on allowance of "horse-corne." The helotry of Mammon are not, in our day, so easily enforced to content themselves as the peasantry of that happy period, as Mr. Southey considers it, which elapsed between the fall of the feudal and the rise of the commercial tyranny.

"The people," says Mr. Southey, "are worse fed than when they were fishers." And yet in another place he complains that they will not eat fish. "They have contracted," says he, "I know not how, some obstinate prejudice against a kind of food at once wholesome and delicate, and everywhere to be obtained cheaply and in abundance, were the demand for it as general as it ought to be." It is true that the lower orders have an obstinate prejudice against fish. But hunger has no such obstinate prejudices. If what was formerly a common diet is now eaten only in times of severe pressure, the inference is plain. The people must be fed with what they at least think better food than that of their ancestors.

The advice and medicine which the poorest labourer can now obtain, in disease, or after an accident, is far superior to what Henry the Eighth could have commanded. Scarcely any part of the country is out of the reach of practitioners, who are probably not so far inferior to Sir Henry Halford as they are superior to Dr. Butts.[6] That there has been a great improvement in this respect, Mr. Southey allows. Indeed he could not well have denied it. "But," says he, "the evils for which these sciences are the palliative, have increased since the time of the Druids, in a proportion that heavily overweighs the benefit of improved therapeutics." We know nothing either of the diseases or the remedies of the Druids. But we are quite sure that the improvement of medicine has far more than kept pace with the increase of disease during the last three centuries. This is proved by the best possible evidence. The term of human life is decidedly longer in England than in any former age, respecting which we possess any information on which we can rely. All the rants in the world about picturesque cottages and temples of Mammon will not shake this argument. No test of the physical well-being of society can be named so decisive as that which is furnished by bills of mortality. That the lives of the people of this country have been gradually lengthening during the course of several generations, is as certain as any fact in statistics;

6 Halford: Royal Physician until his death in 1844; Sir William Butts: physician to Henry VIII.

and that the lives of men should become longer and longer, while their bodily condition during life is becoming worse and worse, is utterly incredible.

Let our readers think over these circumstances. Let them take into the account the sweating sickness and the plague. Let them take into the account that fearful disease which first made its appearance in the generation to which Mr. Southey assigns the palm of felicity, and raged through Europe with a fury at which the physician stood aghast, and before which the people were swept away by myriads. Let them consider the state of the northern counties, constantly the scene of robberies, rapes, massacres, and conflagrations. Let them add to all this the fact that seventy-two thousand persons suffered death by the hands of the executioner during the reign of Henry the Eighth, and judge between the nineteenth and the sixteenth century.

We do not say that the lower orders in England do not suffer severe hardships. But, in spite of Mr. Southey's assertions, and in spite of the assertions of a class of politicians, who, differing from Mr. Southey in every other point, agree with him in this, we are inclined to doubt whether the labouring classes here really suffer greater physical distress than the labouring classes of the most flourishing countries of the Continent.

It will scarcely be maintained that the lazzaroni who sleep under the porticoes of Naples, or the beggars who besiege the convents of Spain, are in a happier situation than the English commonalty. The distress which has lately been experienced in the northern part of Germany, one of the best governed and most prosperous regions of Europe, surpasses, if we have been correctly informed, anything which has of late years been known among us. In Norway and Sweden the peasantry are constantly compelled to mix bark with their bread; and even this expedient has not always preserved whole families and neighbourhoods from perishing together of famine. An experiment has lately been tried in the kingdom of the Netherlands, which has been cited to prove the possibility of establishing agricultural colonies on the waste lands of England, but which proves to our minds nothing so clearly as this, that the rate of subsistence to which the labouring classes are reduced in the Netherlands is miserably low, and very far inferior to that of the English paupers. No distress which the people here have endured for centuries approaches to that which has been felt by the French in our own time. The beginning of the year 1817 was a time of great distress in this island. But the state of the lowest classes here was luxury compared with that of the people of France. We find in Magendie's [7] *Journal de Physiologie Expérimentale* a paper on a point of physiology connected with the distress of that season. It appears that the inhabitants of six departments, Aix, Jura, Doubs, Haute Saone, Vosges, and Saone-et-Loire, were reduced first to oat-

[7] François Magendie (1783–1855), physiologist.

meal and potatoes, and at last to nettles, beanstalks, and other kinds
of herbage fit only for cattle; that when the next harvest enabled them
to eat barley-bread, many of them died from intemperate indulgence in
what they thought an exquisite repast; and that a dropsy of a peculiar
description was produced by the hard fare of the year. Dead bodies
were found on the roads and in the fields. A single surgeon dissected
six of these, and found the stomach shrunk, and filled with the unwholesome aliments which hunger had driven men to share with
beasts. Such extremity of distress as this is never heard of in England,
or even in Ireland. We are, on the whole, inclined to think, though
we would speak with diffidence on a point on which it would be rash
to pronounce a positive judgment without a much longer and closer
investigation than we have bestowed upon it, that the labouring classes
of this island, though they have their grievances and distresses, some
produced by their own improvidence, some by the errors of their rulers, are on the whole better off as to physical comforts than the inhabitants of any equally extensive district of the old world. For this very
reason, suffering is more acutely felt and more loudly bewailed here
than elsewhere. We must take into the account the liberty of discussion, and the strong interest which the opponents of a ministry always
have to exaggerate the extent of the public disasters. There are countries in which the people quietly endure distress that here would shake
the foundations of the State, countries in which the inhabitants of a
whole province turn out to eat grass with less clamour than one Spital-
fields weaver would make here, if the overseers were to put him on
barley-bread. In those new commonwealths in which a civilised population has at its command a boundless extent of the richest soil, the
condition of the labourer is probably happier than in any society which
has lasted for many centuries. But in the old world we must confess
ourselves unable to find any satisfactory record of any great nation,
past or present, in which the working classes have been in a more
comfortable situation than in England during the last thirty years.
When this island was thinly peopled, it was barbarous: there was little
capital; and that little was insecure. It is now the richest and most
highly civilised spot in the world; but the population is dense. Thus
we have never known that golden age which the lower orders in the
United States are now enjoying. We have never known an age of
liberty, of order, and of education, an age in which the mechanical
sciences were carried to a great height, yet in which the people were
not sufficiently numerous to cultivate even the most fertile valleys.
But, when we compare our own condition with that of our ancestors,
we think it clear that the advantages arising from the progress of civilisation have far more than counterbalanced the disadvantages arising
from the progress of population. While our numbers have increased
tenfold, our wealth has increased a hundredfold. Though there are
so many more people to share the wealth now existing in the country

than there were in the sixteenth century, it seems certain that a greater share falls to almost every individual than fell to the share of any of the corresponding class in the sixteenth century. The King keeps a more splendid court. The establishments of the nobles are more magnificent. The esquires are richer; the merchants are richer; the shopkeepers are richer. The serving-man, the artisan, and the husbandman, have a more copious and palatable supply of food, better clothing, and better furniture. This is no reason for tolerating abuses, or for neglecting any means of ameliorating the condition of our poorer countrymen. But it is a reason against telling them, as some of our philosophers are constantly telling them, that they are the most wretched people who ever existed on the face of the earth.

We have already adverted to Mr. Southey's amusing doctrine about national wealth. A state, says he, cannot be too rich; but a people may be too rich. His reason for thinking this is extremely curious.

"A people may be too rich, because it is the tendency of the commercial, and more especially of the manufacturing system, to collect wealth rather than to diffuse it. Where wealth is necessarily employed in any of the speculations of trade, its increase is in proportion to its amount. Great capitalists become like pikes in a fish-pond who devour the weaker fish; and it is but too certain, that the poverty of one part of the people seems to increase in the same ratio as the riches of another. There are examples of this in history. In Portugal, when the high tide of wealth flowed in from the conquests in Africa and the East, the effect of that great influx was not more visible in the augmented splendour of the court, and the luxury of the higher ranks, than in the distress of the people."

Mr. Southey's instance is not a very fortunate one. The wealth which did so little for the Portuguese was not the fruit either of manufactures or of commerce carried on by private individuals. It was the wealth, not of the people, but of the Government and its creatures, of those who, as Mr. Southey thinks, can never be too rich. The fact is, that Mr. Southey's proposition is opposed to all history, and to the phænomena which surround us on every side. England is the richest country in Europe, the most commercial country, and the country in which manufactures flourish most. Russia and Poland are the poorest countries in Europe. They have scarcely any trade, and none but the rudest manufactures. Is wealth more diffused in Russia and Poland than in England? There are individuals in Russia and Poland whose incomes are probably equal to those of our richest countrymen. It may be doubted whether there are not, in those countries, as many fortunes of eighty thousand a year as here. But are there as many fortunes of two thousand a year, or of one thousand a year? There are parishes in England which contain more people of between three hundred and three thousand pounds a year than could be found in all the dominions of the Emperor Nicholas. The neat and commodious houses which have been built in London and its vicinity, for people of this class, within the last thirty years, would of themselves form a city larger than the capitals of some European kingdoms. And this is the state of society in which the great proprietors have devoured a smaller!

The cure which Mr. Southey thinks that he has discovered is worthy of the sagacity which he has shown in detecting the evil. The calamities arising from the collection of wealth in the hands of a few capitalists are to be remedied by collecting it in the hands of one great capitalist, who has no conceivable motive to use it better than other capitalists, the all-devouring State.

It is not strange that, differing so widely from Mr. Southey as to the past progress of society, we should differ from him also as to its probable destiny. He thinks, that to all outward appearance, the country is hastening to destruction; but he relies firmly on the goodness of God. We do not see either the piety or the rationality of thus confidently expecting that the Supreme Being will interfere to disturb the common succession of causes and effects. We, too, rely on his goodness, on his goodness as manifested, not in extraordinary interpositions, but in those general laws which it has pleased him to establish in the physical and in the moral world. We rely on the natural tendency of the human intellect to truth, and on the natural tendency of society to improvement. We know no well-authenticated instance of a people which has decidedly retrograded in civilisation and prosperity, except from the influence of violent and terrible calamities, such as those which laid the Roman Empire in ruins, or those which, about the beginning of the sixteenth century, desolated Italy. We know of no country which, at the end of fifty years of peace and tolerably good government, has been less prosperous than at the beginning of that period. The political importance of a state may decline, as the balance of power is disturbed by the introduction of new forces. Thus the influence of Holland and of Spain is much diminished. But are Holland and Spain poorer than formerly? We doubt it. Other countries have outrun them. But we suspect that they have been positively, though not relatively, advancing. We suspect that Holland is richer than when she sent her navies up the Thames, that Spain is richer than when a French king was brought captive to the footstool of Charles the Fifth.

History is full of the signs of this natural progress of society. We see in almost every part of the annals of mankind how the industry of individuals, struggling up against wars, taxes, famines, conflagrations, mischievous prohibitions, and more mischievous protections, creates faster than governments can squander, and repairs whatever invaders can destroy. We see the wealth of nations increasing, and all the arts of life approaching nearer and nearer to perfection, in spite of the grossest corruption and the wildest profusion on the part of rulers.

The present moment is one of great distress. But how small will that distress appear when we think over the history of the last forty years; a war, compared with which all other wars sink into insignificance; taxation, such as the most heavily taxed people of former times could not have conceived; a debt larger than all the public debts that ever existed in the world added together; the food of the people studiously rendered dear; the currency imprudently debased, and imprudently restored. Yet is the country poorer than in 1790? We firmly believe that, in spite of all the misgovernment of her rulers, she has been almost constantly becoming richer and richer. Now and then there has been a stoppage, now and then a short retrogression; but as to the general tendency there can be no doubt. A single breaker may recede; but the tide is evidently coming in.

If we were to prophesy that in the year 1930 a population of fifty millions, better fed, clad, and lodged than the English of our time, will cover these islands, that Sussex and Huntingdonshire will be wealthier than the wealthiest parts of the West Riding of Yorkshire now are, that cultivation, rich as that of a flower-garden, will be carried up to the very tops of Ben Nevis and Helvellyn, that machines constructed on principles yet undiscovered will be in every house, that there will be no highways but railroads, no travelling but by steam, that our debt, vast as it seems to us, will appear to our great-grandchildren a trifling encumbrance, which might easily be paid off in a year or two, many people would think us insane. We prophesy nothing; but this we say: If any person had told the Parliament which met in perplexity and terror after the crash in 1720 that in 1830 the wealth of England would surpass all their wildest dreams, that the annual revenue would equal the principal of that debt which they considered as an intolerable burden, that for one man of ten thousand pounds then living there would be five men of fifty thousand pounds, that London would be twice as large and twice as populous, and that nevertheless the rate of mortality would have diminished to one-half of what it then was, that the post-office would bring more into the exchequer than the excise and customs had brought in together under Charles the Second, that stage coaches would run from London to York in twenty-four hours, that men would be in the habit of sailing without wind, and would be beginning to ride without horses, our ancestors would have given as much credit to the prediction as they gave to *Gulliver's Travels*. Yet the prediction would have been true; and they would have perceived that it was not altogether absurd, if they had considered that the country was then raising every year a sum which would have purchased the fee-simple of the revenue of the Plantagenets, ten times what supported the Government of Elizabeth, three times what, in the time of Cromwell, had been thought intolerably oppressive. To almost all men the state of things under which they have been used to live seems to be the necessary state of things. We have heard it said that five per cent. is the natural interest of money, that twelve is the natural number of a jury, that forty shillings is the natural qualification of a county voter. Hence it is that, though in every age everybody knows that up to his own time progressive improvement has been taking place, nobody seems to reckon on any improvement during the next generation. We cannot absolutely prove that those are in error who tell us that society has reached a turning point, that we have seen our best days. But so said all who came before us, and with just as much apparent reason. "A million a year will beggar us," said the patriots of 1640. "Two millions a year will grind the country to powder," was the cry in 1660. "Six millions a year, and a debt of fifty millions!" exclaimed Swift, "the high allies have been the ruin of us." "A hundred and forty millions of debt!" said Junius; [8] "well may we say that we owe Lord Chatham more than we shall ever pay, if we owe him such a load as this." "Two hundred and forty millions of debt!" cried all the statesmen of 1783 in chorus; "what abilities, or what economy on the part of a minister, can save a country so burdened?" We know that if, since 1783, no fresh debt had been incurred, the increased resources of the country would have enabled us to defray that debt at which Pitt, Fox, and Burke stood aghast, nay, to defray it over and over again, and that with much lighter taxation than what we have actually borne. In what principle is it that, when we see nothing but improvement behind us, we are to expect nothing but deterioration before us?

It is not by the intermeddling of Mr. Southey's idol, the omniscient and omnipotent State, but by the prudence and energy of the people, that England has hitherto been carried forward in civilisation; and it is to the same prudence and the same energy that we now look with comfort and good hope. Our rulers will best promote the improvement of the nation by strictly confining themselves to their own legitimate duties, by leaving capital to find its most lucrative course, commodities their fair price, industry and intelligence their natural reward, idleness and folly their natural punishment, by maintaining peace, by defending property, by diminishing the price of law, and by observing strict economy in every department of the State. Let the Government do this: the People will assuredly do the rest.

8 Pseudonym of the author of a series of letters (1769–1771) attacking George III and his ministers.

Lord Bacon

◖ This essay, a review of a new (1825–1834) sixteen-volume edition of the works of Francis Bacon edited by Basil Montagu, appeared in the *Edinburgh Review* for July 1837. Macaulay's understanding of Bacon was limited, and students of Bacon now look upon the essay as a curious period piece. Nevertheless, that portion of the essay here printed provides a clear, bold statement of utilitarian liberalism; an important document in the Victorian war between the ancients and the moderns; and the best text for the study of Macaulay's limitations as a philosopher. ◗

. . . What then was the end which Bacon proposed to himself? It was, to use his own emphatic expression, "fruit." It was the multiplying of human enjoyments and the mitigating of human sufferings. It was "the relief of man's estate." It was "commodis humanis inservire." [1] It was "efficaciter operari ad sublevanda vitæ humanæ incommoda." [2] It was "dotare vitam humanam novis inventis et copiis.' [3] It was "genus humanum novis operibus et potestatibus continuo dotare." [4] This was the object of all his speculations in every department of science, in natural philosophy, in legislation, in politics, in morals.

Two words form the key of the Baconian doctrine, Utility and Progress. The ancient philosophy disdained to be useful, and was content to be stationary. It dealt largely in theories of moral perfection, which were so sublime that they never could be more than theories; in attempts to solve insoluble enigmas; in exhortations to the attainment of unattainable frames of mind. It could not condescend to the humble office of. ministering to the comfort of human beings. All the schools contemned that office as degrading; some censured it as immoral. Once indeed Posidonius, a distinguished writer of the age of Cicero and Cæsar, so far forgot himself as to enumerate, among the humbler blessings which mankind owed to philosophy, the discovery of the principle of the arch, and the introduction of the use of metals. This eulogy was considered as an affront, and was taken up with proper spirit. Seneca vehemently disclaims these insulting compliments. Philosophy, according to him, has nothing to do with teaching men to rear arched roofs over their heads. The true philosopher does not care whether he has an arched roof or any roof. Philosophy has nothing to do with teaching men the uses of metals. She teaches

[1] "to advance human comforts." (The translation of the Latin throughout this essay follows that of Professors Walter H. French and Gerald D. Sanders in *The Reader's Macaulay* (New York, 1936).

[2] "to work effectually to remove the discomforts of human life."

[3] "to endow human life with new discoveries and powers."

[4] "ever anew to endow mankind with new achievements and powers."

us to be independent of all material substances, of all mechanical contrivances. The wise man lives according to nature. Instead of attempting to add to the physical comforts of his species, he regrets that his
lot was not cast in that golden age when the human race had no protection against the cold but the skins of wild beasts, no screen from
the sun but a cavern. To impute to such a man any share in the invention or improvement of a plough, a ship, or a mill is an insult. "In
my own time," says Seneca, "there have been inventions of this sort,
transparent windows, tubes for diffusing warmth equally through all
parts of a building, shorthand, which has been carried to such a perfection that a writer can keep pace with the most rapid speaker. But
the inventing of such things is drudgery for the lowest slaves; philosophy lies deeper. It is not her office to teach men how to use their
hands. The object of her lessons is to form the soul. *Non est, inquam,
instrumentorum ad usus necessarios opifex.*" [5] If the *non* were left out,
this last sentence would be no bad description of the Baconian philosophy, and would, indeed, very much resemble several expressions in the
Novum Organum. "We shall next be told," exclaims Seneca, "that the
first shoemaker was a philosopher." For our own part, if we are forced
to make our choice between the first shoemaker and the author of the
three books "On Anger," we pronounce for the shoemaker. It may be
worse to be angry than to be wet. But shoes have kept millions from
being wet; and we doubt whether Seneca ever kept anybody from
being angry.

It is very reluctantly that Seneca can be brought to confess that any
philosopher had ever paid the smallest attention to anything that could
possibly promote what vulgar people would consider as the well-being
of mankind. He labours to clear Democritus from the disgraceful imputation of having made the first arch, and Anacharsis [6] from the
charge of having contrived the potter's wheel. He is forced to own
that such a thing might happen; and it may also happen, he tells us,
that a philosopher may be swift of foot. But it is not in his character
of philosopher that he either wins a race or invents a machine. No,
to be sure. The business of a philosopher was to declaim in praise of
poverty with two millions sterling out at usury, to meditate epigrammatic conceits about the evils of luxury, in gardens which moved the
envy of sovereigns, to rant about liberty, while fawning on the insolent and pampered freedmen of a tyrant, to celebrate the divine
beauty of virtue with the same pen which had just before written a
defence of the murder of a mother by a son.

From the cant of this philosophy, a philosophy meanly proud of
its own unprofitableness, it is delightful to turn to the lessons of the
great English teacher. We can almost forgive all the faults of Bacon's

5 "She is not, I say, the maker of instruments for necessary purposes."
6 A Scythian prince of the 6th century B.C. generally admired in Athens for
his wisdom.

life when we read that singularly graceful and dignified passage: "Ego certe, ut de me ipso, quod res est, loquar, et in iis quæ nunc edo, et in iis quæ in posterum meditor, dignitatem ingenii et nominis mei, si qua sit, sæpius sciens et volens projicio, dum commodis humanis inserviam; quique architectus fortasse in philosophia et scientiis esse debeam, etiam operarius, et bajulus, et quidvis demum fio, cum haud pauca quæ omnino fieri necesse sit, alii autem ob innatam superbiam subterfugiant, ipsi sustineam et exsequar." [7] This *philanthropia*, which, as he said in one of the most remarkable of his early letters, "was so fixed in his mind, as it could not be removed," this majestic humility, this persuasion that nothing can be too insignificant for the attention of the wisest, which is not too insignificant to give pleasure or pain to the meanest, is the great characteristic distinction, the essential spirit of the Baconian philosophy. We trace it in all that Bacon has written on Physics, on Laws, on Morals. And we conceive that from this peculiarity all the other peculiarities of his system directly and almost necessarily sprang.

The spirit which appears in the passage of Seneca to which we have referred tainted the whole body of the ancient philosophy from the time of Socrates downwards, and took possession of intellects with which that of Seneca cannot for a moment be compared. It pervades the dialogues of Plato. It may be distinctly traced in many parts of the works of Aristotle. Bacon has dropped hints from which it may be inferred that, in his opinion, the prevalence of this feeling was in a great measure to be attributed to the influence of Socrates. Our great countryman evidently did not consider the revolution which Socrates effected in philosophy as a happy event, and constantly maintained that the earlier Greek speculators, Democritus in particular, were, on the whole, superior to their more celebrated successors.

Assuredly if the tree which Socrates planted and Plato watered is to be judged of by its flowers and leaves, it is the noblest of trees. But if we take the homely test of Bacon, if we judge of the tree by its fruits, our opinion of it may perhaps be less favourable. When we sum up all the useful truths which we owe to that philosophy, to what do they amount? We find, indeed, abundant proofs that some of those who cultivated it were men of the first order of intellect. We find among their writings incomparable specimens both of dialectical and rhetorical art. We have no doubt that the ancient controversies were of use, in so far as they served to exercise the faculties of the disputants; for there

---

[7] "But I, to say how the matter stands with myself alone, both with respect to what I am now producing and in what I intend hereafter, often advisedly and deliberately throw aside the dignity of my name and wit, if I have any, in my endeavor to advance human comforts; and being one who should properly, perhaps, be an architect in philosophy and the sciences, I turn common laborer, hodman, anything that is wanted; taking upon myself the burden and execution of many things that must needs be done, and that others, through an inborn pride, shrink from and decline."

is no controversy so idle that it may not be of use in this way. But, when we look for something more, for something which adds to the comforts or alleviates the calamities of the human race, we are forced to own ourselves disappointed. We are forced to say with Bacon that this celebrated philosophy ended in nothing but disputation, that it was neither a vineyard nor an olive-ground, but an intricate wood of briars and thistles, from which those who lost themselves in it brought back many scratches and no food.

We readily acknowledge that some of the teachers of this unfruitful wisdom were among the greatest men that the world has ever seen. If we admit the justice of Bacon's censure, we admit it with regret, similar to that which Dante felt when he learned the fate of those illustrious heathens who were doomed to the first circle of Hell:

> "Gran duol mi prese al cuor quando lo 'ntesi,
> Perocché gente di molto valore
> Conobbi che 'n quel limbo eran sospesi." [8]

But in truth the very admiration which we feel for the eminent philosophers of antiquity forces us to adopt the opinion that their powers were systematically misdirected. For how else could it be that such powers should effect so little for mankind? A pedestrian may show as much muscular vigour on a treadmill as on the highway road. But on the road his vigour will assuredly carry him forward; and on the treadmill he will not advance an inch. The ancient philosophy was a treadmill, not a path. It was made up of revolving questions, of controversies which were always beginning again. It was a contrivance for having much exertion and no progress. We must acknowledge that more than once, while contemplating the doctrines of the Academy and the Portico, even as they appear in the transparent splendour of Cicero's incomparable diction, we have been tempted to mutter with the surly centurion in Persius, "Cur quis non prandeat hoc est?" [9] What is the highest good, whether pain be an evil, whether all things be fated, whether we can be certain of anything, whether we can be certain that we are certain of nothing, whether a wise man can be unhappy, whether all departures from right be equally reprehensible; these, and other questions of the same sort, occupied the brains, the tongues, and the pens of the ablest men in the civilised world during several centuries. This sort of philosophy, it is evident, could not be progressive. It might indeed sharpen and invigorate the minds of those who devoted themselves

---

8 As translated by Cary:
> "Sore grief assail'd
> My heart at hearing this, for well I knew
> Suspended in that Limbo many a soul
> Of mighty worth."
9 "Is it for this that one should not dine?"

to it; and so might the disputes of the orthodox Lilliputians and the heretical Blefuscudians about the big ends and the little ends of eggs. But such disputes could add nothing to the stock of knowledge. The human mind accordingly, instead of marching, merely marked time. It took as much trouble as would have sufficed to carry it forward; and yet remained on the same spot. There was no accumulation of truth, no heritage of truth acquired by the labour of one generation and bequeathed to another, to be again transmitted with large additions to a third. Where this philosophy was in the time of Cicero, there it continued to be in the time of Seneca, and there it continued to be in the time of Favorinus.[10] The same sects were still battling with the same unsatisfactory arguments, about the same interminable questions. There had been no want of ingenuity, of zeal, of industry. Every trace of intellectual cultivation was there, except a harvest. There had been plenty of ploughing, harrowing, reaping, threshing. But the garners contained only smut and stubble.

The ancient philosophers did not neglect natural science; but they did not cultivate it for the purpose of increasing the power and ameliorating the condition of man. The taint of barrenness had spread from ethical to physical speculations. Seneca wrote largely on natural philosophy, and magnified the importance of that study. But why? Not because it tended to assuage suffering, to multiply the conveniences of life, to extend the empire of man over the material world; but solely because it tended to raise the mind above low cares, to separate it from the body, to exercise its subtility in the solution of very obscure questions. Thus natural philosophy was considered in the light merely of a mental exercise. It was made subsidiary to the art of disputation; and it consequently proved altogether barren of useful discoveries.

There was one sect which, however absurd and pernicious some of its doctrines may have been, ought, it should seem, to have merited an exception from the general censure which Bacon has pronounced on the ancient schools of wisdom. The Epicurean, who referred all happiness to bodily pleasure, and all evil to bodily pain, might have been expected to exert himself for the purpose of bettering his own physical condition and that of his neighbours. But the thought seems never to have occurred to any member of that school. Indeed their notion, as reported by their great poet, was, that no more improvements were to be expected in the arts which conduce to the comfort of life.

"Ad victum quæ flagitat usus
Omnia jam ferme mortalibus esse parata." [11]

---

10 Greek sophist of the 2nd century A.D.
11 "That mortals had prepared for them almost all that necessity demands for living."

This contented despondency, this disposition to admire what has been done, and to expect that nothing more will be done, is strongly characteristic of all the schools which preceded the school of Fruit and Progress. Widely as the Epicurean and the Stoic differed on most points, they seem to have quite agreed in their contempt for pursuits so vulgar as to be useful. The philosophy of both was a garrulous, declaiming, canting, wrangling philosophy. Century after century they continued to repeat their hostile war-cries, Virtue and Pleasure; and in the end it appeared that the Epicurean had added as little to the quantity of pleasure as the Stoic to the quantity of virtue. It is on the pedestal of Bacon, not on that of Epicurus, that those noble lines ought to be inscribed:

> "O tenebris tantis tam clarum extollere lumen
> Qui primus potuisti, illustrans commoda vitæ." [12]

In the fifth century Christianity had conquered Paganism, and Paganism had infected Christianity. The Church was now victorious and corrupt. The rites of the Pantheon had passed into her worship, the subtilities of the Academy into her creed. In an evil day, though with great pomp and solemnity, — we quote the language of Bacon, — was the ill-starred alliance stricken between the old philosophy and the new faith. Questions widely different from those which had employed the ingenuity of Pyrrho and Carneades,[13] but just as subtle, just as interminable, and just as unprofitable, exercised the minds of the lively and voluble Greeks. When learning began to revive in the West, similar trifles occupied the sharp and vigorous intellects of the Schoolmen. There was another sowing of the wind, and another reaping of the whirlwind. The great work of improving the condition of the human race was still considered as unworthy of a man of learning. Those who undertook that task, if what they effected could be readily comprehended, were despised as mechanics; if not, they were in danger of being burned as conjurers.

There cannot be a stronger proof of the degree in which the human mind had been misdirected than the history of the two greatest events which took place during the middle ages. We speak of the invention of Gunpowder and of the invention of Printing. The dates of both are unknown. The authors of both are unknown. Nor was this because men were too rude and ignorant to value intellectual superiority. The inventor of gunpowder appears to have been contemporary with Petrarch and Boccaccio. The inventor of printing was certainly contemporary with Nicholas the Fifth, with Cosmo de' Medici, and with

---

12 "O you, who first were able from so much darkness to raise up a light, illuminating the comforts of life."
13 Founder of the Pyrrhonian (Skeptical) school of philosophy; a skeptical philosopher of the 3rd century B.C., founder of the New Academy at Athens.

a crowd of distinguished scholars. But the human mind still retained
that fatal bent which it had received two thousand years earlier.
George of Trebisond and Marsilio Ficino [14] would not easily have
been brought to believe that the inventor of the printing-press had
done more for mankind than themselves, or than those ancient writers
of whom they were the enthusiastic votaries.

At length the time arrived when the barren philosophy which had,
during so many ages, employed the faculties of the ablest of men,
was destined to fall. It had worn many shapes. It had mingled itself
with many creeds. It had survived revolutions in which empires,
religions, languages, races, had perished. Driven from its ancient
haunts, it had taken sanctuary in that Church which it had persecuted,
and had, like the daring fiends of the poet, placed its seat

> "next the seat of God,
> And with its darkness dared affront his light."

Words, and more words, and nothing but words, had been all the
fruit of all the toil of all the most renowned sages of sixty generations.
But the days of this sterile exuberance were numbered.

Many causes predisposed the public mind to a change. The study
of a great variety of ancient writers, though it did not give a right
direction to philosophical research, did much towards destroying that
blind reverence for authority which had prevailed when Aristotle ruled
alone. The rise of the Florentine sect of Platonists, a sect to which
belonged some of the finest minds of the fifteenth century, was not an
unimportant event. The mere substitution of the Academic for the
Peripatetic philosophy would indeed have done little good. But
anything was better than the old habit of unreasoning servility. It
was something to have a choice of tyrants. "A spark of freedom," as
Gibbon has justly remarked, "was produced by this collision of adverse servitude."

Other causes might be mentioned. But it is chiefly to the great
reformation of religion that we owe the great reformation of philosophy. The alliance between the Schools and the Vatican had for ages
been so close that those who threw off the dominion of the Vatican
could not continue to recognise the authority of the Schools. Most
of the chiefs of the schism treated the Peripatetic philosophy with
contempt, and spoke of Aristotle as if Aristotle had been answerable
for all the dogmas of Thomas Aquinas. "Nullo apud Lutheranos
philosophiam esse in pretio," [15] was a reproach which the defenders
of the Church of Rome loudly repeated, and which many of the
Protestant leaders considered as a compliment. Scarcely any text

14 George of Trebizond was a 15th century humanist; Marsilio Ficino was
a 15th century Greek scholar.
15 "Among the Lutherans, philosophy has no value."

was more frequently cited by the reformers than that in which St.
Paul cautions the Colossians not to let any man spoil them by philosophy. Luther, almost at the outset of his career, went so far as to
declare that no man could be at once a proficient in the school of
Aristotle and in that of Christ. Zwingli, Bucer, Peter Martyr,[16] Calvin,
held similar language. In some of the Scotch universities, the Aristotelian system was discarded for that of Ramus.[17] Thus, before the
birth of Bacon, the empire of the scholastic philosophy had been
shaken to its foundations. There was in the intellectual world an
anarchy resembling that which in the political world often follows
the overthrow of an old and deeply rooted Government. Antiquity,
prescription, the sound of great names, have ceased to awe mankind.
The dynasty which had reigned for ages was at an end; and the
vacant throne was left to be struggled for by pretenders.

The first effect of this great revolution was, as Bacon most justly
observed, to give for a time an undue importance to the mere graces
of style. The new breed of scholars, the Aschams and Buchanans,[18]
nourished with the finest compositions of the Augustan age, regarded
with loathing the dry, crabbed, and barbarous diction of respondents
and opponents. They were far less studious about the matter of their
writing than about the manner. They succeeded in reforming Latinity;
but they never even aspired to effect a reform in Philosophy.

At this time Bacon appeared. It is altogether incorrect to say, as
has often been said, that he was the first man who rose up against the
Aristotelian philosophy when in the height of his power. The authority
of that philosophy had, as we have shown, received a fatal blow long
before he was born. Several speculators, among whom Ramus is the
best known, had recently attempted to form new sects. Bacon's own
expressions about the state of public opinion in the time of Luther
are clear and strong: "Accedebat," says he, "odium et contemptus, illis
ipsis temporibus ortus erga Scholasticos." [19] And again, "Scholasticorum
doctrina despectui prorsus haberi cœpit tanquam aspera et barbara." [20]
The part which Bacon played in this great change was the part, not
of Robespierre, but of Bonaparte. The ancient order of things had
been subverted. Some bigots still cherished with devoted loyalty the
remembrance of the fallen monarchy, and exerted themselves to effect
a restoration. But the majority had no such feeling. Freed, yet not
knowing how to use their freedom, they pursued no determinate
course, and had found no leader capable of conducting them.

16 Martin Bucer (German) and Peter Martyr (Italian) were early preachers of
the Protestant Reformation.
17 Peter Ramus (1515–1572), a strong critic of the Aristotelian dialectic.
18 George Buchanan (1506–1582) was the tutor of James VI and I.
19 "It befell that hate and contempt rose against the Schoolmen in their own
times."
20 "The doctrine of the Schoolmen, in short, began to be held a contemptible
spectacle, as well as harsh and barbarous."

That leader at length arose. The philosophy which he taught was essentially new. It differed from that of the celebrated ancient teachers, not merely in method, but also in object. Its object was the good of mankind, in the sense in which the mass of mankind always·have understood and always will understand the word good. "Meditor," said Bacon, "instaurationem philosophiæ ejusmodi quæ nihil inanis aut abstracti habeat, quæque vitæ humanæ conditiones in melius provehat." [21]

The difference between the philosophy of Bacon and that of his predecessors cannot, we think, be better illustrated than by comparing his views on some important subjects with those of Plato. We select Plato, because we conceive that he did more than any other person towards giving to the minds of speculative men that bent which they retained till they received from Bacon a new impulse in a diametrically opposite direction.

It is curious to observe how differently these great men estimated the value of every kind of knowledge. Take Arithmetic for example. Plato, after speaking slightly of the convenience of being able to reckon and compute in the ordinary transactions of life, passes to what he considers as a far more important advantage. The study of the properties of numbers, he tells us, habituates the mind to the contemplation of pure truth, and raises us above the material universe. He would have his disciples apply themselves to this study, not that they may be able to buy or sell, not that they may qualify themselves to be shopkeepers or travelling merchants, but that they may learn to withdraw their minds from the ever-shifting spectacle of this visible and tangible world, and to fix them on the immutable essences of things.

Bacon, on the other hand, valued this branch of knowledge, only on account of its uses with reference to that visible and tangible world which Plato so much despised. He speaks with scorn of the mystical arithmetic of the later Platonists, and laments the propensity of mankind to employ, on mere matters of curiosity, powers the whole exertion of which is required for purposes of solid advantage. He advises arithmeticians to leave these trifles, and to employ themselves in framing convenient expressions, which may be of use in physical researches.

The same reasons which led Plato to recommend the study of arithmetic led him to recommend also the study of mathematics. The vulgar crowd of geometricians, he says, will not understand him. They have practice always in view. They do not know that the real use of the science is to lead men to the knowledge of abstract, essential, eternal truth. Indeed, if we are to believe Plutarch, Plato carried

21 "I intend a renewal of philosophy of a sort which shall have nothing abstract or empty, and which shall carry ahead the condition of human life to something better."

this feeling so far that he considered geometry as degraded by being applied to any purpose of vulgar utility. Archytas, it seems, had framed machines of extraordinary power on mathematical principles. Plato remonstrated with his friend, and declared that this was to degrade a noble intellectual exercise into a low craft, fit only for carpenters and wheelwrights. The office of geometry, he said, was to discipline the mind, not to minister to the base wants of the body. His interference was successful; and from that time, according to Plutarch, the science of mechanics was considered as unworthy of the attention of a philosopher.

Archimedes in a later age imitated and surpassed Archytas. But even Archimedes was not free from the prevailing notion that geometry was degraded by being employed to produce anything useful. It was with difficulty that he was induced to stoop from speculation to practice. He was half ashamed of those inventions which were the wonder of hostile nations, and always spoke of them slightingly as mere amusements, as trifles in which a mathematician might be suffered to relax his mind after intense application to the higher parts of his science.

The opinion of Bacon on this subject was diametrically opposed to that of the ancient philosophers. He valued geometry chiefly, if not solely, on account of those uses, which to Plato appeared so base. And it is remarkable that the longer Bacon lived the stronger this feeling became. When in 1605 he wrote the two books on the *Advancement of Learning,* he dwelt on the advantages which mankind derived from mixed mathematics; but he at the same time admitted that the beneficial effect produced by mathematical study on the intellect, though a collateral advantage, was "no less worthy than that which was principal and intended." But it is evident that his views underwent a change. When, near twenty years later, he published the *De Augmentis,* which is the *Treatise on the Advancement of Learning,* greatly expanded and carefully corrected, he made important alterations in the part which related to mathematics. He condemned with severity the high pretensions of the mathematicians, "delicias et fastum mathematicorum." [22] Assuming the well-being of the human race to be the end of knowledge, he pronounced that mathematical science could claim no higher rank than that of an appendage or auxiliary to other sciences. Mathematical science, he says, is the handmaid of natural philosophy; she ought to demean herself as such; and he declares that he cannot conceive by what ill chance it has happened that she presumes to claim precedence over her mistress. He predicts — a prediction which would have made Plato shudder — that as more and more discoveries are made in physics, there will be more and more branches of mixed mathematics. Of that collateral advantage the value of which, twenty years before, he rated

22 "the arrogant dallying of the mathematicians."

so highly, he says not one word. This omission cannot have been the effect of mere inadvertence. His own treatise was before him. From that treatise he deliberately expunged whatever was favourable to the study of pure mathematics, and inserted several keen reflections on the ardent votaries of that study. This fact, in our opinion, admits of only one explanation. Bacon's love of those pursuits which directly tend to improve the condition of mankind, and his jealousy of all pursuits merely curious, had grown upon him, and had, it may be, become immoderate. He was afraid of using any expression which might have the effect of inducing any man of talents to employ in speculations, useful only to the mind of the speculator, a single hour which might be employed in extending the empire of man over matter. If Bacon erred here, we must acknowledge that we greatly prefer his error to the opposite error of Plato. We have no patience with a philosophy which, like those Roman matrons who swallowed abortives in order to preserve their shapes, takes pains to be barren for fear of being homely.

Let us pass to astronomy. This was one of the sciences which Plato exhorted his disciples to learn, but for reasons far removed from common habits of thinking. "Shall we set down astronomy," says Socrates, "among the subjects of study?" "I think so," answers his young friend Glaucon: "to know something about the seasons, the months, and the years is of use for military purposes, as well as for agriculture and navigation." "It amuses me," says Socrates, "to see how afraid you are, lest the common herd of people should accuse you of recommending useless studies." He then proceeds, in that pure and magnificent diction which, as Cicero said, Jupiter would use if Jupiter spoke Greek, to explain, that the use of astronomy is not to add to the vulgar comforts of life, but to assist in raising the mind to the contemplation of things which are to be perceived by the pure intellect alone. The knowledge of the actual motions of the heavenly bodies Socrates considers as of little value. The appearances which make the sky beautiful at night are, he tells us, like the figures which a geometrician draws on the sand, mere examples, mere helps to feeble minds. We must get beyond them; we must neglect them; we must attain to an astronomy which is as independent of the actual stars as geometrical truth is independent of the lines of an ill-drawn diagram. This is, we imagine, very nearly, if not exactly, the astronomy which Bacon compared to the ox of Prometheus, a sleek, well-shaped hide, stuffed with rubbish, goodly to look at, but containing nothing to eat. He complained that astronomy had, to its great injury, been separated from natural philosophy, of which it was one of the noblest provinces, and annexed to the domain of mathematics. The world stood in need, he said, of a very different astronomy, of a living astronomy, of an astronomy which should set forth the nature, the motion, and the influences of the heavenly bodies, as they really are.

On the greatest and most useful of all human inventions, the invention of alphabetical writing, Plato did not look with much complacency. He seems to have thought that the use of letters had operated on the human mind as the use of the go-cart in learning to walk, or of corks in learning to swim, is said to operate on the human body. It was a support which, in his opinion, soon became indispensable to those who used it, which made vigorous exertion first unnecessary and then impossible. The powers of the intellect would, he conceived, have been more fully developed without this delusive aid. Men would have been compelled to exercise the understanding and the memory, and, by deep and assiduous meditation, to make truth thoroughly their own. Now, on the contrary, much knowledge is traced on paper, but little is engraved in the soul. A man is certain that he can find information at a moment's notice when he wants it. He therefore suffers it to fade from his mind. Such a man cannot in strictness be said to know anything. He has the show without the reality of wisdom. These opinions Plato has put into the mouth of an ancient king of Egypt. But it is evident from the context that they were his own; and so they were understood to be by Quinctilian.[23] Indeed they are in perfect accordance with the whole Platonic system.

Bacon's views, as may easily be supposed, were widely different. The powers of the memory, he observes, without the help of writing, can do little towards the advancement of any useful science. He acknowledges that the memory may be disciplined to such a point as to be able to perform very extraordinary feats. But on such feats he sets little value. The habits of his mind, he tells us, are such that he is not disposed to rate highly any accomplishment, however rare, which is of no practical use to mankind. As to these prodigious achievements of the memory, he ranks them with the exhibitions of rope-dancers and tumblers. "These two performances," he says, "are much of the same sort. The one is an abuse of the powers of the body; the other is an abuse of the powers of the mind. Both may perhaps excite our wonder; but neither is entitled to our respect."

To Plato, the science of medicine appeared to be of very disputable advantages. He did not indeed object to quick cures for acute disorders, or for injuries produced by accidents. But the art which resists the slow sap of a chronic disease, which repairs frames enervated by lust, swollen by gluttony, or inflamed by wine, which encourages sensuality by mitigating the natural punishment of the sensualist, and prolongs existence when the intellect has ceased to retain its entire energy, had no share of his esteem. A life protracted by medical skill he pronounced to be a long death. The exercise of the art of medicine ought, he said, to be tolerated, so far as that art may serve to cure the occasional distempers of men whose constitutions are good. As

23 Or Quintilian.

to those who have bad constitutions, let them die; and the sooner the better. Such men are unfit for war, for magistracy, for the management of their domestic affairs, for severe study and speculation. If they engage in any vigorous mental exercise, they are troubled with giddiness and fulness of the head, all which they lay to the account of philosophy. The best thing that can happen to such wretches is to have done with life at once. He quotes mythical authority in support of this doctrine; and reminds his disciples that the practice of the sons of Æsculapius,[24] as described by Homer, extended only to the cure of external injuries.

Far different was the philosophy of Bacon. Of all the sciences, that which he seems to have regarded with the greatest interest was the science which, in Plato's opinion, would not be tolerated in a well-regulated community. To make men perfect was no part of Bacon's plan. His humble aim was to make imperfect men comfortable. The beneficence of his philosophy resembled the beneficence of the common Father, whose sun rises on the evil and the good, whose rain descends for the just and the unjust. In Plato's opinion man was made for philosophy; in Bacon's opinion philosophy was made for man; it was a means to an end; and that end was to increase the pleasures and to mitigate the pains of millions who are not and cannot be philosophers. That a valetudinarian who took pleasure in being wheeled along his terrace, who relished his boiled chicken and his weak wine and water, and who enjoyed a hearty laugh over the Queen of Navarre's tales,[25] should be treated as a *caput lupinum* [26] because he could not read the *Timœus* [27] without a headache, was a notion which the humane spirit of the English school of wisdom altogether rejected. Bacon would not have thought it beneath the dignity of a philosopher to contrive an improved garden chair for such a valetudinarian, to devise some way of rendering his medicines more palatable, to invent repasts which he might enjoy, and pillows on which he might sleep soundly; and this though there might not be the smallest hope that the mind of the poor invalid would ever rise to the contemplation of the ideal beautiful and the ideal good. As Plato had cited the religious legends of Greece to justify his contempt for the more recondite parts of the art of healing, Bacon vindicated the dignity of that art by appealing to the example of Christ, and reminded men that the great Physician of the soul did not disdain to be also the physician of the body.

When we pass from the science of medicine to that of legislation,

24 That is, Machaon and Podalirius, physicians in the Greek army in the war with Troy.
25 Marguerite, Queen of Navarre (1492–1549), author of *Heptameron,* a collection of love stories in imitation of Boccaccio.
26 Outlaw.
27 A Platonic dialogue.

we find the same difference between the systems of these two great men. Plato, at the commencement of the *Dialogue on Laws,* lays it down as a fundamental principle that the end of legislation is to make men virtuous. It is unnecessary to point out the extravagant conclusions to which such a proposition leads. Bacon well knew to how great an extent the happiness of every society must depend on the virtue of its members; and he also knew what legislators can and what they cannot do for the purpose of promoting virtue. The view which he has given of the end of legislation, and of the principal means for the attainment of that end, has always seemed to us eminently happy, even among the many happy passages of the same kind with which his works abound. "Finis et scopus quem leges intueri atque ad quem jussiones et sanctiones suas dirigere debent, non alius est quam ut cives feliciter degant. Id fiet si pietate et religione recte instituti, moribus honesti, armis adversus hostes externos tuti, legum auxilio adversus seditiones et privatas injurias muniti, imperio et magistratibus obsequentes, copiis et opibus locupletes et florentes fuerint." [28] The end is the well-being of the people. The means are the imparting of moral and religious education; the providing of everything necessary for defense against foreign enemies; the maintaining of internal order; the establishing of a judicial, financial, and commercial system, under which wealth may be rapidly accumulated and securely enjoyed.

Even with respect to the form in which laws ought to be drawn, there is a remarkable difference of opinion between the Greek and the Englishman. Plato thought a preamble essential; Bacon thought it mischievous. Each was consistent with himself. Plato, considering the moral improvement of the people as the end of legislation, justly inferred that a law which commanded and threatened, but which neither convinced the reason, nor touched the heart, must be a most imperfect law. He was not content with deterring from theft a man who still continued to be a thief at heart, with restraining a son who hated his mother from beating his mother. The only obedience on which he set much value was the obedience which an enlightened understanding yields to reason, and which a virtuous disposition yields to precepts of virtue. He really seems to have believed that, by prefixing to every law an eloquent and pathetic exhortation, he should, to a great extent, render penal enactments superfluous. Bacon entertained no such romantic hopes; and he well knew the practical inconveniences of the course which Plato recommended. "Neque nobis," says he, "prologi legum qui inepti olim habiti sunt, et leges introducunt disputantes non jubentes, utique placerent, si priscos mores ferre

28 "The end and scope that laws should have in view and to which they should direct their decrees and sanctions is no other than that the citizens should live happily. This will come to pass if the citizens be rightly trained in piety and religion, sound in morality, protected by arms against foreign enemies, obedient to the government and the magistrates, and rich and flourishing in good things and health."

possemus. . . . Quantum fieri potest prologi evitentur, et lex incipiat a jussione." [29]

Each of the great men whom we have compared intended to illustrate his system by a philosophical romance; and each left his romance imperfect. Had Plato lived to finish the *Critias*, a comparison between that noble fiction and the new *Atlantis* would probably have furnished us with still more striking instances than any which we have given. It is amusing to think with what horror he would have seen such an institution as Solomon's House [30] rising in his republic: with what vehemence he would have ordered the brew-houses, the perfume-houses, and the dispensatories to be pulled down; and with what inexorable rigour he would have driven beyond the frontier all the Fellows of the College, Merchants of Light and Depredators, Lamps and Pioneers.

To sum up the whole, we should say that the aim of the Platonic philosophy was to exalt man into a god. The aim of the Baconian philosophy was to provide man with what he requires while he continues to be man. The aim of the Platonic philosophy was to raise us far above vulgar wants. The aim of the Baconian philosophy was to supply our vulgar wants. The former aim was noble; but the latter was attainable. Plato drew a good bow; but like Acestes in Virgil, he aimed at the stars; and therefore, though there was no want of strength or skill, the shot was thrown away. His arrow was indeed followed by a track of dazzling radiance, but it struck nothing.

> "Volans liquidis in nubibus arsit arundo
> Signavitque viam flammis, tenuisque recessit
> Consumpta in ventos." [31]

Bacon fixed his eye on a mark which was placed on the earth, and within bow-shot, and hit it in the white. The philosophy of Plato began in words and ended in words, noble words indeed, words such as were to be expected from the finest of human intellects exercising boundless dominion over the finest of human languages. The philosophy of Bacon began in observations and ended in arts.

The boast of the ancient philosophers was that their doctrine formed the minds of men to a high degree of wisdom and virtue. This was indeed the only practical good which the most celebrated of those teachers even pretended to effect; and undoubtedly, if they had effected this, they would have deserved far higher praise than if they

---

29 "Nor do we approve at all of the preambles to the laws, which were formerly deemed impertinent, and which represent laws disputing and not commanding, if only we could support the ancient practices. But so far as may be, let preambles be avoided, and let the law commence with an enactment."

30 The utopian institution described by Bacon in his *New Atlantis*.

31 "The shaft, as it sped among the steaming clouds, took fire,
Blazing a trail in the sky, then burnt itself out and vanished
Into thin air." (C. Day Lewis' translation.)

had discovered the most salutary medicines or constructed the most powerful machines. But the truth is that, in those very matters in which alone they professed to do any good to mankind, in those very matters for the sake of which they neglected all the vulgar interests of mankind, they did nothing, or worse than nothing. They promised what was impracticable; they despised what was practicable; they filled the world with long words and long beards; and they left it as wicked and as ignorant as they found it.

An acre in Middlesex is better than a principality in Utopia. The smallest actual good is better than the most magnificent promises of impossibilities. The wise man of the Stoics would, no doubt, be a grander object than a steam-engine. But there are steam-engines. And the wise man of the Stoics is yet to be born. A philosophy which should enable a man to feel perfectly happy while in agonies of pain would be better than a philosophy which assuages pain. But we know that there are remedies which will assuage pain; and we know that the ancient sages liked the toothache just as little as their neighbours. A philosophy which should extinguish cupidity would be better than a philosophy which should devise laws for the security of property. But it is possible to make laws which shall, to a very great extent, secure property. And we do not understand how any motives which the ancient philosophy furnished could extinguish cupidity. We know indeed that the philosophers were no better than other men. From the testimony of friends as well as of foes, from the confessions of Epictetus and Seneca, as well as from the sneers of Lucian and the fierce invectives of Juvenal, it is plain that these teachers of virtue had all the vices of their neighbours, with the additional vice of hypocrisy. Some people may think the object of the Baconian philosophy a low object, but they cannot deny that, high or low, it has been attained. They cannot deny that every year makes an addition to what Bacon called "fruit." They cannot deny that mankind have made, and are making, great and constant progress in the road which he pointed out to them. Was there any such progressive movement among the ancient philosophers? After they had been declaiming eight hundred years, had they made the world better than when they began? Our belief is that, among the philosophers themselves, instead of a progressive improvement there was a progressive degeneracy. An abject superstition which Democritus or Anaxagoras would have rejected with scorn, added the last disgrace to the long dotage of the Stoic and Platonic schools. Those unsuccessful attempts to articulate which are so delightful and interesting in a child shock and disgust in an aged paralytic; and in the same way, those wild and mythological fictions which charm us, when we hear them lisped by Greek poetry in its infancy, excite a mixed sensation of pity and loathing, when mumbled by Greek philosophy in its old age. We know that guns, cutlery, spyglasses, clocks, are better in our time than they were in the time of our fathers, and were better in the time of our fathers than they were in the time of our grandfathers. We might, therefore, be inclined to think that, when a philosophy which boasted that its object was the elevation and purification of the mind, and which for this object neglected the sordid office of administering to the comforts of the body, had flourished in the highest honour during many hundreds of years, a vast moral amelioration must have taken place. Was it so? Look at the schools of this wisdom four centuries before the Christian era and four centuries after that era. Compare the men whom those schools formed at those two periods. Compare Plato and Libanius.[32] Compare Pericles and Julian. This philosophy confessed, nay boasted, that for every end but one it was useless. Had it attained that one end?

Suppose that Justinian, when he closed the schools of Athens, had called on the last few sages who still haunted the Portico, and lingered round the ancient planetrees, to show their title to public veneration: suppose that he had said: "A thousand years have elapsed since, in this famous city, Socrates posed Protagoras and Hippias;[33] during those thousand years a large proportion of the ablest men of every genera-tion has been employed in constant efforts to bring to perfection the philosophy which you teach, that philosophy has been munificently patronised by the powerful; its professors have been held in the highest esteem by the public; it has drawn to itself almost all the sap and vigour of the human intellect: and what has it effected? What profit-able truth has it taught us which we should not equally have known without it? What has it enabled us to do which we should not have been equally able to do without it?" Such questions, we suspect, would have puzzled Simplicius and Isidore.[34] Ask a follower of Bacon what the new philosophy, as it was called in the time of Charles the Second, has effected for mankind, and his answer is ready; "It has lengthened life; it has mitigated pain; it has extinguished diseases; it has increased the fertility of the soil; it has given new securities to the mariner; it has furnished new arms to the warrior; it has spanned great rivers and estuaries with bridges of form unknown to our fathers; it has guided the thunderbolt innocuously from heaven to earth; it has lighted up the night with the splendour of day; it has extended the range of the human vision; it has multiplied the power of the human muscles; it has accelerated motion; it has annihilated distance; it has facilitated intercourse, correspondence, all friendly offices, all despatch of business; it has enabled man to descend to the depths of the sea, to soar into the air, to penetrate securely into the noxious recesses of the earth, to traverse the land in cars which whirl along without horses, and the ocean in ships which run ten knots an hour against the wind. These are but a part of its fruits, and of its first fruits. For it is a

32 A Greek sophist of the 4th century A.D.
33 Characters in Plato's *Protagoras*.
34 Neo-Platonists of the 6th century A.D.

philosophy which never rests, which has never attained, which is
never perfect. Its law is progress. A point which yesterday was invisible is its goal to-day, and will be its starting-post to-morrow."

Great and various as the powers of Bacon were, he owes his wide
and durable fame chiefly to this, that all those powers received their
direction from common sense. His love of the vulgar useful, his strong
sympathy with the popular notions of good and evil, and the openness
with which he avowed that sympathy, are the secret of his influence.
There was in his system no cant, no illusion. He had no anointing for
broken bones, no fine theories *de finibus,* no arguments to persuade
men out of their senses. He knew that men, and philosophers as well
as other men, do actually love life, health, comfort, honour, security,
the society of friends, and do actually dislike death, sickness, pain,
poverty, disgrace, danger, separation from those to whom they are
attached. He knew that religion, though it often regulates and moder-
ates these feelings, seldom eradicates them; nor did he think it desirable for mankind that they should be eradicated. The plan of erad-
icating them by conceits like those of Seneca, or syllogisms like those
of Chrysippus,[35] was too preposterous to be for a moment entertained
by a mind like his. He did not understand what wisdom there could
be in changing names where it was impossible to change things; in
denying that blindness, hunger, the gout, the rack, were evils, and
calling them ἀποπροήγμενα;[36] in refusing to acknowledge that health,
safety, plenty, were good things, and dubbing them by the name of
ἀδιάφορα.[37] In his opinions on all these subjects, he was not a Stoic,
nor an Epicurean, nor an Academic, but what would have been called
by Stoics, Epicureans, and Academics a mere ἰδιώτης, a mere common
man. And it was precisely because he was so that his name makes
so great an era in the history of the world. It was because he dug deep
that he was able to pile high. It was because, in order to lay his foundations, he went down into those parts of human nature which lie low,
but which are not liable to change, that the fabric which he reared
has risen to so stately an elevation, and stands with such immovable
strength.

We have sometimes thought that an amusing fiction might be
written, in which a disciple of Epictetus and a disciple of Bacon
should be introduced as fellow-travellers. They come to a village
where the small-pox has just begun to rage, and find houses shut up,
intercourse suspended, the sick abandoned, mothers weeping in terror
over their children. The Stoic assures the dismayed population that
there is nothing bad in the small-pox, and that to a wise man disease,
deformity, death, the loss of friends, are not evils. The Baconian takes
out a lancet and begins to vaccinate. They find a body of miners in

35 Stoic philosopher of the 3rd century B.C.
36 "things relatively evil."
37 "things indifferent."

great dismay. An explosion of noisome vapours has just killed many of those who were at work; and the survivors are afraid to venture into the cavern. The Stoic assures them that such an accident is nothing but a mere ἀποπροήγμενον. The Baconian, who has no such fine word at his command, contents himself with devising a safety-lamp. They find a shipwrecked merchant wringing his hands on the shore. His vessel with an inestimable cargo has just gone down, and he is reduced in a moment from opulence to beggary. The Stoic exhorts him not to seek happiness in things which lie without himself, and repeats the whole chapter of Epictetus πρὸς τοὺς τὴν ἀπορίαν δεδοικότας.[38] The Baconian constructs a diving-bell, goes down in it, and returns with the most precious effects from the wreck. It would be easy to multiply illustrations of the difference between the philosophy of thorns and the philosophy of fruit, the philosophy of words and the philosophy of works. . . .

History of England

❴ Macaulay, for whom history was "a compound of poetry and philosophy," had planned to write "the history of England from the accession of King James the Second [1685] to a time which is within the memory of men still living [c.1830]." Macaulay's hopes to "relate the history of the people as well as the history of the government, to trace the progress of useful and ornamental arts, to describe the rise of religious sects and the changes of literary taste, to portray the manners of successive generations, and not to pass by with neglect even the revolutions which have taken place in dress, furniture, repasts, and public amusements," of course, made it impossible for him to cover a century and a half; and he has left a fragment covering some fifteen years. The third chapter of Volume I (England in 1685), the best remembered of the *History* and the source of the excerpt printed here, goes far to explain the one-time-common characterization of Victorianism as prosperous, optimistic, and complacent and has sometimes earned for Macaulay the title of "Mr. Victorian." ❵

. . . The coffee house must not be dismissed with a cursory mention. It might indeed at that time have been not improperly called a most important political institution. No Parliament had sat for years. The municipal council of the City had ceased to speak the sense of the citizens. Public meetings, harangues, resolutions, and the rest of the modern machinery of agitation had not yet come into fashion. Nothing resembling the modern newspaper existed. In such circumstances

38 "to those who fear poverty."

the coffee houses were the chief organs through which the public opinion of the metropolis vented itself.

The first of these establishments had been set up, in the time of the Commonwealth, by a Turkey merchant, who had acquired among the Mahometans a taste for their favourite beverage. The convenience of being able to make appointments in any part of the town, and of being able to pass evenings socially at a very small charge, was so great that the fashion spread fast. Every man of the upper or middle class went daily to his coffee house to learn the news and to discuss it. Every coffee house had one or more orators to whose eloquence the crowd listened with admiration, and who soon became, what the journalists of our time have been called, a fourth Estate of the realm. The Court had long seen with uneasiness the growth of this new power in the state. An attempt had been made, during Danby's administration,[1] to close the coffee houses. But men of all parties missed their usual places of resort so much that there was an universal outcry. The government did not venture, in opposition to a feeling so strong and general, to enforce a regulation of which the legality might well be questioned. Since that time ten years had elapsed, and during those years the number and influence of the coffee houses had been constantly increasing. Foreigners remarked that the coffee house was that which especially distinguished London from all other cities; that the coffee house was the Londoner's home, and that those who wished to find a gentleman commonly asked, not whether he lived in Fleet Street or Chancery Lane, but whether he frequented the Grecian or the Rainbow. Nobody was excluded from these places who laid down his penny at the bar. Yet every rank and profession, and every shade of religious and political opinion, had its own head-quarters. There were houses near Saint James's Park where fops congregated, their heads and shoulders covered with black or flaxen wigs, not less ample than those which are now worn by the Chancellor and by the Speaker of the House of Commons. The wig came from Paris; and so did the rest of the fine gentleman's ornaments, his embroidered coat, his fringed gloves, and the tassel which upheld his pantaloons. The conversation was in that dialect which, long after it had ceased to be spoken in fashionable circles, continued, in the mouth of Lord Foppington, to excite the mirth of theatres. The atmosphere was like that of a perfumer's shop. Tobacco in any other form than that of richly scented snuff was held in abomination. If any clown, ignorant of the usages of the house, called for a pipe, the sneers of the whole assembly and the short answers of the waiters soon convinced him that he had better go somewhere else. Nor, indeed, would he have had far to go. For, in general, the coffee rooms reeked with tobacco like a guardroom; and strangers sometimes expressed their surprise

[1] Sir Thomas Osborne, Earl of Danby (1631–1712), Lord Treasurer 1673–1678.

that so many people should leave their own firesides to sit in the midst of eternal fog and stench. Nowhere was the smoking more constant than at Will's. That celebrated house, situated between Covent Garden and Bow Street, was sacred to polite letters. There the talk was about poetical justice and the unities of place and time. There was a faction for Perrault and the moderns, a faction for Boileau and the ancients. One group debated whether Paradise Lost ought not to have been in rhyme. To another an envious poetaster demonstrated that Venice Preserved [2] ought to have been hooted from the stage. Under no roof was a greater variety of figures to be seen. There were Earls in stars and garters, clergymen in cassocks and bands, pert Templars, sheepish lads from the Universities, translators and indexmakers in ragged coats of frieze. The great press was to get near the chair where John Dryden sate. In winter that chair was always in the warmest nook by the fire; in summer it stood in the balcony. To bow to the Laureate, and to hear his opinion of Racine's last tragedy or of Bossu's [3] treatise on epic poetry, was thought a privilege. A pinch from his snuff-box was an honour sufficient to turn the head of a young enthusiast. There were coffee houses where the first medical men might be consulted. Doctor John Radcliffe, who, in the year 1685, rose to the largest practice in London, came daily, at the hour when the Exchange was full, from his house in Bow Street, then a fashionable part of the capital, to Garraway's, and was to be found, surrounded by surgeons and apothecaries, at a particular table. There were Puritan coffee houses where no oath was heard, and where lank-haired men discussed election and reprobation through their noses; Jew coffee houses where dark-eyed money changers from Venice and from Amsterdam greeted each other; and Popish coffee houses where, as good Protestants believed, Jesuits planned, over their cups, another great fire, and cast silver bullets to shoot the King.

These gregarious habits had no small share in forming the character of the Londoner of that age. He was, indeed, a different being from the rustic Englishman. There was not then the intercourse which now exists between the two classes. Only very great men were in the habit of dividing the year between town and country. Few esquires came to the capital thrice in their lives. Nor was it yet the practice of all citizens in easy circumstances to breathe the fresh air of the fields and woods during some weeks of every summer. A cockney, in a rural village, was stared at as much as if he had intruded into a Kraal of Hottentots. On the other hand, when the lord of a Lincolnshire or Shropshire manor appeared in Fleet Street, he was as easily distinguished from the resident population as a Turk or a Lascar. His dress, his gait, his accent, the manner in which he gazed at the shops, stumbled into the gutters, ran against the porters, and stood

---

[2] A popular tragedy by Thomas Otway.
[3] René Le Bossu (1631–1680), French critic, admired by Boileau.

under the waterspouts, marked him out as an excellent subject for
the operations of swindlers and banterers. Bullies jostled him into
the kennel. Hackney coachmen splashed him from head to foot.
Thieves explored with perfect security the huge pockets of his horse-
man's coat, while he stood entranced by the splendour of the Lord
Mayor's show. Moneydroppers,[4] sore from the cart's tail,[5] introduced
themselves to him, and appeared to him the most honest friendly
gentlemen that he had ever seen. Painted women, the refuse of Lewk-
ner Lane and Whetstone Park, passed themselves on him for count-
esses and maids of honour. If he asked his way to Saint James's, his
informants sent him to Mile End. If he went into a shop, he was instantly discerned to be a fit purchaser of everything that nobody else
would buy, of secondhand embroidery, copper rings, and watches
that would not go. If he rambled into any fashionable coffee house, he
became a mark for the insolent derision of fops and the grave waggery
of Templars. Enraged and mortified, he soon returned to his mansion,
and there, in the homage of his tenants and the conversation of his
boon companions, found consolation for the vexations and humiliations
which he had undergone. There he was once more a great man, and
saw nothing above himself except when at the assizes he took his seat
on the bench near the Judge, or when at the muster of the militia he
saluted the Lord Lieutenant.

The chief cause which made the fusion of the different elements
of society so imperfect was the extreme difficulty which our ancestors
found in passing from place to place. Of all inventions, the alphabet
and the printing press alone excepted, those inventions which abridge
distance have done most for the civilisation of our species. Every improvement of the means of locomotion benefits mankind morally and
intellectually as well as materially, and not only facilitates the inter-
change of the various productions of nature and art, but tends to
remove national and provincial antipathies, and to bind together all
the branches of the great human family. In the seventeenth century
the inhabitants of London were, for almost every practical purpose,
farther from Reading than they now are from Edinburgh, and farther
from Edinburgh than they now are from Vienna.

The subjects of Charles the Second were not, it is true, quite un-
acquainted with that principle which has, in our own time, produced
an unprecedented revolution in human affairs, which has enabled
navies to advance in face of wind and tide, and brigades of troops,
attended by all their baggage and artillery, to traverse kingdoms at
a pace equal to that of the fleetest race horse. The Marquess of Worcester had recently observed the expansive power of moisture rarefied
by heat. After many experiments he had succeeded in constructing a

4 Confidence men.
5 Public offenders were tied to the tail of a cart and whipped while being
pulled along.

rude steam engine, which he called a fire water work, and which he pronounced to be an admirable and most forcible instrument of propulsion. But the Marquess was suspected to be a madman, and known to be a Papist. His inventions, therefore, found no favourable reception. His fire water work might, perhaps, furnish matter for conversation at a meeting of the Royal Society, but was not applied to any practical purpose. There were no railways, except a few made of timber, on which coals were carried from the mouths of the Northumbrian pits to the banks of the Tyne. There was very little internal communication by water. A few attempts had been made to deepen and embank the natural streams, but with slender success. Hardly a single navigable canal had been even projected. The English of that day were in the habit of talking with mingled admiration and despair of the immense trench by which Lewis the Fourteenth had made a junction between the Atlantic and the Mediterranean. They little thought that their country would, in the course of a few generations, be intersected, at the cost of private adventurers, by artificial rivers making up more than four times the length of the Thames, the Severn, and the Trent together.

It was by the highways that both travellers and goods generally passed from place to place; and those highways appear to have been far worse than might have been expected from the degree of wealth and civilisation which the nation had even then attained. On the best lines of communication the ruts were deep, the descents precipitous, and the way often such as it was hardly possible to distinguish, in the dusk, from the unenclosed heath and fen which lay on both sides. Ralph Thoresby, the antiquary, was in danger of losing his way on the great North road, between Barnby Moor and Tuxford, and actually lost his way between Doncaster and York. Pepys and his wife, travelling in their own coach, lost their way between Newbury and Reading. In the course of the same tour they lost their way near Salisbury, and were in danger of having to pass the night on the plain. It was only in fine weather that the whole breadth of the road was available for wheeled vehicles. Often the mud lay deep on the right and the left; and only a narrow track of firm ground rose above the quagmire. At such times obstructions and quarrels were frequent, and the path was sometimes blocked up during a long time by carriers, neither of whom would break the way. It happened, almost every day, that coaches stuck fast, until a team of cattle could be procured from some neighbouring farm, to tug them out of the slough. But in bad seasons the traveller had to encounter inconveniences still more serious. Thoresby, who was in the habit of travelling between Leeds and the capital, has recorded, in his Diary, such a series of perils and disasters as might suffice for a journey to the Frozen Ocean or to the Desert of Sahara. On one occasion he learned that the floods were out between Ware and London, that passengers had to swim for their lives, and that a higgler [6] had perished in the attempt to cross. In consequence of these tidings he turned out of the high road, and was conducted across some meadows, where it was necessary for him to ride to the saddle skirts in water. In the course of another journey he narrowly escaped being swept away by an inundation of the Trent. He was afterwards detained at Stamford four days, on account of the state of the roads, and then ventured to proceed only because fourteen members of the House of Commons, who were going up in a body to Parliament with guides and numerous attendants, took him into their company. On the roads of Derbyshire, travellers were in constant fear for their necks, and were frequently compelled to alight and lead their beasts. The great route through Wales to Holyhead was in such a state that, in 1685, a viceroy, going to Ireland, was five hours in travelling fourteen miles, from Saint Asaph to Conway. Between Conway and Beaumaris he was forced to walk great part of the way; and his lady was carried in a litter. His coach was, with much difficulty, and by the help of many hands, brought after him entire. In general, carriages were taken to pieces at Conway, and borne, on the shoulders of stout Welsh peasants, to the Menai Straits. In some parts of Kent and Sussex, none but the strongest horses could, in winter, get through the bog, in which, at every step, they sank deep. The markets were often inaccessible during several months. It is said that the fruits of the earth were sometimes suffered to rot in one place, while in another place, distant only a few miles, the supply fell far short of the demand. The wheeled carriages were, in this district, generally pulled by oxen. When Prince George of Denmark visited the stately mansion of Petworth in wet weather, he was six hours in going nine miles; and it was necessary that a body of sturdy hinds should be on each side of his coach, in order to prop it. Of the carriages which conveyed his retinue several were upset and injured. A letter from one of the party has been preserved, in which the unfortunate courtier complains that, during fourteen hours, he never once alighted, except when his coach was overturned or stuck fast in the mud.

One chief cause of the badness of the roads seems to have been the defective state of the law. Every parish was bound to repair the highways which passed through it. The peasantry were forced to give their gratuitous labour six days in the year. If this was not sufficient, hired labour was employed, and the expense was met by a parochial rate. That a route connecting two great towns, which have a large and thriving trade with each other, should be maintained at the cost of the rural population scattered between them is obviously unjust; and this injustice was peculiarly glaring in the case of the great North road, which traversed very poor and thinly inhabited districts, and joined very rich and populous districts. Indeed it was not in the power

[6] A peddler.

of the parishes of Huntingdonshire to mend a highway worn by the constant traffic between the West Riding of Yorkshire and London. Soon after the Restoration this grievance attracted the notice of Parliament; and an act, the first of our many turnpike acts, was passed, imposing a small toll on travellers and goods, for the purpose of keeping some parts of this important line of communication in good repair. This innovation, however, excited many murmurs; and the other great avenues to the capital were long left under the old system. A change was at length effected, but not without much difficulty. For unjust and absurd taxation to which men are accustomed is often borne far more willingly than the most reasonable impost which is new. It was not till many toll bars had been violently pulled down, till the troops had in many districts been forced to act against the people, and till much blood had been shed, that a good system was introduced. By slow degrees reason triumphed over prejudice; and our island is now crossed in every direction by near thirty thousand miles of turnpike road.

On the best highways heavy articles were, in the time of Charles the Second, generally conveyed from place to place by stage waggons. In the straw of these vehicles nestled a crowd of passengers, who could not afford to travel by coach or on horseback, and who were prevented by infirmity, or by the weight of their luggage, from going on foot. The expense of transmitting heavy goods in this way was enormous. From London to Birmingham the charge was seven pounds a ton; from London to Exeter twelve pounds a ton. This was about fifteen pence a ton for every mile, more by a third than was afterwards charged on turnpike roads, and fifteen times what is now demanded by railway companies. The cost of conveyance amounted to a prohibitory tax on many useful articles. Coal in particular was never seen except in the districts where it was produced, or in the districts to which it could be carried by sea, and was indeed always known in the south of England by the name of sea coal.

On byroads, and generally throughout the country north of York and west of Exeter, goods were carried by long trains of packhorses. These strong and patient beasts, the breed of which is now extinct, were attended by a class of men who seem to have borne much resemblance to the Spanish muleteers. A traveller of humble condition often found it convenient to perform a journey mounted on a pack-saddle between two baskets, under the care of these hardy guides. The expense of this mode of conveyance was small. But the caravan moved at a foot's pace; and in winter the cold was often insupportable.

The rich commonly travelled in their own carriages, with at least four horses. Cotton, the facetious poet, attempted to go from London to the Peak with a single pair, but found at Saint Albans that the journey would be insupportably tedious, and altered his plan. A coach and six is in our time never seen, except as part of some pageant.

The frequent mention therefore of such equipages in old books is likely to mislead us. We attribute to magnificence what was really the effect of a very disagreeable necessity. People, in the time of Charles the Second, travelled with six horses, because with a smaller number there was great danger of sticking fast in the mire. Nor were even six horses always sufficient. Vanbrugh, in the succeeding generation, described with great humour the way in which a country gentleman newly chosen a member of Parliament, went up to London. On that occasion all the exertions of six beasts, two of which had been taken from the plough, could not save the family coach from being embedded in a quagmire.

Public carriages had recently been much improved. During the years which immediately followed the Restoration, a diligence ran between London and Oxford in two days. The passengers slept at Beaconsfield. At length, in the spring of 1669, a great and daring innovation was attempted. It was announced that a vehicle, described as the Flying Coach, would perform the whole journey between sunrise and sunset. This spirited undertaking was solemnly considered and sanctioned by the Heads of the University, and appears to have excited the same sort of interest which is excited in our own time by the opening of a new railway. The Vicechancellor, by a notice affixed in all public places, prescribed the hour and place of departure. The success of the experiment was complete. At six in the morning the carriage began to move from before the ancient front of All Souls College; and at seven in the evening the adventurous gentlemen who had run the first risk were safely deposited at their inn in London. The emulation of the sister University was moved; and soon a diligence was set up which in one day carried passengers from Cambridge to the capital. At the close of the reign of Charles the Second, flying carriages ran thrice a week from London to the chief towns. But no stage coach, indeed no stage waggon, appears to have proceeded further north than York, or further west than Exeter. The ordinary day's journey of a flying coach was about fifty miles in the summer; but in winter, when the ways were bad and the nights long, little more than thirty. The Chester coach, the York coach, and the Exeter coach generally reached London in four days during the fine season, but at Christmas not till the sixth day. The passengers, six in number, were all seated in the carriage. For accidents were so frequent that it would have been most perilous to mount the roof. The ordinary fare was about twopence halfpenny a mile in summer, and somewhat more in winter.

This mode of travelling, which by Englishmen of the present day would be regarded as insufferably slow, seemed to our ancestors wonderfully and indeed alarmingly rapid. In a work published a few months before the death of Charles the Second, the flying coaches are extolled as far superior to any similar vehicles ever known in the world. Their velocity is the subject of special commendation, and is triumphantly contrasted with the sluggish pace of the continental posts. But with boasts like these were mingled the sound of complaint and invective. The interests of large classes had been unfavourably affected by the establishment of the new diligences; and, as usual, many persons were, from mere stupidity and obstinacy, disposed to clamour against the innovation, simply because it was an innovation. It was vehemently argued that this mode of conveyance would be fatal to the breed of horses and to the noble art of horsemanship; that the Thames, which had long been an important nursery of seamen, would cease to be the chief thoroughfare from London up to Windsor and down to Gravesend; that saddlers and spurriers would be ruined by hundreds; that numerous inns, at which mounted travellers had been in the habit of stopping, would be deserted, and would no longer pay any rent; that the new carriages were too hot in summer and too cold in winter; that the passengers were grievously annoyed by invalids and crying children; that the coach sometimes reached the inn so late that it was impossible to get supper, and sometimes started so early that it was impossible to get breakfast. On these grounds it was gravely recommended that no public coach should be permitted to have more than four horses, to start oftener than once a week, or to go more than thirty miles a day. It was hoped that, if this regulation were adopted, all except the sick and the lame would return to the old mode of travelling. Petitions embodying such opinions as these were presented to the King in council from several companies of the City of London, from several provincial towns, and from the justices of several counties. We smile at these things. It is not impossible that our descendants, when they read the history of the opposition offered by cupidity and prejudice to the improvements of the nineteenth century, may smile in their turn.

In spite of the attractions of the flying coaches, it was still usual for men who enjoyed health and vigour, and who were not encumbered by much baggage, to perform long journeys on horseback. If the traveller wished to move expeditiously he rode post. French saddle horses and guides were to be procured at convenient distances along all the great lines of road. The charge was threepence a mile for each horse, and fourpence a stage for the guide. In this manner, when the ways were good, it was possible to travel, for a considerable time, as rapidly as by any conveyance known in England, till vehicles were propelled by steam. There were as yet no post chaises; nor could those who rode in their own coaches ordinarily procure a change of horses. The King, however, and the great officers of state were able to command relays. Thus Charles commonly went in one day from Whitehall to Newmarket, a distance of about fifty-five miles through a level country; and this was thought by his subjects a proof of great activity. Evelyn performed the same journey in company with the

Lord Treasurer Clifford. The coach was drawn by six horses, which were changed at Bishop Stortford and again at Chesterford. The travellers reached Newmarket at night. Such a mode of conveyance seems to have been considered as a rare luxury confined to princes and ministers.

Whatever might be the way in which a journey was performed, the travellers, unless they were numerous and well armed, ran considerable risk of being stopped and plundered. The mounted highwayman, a marauder known to our generation only from books, was to be found on every main road. The waste tracts which lay on the great routes near London were especially haunted by plunderers of this class. Hounslow Heath, on the great Western Road, and Finchley Common, on the great Northern Road, were perhaps the most celebrated of these spots. The Cambridge scholars trembled when they approached Epping Forest, even in broad daylight. Seamen who had just been paid off at Chatham were often compelled to deliver their purses on Gadshill, celebrated near a hundred years earlier by the greatest of poets as the scene of the depredations of Falstaff. The public authorities seem to have been often at a loss how to deal with the plunderers. At one time it was announced in the Gazette, that several persons, who were strongly suspected of being highwaymen, but against whom there was not sufficient evidence, would be paraded at Newgate in riding dresses: their horses would also be shown; and all gentlemen who had been robbed were invited to inspect this singular exhibition. On another occasion a pardon was publicly offered to a robber if he would give up some rough diamonds, of immense value, which he had taken when he stopped the Harwich mail. A short time after appeared another proclamation, warning the innkeepers that the eye of the government was upon them. Their criminal connivance, it was affirmed, enabled banditti to infest the roads with impunity. That these suspicions were not without foundation, is proved by the dying speeches of some penitent robbers of that age, who appear to have received from the innkeepers services much resembling those which Farquhar's Boniface rendered to Gibbet.[7]

It was necessary to the success and even to the safety of the highwayman that he should be a bold and skilful rider, and that his manners and appearance should be such as suited the master of a fine horse. He therefore held an aristocratical position in the community of thieves, appeared at fashionable coffee houses and gaming houses, and betted with men of quality on the race ground. Sometimes, indeed, he was a man of good family and education. A romantic interest therefore attached, and perhaps still attaches, to the names of freebooters of this class. The vulgar eagerly drank in tales of their ferocity and audacity, of their occasional acts of generosity and good nature, of their amours, of their miraculous escapes, of their desperate strug-

7 Allusion to Farquhar's *The Beaux' Stratagem.*

gles, and of their manly bearing at the bar and in the cart. Thus it was related of William Nevison, the great robber of Yorkshire, that he levied a quarterly tribute on all the northern drovers, and, in return, not only spared them himself, but protected them against all other thieves; that he demanded purses in the most courteous manner; that he gave largely to the poor what he had taken from the rich; that his life was once spared by the royal clemency, but that he again tempted his fate, and at length died, in 1685, on the gallows of York. It was related how Claude Duval, the French page of the Duke of Richmond, took to the road, became captain of a formidable gang, and had the honour to be named first in a royal proclamation against notorious offenders; how at the head of his troop he stopped a lady's coach, in which there was a booty of four hundred pounds; how he took only one hundred, and suffered the fair owner to ransom the rest by dancing a coranto with him on the heath; how his vivacious gallantry stole away the hearts of all women; how his dexterity at sword and pistol made him a terror to all men; how, at length, in the year 1670, he was seized when overcome by wine; how dames of high rank visited him in prison, and with tears interceded for his life; how the King would have granted a pardon, but for the interference of Judge Morton, the terror of highwaymen, who threatened to resign his office unless the law were carried into full effect; and how, after the execution, the corpse lay in state with all the pomp of scutcheons, wax lights, black hangings and mutes, till the same cruel Judge, who had intercepted the mercy of the crown, sent officers to disturb the obsequies. In these anecdotes there is doubtless a large mixture of fable; but they are not on that account unworthy of being recorded; for it is both an authentic and an important fact that such tales, whether false or true, were heard by our ancestors with eagerness and faith.

All the various dangers by which the traveller was beset were greatly increased by darkness. He was therefore commonly desirous of having the shelter of a roof during the night; and such shelter it was not difficult to obtain. From a very early period the inns of England had been renowned. Our first great poet had described the excellent accommodation which they afforded to the pilgrims of the fourteenth century. Nine and twenty persons, with their horses, found room in the wide chambers and stables of the Tabard in Southwark. The food was of the best, and the wines such as drew the company on to drink largely. Two hundred years later, under the reign of Elizabeth, William Harrison gave a lively description of the plenty and comfort of the great hostelries. The Continent of Europe, he said, could show nothing like them. There were some in which two or three hundred people, with their horses, could without difficulty be lodged and fed. The bedding, the tapestry, above all, the abundance of clean and fine linen was matter of wonder. Valuable plate was often set on the tables. Nay, there were signs which had cost thirty or forty pounds.

In the seventeenth century England abounded with excellent inns of every rank. The traveller sometimes, in a small village, lighted on a public house such as Walton has described, where the brick floor was swept clean, where the walls were stuck round with ballads, where the sheets smelt of lavender, and where a blazing fire, a cup of good ale, and a dish of trouts fresh from the neighbouring brook, were to be procured at small charge. At the larger houses of entertainment were to be found beds hung with silk, choice cookery, and claret equal to the best which was drunk in London. The innkeepers too, it was said, were not like other innkeepers. On the Continent the landlord was the tyrant of those who crossed the threshold. In England he was a servant. Never was an Englishman more at home than when he took his ease in his inn. Even men of fortune, who might in their own mansions have enjoyed every luxury, were often in the habit of passing their evenings in the parlour of some neighbouring house of public entertainment. They seem to have thought that comfort and freedom could in no other place be enjoyed in equal perfection. This feeling continued during many generations to be a national peculiarity. The liberty and jollity of inns long furnished matter to our novelists and dramatists. Johnson declared that a tavern chair was the throne of human felicity; and Shenstone gently complained that no private roof, however friendly, gave the wanderer so warm a welcome as that which was to be found at an inn.

Many conveniences, which were unknown at Hampton Court and Whitehall in the seventeenth century are in all modern hotels. Yet on the whole it is certain that the improvement of our houses of public entertainment has by no means kept pace with the improvement of our roads and of our conveyances. Nor is this strange; for it is evident that, all other circumstances being supposed equal, the inns will be best where the means of locomotion are worst. The quicker the rate of travelling, the less important is it that there should be numerous agreeable resting places for the traveller. A hundred and sixty years ago a person who came up to the capital from a remote county generally required, by the way, twelve or fifteen meals, and lodging for five or six nights. If he were a great man, he expected the meals and lodging to be comfortable, and even luxurious. At present we fly from York or Exeter to London by the light of a single winter's day. At present, therefore, a traveller seldom interrupts his journey merely for the sake of rest and refreshment. The consequence is that hundreds of excellent inns have fallen into utter decay. In a short time no good houses of that description will be found, except at places where strangers are likely to be detained by business or pleasure.

The mode in which correspondence was carried on between distant places may excite the scorn of the present generation; yet it was such as might have moved the admiration and envy of the polished nations of antiquity, or of the contemporaries of Raleigh and Cecil. A rude and imperfect establishment of posts for the conveyance of letters had been set up by Charles the First, and had been swept away by the civil war. Under the Commonwealth the design was resumed. At the Restoration the proceeds of the Post Office, after all expenses had been paid, were settled on the Duke of York. On most lines of road the mails went out and came in only on the alternate days. In Cornwall, in the fens of Lincolnshire, and among the hills and lakes of Cumberland, letters were received only once a week. During a royal progress a daily post was despatched from the capital to the place where the court sojourned. There was also daily communication between London and the Downs; and the same privilege was sometimes extended to Tunbridge Wells and Bath at the seasons when those places were crowded by the great. The bags were carried on horseback day and night at the rate of about five miles an hour.

The revenue of this establishment was not derived solely from the charge for the transmission of letters. The Post Office alone was entitled to furnish post horses; and, from the care with which this monopoly was guarded, we may infer that it was found profitable. If, indeed, a traveller had waited half an hour without being supplied, he might hire a horse wherever he could.

To facilitate correspondence between one part of London and another was not originally one of the objects of the Post Office. But, in the reign of Charles the Second, an enterprising citizen of London, William Dockwray, set up, at great expense, a penny post, which delivered letters and parcels six or eight times a day in the busy and crowded streets near the Exchange, and four times a day in the outskirts of the capital. This improvement was, as usual, strenuously resisted. The porters complained that their interests were attacked, and tore down the placards in which the scheme was announced to the public. The excitement caused by Godfrey's death, and by the discovery of Coleman's papers, was then at the height. A cry was therefore raised that the penny post was a Popish contrivance. The great Doctor Oates,[8] it was affirmed, had hinted a suspicion that the Jesuits were at the bottom of the scheme, and that the bags, if examined, would be found full of treason. The utility of the enterprise was, however, so great and obvious that all opposition proved fruitless. As soon as it became clear that the speculation would be lucrative, the Duke of York complained of it as an infraction of his monopoly; and the courts of law decided in his favour.

The revenue of the Post Office was from the first constantly increasing. In the year of the Restoration a committee of the House of Commons, after strict enquiry, had estimated the net receipt at about twenty thousand pounds. At the close of the reign of Charles the

8 Titus Oates was the fabricator of the "popish plot"; Sir Edmund Godfrey was the Justice of the Peace who received his first depositions; and Edward Coleman was executed as a conspirator who aided English Catholics.

Second, the net receipt was little short of fifty thousand pounds; and
this was then thought a stupendous sum. The gross receipt was about
seventy thousand pounds. The charge for conveying a single letter
was twopence for eighty miles, and threepence for a longer distance.
The postage increased in proportion to the weight of the packet. At
present a single letter is carried to the extremity of Scotland or of Ireland for a penny; and the monopoly of post horses has long ceased
to exist. Yet the gross annual receipts of the department amount to
more than eighteen hundred thousand pounds, and the net receipts
to more than seven hundred thousand pounds. It is, therefore, scarcely
possible to doubt that the number of letters now conveyed by mail is
seventy times the number which was so conveyed at the time of the
accession of James the Second.

No part of the load which the old mails carried out was more important than the newsletters. In 1685 nothing like the London daily
paper of our time existed, or could exist. Neither the necessary capital
nor the necessary skill was to be found. Freedom too was wanting, a
want as fatal as that of either capital or skill. The press was not indeed at that moment under a general censorship. The licensing act,
which had been passed soon after the Restoration, had expired in 1679.
Any person might therefore print, at his own risk, a history, a sermon,
or a poem, without the previous approbation of any officer; but the
Judges were unanimously of opinion that this liberty did not extend
to Gazettes, and that, by the common law of England, no man, not
authorised by the crown, had a right to publish political news. While
the Whig party was still formidable, the government thought it expedient occasionally to connive at the violation of this rule. During
the great battle of the Exclusion Bill,[9] many newspapers were suffered to appear, the Protestant Intelligence, the Current Intelligence,
the Domestic Intelligence, the True News, the London Mercury. None
of these was published oftener than twice a week. None exceeded in
size a single small leaf. The quantity of matter which one of them
contained in a year was not more than is often found in two numbers
of the Times. After the defeat of the Whigs it was no longer necessary
for the King to be sparing in the use of that which all his Judges had
pronounced to be his undoubted prerogative. At the close of his reign
no newspaper was suffered to appear without his allowance: and his allowance was given exclusively to the London Gazette. The London
Gazette came out only on Mondays and Thursdays. The contents generally were a royal proclamation, two or three Tory addresses, notices
of two or three promotions, an account of a skirmish between the imperial troops and the Janissaries on the Danube, a description of a highwayman, an announcement of a grand cockfight between two persons
of honour, and an advertisement offering a reward for a strayed dog.

9 A bill whereby James II would have been excluded from the throne as a
Papist.

The whole made up two pages of moderate size. Whatever was communicated respecting matters of the highest moment was communicated in the most meagre and formal style. Sometimes, indeed, when the government was disposed to gratify the public curiosity respecting an important transaction, a broadside was put forth giving fuller details than could be found in the Gazette: but neither the Gazette nor any supplementary broadside printed by authority ever contained any intelligence which it did not suit the purposes of the Court to publish. The most important parliamentary debates, the most important state trials, recorded in our history, were passed over in profound silence. In the capital the coffee houses supplied in some measure the place of a journal. Thither the Londoners flocked, as the Athenians of old flocked to the market place, to hear whether there was any news. There men might learn how brutally a Whig had been treated the day before in Westminster Hall, what horrible accounts the letters from Edinburgh gave of the torturing of Covenanters, how grossly the Navy Board had cheated the crown in the victualling of the fleet, and what grave charges the Lord Privy Seal had brought against the Treasury in the matter of the hearth money.[10]

But the people who lived at a distance from the great theatre of political contention could be kept regularly informed of what was passing there only by means of newsletters. To prepare such letters became a calling in London, as it now is among the natives of India. The newswriter rambled from coffee room to coffee room, collecting reports, squeezed himself into the Sessions House at the Old Bailey if there was an interesting trial, nay, perhaps obtained admission to the gallery of Whitehall, and noticed how the King and Duke looked. In this way he gathered materials for weekly epistles destined to enlighten some county town or some bench of rustic magistrates. Such were the sources from which the inhabitants of the largest provincial cities, and the great body of the gentry and clergy, learned almost all that they knew of the history of their own time. We must suppose that at Cambridge there were as many persons curious to know what was passing in the world as at almost any place in the kingdom, out of London. Yet at Cambridge, during a great part of the reign of Charles the Second, the Doctors of Laws and the Masters of Arts had no regular supply of news except through the London Gazette. At length the services of one of the collectors of intelligence in the capital were employed. That was a memorable day on which the first newsletter from London was laid on the table of the only coffee room in Cambridge. At the seat of a man of fortune in the country the newsletter was impatiently expected. Within a week after it had arrived it had been thumbed by twenty families. It furnished the neighbouring squires with matter for talk over their October, and the neighbouring

10 A tax of two shillings laid on each hearth in houses paying the church and poor rates.

rectors with topics for sharp sermons against Whiggery or Popery.
Many of these curious journals might doubtless still be detected by
a diligent search in the archives of old families. Some are to be
found in our public libraries; and one series, which is not the least
valuable part of the literary treasures collected by Sir James Mackin-
tosh, will be occasionally quoted in the course of this work.

It is scarcely necessary to say that there were then no provincial
newspapers. Indeed, except in the capital and at the two Universities,
there was scarcely a printer in the kingdom. The only press in England north of Trent appears to have been at York.

It was not only by means of the London Gazette that the government
undertook to furnish political instruction to the people. That journal
contained a scanty supply of news without comment. Another journal, published under the patronage of the court, consisted of comment
without news. This paper, called the Observator, was edited by an old
Tory pamphleteer named Roger Lestrange. Lestrange was by no
means deficient in readiness and shrewdness; and his diction, though
coarse, and disfigured by a mean and flippant jargon which then passed
for wit in the green room and the tavern, was not without keenness
and vigour. But his nature, at once ferocious and ignoble, showed
itself in every line that he penned. When the first Observators appeared there was some excuse for his acrimony. For the Whigs were
then powerful; and he had to contend against numerous adversaries,
whose unscrupulous violence might seem to justify unsparing retalia-
tion. But in 1685 all opposition had been crushed. A generous spirit
would have disdained to insult a party which could not reply, and
to aggravate the misery of prisoners, of exiles, of bereaved families:
but from the malice of Lestrange the grave was no hiding place, and
the house of mourning no sanctuary. In the last month of the reign
of Charles the Second, William Jenkyn, an aged dissenting pastor of
great note, who had been cruelly persecuted for no crime but that
of worshipping God according to the fashion generally followed
throughout Protestant Europe, died of hardships and privations in
Newgate. The outbreak of popular sympathy could not be repressed.
The corpse was followed to the grave by a train of a hundred and
fifty coaches. Even courtiers looked sad. Even the unthinking King
showed some signs of concern. Lestrange alone set up a howl of savage
exultation, laughed at the weak compassion of the Trimmers,[11] proclaimed that the blasphemous old imposter had met with a most
righteous punishment, and vowed to wage war, not only to the death,
but after death, with all the mock saints and martyrs. Such was the
spirit of the paper which was at this time the oracle of the Tory party,
and especially of the parochial clergy.

Literature which could be carried by the post bag then formed the
greater part of the intellectual nutriment ruminated by the country

11 Middle-of-the-roaders politically.

divines and the country justices. The difficulty and expense of conveying large packets from place to place was so great, that an extensive work was longer in making its way from Paternoster Row to Devonshire or Lancashire than it now is in reaching Kentucky. How scantily a rural parsonage was then furnished, even with books the most necessary to a theologian, has already been remarked. The houses of the gentry were not more plentifully supplied. Few knights of the shire had libraries so good as may now perpetually be found in a servants' hall, or in the back parlour of a small shopkeeper. An esquire passed among his neighbours for a great scholar, if Hudibras and Baker's Chronicle, Tarlton's Jests and the Seven Champions of Christendom,[12] lay in his hall window among the fishing rods and fowling pieces. No circulating library, no book society, then existed even in the capital: but in the capital those students who could not afford to purchase largely had a resource. The shops of the great booksellers, near Saint Paul's Churchyard, were crowded every day and all day long with readers; and a known customer was often permitted to carry a volume home. In the country there was no such accommodation; and every man was under the necessity of buying whatever he wished to read.

As to the lady of the manor and her daughters, their literary stores generally consisted of a prayer book and a receipt book. But in truth they lost little by living in rural seclusion. For, even in the highest ranks, and in those situations which afforded the greatest facilities for mental improvement, the English women of that generation were decidedly worse educated than they have been at any other time since the revival of learning. At an earlier period they had studied the masterpieces of ancient genius. In the present day they seldom bestow much attention on the dead languages; but they are familiar with the tongue of Pascal and Molière, with the tongue of Dante and Tasso, with the tongue of Goethe and Schiller; nor is there any purer or more graceful English than that which accomplished women now speak and write. But, during the latter part of the seventeenth century, the culture of the female mind seems to have been almost entirely neglected. If a damsel had the least smattering of literature she was regarded as a prodigy. Ladies highly born, highly bred, and naturally quick witted, were unable to write a line in their mother tongue without solecisms and faults of spelling such as a charity girl would now be ashamed to commit.

The explanation may easily be found. Extravagant licentiousness, the natural effect of extravagant austerity, was now the mode; and licentiousness had produced its ordinary effect, the moral and intel-

12 Hudibras: a verse satire by Samuel Butler; Baker's Chronicle: a chronicle of the kings of England from the Roman period by Sir Richard Baker; Tarlton's Jests: a collection of fictitious jests concerning Richard Tarlton, comic actor; Seven Champions of Christendom: a romance concerning St. George and other national champions by Richard Johnson.

lectual degradation of women. To their personal beauty, it was the
fashion to pay rude and impudent homage. But the admiration and
des.re which they inspired were seldom mingled with respect, with
affection, or with any chivalrous sentiment. The qualities which
fit them to be companions, advisers, confidential friends, rather re-
pelled than attracted the libertines of Whitehall. In that court a maid
of honour, who dressed in such a manner as to do full justice to a
white bosom, who ogled sigrificantly, who danced voluptuously, who
excelled in pert repartee, who was not ashamed to romp with Lords
of the Bedchamber and Captains of the Guards, to sing sly verses with
sly expression, or to put on a page's dress for a frolic, was more likely
to be followed and admired, more likely to be honoured with royal
attentions, more likely to win a rich and noble husband than Jane
Grey or Lucy Hutchinson [13] would have been. In such circumstances
the standard of female attainments was necessarily low; and it was
more dangerous to be above that standard than to be beneath it. Extreme ignorance and frivolity were thought less unbecoming in a
lady than the slightest tincture of pedantry. Of the too celebrated
women whose faces we still admire on the walls of Hampton Court,
few indeed were in the habit of reading anything more valuable than
acrostics, lampoons, and translations of the Clelia and the Grand
Cyrus. [14]

The literary acquirements, even of the accomplished gentlemen of
that generation, seem to have been somewhat less solid and profound
than at an earlier or a later period. Greek learning, at least, did not
flourish among us in the days of Charles the Second, as it had
flourished before the civil war, or as it again flourished long after
the Revolution. There were undoubtedly scholars to whom the whole
Greek literature, from Homer to Photius,[15] was familiar: but such
scholars were to be found almost exclusively among the clergy resident at the Universities, and even at the Universities were few, and
were not fully appreciated. At Cambridge it was not thought by
any means necessary that a divine should be able to read the Gospels in the original. Nor was the standard at Oxford higher. When,
in the reign of William the Third, Christ Church rose up as one
man to defend the genuineness of the Epistles of Phalaris,[16] that
great college, then considered as the first seat of philology in the
kingdom, could not muster such a stock of Attic learning as is now
possessed by several youths at every great public school. It may

13 Lady Jane Grey was a Greek scholar and humanist; Lucy Hutchinson was
the author of the *Life of Colonel Hutchinson* and of *Principles of the Christian
Religion*.
14 Long heroic romances by Madeleine de Scudéry, a popular French writer.
15 Photius was a 9th century scholar and collector of classical authors.
16 That is, 1689–1702, at which time a controversy involving such names as
Sir William Temple, Charles Boyle, and Richard Bentley was waged over certain spurious letters said to be by the tyrant Phalaris (6th century B.C.).

easily be supposed that a dead language, neglected at the Universities, was not much studied by men of the world. In a former age the poetry and eloquence of Greece had been the delight of Raleigh and Falkland. In a later age the poetry and eloquence of Greece were the delight of Pitt and Fox, of Windham and Grenville. But during the latter part of the seventeenth century there was in England scarcely one eminent statesman who could read with enjoyment a page of Sophocles or Plato.

Good Latin scholars were numerous. The language of Rome, indeed, had not altogether lost its imperial prerogatives, and was still, in many parts of Europe, almost indispensable to a traveller or a negotiator. To speak it well was therefore a much more common accomplishment than in our time; and neither Oxford nor Cambridge wanted poets who, on a great occasion, could lay at the foot of the throne happy imitations of the verses in which Virgil and Ovid had celebrated the greatness of Augustus.

Yet even the Latin was giving way to a younger rival. France united at that time almost every species of ascendancy. Her military glory was at the height. She had vanquished mighty coalitions. She had dictated treaties. She had subjugated great cities and provinces. She had forced the Castilian pride to yield her the precedence. She had summoned Italian princes to prostrate themselves at her footstool. Her authority was supreme in all matters of good breeding, from a duel to a minuet. She determined how a gentleman's coat must be cut, how long his peruke must be, whether his heels must be high or low, and whether the lace on his hat must be broad or narrow. In literature she gave law to the world. The fame of her great writers filled Europe. No other country could produce a tragic poet equal to Racine, a comic poet equal to Molière, a trifler so agreeable as La Fontaine, a rhetorician so skilful as Bossuet. The literary glory of Italy and of Spain had set; that of Germany had not yet dawned. The genius, therefore, of the eminent men who adorned Paris shone forth with a splendour which was set off to full advantage by contrast. France, indeed, had at that time an empire over mankind, such as even the Roman Republic never attained. For, when Rome was politically dominant, she was in arts and letters the humble pupil of Greece. France had, over the surrounding countries, at once the ascendancy which Rome had over Greece, and the ascendancy which Greece had over Rome. French was fast becoming the universal language, the language of fashionable society, the language of diplomacy. At several courts princes and nobles spoke it more accurately and politely than their mother tongue. In our island there was less of this servility than on the Continent. Neither our good nor our bad qualities were those of imitators. Yet even here homage was paid, awkwardly indeed and sullenly, to the literary supremacy of our neighbours. The melodious Tuscan, so familiar to

the gallants and ladies of the court of Elizabeth, sank into contempt.
A gentleman who quoted Horace or Terence was considered in good
company as a pompous pedant. But to garnish his conversation with
scraps of French was the best proof which he could give of his parts
and attainments. New canons of criticism, new models of style came
into fashion. The quaint ingenuity which had deformed the verses
of Donne, and had been a blemish on those of Cowley, disappeared
from our poetry. Our prose became less majestic, less artfully involved, less variously musical than that of an earlier age, but more
lucid, more easy, and better fitted for controversy and narrative.
In these changes it is impossible not to recognise the influence of
French precept and of French example. Great masters of our language, in their most dignified compositions, affected to use French
words, when English words, quite as expressive and sonorous, were
at hand: and from France was imported the tragedy in rhyme, an
exotic which, in our soil, drooped, and speedily died.

It would have been well if our writers had also copied the decorum
which their great French contemporaries, with few exceptions, preserved; for the profligacy of the English plays, satires, songs, and
novels of that age is a deep blot on our national fame. The evil may
easily be traced to its source. The wits and the Puritans had never
been on friendly terms. There was no sympathy between the two
classes. They looked on the whole system of human life from different points and in different lights. The earnest of each was the
jest of the other. The pleasures of each were the torments of the
other. To the stern precisian even the innocent sport of the fancy
seemed a crime. To light and festive natures the solemnity of the
zealous brethren furnished copious matter of ridicule. From the
Reformation to the civil war, almost every writer, gifted with a fine
sense of the ludicrous, had taken some opportunity of assailing the
straight-haired, snuffling, whining saints, who christened their children out of the Book of Nehemiah, who groaned in spirit at the
sight of Jack in the Green,[17] and who thought it impious to taste
plum porridge on Christmas day. At length a time came when the
laughers began to look grave in their turn. The rigid, ungainly
zealots, after having furnished much good sport during two generations, rose up in arms, conquered, ruled, and, grimly smiling, trod
down under their feet the whole crowd of mockers. The wounds
inflicted by gay and petulant malice were retaliated with the gloomy
and implacable malice peculiar to bigots who mistake their own
rancour for virtue. The theatres were closed. The players were
flogged. The press was put under the guardianship of austere licens-
ers. The Muses were banished from their own favourite haunts, Cambridge and Oxford. Cowley, Crashaw, and Cleveland were ejected

17 A character in the May-day games.

from their fellowships.[18] The young candidate for academical honours was no longer required to write Ovidian epistles or Virgilian pastorals, but was strictly interrogated by a synod of lowering Supralapsarians as to the day and hour when he experienced the new birth. Such a system was of course fruitful of hypocrites. Under sober clothing and under visages composed to the expression of austerity lay hid during several years the intense desire of license and of revenge. At length that desire was gratified. The Restoration emancipated thousands of minds from a yoke which had become insupportable. The old fight recommenced, but with an animosity altogether new. It was now not a sportive combat, but a war to the death. The Roundhead had no better quarter to expect from those whom he had persecuted than a cruel slavedriver can expect from insurgent slaves still bearing the marks of his collars and his scourges.

The war between wit and Puritanism soon became a war between wit and morality. The hostility excited by a grotesque caricature of virtue did not spare virtue herself. Whatever the canting Roundhead had regarded with reverence was insulted. Whatever he had proscribed was favoured. Because he had been scrupulous about trifles, all scruples were treated with derision. Because he had covered his failings with the mask of devotion, men were encouraged to obtrude with Cynic impudence all their most scandalous vices on the public eye. Because he had punished illicit love with barbarous severity, virgin purity and conjugal fidelity were made a jest. To that sanctimonious jargon which was his Shibboleth, was opposed another jargon not less absurd and much more odious. As he never opened his mouth except in scriptural phrase, the new breed of wits and fine gentlemen never opened their mouths without uttering ribaldry of which a porter would now be ashamed, and without calling on their Maker to curse them, sink them, confound them, blast them, and damn them.

It is not strange, therefore, that our polite literature, when it revived with the revival of the old civil and ecclesiastical polity, should have been profoundly immoral. A few eminent men, who belonged to an earlier and better age, were exempt from the general contagion. The verse of Waller still breathed the sentiments which had animated a more chivalrous generation. Cowley, distinguished as a loyalist and as a man of letters, raised his voice courageously against the immorality which disgraced both letters and loyalty. A mightier poet, tried at once by pain, danger, poverty, obloquy, and blindness, meditated, undisturbed by the obscene tumult which raged all around him, a song so sublime and so holy that it would not have misbecome the lips of those ethereal Virtues whom he saw, with that inner eye which no calamity could darken, flinging down on the jasper pavement their crowns of amaranth and gold. The vigorous and fertile genius of Butler, if it did not altogether escape the prevailing infection, took the disease in

[18] Poets sympathetic with the Royalist cause.

a mild form. But these were men whose minds had been trained in
a world which had passed away. They gave place in no long time to
a younger generation of wits; and of that generation, from Dryden
down to Durfey, the common characteristic was hardhearted, shame-
less, swaggering licentiousness, at once inelegant and inhuman. The
influence of these writers was doubtless noxious, yet less noxious than
it would have been had they been less depraved. The poison which
they administered was so strong that it was, in no long time, rejected
with nausea. None of them understood the dangerous art of associating
images of unlawful pleasure with all that is endearing and ennobling.
None of them was aware that a certain decorum is essential even to
voluptuousness, that drapery may be more alluring than exposure, and
that the imagination may be far more powerfully moved by delicate
hints which impel it to exert itself, than by gross descriptions which
it takes in passively.

The spirit of the Antipuritan reaction pervades almost the whole
polite literature of the reign of Charles the Second. But the very quintessence of that spirit will be found in the comic drama. The play-
houses, shut by the meddling fanatic in the day of his power, were
again crowded. To their old attractions new and more powerful attractions had been added. Scenery, dresses, and decorations, such as
would now be thought mean or absurd, but such as would have been
esteemed incredibly magnificent by those who, early in the seventeenth
century, sat on the filthy benches of the Hope, or under the thatched
roof of the Rose,[19] dazzled the eyes of the multitude. The fascination
of sex was called in to aid the fascination of art: and the young spectator saw, with emotions unknown to the contemporaries of Shakespeare
and Jonson, tender and sprightly heroines personated by lovely women.
From the day on which the theatres were reopened they became semi-
naries of vice; and the evil propagated itself. The profligacy of the
representations soon drove away sober people. The frivolous and dis-
solute who remained required every year stronger and stronger stimu-
lants. Thus the artists corrupted the spectators, and the spectators the
artists, till the turpitude of the drama became such as must astonish all
who are not aware that extreme relaxation is the natural effect of extreme restraint, and that an age of hypocrisy is, in the regular course
of things, followed by an age of impudence.

Nothing is more characteristic of the times than the care with which
the poets contrived to put all their loosest verses into the mouths of
women. The compositions in which the greatest license was taken were
the epilogues. They were almost always recited by favourite actresses;
and nothing charmed the depraved audience so much as to hear lines
grossly indecent repeated by a beautiful girl, who was supposed to
have not yet lost her innocence.

19 Theaters built in 1613 and 1592, respectively, the latter associated with
Shakespeare, the former with Ben Jonson.

Our theatre was indebted in that age for many plots and characters to Spain, to France, and to the old English masters: but whatever our dramatists touched they tainted. In their imitations the houses of Calderón's stately and high-spirited Castilian gentlemen became sties of vice, Shakespeare's Viola a procuress, Molière's Misanthrope a ravisher, Molière's Agnes an adulteress. Nothing could be so pure or so heroic but that it became foul and ignoble by transfusion through those foul and ignoble minds.

Such was the state of the drama; and the drama was the department of polite literature in which a poet had the best chance of obtaining a subsistence by his pen. The sale of books was so small that a man of the greatest name could hardly expect more than a pittance for the copyright of the best performance. There cannot be a stronger instance than the fate of Dryden's last production, the Fables. That volume was published when he was universally admitted to be the chief of living English poets. It contains about twelve thousand lines. The versification is admirable, the narratives and descriptions full of life. To this day Palamon and Arcite, Cymon and Iphigenia, Theodore and Honoria, are the delight both of critics and of schoolboys. The collection includes Alexander's Feast, the noblest ode in our language. For the copyright Dryden received two hundred and fifty pounds, less than in our days has sometimes been paid for two articles in a review. Nor does the bargain seem to have been a hard one. For the book went off slowly; and the second edition was not required till the author had been ten years in his grave. By writing for the theatre it was possible to earn a much larger sum with much less trouble. Southern made seven hundred pounds by one play. Otway was raised from beggary to temporary affluence by the success of his Don Carlos. Shadwell cleared a hundred and thirty pounds by a single representation of the Squire of Alsatia. The consequence was that every man who had to live by his wit wrote plays, whether he had any internal vocation to write plays or not. It was thus with Dryden. As a satirist he has rivalled Juvenal. As a didactic poet he perhaps might, with care and meditation, have rivalled Lucretius. Of lyric poets he is, if not the most sublime, the most brilliant and spirit-stirring. But nature, profuse to him of many rare gifts, had withheld from him the dramatic faculty. Nevertheless all the energies of his best years were wasted on dramatic composition. He had too much judgment not to be aware that in the power of exhibiting character by means of dialogue he was deficient. That deficiency he did his best to conceal, sometimes by surprising and amusing incidents, sometimes by stately declamation, sometimes by harmonious numbers, sometimes by ribaldry but too well suited to the taste of a profane and licentious pit. Yet he never obtained any theatrical success equal to that which rewarded the exertions of some men far inferior to him in general powers. He thought himself fortunate if he cleared a hundred guineas by a play; a scanty remuneration, yet apparently larger than he could have earned in any other way by the same quantity of labour.

The recompense which the wits of that age could obtain from the public was so small, that they were under the necessity of eking out their incomes by levying contributions on the great. Every rich and goodnatured lord was pestered by authors with a mediancy so importunate, and a flattery so abject, as may in our time seem incredible. The patron to whom a work was inscribed was expected to reward the writer with a purse of gold. The fee paid for the dedication of a book was often much larger than the sum which any publisher would give for the copyright. Books were therefore frequently printed merely that they might be dedicated. This traffic in praise produced the effect which might have been expected. Adulation pushed to the verge, sometimes of nonsense, and sometimes of impiety, was not thought to disgrace a poet. Independence, veracity, self-respect, were things not required by the world for him. In truth, he was in morals something between a pandar and a beggar.

To the other vices which degraded the literary character was added, towards the close of the reign of Charles the Second, the most savage intemperance of party spirit. The wits, as a class, had been impelled by their old hatred of Puritanism to take the side of the court, and had been found useful allies. Dryden, in particular, had done good service to the government. His Absalom and Achitophel, the greatest satire of modern times, had amazed the town, had made its way with unprecedented rapidity even into rural districts, and had, wherever it appeared, bitterly annoyed the Exclusionists, and raised the courage of the Tories. But we must not, in the admiration which we naturally feel for noble diction and versification, forget the great distinctions of good and evil. The spirit by which Dryden and several of his compeers were at this time animated against the Whigs deserves to be called fiendish. The servile Judges and Sheriffs of those evil days could not shed blood so fast as the poets cried out for it. Calls for more victims, hideous jests on hanging, bitter taunts on those who, having stood by the King in the hour of danger, now advised him to deal mercifully and generously by his vanquished enemies, were publicly recited on the stage, and, that nothing might be wanting to the guilt and the shame, were recited by women, who, having long been taught to discard all modesty, were now taught to discard all compassion.

It is a remarkable fact that, while the lighter literature of England was thus becoming a nuisance and a national disgrace, the English genius was effecting in science a revolution which will, to the end of time, be reckoned among the highest achievements of the human intellect. Bacon had sown the good seed in a sluggish soil and an ungenial season. He had not expected an early crop, and in his last testament had solemnly bequeathed his fame to the next age. During a whole generation his philosophy had, amidst tumults, wars, and proscriptions, been slowly ripening in a few well constituted minds. While factions were struggling for dominion over each other, a small body of sages had turned away with benevolent disdain from the conflict, and had devoted themselves to the nobler work of extending the dominion of man over matter. As soon as tranquillity was restored, these teachers easily found attentive audience. For the discipline through which the nation had passed had brought the public mind to a temper well fitted for the reception of the Verulamian [20] doctrine. The civil troubles had stimulated the faculties of the educated classes, and had called forth a restless activity and an insatiable curiosity, such as had not before been known among us. Yet the effect of those troubles was that schemes of political and religious reform were generally regarded with suspicion and contempt. During twenty years the chief employment of busy and ingenious men had been to frame constitutions with first magistrates, without first magistrates, with hereditary senates, with senates appointed by lot, with annual senates, with perpetual senates. In these plans nothing was omitted. All the detail, all the nomenclature, all the ceremonial of the imaginary government was fully set forth, Polemarchs and Phylarchs, Tribes and Galaxies, the Lord Archon and the Lord Strategus. Which ballot boxes were to be green and which red, which balls were to be of gold and which of silver, which magistrates were to wear hats and which black velvet caps with peaks, how the mace was to be carried and when the heralds were to uncover, these, and a hundred more such trifles, were gravely considered and arranged by men of no common capacity and learning. But the time for these visions had gone by; and, if any steadfast republican still continued to amuse himself with them, fear of public derision and of a criminal information generally induced him to keep his fancies to himself. It was now unpopular and unsafe to mutter a word against the fundamental laws of the monarchy: but daring and ingenious men might indemnify themselves by treating with disdain what had lately been considered as the fundamental laws of nature. The torrent which had been damned up in one channel rushed violently into another. The revolutionary spirit, ceasing to operate in politics, began to exert itself with unprecedented vigour and hardihood in every department of physics. The year 1660, the era of the restoration of the old constitution, is also the era from which dates the ascendancy of the new philosophy. In that year the Royal Society, destined to be a chief agent in a long series of glorious and salutary reforms, began to exist. In a few months experimental science became all the mode. The transfusion of blood, the ponderation of air, the fixation of mercury, succeeded to that place in the public mind which had been lately occupied by the controversies of the Rota.[21] Dreams of perfect forms of gov-

---

20 That is, Baconian.
21 A political club with republican ideas.

ernment made way for dreams of wings with which men were to fly
from the Tower to the Abbey, and of double-keeled ships which were
never to founder in the fiercest storm. All classes were hurried along
by the prevailing sentiment. Cavalier and Roundhead, Churchman and
Puritan, were for once allied. Divines, jurists, statesmen, nobles,
princes, swelled the triumph of the Baconian philosophy. Poets sang
with emulous fervour the approach of the golden age. Cowley, in lines
weighty with thought and resplendent with wit, urged the chosen seed
to take possession of the promised land flowing with milk and honey,
that land which their great deliverer and lawgiver had seen, as from
the summit of Pisgah, but had not been permitted to enter. Dryden,
with more zeal than knowledge, joined his voice to the general accla-
mation, and foretold things which neither he nor anybody else understood. The Royal Society, he predicted, would soon lead us to the
extreme verge of the globe, and there delight us with a better view
of the moon. Two able and aspiring prelates, Ward, Bishop of Salisbury, and Wilkins, Bishop of Chester, were conspicuous among the
leaders of the movement. Its history was eloquently written by a
younger divine, who was rising to high distinction in his profession,
Thomas Sprat, afterwards Bishop of Rochester. Both Chief Justice
Hale and Lord Keeper Guildford stole some hours from the business
of their courts to write on hydrostatics. Indeed it was under the immediate direction of Guildford that the first barometers ever exposed
to sale in London were constructed. Chemistry divided, for a time,
with wine and love, with the stage and the gaming table, with the
intrigues of a courtier and the intrigues of a demagogue, the attention
of the fickle Buckingham. Rupert has the credit of having invented
mezzotinto; and from him is named that curious bubble of glass which
has long amused children and puzzled philosophers. Charles himself
had a laboratory at Whitehall, and was far more active and attentive
there than at the council board. It was almost necessary to the character of a fine gentleman to have something to say about air-pumps and
telescopes; and even fine ladies, now and then, thought it becoming to
affect a taste for science, went in coaches and six to visit the Gresham
curiosities, and broke forth into cries of delight at finding that a mag-
net really attracted a needle, and that a microscope really made a fly
look as large as a sparrow.

In this, as in every great stir of the human mind, there was doubtless something which might well move a smile. It is the universal law
that whatever pursuit, whatever doctrine, becomes fashionable, shall
lose a portion of that dignity which it had possessed while it was
confined to a small but earnest minority, and was loved for its own
sake alone. It is true that the follies of some persons who, without
any real aptitude for science, professed a passion for it, furnished matter of contemptuous mirth to a few malignant satirists who belonged
to the preceding generation, and were not disposed to unlearn the lore

of their youth. But it is not less true that the great work of interpreting nature was performed by the English of that age as it had never before been performed in any age by any nation. The spirit of Francis Bacon was abroad, a spirit admirably compounded of audacity and sobriety. There was a strong persuasion that the whole world was full of secrets of high moment to the happiness of man, and that man had, by his Maker, been entrusted with the key which, rightly used, would give access to them. There was at the same time a conviction that in physics it was impossible to arrive at the knowledge of general laws except by the careful observation of particular facts. Deeply impressed with these great truths, the professors of the new philosophy applied themselves to their task, and, before a quarter of a century had expired, they had given ample earnest of what has since been achieved. Already a reform of agriculture had been commenced. New vegetables were cultivated. New implements of husbandry were employed. New manures were applied to the soil. Evelyn had, under the formal sanction of the Royal Society, given instruction to his countrymen in planting. Temple, in his intervals of leisure, had tried many experiments in horticulture, and had proved that many delicate fruits, the natives of more favoured climates, might, with the help of art, be grown on English ground. Medicine, which in France was still in abject bondage, and afforded an inexhaustible subject of just ridicule to Molière, had in England become an experimental and progressive science, and every day made some new advance, in defiance of Hippocrates and Galen. The attention of speculative men had been, for the first time, directed to the important subject of sanitary police. The great plague of 1665 induced them to consider with care the defective architecture, draining, and ventilation of the capital. The great fire of 1666 afforded an opportunity for effecting extensive improvements. The whole matter was diligently examined by the Royal Society; and to the suggestions of that body must be partly attributed the changes which, though far short of what the public welfare required, yet made a wide difference between the new and the old London, and probably put a final close to the ravages of pestilence in our country. At the same time one of the founders of the Society, Sir William Petty, created the science of political arithmetic, the humble but indispensable handmaid of political philosophy. No kingdom of nature was left unexplored. To that period belong the chemical discoveries of Boyle, and the earliest botanical researches of Sloane. It was then that Ray made a new classification of birds and fishes, and that the attention of Woodward was first drawn towards fossils and shells. One after another phantoms which had haunted the world through ages of darkness fled before the light. Astrology and alchemy became jests. Soon there was scarcely a county in which some of the Quorum did not smile contemptuously when an old woman was brought before them for riding on broomsticks or giving cattle the murrain.

But it was in those noblest and most arduous departments of knowledge in which induction and mathematical demonstration co-operate
for the discovery of truth, that the English genius won in that age the
most memorable triumphs. John Wallis placed the whole system of
statics on a new foundation. Edmund Halley investigated the prop·
erties of the atmosphere, the ebb and flow of the sea, the laws of
magnetism, and the course of the comets; nor did he shrink from toil,
peril, and exile in the cause of science. While he, on the rock of Saint
Helena, mapped the constellations of the southern hemisphere, our
national observatory was rising at Greenwich; and John Flamsteed, the
first Astronomer Royal, was commencing that long series of observations which is never mentioned without respect and gratitude in any
part of the globe. But the glory of these men, eminent as they were,
is cast into the shade by the transcendent lustre of one immortal name.
In Isaac Newton two kinds of intellectual power, which have little in
common, and which are not often found together in a very high degree
of vigour, but which nevertheless are equally necessary in the most
sublime departments of physics, were united as they have never been
united before or since. There may have been minds as happily constituted as his for the cultivation of pure mathematical science, there
may have been minds as happily constituted for the cultivation of
science purely experimental: but in no other mind have the demonstrative faculty and the inductive faculty coexisted in such supreme
excellence and perfect harmony. Perhaps in the days of Scotists and
Thomists even his intellect might have run to waste, as many intellects
ran to waste which were inferior only to his. Happily the spirit of the
age on which his lot was cast, gave the right direction to his mind;
and his mind reacted with tenfold force on the spirit of the age. In
the year 1685 his fame, though splendid, was only dawning; but his
genius was in the meridian. His great work, that work which effected
a revolution in the most important provinces of natural philosophy,
had been completed, but was not yet published, and was just about
to be submitted to the consideration of the Royal Society. . . .

Thomas Carlyle

THOMAS CARLYLE

CHRONOLOGY

1795   Born December 4 in Dumfriesshire, Scotland.

1809–1814   Attended Edinburgh University.

1814–1818   Served as a reluctant schoolteacher.

1818–1822   Years of acute physical and spiritual distress.

1824   Published a translation of Goethe's *Wilhelm Meister's Apprenticeship*.

1825   Published the *Life of Schiller* in book form.

1830–1831   Wrote *Sartor Resartus*.

1837   Published *The French Revolution,* in three volumes.

1839   Published *Chartism* and *Critical and Miscellaneous Essays* (on Burns, Goethe, Voltaire, and so forth).

1841   Published *Heroes and Hero-Worship*.

1843   Published *Past and Present*.

1845   Published *Oliver Cromwell's Letters and Speeches,* in two volumes.

1850   Published *Latter-Day Pamphlets*.

1851   Published the *Life of John Sterling*.

1858–1865   Published the *History of Friedrich II of Prussia,* in six volumes.

1865   Elected Lord Rector of Edinburgh University.

1874   Received the Prussian Order of Merit.

1875   Published *The Early Kings of Norway* and *Portraits of John Knox*.

1881   Died February 4.

Sartor Resartus

❨ *Sartor Resartus* ("The Tailor Re-tailored") is Carlyle's spiritual auto-biography and contains, explicit or implicit, all the basic teachings of his long life as historian, critic, and prophet. It was first published as a serial in *Fraser's Magazine* (November 1833 to August 1834), was seen through the American press by Emerson, and was published in England as a book in 1838. Here Carlyle wears a mask (he spoke of *Sartor* as a "Didactic Novel . . . . a kind of 'Satirical Extravaganza on Things in General' "), but he has admitted that the book "contains more of my opinions on Art, Politics, Religion, Heaven, Earth, and Air, than all the things I have yet written." The three chapters from Book II printed here describe an intense experience through which Carlyle himself passed. The chapter "Natural Supernaturalism" summarizes the central theme of the volume and posits the fundamental principle of Carlyle's philosophy of life. Teufelsdröckh and the "Editor" are both Carlyle. ❩

BOOK SECOND

CHAPTER VII

The Everlasting No

UNDER the strange nebulous envelopment, wherein our Professor has now shrouded himself, no doubt but his spiritual nature is nevertheless progressive, and growing: for how can the "Son of Time," in any case, stand still? We behold him, through those dim years, in a state of crisis, of transition: his mad Pilgrimings, and general solution into aimless Discontinuity, what is all this but a mad Fermentation; where-from, the fiercer it is, the clearer product will one day evolve itself.

Such transitions are ever full of pain: thus the Eagle when he moults is sickly; and, to attain his new beak, must harshly dash-off the old one upon rocks. What Stoicism soever our Wanderer, in his indi-vidual acts and motions, may affect, it is clear that there is a hot fever of anarchy and misery raging within; coruscations of which flash out: as, indeed, how could there be other? Have we not seen him dis-appointed, bemocked of Destiny, through long years? All that the young heart might desire and pray for has been denied; nay, as in the last worst instance, offered and then snatched away. Ever an "ex-cellent Passivity"; but of useful, reasonable Activity, essential to the former as Food to Hunger, nothing granted: till at length, in this wild Pilgrimage, he must forcibly seize for himself an Activity, though use-less, unreasonable. Alas, his cup of bitterness, which had been filling drop by drop, ever since that first "ruddy morning" in the Hinterschlag Gymnasium, was at the very lip; and then with that poison-drop, of the

Towngood-and-Blumine business, it runs over, and even hisses over in
a deluge of foam.

He himself says once, with more justice than originality: "Man is,
properly speaking, based upon Hope, he has no other possession but
Hope; this world of his is emphatically the Place of Hope." What,
then, was our Professor's possession? We see him, for the present, quite
shut-out from Hope; looking not into the golden orient, but vaguely all
round into a dim copper firmament, pregnant with earthquake and
tornado.

Alas, shut-out from Hope, in a deeper sense than we yet dream of!
For, as he wanders wearisomely through this world, he has now lost
all tidings of another and higher. Full of religion, or at least of re-
ligiosity, as our Friend has since exhibited himself, he hides not that,
in those days, he was wholly irreligious: "Doubt had darkened into
Unbelief," says he; "shade after shade goes grimly over your soul, till
you have the fixed, starless, Tartarean black." To such readers as have
reflected, what can be called reflecting, on man's life, and happily
discovered, in contradiction to much Profit-and-loss Philosophy, speculative and practical, that Soul is *not* synonymous with Stomach; who
understand, therefore, in our Friend's words, "that, for man's well-
being, Faith is properly the one thing needful; how, with it, Martyrs,
otherwise weak, can cheerfully endure the shame and the cross; and
without it, Worldlings puke-up their sick existence, by suicide, in the
midst of luxury": to such it will be clear that, for a pure moral nature,
the loss of his religious Belief was the loss of everything. Unhappy
young man! All wounds, the crush of long-continued Destitution, the
stab of false Friendship and of false Love, all wounds in thy so genial
heart, would have healed again, had not its life-warmth been withdrawn. Well might he exclaim, in his wild way: "Is there no God,
then; but at best an absentee God, sitting idle, ever since the first
Sabbath, at the outside of his Universe, and *seeing* it go? Has the
word Duty no meaning; is what we call Duty no divine Messenger
and Guide, but a false earthly Fantasm, made-up of Desire and Fear,
of emanations from the Gallows and from Dr. Graham's Celestial Bed? [1]
Happiness of an approving Conscience! Did not Paul of Tarsus, whom
admiring men have since named Saint, feel that *he* was 'the chief of
sinners'; and Nero of Rome, jocund in spirit (*wohlgemuth*), spend
much of his time in fiddling? Foolish Word-monger and Motive-
grinder, who in thy Logic-mill hast an earthly mechanism for the
God-like itself, and wouldst fain grind me out Virtue from the husks
of Pleasure, — I tell thee, Nay! To the unregenerate Prometheus
Vinctus [2] of a man, it is ever the bitterest aggravation of his wretchedness that he is conscious of Virtue, that he feels himself the victim not

[1] James Graham (1745–1794), a quack, professed to have invented a bed
to cure sterility in married people.
[2] "Prometheus Bound," title of a play by Æschylus.

of suffering only, but of injustice. What then? Is the heroic inspiration we name Virtue but some Passion; some bubble of the blood, bubbling in the direction others *profit* by? I know not: only this I know, If what thou namest Happiness be our true aim, then are we all astray. With Stupidity and sound Digestion man may front much. But what, in these dull unimaginative days, are the terrors of Conscience to the diseases of the Liver! Not on Morality, but on Cookery, let us build our stronghold: there brandishing our frying-pan, as censer, let us offer sweet incense to the Devil, and live at ease on the fat things *he* has provided for his Elect!"

Thus has the bewildered Wanderer to stand, as so many have done, shouting question after question into the Sibyl-cave of Destiny, and receive no Answer but an Echo. It is all a grim Desert, this once-fair world of his; wherein is heard only the howling of wild-beasts, or the shrieks of despairing, hate-filled men; and no Pillar of Cloud by day, and no Pillar of Fire by night, any longer guides the Pilgrim. To such length has the spirit of Inquiry carried him. "But what boots it (*was thut's*)?" cries he: "it is but the common lot in this era. Not having come to spiritual majority prior to the *Siècle de Louis Quinze*,[3] and not being born purely a Loghead (*Dummkopf*), thou hast no other outlook. The whole world is, like thee, sold to Unbelief; their old Temples of the Godhead, which for long have not been rainproof, crumble down; and men ask now: Where is the Godhead; our eyes never saw him?"

Pitiful enough were it, for all these wild utterances, to call our Diogenes wicked. Unprofitable servants as we all are, perhaps at no era of his life was he more decisively the Servant of Goodness, the Servant of God, than even now when doubting God's existence. "One circumstance I note," says he: "after all the nameless woe that Inquiry, which for me, what it is not always, was genuine Love of Truth, had wrought me, I nevertheless still loved Truth, and would bate no jot of my allegiance to her. 'Truth'! I cried, 'though the Heavens crush me for following her: no Falsehood! though a whole celestial Lubberland were the price of Apostasy.' In conduct it was the same. Had a divine Messenger from the clouds, or miraculous Handwriting on the wall, convincingly proclaimed to me *This thou shalt do*, with what passionate readiness, as I often thought, would I have done it, had it been leaping into the infernal Fire. Thus, in spite of all Motive-grinders, and Mechanical Profit-and-Loss Philosophies, with the sick ophthalmia and hallucination they had brought on, was the Infinite nature of Duty still dimly present to me: living without God in the world, of God's light I was not utterly bereft; if my as yet sealed eyes, with their unspeakable longing, could nowhere see Him, nevertheless in my heart He was present, and His heaven-written Law still stood legible and sacred there."

3 The name of the Age of Reason and of a book by Voltaire.

Meanwhile, under all these tribulations, and temporal and spiritual destitutions, what must the Wanderer, in his silent soul, have endured! "The painfullest feeling," writes he, "is that of your own Feebleness (*Unkraft*); ever, as the English Milton says, to be weak is the true misery. And yet of your Strength there is and can be no clear feeling, save by what you have prospered in, by what you have done. Between vague wavering Capability and fixed indubitable Performance, what a difference! A certain inarticulate Self-consciousness dwells dimly in us; which only our Works can render articulate and decisively discernible. Our works are the mirror wherein the spirit first sees its natural lineaments. Hence, too, the folly of that impossible Precept, *Know thyself;* till it be translated into this partially possible one, *Know what thou canst work-at.*

"But for me, so strangely unprosperous had I been, the net-result of my Workings amounted as yet simply to — Nothing. How then could I believe in my Strength, when there was as yet no mirror to see it in? Ever did this agitating, yet, as I now perceive, quite frivolous question, remain to me insoluble: Hast thou a certain Faculty, a certain Worth, such even as the most have not; or art thou the completest Dullard of these modern times? Alas! the fearful Unbelief is unbelief in yourself; and how could I believe? Had not my first, last Faith in myself, when even to me the Heavens seemed laid open, and I dared to love, been all-too cruelly belied? The speculative Mystery of Life grew ever more mysterious to me: neither in the practical Mystery had I made the slightest progress, but been everywhere buffeted, foiled, and contemptuously cast-out. A feeble unit in the middle of a threatening Infinitude, I seemed to have nothing given me but eyes, whereby to discern my own wretchedness. Invisible yet impenetrable walls, as of Enchantment, divided me from all living: was there, in the wide world, any true bosom I could press trustfully to mine? O Heaven, No, there was none! I kept a lock upon my lips: why should I speak much with that shifting variety of so-called Friends, in whose withered, vain and too-hungry souls Friendship was but an incredible tradition? In such cases, your resource is to talk little, and that little mostly from the Newspapers. Now when I look back, it was a strange isolation I then lived in. The men and women around me, even speaking with me, were but Figures; I had, practically, forgotten that they were alive, that they were not merely automatic. In midst of their crowded streets and assemblages, I walked solitary; and (except as it was my own heart, not another's, that I kept devouring) savage also, as the tiger in his jungle. Some comfort it would have been, could I, like a Faust, have fancied myself tempted and tormented of the Devil; for a Hell, as I imagine, without Life, though only diabolic Life, were more frightful: but in our age of Down-pulling and Disbelief, the very Devil has been pulled down, you cannot so much as believe in a Devil. To me the Universe was all void of Life, of Purpose, of Volition, even of Hostility:

it was one huge, dead, immeasurable Steam-engine, rolling on, in its dead indifference, to grind me limb from limb. O, the vast, gloomy, solitary Golgotha, and Mill of Death! Why was the Living banished thither companionless, conscious? Why, if there is no Devil; nay, unless the Devil is your God?"

A prey incessantly to such corrosions might not, moreover, as the worst aggravation to them, the iron constitution even of a Teufelsdröckh threaten to fail? We conjecture that he has known sickness; and, in spite of his locomotive habits, perhaps sickness of the chronic sort. Hear this, for example: "How beautiful to die of broken-heart, on Paper! Quite another thing in practice; every window of your Feeling, even of your Intellect, as it were, begrimed and mud-bespattered, so that no pure ray can enter; a whole Drugshop in your inwards; the fordone soul drowning slowly in quagmires of Disgust!"

Putting all which external and internal miseries together, may we not find in the following sentences, quite in our Professor's still vein, significance enough? "From Suicide a certain aftershine (*Nachschein*) of Christianity withheld me: perhaps also a certain indolence of character; for, was not that a remedy I had at any time within reach? Often, however, was there a question present to me: Should some one now, at the turning of that corner, blow thee suddenly out of Space, into the other World, or other No-World, by pistol-shot, — how were it? On which ground, too, I have often, in sea-storms and sieged cities and other death-scenes, exhibited an imperturbability, which passed, falsely enough, for courage."

"So had it lasted," concludes the Wanderer, "so had it lasted, as in bitter protracted Death-agony, through long years. The heart within me, unvisited by any heavenly dewdrop, was smouldering in sulphurous, slow-consuming fire. Almost since earliest memory I had shed no tear; or once only when I, murmuring half-audibly, recited Faust's Deathsong, that wild *Selig der den er im Siegesglanze findet* (Happy whom *he* finds in Battle's splendour), and thought that of this last Friend even I was not forsaken, that Destiny itself could not doom me not to die. Having no hope, neither had I any definite fear, were it of Man or of Devil: nay, I often felt as if it might be solacing, could the Arch-Devil himself, though in Tartarean terrors, but rise to me, that I might tell him a little of my mind. And yet, strangely enough, I lived in a continual, indefinite, pining fear; tremulous, pusillanimous, apprehensive of I knew not what: it seemed as if all things in the Heavens above and the Earth beneath would hurt me; as if the Heavens and the Earth were but boundless jaws of a devouring monster, wherein I, palpitating, waited to be devoured.

"Full of such humour, and perhaps the miserablest man in the whole French Capital or Suburbs, was I, one sultry Dogday, after much perambulation, toiling along the dirty little *Rue Saint-Thomas de l'Enfer*, among civic rubbish enough, in a close atmosphere, and over pavements hot as Nebuchadnezzar's Furnace, whereby doubtless my spirits were little cheered; when, all at once, there rose a Thought in me, and I asked myself: 'What *art* thou afraid of? Wherefore, like a coward, dost thou forever pip and whimper, and go cowering and trembling? Despicable biped! what is the sum-total of the worst that lies before thee? Death? Well, Death; and say the pangs of Tophet too, and all that the Devil and Man may, will or can do against thee! Hast thou not a heart; canst thou not suffer whatsoever it be; and, as a Child of Freedom, though outcast, trample Tophet itself under thy feet, while it consumes thee? Let it come, then; I will meet it and defy it!' And as I so thought, there rushed like a stream of fire over my whole soul; and I shook base Fear away from me forever. I was strong, of unknown strength; a spirit, almost a god. Ever from that time, the temper of my misery was changed: not Fear or whining Sorrow was it, but Indignation and grim fire-eyed Defiance.

"Thus had the EVERLASTING NO (*das ewige Nein*) pealed authoritatively through all the recesses of my Being, of my ME; and then was it that my whole ME stood up, in native God-created majesty, and with emphasis recorded its Protest. Such a Protest, the most important transaction in Life, may that same Indignation and Defiance, in a psychological point of view, be fitly called. The Everlasting No had said: 'Behold, thou art fatherless, outcast, and the Universe is mine (the Devil's)'; to which my whole Me now made answer: '*I* am not thine, but Free, and forever hate thee!'

"It is from this hour that I incline to date my Spiritual New-birth, or Baphometic Fire-baptism; perhaps I directly thereupon began to be a Man."

Chapter VIII

Centre of Indifference

Though, after this "Baphometic Fire-baptism" of his, our Wanderer signifies that his Unrest was but increased; as, indeed, "Indignation and Defiance," especially against things in general, are not the most peaceable inmates; yet can the Psychologist surmise that it was no longer a quite hopeless Unrest; that henceforth it had at least a fixed centre to revolve round. For the fire-baptised soul, long so scathed and thunder-riven, here feels its own Freedom, which feeling is its Baphometic Baptism: the citadel of its whole kingdom it has thus gained by assault, and will keep inexpugnable; outwards from which the remaining dominions, not indeed without hard battling, will doubtless by degrees be conquered and pacificated. Under another figure, we might say, if in that great moment, in the *Rue Saint-Thomas de l'Enfer*, the old inward Satanic School was not yet thrown out of doors, it received peremptory judicial notice to quit; — whereby, for the rest, its howl-chantings, Ernulphus-cursings, and rebellious gnashings of teeth, might, in the meanwhile, become only the more tumultuous, and difficult to keep secret.

Accordingly, if we scrutinise these Pilgrimings well, there is perhaps discernible henceforth a certain incipient method in their madness. Not wholly as a Spectre does Teufelsdröckh now storm through the world; at worst a spectre-fighting Man, nay who will one day be a Spectre-queller. If pilgriming restlessly to so many "Saints' Wells," and ever without quenching of his thirst, he nevertheless finds little secular wells, whereby from time to time some alleviation is ministered. In a word, he is now, if not ceasing, yet intermitting to "eat his own heart"; and clutches round him outwardly on the NOT-ME for wholesomer food. Does not the following glimpse exhibit him in a much more natural state?

"Towns also and Cities, especially the ancient, I failed not to look upon with interest. How beautiful to see thereby, as through a long vista, into the remote Time, to have, as it were, an actual section of almost the earliest Past brought safe into the Present, and set before your eyes! There, in that old City, was a live ember of Culinary Fire put down, say only two thousand years ago; and there, burning more or less triumphantly, with such fuel as the region yielded, it has burnt, and still burns, and thou thyself seest the very smoke thereof. Ah! and the far more mysterious live ember of Vital Fire was then also put down there; and still miraculously burns and spreads; and the smoke and ashes thereof (in these Judgment-Halls and Churchyards), and its bellow-engines (in these Churches), thou still seest; and its flame, looking out from every kind countenance, and every hateful one, still warms thee or scorches thee.

"Of Man's Activity and Attainment the chief results are aeriform, mystic, and preserved in Tradition only: such are his Forms of Government, with the Authority they rest on; his Customs, or Fashions both of Cloth-habits and of Soul-habits; much more his collective stock of Handicrafts, the whole Faculty he has acquired of manipulating Nature: all these things, as indispensable and priceless as they are, cannot in any way be fixed under lock and key, but must flit, spirit-like, on impalpable vehicles, from Father to Son; if you demand sight of them, they are nowhere to be met with. Visible Ploughmen and Hammermen there have been, ever from Cain and Tubalcain downwards: but where does your accumulated Agricultural, Metallurgic, and other Manufacturing SKILL lie warehoused? It transmits itself on the atmospheric air, on the sun's rays (by Hearing and by Vision); it is a thing aeriform, impalpable, of quite spiritual sort. In like manner, ask me not, Where are the Laws; where is the GOVERNMENT? In vain wilt thou go to Schönbrunn, to Downing Street, to the Palais Bourbon: thou findest nothing there but brick or stone houses, and some bundles of Papers tied with tape. Where, then, is that same cunningly-devised almighty GOVERNMENT of theirs to be laid hands on? Every-where, yet nowhere: seen only in its works, this too is a thing aeriform, invisible; or if you will, mystic and miraculous. So spiritual (*geistig*) is our whole daily Life: all that we do springs out of Mystery, Spirit, invisible Force; only like a little Cloud-image, or Armida's Palace, air-built, does the Actual body itself forth from the great mystic Deep.

"Visible and tangible products of the Past, again, I reckon-up to the extent of three: Cities, with their Cabinets and Arsenals; then tilled Fields, to either or to both of which divisions Roads with their Bridges may belong; and thirdly — Books. In which third truly, the last in-vented, lies a worth far surpassing that of the two others. Wondrous indeed is the virtue of a true Book. Not like a dead city of stones, yearly crumbling, yearly needing repair; more like a tilled field, but then a spiritual field: like a spiritual tree, let me rather say, it stands from year to year, and from age to age (we have Books that already number some hundred-and-fifty human ages); and yearly comes its new produce of leaves (Commentaries, Deductions, Phil-osophical, Political Systems; or were it only Sermons, Pamphlets, Jour-nalistic Essays), every one of which is talismanic and thaumaturgic, for it can persuade men. O thou who art able to write a Book, which once in the two centuries or oftener there is a man gifted to do, envy not him whom they name City-builder, and inexpressibly pity him whom they name Conqueror or City-burner! Thou too art a Con-queror and Victor: but of the true sort, namely over the Devil: thou too hast built what will outlast all marble and metal, and be a wonder-bringing City of the Mind, a Temple and Seminary and Prophetic Mount, whereto all kindreds of the Earth will pilgrim. — Fool! why journeyest thou wearisomely, in thy antiquarian fervour, to gaze on the stone pyramids of Geeza, or the clay ones of Sacchara? These stand there, as I can tell thee, idle and inert, looking over the Desert, foolishly enough, for the last three-thousand years: but canst thou not open thy Hebrew BIBLE, then, or even Luther's Version thereof?"

No less satisfactory is his sudden appearance not in Battle, yet on some Battlefield; which, we soon gather, must be that of Wagram;[1] so that here, for once, is a certain approximation to distinctness of date. Omitting much, let us impart what follows:

"Horrible enough! A whole Marchfeld [2] strewed with shell-splin-ters, cannon-shot, ruined tumbrils, and dead men and horses; strag-glers still remaining not so much as buried. And those red mould heaps: ay, there lie the Shells of Men, out of which all the Life and Virtue has been blown; and now are they swept together, and crammed-down out of sight, like blown Egg-shells! — Did Nature, when she bade

---

1 A village near Vienna where Napoleon defeated the Austrians.
2 A field near Vienna, where the Austrians defeated the Bohemians in the 13th century and where Napoleon defeated the Austrians in the 19th.

the Donau bring down his mould-cargoes from the Carinthian and Carpathian Heights, and spread them out here into the softest, richest level, — intend thee, O Marchfeld, for a corn-bearing Nursery, whereon her children might be nursed; or for a Cockpit, wherein they might the more commodiously be throttled and tattered? Were thy three broad Highways, meeting here from the ends of Europe, made for Ammunition-wagons, then? Were thy Wagrams and Stillfrieds but so many ready-built Casemates, wherein the house of Hapsburg might batter with artillery, and with artillery be battered? König Ottokar, amid yonder hillocks, dies under Rodolf's truncheon; here Kaiser Franz falls a-swoon under Napoleon's: within which five centuries, to omit the others, how has thy breast, fair Plain, been defaced and defiled! The greensward is torn-up and trampled-down; man's fond care of it, his fruit-trees, hedge-rows, and pleasant dwellings, blown-away with gunpowder; and the kind seedfield lies a desolate, hideous Place of Sculls. — Nevertheless, Nature is at work; neither shall these Powder-Devilkins with their utmost devilry gainsay her: but all that gore and carnage will be shrouded-in, absorbed into manure; and next year the Marchfeld will be green, nay greener. Thrifty unwearied Nature, ever out of our great waste educing some little profit of thy own, — how dost thou, from the very carcass of the Killer, bring Life for the Living!

"What, speaking in quite unofficial language, is the net-purport and upshot of war? To my own knowledge, for example, there dwell and toil, in the British village of Dumdrudge, usually some five-hundred souls. From these, by certain 'Natural Enemies' of the French, there are successively selected, during the French war, say thirty able-bodied men: Dumdrudge, at her own expense, has suckled and nursed them: she has, not without difficulty and sorrow, fed them up to manhood, and even trained them to crafts, so that one can weave, another build, another hammer, and the weakest can stand under thirty stone avoirdupois. Nevertheless, amid much weeping and swearing, they are selected; all dressed in red; and shipped away, at the public charges, some two-thousand miles, or say only to the south of Spain; and fed there till wanted. And now to that same spot, in the south of Spain, are thirty similar French artisans, from a French Dumdrudge, in like manner wending: till at length, after infinite effort, the two parties come into actual juxtaposition; and Thirty stands fronting Thirty, each with a gun in his hand. Straightway the word "Fire!" is given: and they blow the souls out of one another; and in place of sixty brisk useful craftsmen, the world has sixty dead carcasses, which it must bury, and anew shed tears for. Had these men any quarrel? Busy as the Devil is, not the smallest! They lived far enough apart; were the entirest strangers; nay, in so wide a Universe, there was even, unconsciously, by Commerce, some mutual helpfulness between them. How then? Simpleton! their Governors had fallen-out; and, instead of shooting one another, had the cunning to make these poor blockheads shoot. — Alas, so is it in Deutschland, and hitherto in all other lands; still as of old, 'what devilry soever Kings do, the Greeks must pay the piper!' — In that fiction of the English Smollet, it is true, the final Cessation of War is perhaps prophetically shadowed forth; where the two Natural Enemies, in person, take each a Tobacco-pipe, filled with Brimstone; light the same, and smoke in one another's faces, till the weaker gives in: but from such predicted Peace-Era, what blood-filled trenches, and contentious centuries, may still divide us!"

Thus can the Professor, at least in lucid intervals, look away from his own sorrows, over the many-coloured world, and pertinently enough note what is passing there. We may remark, indeed, that for the matter of spiritual culture, if for nothing else, perhaps few periods of his life were richer than this. Internally, there is the most momentous instructive Course of Practical Philosophy, with Experiments, going on; towards the right comprehension of which his Peripatetic habits, favourable to Meditation, might help him rather than hinder. Externally, again, as he wanders to and fro, there are, if for the longing heart little substance, yet for the seeing eye sights enough: in these so boundless Travels of his, granting that the Satanic School was even partially kept down, what an incredible knowledge of our Planet, and its Inhabitants and their Works, that is to say, of all knowable things, might not Teufelsdröckh acquire!

"I have read in most Public Libraries," says he, "including those of Constantinople and Samarcand: in most Colleges, except the Chinese Mandarin ones, I have studied, or seen that there was no studying. Unknown Languages have I oftenest gathered from their natural repertory, the Air, by my organ of Hearing; Statistics, Geographics, Topographics came, through the Eye, almost of their own accord. The ways of Man, how he seeks food, and warmth, and protection for himself, in most regions, are ocularly known to me. Like the great Hadrian I meted-out much of the terraqueous Globe with a pair of Compasses that belonged to myself only.

"Of great Scenes why speak? Three summer days, I lingered reflecting, and even composing (dichtete), by the Pine-chasms of Vaucluse;[3] and in that clear Lakelet moistened my bread. I have sat under the Palm-trees of Tadmor;[4] smoked a pipe among the ruins of Babylon. The great Wall of China I have seen; and can testify that it is of gray brick, coped and covered with granite, and shows only second-rate masonry. — Great Events, also, have not I witnessed? Kings sweated-down (ausgemergelt) into Berlin-and-Milan Customhouse-Officers; the World well won, and the World well lost; oftener than once a hundred-thousand individuals shot (by each other) in one day. All kindreds and peoples and nations dashed together, and

[3] The home of Petrarch in south-east France.
[4] Palmyra.

shifted and shovelled into heaps, that they might ferment there, and in time unite. The birthpangs of Democracy, wherewith convulsed Europe was groaning in cries that reached Heaven, could not escape me.

"For great Men I have ever had the warmest predilection; and can perhaps boast that few such in this era have wholly escaped me. Great Men are the inspired (speaking and acting) Texts of that divine BOOK OF REVELATIONS, whereof a Chapter is completed from epoch to epoch, and by some named HISTORY; to which inspired Texts your numerous talented men, and your innumerable untalented men, are the better or worse exegetic Commentaries, and wagonload of too-stupid, heretical or orthodox, weekly Sermons. For my study the inspired Texts themselves! Thus did not I, in very early days, having disguised me as tavern-waiter, stand behind the field-chairs, under that shady Tree at Treisnitz [5] by the Jena Highway; waiting upon the great Schiller and greater Goethe; and hearing what I have not forgotten. For —— "

—— But at this point the Editor recalls his principle of caution, some time ago laid down, and must suppress much. Let not the sacredness of Laurelled, still more, of Crowned Heads, be tampered with. Should we, at a future day, find circumstances altered, and the time come for Publication, then may these glimpses into the privacy of the Illustrious be conceded; which for the present were little better than treacherous, perhaps traitorous Eavesdroppings. Of Lord Byron, therefore, of Pope Pius, Emperor Tarakwang,[6] and the "White Waterroses" (Chinese Carbonari) with their mysteries, no notice here! Of Napoleon himself we shall only, glancing from afar, remark that Teufelsdröckh's relation to him seems to have been of very varied character. At first we find our poor Professor on the point of being shot as a spy; then taken into private conversation, even pinched on the ear, yet presented with no money; at last indignantly dismissed, almost thrown out of doors, as an "Ideologist." "He himself," says the Professor, "was among the completest Ideologists, at least Ideopraxists: in the Idea (*in der Idee*) he lived, moved and fought. The man was a Divine Missionary, though unconscious of it; and preached, through the cannon's throat, that great doctrine, *La carrière ouverte aux talens* (The Tools to him that can handle them), which is our ultimate Political Evangel, wherein alone can liberty lie. Madly enough he preached, it is true, as Enthusiasts and first Missionaries are wont, with imperfect utterance, amid much frothy rant; yet as articulately perhaps as the case admitted. Or call him, if you will, an American Backwoodsman, who had to fell unpenetrated forests, and battle with innumerable wolves, and did not entirely forbear strong liquor, rioting, and even theft; whom, notwithstanding, the peaceful Sower will follow, and, as he cuts the boundless harvest, bless."

5 Rendezvous of Goethe and Schiller near Jena, Germany.
6 Tao Kuang, reigning emperor of China.

More legitimate and decisively authentic is Teufelsdröckh's appearance and emergence (we know not well whence) in the solitude of the North Cape, on that June Midnight. He has "a light-blue Spanish cloak" hanging round him, as his "most commodious, principal, indeed sole upper garment"; and stands there, on the World-promontory, looking over the infinite Brine, like a little blue Belfry (as we figure), now motionless indeed, yet ready, if stirred, to ring quaintest changes.

"Silence as of death," writes he; "for Midnight, even in the Arctic latitudes, has its character: nothing but the granite cliffs ruddy-tinged, the peaceable gurgle of that slow-heaving Polar Ocean, over which in the utmost North the great Sun hangs low and lazy, as if he too were slumbering. Yet is his cloud-couch wrought of crimson and cloth-of-gold; yet does his light stream over the mirror of waters, like a tremulous fire-pillar, shooting downwards to the abyss, and hide itself under my feet. In such moments, Solitude also is invaluable; for who would speak, or be looked on, when behind him lies all Europe and Africa, fast asleep, except the watchmen; and before him the silent Immensity, and Palace of the Eternal, whereof our Sun is but a porch-lamp?

"Nevertheless, in this solemn moment comes a man, or monster, scrambling from among the rock-hollows; and, shaggy, huge as the Hyperborean Bear, hails me in Russian speech: most probably, therefore, a Russian Smuggler. With courteous brevity, I signify my indifference to contraband trade, my humane intentions, yet strong wish to be private. In vain: the monster, counting doubtless on his superior stature, and minded to make sport for himself, or perhaps profit, were it with murder, continues to advance; ever assailing me with his importunate train-oil breath; and now has advanced, till we stand both on the verge of the rock, the deep Sea rippling greedily down below. What argument will avail? On the thick Hyperborean, cherubic reasoning, seraphic eloquence were lost. Prepared for such extremity, I, deftly enough, whisk aside one step; draw out, from my interior reservoirs, a sufficient Birmingham Horse-pistol, and say, 'Be so obliging as retire, Friend (*Er ziehe sich zurück, Freund*), and with promptitude!' This logic even the Hyperborean understands; fast enough, with apologetic, petitionary growl, he sidles off; and, except for suicidal as well as homicidal purposes, need not return.

"Such I hold to be the genuine use of Gunpowder: that it makes all men alike tall. Nay, if thou be cooler, cleverer than I, if thou have more *Mind* though all but no Body whatever, then canst thou kill me first, and art the taller. Hereby, at last, is the Goliath powerless, and the David resistless; savage Animalism is nothing, inventive Spiritualism is all.

"With respect to Duels, indeed, I have my own ideas. Few things, in this so surprising world, strike me with more surprise. Two little visual Spectra of men, hovering with insecure enough cohesion in the midst of the UNFATHOMABLE, and to dissolve therein, at any rate, very soon, — make pause at the distance of twelve paces asunder; whirl round; and, simultaneously by the cunningest mechanism, explode one another into Dissolution; and off-hand become Air, and Non-extant! Deuce on it (*verdammt*), the little spitfires! — Nay, I think with old Hugo von Trimberg: [7] 'God must needs laugh outright, could such a thing be, to see his wondrous Manikins here below.' "

But amid these specialties, let us not forget the great generality, which is our chief quest here: How prospered the inner man of Teufelsdröckh under so much outward shifting? Does Legion still lurk in him, though repressed; or has he exorcised that Devil's Brood? We can answer that the symptons continue promising. Experience is the grand spiritual Doctor; and with him Teufelsdröckh has now been long a patient, swallowing many a bitter bolus. Unless our poor Friend belong to the numerous class of Incurables, which seems not likely, some cure will doubtless be effected. We should rather say that Legion, or the Satanic School, was now pretty well extirpated and cast out, but next to nothing introduced in its room; whereby the heart remains, for the while, in a quiet but no comfortable state.

"At length, after so much roasting," thus writes our Autobiographer, "I was what you might name calcined. Pray only that it be not rather, as is the more frequent issue, reduced to a *caput-mortuum*! [8] But in any case, by mere dint of practice, I had grown familiar with many things. Wretchedness was still wretched; but I could now partly see through it, and despise it. Which highest mortal, in this inane Existence, had I not found a Shadow-hunter, or Shadow-hunted; and, when I looked through his brave garnitures, miserable enough? Thy wishes have all been sniffed aside, thought I: but what, had they even been all granted? Did not the Boy Alexander weep because he had not two Planets to conquer; or a whole Solar System; or after that, a whole Universe? *Ach Gott,* when I gazed into these Stars, have they not looked down on me as if with pity, from their serene spaces; like Eyes glistening with heavenly tears over the little lot of man! Thousands of human generations, all as noisy as our own, have been swallowed-up of Time, and there remains no wreck of them any more; and Arcturus and Orion and Sirius and the Pleiades are still shining in their courses, clear and young, as when the Shepherd first noted them in the plain of Shinar. Pshaw! what is this paltry little Dog-cage of an Earth; what art thou that sittest whining there? Thou art still Nothing, Nobody: true; but who, then, is Something, Somebody? For thee the Family of Man has no use; it rejects thee; thou art wholly as a dissevered limb: so be it; perhaps it is better so!"

7 One of the Meistersingers.
8 "Death's head."

Too-heavy-laden Teufelsdröckh! Yet surely his bands are loosening; one day he will hurl the burden far from him, and bound forth free and with a second youth.

"This," says our Professor, "was the CENTRE OF INDIFFERENCE I had now reached; through which whoso travels from the Negative Pole to the Positive must necessarily pass."

CHAPTER IX

The Everlasting Yea

"TEMPTATIONS in the Wilderness!" exclaims Teufelsdröckh: "Have we not all to be tried with such? Not so easily can the old Adam, lodged in us by birth, be dispossessed. Our Life is compassed round with Necessity; yet is the meaning of Life itself no other than Freedom, than Voluntary Force: thus have we a warfare; in the beginning, especially, a hard-fought battle. For the God-given mandate, *Work thou in Well-doing,* lies mysteriously written, in Promethean Prophetic Characters, in our hearts; and leaves us no rest, night or day, till it be deciphered and obeyed; till it burn forth, in our conduct, a visible, acted Gospel of Freedom. And as the clay-given mandate, *Eat thou and be filled,* at the same time persuasively proclaims itself through every nerve, — must not there be a confusion, a contest, before the better Influence can become the upper?

"To me nothing seems more natural than that the Son of Man, when such God-given mandate first prophetically stirs within him, and the Clay must now be vanquished, or vanquish, — should be carried of the spirit into grim Solitudes, and there fronting the Tempter do grimmest battle with him; defiantly setting him at naught, till he yield and fly. Name it as we choose: with or without visible Devil, whether in the natural Desert of rocks and sands, or in the populous moral Desert of selfishness and baseness, — to such Temptation are we all called. Unhappy if we are not! Unhappy if we are but Half-men, in whom that divine handwriting has never blazed forth, all-subduing, in true sun-splendour; but quivers dubiously amid meaner lights: or smoulders, in dull pain, in darkness, under earthly vapours! — Our Wilderness is the wide World in an Atheistic Century; our Forty Days are long years of suffering and fasting: nevertheless, to these also comes an end. Yes, to me also was given, if not Victory, yet the consciousness of Battle, and the resolve to persevere therein while life or faculty is left. To me also, entangled in the enchanted forests, demon-peopled, doleful of sight and of sound, it was given, after weariest wanderings, to work out my way into the higher sunlit slopes — of that Mountain which has no summit, or whose summit is in Heaven only!"

He says elsewhere, under a less ambitious figure; as figures are, once for all, natural to him: "Has not thy Life been that of most sufficient men (*tüchtigen Männer*) thou hast known in this generation? An outflush of foolish young Enthusiasm, like the first fallow-crop, wherein are as many weeds as valuable herbs: this all parched away, under the Droughts of practical and spiritual Unbelief, as Disappointment, in thought and act, often-repeated gave rise to Doubt, and Doubt gradually settled into Denial! If I have had a second-crop, and now see the perennial greensward, and sit under umbrageous cedars, which defy all Drought (and Doubt); herein too, be the Heavens praised, I am not without examples, and even exemplars."

So that, for Teufelsdröckh also, there has been a "glorious revolution": these mad shadow-hunting and shadow-hunted Pilgrimings of his were but some purifying "Temptation in the Wilderness," before his Apostolic work (such as it was) could begin; which Temptation is now happily over, and the Devil once more worsted! Was "that high moment in the *Rue de l'Enfer*," then, properly the turning-point of the battle; when the Fiend said, *Worship me or be torn in shreds;* and was answered valiantly with an *Apage Satana?* [1] — Singular Teufelsdröckh, would thou hadst told thy singular story in plain words! But it is fruitless to look there, in those Paper-bags, for such. Nothing but innuendoes, figurative crotchets: a typical Shadow, fitfully wavering, prophetico-satiric; no clear logical Picture. "How paint to the sensual eye," asks he once, "what passes in the Holy-of-Holies of Man's Soul; in what words, known to these profane times, speak even afar-off of the unspeakable?" We ask in turn: Why perplex these times, profane as they are, with needless obscurity, by omission and by commission? Not mystical only is our Professor, but whimsical; and involves himself, now more than ever, in eye-bewildering *chiaroscuro*. Successive glimpses, here faithfully imparted, our more gifted readers must endeavour to combine for their own behoof.

He says: "The hot Harmattan wind had raged itself out; its howl went silent within me; and the long-deafened soul could now hear. I paused in my wild wanderings; and sat me down to wait, and consider; for it was as if the hour of change drew nigh. I seemed to surrender, to renounce utterly, and say: Fly, then, false shadows of Hope; I will chase you no more, I will believe you no more. And ye too, haggard spectres of Fear, I care not for you; ye too are all shadows and a lie. Let me rest here: for I am way-weary and life-weary; I will rest here, were it but to die: to die or to live is alike to me; alike insignificant." — And again: "Here, then, as I lay in that Centre of Indifference; cast, doubtless by benignant upper Influence, into a healing sleep, the heavy dreams rolled gradually away, and I awoke to a new Heaven and a new Earth. The first preliminary moral Act, Annihilation of Self (*Selbsttödtung*), had been happily accomplished; and my mind's eyes were now unsealed, and its hands ungyved."

1 "Get thee hence, Satan!"

Might we not also conjecture that the following passage refers to his Locality, during this same "healing sleep"; that his Pilgrim-staff lies cast aside here, on "the high table-land"; and indeed that the repose is already taking wholesome effect on him? If it were not that the tone, in some parts, has more of riancy, even of levity, than we could have expected! However, in Teufelsdröckh, there is always the strangest Dualism: light dancing, with guitar-music, will be going on in the fore-court, while by fits from within comes the faint whimpering of woe and wail. We transcribe the piece entire:

"Beautiful it was to sit there, as in my skyey Tent, musing and meditating; on the high table-land, in front of the Mountains; over me, as roof, the azure Dome, and around me, for walls, four azure-flowing curtains, — namely, of the Four azure winds, on whose bottom-fringes also I have seen gilding. And then to fancy the fair Castles that stood sheltered in these Mountain hollows; with their green flower-lawns, and white dames and damosels, lovely enough: or better still, the straw-roofed Cottages, wherein stood many a Mother baking bread, with her children round her: — all hidden and protectingly folded-up in the valley-folds; yet there and alive, as sure as if I beheld them. Or to see, as well as fancy, the nine Towns and Villages, that lay round my mountain-seat, which, in still weather, were wont to speak to me (by their steeple-bells) with metal tongue; and, in almost all weather, proclaimed their vitality by repeated Smoke-clouds; whereon, as on a culinary horologe, I might read the hour of the day. For it was the smoke of cookery, as kind housewives at morning, mid-day, eventide, were boiling their husbands' kettles; and ever a blue pillar rose up into the air, successively or simultaneously, from each of the nine, saying, as plainly as smoke could say: Such and such a meal is getting ready here. Not uninteresting! For you have the whole Borough, with all its love-makings and scandal-mongeries, contentions and contentments, as in miniature, and could cover it all with your hat. — If, in my wide Wayfarings, I had learned to look into the business of the World in its details, here perhaps was the place for combining it into general propositions, and deducing inferences therefrom.

"Often also could I see the black Tempest marching in anger through the Distance: round some Schreckhorn, as yet grim-blue, would the eddying vapour gather, and there tumultuously eddy, and flow down like a mad witch's hair; till, after a space, it vanished, and, in the clear sunbeam, your Schreckhorn stood smiling grim-white, for the vapour had held snow. How thou fermentest and elaboratest, in thy great fermenting-vat and laboratory of an Atmosphere, of a World, O Nature! — Or what is Nature? Ha! why do I not name thee GOD? Art not thou the 'Living Garment of God'? O Heavens, is it, in very deed, HE, then, that ever speaks through thee; that lives and loves in thee, that lives and loves in me?

"Fore-shadows, call them rather fore-splendours, of that Truth, and Beginning of Truths, fell mysteriously over my soul. Sweeter than Dayspring to the Shipwrecked in Nova Zembla; ah, like the mother's voice to her little child that strays bewildered, weeping, in unknown tumults; like soft streamings of celestial music to my too-exasperated heart, came that Evangel. The Universe is not dead and demoniacal, a charnel-house with spectres; but godlike, and my Father's!

"With other eyes, too, could I now look upon my fellow man; with an infinite Love, an infinite Pity. Poor, wandering, wayward man! Art thou not tired, and beaten with stripes, even as I am? Ever, whether thou bear the royal mantle or the beggar's gabardine, art thou not so weary, so heavy-laden; and thy Bed of Rest is but a Grave. O my Brother, my Brother, why cannot I shelter thee in my bosom, and wipe away all tears from thy eyes! Truly, the din of many-voiced Life, which, in this solitude, with the mind's organ, I could hear, was no longer a maddening discord, but a melting one; like inarticulate cries, and sobbings of a dumb creature, which in the ear of Heaven are prayers. The poor Earth, with her poor joys, was now my needy Mother, not my cruel Stepdame; man, with his so mad Wants and so mean Endeavours, had become the dearer to me; and even for his sufferings and his sins, I now first named him Brother. Thus I was standing in the porch of that 'Sanctuary of Sorrow'; by strange, steep ways had I too been guided thither; and ere long its sacred gates would open, and the 'Divine Depth of Sorrow' lie disclosed to me."

The Professor says, he here first got eye on the Knot that had been strangling him, and straightway could unfasten it, and was free. "A vain interminable controversy," writes he, "touching what is at present called Origin of Evil, or some such thing, arises in every soul, since the beginning of the world; and in every soul, that would pass from idle Suffering into actual Endeavouring, must first be put an end to. The most, in our time, have to go content with a simple, incomplete enough Suppression of this controversy; to a few some Solution of it is indispensable. In every new era, too, such Solution comes-out in different terms; and ever the Solution of the last era has become obsolete, and is found unserviceable. For it is man's nature to change his Dialect from century to century; he cannot help it though he would. The authentic *Church-Catechism* of our present century has not yet fallen into my hands: meanwhile, for my own private behoof, I attempt to elucidate the matter so. Man's Unhappiness, as I construe, comes of his Greatness; it is because there is an Infinite in him, which with all his cunning he cannot quite bury under the Finite. Will the whole Finance Ministers and Upholsterers and Confectioners of modern Europe undertake, in joint-stock company, to make one Shoeblack HAPPY? They cannot accomplish it, above an hour or two; for the Shoeblack also has a Soul quite other than his Stomach; and would require, if you consider it, for his permanent satisfaction and saturation, simply this allotment, no more, and no less: *God's infinite Universe altogether to himself,* therein to enjoy indefinitely, and fill every wish as fast as it rose. Oceans of Hochheimer, a Throat like that of Ophiuchus: speak not of them; to the infinite Shoeblack they are as nothing. No sooner is your ocean filled, than he grumbles that it might have been of better vintage. Try him with half of a Universe, of an Omnipotence, he sets to quarrelling with the proprietor of the other half, and declares himself the most maltreated of men. — Always there is a black spot in our sunshine: it is even as I said, the *Shadow of Ourselves.*

"But the whim we have of Happiness is somewhat thus. By certain valuations, and averages, of our own striking, we come upon some sort of average terrestrial lot; this we fancy belongs to us by nature, and of indefeasible right. It is simple payment of our wages, of our deserts; requires neither thanks nor complaint; only such *overplus* as there may be do we account Happiness; any *deficit* again is Misery. Now consider that we have the valuation of our own deserts ourselves, and what a fund of Self-conceit there is in each of us, — do you wonder that the balance should so often dip the wrong way, and many a Blockhead cry: See there, what a payment; was ever worthy gentleman so used! — I tell thee, Blockhead, it all comes of thy Vanity; of what thou *fanciest* those same deserts of thine to be. Fancy that thou deservest to be hanged (as is most likely), thou wilt feel it happiness to be only that: fancy that thou deservest to be hanged in a hair-halter, it will be a luxury to die in hemp.

"So true is it, what I then say, that *the Fraction of Life can be increased in value not so much by increasing your Numerator as by lessening your Denominator.* Nay, unless my Algebra deceive me, *Unity* itself divided by Zero will give *Infinity.* Make thy claims of wages a zero, then; thou hast the world under thy feet. Well did the Wisest of our time [2] write: 'It is only with Renunciation (*Entsagen*) that Life, properly speaking, can be said to begin.'

"I asked myself: What is this that, ever since earliest years, thou hast been fretting and fuming, and lamenting and self-tormenting, on account of? Say it in a word: is it not because thou art not HAPPY? Because the THOU (sweet gentleman) is not sufficiently honoured, nourished, soft-bedded, and lovingly cared for? Foolish soul! What Act of Legislature was there that *thou* shouldst be Happy? A little while ago thou hadst no right to *be* at all. What if thou wert born and predestined not to be Happy, but to be Unhappy! Art thou nothing other than a Vulture, then, that fliest through the Universe seeking after somewhat to *eat;* and shrieking dolefully because carrion enough is not given thee? Close thy *Byron;* open thy *Goethe.*"

"*Es leuchtet mir ein,* I see a glimpse of it!" cries he elsewhere: "there is in man a HIGHER than Love of Happiness: he can do without Hap-

[2] Goethe.

piness, and instead thereof find Blessedness! Was it not to preach-
forth this same HIGHER that sages and martyrs, the Poet and the Priest,
in all times, have spoken and suffered; bearing testimony, through life
and through death, of the Godlike that is in Man, and how in the
Godlike only has he Strength and Freedom? Which God-inspired
Doctrine art thou also honoured to be taught; O Heavens! and broken
with manifold merciful Afflictions, even till thou become contrite, and
learn it! O, thank thy Destiny for these; thankfully bear what yet remain: thou hadst need of them; the Self in thee needed to be annihilated. By benignant fever-paroxysms is Life rooting out the deep-
seated chronic Diseases, and triumphs over Death. On the roaring
billows of Time, thou art not engulfed, but borne aloft into the azure
of Eternity. Love not Pleasure; love God. This is the EVERLASTING
YEA, wherein all contradiction is solved: wherein whoso walks and
works, it is well with him."

And again: "Small is it that thou canst trample the Earth with its
injuries under thy feet, as old Greek Zeno trained thee: thou canst
love the Earth while it injures thee, and even because it injures thee;
for this a Greater than Zeno was needed, and he too was sent. Knowest thou that 'Worship of Sorrow'? The Temple whereof, founded
some eighteen centuries ago, now lies in ruins, overgrown with jungle, the habitation of doleful creatures: nevertheless, venture forward;
in a low crypt, arched out of falling fragments, thou findest the Altar
still there, and its sacred Lamp perennially burning."

Without pretending to comment on which strange utterances, the
Editor will only remark, that there lies beside them much of a still
more questionable character; unsuited to the general apprehension;
nay wherein he himself does not see his way. Nebulous disquisitions
on Religion, yet not without bursts of splendour; on the "perennial continuance of Inspiration"; on Prophecy; that there are "true Priests, as
well as Baal-Priests, in our own day": with more of the like sort. We
select some fractions, by way of finish to this farrago.

"Cease, my much-respected Herr von Voltaire," thus apostrophises
the Professor: "shut thy sweet voice; for the task appointed thee seems
finished. Sufficiently hast thou demonstrated this proposition, considerable or otherwise: That the Mythus of the Christian Religion
looks not in the eighteenth century as it did in the eighth. Alas, were
thy six-and-thirty quartos, and the six-and-thirty thousand other
quartos and folios, and flying sheets or reams, printed before and
since on the same subject, all needed to convince us of so little! But
what next? Wilt thou help us to embody the divine Spirit of that Religion in a new Mythus, in a new vehicle and vesture, that our Souls,
otherwise too like perishing, may live? What! thou hast no faculty in
that kind? Only a torch for burning, no hammer for building? Take
our thanks, then, and — thyself away.

"Meanwhile what are antiquated Mythuses to me? Or is the God present, felt in my own heart, a thing which Herr von Voltaire will dispute out of me; or dispute into me? To the 'Worship of Sorrow' ascribe what origin and genesis thou pleasest, has not that Worship originated, and been generated; is it not here? Feel it in thy heart, and then say whether it is of God! This is Belief; all else is Opinion, — for which latter whoso will let him worry and be worried."

"Neither," observes he elsewhere, "shall ye tear-out one another's eyes, struggling over 'Plenary Inspiration,' and such-like: try rather to get a little even Partial Inspiration, each of you for himself. One BIBLE I know, of whose Plenary Inspiration doubt is not so much as possible; nay with my own eyes I saw the God's-Hand writing it: thereof all other Bibles are but leaves, — say, in Picture-Writing to assist the weaker faculty."

Or, to give the wearied reader relief, and bring it to an end, let him take the following perhaps more intelligible passage:

"To me, in this our life," says the Professor, "which is an internecine warfare with the Time-spirit, other warfare seems questionable. Hast thou in any way a Contention with thy brother, I advise thee, think well what the meaning thereof is. If thou gauge it to the bottom, it is simply this: 'Fellow, see! thou art taking more than thy share of Happiness in the world, something from my share: which, by the Heavens, thou shalt not; nay I will fight thee rather.' — Alas, and the whole lot to be divided is such a beggarly matter, truly a 'feast of shells,' for the substance has been spilled out: not enough to quench one Appetite; and the collective human species clutching at them! — Can we not, in all such cases, rather say: 'Take it, thou too-ravenous individual; take that pitiful additional fraction of a share, which I reckoned mine, but which thou so wantest; take it with a blessing: would to Heaven I had enough for thee!' — If Fichte's Wissenschaftslehre be, 'to a certain extent, Applied Christianity,' surely to a still greater extent, so is this. We have here not a Whole Duty of Man, yet a Half Duty, namely the Passive half: could we but do it, as we can demonstrate it!

"But indeed Conviction, were it never so excellent, is worthless till it convert itself into Conduct. Nay properly Conviction is not possible till then; inasmuch as all Speculation is by nature endless, formless, a vortex amid vortices: only by a felt indubitable certainty of Experience does it find any centre to revolve round, and so fashion itself into a system. Most true is it, as a wise man teaches us, that 'Doubt of any sort cannot be removed except by Action.' On which ground, too, let him who gropes painfully in darkness or uncertain light, and prays vehemently that the dawn may ripen into day, lay this other precept well to heart, which to me was of invaluable service: 'Do the Duty which lies nearest thee,' which thou knowest to be a Duty! Thy second Duty will already have become clearer.

"May we not say, however, that the hour of Spiritual Enfranchisement is even this: When your Ideal World, wherein the whole man has been dimly struggling and inexpressibly languishing to work, becomes revealed, and thrown open; and you discover, with amazement enough, like the Lothario in *Wilhelm Meister*, that your 'America is here or nowhere'? The Situation that has not its Duty, its Ideal, was never yet occupied by man. Yes here, in this poor, miserable, hampered, despicable Actual, wherein thou even now standest, here or nowhere is thy Ideal: work it out therefrom; and working, believe, live, be free. Fool! the Ideal is in thyself, the impediment too is in thyself: thy Condition is but the stuff thou art to shape that same Ideal out of: what matters whether such stuff be of this sort or that, so the Form thou give it be heroic, be poetic? O thou that pinest in the imprisonment of the Actual, and criest bitterly to the gods for a kingdom wherein to rule and create, know this of a truth: the thing thou seekest is already with thee, 'here or nowhere,' couldst thou only see!

"But it is with man's Soul as it was with Nature: the beginning of Creation is — Light. Till the eye have vision, the whole members are in bonds. Divine moment, when over the tempest-tost Soul, as once over the wild-weltering Chaos, it is spoken: Let there be Light! Ever to the greatest that has felt such moment, is it not miraculous and God-announcing; even as, under simpler figures, to the simplest and least. The mad primeval Discord is hushed; the rudely-jumbled conflicting elements bind themselves into separate Firmaments: deep silent rock-foundations are built beneath; and the skyey vault with its everlasting Luminaries above: instead of a dark wasteful Chaos, we have a blooming, fertile, heaven-encompassed World.

"I too could now say to myself: Be no longer a Chaos, but a World, or even Worldkin. Produce! Produce! Were it but the pitifullest infinitesimal fraction of a Product, produce it, in God's name! 'Tis the utmost thou hast in thee: out with it, then. Up, up! Whatsoever thy hand findeth to do, do it with thy whole might. Work while it is called Today; for the Night cometh, wherein no man can work."

BOOK THIRD

CHAPTER VIII

Natural Supernaturalism

IT is in his stupendous Section, headed *Natural Supernaturalism*, that the Professor first becomes a Seer; and, after long effort, such as we have witnessed, finally subducs under his feet this refractory Clothes-Philosophy, and takes victorious possession thereof. Phantasms enough he has had to struggle with; "Cloth-webs and Cob-webs," of Imperial Mantles, Superannuated Symbols, and what not: yet still did he courageously pierce through. Nay, worst of all, two quite mysterious, world-embracing Phantasms, TIME and SPACE, have ever hovered round him, perplexing and bewildering: but with these also he now resolutely grapples, these also he victoriously rends asunder. In a word, he has looked fixedly on Existence, till, one after the other, its earthly hulls and garnitures have all melted away; and now, to his rapt vision, the interior celestial Holy of Holies lies disclosed.

Here, therefore, properly it is that the Philosophy of Clothes attains to Transcendentalism; this last leap, can we but clear it, takes us safe into the promised land, where *Palingenesia*,[1] in all senses, may be considered as beginning. "Courage, then!" may our Diogenes exclaim, with better right than Diogenes the First once did.[2] This stupendous Section we, after long painful meditation, have found not to be unintelligible; but, on the contrary, to grow clear, nay radiant, and all-illuminating. Let the reader, turning on it what utmost force of speculative intellect is in him, do his part; as we, by judicious selection and adjustment, shall study to do ours:

"Deep has been, and is, the significance of Miracles," thus quietly begins the Professor; "far deeper perhaps than we imagine. Meanwhile, the question of questions were: What specially is a Miracle? To that Dutch King of Siam, an icicle had been a miracle; whoso had carried with him an air-pump, and vial of vitriolic ether, might have worked a miracle. To my Horse, again, who unhappily is still more unscientific, do not I work a miracle, and magical *'Open sesame!'* every time I please to pay twopence, and open for him an impassable *Schlagbaum,* or shut Turnpike?

" 'But is not a real Miracle simply a violation of the Laws of Nature?' ask several. Whom I answer by this new question: What are the Laws of Nature? To me perhaps the rising of one from the dead were no violation of these Laws, but a confirmation; were some far deeper Law, now first penetrated into, and by Spiritual Force, even as the rest have all been, brought to bear on us with its Material Force.

"Here too may some inquire, not without astonishment: On what ground shall one, that can make Iron swim, come and declare that therefore he can teach Religion? To us, truly, of the Nineteenth Century, such declaration were inept enough; which nevertheless to our fathers, of the First Century, was full of meaning.

" 'But is it not the deepest Law of Nature that she be constant?' cries an illuminated class: 'Is not the Machine of the Universe fixed to move by unalterable rules?' Probable enough, good friends: nay I, too, must believe that the God, whom ancient inspired men assert to be 'without variableness or shadow of turning,' does indeed never change; that Nature, that the Universe, which no one whom it so pleases can be prevented from calling a Machine, does move by the most unalter-

---

1 Re-birth.
2 Diogenes, toward the end of a wearisome lecture, cried, "Courage, friends! I see land!"

able rules. And now of you, too, I make the old inquiry: What those same unalterable rules, forming the complete Statute-Book of Nature, may possibly be?

"They stand written in our Works of Science, say you; in the accumulated records of Man's Experience? — Was Man with his Experience present at the Creation, then, to see how it all went on? Have any deepest scientific individuals yet dived-down to the foundations of the Universe, and gauged everything there? Did the Maker take them into His counsel; that they read His ground-plan of the incomprehensible All; and can say, This stands marked therein, and no more than this? Alas, not in anywise! These scientific individuals have been nowhere but where we also are; have seen some handbreadths deeper than we see into the Deep that is infinite, without bottom as without shore.

"Laplace's Book on the Stars, wherein he exhibits that certain Planets, with their Satellites, gyrate round our worthy Sun, at a rate and in a course, which, by greatest good fortune, he and the like of him have succeeded in detecting, — is to me as precious as to another. But is this what thou namest 'Mechanism of the Heavens,' and 'System of the World'; this, wherein Sirius and the Pleiades, and all Herschel's Fifteen-thousand Suns per minute, being left out, some paltry handful of Moons, and inert Balls, had been — looked at, nicknamed, and marked in the Zodiacal Way-bill; so that we can now prate of their Whereabout; their How, their Why, their What, being hid from us, as in the signless Inane?

"System of Nature! To the wisest man, wide as is his vision, Nature remains of quite *infinite* depth, of quite infinite expansion; and all Experience thereof limits itself to some few computed centuries and measured square-miles. The course of Nature's phases, on this our little fraction of a Planet, is partially known to us: but who knows what deeper courses these depend on; what infinitely larger Cycle (of causes) our little Epicycle revolves on? To the Minnow every cranny and pebble, and quality and accident, of its little native Creek may have become familiar: but does the Minnow understand the Ocean Tides and periodic Currents, the Trade-winds, and Monsoons, and Moon's Eclipses; by all which the condition of its little Creek is regulated, and may, from time to time (*un*miraculously enough), be quite overset and reversed? Such a Minnow is Man; his Creek this Planet Earth; his ocean the immeasurable All; his Monsoons and periodic Currents the mysterious Course of Providence through Æons of Æons.

"We speak of the Volume of Nature: and truly a Volume it is, — whose Author and Writer is God. To read it! Dost thou, does man, so much as well know the Alphabet thereof? With its Words, Sentences, and grand descriptive Pages, poetical and philosophical, spread out through Solar Systems, and Thousands of Years, we shall not try thee. It is a Volume written in celestial hieroglyphs, in the true Sacred-writing; of which even Prophets are happy that they can read here a line

and there a line. As for your Institutes, and Academies of Science, they
strive bravely; and, from amid the thick crowded, inextricably inter-
twisted hieroglyphic writing, pick-out, by dextrous combination, some
Letters in the vulgar Character, and therefrom put together this and
the other economic Recipe, of high avail in Practice. That Nature is
more than some boundless Volume of such Recipes, or huge, well-
nigh inexhaustible Domestic-Cookery Book, of which the whole secret
will in this manner one day evolve itself, the fewest dream.

"Custom," continues the Professor, "doth make dotards of us all.
Consider well, thou wilt find that Custom is the greatest of Weavers;
and weaves air-raiment for all the Spirits of the Universe; whereby
indeed these dwell with us visibly, as ministering servants, in our
houses and workshops; but their spiritual nature becomes, to the
most, forever hidden. Philosophy complains that Custom has hood-
winked us, from the first; that we do everything by Custom, even
Believe by it; that our very Axioms, let us boast of Free-thinking as
we may, are oftenest simply such Beliefs as we have never heard
questioned. Nay, what is Philosophy throughout but a continual
battle against Custom; an ever-renewed effort to *transcend* the sphere
of blind Custom, and so become Transcendental?

"Innumerable are the illusions and legerdemain-tricks of Custom:
but of all these, perhaps the cleverest is her knack of persuading us
that the Miraculous, by simple repetition, ceases to be Miraculous.
True, it is by this means we live; for man must work as well as wonder:
and herein is Custom so far a kind nurse, guiding him to his true benefit. But she is a fond foolish nurse, or rather we are false foolish nurs-
lings, when, in our resting and reflecting hours, we prolong the same
deception. Am I to view the Stupendous with stupid indifference, because I have seen it twice, or two-hundred, or two-million times? There
is no reason in Nature or in Art why I should: unless, indeed, I am a
mere Work-Machine, for whom the divine gift of Thought were no
other than the terrestrial gift of Steam is to the Steam-engine; a power
whereby Cotton might be spun, and money and money's worth realised.

"Notable enough too, here as elsewhere, wilt thou find the potency
of Names; which indeed are but one kind of such custom-woven, won-
der-hiding Garments. Witchcraft, and all manner of Spectre-work, and
Demonology, we have now named Madness and Diseases of the
Nerves. Seldom reflecting that still the new question comes upon us:
What is Madness, what are Nerves? Ever, as before, does Madness
remain a mysterious-terrific, altogether *infernal* boiling-up of the Nether
Chaotic Deep, through this fair-painted Vision of Creation, which
swims thereon, which we name the Real. Was Luther's Picture of the
Devil less a Reality, whether it were formed within the bodily eye,
or without it? In every the wisest Soul lies a whole world of internal

Madness, an authentic Demon Empire; out of which, indeed, his world of Wisdom has been creatively built together, and now rests there, as on its dark foundations does a habitable flowery Earth-rind.

"But deepest of all illusory Appearances, for hiding Wonder, as foi many other ends, are your two grand fundamental world-enveloping Appearances, SPACE and TIME. These, as spun and woven for us from before Birth itself, to clothe our celestial ME for dwelling here, and yet to blind it, — lie all embracing, as the universal canvas, or warp and woof, whereby all minor Illusions, in this Phantom Existence, weave and paint themselves. In vain, while here on Earth, shall you endeavour to strip them off; you can, at best, but rend them asunder for moments, and look through.

"Fortunatus had a wishing Hat, which when he put on, and wished himself Anywhere, behold he was There. By this means had Fortunatus triumphed over Space, he had annihilated Space; for him there was no Where, but all was Here. Were a Hatter to establish himself, in the Wahngasse of Weissnichtwo, and make felts of this sort for all mankind, what a world we should have of it! Still stranger, should, on the opposite side of the street, another Hatter establish himself; and as his fellow-craftsman made Space-annihilating Hats, make Time-annihilating! Of both would I purchase, were it with my last groschen; but chiefly of this latter. To clap-on your felt, and, simply by wishing that you were, Any*where*, straightway to be *There!* Next to clap-on your other felt, and, simply by wishing that you were Any*when*, straightway to be *Then!* This were indeed the grander: shooting at will from the Fire-Creation of the World to its Fire-Consummation; here historically present in the First Century, conversing face to face with Paul and Seneca; there prophetically in the Thirty-first, conversing also face to face with other Pauls and Senecas, who as yet stand hidden in the depth of that late Time!

"Or thinkest thou it were impossible, unimaginable? Is the Past annihilated, then, or only past; is the Future non-extant, or only future? Those mystic faculties of thine, Memory and Hope, already answer: already through those mystic avenues, thou the Earth-blinded summonest both Past and Future, and communest with them, though as yet darkly, and with mute beckonings. The curtains of Yesterday drop down, the curtains of Tomorrow roll up; but Yesterday and Tomorrow both *are*. Pierce through the Time-element, glance into the Eternal. Believe what thou findest written in the sanctuaries of Man's Soul, even as all Thinkers, in all ages, have devoutly read it there: that Time and Space are not God, but creations of God; that with God as it is a universal HERE, so is it an everlasting Now.

"And seest thou therein any glimpse of IMMORTALITY? — O Heaven! Is the white Tomb of our Loved One, who died from our arms, and had to be left behind us there, which rises in the distance, like a pale, mournfully receding Milestone, to tell how many toilsome uncheered miles we have journeyed on alone, — but a pale spectral Illusion! Is the lost Friend still mysteriously Here, even as we are Here mysteriously, with God! — Know of a truth that only the Time-shadows have perished, or are perishable; that the real Being of whatever was, and whatever is, and whatever will be, *is* even now and forever. This, should it unhappily seem new, thou mayest ponder at thy leisure; for the next twenty years, or the next twenty centuries: believe it thou must; understand it thou canst not.

"That the Thought-forms, Space and Time, wherein, once for all, we are sent into this Earth to live, should condition and determine our whole Practical reasonings, conceptions, and imagings or imaginings, — seems altogether fit, just, and unavoidable. But that they should, furthermore, usurp such sway over pure spiritual Meditation, and blind us to the wonder everywhere lying close on us, seems no-wise so. Admit Space and Time to their due rank as Forms of Thought; nay even, if thou wilt, to their quite undue rank of Realities: and consider, then, with thyself how their thin disguises hide from us the brightest God-effulgences! Thus, were it not miraculous, could I stretch forth my hand and clutch the Sun? Yet thou seest me daily stretch forth my hand and therewith clutch many a thing, and swing it hither and thither. Art thou a grown baby, then, to fancy that the Miracle lies in miles of distance, or in pounds avoirdupois of weight; and not to see that the true inexplicable God-revealing Miracle lies in this, that I can stretch forth my hand at all; that I have free Force to clutch aught therewith? Innumerable other of this sort are the deceptions, and wonder-hiding stupefactions, which Space practises on us.

"Still worse is it with regard to Time. Your grand anti-magician, and universal wonder-hider, is this same lying Time. Had we but the Time-annihilating Hat, to put on for only once, we should see ourselves in a World of Miracles, wherein all fabled or authentic Thaumaturgy, and feats of Magic, were outdone. But unhappily we have not such a Hat; and man, poor fool that he is, can seldom and scantily help himself without one.

"Were it not wonderful, for instance, had Orpheus, or Amphion, built the walls of Thebes by the mere sound of his Lyre? Yet tell me, Who built these walls of Weissnichtwo; summoning-out all the sandstone rocks, to dance along from the *Steinbruch* (now a huge Troglodyte [3] Chasm, with frightful green-mantled pools); and shape themselves into Doric and Ionic pillars, squared ashlar houses and noble streets? Was it not the still higher Orpheus, or Orpheuses, who, in past centuries, by the divine Music of Wisdom, succeeded in civilising Man? Our highest Orpheus walked in Judea, eighteen hundred years ago: his sphere-melody, flowing in wild native tones, took captive the ravished souls of men; and, being of a true sphere-melody, still flows

3 *Steinbruch*: quarry; *Troglodyte*: cave-dweller.

and sounds, though now with thousandfold accompaniments, and rich symphonies, through all our hearts; and modulates, and divinely leads them. Is that a wonder, which happens in two hours; and does it cease to be wonderful if happening in two million? Not only was Thebes built by the music of an Orpheus; but without the music of some inspired Orpheus was no city ever built, no work that man glories-in ever done.

"Sweep away the Illusion of Time; glance, if thou hast eyes, from the near moving-cause to its far-distant Mover: The stroke that came transmitted through a whole galaxy of elastic balls, was it less a stroke than if the last ball only had been struck, and sent flying? O, could I (with the Time-annihilating Hat) transport thee direct from the Beginnings to the Endings, how were thy eyesight unsealed, and thy heart set flaming in the Light-sea of celestial wonder! Then sawest thou that this fair Universe, were it in the meanest province thereof, is in very deed the star-domed City of God; that through every star, through every grass-blade, and most through every Living Soul, the glory of a present God still beams. But Nature, which is the Time-vesture of God, and reveals Him to the wise, hides Him from the foolish.

"Again, could anything be more miraculous than an authentic Ghost? The English Johnson longed, all his life, to see one; but could not, though he went to Cock Lane, and thence to the church-vaults, and tapped on coffins. Foolish Doctor! Did he never, with the mind's eye as well as with the body's, look round him into that full tide of human Life he so loved; did he never so much as look into Himself? The good Doctor was a Ghost, as actual and authentic as heart could wish; well-nigh a million of Ghosts were travelling the streets by his side. Once more I say, sweep away the illusion of Time; compress the threescore years into three minutes: what else was he, what else are we? Are we not Spirits, that are shaped into a body, into an Appearance; and that fade-away again into air and Invisibility? This is no metaphor, it is a simple scientific *fact*: we start out of Nothingness, take figure, and are Apparitions; round us, as round the veriest spectre, is Eternity; and to Eternity minutes are as years and æons. Come there not tones of Love and Faith, as from celestial harp-strings, like the Song of beatified Souls? And again, do not we squeak and jibber (in our discordant, screech-owlish debatings and recriminatings); and glide bodeful, and feeble, and fearful; or uproar (*poltern*), and revel in our mad Dance of the Dead, — till the scent of the morning air summons us to our still Home; and dreamy Night becomes awake and Day? Where now is Alexander of Macedon: does the steel Host, that yelled in fierce battle-shouts at Issus and Arbela, remain behind him; or have they all vanished utterly, even as perturbed Goblins must? Napoleon too, and his Moscow Retreats and Austerlitz Campaigns! Was it all other than the veriest Spectre-hunt; which has now, with its howling tumult that made Night hideous, flitted away? — Ghosts! There are nigh a thousand-million walking the Earth openly at noontide; some half-hundred have vanished from it, some half-hundred have arisen in it, ere thy watch ticks once.

"O Heaven, it is mysterious, it is awful to consider that we not only carry each a future Ghost within him; but are, in very deed, Ghosts! These Limbs, whence had we them; this stormy Force; this life-blood with its burning Passion? They are dust and shadow; a Shadow-system gathered round our ME; wherein, through some moments or years, the Divine Essence is to be revealed in the Flesh. That warrior on his strong war-horse, fire flashes through his eyes; force dwells in his arm and heart: but warrior and war-horse are a vision; a revealed Force, nothing more. Stately they tread the Earth, as if it were a firm substance: fool! the earth is but a film; it cracks in twain, and warrior and war-horse sink beyond plummet's sounding. Plummet's? Fantasy herself will not follow them. A little while ago, they were not; a little while, and they are not, their very ashes are not.

"So has it been from the beginning, so will it be to the end. Generation after generation takes to itself the Form of a Body; and forth-issuing from Cimmerian Night, on Heaven's mission APPEARS. What Force and Fire is in each he expends: one grinding in the mill of Industry; one hunter-like climbing the giddy Alpine heights of Science; one madly dashed in pieces on the rocks of Strife, in war with his fellow: — and then the Heaven-sent is recalled; his earthly Vesture falls away, and soon even to Sense becomes a vanished Shadow. Thus, like some wild-flaming, wild-thundering train of Heaven's Artillery, does this mysterious MANKIND thunder and flame, in long-drawn, quick-succeeding grandeur, through the unknown Deep. Thus, like a God-created, fire-breathing Spirit-host, we emerge from the Inane; haste stormfully across the astonished Earth; then plunge again into the Inane. Earth's mountains are levelled, and her seas filled up, in our passage: can the Earth, which is but dead and a vision, resist Spirits which have reality and are alive? On the hardest adamant some footprint of us is stamped-in; the last Rear of the host will read traces of the earliest Van. But whence? — O Heaven, whither? Sense knows not; Faith knows not; only that it is through Mystery to Mystery, from God to God.

'We *are such stuff*
As Dreams are made of, and our little Life
Is rounded with a sleep!' "

On Heroes, Hero-Worship, and The Heroic in History

LECTURE III

The Hero as Poet. Dante; Shakspeare

❲ *Heroes and Hero-Worship* was delivered as a series of six lectures in May 1840 — "The Hero as Poet" coming on Tuesday, 12 May. Other titles in the series of lectures were as follows: I. "The Hero as Divinity. Odin. Paganism: Scandinavian Mythology"; II. "The Hero as Prophet. Mahomet: Islam"; IV. "The Hero as Priest. Luther; Reformation: Knox; Puritanism"; V. "The Hero as Man of Letters. Johnson, Rousseau, Burns"; VI. "The Hero as King. Cromwell, Napoleon: Modern Revolutionism." "The History of the world," Carlyle said in his first lecture, "is but the Biography of great men . . . . Could we see *them,* we should get some glimpses into the very marrow of the world's history." It is instructive to compare the critical assumptions of Macaulay and Carlyle as they are revealed in their judgments of Dante. ❳

THE Hero as Divinity, the Hero as Prophet, are productions of old ages; not to be repeated in the new. They presuppose a certain rudeness of conception, which the progress of mere scientific knowledge puts an end to. There needs to be, as it were, a world vacant, or almost vacant of scientific forms, if men in their loving wonder are to fancy their fellow-man either a god or one speaking with the voice of a god. Divinity and Prophet are past. We are now to see our Hero in the less ambitious, but also less questionable, character of Poet; a character which does not pass. The Poet is a heroic figure belonging to all ages; whom all ages possess, when once he is produced, whom the newest age as the oldest may produce; — and will produce, always when Nature pleases. Let Nature send a Hero-soul; in no age is it other than possible that he may be shaped into a Poet.

Hero, Prophet, Poet, — many different names, in different times and places, do we give to Great Men; according to varieties we note in them, according to the sphere in which they have displayed themselves! We might give many more names, on this same principle. I will remark again, however, as a fact not unimportant to be understood, that the different *sphere* constitutes the grand origin of such distinction; that the Hero can be Poet, Prophet, King, Priest or what you will, according to the kind of world he finds himself born into. I confess, I have no notion of a truly great man that could not be *all* sorts of men. The Poet who could merely sit on a chair, and com-

pose stanzas, would never make a stanza worth much. He could not
sing the Heroic warrior, unless he himself were at least a Heroic warrior too. I fancy there is in him the Politician, the Thinker, Legislator,
Philosopher; — in one or the other degree, he could have been, he
is all these. So too I cannot understand how a Mirabeau, with that
great glowing heart, with the fire that was in it, with the bursting tears
that were in it, could not have written verses, tragedies, poems, and
touched all hearts in that way, had his course of life and education
led him thitherward. The grand fundamental character is that of Great
Man; that the man be great. Napoleon has words in him which are
like Austerlitz Battles. Louis Fourteenth's Marshals are a kind of poetical men withal; the things Turenne says are full of sagacity and genial-
ity, like sayings of Samuel Johnson. The great heart, the clear deep-
seeing eye: there it lies; no man whatever, in what province soever,
can prosper at all without these. Petrarch and Boccaccio did diplo-
matic messages, it seems, quite well: one can easily believe it; they
had done things a little harder than these! Burns, a gifted song-
writer, might have made a still better Mirabeau. Shakspeare, — one
knows not what *he* could not have made, in the supreme degree.

True, there are aptitudes of Nature, too. Nature does not make all
great men, more than all other men, in the self-same mould. Varieties
of aptitude doubtless; but infinitely more of circumstance; and far
oftenest it is the *latter* only that are looked to. But it is as with common men in the learning of trades. You take any man, as yet a vague
capability of a man, who could be any kind of craftsman; and make
him into a smith, a carpenter, a mason: he is then and thenceforth that
and nothing else. And if, as Addison complains, you sometimes see a
street-porter staggering under his load on spindle-shanks, and near at
hand a tailor with the frame of a Samson handling a bit of cloth and
small Whitechapel needle, — it cannot be considered that aptitude of
Nature alone has been consulted here either! — The Great Man also,
to what shall he be bound apprentice? Given your Hero, is he to become Conqueror, King, Philosopher, Poet? It is an inexplicably complex controversial-calculation between the world and him! He will
read the world and its laws; the world with its laws will be there to
be read. What the world, on *this* matter, shall permit and bid is, as we
said, the most important fact about the world. —

Poet and Prophet differ greatly in our loose modern notions of them.
In some old languages, again, the titles are synonymous; *Vates* means
both Prophet and Poet: and indeed at all times, Prophet and Poet, well
understood, have much kindred of meaning. Fundamentally indeed
they are still the same; in this most important respect especially, That
they have penetrated both of them into the sacred mystery of the Universe; what Goethe calls "the open secret." "Which is the great secret?"
asks one. — "The *open* secret," — open to all, seen by almost none!
That divine mystery, which lies everywhere in all Beings, "the Divine

Idea of the World, that which lies at the bottom of Appearance," as Fichte styles it; of which all Appearance, from the starry sky to the grass of the field, but especially the Appearance of Man and his work, is but the *vesture*, the embodiment that renders it visible. This divine mystery *is* in all times and in all places; veritably is. In most times and places it is greatly overlooked; and the Universe, definable always in one or the other dialect, as the realised Thought of God, is considered a trivial, inert, commonplace matter, — as if, says the Satirist,[1] it were a dead thing, which some upholsterer had put together! It could do no good, at present, to *speak* much about this; but it is a pity for every one of us if we do not know it, live ever in the knowledge of it. Really a most mournful pity; — a failure to live at all, if we live otherwise!

But now, I say, whoever may forget this divine mystery, the *Vates*, whether Prophet or Poet, has penetrated into it; is a man sent hither to make it more impressively known to us. That always is his message; he is to reveal that to us, — that sacred mystery which he more than others lives ever present with. While others forget it, he knows it; — I might say, he has been driven to know it; without consent asked of *him*, he finds himself living in it, bound to live in it. Once more, here is no Hearsay, but a direct Insight and Belief; this man too could not help being a sincere man! Whosoever may live in the shows of things, it is for him a necessity of nature to live in the very fact of things. A man once more, in earnest with the Universe, though all others were but toying with it. He is a *Vates*, first of all, in virtue of being sincere. So far Poet and Prophet, participators in the "open secret," are one.

With respect to their distinction again: the *Vates* Prophet, we might say, has seized that sacred mystery rather on the moral side, as Good and Evil, Duty and Prohibition; the *Vates* Poet on what the Germans call the æsthetic side, as Beautiful, and the like. The one we may call a revealer of what we are to do, the other of what we are to love. But indeed these two provinces run into one another, and cannot be disjoined. The Prophet too has his eye on what we are to love: how else shall he know what it is we are to do? The highest Voice ever heard on this earth said withal, "Consider the lilies of the field; they toil not, neither do they spin: yet Solomon in all his glory was not arrayed like one of these." A glance, that, into the deepest deep of Beauty. "The lilies of the field," — dressed finer than earthly princes, springing-up there in the humble furrow-field; a beautiful *eye* looking-out on you, from the great inner Sea of Beauty! How could the rude Earth make these if her Essence, rugged as she looks and is, were not inwardly Beauty? In this point of view, too, a saying of Goethe's, which has staggered several, may have meaning: "The Beautiful," he intimates, "is higher than the Good; the Beautiful includes in it the Good." The *true* Beautiful; which however, I have said somewhere, "differs from

[1] Carlyle himself.

the *false* as Heaven does from Vauxhall!" So much for the distinction and identity of Poet and Prophet. —

In ancient and also in modern periods we find a few Poets who are accounted perfect; whom it were a kind of treason to find fault with. This is noteworthy; this is right: yet in strictness it is only an illusion. At bottom, clearly enough, there is no perfect Poet! A vein of Poetry exists in the hearts of all men; no man is made altogether of Poetry. We are all poets when we *read* a poem well. The "imagination that shudders at the Hell of Dante," is not that the same faculty, weaker in degree, as Dante's own? No one but Shakspeare can embody, out of *Saxo Grammaticus,* the story of *Hamlet* as Shakspeare did: but every one models some kind of story out of it; every one embodies it better or worse. We need not spend time in defining. Where there is no specific difference, as between round and square, all definition must be more or less arbitrary. A man that has *so* much more of the poetic element developed in him as to have become noticeable, will be called Poet by his neighbours. World-Poets too, those whom we are to take for perfect Poets, are settled by critics in the same way. One who rises *so* far above the general level of Poets will, to such and such critics, seem a Universal Poet; as he ought to do. And yet it is, and must be, an arbitrary distinction. All Poets, all men, have some touches of the Universal; no man is wholly made of that. Most Poets are very soon forgotten: but not the noblest Shakspeare or Homer of them can be remembered *forever*; — a day comes when he too is not!

Nevertheless, you will say, there must be a difference between true Poetry and true speech not poetical: what is the difference? On this point many things have been written, especially by late German Critics, some of which are not very intelligible at first. They say, for example, that the Poet has an *infinitude* in him; communicates an *Unendlichkeit,* a certain character of "infinitude," to whatsoever he delineates. This, though not very precise, yet on so vague a matter is worth remembering: if well meditated, some meaning will gradually be found in it. For my own part, I find considerable meaning in the old vulgar distinction of Poetry being *metrical,* having music in it, being a Song. Truly, if pressed to give a definition, one might say this as soon as anything else: If your delineation be authentically *musical,* musical not in word only, but in heart and substance, in all the thoughts and utterances of it, in the whole conception of it, then it will be poetical; if not, not. — Musical: how much lies in that! A *musical* thought is one spoken by a mind that has penetrated into the inmost heart of the thing; detected the inmost mystery of it, namely the *melody* that lies hidden in it; the inward harmony of coherence which is its soul, whereby it exists, and has a right to be, here in this world. All inmost things, we may say, are melodious; naturally utter themselves in Song. The meaning of Song goes deep. Who is there that, in logical words, can express the effect music has on us? A kind of inarticulate unfathomable speech, which leads us to the edge of the Infinite, and lets us for moments gaze into that!

Nay all speech, even the commonest speech, has something of song in it: not a parish in the world but has its parish-accent; — the rhythm or *tune* to which the people there *sing* what they have to say! Accent is a kind of chanting; all men have accent of their own, — though they only *notice* that of others. Observe too how all passionate language does of itself become musical, — with a finer music than the mere accent; the speech of a man even in zealous anger becomes a chant, a song. All deep things are Song. It seems somehow the very central essence of us, Song; as if all the rest were but wrappages and hulls! The primal element of us; of us, and of all things. The Greeks fabled of Sphere-Harmonies: it was the feeling they had of the inner structure of Nature: that the soul of all her voices and utterances was perfect music. Poetry, therefore, we will call *musical Thought*. The Poet is he who *thinks* in that manner. At bottom, it turns still on power of intellect; it is a man's sincerity and depth of vision that makes him a Poet. See deep enough, and you see musically; the heart of Nature *being* everywhere music, if you can only reach it. . . .

Nay here in these ages, such as they are, have we not two mere Poets, if not deified, yet we may say beatified? Shakspeare and Dante are Saints of Poetry; really, if we will think of it, *canonised*, so that it is impiety to meddle with them. The unguided instinct of the world, working across all these perverse impediments, has arrived at such result. Dante and Shakspeare are a peculiar Two. They dwell apart, in a kind of royal solitude; none equal, none second to them: in the general feeling of the world, a certain transcendentalism, a glory as of complete perfection, invests these two. They *are* canonised, though no Pope or Cardinals took hand in doing it! Such, in spite of every perverting influence, in the most unheroic times, is still our indestructible reverence for heroism. — We will look a little at these Two, the Poet Dante and the Poet Shakspeare: what little it is permitted us to say here of the Hero as Poet will most fitly arrange itself in that fashion.

Many volumes have been written by way of commentary on Dante and his Book; yet, on the whole, with no great result. His Biography is, as it were, irrecoverably lost for us. An unimportant, wandering, sorrow-stricken man, not much note was taken of him while he lived; and the most of that has vanished, in the long space that now intervenes. It is five centuries since he ceased writing and living here. After all commentaries, the Book itself is mainly what we know of him. The Book; — and one might add that Portrait commonly attributed to Giotto, which, looking on it, you cannot help inclining to think genuine, whoever did it. To me it is a most touching face; perhaps of all faces that I know, the most so. Lonely there, painted as on vacancy, with the simple laurel wound round it; the deathless sorrow and pain, the known victory which is also deathless; — significant of the whole history of Dante! I think it is the mournfulest face that ever was painted from reality; an altogether tragic, heart-affecting face. There is in it, as a foundation of it, the softness, tenderness, gentle affection as of a child; but all this is as if congealed into sharp contradiction, into abnegation, isolation, proud hopeless pain. A soft ethereal soul looking-out so stern, implacable, grim-trenchant, as from imprisonment of thick-ribbed ice! Withal it is a silent pain too, a silent scornful one: the lip is curled in a kind of godlike disdain of the thing that is eating-out his heart, — as if it were withal a mean insignificant thing, as if he whom it had power to torture and strangle were greater than it. The face of one wholly in protest, and life-long unsurrendering battle, against the world. Affection all converted into indignation: an implacable indignation; slow, equable, silent, like that of a god! The eye too, it looks-out as in a kind of *surprise,* a kind of inquiry, Why the world was of such a sort? This is Dante: so he looks, this "voice of ten silent centuries," and sings us "his mystic unfathomable song."

The little that we know of Dante's Life corresponds well enough with this Portrait and this Book. He was born at Florence, in the upper class of society, in the year 1265. His education was the best then going; much school-divinity, Aristotelian logic, some Latin classics, — no inconsiderable insight into certain provinces of things: and Dante, with his earnest intelligent nature, we need not doubt, learned better than most all that was learnable. He has a clear cultivated understanding, and of great subtlety; this best fruit of education he had contrived to realise from these scholastics. He knows accurately and well what lies close to him; but, in such a time, without printed books or free intercourse, he could not know well what was distant: the small clear light, most luminous for what is near, breaks itself into singular *chiaroscuro* striking on what is far off. This was Dante's learning from the schools. In life, he had gone through the usual destinies; been twice out campaigning as a soldier for the Florentine State, been on embassy; had in his thirty-fifth year, by natural gradation of talent and service, become one of the Chief Magistrates of Florence. He had met in boyhood a certain Beatrice Portinari, a beautiful little girl of his own age and rank, and grown-up thenceforth in partial sight of her, in some distant intercourse with her. All readers know his graceful affecting account of this; and then of their being parted; of her being wedded to another, and of her death soon after. She makes a great figure in Dante's Poem; seems to have made a great figure in his life. Of all beings it might seem as if she, held apart from him, far apart at last in the dim Eternity, were the only one he had ever with his whole strength of affection loved. She died: Dante himself was wedded; but it seems not happily, far from happily. I fancy, the rigorous earnest man, with his keen excitabilities, was not altogether easy to make happy. . . .

I said, Dante's Poem was a Song: it is Tieck who calls it "a mystic unfathomable Song"; and such is literally the character of it. Coleridge remarks very pertinently somewhere, that wherever you find a sentence musically worded, of true rhythm and melody in the words, there is something deep and good in the meaning too. For body and soul, word and idea, go strangely together here as everywhere. Song: we said before, it was the Heroic of Speech! All *old* Poems, Homer's and the rest, are authentically Songs. I would say, in strictness, that all right Poems are; that whatsoever is not *sung* is properly no Poem, but a piece of Prose cramped into jingling lines, — to the great injury of the grammar, to the great grief of the reader, for most part! What we want to get at is the *thought* the man had, if he had any: why should he twist it into jingle, if he *could* speak it out plainly? It is only when the heart of him is rapt into true passion of melody, and the very tones of him, according to Coleridge's remark, become musical by the greatness, depth and music of his thoughts, that we can give him right to rhyme and sing; that we call him a Poet, and listen to him as the Heroic of Speakers, — whose speech *is* Song. Pretenders to this are many; and to an earnest reader, I doubt, it is for most part a very melancholy, not to say an insupportable business, that of reading rhyme! Rhyme that had no inward necessity to be rhymed: — it ought to have told us plainly, without any jingle, what it was aiming at. I would advise all men who *can* speak their thought, not to sing it; to understand that, in a serious time, among serious men, there is no vocation in them for singing it. Precisely as we love the true song, and are charmed by it as by something divine, so shall we hate the false song, and account it a mere wooden noise, a thing hollow, superfluous, altogether an insincere and offensive thing.

I give Dante my highest praise when I say of his *Divine Comedy* that it is, in all senses, genuinely a Song. In the very sound of it there is a *canto fermo;* it proceeds as by a chant. The language, his simple *terza rima,* doubtless helped him in this. One reads along naturally with a sort of *lilt.* But I add, that it could not be otherwise; for the essence and material of the work are themselves rhythmic. Its depth, and rapt passion and sincerity, makes it musical; — go *deep* enough, there is music everywhere. A true inward symmetry, what one calls an architectural harmony, reigns in it, proportionates it all: architectural; which also partakes of the character of music. The three kingdoms, *Inferno, Purgatorio, Paradiso,* look-out on one another like compartments of a great edifice; a great supernatural world-cathedral, piled-up there, stern, solemn, awful; Dante's World of Souls! It is, at bottom, the *sincerest* of all Poems; sincerity, here too, we find to be the measure of worth. It came deep out of the author's heart of hearts; and it goes deep, and through long generations, into ours. The people of Verona, when they saw him on the streets, used to say, *"Eccovi l' uom ch' è stato all' Inferno,* See, there is the man that was

in Hell!" Ah yes, he had been in Hell; — in Hell enough, in long
severe sorrow and struggle; as the like of him is pretty sure to have
been. Commedias that come-out *divine* are not accomplished otherwise. Thought, true labour of any kind, highest virtue itself, is it not
the daughter of Pain? Born as out of the black whirlwind; — true
effort, in fact, as of a captive struggling to free himself: that is
Thought. In all ways we are "to become perfect through *suffering."*
— But, as I say, no work known to me is so elaborated as this of
Dante's. It has all been as if molten, in the hottest furnace of his soul.
It had made him "lean" for many years. Not the general whole only;
every compartment of it is worked-out, with intense earnestness, into
truth, into clear visuality. Each answers to the other; each fits in its
place, like a marble stone accurately hewn and polished. It is the
soul of Dante, and in this the soul of the middle ages, rendered forever
rhythmically visible there. No light task; a right intense one: but a
task which is *done.*

Perhaps one would say, *intensity,* with the much that depends on
it, is the prevailing character of Dante's genius. Dante does not come
before us as a large catholic mind, rather a narrow, and even sectarian
mind: it is partly the fruit of his age and position, but partly too of
his own nature. His greatness has, in all senses, concentered itself
into fiery emphasis and depth. He is world-great not because he is
world-wide, but because he is world-deep. Through all objects he
pierces as it were down into the heart of Being. I know nothing so intense as Dante. Consider, for example, to begin with the outermost
development of his intensity, consider how he paints. He has a great
power of vision; seizes the very type of a thing; presents that and
nothing more. You remember that first view he gets of the Hall of
Dite: *red* pinnacle, redhot cone of iron glowing through the dim immensity of gloom; — so vivid, so distinct, visible at once and forever!
It is as an emblem of the whole genius of Dante. There is a brevity,
an abrupt precision in him: Tacitus is not briefer, more condensed; and
then in Dante it seems a natural condensation, spontaneous to the
man. One smiting word; and then there is silence, nothing more said.
His silence is more eloquent than words. It is strange with what a
sharp decisive grace he snatches the true likeness of a matter: cuts into
the matter as with a pen of fire. Plutus, the blustering giant, collapses
at Virgil's rebuke; it is "as the sails sink, the mast being suddenly
broken." Or that poor Brunetto Latini, with the *cotto aspetto,* "face
baked," parched brown and lean; and the "fiery snow" that falls on
them there, a "fiery snow without wind," slow, deliberate, never-ending! Or the lids of those Tombs; square sarcophaguses, in that silent
dim-burning Hall, each with its Soul in torment; the lids laid open
there; they are to be shut at the Day of Judgment, through Eternity.
And how Farinata rises; and how Cavalcante falls — at hearing of his
Son, and the past tense *"fue"!* The very movements in Dante have

something brief; swift, decisive, almost military. It is of the inmost essence of his genius, this sort of painting. The fiery, swift Italian nature of the man, so silent, passionate, with its quick abrupt movements, its silent "pale rages," speaks itself in these things. . . .

Dante's Hell, Purgatory, Paradise, are a symbol withal, an emblematic representation of his Belief about this Universe: — some Critic in a future age, like those Scandinavian ones the other day, who has ceased altogether to think as Dante did, may find this too all an "Allegory," perhaps an idle Allegory! It is a sublime embodiment, or sublimest, of the soul of Christianity. It expresses, as in huge worldwide architectural emblems, how the Christian Dante felt Good and Evil to be the two polar elements of this Creation, on which it all turns; that these two differ not by *preferability* of one to the other, but by incompatibility absolute and infinite; that the one is excellent and high as light and Heaven, the other hideous, black as Gehenna and the Pit of Hell! Everlasting Justice, yet with Penitence, with everlasting Pity, — all Christianism, as Dante and the Middle Ages had it, is emblemed here. Emblemed: and yet, as I urged the other day, with what entire truth of purpose; how unconscious of any embleming! Hell, Purgatory, Paradise: these things were not fashioned as emblems; was there, in our Modern European Mind, any thought at all of their being emblems! Were they not indubitable awful facts; the whole heart of man taking them for practically true, all Nature everywhere confirming them? So is it always in these things. Men do not believe an Allegory. The future Critic, whatever his new thought may be, who considers this of Dante to have been all got-up as an Allegory, will commit one sore mistake! — Paganism we recognised as a veracious expression of the earnest awe-struck feeling of man towards the Universe; veracious, true once, and still not without worth for us. But mark here the difference of Paganism and Christianism; one great difference. Paganism emblemed chiefly the Operations of Nature; the destinies, efforts, combinations, vicissitudes of things and men in this world; Christianism emblemed the Law of Human Duty, the Moral Law of Man. One was for the sensuous nature: a rude helpless utterance of the *first* Thought of men, — the chief recognised virtue, Courage, Superiority to Fear. The other was not for the sensuous nature, but for the moral. What a progress is here, if in that one respect only! —

And so in this Dante, as we said, had ten silent centuries, in a very strange way, found a voice. The *Divina Commedia* is of Dante's writing; yet in truth *it* belongs to ten Christian centuries, only the finishing of it is Dante's. So always. The craftsman there, the smith with that metal of his, with these tools, with these cunning methods, — how little of all he does is properly *his* work! All past inventive men work there with him; — as indeed with all of us, in all things. Dante is the spokesman of the Middle Ages; the Thought they lived by stands here, in everlasting music. These sublime ideas of his, terrible and beautiful, are the fruit of the Christian Meditation of all the good men who had gone before him. Precious they; but also is not he precious? Much, had not he spoken, would have been dumb; not dead, yet living voiceless. . . .

As Dante, the Italian man, was sent into our world to embody musically the Religion of the Middle Ages, the Religion of our Modern Europe, its Inner Life; so Shakspeare, we may say, embodies for us the Outer Life of our Europe as developed then, its chivalries, courtesies, humours, ambitions, what practical way of thinking, acting, looking at the world, men then had. As in Homer we may still construe Old Greece; so in Shakspeare and Dante, after thousands of years, what our modern Europe was, in Faith and in Practice, will still be legible. Dante has given us the Faith or Soul; Shakspeare, in a not less noble way, has given us the Practice or body. This latter also we were to have; a man was sent for it, the man Shakspeare. Just when that chivalry way of life had reached its last finish, and was on the point of breaking down into slow or swift dissolution, as we now see it everywhere, this other sovereign Poet, with his seeing eye, with his perennial singing voice, was sent to take note of it, to give long-enduring record of it. Two fit men: Dante, deep, fierce as the central fire of the world; Shakspeare, wide, placid, far-seeing, as the Sun, the upper light of the world. Italy produced the one world-voice; we English had the honour of producing the other.

Curious enough how, as it were by mere accident, this man came to us. I think always, so great, quiet, complete and self-sufficing is this Shakspeare, had the Warwickshire Squire not prosecuted him for deer-stealing, we had perhaps never heard of him as a Poet! The woods and skies, the rustic Life of Man in Stratford there, had been enough for this man! But indeed that strange outbudding of our whole English Existence, which we call the Elizabethan Era, did not it too come as of its own accord? The "Tree Igdrasil" buds and withers by its own laws, — too deep for our scanning. Yet it does bud and wither, and every bough and leaf of it is there, by fixed eternal laws; not a Sir Thomas Lucy [2] but comes at the hour fit for him. Curious, I say, and not sufficiently considered: how everything does coöperate with all; not a leaf rotting on the highway but is indissoluble portion óf solar and stellar systems; no thought, word or act of man but has sprung withal out of all men, and works sooner or later, recognisably or irrecognisably, on all men! It is all a Tree: circulation of sap and influences, mutual communication of every minutest leaf with the lowest talon of a root, with every other greatest and minutest portion of the whole. The Tree Igdrasil, that has its roots down in the

2 (1532–1600), said to have prosecuted Shakespeare for deer-stealing.

Kingdoms of Hela and Death, and whose boughs overspread the highest Heaven! —

In some sense it may be said that this glorious Elizabethan Era with its Shakspeare, as the outcome and flowerage of all which had preceded it, is itself attributable to the Catholicism of the Middle Ages. The Christian Faith, which was the theme of Dante's Song, had produced this Practical Life which Shakspeare was to sing. For Religion then, as it now and always is, was the soul of Practice; the primary vital fact in men's life. And remark here, as rather curious, that Middle-Age Catholicism was abolished, so far as Acts of Parliament could abolish it, before Shakspeare, the noblest product of it, made his appearance. He did make his appearance nevertheless. Nature at her own time, with Catholicism or what else might be necessary, sent him forth; taking small thought of Acts of Parliament. King-Henrys, Queen-Elizabeths go their way; and Nature too goes hers. Acts of Parliament, on the whole, are small, notwithstanding the noise they make. What Act of Parliament, debate at St. Stephen's, on the hustings or elsewhere, was it that brought this Shakspeare into being? No dining at Freemasons' Tavern, opening subscription-lists, selling of shares, and infinite other jangling and true or false endeavouring! This Elizabethan Era, and all its nobleness and blessedness, came without proclamation, preparation of ours. Priceless Shakspeare was the free gift of Nature; given altogether silently; — received altogether silently, as if it had been a thing of little account. And yet, very literally, it is a priceless thing. One should look at that side of matters too.

Of this Shakspeare of ours, perhaps the opinion one sometimes hears a little idolatrously expressed is, in fact, the right one; I think the best judgment not of this country only, but of Europe at large, is slowly pointing to the conclusion, That Shakspeare is the chief of all Poets hitherto; the greatest intellect who, in our recorded world, has left record of himself in the way of Literature. On the whole, I know not such a power of vision, such a faculty of thought, if we take all the characters of it, in any other man. Such a calmness of depth; placid joyous strength; all things imaged in that great soul of his so true and clear, as in a tranquil unfathomable sea! It has been said,[3] that in the constructing of Shakspeare's Dramas there is, apart from all other "faculties" as they are called, an understanding manifested, equal to that in Bacon's *Novum Organum*. That is true; and it is not a truth that strikes every one. It would become more apparent if we tried, any of us for himself, how, out of Shakspeare's dramatic materials, *we* could fashion such a result! The built house seems all so fit, — everyway as it should be, as if it came there by its own law and the nature of things, — we forget the rude disorderly quarry

[3] By Carlyle himself.

it was shaped from. The very perfection of the house, as if Nature herself had made it, hides the builder's merit. Perfect, more perfect than any other man, we may call Shakspeare in this: he discerns, knows as by instinct, what condition he works under, what his materials are, what his own force and its relation to them is. It is not a transitory glance of insight that will suffice; it is deliberate illumination of the whole matter; it is a calmly *seeing* eye; a great intellect, in short. How a man, of some wide thing that he has witnessed, will construct a narrative, what kind of picture and delineation he will give of it, — is the best measure you could get of what intellect is in the man. Which circumstance is vital and shall stand prominent; which unessential, fit to be suppressed; where is the true *beginning*, the true sequence and ending? To find out this, you task the whole force of insight that is in the man. He must *understand* the thing; according to the depth of his understanding, will the fitness of his answer be. You will try him so. Does like join itself to like; does the spirit of method stir in that confusion, so that its embroilment becomes order? Can the man say, *Fiat lux*, Let there be light; and out of chaos make a world? Precisely as there is *light* in himself, will he accomplish this.

Or indeed we may say again, it is in what I called Portrait-painting, delineating of men and things, especially of men, that Shakspeare is great. All the greatness of the man comes out decisively here. It is unexampled, I think, that calm creative perspicacity of Shakspeare. The thing he looks at reveals not this or that face of it, but its inmost heart, and generic secret: it dissolves itself as in light before him, so that he discerns the perfect structure of it. Creative, we said: poetic creation, what is this too but *seeing* the thing sufficiently? The *word* that will describe the thing, follows of itself from such clear intense sight of the thing. And is not Shakspeare's *morality*, his valour, candour, tolerance, truthfulness; his whole victorious strength and greatness, which can triumph over such obstructions, visible there too? Great as the world! No *twisted*, poor convex-concave mirror, reflecting all objects with its own convexities and concavities; a perfectly *level* mirror; — that is to say withal, if we will understand it, a man justly related to all things and men, a good man. It is truly a lordly spectacle how this great soul takes-in all kinds of men and objects, a Falstaff, an Othello, a Juliet, a Coriolanus; sets them all forth to us in their round completeness; loving, just, the equal brother of all. *Novum Organum*, and all the intellect you will find in Bacon, is of a quite secondary order; early, material, poor in comparison with this. Among modern men, one finds, in strictness, almost nothing of the same rank. Goethe alone, since the days of Shakspeare, reminds me of it. Of him too you say that he *saw* the object; you may say what he himself says of Shakspeare: "His characters are like watches with dial-plates of transparent crystal; they show you the hour like others, and the inward mechanism also is all visible."

The seeing eye! It is this that discloses the inner harmony of things; what Nature meant, what musical idea Nature has wrapped-up in these often rough embodiments. Something she did mean. To the seeing eye that something were discernible. Are they base, miserable things? You can laugh over them, you can weep over them; you can in some way or other genially relate yourself to them; — you can, at lowest, hold your peace about them, turn away your own and others' face from them, till the hour come for practically exterminating and extinguishing them! At bottom, it is the Poet's first gift, as it is all men's, that he have intellect enough. He will be a Poet if he have: a Poet in word; or failing that, perhaps still better, a Poet in act. Whether he write at all; and if so, whether in prose or in verse, will depend on accidents: who knows on what extremely trivial accidents, — perhaps on his having had a singing-master, on his being taught to sing in his boyhood! But the faculty which enables him to discern the inner heart of things, and the harmony that dwells there (for whatsoever exists has a harmony in the heart of it, or it would not hold together and exist), is not the result of habits or accidents, but the gift of Nature herself; the primary outfit for a Heroic Man in what sort soever. To the Poet, as to every other, we say first of all, *See*. If you cannot do that, it is of no use to keep stringing rhymes together, jingling sensibilities against each other, and *name* yourself a Poet; there is no hope for you. If you can, there is, in prose or verse, in action or speculation, all manner of hope. The crabbed old Schoolmaster used to ask, when they brought him a new pupil, "But are ye sure he's *not a dunce?*" Why, really one might ask the same thing, in regard to every man proposed for whatsoever function; and consider it as the one inquiry needful: Are ye sure he's not a dunce? There is, in this world, no other entirely fatal person. . . .

If I say, therefore, that Shakspeare is the greatest of Intellects, I have said all concerning him. But there is more in Shakspeare's intellect than we have yet seen. It is what I call an unconscious intellect; there is more virtue in it than he himself is aware of. Novalis beautifully remarks of him, that those Dramas of his are Products of Nature too, deep as Nature herself. I find a great truth in this saying. Shakspeare's Art is not Artifice; the noblest worth of it is not there by plan or precontrivance. It grows-up from the deeps of Nature, through this noble sincere soul, who is a voice of Nature. The latest generations of men will find new meanings in Shakspeare, new elucidations of their own human being; "new harmonies with the infinite structure of the Universe; concurrences with later ideas, affinities with the higher powers and senses of man." This well deserves meditating. It is Nature's highest reward to a true simple great soul, that he get thus to be *a part of herself*. Such a man's works, whatsoever he with utmost conscious exertion and forethought shall accomplish, grow up withal *un*consciously, from the unknown deeps in him; — as the oak-tree

grows from the Earth's bosom, as the mountains and waters shape
themselves; with a symmetry grounded on Nature's own laws, conformable to all Truth whatsoever. How much in Shakspeare lies
hid; his sorrows, his silent struggles known to himself; much that was
not known at all, not speakable at all: like *roots*, like sap and forces
working underground! Speech is great; but Silence is greater.

Withal the joyful tranquillity of this man is notable. I will not
blame Dante for his misery: it is as battle without victory; but true
battle, — the first, indispensable thing. Yet I call Shakspeare greater
than Dante, in that he fought truly, and did conquer. Doubt it not,
he had his own sorrows: those *Sonnets* of his will even testify expressly
in what deep waters he had waded, and swum struggling for his
life; — as what man like him ever failed to have to do? It seems to
me a heedless notion, our common one, that he sat like a bird on the
bough; and sang forth, free and off-hand, never knowing the troubles
of other men. Not so; with no man is it so. How could a man travel
forward from rustic deer-poaching to such tragedy-writing, and not
fall-in with sorrows by the way? Or, still better, how could a man
delineate a Hamlet, a Coriolanus, a Macbeth, so many suffering heroic
hearts, if his own heroic heart had never suffered? — And now, in
contrast with all this, observe his mirthfulness, his genuine overflowing love of laughter! You would say, in no point does he *exaggerate*
but only in laughter. Fiery objurgations, words that pierce and burn,
are to be found in Shakspeare; yet he is always in measure here;
never what Johnson would remark as a specially "good hater." But
his laughter seems to pour from him in floods; he heaps all manner of
ridiculous nicknames on the butt he is bantering, tumbles and tosses
him in all sorts of horse-play; you would say, with his whole heart
laughs. And then, if not always the finest, it is always a genial
laughter. Not at mere weakness, at misery or poverty; never. No
man who *can* laugh, what we call laughing, will laugh at these things.
It is some poor character only *desiring* to laugh, and have the credit
of wit, that does so. Laughter means sympathy; good laughter is not
"the crackling of thorns under the pot." Even at stupidity and pretension this Shakspeare does not laugh otherwise than genially. Dog-
berry and Verges tickle our very hearts; and we dismiss them covered
with explosions of laughter: but we like the poor fellows only the
better for our laughing; and hope they will get on well there, and
continue Presidents of the City-watch. Such laughter, like sunshine
on the deep sea, is very beautiful to me. . . .

Shakspeare's works . . . are so many windows, through which we
see a glimpse of the world that was in him. All his works seem,
comparatively speaking, cursory, imperfect, written under cramping
circumstances; giving only here and there a note of the full utterance
of the man. Passages there are that come upon you like splendour
out of Heaven; bursts of radiance, illuminating the very heart of the

thing: you say, "That is *true,* spoken once and forever; wheresoever and whensoever there is an open human soul, that will be recognised as true!" Such bursts, however, make us feel that the surrounding matter is not radiant; that it is, in part, temporary, conventional. Alas, Shakspeare had to write for the Globe Playhouse: his great soul had to crush itself, as it could, into that and no other mould. It was with him, then, as it is with us all. No man works save under conditions. The sculptor cannot set his own free Thought before us; but his Thought as he could translate it into the stone that was given, with the tools that were given. *Disjecta membra* are all that we find of any Poet, or of any man.

Whoever looks intelligently at this Shakspeare may recognise that he too was a *Prophet,* in his way; of an insight analogous to the Prophetic, though he took it up in another strain. Nature seemed to this man also divine; *un*speakable, deep as Tophet, high as Heaven: "We are such stuff as Dreams are made of!" That scroll in Westminster Abbey, which few read with understanding, is of the depth of any seer. But the man sang; did not preach, except musically. We called Dante the melodious Priest of Middle-Age Catholicism. May we not call Shakspeare the still more melodious Priest of a *true* Catholicism, the "Universal Church" of the Future and of all times? No narrow superstition, harsh asceticism, intolerance, fanatical fierceness or perversion: a Revelation, so far as it goes, that such a thousandfold hidden beauty and divineness dwells in all Nature; which let all men worship as they can! We may say without offence, that there rises a kind of universal Psalm out of this Shakspeare too; not unfit to make itself heard among the still more sacred Psalms. Not in disharmony with these, if we understood them, but in harmony! — I cannot call this Shakspeare a "Sceptic," as some do; his indifference to the creeds and theological quarrels of his time misleading them. No: neither unpatriotic, though he says little about his Patriotism; nor sceptic, though he says little about his Faith. Such "indifference" was the fruit of his greatness withal: his whole heart was in his own grand sphere of worship (we may call it such); these other controversies, vitally important to other men, were not vital to him.

But call it worship, call it what you will, is it not a right glorious thing, and set of things, this that Shakspeare has brought us? For myself, I feel that there is actually a kind of sacredness in the fact of such a man being sent into this Earth. Is he not an eye to us all; a blessed heaven-sent Bringer of Light? — And, at bottom, was it not perhaps far better that this Shakspeare, everyway an unconscious man, was *conscious* of no Heavenly message? He did not feel, like Mahomet, because he saw into those internal Splendours, that he specially was the "Prophet of God": and was he not greater than Mahomet in that? Greater; and also, if we compute strictly, as we did in Dante's case, more successful. It was intrinsically an error that notion of Mahomet's, of his supreme Prophethood; and has come down to us inextricably involved in error to this day; dragging along with it such a coil of fables, impurities, intolerances, as makes it a questionable step for me here and now to say, as I have done, that Mahomet was a true Speaker at all, and not rather an ambitious charlatan, perversity and simulacrum; ao Speaker, but a Babbler! Even in Arabia, as I compute, Mahomet will have exhausted himself and become obsolete, while this Shakspeare, this Dante may still be young; — while this Shakspeare may still pretend to be a Priest of Mankind, of Arabia as of other places, for unlimited periods to come!

Compared with any speaker or singer one knows, even with Æschylus or Homer, why should he not, for veracity and universality, last like them? He is *sincere* as they; reaches deep down like them, to the universal and perennial. But as for Mahomet, I think it had been better for him *not* to be so conscious! Alas, poor Mahomet; all that he was *conscious* of was a mere error; a futility and triviality, — as indeed such ever is. The truly great in him too was the unconscious: that he was a wild Arab lion of the desert, and did speak-out with that great thunder-voice of his, not by words which he *thought* to be great, but by actions, by feelings, by a history which *were* great! His Koran has become a stupid piece of prolix absurdity; we do not believe, like him, that God wrote that! The Great Man here too, as always, is a Force of Nature: whatsoever is truly great in him springs-up from the *in*articulate deeps.

Well: this is our poor Warwickshire Peasant, who rose to be Manager of a Playhouse, so that he could live without begging; whom the Earl of Southampton [4] cast some kind glances on; whom Sir Thomas Lucy, many thanks to him, was for sending to the Treadmill! We did not account him a god, like Odin, while he dwelt with us; — on which point there were much to be said. But I will say rather, or repeat: In spite of the sad state Hero-worship now lies in, consider what this Shakspeare has actually become among us. Which Englishman we ever made, in this land of ours, which million of Englishmen, would we not give-up rather than the Stratford Peasant? There is no regiment of highest Dignitaries that we would sell him for. He is the grandest thing we have yet done. For our honour among foreign nations, as an ornament to our English Household, what item is there that we would not surrender rather than him? Consider now, if they asked us, Will you give-up your Indian Empire or your Shakspeare, you English; never have had any Indian Empire, or never have had any Shakspeare? Really it were a grave question. Official persons would answer doubtless in official language; but we, for our

4 (1573–1624), Shakespeare's patron.

part too, should not we be forced to answer: Indian Empire, or no Indian Empire; we cannot do without Shakspeare! Indian Empire will go, at any rate, some day; but this Shakspeare does not go, he lasts forever with us; we cannot give-up our Shakspeare! . . .

Yes, truly, it is a great thing for a Nation that it get an articulate voice; that it produce a man who will speak-forth melodiously what the heart of it means! Italy, for example, poor Italy lies dismembered, scattered asunder, not appearing in any protocol or treaty as a unity at all; yet the noble Italy is actually *one*: Italy produced its Dante; Italy can speak! The Czar of all the Russias, he is strong with so many bayonets, Cossacks and cannons; and does a great feat in keeping such a tract of Earth politically together; but he cannot yet speak. Something great in him, but it is a dumb greatness. He has had no voice of genius, to be heard of all men and times. He must learn to speak. He is a great dumb monster hitherto. His cannons and Cossacks will all have rusted into nonentity, while that Dante's voice is still audible. The Nation that has a Dante is bound together as no dumb Russia can be. — We must here end what we had to say of the *Hero-Poet*.

Past and Present

❲ *Past and Present* contains Carlyle's principal contemporary social criticism. In the middle of composing the volume (we are told that it "was written off with singular ease in the first seven weeks of 1843") Carlyle wrote to a friend: "The thing I am upon is a volume to be called 'Past and Present.' It is a moral, political, historical, and a most questionable red-hot indignant thing, for my heart is sick to look at the things now going on in England." The volume is divided into four books: I. "Proem"; II. "The Ancient Monk"; III. "The Modern Worker"; IV. "Horoscope." No single chapter from Book II, admittedly, can give an adequate idea of Carlyle's method and philosophy of history, but the first chapter is offered as at least suggestive thereof. Sauerteig, "Sour dough," is an imaginary German used as a formal device by Carlyle. ❳

BOOK II — THE ANCIENT MONK

CHAPTER I

Jocelin of Brakelond

We will, in this Second Portion of our Work, strive to penetrate a little, by means of certain confused Papers, printed and other, into a somewhat remote Century; and to look face to face on it, in hope of perhaps illustrating our own poor Century thereby. It seems a circuitous way; but it may prove a way nevertheless. For man has ever been a striving, struggling, and, in spite of wide-spread calumnies to the contrary, a veracious creature: the Centuries too are all lineal children of one another; and often, in the portrait of early grandfathers, this and the other enigmatic feature of the newest grandson shall disclose itself, to mutual elucidation. This Editor will venture on such a thing.

Besides, in Editors' Books, and indeed everywhere else in the world of To-day, a certain latitude of movement grows more and more becoming for the practical man. Salvation lies not in tight lacing, in these times; — how far from that, in any province whatsoever! Readers and men generally are getting into strange habits of asking all persons and things, from poor Editors' Books up to Church Bishops and State Potentates, not, By what designation art thou called; in what wig and black triangle dost thou walk abroad? Heavens, I know thy designation and black triangle well enough! But, in God's name, what *art* thou? Not Nothing, sayest thou! Then, How much and what? This is the thing I would know; and even *must* soon know, such a pass am I come to! —— What weather-symptoms, — not for the poor Editor of Books alone! The Editor of Books may understand withal that if, as is said, "many kinds are permissible," there is one kind not permissible, "the kind that has nothing in it, *le genre ennuyeux*"; and go on his way accordingly.

A certain Jocelinus de Brakelonda, a natural-born Englishman, has left us an extremely foreign Book,[1] which the labours of the Camden Society have brought to light in these days. Jocelin's Book, the "Chronicle," or private Boswellean Notebook, of Jocelin, a certain old St. Edmundsbury Monk and Boswell, now seven centuries old, how remote is it from us; exotic, extraneous; in all ways, coming from far abroad! The language of it is not foreign only but dead: Monk-Latin lies across not the British Channel, but the nine-fold Stygian Marshes, Stream of Lethe, and one knows not where! Roman Latin itself, still alive for us in the Elysian Fields of Memory, is domestic in comparison. And then the ideas, life-furniture, whole workings and ways of this worthy Jocelin; covered deeper than Pompeii with the lava-ashes and inarticulate wreck of seven hundred years!

Jocelin of Brakelond cannot be called a conspicuous literary character; indeed few mortals that have left so visible a work, or footmark, behind them can be more obscure. One other of those vanished Existences, whose work has not yet vanished; — almost a pathetic phenomenon, were not the whole world full of such! The builders

---

[1] *Chronica Jocelini de Brakelonda, de rebus gestis Samsonis Abbatis Monasterii Sancti Edmundi: nunc primum typis mandata, curante Johanne Gage Rokewood.* (Camden Society, London, 1840.) [Carlyle's note.]

of Stonehenge, for example: — or alas, what say we, Stonehenge and builders? The writers of the *Universal Review* and *Homer's Iliad;* the paviours of London streets; — sooner or later, the entire Posterity of Adam! It is a pathetic phenomenon; but an irremediable, nay, if well meditated, a consoling one.

By his dialect of Monk-Latin, and indeed by his name, this Jocelin seems to have been a Norman Englishman; the surname *de Brake-londa* indicates a native of St. Edmundsbury itself, *Brakelond* being the known old name of a street or quarter in that venerable Town. Then farther, sure enough, our Jocelin was a Monk of St. Edmundsbury Convent; held some *"obedientia,"* subaltern officiality there, or rather, in succession several; was, for one thing, "chaplain to my Lord Abbot, living beside him night and day for the space of six years"; — which last, indeed, is the grand fact of Jocelin's existence, and properly the origin of this present Book, and of the chief meaning it has for us now. He was, as we have hinted, a kind of born *Boswell,* though an infinitesimally small one; neither did he altogether want his *Johnson* even there and then. Johnsons are rare; yet, as has been asserted, Boswells perhaps still rarer, — the more is the pity on both sides! This Jocelin, as we can discern well, was an ingenious and ingenuous, a cheery-hearted, innocent, yet withal shrewd, noticing, quick-witted man; and from under his monk's cowl has looked out on that narrow section of the world in a really *human* manner; not in any *simial,* canine, ovine, or otherwise *in*human manner, — afflictive to all that have humanity! The man is of patient, peaceable, loving, clear-smiling nature; open for this and that. A wise simplicity is in him; much natural sense; *a veracity* that goes deeper than words. Veracity: it is the basis of all; and, some say, means genius itself; the prime essence of all genius whatsoever. Our Jocelin, for the rest, has read his classical manuscripts, his Virgilius, his Flaccus, Ovidius Naso; of course still more, his Homilies and Breviaries, and if not the Bible, considerable extracts of the Bible. Then also he has a pleasant wit; and loves a timely joke, though in mild subdued manner: very amiable to see. A learned grown man, yet with the heart of a good child; whose whole life indeed has been that of a child, — St. Edmundsbury Monastery a larger kind of cradle for him, in which his whole prescribed duty was to *sleep* kindly, and love his mother well! This is the Biography of Jocelin; "a man of excellent religion," says one of his contemporary Brother Monks, *"eximiae religionis, potens sermone et opere."*

For one thing, he had learned to write a kind of Monk or Dog-Latin, still readable to mankind; and, by good luck for us, had be-thought him of noting down thereby what things seemed notablest to him. Hence gradually resulted a *Chronica Jocelini;* new Manuscript in the *Liber Albus* of St. Edmundsbury. Which Chronicle, once written in its childlike transparency, in its innocent good humour, not without touches of ready pleasant wit and many kinds of worth, other men liked naturally to read: whereby it failed not to be copied, to be multiplied, to be inserted in the *Liber Albus;* and so surviving Henry the Eighth, Putney Cromwell,[2] the Dissolution of Monasteries, and all accidents of malice and neglect for six centuries or so, it got into the *Harleian Collection,*[3] — and has now therefrom, by Mr. Rokewood of the Camden Society, been deciphered into clear print; and lies before us, a dainty thin quarto, to interest for a few minutes whomsoever it can.

Here too it will behove a just Historian gratefully to say that Mr. Rokewood, Jocelin's Editor, has done his editorial function well. Not only has he deciphered his crabbed Manuscript into clear print; but he has attended, what his fellow editors are not always in the habit of doing, to the important truth that the Manuscript so deciphered ought to have a meaning for the reader. Standing faithfully by his text, and printing its very errors in spelling, in grammar or otherwise, he has taken care by some note to indicate that they are errors, and what the correction of them ought to be. Jocelin's Monk-Latin is generally transparent, as shallow limpid water. But at any stop that may occur, of which there are a few, and only a very few, we have the comfortable assurance that a meaning does lie in the passage, and may by industry be got at; that a faithful editor's industry had already got at it before passing on. A compendious useful Glossary is given; nearly adequate to help the uninitiated through: sometimes one wishes it had been a trifle larger; but, with a Spelman and Ducange [4] at your elbow, how easy to have made it far too large! Notes are added, generally brief; sufficiently explanatory of most points. Lastly, a copious correct Index; which no such Book should want, and which unluckily very few possess. And so, in a word, the *Chronicle of Jocelin* is, as it professes to be, unwrapped from its thick cerements, and fairly brought forth into the common daylight, so that he who runs, and has a smattering of grammar, may read.

We have heard so much of Monks; everywhere, in real and fictitious History, from Muratori Annals [5] to Radcliffe Romances,[6] these singular two-legged animals, with their rosaries and breviaries, with their shaven crowns, hair-cilices, and vows of poverty, masquerade so strangely through our fancy; and they are in fact so very strange an

2 Thomas Cromwell, Earl of Sussex (1485–1540), born at Putney; not Oliver Cromwell.

3 *The Harleian Miscellany* — a collection of rare manuscripts first made by Robert Harley (1661–1724).

4 A dictionary published in 1840 containing the Anglo-Saxon glossary of Sir Henry Spelman (1564–1641) and the Latin and Greek glossaries of Charles D. Ducange (1610–1688).

5 A collection of the chronicles of Italy from the 5th to the 16th century by Ludovico Antonio Muratori (1672–1750).

6 "Gothic" romances by Mrs. Ann Radcliffe (1764–1823).

extinct species of the human family, — a veritable Monk of Bury St. Edmunds is worth attending to, if by chance made visible and audible. Here he is; and in his hand a magical speculum, much gone to rust indeed, yet in fragments still clear; wherein the marvellous image of his existence does still shadow itself, though fitfully, and as with an intermittent light! Will not the reader peep with us into this singular *camera lucida*, where an extinct species, though fitfully, can still be seen alive? Extinct species, we say; for the live specimens which still go about under that character are too evidently to be classed as spurious in Natural History: the Gospel of Richard Arkwright once promulgated, no Monk of the old sort is any longer possible in this world. But fancy a deep-buried Mastodon, some fossil Megatherion, Ichthyosaurus, were to begin to *speak* from amid its rock-swathings, never so indistinctly! The most extinct fossil species of Men or Monks can do, and does, this miracle, — thanks to the Letters of the Alphabet, good for so many things.

Jocelin, we said, was somewhat of a Boswell; but unfortunately, by Nature, he is none of the largest, and distance has now dwarfed him to an extreme degree. His light is most feeble, intermittent, and requires the intensest kindest inspection; otherwise it will disclose mere vacant haze. It must be owned, the good Jocelin, spite of his beautiful childlike character, is but an altogether imperfect "mirror" of these old-world things! The good man, he looks on us so clear and cheery, and in his neighbourly soft-smiling eyes we see so well our *own* shadow, — we have a longing always to cross-question him, to force from him an explanation of much. But no; Jocelin, though he talks with such clear familiarity, like a next-door neighbour, will not answer any question: that is the peculiarity of him, dead these six hundred and fifty years, and quite deaf to us, though still so audible! The good man, he cannot help it, nor can we.

But truly it is a strange consideration this simple one, as we go on with him, or indeed with any lucid simple-hearted soul like him: Behold therefore, this England of the Year 1200 was no chimerical vacuity or dreamland, peopled with mere vaporous Phantasms, Rymer's Foedera,[7] and Doctrines of the Constitution; but a green solid place, that grew corn and several other things. The Sun shone on it; the vicissitude of seasons and human fortunes. Cloth was woven and worn; ditches were dug, furrow-fields ploughed, and houses built. Day by day all men and cattle rose to labour, and night by night returned home weary to their several lairs. In wondrous Dualism, then as now, lived nations of breathing men; alternating, in all ways, between Light and Dark; between joy and sorrow, between rest and toil, — between hope, hope reaching high as Heaven, and fear deep as very Hell. Not vapour Phantasms, Rymer's Foedera at all! Cœur-

---

7 A collection of documents relating to England's foreign relations from the 12th to the 17th century made by Thomas Rymer (1641–1713), English antiquarian.

de-Lion was not a theatrical popinjay with greaves and steel-cap on it, but a man living upon victuals, — *not* imported by Peel's Tariff. Cœur-de-Lion came palpably athwart this Jocelin at St. Edmundsbury; and had almost peeled the sacred gold *"Feretrum,"* or St. Edmund Shrine itself, to ransom him out of the Danube Jail.

These clear eyes of neighbour Jocelin looked on the bodily presence of King John; the very John *Sansterre,* or Lackland, who signed *Magna Charta* afterwards in Runnymead. Lackland, with a great retinue, boarded once, for the matter of a fortnight, in St. Edmundsbury Convent; daily in the very eyesight, palpable to the very fingers of our Jocelin: O Jocelin, what did he say, what did he do; how looked he, lived he, — at the very lowest, what coat or breeches had he on? Jocelin is obstinately silent. Jocelin marks down what interests *him;* entirely deaf to *us.* With Jocelin's eyes we discern almost nothing of John Lackland. As through a glass darkly, we with our own eyes and appliances, intensely looking, discern at most: A blustering, dissipated human figure, with a kind of blackguard quality air, in cramoisy velvet, or other uncertain texture, uncertain cut, with much plumage and fringing; amid numerous other human figures of the like; riding abroad with hawks; talking noisy nonsense; — tearing out the bowels of St. Edmundsbury Convent (its larders namely and cellars) in the most ruinous way, by living at rack and manger there. Jocelin notes only, with a slight subacidity of manner, that the King's Majesty, *Dominus Rex,* did leave, as gift for our St. Edmund Shrine, a handsome enough silk cloak, — or rather pretended to leave, for one of his retinue borrowed it of us, and *we* never got sight of it again; and, on the whole, that the *Dominus Rex,* at departing, gave us "thirteen *sterlingii,"* one shilling and one penny, to say a mass for him; and so departed, — like a shabby Lackland as he was! "Thirteen pence sterling," this was what the Convent got from Lackland, for all the victuals he and his had made away with. We of course said our mass for him, having covenanted to do it, — but let impartial posterity judge with what degree of fervour!

And in this manner vanishes King Lackland; traverses swiftly our strange intermittent magic-mirror, jingling the shabby thirteen pence merely; and rides with his hawks into Egyptian night again. It is Jocelin's manner with all things; and it is men's manner and men's necessity. How intermittent is our good Jocelin; marking down, without eye to *us,* what *he* finds interesting! How much in Jocelin, as in all History, and indeed in all Nature, is at once inscrutable and certain; so dim, yet so indubitable; exciting us to endless considerations. For King Lackland *was* there, verily he; and did leave these *tredecim sterlingii,* if nothing more, and did live and look in one way or the other, and a whole world was living and looking along with him! There, we say, is the grand peculiarity; the immeasurable one; distinguishing, to a really infinite degree, the poorest historical Fact from all

Fiction whatsoever. Fiction, "Imagination," "Imaginative Poetry," &c.,
&c., except as the vehicle for truth, or *fact* of some sort, — which
surely a man should first try various other ways of vehiculating, and
conveying safe, — what is it? Let the Minerva and other Presses
respond! —

But it is time we were in St. Edmundsbury Monastery, and Seven
good Centuries off. If indeed it be possible, by any aid of Jocelin,
by any human art, to get thither, with a reader or two still following
us?

BOOK III — THE MODERN WORKER

CHAPTER II

Gospel of Mammonism

READER, even Christian Reader as thy title goes, hast thou any notion
of Heaven and Hell? I rather apprehend, not. Often as the words are
on our tongue, they have got a fabulous or semi-fabulous character
for most of us, and pass on like a kind of transient similitude, like a
sound signifying little.

Yet it is well worth while for us to know, once and always, that they
are not a similitude, nor a fable nor semi-fable; that they are an
everlasting highest fact! "No Lake of Sicilian or other sulphur burns
now anywhere in these ages," sayest thou? Well, and if there did
not! Believe that there does not; believe it if thou wilt, nay hold by
it as a real increase, a rise to higher stages, to wider horizons and
empires. All this has vanished, or has not vanished; believe as thou
wilt as to all this. But that an Infinite of Practical Importance, speaking with strict arithmetical exactness, an *Infinite* has vanished or can
vanish from the Life of any Man: this thou shalt not believe! O
brother, the Infinite of Terror, of Hope, of Pity, did it not at any moment disclose itself to thee, indubitable, unnameable? Came it never,
like the gleam of *preter*-natural Oceans, like the voice of old Eternities,
far-sounding through thy heart of hearts? Never? Alas, it was not
thy Liberalism then; it was thy Animalism! The Infinite is more sure
than any other fact. But only men can discern it; mere building beavers, spinning arachnes, much more the predatory vulturous and vul-
pine species, do not discern it well! —

"The word Hell," says Sauerteig, "is still frequently in use among
the English People: but I could not without difficulty ascertain what
they meant by it. Hell generally signifies the Infinite Terror, the thing
a man *is* infinitely afraid of, and shudders and shrinks from, struggling
with his whole soul to escape from it. There is a Hell therefore, if
you will consider, which accompanies man, in all stages of his history, and religious or other development: but the Hells of men and

Peoples differ notably. With Christians it is the infinite terror of being found guilty before the Just Judge. With old Romans, I conjecture, it was the terror not of Pluto, for whom probably they cared
little, but of doing unworthily, doing unvirtuously, which was their
word for un*man*fully. And now what is it, if you pierce through his
Cants, his oft-repeated Hearsays, what he calls his Worships and so
forth, — what is it that the modern English soul does, in very truth,
dread infinitely, and contemplate with entire despair? What *is* his Hell,
after all these reputable, oft-repeated Hearsays, what is it? With hesitation, with astonishment, I pronounce it to be: The terror of 'Not
succeeding'; of not making money, fame, or some other figure in the
world, — chiefly of not making money! Is not that a somewhat singular Hell?"

Yes, O Sauerteig, it is very singular. If we do not "succeed," where
is the use of us? We had better never have been born. "Tremble intensely," as our friend the Emperor of China says: *there* is the black
Bottomless of Terror; what Sauerteig calls the "Hell of the English!"
— But indeed this Hell belongs naturally to the Gospel of Mammonism, which also has its corresponding Heaven. For there *is* one Reality among so many Phantasms; about one thing we are entirely in
earnest: The making of money. Working Mammonism does divide the
world with the idle game-preserving Dilettantism: — thank Heaven
that there is even a Mammonism, *any*thing we are in earnest about!
Idleness is worst, Idleness alone is without hope: work earnestly at
anything, you will by degrees learn to work at almost all things.
There is endless hope in work, were it even work at making money.

True, it must be owned, we for the present, with our Mammon-Gos-
pel, have come to strange conclusions. We call it a Society; and go
about professing openly the totallest separation, isolation. Our life
is not a mutual helpfulness; but rather, cloaked under due laws-of-war,
named "fair competition" and so forth, it is a mutual hostility. We
have profoundly forgotten everywhere that *Cash-payment* is not the
sole relation of human beings; we think, nothing doubting, that *it*
absolves and liquidates all engagements of man. "My starving workers?" answers the rich Millowner: "Did not I hire them fairly in the
market? Did I not pay them, to the last sixpence, the sum covenanted
for? What have I to do with them more?" — Verily Mammon-worship
is a melancholy creed. When Cain, for his own behoof, had killed
Abel, and was questioned, "Where is thy brother?" he too made
answer, "Am I my brother's keeper?" Did I not pay my brother *his*
wages, the thing he had merited from me?

O sumptuous Merchant-Prince, illustrious game-preserving Duke,
is there no way of "killing" thy brother but Cain's rude way! "A good
man by the very look of him, by his very presence with us as a fellow
wayfarer in this Life-pilgrimage, *promises* so much": woe to him if
he forget all such promises, if he never know that they are given! To

a deadened soul, seared with the brute Idolatry of the Sense, to whom
going to Hell is equivalent to not making money, all "promises," and
moral duties, that cannot be pleaded for in Courts of Requests, address themselves in vain. Money he can be ordered to pay, but nothing more. I have not heard in all Past History, and expect not to hear
in all Future History, of any Society anywhere under God's Heaven
supporting itself on such Philosophy. The Universe is not made so;
it is made otherwise than so. The man or nation of men that thinks
it is made so, marches forward nothing doubting, step after step; but
marches — whither we know! In these last two centuries of Atheistic
Government (near two centuries now, since the blessed restoration
of his Sacred Majesty, and Defender of the Faith, Charles Second),
I reckon that we have pretty well exhausted what of "firm earth" there
was for us to march on; — and are now, very ominously, shuddering,
reeling, and let us hope trying to recoil, on the cliff's edge! —

For out of this that we call Atheism come so many other *isms* and
falsities, each falsity with its misery at its heels! — A soul is not like
wind (*spiritus*, or breath) contained within a capsule; the Almighty
Maker is not like a Clockmaker that once, in old immemorial ages,
having *made* his Horologe of a Universe, sits ever since and sees it
go! Not at all. Hence comes Atheism; come, as we say, many other
isms; and as the sum of all, comes Valetism, the *reverse* of Heroism;
sad root of all woes whatsoever. For indeed, as no man ever saw
the above-said wind-element enclosed within its capsule, and finds
it at bottom more deniable than conceivable; so too he finds, in spite
of Bridgewater Bequests,[1] your Clockmaker Almighty an entirely questionable affair, a deniable affair; — and accordingly denies it, and
along with it so much else. Alas, one knows not what and how much
else! For the faith in an Invisible, Unnameable, Godlike, present
everywhere in all that we see and work and suffer, is the essence of
all faith whatsoever; and that once denied, or still worse, asserted
with lips only, and out of bound prayerbooks only, what other thing
remains believable? That Cant well-ordered is marketable Cant; that
Heroism means gas-lighted Histrionism; that seen with "clear eyes"
(as they call Valet-eyes), no man is a Hero, or ever was a Hero, but
all men are Valets and Varlets. The accursed practical quintessence
of all sorts of Unbelief! For if there be now no Hero, and the Histrio
himself begin to be seen into, what hope is there for the seed of
Adam here below? We are the doomed everlasting prey of the Quack;
who, now in this guise, now in that, is to filch us, to pluck and eat
us, by such modes as are convenient for him. For the modes and
guises I care little. The Quack once inevitable, let him come swiftly,
let him pluck and eat me; — swiftly, that I may at least have done

[1] Bequests from the £ 8000 left by Francis Henry Egerton (1756–1829),
8th Earl of Bridgewater, to the authors of the "Bridgewater Treatises" on "The
Goodness of God as manifested in the Creation."

with him; for in his Quack-world I can have no wish to linger. Though he slay me, yet will I *not* trust in him. Though he conquer nations, and have all the Flunkeys of the Universe shouting at his heels, yet will I know well that *he* is an Inanity; that for him and his there is no continuance appointed, save only in Gehenna and the Pool. Alas, the Atheist world, from its utmost summits of Heaven and Westminster Hall, downwards through poor seven-foot Hats and "Unveracities fallen hungry," down to the lowest cellars and neglected hunger-dens of it, is very wretched.

One of Dr. Alison's Scotch facts struck us much.[2] A poor Irish Widow, her husband having died in one of the Lanes of Edinburgh, went forth with her three children, bare of all resource, to solicit help from the Charitable Establishments of that City. At this Charitable Establishment and then at that she was refused; referred from one to the other, helped by none; — till she had exhausted them all; till her strength and heart failed her: she sank down in typhus-fever; died, and infected her Lane with fever, so that "seventeen other persons" died of fever there in consequence. The humane Physician asks thereupon, as with a heart too full for speaking, Would it not have been *economy* to help this poor Widow? She took typhus-fever, and killed seventeen of you! — Very curious. The forlorn Irish Widow applies to her fellow-creatures, as if saying, "Behold I am sinking, bare of help: ye must help me! I am your sister, bone of your bone; one God made us: ye must help me!" They answer, "No; impossible; thou art no sister of ours." But she proves her sisterhood; her typhus-fever kills *them*: they actually were her brothers, though denying it! Had human creature ever to go lower for a proof?

For, as indeed was very natural in such case, all government of the Poor by the Rich has long ago been given over to Supply-and-demand, Laissez-faire and such like, and universally declared to be "impossible." "You are no sister of ours; what shadow of proof is there? Here are our parchments, our padlocks, proving indisputably our money-safes to be *ours*, and you have no business with them. Depart! It is impossible!" — Nay, what wouldst thou thyself have us do? cry indignant readers. Nothing, my friends, — till you have got a soul for yourselves again. Till then all things are "impossible." Till then I cannot even bid you buy, as the old Spartans would have done, twopence worth of powder and lead, and compendiously shoot to death this poor Irish Widow: even that is "impossible" for you. Nothing is left but that she prove her sisterhood by dying, and infecting you with typhus. Seventeen of you lying dead will not deny such proof that she *was* flesh of your flesh; and perhaps some of the living may lay it to heart.

2 Observations on the Management of the Poor in Scotland: By William Pulteney Alison, M. D. (Edinburgh, 1840). [Carlyle's note.]

"Impossible": of a certain two-legged animal with feathers it is said, if you draw a distinct chalk-circle round him, he sits imprisoned, as if girt with the iron ring of Fate; and will die there, though within sight of victuals, — or sit in sick misery there, and be fatted to death. The name of this poor two-legged animal is — Goose; and they make of him, when well fattened, *Pâté de foie gras,* much prized by some!

CHAPTER III

Gospel of Dilettantism

BUT after all, the Gospel of Dilettantism, producing a Governing Class who do not govern, nor understand in the least that they are bound or expected to govern, is still mournfuller than that of Mammonism. Mammonism, as we said, at least works; this goes idle. Mammonism has seized some portion of the message of Nature to man; and seizing that, following it, will seize and appropriate more and more of Nature's message: but Dilettantism has missed it wholly. "Make money": that will mean withal, "Do work in order to make money." But, "Go gracefully idle in Mayfair," what does or can that mean? An idle, game-preserving and even corn-lawing Aristocracy, in such an England as ours: has the world, if we take thought of it, ever seen such a phenomenon till very lately? Can it long continue to see such?

Accordingly the impotent, insolent Donothingism in Practice, and Saynothingism in Speech, which we have to witness on that side of our affairs, is altogether amazing. A Corn-Law demonstrating itself openly, for ten years or more, with "arguments" to make the angels, and some other classes of creatures, weep! For men are not ashamed to rise in Parliament and elsewhere, and speak the things they do *not* think. "Expediency," "Necessities of Party," &c. &c! It is not known that the Tongue of Man is a sacred organ; that Man himself is definable in Philosophy as an "Incarnate *Word*"; the Word not there, you have no Man there either, but a Phantasm instead! In this way it is that Absurdities may live long enough, — still walking, and talking for themselves, years and decades after the brains are quite out! How are "the knaves and dastards" ever to be got "arrested" at that rate? —

"No man in this fashionable London of yours," friend Sauerteig would say, "speaks a plain word to me. Every man feels bound to be something more than plain; to be pungent withal, witty, ornamental. His poor fraction of sense has to be perked into some epigrammatic shape, that it may prick into me; — perhaps (this is the commonest) to be topsy-turvied, left standing on its head, that I may remember it the better! Such grinning inanity is very sad to the soul of man. Human faces should not grin on one like masks; they should look on one like faces! I love honest laughter, as I do sunlight; but not dishonest: most kinds of dancing too; but the St. Vitus kind not at all! A fashionable wit, *ach Himmel,* if you ask, Which, he or a Death's-head, will be the cheerier company for me? pray send *not* him!"

Insincere Speech, truly, is the prime material of insincere Action. Action hangs, as it were, *dissolved* in Speech, in Thought whereof Speech is the shadow; and precipitates itself therefrom. The kind of Speech in a man betokens the kind of Action you will get from him. Our Speech, in these modern days, has become amazing. Johnson complained, "Nobody speaks in earnest, Sir; there is no serious conversation." To us all serious speech of men, as that of Seventeenth-Century Puritans, Twelfth-Century Catholics, German Poets of this Century, has become jargon, more or less insane. Cromwell was mad and a quack; Anselm, Becket, Goethe, *ditto ditto.*

Perhaps a few narratives in History or Mythology are more significant than that Moslem one, of Moses and the Dwellers by the Dead Sea. A tribe of men dwelt on the shores of that same Asphaltic Lake; and having forgotten, as we are all too prone to do, the inner facts of Nature, and taken up with the falsities and outer semblances of it, were fallen into sad conditions, — verging indeed towards a certain far deeper Lake. Whereupon it pleased kind Heaven to send them the Prophet Moses, with an instructive word of warning, out of which might have sprung "remedial measures" not a few. But no: the men of the Dead Sea discovered, as the valet-species always does in heroes or prophets, no comeliness in Moses; listened with real tedium to Moses, with light grinning, or with splenetic sniffs and sneers, affecting even to yawn; and signified, in short, that they found him a humbug, and even a bore. Such was the candid theory these men of the Asphalt Lake formed to themselves of Moses, That probably he was a humbug, that certainly he was a bore.

Moses withdrew; but Nature and her rigorous veracities did not withdraw. The men of the Dead Sea, when we next went to visit them, were all "changed into Apes"; sitting on the trees there, grinning now in the most *un*affected manner; gibbering and chattering very genuine nonsense; finding the whole Universe now a most indisputable Humbug! The Universe has *become* a Humbug to these Apes who thought it one. There they sit and chatter, to this hour: only, I believe, every Sabbath there returns to them a bewildered half-consciousness, half-reminiscence; and they sit, with their wizened smoke-dried visages, and such an air of supreme tragicality as Apes may; looking out through those blinking smoke-bleared eyes of theirs, into the wonderfullest universal smoky Twilight and undecipherable disordered Dusk of Things; wholly an Uncertainty, Unintelligibility, they and it; and for commentary thereon, here and there an unmusical chatter or mew: — truest, tragicallest Humbug conceivable by the mind of man or ape! They made no use of their souls; and so have lost them. Their worship on the Sabbath now is to roost there, with unmusical screeches, and half-remember that they had souls.

Didst thou never, O Traveller, fall in with parties of this tribe? Meseems they are grown somewhat numerous in our day.

CHAPTER IV

Happy

ALL work, even cotton-spinning, is noble; work is alone noble: be that here said and asserted once more. And in like manner, too, all dignity is painful; a life of ease is not for any man, nor for any god. The life of all gods figures itself to us as a Sublime Sadness, — earnestness of Infinite Battle against Infinite Labour. Our highest religion is named the "Worship of Sorrow." For the son of man there is no noble crown, well worn, or even ill worn, but is a crown of thorns! — These things, in spoken words, or still better, in felt instincts alive in every heart, were once well known.

Does not the whole wretchedness, the whole *Atheism* as I call it, of man's ways, in these generations, shadow itself for us in that unspeakable Life-philosophy of his: The pretension to be what he calls "happy"? Every pitifullest whipster that walks within a skin has his head filled with the notion that he is, shall be, or by all human and divine laws ought to be, "happy." His wishes, the pitifullest whipster's, are to be fulfilled for him; his days, the pitifullest whipster's, are to flow on in ever-gentle current of enjoyment, impossible even for the gods. The prophets preach to us, Thou shalt be happy; thou shalt love pleasant things, and find them. The people clamour, Why have we not found pleasant things?

We construct our theory of Human Duties, not on any Greatest-Nobleness Principle, never so mistaken; no, but on a Greatest-Happiness Principle. "The word *Soul* with us, as in some Slavonic dialects, seems to be synonymous with *Stomach*." We plead and speak, in our Parliaments and elsewhere, not as from the Soul, but from the Stomach; — wherefore, indeed, our pleadings are so slow to profit. We plead not for God's Justice; we are not ashamed to stand clamouring and pleading for our own "interests," our own rents and trade-profits; we say, They are the "interests" of so many; there is such an intense desire in us for them! We demand Free-Trade, with much just vociferation and benevolence, That the poorer classes, who are terribly ill-off at present, may have cheaper New-Orleans bacon. Men ask on Free-trade platforms, How can the indomitable spirit of Englishmen be kept up without plenty of bacon? We shall become a ruined Nation! — Surely, my friends, plenty of bacon is good and indispensable: but, I doubt, you will never get even bacon by aiming only at that. You are men, not animals of prey, well-used or illused! Your Greatest-Happiness Principle seems to me fast becoming a rather unhappy one. — What if we should cease babbling about "happiness," and leave *it* resting on its own basis, as it used to do!

A gifted Byron rises in his wrath; and feeling too surely that he for his part is not "happy," declares the same in very violent language, as a piece of news that may be interesting. It evidently has surprised him much. One dislikes to see a man and poet reduced to proclaim on the streets such tidings: but on the whole, as matters go, that is not the most dislikable. Byron speaks the *truth* in his matter. Byron's large audience indicates how true it is felt to be.

"Happy," my brother? First of all, what difference is it whether thou art happy or not? To-day becomes Yesterday so fast, all To-morrows become Yesterdays; and then there is no question whatever of thy "happiness," but quite another question. Nay, thou hast such a sacred pity left at least for thyself, thy very pains, once gone over into Yesterday, become joys to thee. Besides, thou knowest not what heavenly blessedness and indispensable sanative virtue was in them; thou shalt only know it after many days, when thou art wiser! — A benevolent old Surgeon sat once in our company, with a Patient fallen sick by gormandizing, whom he had just, too briefly in the Patient's judgment, been examining. The foolish Patient still at intervals continued to break in on our discourse, which rather promised to take a philosophic turn: "But I have lost my appetite," said he, objurgatively, with a tone of irritated pathos; "I have no appetite; I can't eat!" — "My dear fellow," answered the Doctor in mildest tone, "it isn't of the slightest consequence"; — and continued his philosophical discoursings with us!

Or does the reader not know the history of that Scottish iron Misanthrope? The inmates of some town-mansion, in those Northern parts, were thrown into the fearfullest alarm by indubitable symptoms of a ghost inhabiting the next house, or perhaps even the partition-wall! Ever at a certain hour, with preternatural gnarring, growling and screeching, which attended as running bass, there began, in a horrid, semi-articulate, unearthly voice, this song: "Once I was hap-hap-happy, but now I'm *mees*-erable! Clack-clack-clack, gnarr-r-r, whuz-z: Once I was hap-hap-happy, but now I'm *mees*-erable!" — Rest, rest, perturbed spirit; — or indeed, as the good old Doctor said: My dear fellow, it isn't of the slightest consequence! But no; the perturbed spirit could not rest; and to the neighbours, fretted, affrighted, or at least insufferably bored by him, it *was* of such consequence that they had to go and examine in his haunted chamber. In his haunted chamber, they find that the perturbed spirit is an unfortunate — Imitator of Byron? No, is an unfortunate rusty Meat-jack, gnarring and creaking with rust and work; and this, in Scottish dialect, is *its* Byronian musical Life-philosophy, sung according to ability!

Truly, I think the man who goes about pothering and uproaring for his "happiness," — pothering, and were it ballot-boxing, poem-making, or in what way soever fussing and exerting himself, — he is not the man that will help us to "get our knaves and dastards arrested"! No; he rather is on the way to increase the number, — by at least one unit and his tail! Observe, too, that this is all a modern affair; belongs not to the old heroic times, but to these dastard new times. "Happiness our being's end and aim," all that very paltry speculation, is at bottom, if we will count well, not yet two centuries old in the world.

The only happiness a brave man ever troubled himself with asking much about was, happiness enough to get his work done. Not "I can't eat!" but "I can't work!" that was the burden of all wise complaining among men. It is, after all, the one unhappiness of a man. That he cannot work; that he cannot get his destiny as a man fulfilled. Behold, the day is passing swiftly over, our life is passing swiftly over; and the night cometh, wherein no man can work. The night once come, our happiness, our unhappiness, — it is all abolished; vanished, clean gone; a thing that has been; "not of the slightest consequence" whether we were happy as eupeptic Curtis,[1] as the fattest pig of Epicurus, or unhappy as Job with potsherds, as musical Byron with Giaours and sensibilities of the heart; as the unmusical Meat-jack with hard labour and rust! But our work, — behold that is not abolished, that has not vanished: our work, behold, it remains, or the want of it remains; — for endless Times and Eternities, remains; and that is now the sole question with us for evermore! Brief brawling Day, with its noisy phantoms, its poor paper-crowns tinsel-gilt, is gone; and divine everlasting Night, with her star-diadems, with her silences and her veracities, is come! What hast thou done, and how? Happiness, unhappiness: all that was but the *wages* thou hadst; thou hast spent all that, in sustaining thyself hitherward; not a coin of it remains with thee, it is all spent, eaten: and now thy work, where is thy work? Swift, out with it, let us see thy work!

Of a truth, if man were not a poor hungry dastard, and even much of a blockhead withal, he would cease criticizing his victuals to such extent; and criticize himself rather, what he does with his victuals!

1 Sir William Curtis (1752–1829), epicurean politician and banker.

CHAPTER XI

Labour

FOR there is a perennial nobleness, and even sacredness, in Work. Were he never so benighted, forgetful of his high calling, there is always hope in a man that actually and earnestly works: in Idleness alone is there perpetual despair. Work, never so Mammonish, mean, *is* in communication with Nature; the real desire to get Work done will itself lead one more and more to truth, to Nature's appointments and regulations which are truth.

The latest Gospel in this world is, Know thy work and do it. "Know thyself:" long enough has that poor "self" of thine tormented thee; thou wilt never get to "know" it, I believe! Think it not thy business, this of knowing thyself; thou art an unknowable individual: know what thou canst work at; and work at it, like a Hercules! That will be thy better plan.

It has been written, "an endless significance lies in Work"; a man perfects himself by working. Foul jungles are cleared away, fair seed-fields rise instead, and stately cities; and withal the man himself first ceases to be a jungle and foul unwholesome desert thereby. Consider how, even in the meanest sorts of Labour, the whole soul of a man is composed into a kind of real harmony, the instant he sets himself to work! Doubt, Desire, Sorrow, Remorse, Indignation, Despair itself, all these like helldogs lie beleaguering the soul of the poor dayworker, as of every man: but he bends himself with free valour against his task, and all these are stilled, all these shrink murmuring far off into their caves. The man is now a man. The blessed glow of Labour in him, is it not as purifying fire, wherein all poison is burnt up, and of sour smoke itself there is made bright blessed flame!

Destiny, on the whole, has no other way of cultivating us. A formless Chaos, once set it *revolving*, grows round and ever rounder; ranges itself, by mere force of gravity, into strata, spherical courses; is no longer a Chaos, but a round compacted World. What would become of the Earth, did she cease to revolve? In the poor old Earth, so long as she revolves, all inequalities, irregularities, disperse themselves; all irregularities are incessantly becoming regular. Hast thou looked on the Potter's wheel, — one of the venerablest objects; old as the Prophet Ezekiel and far older? Rude lumps of clay, how they spin themselves up, by mere quick whirling, into beautiful circular dishes. And fancy the most assiduous Potter, but without his wheel; reduced to make dishes, or rather amorphous botches, by mere kneading and baking! Even such a Potter were Destiny, with a human soul that would rest and lie at ease, that would not work and spin! Of an idle unrevolving man the kindest Destiny, like the most assiduous

Potter without wheel, can bake and knead nothing other than a botch; let her spend on him what expensive colouring, what gilding and enamelling she will, he is but a botch. Not a dish; no, a bulging, kneaded, crooked, shambling, squint-cornered, amorphous botch, — a mere enamelled vessel of dishonour! Let the idle think of this.

Blessed is he who has found his work; let him ask no other blessedness. He has a work, a life-purpose; he has found it, and will follow it! How, as a free-flowing channel, dug and torn by noble force through the sour mud-swamp of one's existence, like an ever-deepening river there, it runs and flows; — draining off the sour festering water, gradually from the root of the remotest grass-blade; making, instead of pestilential swamp, a green fruitful meadow with its clear-flowing stream. How blessed for the meadow itself, let the stream and *its* value be great or small! Labour is Life: from the inmost heart of the Worker rises his god-given Force, the sacred celestial Life-essence breathed into him by Almighty God; from his inmost heart awakens him to all nobleness, — to all knowledge, "self-knowledge" and much else, so soon as Work fitly begins. Knowledge? The knowledge that will hold good in working, cleave thou to that; for Nature herself accredits that, says Yea to that. Properly thou hast no other knowledge but what thou hast got by working: the rest is yet all a hypothesis of knowledge; a thing to be argued of in schools, a thing floating in the clouds, in endless logic-vortices, till we try it and fix it. "Doubt, of whatever kind, can be ended by Action alone."

And again, hast thou valued Patience, Courage, Perseverance, Openness to light; readiness to own thyself mistaken, to do better next time? All these, all virtues, in wrestling with the dim brute Powers of Fact, in ordering of thy fellows in such wrestle, there and elsewhere not at all, thou wilt continually learn. Set down a brave Sir Christopher [1] in the middle of black ruined Stone-heaps, of foolish unarchitectural Bishops, redtape Officials, idle Nell-Gwyn Defenders of the Faith; and see whether he will ever raise a Paul's Cathedral out of all that, yea or no! Rough, rude, contradictory are all things and persons, from the mutinous masons and Irish hodmen, up to the idle Nell-Gwyn Defenders, to blustering redtape Officials, foolish unarchitectural Bishops. All these things and persons are there not for Christopher's sake and his Cathedral's; they are there for their own sake mainly! Christopher will have to conquer and constrain all these, — if he be able. All these are against him. Equitable Nature herself, who carries her mathematics and architectonics not on the face of her, but deep in the hidden heart of her, — Nature herself is but partially for him; will be wholly against him, if he constrain her not! His very money, where is it to come from? The pious munif-

1 Sir Christopher Wren (1632–1723), architect of many of the public buildings and churches of London after the Great Fire of 1666.

icence of England lies far-scattered, distant, unable to speak, and say,
"I am here"; — must be spoken to before it can speak. Pious munificence, and all help, is so silent, invisible like the gods; impediment,
contradictions manifold are so loud and near! O brave Sir Christopher,
trust thou in those, notwithstanding, and front all these; understand
all these; by valiant patience, noble effort, insight, by man's-strength,
vanquish and compel all these, — and, on the whole, strike down
victoriously the last topstone of that Paul's Edifice; thy monument
for certain centuries, the stamp "Great Man" impressed very legibly
on Portland stone there! —

Yes, all manner of help, and pious response from Men or Nature,
is always what we call silent; cannot speak or come to light, till it
be seen, till it be spoken to. Every noble work is at first "impossible."
In very truth, for every noble work the possibilities will lie diffused
through Immensity; inarticulate, undiscoverable except to faith. Like
Gideon thou shalt spread out thy fleece at the door of thy tent; see
whether under the wide arch of Heaven there be any bounteous
moisture, or none. Thy heart and life-purpose shall be as a miraculous
Gideon's fleece, spread out in silent appeal to Heaven; and from the
kind Immensities, what from the poor unkind Localities and town
and country Parishes there never could, blessed dew-moisture to suffice thee shall have fallen!

Work is of a religious nature: — work is of a *brave* nature; which
it is the aim of all religion to be. All work of man is as the swim-
mer's: a waste ocean threatens to devour him; if he front it not
bravely, it will keep its word. By incessant wise defiance of it, lusty
rebuke and buffet of it, behold how it loyally supports him, bears him
as its conqueror along. "It is so," says Goethe, "with all things that
man undertakes in this world."

Brave Sea-captain, Norse Sea-king, — Columbus, my hero, royal-
lest Sea-king of all! it is no friendly environment this of thine, in the
waste deep waters; around thee mutinous discouraged souls, behind
thee disgrace and ruin, before thee the unpenetrated veil of Night.
Brother, these wild water-mountains, bounding from their deep bases
(ten miles deep, I am told), are not entirely there on thy behalf!
Meseems *they* have other work than floating thee forward: — and
the huge Winds, that sweep from Ursa Major to the Tropics and
Equators, dancing their giant-waltz through the kingdoms of Chaos
and Immensity, they care little about filling rightly or filling wrongly
the small shoulder-of-mutton sails in this cockle-skiff of thine! Thou
are not among articulate-speaking friends, my brother; thou art among
immeasurable dumb monsters, tumbling, howling wide as the world
here. Secret, far off, invisible to all hearts but thine, there lies a help
in them: see how thou wilt get at that. Patiently thou wilt wait till
the mad South-wester spend itself, saving thyself by dexterous science
of defence, the while: valiantly, with swift decision, wilt thou strike

in, when the favouring East, the Possible, springs up. Mutiny of men thou wilt sternly repress; weakness, despondency, thou wilt cheerily encourage: thou wilt swallow down complaint, unreason, weariness, weakness of others and thyself; — how much wilt thou swallow down! There shall be a depth of Silence in thee, deeper than this Sea, which is but ten miles deep: a Silence unsoundable; known to God only. Thou shalt be a Great Man. Yes, my World-Soldier, thou of the World Marine-service, — thou wilt have to be *greater* than this tumultuous unmeasured World here round thee is: thou, in thy strong soul, as with wrestler's arms, shalt embrace it, harness it down; and make it bear thee on, — to new Americas, or whither God wills!

CHAPTER XII

Reward

"RELIGION," I said; for, properly speaking, all true Work is Religion: and whatsoever Religion is not Work may go and dwell among the Brahmins, Antinomians, Spinning Dervishes, or where it will; with me it shall have no harbour. Admirable was that of the old Monks, *"Laborare est Orare,* Work is Worship."

Older than all preached Gospels was this unpreached, inarticulate, but ineradicable, forever-enduring Gospel: Work, and therein have wellbeing. Man, Son of Earth and of Heaven, lies there not, in the innermost heart of thee, a Spirit of active Method, a Force for Work; — and burns like a painfully smouldering fire, giving thee no rest till thou unfold it, till thou write it down in beneficent Facts around thee! What is immethodic, waste, thou shalt make methodic, regulated, arable; obedient and productive to thee. Wheresoever thou findest Disorder, there is thy eternal enemy; attack him swiftly, subdue him; make Order of him, the subject not of Chaos, but of Intelligence, Divinity and Thee! The thistle that grows in thy path, dig it out, that a blade of useful grass, a drop of nourishing milk, may grow there instead. The waste cotton-shrub, gather its waste white down, spin it, weave it; that, in place of idle litter, there may be folded webs, and the naked skin of man be covered.

But above all, where thou findest Ignorance, Stupidity, Brutemindedness, — yes, there, with or without Church-tithes and Shovelhat, with or without Talfourd-Mahon Copyrights,[1] or were it with mere dungeons and gibbets and crosses, attack it, I say; smite it wisely, unweariedly, and rest not while thou livest and it lives; but smite, smite, in the name of God! The Highest God, as I understand it, does audibly so command thee; still audibly, if thou have ears to hear.

1 Sir Thomas Noon Talfourd (1795–1854) and Philip Henry, 5th Earl of Stanhope (1805–1875) were ardent supporters of the Copyright Act of 1842.

He, even He, with his *un*spoken voice, awfuller than any Sinai thunders or syllabled speech of Whirlwinds; for the SILENCE of deep Eternities, of Worlds from beyond the morning-stars, does it not speak to thee? The unborn Ages; the old Graves, with their long-mouldering dust, the very tears that wetted it now all dry, — do not these speak to thee, what our ear hath not heard? The deep Death-kingdoms, the Stars in their never-resting courses, all Space and all Time, proclaim it to thee in continual silent admonition. Thou too, if ever man should, shalt work while it is called Today. For the Night cometh, wherein no man can work.

All true Work is sacred; in all true Work, were it but true hand-labour, there is something of divineness. Labour, wide as the Earth, has its summit in Heaven. Sweat of the brow; and up from that to sweat of the brain, sweat of the heart; which includes all Kepler calculations, Newton meditations, all Sciences, all spoken Epics, all acted Heroisms, Martyrdoms, — up to that "Agony of bloody sweat," which all men have called divine! O brother, if this is not "worship," then I say, the more pity for worship; for this is the noblest thing yet discovered under God's sky. Who art thou that complainest of thy life of toil? Complain not. Look up, my wearied brother; see thy fellow Workmen there, in God's Eternity; surviving there, they alone surviving: sacred Band of the Immortals, celestial Bodyguard of the Empire of Mankind. Even in the weak Human Memory they survive so long, as saints, as heroes, as gods; they alone surviving; peopling, they alone, the unmeasured solitudes of Time! To thee Heaven, though severe, is *not* unkind; Heaven is kind, — as a nobler Mother; as that Spartan Mother, saying, while she gave her son his shield, "With it, my son, or upon it!" Thou too shalt return *home* in honour; to thy far-distant Home, in honour; doubt it not, — if in the battle thou keep thy shield! Thou, in the Eternities and deepest Death-kingdoms, art not an alien; thou everywhere art a denizen! Complain not; the very Spartans did not *complain*.

And who art thou that braggest of thy life of Idleness; complacently showest thy bright gilt equipages; sumptuous cushions; appliances for folding of the hands to mere sleep? Looking up, looking down, around, behind or before, discernest thou, if it be not in Mayfair alone, any *idle* hero, saint, god, or even devil? Not a vestige of one. In the Heavens, in the Earth, in the Waters under the Earth, is none like unto thee. Thou art an original figure in this Creation; a denizen in Mayfair alone, in this extraordinary Century or Half-Century alone! One monster there is in the world: the idle man. What is his "Religion"? That Nature is a Phantasm, where cunning beggary or thievery may sometimes find good victual. That God is a lie; and that Man and his Life are a lie. — Alas, alas, who of us *is* there that can say, I have worked? The faithfullest of us are unprofitable servants; the faithfullest of us know that best. The faithfullest of us may say, with sad and true old Samuel. "Much of my life has been trifled away!" But he that has, and except "on public occasions" professes to have, no function but that of going idle in a graceful or graceless manner; and of begetting sons to go idle; and to address Chief Spinners and Diggers, who at least *are* spinning and digging, "Ye scandalous persons who produce too much" — My Corn-Law friends, on what imaginary still richer Eldorados, and true iron-spikes with law of gravitation, are ye rushing!

As to the Wages of Work there might innumerable things be said; there will and must yet innumerable things be said and spoken, in St. Stephen's and out of St. Stephen's; and gradually not a few things be ascertained and written, on Law-parchment, concerning this very matter: — "Fair day's-wages for a fair day's-work" is the most unrefusable demand! Money-wages "to the extent of keeping your worker alive that he may work more"; these, unless you mean to dismiss him straightway out of this world, are indispensable alike to the noblest Worker and to the least noble!

One thing only I will say here, in special reference to the former class, the noble and noblest; but throwing light on all the other classes and their arrangements of this difficult matter: The "wages" of every noble Work do yet lie in Heaven or else Nowhere. Not in Bank-of-England bills, in Owen's Labour-bank,[2] or any the most improved establishment of banking and money-changing, needest thou, heroic soul, present thy account of earnings. Human banks and labour-banks know thee not; or know thee after generations and centuries have passed away, and thou art clean gone from "rewarding," — all manner of bank-drafts, shop-tills, and Downing-street Exchequers lying very invisible, so far from thee! Nay, at bottom, dost thou need any reward? Was it thy aim and life-purpose to be filled with good things for thy heroism; to have a life of pomp and ease, and be what men call "happy," in this world, or in any other world? I answer for thee deliberately, No. The whole spiritual secret of the new epoch lies in this, that thou canst answer for thyself, with thy whole clearness of head and heart, deliberately, No!

My brother, the brave man has to give his Life away. Give it, I advise thee; — thou dost not expect to *sell* thy Life in an adequate manner? What price, for example, would content thee? The just price of thy LIFE to thee, — why, God's entire Creation to thyself, the whole Universe of Space, the whole Eternity of Time, and what they hold: that is the price which would content thee; that, and if thou wilt be candid, nothing short of that! It is thy all; and for it thou wouldst have all. Thou art an unreasonable mortal; — or rather thou art a poor *infinite* mortal, who, in thy narrow clay-prison here, *seemest*

2 Robert Owen (1771–1858), socialist reformer, founded the "Equitable Labour Exchange" in 1832 at which "Labour Notes" were used as currency.

so unreasonable! Thou wilt never sell thy Life, or any part of thy
Life, in a satisfactory manner. Give it, like a royal heart; let the price
be Nothing: thou *hast* then, in a certain sense, got All for it! The
heroic man, — and is not every man, God be thanked, a potential
hero? — has to do so, in all times and circumstances. In the most
heroic age, as in the most unheroic, he will have to say, as Burns said
proudly and humbly of his little Scottish Songs, little dewdrops of
Celestial Melody in an age when so much was unmelodious: "By
Heaven, they shall either be invaluable or of no value; I do not need
your guineas for them!" It is an element which should, and must,
enter deeply into all settlements of wages here below. They never
will be "satisfactory" otherwise; they cannot, O Mammon Gospel, they
never can! Money for my little piece of work "to the extent that
will allow me to keep working"; yes, this, — unless you mean that I
shall go my ways *before* the work is all taken out of me: but as to
"wages" — ! —

On the whole, we do entirely agree with those old Monks, *Laborare
est Orare*. In a thousand senses, from one end of it to the other, true
Work *is* Worship. He that works, whatsoever be his work, he bodies
forth the form of Things Unseen; a small Poet every Worker is. The
idea, were it but of his poor Delf Platter, how much more of his Epic
Poem, is as yet "seen," half-seen, only by himself; to all others it is
a thing unseen, impossible; to Nature herself it is a thing unseen, a
thing which never hitherto was; — very "impossible," for it is as yet
a No-thing! The Unseen Powers had need to watch over such a man;
he works in and for the Unseen. Alas, if he look to the Seen Powers
only, he may as well quit the business; his No-thing will never rightly
issue as a Thing, but as a Deceptivity, a Sham-thing, — which it had
better not do!

Thy No-thing of an Intended Poem, O Poet who hast looked merely
to reviewers, copyrights, booksellers, popularities, behold it has not
yet become a Thing; for the truth is not in it! Though printed, hot-
pressed, reviewed, celebrated, sold to the twentieth edition: what is
all that? The Thing, in philosophical uncommercial language, is still
a No-thing, mostly semblance, and deception of the sight; — benign
Oblivion incessantly gnawing at it, impatient till Chaos, to which it
belongs, do reabsorb it! —

He who takes not counsel of the Unseen and Silent, from him will
never come real visibility and speech. Thou must descend to the
Mothers, to the *Manes*, and Hercules-like long suffer and labour there,
wouldst thou emerge with victory into the sunlight. As in battle and
the shock of war, — for is not this a battle? — thou too shalt fear no
pain or death, shalt love no ease or life; the voice of festive Lubber-
lands,[3] the noise of greedy Acheron shall alike lie silent under thy
victorious feet. Thy work, like Dante's, shall "make thee lean for many

3 Lands of Plenty.

years." The world and its wages, its criticisms, counsels, helps, impediments, shall be as a waste ocean-flood; the chaos through which thou art to swim and sail. Not the waste waves and their weedy gulf-streams, shalt thou take for guidance: thy star alone, — "*Se tu segui tua stella!*" Thy star alone, now clear-beaming over Chaos, nay now by fits gone out, disastrously eclipsed: this only shalt thou strive to follow. O, it is a business, as I fancy, that of weltering your way through Chaos and the murk of Hell! Green-eyed dragons watching you, three-headed Cerberuses, — not without sympathy of *their* sort! "*Eccovi l' uom ch' è stato all' Inferno.*" [4] For in fine, as Poet Dryden says, you do walk hand in hand with sheer Madness, all the way, — who is by no means pleasant company! You look fixedly into Madness, and *her* undiscovered, boundless, bottomless Night-empire; that you may extort new Wisdom out of it, as an Eurydice from Tartarus. The higher the Wisdom, the closer was its neighbourhood and kindred with mere Insanity; literally so; — and thou wilt, with a speechless feeling, observe how highest Wisdom, struggling up into this world, has oftentimes carried such tinctures and adhesions of Insanity still cleaving to it hither!

All Works, each in their degree, are a making of Madness sane; — truly enough a religious operation; which cannot be carried on without religion. You have not work otherwise; you have eye-service, greedy grasping of wages, swift and ever swifter manufacture of semblances to get hold of wages. Instead of better felt-hats to cover your head, you have bigger lath-and-plaster hats set travelling the streets on wheels. Instead of heavenly and earthly Guidance for the souls of men, you have "Black or White Surplice" Controversies, stuffed hair-and-leather Popes; — terrestrial *Law-wards*, Lords and Law-bringers, "organizing Labour" in these years, by passing Corn-Laws. With all which, alas, this distracted Earth is now full, nigh to bursting. Semblances most smooth to the touch and eye; most accursed nevertheless to body and soul. Semblances, be they of Sham-woven Cloth or of Dilettante Legislation, which are *not* real wool or substance, but Devil's-dust, accursed of God and man! No man has worked, or can work, except religiously; not even the poor day-labourer, the weaver of your coat, the sewer of your shoes. All men, if they work not as in a Great Taskmaster's eye, will work wrong, work unhappily for themselves and you.

Industrial work, still under bondage to Mammon, the rational soul of it not yet awakened, is a tragic spectacle. Men in the rapidest motion and self-motion; restless, with convulsive energy, as if driven by Galvanism, as if possessed by a Devil; tearing asunder mountains, — to no purpose, for Mammonism is always Midas-eared! This is sad, on the face of it. Yet courage: the beneficent Destinies, kind in

4 "Behold the man who has been in Hell."

their sternness, are apprising us that this cannot continue. Labour
is not a devil, even while encased in Mammonism; Labour is ever
an imprisoned god, writhing unconsciously or consciously to escape
out of Mammonism! Plugson of Unc-rshot, like Taillefer of Nor-
mandy,[5] wants victory; how much happier will even Plugson be to
have a Chivalrous victory than a Chactaw one! The unredeemed
ugliness is that of a slothful People. Show me a People energetically
busy; heaving, struggling, all shoulders at the wheel; their heart puls-
ing, every muscle swelling, with man's energy and will; — I show
you a People of whom great good is already predicable; to whom
all manner of good is yet certain, if their energy endure. By very
working, they will learn; they have, Antaeus-like, their foot on Mother
Fact: how can they but learn?

The vulgarest Plugson of a Master-Worker, who can command
Workers, and get work out of them, is already a considerable man.
Blessed and thrice-blessed symptoms I discern of Master-Workers
who are not vulgar men; who are Nobles, and begin to feel that they
must act as such: all speed to these, they are England's hope at present! But in this Plugson himself, conscious of almost no nobleness
whatever, how much is there! Not without man's faculty, insight,
courage, hard energy, is this rugged figure. His words none of the
wisest; but his actings cannot be altogether foolish. Think, how
were it, stoodst thou suddenly in his shoes! He has to command a
thousand men. And not imaginary commanding; no, it is real, incessantly practical. The evil passions of so many men (with the Devil
in them, as in all of us) he has to vanquish; by manifold force of
speech and of silence, to repress or evade. What a force of silence,
to say nothing of the others, is in Plugson! For these his thousand
men he has to provide raw-material, machinery, arrangement, house-
room; and ever at the week's end, wages by due sale. No Civil-List,
or Goulburn-Baring Budget [6] has he to fall back upon, for paying of
his regiment; he has to pick his supplies from this confused face of
the whole Earth and Contemporaneous History, by his dexterity
alone. There will be dry eyes if he fail to do it! — He exclaims, at
present, "black in the face," near strangled with Dilettante Legislation: "Let me have elbow-room, throat-room, and I will not fail! No,
I will spin yet, and conquer like a giant: what 'sinews of war' lie
in me, untold resources towards the Conquest of this Planet, if instead
of hanging me, you husband them, and help me!" — My indomitable
friend, it is *true;* and thou shalt and must be helped.

This is not a man I would kill and strangle by Corn-Laws, even if
I could! No, I would fling my Corn-Laws and Shotbelts to the Devil;

5 A Minstrel in the army of William the Conqueror who sang the deeds of
Roland to encourage the Normans.
6 Henry Goulburn (1784–1856) and Francis Thornhill Baring (1796–1866),
respectively, present and past chancellors of the exchequer.

and try to help this man. I would teach him, by noble precept and law-precept, by noble example most of all, that Mammonism was not the essence of his or of my station in God's Universe; but the ad-scititious excrescence of it; the gross, terrene, godless embodiment of it; which would have to become, more or less, a godlike one. By noble *real* legislation, by true *noble's*-work, by unwearied, valiant, and were it wageless effort, in my Parliament and in my Parish, I would aid, constrain, encourage him to effect more or less this blessed change. I should know that it would have to be effected; that unless it were in some measure effected, he and I and all of us, I first and soonest of all, were doomed to perdition! — Effected it will be; un-less it were a Demon that made this Universe; which I, for my own part, do at no moment, under no form, in the least believe.

May it please your Serene Highnesses, your Majesties, Lordships and Law-wardships, the proper Epic of this world is not now "Arms and the Man"; how much less, "Shirt-frills and the Man": no, it is now "Tools and the Man": that, henceforth to all time, is now our Epic; — and you, first of all others, I think, were wise to take note of that!

CHAPTER XIII

Democracy

IF the Serene Highnesses and Majesties do not take note of that, then, as I perceive, *that* will take note of itself! The time for levity, in-sincerity, and idle babble and play-acting, in all kinds, is gone by; it is a serious, grave time. Old long-vexed questions, not yet solved in logical words or parliamentary laws, are fast solving themselves in facts, somewhat unblessed to behold! This largest of questions, this question of Work and Wages, which ought, had we heeded Heaven's voice, to have begun two generations ago or more, cannot be delayed longer without hearing Earth's voice. "Labour" will verily need to be somewhat "organized," as they say, — God knows with what dif-ficulty. Man will actually need to have his debts and earnings a little better paid by man; which, let Parliaments speak of them, or be silent of them, are eternally his due from man, and cannot, without penalty and at length not without death-penalty, be withheld. How much ought to cease among us straightway; how much ought to be-gin straightway, while the hours yet are!

Truly they are strange results to which this of leaving all to "Cash"; of quietly shutting up the God's Temple, and gradually opening wide-open the Mammon's Temple, with "Laissez-faire, and Every man for himself," — have led us in these days! We have Upper, speaking Classes, who indeed do "speak" as never man spake before;

the withered flimsiness, godless baseness and barrenness of whose Speech might of itself indicate what kind of Doing and practical Governing went on under it! For Speech is the gaseous element out of which most kinds of Practice and Performance, especially all kinds of moral Performance, condense themselves, and take shape; as the one is, so will the other be. Descending, accordingly, into the Dumb Class in its Stockport Cellars and Poor-Law Bastilles, have we not to announce that they are hitherto unexampled in the History of Adam's Posterity?

Life was never a May-game for men: in all times the lot of the dumb millions born to toil was defaced with manifold sufferings, injustices, heavy burdens, avoidable and unavoidable; not play at all, but hard work that made the sinews sore and the heart sore. As bond-slaves, *villani, bordarii, sochemanni,* nay indeed as dukes, earls and kings, men were oftentimes made weary of their life; and had to say, in the sweat of their brow and of their soul, Behold, it is not sport, it is grim earnest, and our back can bear no more! Who knows not what massacrings and harryings there have been; grinding, long-continuing, unbearable injustices, — till the heart had to rise in madness, and some *"Eu Sachsen, nimith euer sachses,* You Saxons, out with your gully-knives, then!" You Saxons, some "arrestment," partial "arrestment of the Knaves and Dastards" has become indispensable! — The page of Dryasdust is heavy with such details.

And yet I will venture to believe that in no time, since the beginnings of Society, was the lot of those same dumb millions of toilers so entirely unbearable as it is even in the days now passing over us. It is not to die, or even to die of hunger, that makes a man wretched; many men have died; all men must die, — the last exit of us all is in a Fire-Chariot of Pain. But it is to live miserable we know not why; to work sore and yet gain nothing; to be heart-worn, weary, yet isolated, unrelated, girt-in with a cold universal Laissez-faire: it is to die slowly all our life long, imprisoned in a deaf, dead, Infinite Injustice, as in the accursed iron belly of a Phalaris' Bull! [1] This is and remains for ever intolerable to all men whom God has made. Do we wonder at French Revolutions, Chartisms, Revolts of Three Days? The times, if we will consider them, are really unexampled.

Never before did I hear of an Irish Widow reduced to "prove her sisterhood by dying of typhus-fever and infecting seventeen persons," — saying in such undeniable way, "You *see,* I was your sister!" Sisterhood, brotherhood, was often forgotten; but not till the rise of these ultimate Mammon and Shotbelt Gospels did I ever see it so expressly denied. If no pious Lord or *Law-ward* would remember it, always some pious Lady (*"Hlaf dig,"* Benefactress, *"Loaf-giveress,"* they say she is, — blessings on her beautiful heart!) was there, with

---

[1] A brazen bull in which Phalaris, tyrant of Agrigentum, punished criminals by burning a fire beneath it.

mild mother-voice and hand, to remember it; some pious thoughtful *Elder*, what we now call "Prester," *Presbyter* or "Priest," was there to put all men in mind of it, in the name of the God who had made all.

Not even in Black Dahomey [2] was it ever, I think, forgotten to the typhus-fever length. Mungo Park, resourceless, had sunk down to die under the Negro Village-Tree, a horrible White object in the eyes of all. But in the poor Black Woman, and her daughter who stood aghast at him, whose earthly wealth and funded capital consisted of one small calabash of rice, there lived a heart richer than *"Laissez-faire"*: they, with a royal munificence, boiled their rice for him; they sang all night to him, spinning assiduous on their cotton distaffs, as he lay to sleep: "Let us pity the poor white man; no mother has he to fetch him milk, no sister to grind him corn!" Thou poor black Noble One, — thou *Lady* too: did not a God make thee too; was there not in thee too something of a God! —

Gurth, born thrall of Cedric the Saxon, has been greatly pitied by Dryasdust and others. Gurth, with the brass collar round his neck, tending Cedric's pigs in the glades of the wood, is not what I call an exemplar of human felicity: but Gurth, with the sky above him, with the free air and tinted boscage and umbrage round him, and in him at least the certainty of supper and social lodging when he came home; Gurth to me seems happy, in comparison with many a Lancashire and Buckinghamshire man, of these days, not born thrall of anybody! Gurth's brass collar did not gall him: Cedric *deserved* to be his Master. The pigs were Cedric's, but Gurth too would get his parings of them. Gurth had the inexpressible satisfaction of feeling himself related indissolubly, though in a rude brass-collar way, to his fellow-mortals in this Earth. He had superiors, inferiors, equals. — Gurth is now "emancipated" long since; has what we call "Liberty." Liberty, I am told, is a Divine thing. Liberty when it becomes the "Liberty to die by starvation" is not so divine!

Liberty? The true liberty of a man, you would say, consisted in his finding out, or being forced to find out, the right path, and to walk thereon. To learn, or to be taught, what work he actually was able for; and then by permission, persuasion, and even compulsion, to set about doing of the same! That is his true blessedness, honour, "liberty" and maximum of wellbeing: if liberty be not that, I for one have small care about liberty. You do not allow a palpable madman to leap over precipices; you violate his liberty, you that are wise; and keep him, were it in strait-waistcoats, away from the precipices! Every stupid, every cowardly and foolish man is but a less palpable madman: his true liberty were that a wiser man, that any and every wiser man, could, by brass collars, or in whatever milder or sharper way, lay hold of him when he was going wrong, and order and compel him to

2 A cannibalistic West African state.

go a little righter. O, if thou really art my *Senior,* Seigneur, my *Elder,* Presbyter or Priest, — if thou art in very deed my *Wiser,* may a beneficent instinct lead and impel thee to "conquer" me, to command me! If thou do know better than I what is good and right, I conjure thee in the name of God, force me to do it; were it by never such brass collars, whips and handcuffs, leave me not to walk over precipices! That I have been called, by all the Newspapers, a "free man" will avail me little, if my pilgrimage have ended in death and wreck. O that the Newspapers had called me slave, coward, fool, or what it pleased their sweet voices to name me, and I had attained not death, but life! — Liberty requires new definitions.

A conscious abhorrence and intolerance of Folly, of Baseness, Stupidity, Poltroonery and all that brood of things, dwells deep in some men: still deeper in others an *un*conscious abhorrence and intolerance, clothed moreover by the beneficent Supreme Powers in what stout appetites, energies, egoisms so-called, are suitable to it; — these latter are your Conquerors, Romans, Normans, Russians, Indo-English; Founders of what we call Aristocracies. Which indeed have they not the most "divine right" to found; — being themselves very truly Ἄριστοι, BRAVEST, BEST; and conquering generally a confused rabble of WORST, or at lowest, clearly enough, of WORSE? I think their divine right, tried, with affirmatory verdict, in the greatest Law-Court known to me, was good! A class of men who are dreadfully exclaimed against by Dryasdust; of whom nevertheless beneficent Nature has oftentimes had need; and may, alas, again have need.

When, across the hundredfold poor scepticisms, trivialisms, and constitutional cob-webberies of Dryasdust, you catch any glimpse of a William the Conqueror, a Tancred of Hauteville or such like, — do you not discern veritably some rude outline of a true God-made King; whom not the Champion of England cased in tin, but all Nature and the Universe were calling to the throne? It is absolutely necessary that he get thither. Nature does not mean her poor Saxon children to perish, of obesity, stupor or other malady, as yet: a stern Ruler and Line of Rulers therefore is called in, — a stern but most beneficent *perpetual House-Surgeon* is by Nature herself called in, and even the appropriate *fees* are provided for him! Dryasdust talks lamentably about Hereward [3] and the Fen Counties; fate of Earl Waltheof; [4] Yorkshire and the North reduced to ashes; all of which is undoubtedly lamentable. But even Dryasdust apprises me of one fact: "A child, in this William's reign, might have carried a purse of gold from end to end of England." My erudite friend, it is a fact which outweighs a thousand! Sweep away thy constitutional, sentimental, and other cob-webberies; look eye to eye, if thou still

---

[3] A romantic outlaw-hero of the 11th century.
[4] A contemporary of Hereward's executed by William the Conqueror and regarded as a martyr by the English.

have any eye, in the face of this big burly William Bastard: thou wilt
see a fellow of most flashing discernment, of most strong lion-heart;
— in whom, as it were, within a frame of oak and iron, the gods
have planted the soul of "a man of genius"! Dost thou call that nothing? I call it an immense thing! — Rage enough was in this Willelmus
Conquæstor, rage enough for his occasions; — and yet the essential
element of him, as of all such men, is not scorching *fire,* but shining
illuminative *light.* Fire and light are strangely interchangeable; nay,
at bottom, I have found them different forms of the same most godlike "elementary substance" in our world: a thing worth stating in
these days. The essential element of this Conquæstor is, first of all,
the most sun-eyed perception of what *is* really what on this God's-
Earth; — which, thou wilt find, does mean at bottom "Justice," and
"Virtues" not a few: *Conformity* to what the Maker has seen good to
make; that, I suppose, will mean Justice and a Virtue or two? —

Dost thou think Willelmus Conquæstor would have tolerated ten
years' jargon, one hour's jargon, on the propriety of killing Cotton-
manufactures by partridge Corn-Laws? I fancy, this was not the man
to knock out of his night's-rest with nothing but a noisy bedlamism
in your mouth! "Assist us still better to bush the partridges; strangle
Plugson who spins the shirts?" — *"Par la Splendeur de Dieu!"* ——
Dost thou think Willelmus Conquæstor, in this new time, with Steam-
engine Captains of Industry on one hand of him, and Joe-Manton
Captains of Idleness [5] on the other, would have doubted which *was*
really the BEST; which did deserve strangling, and which not?

I have a certain indestructible regard for Willelmus Conquæstor.
A resident House-Surgeon, provided by Nature for her beloved English People, and even furnished with the requisite fees, as I said; for
he by no means felt himself doing Nature's work, this Willelmus, but
his own work exclusively! And his own work withal it was; informed
"par la Splendeur de Dieu." — I say, it is necessary to get the work
out of such a man, however harsh that be! When a world, not yet
doomed for death, is rushing down to ever-deeper Baseness and
Confusion, it is a dire necessity of Nature's to bring in her ARISTOC-
RACIES, her BEST, even by forcible methods. When their descendants
or representatives cease entirely to *be* the Best, Nature's poor world
will very soon rush down again to Baseness; and it becomes a dire
necessity of Nature's to cast them out. Hence French Revolutions,
Five-point Charters, Democracies, and a mournful list of *Etceteras,*
in these our afflicted times.

To what extent Democracy has now reached, how it advances irresistible with ominous, ever-increasing speed, he that will open his
eyes on any province of human affairs may discern. Democracy is
everywhere the inexorable demand of these ages, swiftly fulfilling it-

5 Joseph Manton was a London gunsmith from whom the aristocrats bought
their hunting-pieces; thus, idle aristocracy.

self. From the thunder of Napoleon battles, to the jabbering of Open-
vestry in St. Mary Axe, all things announce Democracy. A distinguished man, whom some of my readers will hear again with pleasure,
thus writes to me what in these days he notes from the Wahngasse
of Weissnichtwo, where our London fashions seem to be in full vogue.
Let us hear the Herr Teufelsdröckh again, were it but the smallest
word!

"Democracy, which means despair of finding any Heroes to govern
you, and contented putting up with the want of them, — alas, thou
too, *mein Lieber,* seest well how close it is of kin to *Atheism,* and
other sad *Isms:* he who discovers no God whatever, how shall he
discover Heroes, the visible Temples of God? — Strange enough
meanwhile it is, to observe with what thoughtlessness, here in our
rigidly Conservative Country, men rush into Democracy with full cry.
Beyond doubt, his Excellenz the Titular-Herr Ritter Kauderwälsch
von Pferdefuss-Quacksalber,[6] he our distinguished Conservative Premier himself, and all but the thicker-headed of his Party, discern
Democracy to be inevitable as death, and are even desperate of delaying it much!

"You cannot walk the streets without beholding Democracy announce itself: the very Tailor has become, if not properly Sansculottic,
which to him would be ruinous, yet a Tailor unconsciously symbolizing, and prophesying with his scissors, the reign of Equality. What
now is our fashionable coat? A thing of superfinest texture, of deeply
meditated cut; with Malines-lace cuffs; quilted with gold; so that a
man can carry, without difficulty, an estate of land on his back?
Keineswegs, By no manner of means! The Sumptuary Laws [7] have
fallen into such a state of desuetude as was never before seen. Our
fashionable coat is an amphibium between barn-sack and drayman's
doublet. The cloth of it is studiously coarse; the colour a speckled
soot-black or rust-brown grey; — the nearest approach to a Peasant's.
And for shape, — thou shouldst see it! The last consummation of the
year now passing over us is definable as Three Bags; a big bag for the
body, two small bags for the arms, and by way of collar a hem! The
first Antique Cheruscan [8] who, of felt-cloth or bear's-hide, with bone
or metal needle, set about making himself a coat, before Tailors had
yet awakened out of Nothing, — did not he make it even so? A
loose wide poke for body, with two holes to let out the arms; this
was his original coat: to which holes it was soon visible that two small
loose pokes, or sleeves, easily appended, would be an improvement.

"Thus has the Tailor-art, so to speak, overset itself, like most other
things; changed its centre-of-gravity; whirled suddenly over from

6 *Kauderwälsch von Pferdefuss-Quacksalber:* Gibberish von Horsefoot-Quack-
doctor. The Premier is Peel, in his second ministry.
7 Laws limiting expenditures for too-sumptuous private living.
8 Member of an ancient German tribe.

zenith to nadir. Your Stulz, with huge somerset, vaults from his high shop-board down to the depths of primal savagery, — carrying much along with him! For I will invite thee to reflect that the Tailor, as topmost ultimate froth of Human Society, is indeed swift-passing, evanescent, slippery to decipher; yet significant of much, nay of all. Topmost evanescent froth, he is churned up from the very lees, and from all intermediate regions of the liquor. The general outcome he, visible to the eye, of what men aimed to do, and were obliged and enabled to do, in this one public department of symbolizing themselves to each other by covering of their skins. A smack of all Human Life lies in the Tailor: its wild struggles towards beauty, dignity, freedom, victory; and how, hemmed in by Sedan and Huddersfield, by Nescience, Dullness, Prurience, and other sad necessities and laws of Nature, it has attained just to this: Grey savagery of Three Sacks with a hem!

"When the very Tailor verges towards Sansculottism, is it not ominous? The last Divinity of poor mankind dethroning himself; sinking *his* taper too, flame downmost, like the Genius of Sleep or of Death; admonitory that Tailor-time shall be no more! — For, little as one could advise Sumptuary Laws at the present epoch, yet nothing is clearer than that where ranks do actually exist, strict division of costumes will also be enforced; that if we ever have a new Hierarchy and Aristocracy, acknowledged veritably as such, for which I daily pray Heaven, the Tailor will re-awaken; and be, by volunteering and appointment, consciously and unconsciously, a safeguard of that same." — Certain farther observations, from the same invaluable pen, on our never-ending changes of mode, our "perpetual nomadic and even ape-like appetite for change and mere change" in all the equipments of our existence, and the "fatal revolutionary character" thereby manifested, we suppress for the present. It may be admitted that Democracy, in all meanings of the word, is in full career; irresistible by any Ritter Kauderwälsch or other Son of Adam, as times go. "Liberty" is a thing men are determined to have.

But truly, as I had to remark in the mean while, "the liberty of not being oppressed by your fellow man" is an indispensable, yet one of the most insignificant fractional parts of Human Liberty. No man oppresses thee, can bid thee fetch or carry, come or go, without reason shown. True; from all men thou art emancipated: but from Thyself and from the Devil — ? No man, wiser, unwiser, can make thee come or go: but thy own futilities, bewilderments, thy false appetites for Money, Windsor Georges and such like? No man oppresses thee, O free and independent Franchiser: but does not this stupid Porter-pot oppress thee? No Son of Adam can bid thee come or go; but this absurd Pot of Heavy-wet,[9] this can and does! Thou art the thrall not

9 Strong malt liquor.

of Cedric the Saxon, but of thy own brutal appetites, and this scoured
dish of liquor. And thou pratest of thy "liberty"? Thou entire blockhead!

Heavy-wet and gin: alas, these are not the only kinds of thraldom.
Thou who walkest in a vain show, looking out with ornamental dilettante sniff, and serene supremacy, at all Life and all Death; and am-
blest jauntily; perking up thy poor talk into crotchets, thy poor conduct into fatuous somnambulisms; — and *art* as an "enchanted Ape"
under God's sky, where thou mightest have been a man, had proper
Schoolmasters and Conquerors, and Constables with cat-o'-nine tails,
been vouch-safed thee: dost thou call that "liberty"? Or your un-
reposing Mammon-worshipper, again, driven, as if by Galvanisms,
by Devils and Fixed-Ideas, who rises early and sits late, chasing the
impossible; straining every faculty to "fill himself with the east wind,"
— how merciful were it, could you, by mild persuasion or by the
severest tyranny so-called, check him in his mad path, and turn him
into a wiser one! All painful tyranny, in that case again, were but
mild "surgery"; the pain of it cheap, as health and life, instead of
galvanism and fixed-idea, are cheap at any price.

Sure enough, of all paths a man could strike into, there *is*, at any
given moment, a *best path* for every man; a thing which, here and now,
it were of all things *wisest* for him to do; — which could he be but
led or driven to do, he were then doing "like a man," as we phrase it; all
men and gods agreeing with him, the whole Universe virtually exclaim-
ing Well-done to him! His success, in such case, were complete; his
felicity a maximum. This path, to find this path and walk in it, is the
one thing needful for him. Whatsoever forwards him in that, let it
come to him even in the shape of blows and spurnings, is liberty: whatsoever hinders him, were it wardmotes, open-vestries, poll-booths, tremendous cheers, rivers of heavy-wet, is slavery.

The notion that a man's liberty consists in giving his vote at elec-
tion-hustings, and saying, "Behold now I too have my twenty-thousandth part of a Talker in our National Palaver; will not all the gods
be good to me?" — is one of the pleasantest! Nature nevertheless is
kind at present; and puts it into the heads of many, almost all. The
liberty especially which has to purchase itself by social isolation, and
each man standing separate from the other, having "no business with
him" but a cash-account: this is such a liberty as the Earth seldom
saw; — as the Earth will not long put up with, recommend it how
you may. This liberty turns out, before it have long continued in action, with all men flinging up their caps round it, to be, for the Working Millions, a liberty to die by want of food; for the Idle Thousands
and Units, alas, a still more fatal liberty to live in want of work; to
have no earnest duty to do in this God's-World any more. What becomes of a man in such predicament? Earth's Laws are silent; and
Heaven's speak in a voice which is not heard. No work, and the in-

eradicable need of work, give rise to new very wondrous life-philos-
ophies, new very wondrous life-practices! Dilettantism, Pococurantism,
Beau-Brummelism, with perhaps an occasional, half-mad, pro-
testing burst of Byronism, establish themselves: at the end of a cer-
tain period, — if you go back to "the Dead Sea," there is, say our
Moslem friends, a very strange "Sabbath-day" transacting itself there!
— Brethren, we know but imperfectly yet, after ages of Constitutional
Government, what Liberty and Slavery are.

Democracy, the chase of Liberty in that direction, shall go its full
course; unrestrained by him of Pferdefuss-Quacksalber, or any of *his*
household. The Toiling Millions of Mankind, in most vital need and
passionate instinctive desire of Guidance, shall cast away False-Guid-
ance; and hope, for an hour, that No-Guidance will suffice them: but it
can be for an hour only. The smallest item of human Slavery is the
oppression of man by his Mock-Superiors; the palpablest, but I say
at bottom the smallest. Let him shake off such oppression, trample
it indignantly under his feet; I blame him not, I pity and commend
him. But oppression by your Mock-Superiors well shaken off, the
grand problem yet remains to solve: That of finding government by
your Real-Superiors! Alas, how shall we ever learn the solution of
that, benighted, bewildered, sniffing, sneering, godforgetting unfortunates as we are? It is a work for centuries; to be taught us by tribulations, confusions, insurrections, obstructions; who knows if not by
conflagration and despair! It is a lesson inclusive of all other lessons;
the hardest of all lessons to learn.

One thing I do know: Those Apes, chattering on the branches by the
Dead Sea, never got it learned; but chatter there to this day. To them
no Moses need come a second time; a thousand Moseses would be but
so many painted Phantasms, interesting Fellow-Apes of new strange
aspect, — whom they would "invite to dinner," be glad to meet with
in lion-soirées. To them the voice of Prophecy, of heavenly monition,
is quite ended. They chatter there, all Heaven shut to them, to the
end of the world. The unfortunates! Oh, what is dying of hunger,
with honest tools in your hand, with a manful purpose in your heart,
and much real labour lying round you done, in comparison? You
honestly quit your tools; quit a most muddy confused coil of sore
work, short rations, of sorrows, dispiritments and contradictions, having now honestly done with it all; — and await, not entirely in a distracted manner, what the Supreme Powers, and the Silences and the
Eternities may have to say to you.

A second thing I know: This lesson will have to be learned, — under
penalties! England will either learn it, or England also will cease to
exist among Nations. England will either learn to reverence its Heroes,
and discriminate them from its Sham-Heroes and Valets and gas-
lighted Histrios; and to prize them as the audible God's-voice, amid
all inane jargons and temporary market-cries, and say to them with

heart-loyalty, "Be ye King and Priest, and Gospel and Guidance for
us": or else England will continue to worship new and ever-new forms
of Quackhood, — and so, with what resiliences and reboundings matters little, go down to the Father of Quacks! Can I dread such things
of England? Wretched, thick-eyed, gross-hearted mortals, why will
ye worship lies, and "Stuffed Clothes-suits, created by the ninth-parts
of men!" It is not your purses that suffer; your farm-rents, your com-
merces, your mill-revenues, loud as ye lament over these; no, it is not
these alone, but a far deeper than these: it is your souls that lie dead,
crushed down under despicable Nightmares, Atheisms, Brain-fumes;
and are not souls at all, but mere succedanea for *salt* to keep your
bodies and their appetites from putrefying! Your cotton-spinning and
thrice-miraculous mechanism, what is this too, by itself, but a larger
kind of Animalism? Spiders can spin, Beavers can build and show
contrivance: the Ant lays up accumulation of capital, and has, for
aught I know, a Bank of Antland. If there is no soul in man higher
than all that, did it reach to sailing on the cloud-rack and spinning
sea-sand; then I say, man is but an animal, a more cunning kind of
brute: he has no soul, but only a succedaneum for salt. Whereupon,
seeing himself to be truly of the beasts that perish, he ought to admit
it, I think; — and also straightway universally to kill himself; and so,
in a manlike manner, at least, *end,* and wave these brute-worlds *his*
dignified farewell! —

BOOK IV — HOROSCOPE

Chapter IV

Captains of Industry

IF I believed that Mammonism with its adjuncts was to continue henceforth the one serious principle of our existence, I should reckon it
idle to solicit remedial measures from any Government, the disease
being insusceptible of remedy. Government can do much, but it can
in no wise do all. Government, as the most conspicuous object in
Society, is called upon to give signal of what shall be done; and, in
many ways, to preside over, further, and command the doing of it.
But the Government cannot do, by all its signalling and commanding,
what the Society is radically indisposed to do. In the long-run every
Government is the exact symbol of its People, with their wisdom and
unwisdom; we have to say, Like People like Government. — The
main substance of this immense Problem of Organizing Labour, and
first of all of Managing the Working Classes, will, it is very clear, have to
be solved by those who stand practically in the middle of it; by those
who themselves work and preside over work. Of all that can be en-

acted by any Parliament in regard to it, the germs must already lie potentially extant in those two Classes, who are to obey such enactment. A Human Chaos *in* which there is no light, you vainly attempt to irradiate by light shed *on* it: order never can arise there.

But it is my firm conviction that the "Hell of England" will *cease* to be that of "not making money"; that we shall get a nobler Hell and a nobler Heaven! I anticipate light *in* the Human Chaos, glimmering, shining more and more; under manifold true signals from without That light shall shine. Our deity no longer being Mammon, — O Heavens, each man will then say to himself: "Why such deadly haste to make money? I shall not go to Hell, even if I do not make money! There is another Hell, I am told!" Competition, at railway-speed, in all branches of commerce and work will then abate: — good felt-hats for the head, in every sense, instead of seven-feet lath-and-plaster hats on wheels, will then be discoverable! Bubble-periods, with their panics and commercial crises, will again become infrequent; steady modest industry will take the place of gambling speculation. To be a noble Master, among noble Workers, will again be the first ambition with some few; to be a rich Master only the second. How the Inventive Genius of England, with the whirr of its bobbins and billy-rollers shoved somewhat into the backgrounds of the brain, will contrive and devise, not cheaper produce exclusively, but fairer distribution of the produce at its present cheapness! By degrees, we shall again have a Society with something of Heroism in it, something of Heaven's Blessing on it; we shall again have, as my German-friend asserts, "instead of Mammon-Feudalism with unsold cotton-shirts and Preservation of the Game, noble just Industrialism and Government by the Wisest!"

It is with the hope of awakening here and there a British man to know himself for a man and divine soul, that a few words of parting admonition, to all persons to whom the Heavenly Powers have lent power of any kind in this land, may now be addressed. And first to those same Master-Workers, Leaders of Industry; who stand nearest, and in fact powerfullest, though not most prominent, being as yet in too many senses a Virtuality rather than an Actuality.

The Leaders of Industry, if Industry is ever to be led, are virtually the Captains of the World; if there be no nobleness in them, there will never be an Aristocracy more. But let the Captains of Industry consider: once again, are they born of other clay than the old Captains of Slaughter; doomed for ever to be not Chivalry, but a mere gold-plated *Doggery,* — what the French well name *Canaille,* "Doggery" with more or less gold carrion at its disposal? Captains of Industry are the true Fighters, henceforth recognizable as the only true ones: Fighters against Chaos, Necessity and the Devils and Jötuns; and lead on Mankind in that great, and alone true, and universal warfare; the stars in their courses fighting for them, and all Heaven and Earth saying audibly, Well done! Let the Captains of Industry retire into their own hearts, and ask solemnly, If there is nothing but vulturous hunger for fine wines, valet reputation and gilt carriages, discoverable there? Of hearts made by the Almighty God I will not believe such a thing. Deep-hidden under wretchedest god-forgetting Cants, Epicurisms, Dead-Sea Apisms; forgotten as under foullest fat Lethe mud and weeds, there is yet, in all hearts born into this God's-World, a spark of the Godlike slumbering. Awake, O nightmare sleepers; awake, arise, or be for ever fallen! This is not playhouse poetry; it is sober fact. Our England, our world cannot live as it is. It will connect itself with a God again, or go down with nameless throes and fire-consummation to the Devils. Thou who feelest aught of such Godlike stirring in thee, any faintest intimation of it as through heavy-laden dreams, follow *it*, I conjure thee. Arise, save thyself, be one of those that save thy country.

Bucaniers, Chactaw Indians, whose supreme aim in fighting is that they may get the scalps, the money, that they may amass scalps and money; out of such came no Chivalry, and never will! Out of such came only gore and wreck, infernal rage and misery; desperation quenched in annihilation. Behold it, I bid thee, behold there, and consider! What is it that thou have a hundred thousand-pound bills laid up in thy strong-room, a hundred scalps hung up in thy wigwam? I value not them or thee. Thy scalps and thy thousand-pound bills are as yet nothing, if no nobleness from within irradiate them; if no Chivalry, in action, or in embryo ever struggling towards birth and action, be there.

Love of men cannot be bought by cash-payment; and without love, men cannot endure to be together. You cannot lead a Fighting World without having it regimented, chivalried: the thing, in a day, becomes impossible; all men in it, the highest at first, the very lowest at last, discern consciously, or by a noble instinct, this necessity. And can you any more continue to lead a Working World unregimented, anarchic? I answer, and the Heavens and Earth are now answering, No! The thing becomes not "in a day" impossible; but in some two generations it does. Yes, when fathers and mothers, in Stockport hunger-cellars, begin to eat their children, and Irish widows have to prove their relationship by dying of typhus-fever; and amid Governing "Corporations of the Best and Bravest," busy to preserve their game by "bushing," dark millions of God's human creatures start up in mad Chartisms, impracticable Sacred-Months, and Manchester Insurrections; — and there is a virtual Industrial Aristocracy as yet only half-alive, spellbound amid money-bags and ledgers; and an actual Idle Aristocracy seemingly near dead in somnolent delusions, in trespasses and double-barrels; "sliding," as on inclined-planes, which every new year they *soap* with new Hansard's-jargon [1] under God's sky, and so are "sliding" ever faster, towards a "scale" and balance-scale whereon is written *Thou art found Wanting*: — in such days, after a generation or two, I say, it does become, even to the low and simple, very palpably impossible! No Working World, any more than a Fighting World, can be led on without a noble Chivalry of Work, and laws and fixed rules which follow out of that, — far nobler than any Chivalry of Fighting was. As an anarchic multitude on mere Supply-and-demand, it is becoming inevitable that we dwindle in horrid suicidal convulsion, and self-abrasion, frightful to the imagination, into *Chactaw* Workers. With wigwams and scalps, — with palaces and thousand-pound bills; with savagery, depopulation, chaotic desolation! Good Heavens, will not one French Revolution and Reign of Terror suffice us, but must there be two? There will be two if needed; there will be twenty if needed; there will be precisely as many as are needed. The Laws of Nature will have themselves fulfilled. That is a thing certain to me.

Your gallant battle-hosts and work-hosts, as the others did, will need to be made loyally yours; they must and will be regulated, methodically secured in their just share of conquest under you; — joined with you in veritable brotherhood, sonhood, by quite other and deeper ties than those of temporary day's wages! How would mere red-coated regiments, to say nothing of chivalries, fight for you, if you could discharge them on the evening of the battle, on payment of the stipulated shillings, — and they discharge you on the morning of it! Chelsea Hospitals, pensions, promotions, rigorous lasting covenant on the one side and on the other, are indispensable even for a hired fighter. The Feudal Baron, much more, — how could he subsist with mere temporary mercenaries round him, at sixpence a day; ready to go over to the other side, if sevenpence were offered? He could not have subsisted; — and his noble instinct saved him from the necessity of even trying! The Feudal Baron had a Man's Soul in him; to which anarchy, mutiny, and the other fruits of temporary mercenaries, were intolerable: he had never been a Baron otherwise, but had continued a Chactaw and Bucanier. He felt it precious, and at last it became habitual, and his fruitful enlarged existence included it as a necessity, to have men round him who in heart loved him; whose life he watched over with rigour yet with love; who were prepared to give their life for him, if need came. It was beautiful; it was human! Man lives not otherwise, nor can live contented, anywhere or anywhen. Isolation is the sum-total of wretchedness to man. To be cut off, to be left solitary: to have a world alien, not your world; all a hostile camp for you; not a home at all, of hearts and faces who are yours, whose you are! It is the frightfullest enchantment; too truly a work of the Evil

[1] Luke Hansard (1752–1828) began printing the parliamentary record in 1774.

One. To have neither superior, nor inferior, nor equal, united manlike to you. Without father, without child, without brother. Man knows no sadder destiny. "How is each of us," exclaims Jean Paul, "so lonely in the wide bosom of the All!" [2] Encased each as in his transparent "ice-palace"; our brother visible in his, making signals and gesticulations to us; — visible, but for ever unattainable: on his bosom we shall never rest, nor he on ours. It was not a God that did this; no!

Awake, ye noble Workers, warriors in the one true war: all this must be remedied. It is you who are already half-alive, whom I will welcome into life; whom I will conjure in God's name to shake off your enchanted sleep, and live wholly! Cease to count scalps, gold-purses; not in these lies your or our salvation. Even these, if you count only these, will not be left. Let bucaniering be put far from you; alter, speedily abrogate all laws of the bucaniers, if you would gain any victory that shall endure. Let God's justice, let pity, nobleness and manly valour, with more gold-purses or with fewer, testify themselves in this your brief Life-transit to all the Eternities, the Gods and Silences. It is to you I call; for ye are not dead, ye are already half-alive: there is in you a sleepless dauntless energy, the prime-matter of all nobleness in man. Honour to you in your kind. It is to you I call: ye know at least this, That the mandate of God to His creature man is: Work! The future Epic of the World rests not with those that are near dead, but with those that are alive, and those that are coming into life.

Look around you. Your world-hosts are all in mutiny, in confusion, destitution; on the eve of fiery wreck and madness! They will not march farther for you, on the sixpence a day and supply-and-demand principle: they will not; nor ought they, nor can they. Ye shall reduce them to order, begin reducing them. To order, to just subordination; noble loyalty in return for noble guidance. Their souls are driven nigh mad; let yours be sane and ever saner. Not as a bewildered bewildering mob; but as a firm regimented mass, with real captains over them, will these men march any more. All human interests, combined human endeavours, and social growths in this world, have, at a certain stage of their development, required organizing: and Work, the grandest of human interests, does now require it.

God knows, the task will be hard: but no noble task was ever easy. This task will wear away your lives, and the lives of your sons and grandsons: but for what purpose, if not for tasks like this, were lives given to men? Ye shall cease to count your thousand-pound scalps, the noble of you shall cease! Nay, the very scalps, as I say, will not long be left if you count on these. Ye shall cease wholly to be barbarous vulturous Chactaws, and become noble European Nineteenth-Century Men. Ye shall know that Mammon, in never such gigs and flunkey

2 Jean Paul Richter (1763–1825), German romantic humorist whom Carlyle greatly admired.

"respectabilities," is not the alone God; that of himself he is but a Devil, and even a Brute-god.

Difficult? Yes, it will be difficult. The short-fibre cotton; that too was difficult. The waste cotton-shrub, long useless, disobedient, as the thistle by the wayside, — have ye not conquered it; made it into beautiful bandana webs; white woven shirts for men; bright-tinted air-garments wherein flit goddesses? Ye have shivered mountains asunder, made the hard iron pliant to you as soft putty: the Forest-giants, Marsh-jötuns bear sheaves of golden grain; Ægir the Sea-demon himself stretches his back for a sleek highway to you, and on Firehorses and Windhorses ye career. Ye are most strong. Thor red-bearded, with his blue sun-eyes, with his cheery heart and strong thunder-hammer, he and you have prevailed. Ye are most strong, ye Sons of the icy North, of the far East, — far marching from your rugged Eastern Wildernesses, hitherward from the grey Dawn of Time! Ye are Sons of the *Jötun*-land; the land of Difficulties Conquered. Difficult? You must try this thing. Once try it with the understanding that it will and shall have to be done. Try it as ye try the paltrier thing, making of money! I will bet on you once more, against all Jötuns, Tailor-gods, Double-barrelled Law-wards, and Denizens of Chaos whatsoever!

Shooting Niagara: and After?

❰ "Shooting Niagara" was first published in *Macmillan's Magazine* for August 1867. The second great Reform Bill was finally put through by the Tory government under Disraeli in August 1867, and this essay-pamphlet was Carlyle's final blow at, in Froude's words, "the longest plunge yet ventured into the whirlpool of democracy." Carlyle himself called the piece "very fierce, exaggerative, ragged, unkempt, and defective." There are ten divisions to the essay, and only a sampling is printed here. ❱

I

THERE probably never was since the Heptarchy ended, or almost since it began, so hugely critical an epoch in the history of England as this we have now entered upon, with universal self-congratulation and flinging-up of caps; nor one in which, — with no Norman Invasion now ahead, to lay hold of it, to bridle and regulate it for us (little thinking it was *for us*), and guide it into higher and wider regions, — the question of utter death or of nobler new life for the poor Country was so uncertain. Three things seem to be agreed upon by Gods and men, at least by English men and gods; certain to happen, and are now in visible course of fulfilment.

1° *Democracy* to complete itself; to go the full length of its course, towards the Bottomless or into it, no power now extant to prevent it or even considerably retard it, — till we have seen where it will lead us to, and whether there will *then* be any return possible, or none. Complete "liberty" to all persons; Count of Heads to be the Divine Court of Appeal on every question and interest of mankind; Count of Heads to choose a Parliament according to its own heart at last, and sit with Penny Newspapers zealously watching the same; said Parliament, so chosen and so watched, to do what trifle of legislating and administering may still be needed in such an England, with its hundred-and-fifty millions "free" more and more to follow each his own nose, by way of guide-post in this intricate world.

2° That, in a limited time, say fifty years hence, the Church, all Churches and so-called religions, the Christian Religion itself, shall have deliquesced, — into "Liberty of Conscience," Progress of Opinion, Progress of Intellect, Philanthropic Movement, and other aqueous residues, of a vapid badly-scented character; — and shall, like water spilt upon the ground, trouble nobody considerably thenceforth, but evaporate at its leisure.

3° That, in lieu thereof, there shall be Free Trade, in all senses, and to all lengths: unlimited Free Trade, — which some take to mean, "Free racing, ere long with unlimited speed, in the career of *Cheap and Nasty*"; — this beautiful career, not in shop-goods only, but in all things temporal, spiritual and eternal, to be flung generously open, wide as the portals of the Universe; so that everybody shall start free, and everywhere, "under enlightened popular suffrage," the race shall be to the swift, and the high office shall fall to him who is ablest if not to do it, at least to get elected for doing it.

These are three altogether new and very considerable achievements, lying visibly ahead of us, not far off, — and so extremely considerable, that every thinking English creature is tempted to go into manifold reflections and inquiries upon them. My own have not been wanting, any time these thirty years past, but they have not been of a joyful or triumphant nature; not prone to utter themselves; indeed expecting, till lately, that they might with propriety lie unuttered altogether. But the series of events comes swifter and swifter, at a strange rate; and hastens unexpectedly, — "velocity increasing" (if you will consider, for this too is as when the little stone has been loosened, which sets the whole mountain-side in motion) "as the *square* of the time"; — so that the wisest Prophecy finds it was quite wrong as to date; and, patiently, or even indolently waiting, is astonished to see itself fulfilled, not in centuries as anticipated, but in decades and years. It was a clear prophecy, for instance, that Germany would either become honourably Prussian or go to gradual annihilation: but who of us ex-

pected that we ourselves, instead of our children's children, should
live to behold it; that a magnanimous and fortunate Herr von Bis-
marck, whose dispraise was in all the Newspapers, would, to his own
amazement, find the thing now doable; and would do it, do the essential of it, in a few of the current weeks? That England would have
to take the Niagara leap of completed Democracy one day, was also
a plain prophecy, though uncertain as to time. . . .

V

I almost think, when once we have made the Niagara leap, the better kind of Nobility, perhaps after experimenting, will more and more
withdraw themselves from the Parliamentary, Oratorical or Political
element; leaving that to such Cleon the Tanner [1] and Company as it
rightfully belongs to; and be far more chary of their speech than now.
Speech issuing in no deed is hateful and contemptible: — how can
a man have any nobleness who knows not that? In God's name, let
us find out what of noble and profitable we can *do;* if it be nothing,
let us at least keep silence, and bear gracefully our strange lot! —
The English Nobleman has still left in him, after such sorrowful
erosions, something considerable of chivalry and magnanimity: polite
he is, in the finest form; politeness, modest, simple, veritable, ineradicable, dwells in him to the bone; I incline to call him the politest
kind of nobleman or man (especially his wife the politest and grace-
fulest kind of woman) you will find in any country. An immense endowment this, if you consider it well! A very great and indispensable
help to whatever other faculties of *kingship* a man may have. Indeed
it springs from them all (its sources, every kingly faculty lying in
you); and is as the beautiful natural skin, and visible sanction, index
and outcome of them all. No king can rule without it; none but
potential kings can really have it. In the crude, what we call unbred
or *Orson* [2] form, all "men of genius" have it; but see what it avails
some of them, — your Samuel Johnson, for instance, — in that crude
form, who was so rich in it, too, in the crude way!

Withal it is perhaps a fortunate circumstance, that the population
has no wild notions, no political enthusiasms of a "New Era" or the
like. This, though in itself a dreary and ignoble item, in respect of
the revolutionary Many, may nevertheless be for good, if the Few
shall be really high and brave, as things roll on.
Certain it is, there is nothing but vulgarity in our People's expectations, resolutions or desires, in this Epoch. It is all a peaceable
mouldering or tumbling down from mere rottenness and decay;
whether slowly mouldering or rapidly tumbling, there will be nothing

1 Greek demagogue of the Age of Pericles, originally a tanner.
2 An "unbred" nobleman in early French romance; Orson's brother Valentine
was raised at court and hence Carlyle's later reference to *Valentinism.*

found of real or true in the rubbish-heap, but a most true desire of
making money easily, and of eating it pleasantly. A poor ideal for
"reformers," sure enough. But it is the fruit of long antecedents, too;
and from of old, our habits in regard to "reformation," or repairing
what went wrong (as something is always doing), have been strangely
didactic! And to such length have we at last brought it, by our wilful, conscious, and now long-continued method of using *varnish*, instead of actual repair by honest *carpentry*, of what we all knew and
saw to have gone undeniably wrong in our procedures and affairs!
Method deliberately, steadily, and even solemnly continued, with
much admiration of it from ourselves and others, as the best and only
good one, for above two hundred years.

Ever since that *annus mirabilis* of 1660, when Oliver Cromwell's
dead clay was hung on the gibbet, and a much easier "reign of Christ"
under the divine gentleman called Charles II. was thought the fit
thing, this has been our steady method: varnish, varnish; if a thing
have grown so rotten that it yawns palpable, and is so inexpressibly
ugly that the eyes of the very populace discern it and detest it, —
bring out a new pot of varnish, with the requisite supply of putty;
and lay it on handsomely. Don't spare varnish; how well it will all
look in a few days, if laid on well! Varnish alone is cheap and is safe;
avoid carpentering, chiselling, sawing and hammering on the old quiet
House; — dry-rot is in it, who knows how deep; don't disturb the old
beams and junctures; varnish, varnish, if you will be blessed by gods
and men! This is called the Constitutional System, Conservative
System, and other fine names; and this at last has its fruits, — such
as we see. Mendacity hanging in the very air we breathe; all men
become, unconsciously or half or wholly consciously, *liars* to their own
souls and to other men's; grimacing, finessing, periphrasing, in continual hypocrisy of *word*, by way of varnish to continual past, present,
future misperformance of *thing*: — clearly sincere about nothing
whatever, except in silence, about the appetites of their own huge
belly, and the readiest method of assuaging these. From a Population of that sunk kind, ardent only in pursuits that are low and in
industries that are sensuous and *beaverish*, there is little peril of
human enthusiasms, or revolutionary transports, such as occurred in
1789, for instance. A low-minded *pecus* all that; essentially torpid
and *ignavum*,[3] on all that is high or nobly human in revolutions.

It is true there is in such a population, of itself, no *help* at all towards reconstruction of the wreck of your Niagara plunge; of themselves they, with whatever cry of "liberty" in their mouths, are in-
exorably marked by Destiny as *slaves;* and not even the immortal gods
could make them free, — except by making them anew and on a different pattern. No help in them at all, to your model Aristocrat, or
to any noble man or thing. But then likewise there is no hindrance,

3 *pecus ignavum:* slothful herd.

or a minimum of it! Nothing there in *bar* of the noble Few, who we always trust will be born to us, generation after generation; and on whom and whose living of a noble and valiantly cosmic life amid the worst impediments and hugest anarchies, the whole of our hope depends. Yes, on them only! If amid the thickest welter of surrounding gluttony and baseness, and what must be reckoned bottomless anarchy from shore to shore, there be found no man, no small but invincible minority of men, capable of keeping themselves free from all that, and of living a heroically human life, while the millions round them are noisily living a mere beaverish or doglike one, then truly all hope is gone. But we always struggle to believe Not. Aristocracy by title, by fortune and position, who can doubt but there are still precious possibilities among the chosen of that class? And if that fail us, there is still, we hope, the unclassed Aristocracy by nature, not inconsiderable in numbers, and supreme in faculty, in wisdom, human talent, nobleness and courage, "who derive their patent of nobility direct from Almighty God." . . .

VI

What we can expect this Aristocracy of Nature to do for us? They are of two kinds: the Speculative, speaking or vocal; and the Practical or industrial, whose function is silent. These are of brother quality; but they go very different roads: "men of *genius*" they all emphatically are, the "inspired Gift of God" lodged in each of them. . . .

On the whole, I hope our Hero will, by heroic word, and heroic thought and *act*, make manifest to mankind that "Reverence for God and for Man" is not yet extinct, but only fallen into disastrous comatose sleep, and hideously dreaming; that the "Christian Religion itself is not dead," that the soul of it is alive forevermore, — and only the dead and rotting *body* of it is now getting burial. The noblest of modern Intellects, by far the noblest we have had since Shakspeare left us, has said of this Religion: "It is a Height to which the Human Species were fitted and destined to attain; and from which, having once attained it, they can never retrograde." Permanently, never. Never, *they;* — though individual Nations of them fatally *can;* of which I hope poor England is not one? Though, here as elsewhere, the *burial*-process does offer ghastly enough phenomena: Ritualisms, Puseyisms,[4] Arches-Court Lawsuits, Cardinals of Westminster, etc., etc.; — making night hideous! For a time and times and half a time, as the old Prophets used to say.

One of my hoping friends, yet more sanguine than I fully dare to be, has these zealous or enthusiast words: "A very great 'work,' surely, is going on in these days, — has been *begun*, and is silently proceeding, and cannot easily *stop*, under all the flying dungheaps of this new

4 After Edward Pusey, one of the leaders of the Oxford Movement.

'Battle of the Giants' flinging their *Dung*-Pelion on their Dung-Ossa, in these ballot-boxing, Nigger-emancipating, empty, dirt-eclipsed days: — no less a 'work' than that of restoring GOD and whatever was Godlike in the traditions and recorded doings of Mankind; dolefully forgotten, or sham-remembered, as it has been, for long degraded and degrading hundreds of years, latterly! Actually this, if you understand it well. The essential, still awful and ever-blessed Fact of all that was meant by 'God and the Godlike' to men's souls is again struggling to become clearly revealed; will extricate itself from what some of us, too irreverently in our impatience, call 'Hebrew old-clothes'; and will again bless the Nations; and heal them from their basenesses, and unendurable woes, and wanderings in the company of madness! This Fact lodges, not exclusively or specially in Hebrew Garnitures, Old or New; but in the Heart of Nature and of Man forevermore. And is not less certain, here at this hour, than it ever was at any Sinai whatsoever. Kant's 'Two things that strike me *dumb*'; — these are perceptible at Königsberg in Prussia, or at Charing-cross in London. And all eyes shall yet see them *better;* and the heroic Few, who are the salt of the earth, shall at length see them *well.* With results for everybody. A great 'work' indeed; the greatness of which beggars all others!"

VII

Of the second, or silent Industrial Hero, I may now say something, as more within my limits and the reader's.

This Industrial hero, here and there recognisable and known to me, as developing himself, and as an opulent and dignified kind of man, is already almost an Aristocrat by class. And if his chivalry is still somewhat in the *Orson* form, he is already by intermarriage and otherwise coming into contact with the Aristocracy by title; and by degrees will acquire the fit *Valentinism,* and other more important advantages there. He cannot do better than unite with this naturally noble kind of Aristocrat by title; the Industrial noble and this one are brothers born; called and impelled to coöperate and go together. Their united result is what we want from both. And the Noble of the Future, — if there be any such, as I well discern there must, — will have grown out of both. A new "Valentine"; and perhaps a considerably improved, — by such recontact with his wild Orson kinsman, and with the earnest veracities this latter has learned in the Woods and the Dens of Bears.

The Practical "man of genius" will probably *not* be altogether absent from the Reformed Parliament: — his *Make-believe,* the vulgar millionaire (truly a "bloated" specimen, this!), is sure to be frequent there; and along with the multitude of *brass* guineas, it will be very salutary to have a *gold* one or two! — In or out of Parliament, our Practical hero will find no end of work ready for him. It is he that

has to recivilise, out of its now utter savagery, the world of Industry;
— think what a set of items: To change *nomadic* contract into *permanent;* to annihilate the soot and dirt and squalid horror now defacing this England, once so clean and comely while it was poor; matters sanitary (and that not to the *body* only) for his people; matters governmental for them; matters etc., etc.: — no want of work for this Hero, through a great many generations yet! . . .

IX

I always fancy there might much be done in the way of military Drill withal. Beyond all other schooling, and as supplement or even as succedaneum for all other, one often wishes the entire Population could be thoroughly drilled; into cooperative movement, into individual behavior, correct, precise, and at once habitual and orderly as mathematics, in all or in very many points, — and ultimately in the point of actual *Military Service,* should such be required of it!

That of commanding and obeying, were there nothing more, is it not the basis of all human culture; ought not all to have it; and how many ever do? I often say, The one Official Person, royal, sacerdotal, scholastic, governmental, of our times, who is still thoroughly a truth and a reality, and *not* in great part a hypothesis and worn-out humbug, proposing and attempting a duty which he fails to do, — is the Drill-Sergeant who is master of his work, and who will perform it. By Drill-Sergeant understand, not the man in three stripes alone; understand him as meaning all such men, up to the Turenne, to the Friedrich of Prussia; — *he* does his function, he is genuine; and from the highest to the lowest no one else does. Ask your poor King's Majesty, Captain-General of England, Defender of the Faith, and so much else; ask your poor Bishop, sacred Overseer of souls; your poor Lawyer, sacred Dispenser of justice; your poor Doctor, ditto of health: they will all answer, "Alas, no, worthy sir, we are all of us unfortunately fallen not a little, some of us altogether, into the imaginary or quasi-humbug condition, and cannot help ourselves; he alone of the three stripes, or of the gorget and baton, *does* what he pretends to!" That is the melancholy fact; well worth considering at present. — Nay, I often consider farther, If, in any Country, the Drill-Sergeant himself fall into the partly imaginary or humbug condition (as is my frightful apprehension of him here in England, on survey of him in his marvellous Crimean expeditions, marvellous Court-martial revelations, Newspaper controversies, and the like), what is to become of that Country and its thrice-miserable Drill-Sergeant? Reformed Parliament, I hear, has decided on a "thorough Army reform," as one of the first things. So that we shall at length have a perfect Army, field-worthy and correct in all points, thinks Reformed Parliament? Alas, yes; — and if the sky fall, we shall catch larks, too! —

But now, what is to hinder the acknowledged King in all corners of his territory, to introduce wisely a universal system of Drill, not military only, but human in all kinds; so that no child or man born in *his* territory might miss the benefit of it, — which would be immense to man, woman and child? I would begin with it, in mild, soft forms, so soon almost as my children were able to stand on their legs; and I would never wholly remit it till they had done with the world and me. Poor Wilderspin [5] knew something of this; the great Goethe evidently knew a great deal! This of outwardly combined and plainly consociated Discipline, in simultaneous movement and action, which may be practical, symbolical, artistic, mechanical in all degrees and modes, — is one of the noblest capabilities of man (most sadly undervalued hitherto); and one he takes the greatest pleasure in exercising and unfolding, not to mention at all the invaluable benefit it would afford him if unfolded. From correct marching in line, to rhythmic dancing in cotillon or minuet, — and to infinitely higher degrees (that of symboling in concert your "first reverence," for instance, supposing reverence and symbol of it to be both sincere!) — there is a natural charm in it; the fulfilment of a deep-seated, universal desire, to all rhythmic social creatures! In man's heaven-born Docility, or power of being Educated, it is estimable as perhaps the deepest and richest element; or the next to that of music, of Sensibility to Song, to Harmony and Number, which some have reckoned the deepest of all. A richer mine than any in California for poor human creatures; richer by what a multiple; and hitherto as good as never opened, — worked only for the Fighting purpose. Assuredly I would not neglect the Fighting purpose; no, from sixteen to sixty, not a son of mine but should know the Soldier's function too, and be able to defend his native soil and self, in best perfection, when need came. But I should not begin with this; I should carefully end with this, after careful travel in innumerable fruitful fields by the way leading to this.

It is strange to me, stupid creatures of routine as we mostly are, how in all education of mankind, this of simultaneous Drilling into combined rhythmic action, for almost all good purposes, has been overlooked and left neglected by the elaborate and many-sounding Pedagogues and Professorial Persons we have had, for the long centuries past! It really should be set on foot a little; and developed gradually into the multiform opulent results it holds for us. As might well be done by an acknowledged king in his own territory, if he were wise. To all children of men it is such an entertainment, when you set them to it. I believe the vulgarest Cockney crowd, flung out millionfold on a Whit-Monday, with nothing but beer and dull folly to depend on for amusement, would at once kindle into something

5 Samuel Wilderspin (1792?–1866), writer on and developer of schools for the very young.

human, if you set them to do almost any regulated act in common. And would dismiss their beer and dull foolery, in the silent charm of rhythmic human companionship, in the practical feeling, probably new, that all of us are made on one pattern, and are, in an unfathomable way, brothers to one another. . . .

X

. . . The Aristocracy, as a class, has as yet no thought of giving-up the game, or ceasing to be what in the language of flattery is called "Governing Class"; nor should, till it have seen farther. In the better heads among them are doubtless grave misgivings; serious enough reflections rising, — perhaps not sorrowful altogether; for there must be questions withal, "Was it so very blessed a function, then, that of 'Governing' on the terms given?" But beyond doubt the vulgar Noble Lord intends fully to continue the game, — with doubly severe study of the new rules issued on it; — and will still, for a good while yet, so as heretofore into Electioneering, Parliamentary Engineering; and hope against hope to keep weltering atop by some method or other, and to make a fit existence for himself in that miserable old way. An existence filled with labour and anxiety, with disappointments and disgraces and futilities I can promise him, but with little or nothing else. Let us hope he will be wise to discern, and not continue the experiment too long!

He has lost his place in that element; nothing but services of a sordid and dishonourable nature, betrayal of his own Order, and of the noble interests of England, can gain him even momentary favour there. He cannot bridle the wild horse of a Plebs any longer: — for a generation past, he has not even tried to bridle it; but has run panting and trotting meanly by the side of it, patting its stupid neck; slavishly plunging with it into any "Crimean" or other slough of black platitudes it might reel towards, — anxious he, only not to be kicked away, not just yet; oh, not yet for a little while! Is this an existence for a man of any honour; for a man ambitious of more honour? I should say, not. And he still thinks to hang by the bridle, now when his Plebs is getting into the gallop? Hanging by its bridle, through what steep brambly places (scratching out the very *eyes* of him, as is often enough observable), through what malodorous quagmires and ignominious pools will the wild horse drag him, — till he quit hold! Let him quit, in Heaven's name. Better he should go yachting to Algeria, and shoot lions for an occupied existence: — or stay at home, and hunt rats? Why not? Is not, in strict truth, the Ratcatcher our one *real* British Nimrod now! — Game-preserving, Highland deer-stalking, and the like, will soon all have ceased in this over-crowded Country; and I can see no other business for the vulgar Noble Lord, if he will continue vulgar! —

John Henry Newman

JOHN HENRY NEWMAN

CHRONOLOGY

1801   Born February 21 in London.

1816   Entered Trinity College, Oxford.

1822   Became Fellow of Oriel College, Oxford.

1824   Took Holy Orders; accepted the curacy of St. Clements, Oxford.

1826   Became Tutor at Oriel; resigned curacy.

1828   Became Vicar of St. Mary's, Oxford.

1832–1833   Resigned Tutorship; made a Mediterranean tour with Hurrell Froude.

1833   Began *Tracts for the Times* in September.

1835–1839   Gained great attention as a preacher at Oxford.

1841   Published *Tract XC; Tracts* discontinued.

1842   Retired to Littlemore and a semi-monastic life.

1845   Resigned Fellowship at Oriel; was received into Roman Catholic Church; published *The Development of Christian Doctrine*.

1846   Went to Rome; was ordained priest and received degree of D. D. from the Pope.

1847   Returned to England; became head of the Oratory at Edgbaston, near Birmingham.

1851   Published *The Present Position of Catholics in England*.

1852   Made Rector-elect of a projected Catholic University in Dublin; began lectures on *The Idea of a University*.

1855   Published *Callista*.

1864   Published the *Apologia pro Vita Sua*.

1865   Published *The Dream of Gerontius and Other Poems*.

1870   Published *A Grammar of Assent*.

1871–1872   Published *Essays, Critical and Historical* (1828–1846), in two volumes; *Discussions and Arguments* (1836–1866); *Historical Sketches* (1824–1860), in three volumes.

1878   Elected Honorary Fellow of Trinity College, Oxford.

1879   Created Cardinal by Pope Leo XIII.

1890   Died August 11.

The Idea of a University

(From May 10 to June 7, 1852, Newman delivered nine lectures to the Catholics of Dublin. In the same year these lectures were published as *Discourses on the Scope and Nature of a University Education*. Afterwards they were republished, with some alterations, together with a series of "Occasional Lectures and Essays on University Subjects," as *The Idea of a University* (1852, 1873). Newman's object was to define "the *aims* and *principles*" of higher education, and in so doing he evolved a classic statement of liberal education and the most universally appreciated of all his works. The student is advised, in contrasting Newman with writers like Macaulay, to note carefully the various uses Newman makes of the word "liberal.")

DISCOURSE V

Knowledge Its Own End

A UNIVERSITY may be considered with reference either to its Students or to its Studies; and the principle, that all Knowledge is a whole and the separate Sciences parts of one, which I have hitherto been using in behalf of its studies, is equally important when we direct our attention to its students. Now then I turn to the students, and shall consider the education which, by virtue of this principle, a University will give them; and thus I shall be introduced, Gentlemen, to the second question, which I proposed to discuss, viz. whether and in what sense its teaching, viewed relatively to the taught, carries the attribute of Utility along with it.

1

I have said that all branches of knowledge are connected together, because the subject-matter of knowledge is intimately united in itself, as being the acts and the work of the Creator. Hence it is that the Sciences, into which our knowledge may be said to be cast, have multiplied bearings one on another, and an internal sympathy, and admit, or rather demand, comparison and adjustment. They complete, correct, balance each other. This consideration, if well-founded, must be taken into account, not only as regards the attainment of truth, which is their common end, but as regards the influence which they exercise upon those whose education consists in the study of them. I have said already, that to give undue prominence to one is to be unjust to another; to neglect or supersede these is to divert those from their proper object. It is to unsettle the boundary lines between science and science, to disturb their action, to destroy the harmony which binds them together. Such a proceeding will have

179

a corresponding effect when introduced into a place of education. There is no science but tells a different tale, when viewed as a portion of a whole, from what it is likely to suggest when taken by itself, without the safeguard, as I may call it, of others.

Let me make use of an illustration. In the combination of colours, very different effects are produced by a difference in their selection and juxtaposition; red, green, and white change their shades, according to the contrast to which they are submitted. And, in like manner, the drift and meaning of a branch of knowledge varies with the company in which it is introduced to the student. If his reading is confined simply to one subject, however such division of labour may favour the advancement of a particular pursuit, a point into which I do not here enter, certainly it has a tendency to contract his mind. If it is incorporated with others, it depends on those others as to the kind of influence which it exerts upon him. Thus the Classics, which in England are the means of refining the taste, have in France subserved the spread of revolutionary and deistical doctrines. In Metaphysics, again, Butler's [1] *Analogy of Religion,* which has had so much to do with the conversion to the Catholic faith of members of the University of Oxford, appeared to Pitt and others, who had received a different training, to operate only in the direction of infidelity. And so again, Watson, Bishop of Llandaff,[2] as I think he tells us in the narrative of his life, felt the science of Mathematics to indispose the mind to religious belief, while others see in its investigations the best parallel, and thereby defence, of the Christian Mysteries. In like manner, I suppose, Arcesilaus [3] would not have handled logic as Aristotle, nor Aristotle have criticized poets as Plato; yet reasoning and poetry are subject to scientific rules.

It is a great point then to enlarge the range of studies which a University professes, even for the sake of the students; and, though they cannot pursue every subject which is open to them, they will be the gainers by living among those and under those who represent the whole circle. This I conceive to be the advantage of a seat of universal learning, considered as a place of education. An assemblage of learned men, zealous for their own sciences, and rivals of each other, are brought, by familiar intercourse and for the sake of intellectual peace, to adjust together the claims and relations of their respective subjects of investigation. They learn to respect, to consult, to aid each other. Thus is created a pure and clear atmosphere of thought, which the student also breathes, though in his own case he only pursues a few sciences out of the multitude. He profits by an intellectual tradition, which is independent of particular teachers,

---

1 Joseph Butler (1692–1752), Anglican divine.
2 Richard Watson (1737–1816), defender of Christianity against Edward Gibbon and Tom Paine.
3 Greek philosopher of the 3rd century B.C.

which guides him in his choice of subjects, and duly interprets for him those which he chooses. He apprehends the great outlines of knowledge, the principles on which it rests, the scale of its parts, its lights and its shades, its great points and its little, as he otherwise cannot apprehend them. Hence it is that his education is called "Liberal." A habit of mind is formed which lasts through life, of which the attributes are, freedom, equitableness, calmness, moderation, and wisdom; or what in a former Discourse I have ventured to call a philosophical habit. This then I would assign as the special fruit of the education furnished at a University, as contrasted with other places of teaching or modes of teaching. This is the main purpose of a University in its treatment of its students.

And now the question is asked me, What is the *use* of it? and my answer will constitute the main subject of the Discourses which are to follow.

2

Cautious and practical thinkers, I say, will ask of me, what, after all, is the gain of this Philosophy of which I make such account, and from which I promise so much. Even supposing it to enable us to exercise the degree of trust exactly due to every science respectively, and to estimate precisely the value of every truth which is anywhere to be found, how are we better for this master view of things, which I have been extolling? Does it not reverse the principle of the division of labour? will practical objects be obtained better or worse by its cultivation? to what then does it lead? where does it end? what does it do? how does it profit? what does it promise? Particular sciences are respectively the basis of definite arts, which carry on to results tangible and beneficial the truths which are the subjects of the knowledge attained; what is the Art of this science of sciences? what is the fruit of such a Philosophy? what are we proposing to effect, what inducements do we hold out to the Catholic community, when we set about the enterprise of founding a University?

I am asked what is the end of University Education, and of the Liberal or Philosophical Knowledge which I conceive it to impart: I answer, that what I have already said has been sufficient to show that it has a very tangible, real, and sufficient end, though the end cannot be divided from that knowledge itself. Knowledge is capable of being its own end. Such is the constitution of the human mind, that any kind of knowledge, if it be really such, is its own reward. And if this is true of all knowledge, it is true also of that special Philosophy, which I have made to consist in a comprehensive view of truth in all its branches, of the relations of science to science, of their mutual bearings, and their respective values. What the worth of such an acquirement is, compared with other objects which we seek, — wealth or power or honour or the conveniences and comforts of life, I do not profess here to discuss; but I would maintain, and mean to show, that it is an object, in its own nature so really and undeniably good, as to be the compensation of a great deal of thought in the compassing, and a great deal of trouble in the attaining.

Now, when I say that Knowledge is, not merely a means to something beyond it, or the preliminary of certain arts into which it naturally resolves, but an end sufficient to rest in and to pursue for its own sake, surely I am uttering no paradox, for I am stating what is both intelligible in itself, and has ever been the common judgment of philosophers and the ordinary feeling of mankind. I am saying what at least the public opinion of this day ought to be slow to deny, considering how much we have heard of late years, in opposition to Religion, of entertaining, curious, and various knowledge. I am but saying what whole volumes have been written to illustrate, viz. by a "selection from the records of Philosophy, Literature, and Art, in all ages and countries, of a body of examples, to show how the most unpropitious circumstances have been unable to conquer an ardent desire for the acquisition of knowledge." That further advantages accrue to us and redound to others by its possession, over and above what it is in itself, I am very far indeed from denying; but, independent of these, we are satisfying a direct need of our nature in its very acquisition; and, whereas our nature, unlike that of the inferior creation, does not at once reach its perfection, but depends, in order to it, on a number of external aids and appliances, Knowledge, as one of the principal of these, is valuable for what its very presence in us does for us after the manner of a habit, even though it be turned to no further account, nor subserve any direct end.

3

Hence it is that Cicero, in enumerating the various heads of mental excellence, lays down the pursuit of Knowledge for its own sake, as the first of them. "This pertains most of all to human nature," he says, "for we are all of us drawn to the pursuit of Knowledge; in which to excel we consider excellent, whereas to mistake, to err, to be ignorant, to be deceived, is both an evil and a disgrace." And he considers Knowledge the very first object to which we are attracted, after the supply of our physical wants. After the calls and duties of our animal existence, as they may be termed, as regards ourselves, our family, and our neighbours, follows, he tells us, "the search after truth. Accordingly, as soon as we escape from the pressure of necessary cares, forthwith we desire to see, to hear, and to learn; and consider the knowledge of what is hidden or is wonderful a condition of our happiness."

This passage, though it is but one of many similar passages in a multitude of authors, I take for the very reason that it is so familiarly known to us; and I wish you to observe, Gentlemen, how distinctly it separates the pursuit of Knowledge from those ulterior objects to which certainly it can be made to conduce, and which are, I suppose, solely contemplated by the persons who would ask of me the use of a University or Liberal Education. So far from dreaming of the cultivation of Knowledge directly and mainly in order to our physical comfort and enjoyment, for the sake of life and person, of health, of the conjugal and family union, of the social tie and civil security, the great Orator implies, that it is only after our physical and political needs are supplied, and when we are "free from necessary duties and cares," that we are in a condition for "desiring to see, to hear, and to learn." Nor does he contemplate in the least degree the reflex or subsequent action of Knowledge, when acquired, upon those material goods which we set out by securing before we seek it; on the contrary, he expressly denies its bearing upon social life altogether, strange as such a procedure is to those who live after the rise of the Baconian philosophy, and he cautions us against such a cultivation of it as will interfere with our duties to our fellow-creatures. "All these methods," he says, "are engaged in the investigation of truth; by the pursuit of which to be carried off from public occupations is a transgression of duty. For the praise of virtue lies altogether in action; yet intermissions often occur, and then we recur to such pursuits; not to say that the incessant activity of the mind is vigorous enough to carry us on in the pursuit of knowledge, even without any exertion of our own." The idea of benefiting society by means of "the pursuit of science and knowledge," did not enter at all into the motives which he would assign for their cultivation.

This was the ground of the opposition which the elder Cato made to the introduction of Greek Philosophy among his countrymen, when Carneades [4] and his companions, on occasion of their embassy, were charming the Roman youth with their eloquent expositions of it. The fit representative of a practical people, Cato estimated everything by what it produced; whereas the Pursuit of Knowledge promised nothing beyond Knowledge itself. He despised that refinement or enlargement of mind of which he had no experience.

4

Things, which can bear to be cut off from everything else and yet persist in living, must have life in themselves; pursuits, which issue in nothing, and still maintain their ground for ages, which are regarded as admirable, though they have not as yet proved themselves to be useful, must have their sufficient end in themselves, whatever it turn out to be. And we are brought to the same conclusion by considering the force of the epithet, by which the knowledge under consideration is popularly designated. It is common to speak of "lib-

[4] Skeptic philosopher of the 3rd century B.C. who held that man has no criterion for truth.

eral knowledge," of the "*liberal* arts and studies," and of a "*liberal*
education," as the especial characteristic or property of a University
and of a gentleman; what is really meant by the word? Now, first,
in its grammatical sense it is opposed to *servile;* and by "servile work"
is understood, as our catechisms inform us, bodily labour, mechanical
employment, and the like, in which the mind has little or no part.
Parallel to such servile works are those arts, if they deserve the name,
of which the poet speaks, which owe their origin and their method
to hazard, not to skill; as, for instance, the practice and operations
of an empiric. As far as this contrast may be considered as a guide
into the meaning of the word, liberal education and liberal pursuits
are exercises of mind, of reason, of reflection.

But we want something more for its explanation, for there are
bodily exercises which are liberal, and mental exercises which are
not so. For instance, in ancient times the practitioners in medicine
were commonly slaves; yet it was an art as intellectual in its nature,
in spite of the pretence, fraud and quackery with which it might
then, as now, be debased, as it was heavenly in its aim. And so in
like manner, we contrast a liberal education with a commercial education or a professional; yet no one can deny that commerce and
the professions afford scope for the highest and most diversified
powers of mind. There is then a great variety of intellectual exercises,
which are not technically called "liberal"; on the other hand, I say,
there are exercises of the body which do receive that appellation.
Such, for instance, was the palæstra, in ancient times; such the Olym-
pic games, in which strength and dexterity of body as well as of mind
gained the prize. In Xenophon we read of the young Persian nobility
being taught to ride on horseback and to speak the truth; both being
among the accomplishments of a gentleman. War, too, however rough
a profession, has ever been accounted liberal, unless in cases when
it becomes heroic, which would introduce us to another subject.

Now comparing these instances together, we shall have no difficulty
in determining the principle of this apparent variation in the application of the term which I am examining. Manly games, or games
of skill, or military prowess, though bodily, are, it seems, accounted
liberal; on the other hand, what is merely professional, though
highly intellectual, nay, though liberal in comparison of trade and
manual labour, is not simply called liberal, and mercantile occupations are not liberal at all. Why this distinction? because that alone
is liberal knowledge, which stands on its own pretensions, which is
independent of sequel, expects no complement, refuses to be *informed*
(as it is called) by any end, or absorbed into any art, in order duly
to present itself to our contemplation. The most ordinary pursuits
have this specific character, if they are self-sufficient and complete;
the highest lose it, when they minister to something beyond them.
It is absurd to balance, in point of worth and importance, a treatise

on reducing fractures with a game of cricket or a fox-chase; yet of the two the bodily exercise has that quality which we call "liberal," and the intellectual has not. And so of the learned professions altogether, considered merely as professions; although one of them be the most popularly beneficial, and another the most politically important, and the third the most intimately divine of all human pursuits, yet the very greatness of their end, the health of the body, or of the commonwealth, or of the soul, diminishes, not increases, their claim to the appellation "liberal," and that still more, if they are cut down to the strict exigencies of that end. If, for instance, Theology instead of being cultivated as a contemplation, be limited to the purposes of the pulpit or be represented by the catechism, it loses — not its usefulness, not its divine character, not its meritoriousness, (rather it gains a claim upon these titles by such charitable condescension), — but it does lose the particular attribute which I am illustrating; just as a face worn by tears and fasting loses its beauty, or a labourer's hand loses its delicateness; — for Theology thus exercised is not simple knowledge, but rather is an art or a business making use of Theology. And thus it appears that even what is supernatural need not be liberal, nor need a hero be a gentleman, for the plain reason that one idea is not another idea. And in like manner the Baconian Philosophy, by using its physical sciences in the service of man, does thereby transfer them from the order of Liberal Pursuits to, I do not say the inferior, but the distinct class of the Useful. And, to take a different instance, hence again, as is evident, whenever personal gain is the motive, still more distinctive an effect has it upon the character of a given pursuit; thus racing, which was a liberal exercise in Greece, forfeits its rank in times like these, so far as it is made the occasion of gambling.

All that I have been now saying is summed up in a few characteristic words of the great Philosopher.[5] "Of possessions," he says, "those rather are useful, which bear fruit; those *liberal, which tend to enjoyment.* By fruitful, I mean, which yield revenue; by enjoyable, where *nothing accrues of consequence beyond the using.*"

5

Do not suppose, that in thus appealing to the ancients, I am throwing back the world two thousand years, and fettering Philosophy with the reasonings of paganism. While the world lasts, will Aristotle's doctrine on these matters last, for he is the oracle of nature and of truth. While we are men, we cannot help, to a great extent, being Aristotelians, for the great Master does but analyze the thoughts, feelings, views, and opinions of human kind. He has told us the meaning of our own words and ideas, before we were born. In many subject-matters, to think correctly, is to think like Aristotle; and we are his

5 Aristotle.

disciples whether we will or no, though we may not know it. Now, as to the particular instance before us, the word "liberal" as applied to Knowledge and Education, expresses a specific idea, which ever has been, and ever will be, while the nature of man is the same, just as the idea of the Beautiful is specific, or of the Sublime, or of the Ridiculous, or of the Sordid. It is in the world now, it was in the world then; and, as in the case of the dogmas of faith, it is illustrated by a continuous historical tradition, and never was out of the world, from the time it came into it. There have indeed been differences of opinion from time to time, as to what pursuits and what arts came under that idea, but such differences are but an additional evidence of its reality. That idea must have a substance in it, which has maintained its ground amid these conflicts and changes, which has ever served as a standard to measure things withal, which has passed from mind to mind unchanged, when there was so much to colour, so much to influence any notion or thought whatever, which was not founded in our very nature. Were it a mere generalization, it would have varied with the subjects from which it was generalized: but though its subjects vary with the age, it varies not itself. The palæstra may seem a liberal exercise to Lycurgus, an illiberal to Seneca; coach-driving and prize-fighting may be recognized in Elis, and be condemned in England; music may be despicable in the eyes of certain moderns, and be in the highest place with Aristotle and Plato, — (and the case is the same in the particular application of the idea of Beauty, or of Goodness, or of Moral Virtue, there is a difference of tastes, a difference of judgments) — still these variations imply, instead of discrediting, the archetypal idea, which is but a previous hypothesis or condition, by means of which issue is joined between contending opinions and without which there would be nothing to dispute about.

I consider, then, that I am chargeable with no paradox, when I speak of a Knowledge which is its own end, when I call it liberal knowledge, or a gentleman's knowledge, when I educate for it, and make it the scope of a University. And still less am I incurring such a charge, when I make this acquisition consist, not in Knowledge in a vague and ordinary sense, but in that Knowledge which I have especially called Philosophy, or, in an extended sense of the word, Science; for whatever claims Knowledge has to be considered as a good, these it has in a higher degree when it is viewed not vaguely, not popularly, but precisely and transcendently as Philosophy. Knowledge, I say, is then especially liberal, or sufficient for itself, apart from every external and ulterior object, when and so far as it is philosophical, and this I proceed to show.

6

Now bear with me, Gentlemen, if what I am about to say, has at first sight a fanciful appearance. Philosophy, then, or Science, is related to Knowledge in this way: — Knowledge is called by the name of

Science or Philosophy, when it is acted upon, informed, or if I may use a strong figure, impregnated by Reason. Reason is the principle of that intrinsic fecundity of Knowledge, which, to those who possess it, is its especial value, and which dispenses with the necessity of their looking abroad for any end to rest upon external to itself. Knowledge, indeed, when thus exalted into a scientific form, is also power; not only is it excellent in itself, but whatever such excellence may be, it is something more, it has a result beyond itself. Doubtless; but that is a further consideration, with which I am not concerned. I only say that, prior to its being a power, it is a good; that it is, not only an instrument, but an end. I know well it may resolve itself into an art, and terminate in a mechanical process, and in tangible fruit; but it also may fall back upon that Reason which informs it, and resolve itself into Philosophy. In one case it is called Useful Knowledge; in the other Liberal. The same person may cultivate it in both ways at once; but this again is a matter foreign to my subject; here I do but say that there are two ways of using Knowledge, and in matter of fact those who use it in one way are not likely to use it in the other, or at least in a very limited measure. You see, then, here are two methods of Education; the end of the one is to be philosophical, of the other to be mechanical; the one rises towards general ideas, the other is exhausted upon what is particular and external. Let me not be thought to deny the necessity, or to decry the benefit, of such attention to what is particular and practical, as belongs to the useful or mechanical arts; life could not go on without them; we owe our daily welfare to them; their exercise is the duty of the many, and we owe to the many a debt of gratitude for fulfilling that duty. I only say that Knowledge, in proportion as it tends more and more to be particular, ceases to be Knowledge. It is a question whether Knowledge can in any proper sense be predicated of the brute creation; without pretending to metaphysical exactness of phraseology, which would be unsuitable to an occasion like this, I say, it seems to me improper to call that passive sensation, or perception of things, which brutes seem to possess, by the name of Knowledge. When I speak of Knowledge, I mean something intellectual, something which grasps what it perceives through the senses; something which takes a view of things; which sees more than the senses convey; which reasons upon what it sees, and while it sees; which invests it with an idea. It expresses itself, not in a mere enunciation, but by an enthymeme: it is of the nature of science from the first, and in this consists its dignity. The principle of real dignity in Knowledge, its worth, its desirableness, considered irrespectively of its results, is this germ within it of a scientific or a philosophical process. This is how it comes to be an end in itself; this is why it admits of being called Liberal. Not to know the relative disposition of things is the state of slaves or children; to have mapped out the Universe is the boast, or at least the ambition, of Philosophy.

Moreover, such knowledge is not a mere extrinsic or accidental advantage, which is ours to-day and another's to-morrow, which may be got up from a book, and easily forgotten again, which we can command or communicate at our pleasure, which we can borrow for the occasion, carry about in our hand, and take into the market; it is an acquired illumination, it is a habit, a personal possession, and an inward endowment. And this is the reason, why it is more correct, as well as more usual, to speak of a University as a place of education, than of instruction, though, when knowledge is concerned, instruction would at first sight have seemed the more appropriate word. We are instructed, for instance, in manual exercises, in the fine and useful arts, in trades, and in ways of business; for these are methods, which have little or no effect upon the mind itself, are contained in rules committed to memory, to tradition, or to use, and bear upon an end external to themselves. But education is a higher word; it implies an action upon our mental nature, and the formation of a character; it is something individual and permanent, and is commonly spoken of in connexion with religion and virtue. When, then, we speak of the communication of Knowledge as being Education, we thereby really imply that that Knowledge is a state or condition of mind; and since cultivation of mind is surely worth seeking for its own sake, we are thus brought once more to the conclusion, which the word "Liberal" and the word "Philosophy" have already suggested, that there is a Knowledge which is desirable, though nothing come of it, as being of itself a treasure, and a sufficient remuneration of years of labour.

7

This, then, is the answer which I am prepared to give to the question with which I opened this Discourse. Before going on to speak of the object of the Church in taking up Philosophy, and the uses to which she puts it, I am prepared to maintain that Philosophy is its own end, and, as I conceive, I have now begun the proof of it. I am prepared to maintain that there is a knowledge worth possessing for what it is, and not merely for what it does; and what minutes remain to me today I shall devote to the removal of some portion of the indistinctness and confusion with which the subject may in some minds be surrounded.

It may be objected then, that, when we profess to seek Knowledge for some end or other beyond itself, whatever it be, we speak intelligibly; but that, whatever men may have said, however obstinately the idea may have kept its ground from age to age, still it is simply unmeaning to say that we seek Knowledge for its own sake, and for nothing else; for that it ever leads to something beyond itself, which therefore is its end, and the cause why it is desirable; — moreover, that this end is two-fold, either of this world or of the next; that all knowledge is cultivated either for secular objects or for eternal; that if it is directed to secular objects, it is called Useful Knowledge, if to eternal, Religious or Christian Knowledge; — in consequence, that if, as I have allowed, this Liberal Knowledge does not benefit the body or estate, it ought to benefit the soul; but if the fact be really so, that it is neither a physical or a secular good on the one hand, nor a moral good on the other, it cannot be a good at all, and is not worth the trouble which is necessary for its acquisition.

And then I may be reminded that the professors of this Liberal or Philosophical Knowledge have themselves, in every age, recognized this exposition of the matter, and have submitted to the issue in which it terminates; for they have ever been attempting to make men virtuous; or, if not, at least have assumed that refinement of mind was virtue, and that they themselves were the virtuous portion of mankind. This they have professed on the one hand; and on the other, they have utterly failed in their professions, so as ever to make themselves a proverb among men, and a laughing-stock both to the grave and the dissipated portion of mankind, in consequence of them. Thus they have furnished against themselves both the ground and the means of their own exposure, without any trouble at all to anyone else. In a word, from the time that Athens was the University of the world, what has Philosophy taught men, but to promise without practising, and to aspire without attaining. What has the deep and lofty thought of its disciples ended in but eloquent words? Nay, what has its teaching ever meditated, when it was boldest in its remedies for human ill, beyond charming us to sleep by its lessons, that we might feel nothing at all? like some melodious air, or rather like those strong and transporting perfumes, which at first spread their sweetness over everything they touch, but in a little while do but offend in proportion as they once pleased us. Did Philosophy support Cicero under the disfavour of the fickle populace, or nerve Seneca to oppose an imperial tyrant? It abandoned Brutus, as he sorrowfully confessed, in his greatest need, and it forced Cato, as his panegyrist strangely boasts, into the false position of defying heaven. How few can be counted among its professors, who, like Polemon,[6] were thereby converted from a profligate course, or like Anaxagoras, thought the world well lost in exchange for its possession? The philosopher in *Rasselas* [7] taught a superhuman doctrine, and then succumbed without an effort to a trial of human affection.

"He had discoursed," we are told, "with great energy on the government of the passions. His look was venerable, his action graceful, his pronunciation clear, and his diction elegant. He showed, with great strength of sentiment and variety of illustration, that human nature is degraded and debased, when the lower faculties predominate over the higher. He communicated the various precepts given, from time to time, for the conquest of passion, and displayed the happiness

---

6 Platonic philosopher of the 3rd and 4th centuries B.C.
7 A didactic romance by Samuel Johnson.

of those who had obtained the important victory, after which man is no longer the slave of fear, nor the fool of hope. . . . He enumerated many examples of heroes immovable by pain or pleasure, who looked with indifference on those modes or accidents to which the vulgar give the names of good and evil."

Rasselas in a few days found the philosopher in a room half darkened, with his eyes misty, and his face pale. "Sir," said he, "you have come at a time when all human friendship is useless; what I suffer cannot be remedied, what I have lost cannot be supplied. My daughter, my only daughter, from whose tenderness I expected all the comforts of my age, died last night of a fever." "Sir," said the prince, "mortality is an event by which a wise man can never be surprised; we know that death is always near, and it should therefore always be expected." "Young man," answered the philosopher, "you speak like one who has never felt the pangs of separation." "Have you, then, forgot the precept," said Rasselas, "which you so powerfully enforced? . . . consider that external things are naturally variable, but truth and reason are always the same." "What comfort," said the mourner, "can truth and reason afford me? Of what effect are they now, but to tell me that my daughter will not be restored?"

8

Better, far better, to make no professions, you will say, than to cheat others with what we are not, and to scandalize them with what we are. The sensualist, or the man of the world, at any rate, is not the victim of fine words, but pursues a reality and gains it. The Philosophy of Utility, you will say, Gentlemen, has at least done its work; and I grant it, — it aimed low, but it has fulfilled its aim. If that man of great intellect who has been its Prophet in the conduct of life played false to his own professions,[8] he was not bound by his philosophy to be true to his friend or faithful in his trust. Moral virtue was not the line in which he undertook to instruct men; and though, as the poet calls him, he were the "meanest" of mankind, he was so in what may be called his private capacity and without any prejudice to the theory of induction. He had a right to be so, if he chose, for anything that the Idols of the den or the theatre had to say to the contrary. His mission was the increase of physical enjoyment and social comfort;[9] and most wonderfully, most awfully has he fulfilled his conception and his design. Almost day by day have we fresh and fresh shoots, and buds, and blossoms, which are to ripen into fruit, on that magical tree of Knowledge which he planted, and to which none of us perhaps, except the very poor, but owes, if not his present life,

    8 Francis Bacon, who confessed to corruption as Lord Chancellor; Pope called him "The wisest, brightest, meanest of mankind."
    9 It will be seen that on the whole I agree with Lord Macaulay in his Essay on Bacon's Philosophy. I do not know whether he would agree with me. [Newman's note.]

at least his daily food, his health, and general well-being. He was the divinely provided minister of temporal benefits to all of us so great, that, whatever I am forced to think of him as a man, I have not the heart, from mere gratitude, to speak of him severely. And, in spite of the tendencies of his philosophy, which are, as we see at this day, to depreciate, or to trample on Theology, he has himself, in his writings, gone out of his way, as if with a prophetic misgiving of those tendencies, to insist on it as the instrument of that beneficent Father, who, when He came on earth in visible form, took on Him first and most prominently the office of assuaging the bodily wounds of human nature. And truly, like the old mediciner in the tale, "he sat diligently at his work, and hummed, with cheerful countenance, a pious song"; and then in turn "went out singing into the meadows so gaily, that those who had seen him from afar might well have thought it was a youth gathering flowers for his beloved, instead of an old physician gathering healing herbs in the morning dew."

Alas, that men, in the action of life or in their heart of hearts, are not what they seem to be in their moments of excitement, or in their trances or intoxications of genius, — so good, so noble, so serene! Alas, that Bacon too in his own way should after all be but the fellow of those heathen philosophers who in their disadvantages had some excuse for their inconsistency, and who surprise us rather in what they did say than in what they did not do! Alas, that he too, like Socrates or Seneca, must be stripped of his holy-day coat, which looks so fair, and should be but a mockery amid his most majestic gravity of phrase; and, for all his vast abilities, should, in the littleness of his own moral being, but typify the intellectual narrowness of his school! However, granting all this, heroism after all was not his philosophy: — I cannot deny he has abundantly achieved what he proposed. His is simply a Method whereby bodily discomforts and temporal wants are to be most effectually removed from the greatest number; and already, before it has shown any signs of exhaustion, the gifts of nature, in their most artificial shapes and luxurious profusion and diversity, from all quarters of the earth, are, it is undeniable, by its means brought even to our doors, and we rejoice in them.

9

Useful Knowledge, then, I grant, has done its work; and Liberal Knowledge as certainly has not done its work, — that is, supposing, as the objectors assume, its direct end, like Religious Knowledge, is to make men better; but this, I will not for an instant allow, and, unless I allow it, those objectors have said nothing to the purpose. I admit, rather I maintain, what they have been urging, for I consider Knowledge to have its end in itself. For all its friends, or its enemies, may say, I insist upon it, that it is as real a mistake to burden it with virtue or religion as with the mechanical arts. Its direct business is not to steel the soul against temptation or to console it in affliction, any more than to set the loom in motion, or to direct the steam carriage; be it ever so much the means or the condition of both material and moral advancement, still, taken by and in itself, it as little mends our hearts as it improves our temporal circumstances. And if its eulogists claim for it such a power, they commit the very same kind of encroachment on a province not their own as the political economist who should maintain that his science educated him for casuistry or diplomacy. Knowledge is one thing, virtue is another; good sense is not conscience, refinement is not humility, nor is largeness and justness of view faith. Philosophy, however enlightened, however profound, gives no command over the passions, no influential motives, no vivifying principles. Liberal Education makes not the Christian, not the Catholic, but the gentleman. It is well to be a gentleman, it is well to have a cultivated intellect, a delicate taste, a candid, equitable, dispassionate mind, a noble and courteous bearing in the conduct of life; — these are the connatural qualities of a large knowledge; they are the objects of a University; I am advocating, I shall illustrate and insist upon them; but still, I repeat, they are no guarantee for sanctity or even for conscientiousness, they may attach to the man of the world, to the profligate, to the heartless, — pleasant, alas, and attractive as he shows when decked out in them. Taken by themselves, they do but seem to be what they are not; they look like virtue at a distance, but they are detected by close observers, and on the long run; and hence it is that they are popularly accused of pretence and hypocrisy, not, I repeat, from their own fault, but because their professors and their admirers persist in taking them for what they are not, and are officious in arrogating for them a praise to which they have no claim. Quarry the granite rock with razors, or moor the vessel with a thread of silk; then may you hope with such keen and delicate instruments as human knowledge and human reason to contend against those giants, the passion and the pride of man.

Surely we are not driven to theories of this kind, in order to vindicate the value and dignity of Liberal Knowledge. Surely the real grounds on which its pretensions rest are not so very subtle or abstruse, so very strange or improbable. Surely it is very intelligible to say, and that is what I say here, that Liberal Education, viewed in itself, is simply the cultivation of the intellect, as such, and its object is nothing more or less than intellectual excellence. Everything has its own perfection, be it higher or lower in the scale of things; and the perfection of one is not the perfection of another. Things animate, inanimate, visible, invisible, all are good in their kind, and have a *best* of themselves, which is an object of pursuit. Why do you take such pains with your garden or your park? You see to your walks and turf and shrubberies; to your trees and drives; not as if you meant to make an orchard of the one, or corn or pasture land of the other, but because there is a special beauty in all that is goodly in wood, water, plain, and slope, brought all together by art into one shape, and grouped into one whole. Your cities are beautiful, your palaces, your public buildings, your territorial mansions, your churches; and their beauty leads to nothing beyond itself. There is a physical beauty and a moral: there is a beauty of person, there is a beauty of our moral being, which is natural virtue; and in like manner there is a beauty, there is a perfection, of the intellect. There is an ideal perfection in these various subject-matters, towards which individual instances are seen to rise, and which are the standards for all instances whatever. The Greek divinities and demigods, as the statuary has moulded them, with their symmetry of figure and their high forehead and their regular features, are the perfection of physical beauty. The heroes, of whom history tells, Alexander, or Cæsar, or Scipio, or Saladin, are the representatives of that magnanimity or self-mastery which is the greatness of human nature. Christianity too has its heroes, and in the supernatural order, and we call them Saints. The artist puts before him beauty of feature and form; the poet, beauty of mind; the preacher, the beauty of grace: then intellect too, I repeat, has its beauty, and it has those who aim at it. To open the mind, to correct it, to refine it, to enable it to know, and to digest, master, rule, and use its knowledge, to give it power over its own faculties, application, flexibility, method, critical exactness, sagacity, resource, address, eloquent expression, is an object as intelligible (for here we are inquiring, not what the object of a Liberal Education is worth, nor what use the Church makes of it, but what it is in itself), I say, an object as intelligible as the cultivation of virtue, while, at the same time, it is absolutely distinct from it.

10

This indeed is but a temporal object, and a transitory possession; but so are other things in themselves which we make much of and pursue. The moralist will tell us that man, in all his functions, is but a flower which blossoms and fades, except so far as a higher principle breathes upon him, and makes him and what he is immortal. Body and mind are carried on into an eternal state of being by the gifts of Divine Munificence; but at first they do but fail in a failing world; and if the powers of intellect decay, the powers of the body have decayed before them, and, as an Hospital or an Almshouse, though its end be ephemeral, may be sanctified to the service of religion, so surely may a University, even were it nothing more than I have as yet described it. We attain to heaven by using this world well, though it is to pass away; we perfect our nature, not by undoing it, but by adding to it what is more than nature, and directing it towards aims higher than its own.

DISCOURSE VI

Knowledge Viewed in Relation to Learning

1

IT were well if the English, like the Greek language, possessed some definite word to express, simply and generally, intellectual proficiency or perfection, such as "health," as used with reference to the animal frame, and "virtue," with reference to our moral nature. I am not able to find such a term; — talent, ability, genius, belong distinctly to the raw material, which is the subject-matter, not to that excellence which is the result of exercise and training. When we turn, indeed, to the particular kinds of intellectual perfection, words are forthcoming for our purpose, as, for instance, judgment, taste, and skill; yet even these belong, for the most part, to powers or habits bearing upon practice or upon art, and not to any perfect condition of the intellect, considered in itself. Wisdom, again, is certainly a more comprehensive word than any other, but it has a direct relation to conduct and to human life. Knowledge, indeed, and Science express purely intellectual ideas, but still not a state or quality of the intellect; for knowledge, in its ordinary sense, is but one of its circumstances, denoting a possession or a habit; and science has been appropriated to the subject-matter of the intellect, instead of belonging in English, as it ought to do, to the intellect itself. The consequence is that, on an occasion like this, many words are necessary, in order, first, to bring out and convey what surely is no difficult idea in itself, — that of the cultivation of the intellect as an end; next, in order to recommend what surely is no unreasonable object; and lastly, to describe and make the mind realize the particular perfection in which that object consists. Every one knows practically what are the constituents of health or of virtue; and every one recognizes health and virtue as ends to be pursued; it is otherwise with intellectual excellence, and this must be my excuse, if I seem to any one to be bestowing a good deal of labour on a preliminary matter.

In default of a recognized term, I have called the perfection or virtue of the intellect by the name of philosophy, philosophical knowledge, enlargement of mind, or illumination; terms which are not uncommonly given to it by writers of this day; but, whatever name we bestow on it, it is, I believe, as a matter of history, the business of a University to make this intellectual culture its direct scope, or to employ itself in the education of the intellect, — just as the work of a Hospital lies in healing the sick or wounded, of a Riding or Fencing School, or of a Gymnasium, in exercising the limbs, of an Almshouse, in aiding and solacing the old, of an Orphanage, in protecting innocence, of a Penitentiary, in restoring the guilty. I say, a University, taken in its bare idea, and before we view it as an instrument of the Church, has this object and this mission; it contemplates neither moral impression nor mechanical production; it professes to exercise the mind neither in art nor in duty; its function is intellectual culture; here it may leave its scholars, and it has done its work when it has done as much as this. It educates the intellect to reason well in all matters, to reach out towards truth, and to grasp it.

2

This, I said in my foregoing Discourse, was the object of a University, viewed in itself, and apart from the Catholic Church, or from the State, or from any other power which may use it; and I illustrated this in various ways. I said that the intellect must have an excellence of its own, for there was nothing which had not its specific good; that the word "educate" would not be used of intellectual culture, as it is used, had not the intellect had an end of its own; that, had it not such an end, there would be no meaning in calling certain intellectual exercises "liberal," in contrast with "useful," as is commonly done; that the very notion of a philosophical temper implied it, for it threw us back upon research and system as ends in themselves, distinct from effects and works of any kind; that a philosophical scheme of knowledge, or system of sciences, could not, from the nature of the case, issue in any one definite art or pursuit, as its end; and that, on the other hand, the discovery and contemplation of truth, to which research and systematizing led, were surely sufficient ends, though nothing beyond them were added, and that they had ever been accounted sufficient by mankind.

Here then I take up the subject; and, having determined that the cultivation of the intellect is an end distinct and sufficient in itself, and that, so far as words go it is an enlargement or illumination, I proceed to inquire what this mental breadth, or power, or light, or philosophy consists in. A Hospital heals a broken limb or cures a fever: what does an Institution effect, which professes the health, not of the body, not of the soul, but of the intellect? What is this good, which in former times, as well as our own, has been found worth the notice, the appropriation, of the Catholic Church?

I have then to investigate, in the Discourses which follow, those qualities and characteristics of the intellect in which its cultivation issues or rather consists; and, with a view of assisting myself in this undertaking, I shall recur to certain questions which have already been touched upon. These questions are three: viz. the relation of intellectual culture, first, to *mere* knowledge; secondly, to *professional* knowledge; and thirdly, to *religious* knowledge. In other words, are *acquirements* and *attainments* the scope of a University Education? or *expertness in particular arts and pursuits?* or *moral and religious proficiency?* or something besides these three? These questions I shall

examine in succession, with the purpose I have mentioned; and I hope
to be excused, if, in this anxious undertaking, I am led to repeat what,
either in these Discourses or elsewhere, I have already put upon
paper. And first, of *Mere Knowledge,* or Learning, and its connexion
with intellectual illumination or Philosophy.

3

I suppose the *primâ-facie* view which the public at large would
take of a University, considering it as a place of Education, is nothing
more or less than a place for acquiring a great deal of knowledge
on a great many subjects. Memory is one of the first developed of the
mental faculties; a boy's business when he goes to school is to learn,
that is, to store up things in his memory. For some years his intellect
is little more than an instrument for taking in facts, or a receptacle
for storing them; he welcomes them as fast as they come to him; he
lives on what is without; he has his eyes ever about him; he has a
lively susceptibility of impressions; he imbibes information of every
kind; and little does he make his own in a true sense of the word,
living rather upon his neighbours all around him. He has opinions,
religious, political, and literary, and, for a boy, is very positive in
them and sure about them; but he gets them from his schoolfellows, or
his masters, or his parents, as the case may be. Such as he is in his
other relations, such also is he in his school exercises; his mind is observant, sharp, ready, retentive; he is almost passive in the acquisition
of knowledge. I say this in no disparagement of the idea of a clever
boy. Geography, chronology, history, language, natural history, he
heaps up the matter of these studies as treasures for a future day. It
is the seven years of plenty with him: he gathers in by handfuls, like
the Egyptians, without counting; and though, as time goes on, there
is exercise for his argumentative powers in the Elements of Mathematics, and for his taste in the Poets and Orators, still, while at school,
or at least, till quite the last years of his time, he acquires, and little
more; and when he is leaving for the University, he is mainly the creature of foreign influences and circumstances, and made up of accidents,
homogeneous or not, as the case may be. Moreover, the moral habits,
which are a boy's praise, encourage and assist this result; that is, diligence, assiduity, regularity, despatch, persevering application; for
these are the direct conditions of acquisition, and naturally lead to
it. Acquirements, again, are emphatically producible, and at a moment; they are a something to show, both for master and scholar; an
audience, even though ignorant themselves of the subjects of an examination, can comprehend when questions are answered and when
they are not. Here again is a reason why mental culture is in the
minds of men identified with the acquisition of knowledge.

The same notion possesses the public mind, when it passes on from
the thought of a school to that of a University: and with the best of

reasons so far as this, that there is no true culture without acquirements, and that philosophy presupposes knowledge. It requires a great deal of reading, or a wide range of information, to warrant us in putting forth our opinions on any serious subject; and without such learning the most original mind may be able indeed to dazzle, to amuse, to refute, to perplex, but not to come to any useful result or any trustworthy conclusion. There are indeed persons who profess a different view of the matter, and even act upon it. Every now and then you will find a person of vigorous or fertile mind, who relies upon his own resources, despises all former authors, and gives the world, with the utmost fearlessness, his views upon religion, or history, or any other popular subject. And his works may sell for a while; he may get a name in his day; but this will be all. His readers are sure to find in the long run that his doctrines are mere theories, and not the expression of facts, that they are chaff instead of bread, and then his popularity drops as suddenly as it rose.

Knowledge, then, is the indispensable condition of expansion of mind, and the instrument of attaining to it; this cannot be denied, it is ever to be insisted on; I begin with it as a first principle; however, the very truth of it carries men too far, and confirms to them the notion that it is the whole of the matter. A narrow mind is thought to be that which contains little knowledge; and an enlarged mind, that which holds a great deal; and what seems to put the matter beyond dispute is, the fact of the great number of studies which are pursued in a University, by its very profession. Lectures are given on every kind of subject; examinations are held; prizes awarded. There are moral, metaphysical, physical Professors; Professors of languages, of history, of mathematics, of experimental science. Lists of questions are published, wonderful for their range and depth, variety and difficulty; treatises are written, which carry upon their very face the evidence of extensive reading or multifarious information; what then is wanting for mental culture to a person of large reading and scientific attainments? what is grasp of mind but acquirement? where shall philosophical repose be found, but in the consciousness and enjoyment of large intellectual possessions?

And yet this notion is, I conceive, a mistake, and my present business is to show that it is one, and that the end of a Liberal Education is not mere knowledge, or knowledge considered in its *matter;* and I shall best attain my object, by actually setting down some cases, which will be generally granted to be instances of the process of enlightenment or enlargement of mind, and others which are not, and thus, by the comparison, you will be able to judge for yourselves, Gentlemen, whether Knowledge, that is, acquirement, is after all the real principle of the enlargement, or whether that principle is not rather something beyond it.

4

For instance, let a person, whose experience has hitherto been confined to the more calm and unpretending scenery of these islands, whether here or in England, go for the first time into parts where physical nature puts on her wilder and more awful forms, whether at home or abroad, as into mountainous districts; or let one, who has ever lived in a quiet village, go for the first time to a great metropolis, — then I suppose he will have a sensation which perhaps he never had before. He has a feeling not in addition or increase of former feelings, but of something different in its nature. He will perhaps be borne forward, and find for a time that he has lost his bearings. He has made a certain progress, and he has a consciousness of mental enlargement; he does not stand where he did, he has a new centre, and a range of thoughts to which he was before a stranger.

Again, the view of the heavens which the telescope opens upon us, if allowed to fill and possess the mind, may almost whirl it round and make it dizzy. It brings in a flood of ideas, and is rightly called an intellectual enlargement, whatever is meant by the term.

And so again, the sight of beasts of prey and other foreign animals, their strangeness, the originality (if I may use the term) of their forms and gestures and habits and their variety and independence of each other, throw us out of ourselves into another creation, and as if under another Creator, if I may so express the temptation which may come on the mind. We seem to have new faculties, or a new exercise for our faculties, by this addition to our knowledge; like a prisoner, who, having been accustomed to wear manacles or fetters, suddenly finds his arms and legs free.

Hence Physical Science generally, in all its departments, as bringing before us the exuberant riches and resources, yet the orderly course, of the Universe, elevates and excites the student, and at first, I may say, almost takes away his breath, while in time it exercises a tranquilizing influence upon him.

Again, the study of history is said to enlarge and enlighten the mind, and why? because, as I conceive, it gives it a power of judging of passing events, and of all events, and a conscious superiority over them, which before it did not possess.

And in like manner, what is called seeing the world, entering into active life, going into society, travelling, gaining acquaintance with the various classes of the community, coming into contact with the principles and modes of thought of various parties, interests, and races, their views, aims, habits and manners, their religious creeds and forms of worship, — gaining experience how various yet how alike men are, how low-minded, how bad, how opposed, yet how confident in their opinions; all this exerts a perceptible influence upon the mind, which it is impossible to mistake, be it good or be it bad, and is popularly called its enlargement.

And then again, the first time the mind comes across the arguments and speculations of unbelievers, and feels what a novel light they cast upon what he has hitherto accounted sacred; and still more, if it gives in to them and embraces them, and throws off as so much prejudice what it has hitherto held, and, as if waking from a dream, begins to realize to its imagination that there is now no such thing as law and the transgression of law, that sin is a phantom, and punishment a bugbear, that it is free to sin, free to enjoy the world and the flesh; and still further, when it does enjoy them, and reflects that it may think and hold just what it will, that "the world is all before it where to choose," and what system to build up as its own private persuasion; when this torrent of wilful thoughts rushes over and inundates it, who will deny that the fruit of the tree of knowledge, or what the mind takes for knowledge, has made it one of the gods, with a sense of expansion and elevation, — an intoxication in reality, still, so far as the subjective state of the mind goes, an illumination? Hence the fanaticism of individuals or nations, who suddenly cast off their Maker. Their eyes are opened; and, like the judgment-stricken king in the Tragedy, they see two suns, and a magic universe, out of which they look back upon their former state of faith and innocence with a sort of contempt and indignation, as if they were then but fools, and the dupes of imposture.

On the other hand, Religion has its own enlargement, and an enlargement, not of tumult, but of peace. It is often remarked of uneducated persons, who have hitherto thought little of the unseen world, that, on their turning to God, looking into themselves, regulating their hearts, reforming their conduct, and meditating on death and judgment, heaven and hell, they seem to become, in point of intellect, different beings from what they were. Before, they took things as they came, and thought no more of one thing than another. But now every event has a meaning; they have their own estimate of whatever happens to them; they are mindful of times and seasons, and compare the present with the past; and the world, no longer dull, monotonous, unprofitable, and hopeless, is a various and complicated drama, with parts and an object, and an awful moral.

5

Now from these instances, to which many more might be added, it is plain, first, that the communication of knowledge certainly is either a condition or the means of that sense of enlargement or enlightenment, of which at this day we hear so much in certain quarters: this cannot be denied; but next, it is equally plain, that such communication is not the whole of the process. The enlargement consists, not merely in the passive reception into the mind of a number of ideas

hitherto unknown to it, but in the mind's energetic and simultaneous
action upon and towards and among those new ideas, which are rushing in upon it. It is the action of a formative power, reducing to
order and meaning the matter of our acquirements; it is a making
the objects of our knowledge subjectively our own, or, to use a
familiar word, it is a digestion of what we receive, into the substance of our previous state of thought; and without this no enlargement is said to follow. There is no enlargement, unless there be a
comparison of ideas one with another, as they come before the mind,
and a systematizing of them. We feel our minds to be growing and
expanding *then*, when we not only learn, but refer what we learn to
what we know already. It is not the mere addition to our knowledge
that is the illumination; but the locomotion, the movement onwards,
of that mental centre, to which both what we know, and what we
are learning, the accumulating mass of our acquirements, gravitates.
And therefore a truly great intellect, and recognized to be such by the
common opinion of mankind, such as the intellect of Aristotle, or of
St. Thomas, or of Newton, or of Goethe, (I purposely take instances
within and without the Catholic pale, when I would speak of the intellect as such,) is one which takes a connected view of old and new,
past and present, far and near, and which has an insight into the
influence of all these one on another; without which there is no whole,
and no centre. It possesses the knowledge, not only of things, but
also of their mutual and true relations; knowledge, not merely considered as acquirement, but as philosophy.

Accordingly, when this analytical, distributive, harmonizing process is away, the mind experiences no enlargement, and is not reckoned
as enlightened or comprehensive, whatever it may add to its knowledge. For instance, a great memory, as I have already said, does not
make a philosopher, any more than a dictionary can be called a grammar. There are men who embrace in their minds a vast multitude
of ideas, but with little sensibility about their real relations towards
each other. These may be antiquarians, annalists, naturalists; they
may be learned in the law; they may be versed in statistics; they are
most useful in their own place; I should shrink from speaking dis-
respectfully of them; still, there is nothing in such attainments to
guarantee the absence of narrowness of mind. If they are nothing
more than well-read men, or men of information, they have not
what specially deserves the name of culture of mind, or fulfils the
type of Liberal Education.

In like manner, we sometimes fall in with persons who have seen
much of the world, and of the men who, in their day, have played
a conspicuous part in it, but who generalize nothing, and have no observation, in the true sense of the word. They abound in information
in detail, curious and entertaining, about men and things; and, having lived under the influence of no very clear or settled principles,

religious or political, they speak of every one and every thing, only as so many phenomena, which are complete in themselves, and lead to nothing, not discussing them, or teaching any truth, or instructing the hearer, but simply talking. No one would say that these persons, well informed as they are, had attained to any great culture of intellect or to philosophy.

The case is the same still more strikingly where the persons in question are beyond dispute men of inferior powers and deficient education. Perhaps they have been much in foreign countries, and they receive, in a passive, otiose, unfruitful way, the various facts which are forced upon them there. Seafaring men, for example, range from one end of the earth to the other; but the multiplicity of external objects, which they have encountered, forms no symmetrical and consistent picture upon their imagination; they see the tapestry of human life, as it were on the wrong side, and it tells no story. They sleep, and they rise up, and they find themselves, now in Europe, now in Asia; they see visions of great cities and wild regions; they are in the marts of commerce, or amid the islands of the South; they gaze on Pompey's Pillar,[1] or on the Andes; and nothing which meets them carries them forward or backward, to any idea beyond itself. Nothing has a drift or relation; nothing has a history or a promise. Every thing stands by itself, and comes and goes in its turn, like the shifting scenes of a show, which leave the spectator where he was. Perhaps you are near such a man on a particular occasion, and expect him to be shocked or perplexed at something which occurs; but one thing is much the same to him as another, or, if he is perplexed, it is as not knowing what to say, whether it is right to admire, or to ridicule, or to disapprove, while conscious that some expression of opinion is expected from him; for in fact he has no standard of judgment at all, and no landmarks to guide him to a conclusion. Such is mere acquisition, and, I repeat, no one would dream of calling it philosophy.

6

Instances, such as these, confirm, by the contrast, the conclusion I have already drawn from those which preceded them. That only is true enlargement of mind which is the power of viewing many things at once as one whole, of referring them severally to their true place in the universal system, of understanding their respective values, and determining their mutual dependence. Thus is that form of Universal Knowledge, of which I have on a former occasion spoken, set up in the individual intellect, and constitutes its perfection. Possessed of this real illumination, the mind never views any part of the extended subject-matter of Knowledge without recollecting that it is but a part, or without the associations which spring from this recol-

[1] At Alexandria, erected in honor of Diocletian.

lection. It makes every thing in some sort lead to every thing else; it would communicate the image of the whole to every separate portion, till that whole becomes in imagination like a spirit, every where pervading and penetrating its component parts, and giving them one definite meaning. Just as our bodily organs, when mentioned, recall their function in the body, as the word "creation" suggests the Creator, and "subjects" a sovereign, so, in the mind of the Philosopher, as we are abstractedly conceiving of him, the elements of the physical and moral world, sciences, arts, pursuits, ranks, offices, events, opinions, individualities, are all viewed as one, with correlative functions and as gradually by successive combinations converging, one and all, to the true centre.

To have even a portion of this illuminative reason and true philosophy is the highest state to which nature can aspire, in the way of intellect; it puts the mind above the influences of chance and necessity, above anxiety, suspense, unsettlement, and superstition, which is the lot of the many. Men, whose minds are possessed with some one object, take exaggerated views of its importance, are feverish in the pursuit of it, make it the measure of things which are utterly foreign to it, and are startled and despond if it happens to fail them. They are ever in alarm or in transport. Those, on the other hand, who have no object or principle whatever to hold by, lose their way, every step they take. They are thrown out, and do not know what to think or say, at every fresh juncture; they have no view of persons, or occurrences, or facts, which come suddenly upon them, and they hang upon the opinion of others, for want of internal resources. But the intellect, which has been disciplined to the perfection of its powers, which knows, and thinks while it knows, which has learned to leaven the dense mass of facts and events with the elastic force of reason, such an intellect cannot be partial, cannot be exclusive, cannot be impetuous, cannot be at a loss, cannot but be patient, collected, and majestically calm, because it discerns the end in every beginning, the origin in every end, the law in every interruption, the limit in each delay; because it ever knows where it stands, and how its path lies from one point to another. It is the τετράγωνος[2] of the Peripatetic, and has the "nil admirari"[3] of the Stoic, —

> Felix qui potuit rerum cognoscere causas,
> Atque metus omnes, et inexorabile fatum
> Subjecit pedibus, strepitumque Acherontis avari.[4]

There are men who, when in difficulties, originate at the moment vast ideas or dazzling projects; who, under the influence of excitement,

2 Square.
3 "to wonder, or be astonished, at nothing."
4 "Happy the man who could understand the causes of things and trample underfoot all fears and inexorable doom and the din of hungry Acheron."

are able to cast a light, almost as if from inspiration, on a subject or course of action which comes before them; who have a sudden presence of mind equal to any emergency, rising with the occasion, and an undaunted magnanimous bearing, and an energy and keenness which is but made intense by opposition. This is genius, this is heroism; it is the exhibition of a natural gift, which no culture can teach, at which no Institution can aim; here, on the contrary, we are concerned, not with mere nature, but with training and teaching. That perfection of the Intellect, which is the result of Education, and its *beau idéal*, to be imparted to individuals in their respective measures, is the clear, calm, accurate vision and comprehension of all things, as far as the finite mind can embrace them, each in its place, and with its own characteristics upon it. It is almost prophetic from its knowledge of history; it is almost heart-searching from its knowledge of human nature; it has almost supernatural charity from its freedom from littleness and prejudice; it has almost the repose of faith, because nothing can startle it; it has almost the beauty and harmony of heavenly contemplation, so intimate is it with the eternal order of things and the music of the spheres.

7

And now, if I may take for granted that the true and adequate end of intellectual training and of a University is not Learning or Acquirement, but rather, is Thought or Reason exercised upon Knowledge, or what may be called Philosophy, I shall be in a position to explain the various mistakes which at the present day beset the subject of University Education.

I say then, if we would improve the intellect, first of all, we must ascend; we cannot gain real knowledge on a level; we must generalize, we must reduce to method, we must have a grasp of principles, and group and shape our acquisitions by means of them. It matters not whether our field of operation be wide or limited; in every case, to command it, is to mount above it. Who has not felt the irritation of mind and impatience created by a deep, rich country, visited for the first time, with winding lanes, and high hedges, and green steeps, and tangled woods, and every thing smiling indeed, but in a maze? The same feeling comes upon us in a strange city, when we have no map of its streets. Hence you hear of practised travellers, when they first come into a place, mounting some high hill or church tower, by way of reconnoitring its neighbourhood. In like manner, you must be above your knowledge, not under it, or it will oppress you; and the more you have of it, the greater will be the load. The learning of a Salmasius or a Burman,[5] unless you are

---

5 Claude de Saumaise (1588–1653), French scholar and professor; and two Dutch classical scholars (Burmann): Pieter the Elder (1668–1741) and Pieter the Younger (1714–1778).

its master, will be your tyrant. "Imperat aut servit;" [6] if you can wield
it with a strong arm, it is a great weapon; otherwise,

> Vis consili expers
> Mole ruit suâ.[7]

You will be overwhelmed, like Tarpeia,[8] by the heavy wealth which
you have exacted from tributary generations.

Instances abound; there are authors who are as pointless as they
are inexhaustible in their literary resources. They measure knowledge
by bulk, as it lies in the rude block, without symmetry, without design. How many commentators are there on the Classics, how many
on Holy Scripture, from whom we rise up, wondering at the learning which has passed before us, and wondering why it passed! How
many writers are there of Ecclesiastical History, such as Mosheim
or Du Pin,[9] who, breaking up their subject into details, destroy its
life, and defraud us of the whole by their anxiety about the parts!
The Sermons, again, of the English Divines in the seventeenth century, how often are they mere repertories of miscellaneous and officious
learning! Of course Catholics also may read without thinking; and
in their case, equally as with Protestants, it holds good, that such
knowledge is unworthy of the name, knowledge which they have
not thought through, and thought out. Such readers are only possessed
by their knowledge, not possessed of it; nay, in matter of fact they
are often even carried away by it, without any volition of their own.
Recollect, the Memory can tyrannize, as well as the Imagination.
Derangement, I believe, has been considered as a loss of control
over the sequence of ideas. The mind, once set in motion, is henceforth deprived of the power of initiation, and becomes the victim
of a train of associations, one thought suggesting another, in the
way of cause and effect, as if by a mechanical process, or some
physical necessity. No one, who has had experience of men of studious
habits, but must recognize the existence of a parallel phenomenon
in the case of those who have overstimulated the Memory. In such
persons Reason acts almost as feebly and as impotently as in the madman; once fairly started on any subject whatever, they have no power
of self-control; they passively endure the succession of impulses
which are evolved out of the original exciting cause; they are passed
on from one idea to another and go steadily forward, plodding along

---

6 "It commands or it serves."

7 "Strength without wisdom falls by its own weight."

8 Daughter of Tarpeius, who exacted a promise from the Sabines that if she
opened the gates to the Roman citadel they would give her whatever they carried in their left hands. For her treachery, she was crushed by the shields of
the Sabines when they entered.

9 Johann Lorenz von Mosheim (1693–1755), German Lutheran divine and
historian; and Louis Ellies Dupin (1657–1719), French ecclesiastical historian.

one line of thought in spite of the amplest concessions of the hearer, or wandering from it in endless digression in spite of his remonstrances. Now, if, as is very certain, no one would envy the madman the glow and originality of his conceptions, why must we extol the cultivation of that intellect, which is the prey, not indeed of barren fancies but of barren facts, of random intrusions from without, though not of morbid imaginations from within? And in thus speaking, I am not denying that a strong and ready memory is in itself a real treasure; I am not disparaging a well-stored mind, though it be nothing besides, provided it be sober, any more than I would despise a bookseller's shop: — it is of great value to others, even when not so to the owner. Nor am I banishing, far from it, the possessors of deep and multifarious learning from my ideal University; they adorn it in the eyes of men; I do but say that they constitute no type of the results at which it aims; that it is no great gain to the intellect to have enlarged the memory at the expense of faculties which are indisputably higher.

8

Nor, indeed, am I supposing that there is any great danger, at least in this day, of over-education; the danger is on the other side. I will tell you, Gentlemen, what has been the practical error of the last twenty years, — not to load the memory of the student with a mass of undigested knowledge, but to force upon him so much that he has rejected all. It has been the error of distracting and enfeebling the mind by an unmeaning profusion of subjects; of implying that a smattering in a dozen branches of study is not shallowness, which it really is, but enlargement, which it is not; of considering an acquaintance with the learned names of things and persons, and the possession of clever duo-decimos, and attendance on eloquent lecturers, and membership with scientific institutions, and the sight of the experiments of a platform and the specimens of a museum, that all this was not dissipation of mind, but progress. All things now are to be learned at once, not first one thing, then another, not one well, but many badly. Learning is to be without exertion, without attention, without toil; without grounding, without advance, without finishing. There is to be nothing individual in it; and this, forsooth, is the wonder of the age. What the steam engine does with matter, the printing press is to do with mind; it is to act mechanically, and the population is to be passively, almost unconsciously enlightened, by the mere multiplication and dissemination of volumes. Whether it be the school boy, or the school girl, or the youth at college, or the mechanic in the town, or the politician in the senate, all have been the victims in one way or other of this most preposterous and pernicious of delusions. Wise men have lifted up their voices in vain; and at length,

lest their own institutions should be outshone and should disappear
in the folly of the hour, they have been obliged, as far as they could
with a good conscience, to humour a spirit which they could not
withstand, and make temporizing concessions at which they could
not but inwardly smile.

It must not be supposed that, because I so speak, therefore I have
some sort of fear of the education of the people: on the contrary, the
more education they have, the better, so that it is really education.
Nor am I an enemy to the cheap publication of scientific and literary
works, which is now in vogue: on the contrary, I consider it a great
advantage, convenience, and gain; that is, to those to whom education
has given a capacity for using them. Further, I consider such innocent recreations as science and literature are able to furnish will be
a very fit occupation of the thoughts and the leisure of young persons, and may be made the means of keeping them from bad employments and bad companions. Moreover, as to that superficial acquaintance with chemistry, and geology, and astronomy, and political
economy, and modern history, and biography, and other branches of
knowledge, which periodical literature and occasional lectures and
scientific institutions diffuse through the community, I think it a
graceful accomplishment, and a suitable, nay, in this day a necessary
accomplishment, in the case of educated men. Nor, lastly, am I disparaging or discouraging the thorough acquisition of any one of these
studies, or denying that, as far as it goes, such thorough acquisition is
a real education of the mind. All I say is, call things by their right
names, and do not confuse together ideas which are essentially different. A thorough knowledge of one science and a superficial acquaintance with many, are not the same thing; a smattering of a hundred things or a memory for detail, is not a philosophical or comprehensive view. Recreations are not education; accomplishments are not
education. Do not say, the people must be educated, when, after all,
you only mean, amused, refreshed, soothed, put into good spirits and
good humour, or kept from vicious excesses. I do not say that such
amusements, such occupations of mind, are not a great gain; but they
are not education. You may as well call drawing and fencing education, as a general knowledge of botany or conchology. Stuffing birds
or playing stringed instruments is an elegant pastime, and a resource
to the idle, but it is not education; it does not form or cultivate the
intellect. Education is a high word; it is the preparation for knowledge, and it is the imparting of knowledge in proportion to that preparation. We require intellectual eyes to know withal, as bodily eyes
for sight. We need both objects and organs intellectual; we cannot
gain them without setting about it; we cannot gain them in our sleep,
or by hap-hazard. The best telescope does not dispense with eyes;
the printing press or the lecture room will assist us greatly, but we
must be true to ourselves, we must be parties in the work. A Uni-

versity is, according to the usual designation, an Alma Mater, knowing her children one by one, not a foundry, or a mint, or a treadmill.

9

I protest to you, Gentlemen, that if I had to choose between a so-called University, which dispensed with residence and tutorial superintendence, and gave its degrees to any person who passed an examination in a wide range of subjects, and a University which had no professors or examinations at all, but merely brought a number of young men together for three or four years, and then sent them away as the University of Oxford is said to have done some sixty years since, if I were asked which of these two methods was the better discipline of the intellect, — mind, I do not say which is *morally* the better, for it is plain that compulsory study must be a good and idleness an intolerable mischief, — but if I must determine which of the two courses was the more successful in training, moulding, enlarging the mind, which sent out men the more fitted for their secular duties, which produced better public men, men of the world, men whose names would descend to posterity, I have no hesitation in giving the preference to that University which did nothing, over that which exacted of its members an acquaintance with every science under the sun. And, paradox as this may seem, still if results be the test of systems, the influence of the public schools and colleges of England, in the course of the last century, at least will bear out one side of the contrast as I have drawn it. What would come, on the other hand, of the ideal systems of education which have fascinated the imagination of this age, could they ever take effect, and whether they would not produce a generation frivolous, narrow-minded, and resourceless, intellectually considered, is a fair subject for debate; but so far is certain, that the Universities and scholastic establishments, to which I refer, and which did little more than bring together first boys and then youths in large numbers, these institutions, with miserable deformities on the side of morals, with a hollow profession of Christianity, and a heathen code of ethics, — I say, at least they can boast of a succession of heroes and statesmen, of literary men and philosophers, of men conspicuous for great natural virtues, for habits of business, for knowledge of life, for practical judgment, for cultivated tastes, for accomplishments, who have made England what it is, — able to subdue the earth, able to domineer over Catholics.

How is this to be explained? I suppose as follows: When a multitude of young men, keen, open-hearted, sympathetic, and observant, as young men are, come together and freely mix with each other, they are sure to learn one from another, even if there be no one to teach them; the conversation of all is a series of lectures to each, and they gain for themselves new ideas and views, fresh matter of thought, and distinct principles for judging and acting, day by day. An infant has to learn the meaning of the information which its senses convey to it, and this seems to be its employment. It fancies all that the eye presents to it to be close to it, till it actually learns the contrary, and thus by practice does it ascertain the relations and uses of those first elements of knowledge which are necessary for its animal existence. A parallel teaching is necessary for our social being, and it is secured by a large school or a college; and this effect may be fairly called in its own department an enlargement of mind. It is seeing the world on a small field with little trouble; for the pupils or students come from very different places, and with widely different notions, and there is much to generalize, much to adjust, much to eliminate, there are inter-relations to be defined, and conventional rules to be established, in the process, by which the whole assemblage is moulded together, and gains one tone and one character.

Let it be clearly understood, I repeat it, that I am not taking into account moral or religious considerations; I am but saying that that youthful community will constitute a whole, it will embody a specific idea, it will represent a doctrine, it will administer a code of conduct, and it will furnish principles of thought and action. It will give birth to a living teaching, which in course of time will take the shape of a self-perpetuating tradition, or a *genius loci,* as it is sometimes called; which haunts the home where it has been born, and which imbues and forms, more or less, and one by one, every individual who is successively brought under its shadow. Thus it is that, independent of direct instruction on the part of Superiors, there is a sort of self-education in the academic institutions of Protestant England; a characteristic tone of thought, a recognized standard of judgment is found in them, which, as developed in the individual who is submitted to it, becomes a two-fold source of strength to him, both from the distinct stamp it impresses on his mind, and from the bond of union which it creates between him and others, — effects which are shared by the authorities of the place, for they themselves have been educated in it, and at all times are exposed to the influence of its ethical atmosphere. Here then is a real teaching, whatever be its standards and principles, true or false; and it at least tends towards cultivation of the intellect; it at least recognizes that knowledge is something more than a sort of passive reception of scraps and details; it is a something, and it does a something, which never will issue from the most strenuous efforts of a set of teachers, with no mutual sympathies and no inter-communion, of a set of examiners with no opinions which they dare profess, and with no common principles, who are teaching or questioning a set of youths who do not know them, and do not know each other, on a large number of subjects, different in kind, and connected by no wide philosophy, three times a week, or three times a year, or once in three years, in chill lecture-rooms or on a pompous anniversary.

10

Nay, self-education in any shape, in the most restricted sense, is preferable to a system of teaching which, professing so much, really does so little for the mind. Shut your College gates against the votary of knowledge, throw him back upon the searchings and the efforts of his own mind; he will gain by being spared an entrance into your Babel. Few, indeed, there are who can dispense with the stimulus and support of instructors, or will do any thing at all, if left to themselves. And fewer still (though such great minds are to be found), who will not, from such unassisted attempts, contract a self-reliance and a self-esteem, which are not only moral evils, but serious hindrances to the attainment of truth. And next to none, perhaps, or none, who will not be reminded from time to time of the disadvantage under which they lie, by their imperfect grounding, by the breaks, deficiencies, and irregularities of their knowledge, by the eccentricity of opinion and the confusion of principle which they exhibit. They will be too often ignorant of what every one knows and takes for granted, of that multitude of small truths which fall upon the mind like dust, impalpable and ever accumulating; they may be unable to converse, they may argue perversely, they may pride themselves on their worst paradoxes or their grossest truisms, they may be full of their own mode of viewing things, unwilling to be put out of their way, slow to enter into the minds of others; — but, with these and whatever other liabilities upon their heads, they are likely to have more thought, more mind, more philosophy, more true enlargement, than those earnest but ill-used persons, who are forced to load their minds with a score of subjects against an examination, who have too much on their hands to indulge themselves in thinking or investigation, who devour premiss and conclusion together with indiscriminate greediness, who hold whole sciences on faith, and commit demonstrations to memory, and who too often, as might be expected, when their period of education is passed, throw up all they have learned in disgust, having gained nothing really by their anxious labours, except perhaps the habit of application.

Yet such is the better specimen of the fruit of that ambitious system which has of late years been making way among us: for its result on ordinary minds, and on the common run of students, is less satisfactory still; they leave their place of education simply dissipated and relaxed by the multiplicity of subjects, which they have never really mastered, and so shallow as not even to know their shallowness. How much better, I say, is it for the active and thoughtful intellect, where such is to be found, to eschew the College and the University altogether, than to submit to drudgery so ignoble, a mockery so contumelious! How much more profitable for the independent mind, after the mere rudiments of education, to range through a library at random,

taking down books as they meet him, and pursuing the trains of
thought which his mother wit suggests! How much healthier to
wander into the fields, and there with the exiled Prince to find
"tongues in the trees, books in the running brooks!" How much more
genuine an education is that of the poor boy in the Poem [10] — a
Poem, whether in conception or in execution, one of the most touching in our language — who, not in the wide world, but ranging day
by day around his widowed mother's home, "a dexterous gleaner" in
a narrow field, and with only such slender outfit

> as the village school and books a few
> Supplied,

contrived from the beach, and the quay, and the fisher's boat, and
the inn's fireside, and the tradesman's shop, and the shepherd's walk,
and the smuggler's hut, and the mossy moor, and the screaming gulls,
and the restless waves, to fashion for himself a philosophy and a poetry
of his own!

But in a large subject, I am exceeding my necessary limits. Gentlemen, I must conclude abruptly; and postpone any summing up of
my argument, should that be necessary, to another day.

DISCOURSE VII

Knowledge Viewed in Relation to Professional Skill

1

I HAVE been insisting, in my two preceding Discourses, first, on the
cultivation of the intellect, as an end which may reasonably be pursued for its own sake; and next, on the nature of that cultivation, or
what that cultivation consists in. Truth of whatever kind is the proper
object of the intellect; its cultivation then lies in fitting it to apprehend
and contemplate truth. Now the intellect in its present state, with
exceptions which need not here be specified, does not discern truth
intuitively, or as a whole. We know, not by a direct and simple vision,
not at a glance, but, as it were, by piecemeal and accumulation, by
a mental process, by going round an object, by the comparison, the
combination, the mutual correction, the continual adaptation, of many
partial notions, by the employment, concentration, and joint action
of many faculties and exercises of mind. Such a union and concert of
the intellectual powers, such an enlargement and development, such
a comprehensiveness, is necessarily a matter of training. And again,
such a training is a matter of rule; it is not mere application, however
exemplary, which introduces the mind to truth, nor the reading many

10 George Crabbe's *Tales of the Hall.*

books, nor the getting up many subjects, nor the witnessing many experiments, nor the attending many lectures. All this is short of enough; a man may have done it all, yet be lingering in the vestibule of knowledge: — he may not realize what his mouth utters; he may not see with his mental eye what confronts him; he may have no grasp of things as they are; or at least he may have no power at all of advancing one step forward of himself, in consequence of what he has already acquired, no power of discriminating between truth and falsehood, of sifting out the grains of truth from the mass, of arranging things according to their real value, and, if I may use the phrase, of building up ideas. Such a power is the result of a scientific formation of mind; it is an acquired faculty of judgment, of clear-sightedness, of sagacity, of wisdom, of philosophical reach of mind, and of intellectual self-possession and repose, — qualities which do not come of mere acquirement. The bodily eye, the organ for apprehending material objects, is provided by nature; the eye of the mind, of which the object is truth, is the work of discipline and habit.

This process of training, by which the intellect, instead of being formed or sacrificed to some particular or accidental purpose, some specific trade or profession, or study or science, is disciplined for its own sake, for the perception of its own proper object, and for its own highest culture, is called Liberal Education; and though there is no one in whom it is carried as far as is conceivable, or whose intellect would be a pattern of what intellects should be made, yet there is scarcely any one but may gain an idea of what real training is, and at least look towards it, and make its true scope and result, not something else, his standard of excellence; and numbers there are who may submit themselves to it, and secure it to themselves in good measure. And to set forth the right standard, and to train according to it, and to help forward all students towards it according to their various capacities, this I conceive to be the business of a University.

2

Now this is what some great men are very slow to allow; they insist that Education should be confined to some particular and narrow end, and should issue in some definite work, which can be weighed and measured. They argue as if everything, as well as every person, had its price; and that where there has been a great outlay, they have a right to expect a return in kind. This they call making Education and Instruction "useful," and "Utility" becomes their watchword. With a fundamental principle of this nature, they very naturally go on to ask, what there is to show for the expense of a University; what is the real worth in the market of the article called "a Liberal Education," on the supposition that it does not teach us definitely how to advance our manufactures, or to improve our lands, or to better our civil economy; or again, if it does not at once make

this man a lawyer, that an engineer, and that a surgeon; or at least if
it does not lead to discoveries in chemistry, astronomy, geology, magnetism, and science of every kind.

This question, as might have been expected, has been keenly debated in the present age, and formed one main subject of the controversy, to which I referred in the Introduction to the present Discourses, as having been sustained in the first decade of this century
by a celebrated Northern Review on the one hand, and defenders of
the University of Oxford on the other. Hardly had the authorities of
that ancient seat of learning, waking from their long neglect, set
on foot a plan for the education of the youth committed to them,
than the representatives of science and literature in the city, which
has sometimes been called the Northern Athens,[1] remonstrated, with
their gravest arguments and their most brilliant satire, against the
direction and shape which the reform was taking. Nothing would
content them, but that the University should be set to rights on the
basis of the philosophy of Utility; a philosophy, as they seem to have
thought, which needed but to be proclaimed in order to be embraced.
In truth, they were little aware of the depth and force of the principles on which the academical authorities were proceeding, and, this
being so, it was not to be expected that they would be allowed to
walk at leisure over the field of controversy which they had selected.
Accordingly they were encountered in behalf of the University by
two men of great name and influence in their day, of very different
minds, but united, as by Collegiate ties, so in the clear-sighted and
large view which they took of the whole subject of Liberal Education;
and the defence thus provided for the Oxford studies has kept its
ground to this day. . . .

5

Now, I am not at present concerned with the specific question of
classical education; else, I might reasonably question the justice of
calling an intellectual discipline, which embraces the study of Aristotle,
Thucydides, and Tacitus, which involves Scholarship and Antiquities,
imaginative; still so far I readily grant, that the cultivation of the
"understanding," of a "talent for speculation and original inquiry,"
and of "the habit of pushing things up to their first principles," is a
principal portion of a *good* or *liberal* education. If then the Reviewers
consider such cultivation the characteristic of a *useful* education,
as they seem to do in the foregoing passage,[2] it follows, that what

1 Edinburgh. Critics in the *Edinburgh Review* had launched an attack on
Oxford's "classical education."

2 A passage in section 4: " . . . The matter of fact is, that a classical scholar
of twenty-three or twenty-four is a man principally conversant with works of
imagination. His feelings are quick, his fancy lively, and his taste good. Talents
for *speculation* and *original inquiry* he has none, nor has he formed the invaluable *habit of pushing things up to their first principles,* or of collecting dry
and unamusing facts as the materials for reasoning. . . ."

they mean by "useful" is just what I mean by "good" or "liberal": and Locke's question becomes a verbal one.[3] Whether youths are to be taught Latin or verse-making will depend on the *fact*, whether these studies tend to mental culture; but, however this is determined, so far is clear, that in that mental culture consists what I have called a liberal or non-professional, and what the Reviewers call a useful education.

This is the obvious answer which may be made to those who urge upon us the claims of Utility in our plans of Education; but I am not going to leave the subject here: I mean to take a wider view of it. Let us take "useful," as Locke takes it, in its proper and popular sense, and then we enter upon a large field of thought, to which I cannot do justice in one Discourse, though today's is all the space that I can give to it. I say, let us take "useful" to mean, not what is simply good, but what *tends* to good, or is the *instrument* of good; and in this sense also, Gentlemen, I will show you how a liberal education is truly and fully a useful, though it be not a professional, education. "Good" indeed means one thing, and "useful" means another; but I lay it down as a principle, which will save us a great deal of anxiety, that, though the useful is not always good, the good is always useful. Good is not only good, but reproductive of good; this is one of its attributes; nothing is excellent, beautiful, perfect, desirable for its own sake, but it overflows, and spreads the likeness of itself all around it. Good is prolific; it is not only good to the eye, but to the taste; it not only attracts us, but it communicates itself; it excites first our admiration and love, then our desire and our gratitude, and that, in proportion to its intenseness and fulness in particular instances. A great good will impart great good. If then the intellect is so excellent a portion of us, and its cultivation so excellent, it is not only beautiful, perfect, admirable, and noble in itself, but in a true and high sense it must be useful to the possessor and to all around him; not useful in any low, mechanical, mercantile sense, but as diffusing good, or as a blessing, or a gift, or power, or a treasure, first to the owner, then through him to the world. I say then, if a liberal education be good, it must necessarily be useful too.

6

You will see what I mean by the parallel of bodily health. Health is a good in itself, though nothing came of it, and is especially worth seeking and cherishing; yet, after all, the blessings which attend its presence are so great, while they are so close to it and so redound back upon it and encircle it, that we never think of it except as use-

---

3 Locke's question is quoted by Newman in section 4: " 'Could it be believed, unless we have every where amongst us examples of it, that a child should be forced to learn the rudiments of a language which *he is never to use in the course of life that he is designed to*, and neglect all the while the writing a good hand, and casting accounts, which are of great advantage in all conditions of life, and to most trades indispensably necessary?' "

ful as well as good, and praise and prize it for what it does, as well
as for what it is, though at the same time we cannot point out any
definite and distinct work or production which it can be said to effect.
And so as regards intellectual culture, I am far from denying utility
in this large sense as the end of Education, when I lay it down, that
the culture of the intellect is a good in itself and its own end; I do
not exclude from the idea of intellectual culture what it cannot but
be, from the very nature of things; I only deny that we must be
able to point out, before we have any right to call it useful, some
art, or business, or profession, or trade, or work, as resulting from it,
and as its real and complete end. The parallel is exact: — As the
body may be sacrificed to some manual or other toil, whether moderate
or oppressive, so may the intellect be devoted to some specific profession; and I do not call *this* the culture of the intellect. Again,
as some member or organ of the body may be inordinately used and
developed, so may memory, or imagination, or the reasoning faculty;
and *this* again is not intellectual culture. On the other hand, as the
body may be tended, cherished, and exercised with a simple view
to its general health, so may the intellect also be generally exercised
in order to its perfect state; and this *is* its cultivation.

Again, as health ought to precede labour of the body, and as a man
in health can do what an unhealthy man cannot do, and as of his
health the properties are strength, energy, agility, graceful carriage
and action, manual dexterity, and endurance of fatigue, so in like
manner general culture of mind is the best aid to professional and
scientific study, and educated men can do what illiterate cannot;
and the man who has learned to think and to reason and to compare
and to discriminate and to analyse, who has refined his taste, and
formed his judgment, and sharpened his mental vision, will not indeed at once be a lawyer, or a pleader, or an orator, or a statesman,
or a physician, or a good landlord, or a man of business, or a soldier,
or an engineer, or a chemist, or a geologist, or an antiquarian, but
he will be placed in that state of intellect in which he can take up
any one of the sciences or callings I have referred to, or any other
for which he has a taste or special talent, with an ease, a grace, a
versatility, and a success, to which another is a stranger. In this sense
then, and as yet I have said but a very few words on a large subject,
mental culture is emphatically *useful*.

If then I am arguing, and shall argue, against Professional or
Scientific knowledge as the sufficient end of a University Education,
let me not be supposed, Gentlemen, to be disrespectful towards particular studies, or arts, or vocations, and those who are engaged in
them. In saying that Law or Medicine is not the end of a University
course, I do not mean to imply that the University does not teach Law
or Medicine. What indeed can it teach at all, if it does not teach
something particular? It teaches *all* knowledge by teaching all

branches of knowledge, and in no other way. I do but say that there will be this distinction as regards a Professor of Law, or of Medicine, or of Geology, or of Political Economy, in a University and out of it, that out of a University he is in danger of being absorbed and narrowed by his pursuit, and of giving Lectures which are the Lectures of nothing more than a lawyer, physician, geologist, or political economist; whereas in a University he will just know where he and his science stand, he has come to it, as it were, from a height, he has taken a survey of all knowledge, he is kept from extravagance by the very rivalry of other studies, he has gained from them a special illumination and largeness of mind and freedom and self-possession, and he treats his own in consequence with a philosophy and a resource, which belongs not to the study itself, but to his liberal education.

This then is how I should solve the fallacy, for so I must call it, by which Locke and his disciples would frighten us from cultivating the intellect, under the notion that no education is useful which does not teach us some temporal calling, or some mechanical art, or some physical secret. I say that a cultivated intellect, because it is a good in itself, brings with it a power and a grace to every work and occupation which it undertakes, and enables us to be more useful, and to a greater number. There is a duty we owe to human society as such, to the state to which we belong, to the sphere in which we move, to the individuals towards whom we are variously related, and whom we successively encounter in life; and that philosophical or liberal education, as I have called it, which is the proper function of a University, if it refuses the foremost place to professional interests, does but postpone them to the formation of the citizen, and, while it subserves the larger interests of philanthropy, prepares also for the successful prosecution of those merely personal objects, which at first sight it seems to disparage. . . .

10

But I must bring these extracts [4] to an end. Today I have confined myself to saying that that training of the intellect, which is best for the individual himself, best enables him to discharge his duties to society. The Philosopher, indeed, and the man of the world differ in their very notion, but the methods, by which they are respectively formed, are pretty much the same. The Philosopher has the same command of matters of thought, which the true citizen and gentleman has of matters of business and conduct. If then a practical end must be assigned to a University course, I say it is that of training good members of society. Its art is the art of social life, and its end is fitness for the world. It neither confines its views to particular professions on the one hand, nor creates heroes or inspires genius on the

[4] Quoted in sections 8 and 9, in reply to the Edinburgh reviewers.

other. Works indeed of genius fall under no art; heroic minds come under no rule; a University is not a birthplace of poets or of immortal authors, of founders of schools, leaders of colonies, or conquerors of nations. It does not promise a generation of Aristotles or Newtons, of Napoleons or Washingtons, of Raphaels or Shakespeares, though such miracles of nature it has before now contained within its precincts. Nor is it content on the other hand with forming the critic or the experimentalist, the economist or the engineer, though such too it includes within its scope. But a University training is the great ordinary means to a great but ordinary end; it aims at raising the intellectual tone of society, at cultivating the public mind, at purifying the national taste, at supplying true principles to popular enthusiasm and fixed aims to popular aspiration, at giving enlargement and sobriety to the ideas of the age, at facilitating the exercise of political power, and refining the intercourse of private life. It is the education which gives a man a clear conscious view of his own opinions and judgments, a truth in developing them, an eloquence in expressing them, and a force in urging them. It teaches him to see things as they are, to go right to the point, to disentangle a skein of thought, to detect what is sophistical, and to discard what is irrelevant. It prepares him to fill any post with credit, and to master any subject with facility. It shows him how to accommodate himself to others, how to throw himself into their state of mind, how to bring before them his own, how to influence them, how to come to an understanding with them, how to bear with them. He is at home in any society, he has common ground with every class; he knows when to speak and when to be silent; he is able to converse, he is able to listen; he can ask a question pertinently, and gain a lesson seasonably, when he has nothing to impart himself; he is ever ready, yet never in the way; he is a pleasant companion, and a comrade you can depend upon; he knows when to be serious and when to trifle, and he has a sure tact which enables him to trifle with gracefulness and to be serious with effect. He has the repose of a mind which lives in itself, while it lives in the world, and which has resources for its happiness at home when it cannot go abroad. He has a gift which serves him in public, and supports him in retirement, without which good fortune is but vulgar, and with which failure and disappointment have a charm. The art which tends to make a man all this, is in the object which it pursues as useful as the art of wealth or the art of health, though it is less susceptible of method, and less tangible, less certain, less complete in its result.

DISCOURSE VIII

Knowledge Viewed in Relation to Religion

3

... Now, on opening the subject, we see at once a momentous benefit which the philosopher is likely to confer on the pastors of the Church. It is obvious that the first step which they have to effect in the conversion of man and the renovation of his nature, is his rescue from that fearful subjection to sense which is his ordinary state. To be able to break through the meshes of that thraldom, and to disentangle and to disengage its ten thousand holds upon the heart, is to bring it, I might almost say, half way to Heaven. Here, even divine grace, to speak of things according to their appearances, is ordinarily baffled, and retires, without expedient or resource, before this giant fascination. Religion seems too high and unearthly to be able to exert a continued influence upon us: its effort to rouse the soul, and the soul's effort to co-operate, are too violent to last. It is like holding out the arm at full length, or supporting some great weight, which we manage to do for a time, but soon are exhausted and succumb. Nothing can act beyond its own nature; when then we are called to what is supernatural, though those extraordinary aids from Heaven are given us, with which obedience becomes possible, yet even with them it is of transcendent difficulty. We are drawn down to earth every moment with the ease and certainty of a natural gravitation, and it is only by sudden impulses and, as it were, forcible plunges that we attempt to mount upwards. Religion indeed enlightens, terrifies, subdues; it gives faith, it inflicts remorse, it inspires resolutions, it draws tears, it inflames devotion, but only for the occasion. I repeat, it imparts an inward power which ought to effect more than this; I am not forgetting either the real sufficiency of its aids, nor the responsibility of those in whom they fail. I am not discussing theological questions at all, I am looking at phenomena as they lie before me, and I say that, in matter of fact, the sinful spirit repents, and protests it will never sin again, and for a while is protected by disgust and abhorrence from the malice of its foe. But that foe knows too well that such seasons of repentance are wont to have their end: he patiently waits, till nature faints with the effort of resistance, and lies passive and hopeless under the next access of temptation. What we need then is some expedient or instrument, which at least will obstruct and stave off the approach of our spiritual enemy, and which is sufficiently congenial and level with our nature to maintain as firm a hold upon us as the inducements of sensual gratification. It will be our wisdom to employ nature against itself. Thus sorrow, sickness, and care are providential antagonists to our inward disorders; they come upon us as years pass on, and generally produce their natural effects on us, in proportion as we are subjected to their influence. These, however, are God's instruments, not ours; we need a similar remedy, which we can make our own, the object of some legitimate faculty, or the aim of some natural affection, which is capable of resting on the mind, and taking up its familiar lodging with it, and engrossing it, and which thus becomes a match for the besetting power of sensuality, and a sort of homœopathic medicine for the disease. Here then I think is the important aid which intellectual cultivation furnishes to us in rescuing the victims of passion and self-will. It does not supply religious motives; it is not the cause or proper antecedent of any thing supernatural; it is not meritorious of heavenly aid or reward; but it does a work, at least *materially* good (as theologians speak), whatever be its real and formal character. It expels the excitements of sense by the introduction of those of the intellect.

This then is the *primâ facie* advantage of the pursuit of Knowledge; it is the drawing the mind off from things which will harm it to subjects which are worthy a rational being; and, though it does not raise it above nature, nor has any tendency to make us pleasing to our Maker, yet is it nothing to substitute what is in itself harmless for what is, to say the least, inexpressibly dangerous? is it a little thing to exchange a circle of ideas which are certainly sinful, for others which are certainly not so? You will say, perhaps, in the words of the Apostle, "Knowledge puffeth up:" and doubtless this mental cultivation, even when it is successful for the purpose for which I am applying it, may be from the first nothing more than the substitution of pride for sensuality. I grant it, I think I shall have something to say on this point presently; but this is not a necessary result, it is but an incidental evil, a danger which may be realized or may be averted, whereas we may in most cases predicate guilt, and guilt of a heinous kind, where the mind is suffered to run wild and indulge its thoughts without training or law of any kind; and surely to turn away a soul from mortal sin is a good and a gain so far, whatever comes of it. And therefore, if a friend in need is twice a friend, I conceive that intellectual employments, though they do no more than occupy the mind with objects naturally noble or innocent, have a special claim upon our consideration and gratitude.

4

Nor is this all: Knowledge, the discipline by which it is gained, and the tastes which it forms, have a natural tendency to refine the mind, and to give it an indisposition, simply natural, yet real, nay, more than this, a disgust and abhorrence, towards excesses and enormities of evil, which are often or ordinarily reached at length by those who are not careful from the first to set themselves against what is vicious and criminal. It generates within the mind a fastidiousness, analogous to the delicacy or daintiness which good nurture or a sickly habit induces in respect of food; and this fastidiousness, though arguing no high principle, though no protection in the case of violent temptation, nor sure in its operation, yet will often or generally be lively enough to create an absolute loathing of certain offences, or a detestation and scorn of them as ungentlemanlike, to which ruder natures, nay, such as have far more of real religion in them, are tempted, or even betrayed. Scarcely can we exaggerate the value, in its place, of a safeguard such as this, as regards those multitudes who are thrown upon the open field of the world, or are withdrawn from its eye and from the restraint of public opinion. In many cases, where it exists, sins, familiar to those who are otherwise circumstanced, will not even occur to the mind: in others, the sense of shame and the quickened apprehension of detection will act as a sufficient obstacle to them, when they do present themselves before it. Then, again, the fastidiousness I am speaking of will create a simple hatred of that miserable tone of conversation which, obtaining as it does in the world, is a constant fuel of evil, heaped up round about the soul: moreover, it will create an irresolution and indecision in doing wrong, which will act as a *remora* [1] till the danger is past away. And though it has no tendency, I repeat, to mend the heart, or to secure it from the dominion in other shapes of those very evils which it repels in the particular modes of approach by which they prevail over others, yet cases may occur when it gives birth, after sins have been committed, to so keen a remorse and so intense a self-hatred, as are even sufficient to cure the particular moral disorder, and to prevent its accesses ever afterwards; — as the spendthrift in the story, who, after gazing on his lost acres from the summit of an eminence, came down a miser, and remained a miser to the end of his days.

And all this holds good in a special way, in an age such as ours, when, although pain of body and mind may be rife as heretofore, yet other counteractions of evil, of a penal character, which are present at other times, are away. In rude and semibarbarous periods, at least in a climate such as our own, it is the daily, nay, the principal business of the senses, to convey feelings of discomfort to the mind, as far as they convey feelings at all. Exposure to the elements, social disorder and lawlessness, the tyranny of the powerful, and the inroads of enemies, are a stern discipline, allowing brief intervals, or awarding a sharp penance, to sloth and sensuality. The rude food, the scanty clothing, the violent exercise, the vagrant life, the military constraint, the imperfect pharmacy, which now are the trials of only particular classes of the community, were once the lot more or less of all. In the deep woods or the wild solitudes of the medieval era, feelings of religion or superstition were naturally present to the population, which in various ways co-operated with the missionary or

[1] Hindrance.

pastor, in retaining it in a noble simplicity of manners. But, when in the advancement of society men congregate in towns, and multiply in contracted spaces, and law gives them security, and art gives them comforts, and good government robs them of courage and manliness, and monotony of life throws them back upon themselves, who does not see that diversion or protection from evil they have none, that vice is the mere reaction of unhealthy toil, and sensual excess the holyday of resourceless ignorance? This is so well understood by the practical benevolence of the day, that it has especially busied itself in plans for supplying the masses of our town population with intellectual and honourable recreations. Cheap literature, libraries of useful and entertaining knowledge, scientific lectureships, museums, zoological collections, buildings and gardens to please the eye and to give repose to the feelings, external objects of whatever kind, which may take the mind off itself, and expand and elevate it in liberal contemplations, these are the human means, wisely suggested, and good as far as they go, for at least parrying the assaults of moral evil, and keeping at bay the enemies, not only of the individual soul, but of society at large.

Such are the instruments by which an age of advanced civilization combats those moral disorders, which Reason as well as Revelation denounces; and I have not been backward to express my sense of their serviceableness to Religion. Moreover, they are but the foremost of a series of influences, which intellectual culture exerts upon our moral nature, and all upon the type of Christianity, manifesting themselves in veracity, probity, equity, fairness, gentleness, benevolence, and amiableness; so much so, that a character more noble to look at, more beautiful, more winning, in the various relations of life and in personal duties, is hardly conceivable, than may, or might be, its result, when that culture is bestowed upon a soil naturally adapted to virtue. If you would obtain a picture for contemplation which may seem to fulfil the ideal, which the Apostle has delineated under the name of charity, in its sweetness and harmony, its generosity, its courtesy to others, and its depreciation of self, you could not have recourse to a better furnished *studio* than to that of Philosophy, with the specimens of it, which with greater or less exactness are scattered through society in a civilized age. It is enough to refer you, Gentlemen, to the various Biographies and Remains of contemporaries and others, which from time to time issue from the press, to see how striking is the action of our intellectual upon our moral nature, where the moral material is rich, and the intellectual cast is perfect. Individuals will occur to all of us, who deservedly attract our love and admiration, and whom the world almost worships as the work of its own hands. Religious principle, indeed, — that is, faith, — is, to all appearance, simply away; the work is as certainly not supernatural as it is certainly noble and beautiful. This must be insisted on, that the

Intellect may have its due; but it also must be insisted on for the sake of conclusions to which I wish to conduct our investigation. The radical difference indeed of this mental refinement from genuine religion, in spite of its seeming relationship, is the very cardinal point on which my present discussion turns; yet, on the other hand, such refinement may readily be assigned to a Christian origin by hasty or distant observers, or by those who view it in a particular light. And as this is the case, I think it advisable, before proceeding with the delineation of its characteristic features, to point out to you distinctly the elementary principles on which its morality is based. . . .

8

Taking these passages [2] as specimens of what I call the Religion of Philosophy, it is obvious to observe that there is no doctrine contained in them which is not in a certain sense true; yet, on the other hand, that almost every statement is perverted and made false, because it is not the whole truth. They are exhibitions of truth under one aspect, and therefore insufficient; conscience is most certainly a moral sense, but it is more; vice again, is a deformity, but it is worse. Lord Shaftesbury may insist, if he will, that simple and solitary fear cannot effect a moral conversion, and we are not concerned to answer him; but he will have a difficulty in proving that any real conversion follows from a doctrine which makes virtue a mere point of good taste, and vice vulgar and ungentlemanlike.

Such a doctrine is essentially superficial, and such will be its effects. It has no better measure of right and wrong than that of visible beauty and tangible fitness. Conscience indeed inflicts an acute pang, but that pang, forsooth, is irrational, and to reverence it is an illiberal superstition. But, if we will make light of what is deepest within us, nothing is left but to pay homage to what is more upon the surface. To *seem* becomes to *be;* what looks fair will be good, what causes offence will be evil; virtue will be what pleases, vice what pains. As well may we measure virtue by utility as by such a rule. Nor is this an imaginary apprehension; we all must recollect the celebrated sentiment into which a great and wise man was betrayed, in the glowing eloquence of his valediction to the spirit of chivalry. "It is gone," cries Mr. Burke; "that sensibility of principle, that chastity of honour, which felt a stain like a wound; which inspired courage, while it mitigated ferocity; which ennobled whatever it touched, and under which *vice lost half its evil by losing all its grossness.*" In the last clause of this beautiful sentence we have too apt an illustration of the ethical temperament of a civilized age. It is detection, not the sin, which is the crime; private life is sacred, and inquiry into it is intolerable; and decency is virtue. Scandals, vulgarities, whatever shocks, whatever disgusts, are offences of the first order. Drinking

2 Quoted in sections 6 and 7, from Edward Gibbon and Lord Shaftesbury.

and swearing, squalid poverty, improvidence, laziness, slovenly disorder, make up the idea of profligacy: poets may say any thing, however wicked, with impunity; works of genius may be read without danger or shame, whatever their principles; fashion, celebrity, the beautiful, the heroic, will suffice to force any evil upon the community. The splendours of a court, and the charms of good society, wit, imagination, taste, and high breeding, the *prestige* of rank, and the resources of wealth are a screen, an instrument, and an apology for vice and irreligion. And thus at length we find, surprising as the change may be, that that very refinement of Intellectualism, which began by repelling sensuality, ends by excusing it. Under the shadow indeed of the Church, and in its due development, Philosophy does service to the cause of morality; but, when it is strong enough to have a will of its own, and is lifted up with an idea of its own importance, and attempts to form a theory, and to lay down a principle, and to carry out a system of ethics, and undertakes the moral education of the man, then it does but abet evils to which at first it seemed instinctively opposed. True Religion is slow in growth, and, when once planted, is difficult of dislodgement; but its intellectual counterfeit has no root in itself: it springs up suddenly, it suddenly withers. It appeals to what is in nature, and it falls under the dominion of the old Adam. Then, like dethroned princes, it keeps up a state and majesty, when it has lost the real power. Deformity is its abhorrence; accordingly, since it cannot dissuade men from vice, therefore in order to escape the sight of its deformity, it embellishes it. It "skins and films the ulcerous place," which it cannot probe or heal,

> Whiles rank corruption, mining all within,
> Infects unseen.

And from this shallowness of philosophical Religion it comes to pass that its disciples seem able to fulfil certain precepts of Christianity more readily and exactly than Christians themselves. St. Paul, as I have said, gives us a pattern of evangelical perfection; he draws the Christian character in its most graceful form, and its most beautiful hues. He discourses of that charity which is patient and meek, humble and single-minded, distinterested, contented, and persevering. He tells us to prefer each the other before himself, to give way to each other, to abstain from rude words and evil speech, to avoid self-conceit, to be calm and grave, to be cheerful and happy, to observe peace with all men, truth and justice, courtesy and gentleness, all that is modest, amiable, virtuous, and of good repute. Such is St. Paul's exemplar of the Christian in his external relations; and, I repeat, the school of the world seems to send out living copies of this typical excellence with greater success than the Church. At this day the "gentleman" is the creation, not of Christianity, but of civilization. But the reason is obvious. The world is content with setting right the surface of things; the Church aims at regenerating the very ⚹ depths of the heart. She ever begins with the beginning; and, as regards the multitude of her children, is never able to get beyond the beginning, but is continually employed in laying the foundation. She is engaged with what is essential, as previous and as introductory to the ornamental and the attractive. She is curing men and keeping them clear of mortal sin; she is "treating of justice and chastity, and the judgment to come:" she is insisting on faith and hope, and devotion, and honesty, and the elements of charity; and has so much to do with precept, that she almost leaves it to inspirations from Heaven to suggest what is of counsel and perfection. She aims at what is necessary rather than at what is desirable. She is for the many as well as for the few. She is putting souls in the way of salvation, that they may then be in a condition, if they shall be called upon, to aspire to the heroic, and to attain the full proportions, as well as the rudiments, of the beautiful. . . .

10

Hence it is that it is almost a definition of a gentleman to say he is one who never inflicts pain. This description is both refined and, as far as it goes, accurate. He is mainly occupied in merely removing the obstacles which hinder the free and unembarrassed action of those about him; and he concurs with their movements rather than takes the initiative himself. His benefits may be considered as parallel to what are called comforts or conveniences in arrangements of a personal nature: like an easy chair or a good fire, which do their part in dispelling cold and fatigue, though nature provides both means of rest and animal heat without them. The true gentleman in like manner carefully avoids whatever may cause a jar or a jolt in the minds of those with whom he is cast; — all clashing of opinion, or collision of feeling, all restraint, or suspicion, or gloom, or resentment; his great concern being to make every one at their ease and at home. He has his eyes on all his company; he is tender towards the bashful, gentle towards the distant, and merciful towards the absurd; he can recollect to whom he is speaking; he guards against unseasonable allusions, or topics which may irritate; he is seldom prominent in conversation, and never wearisome. He makes light of favours while he does them, and seems to be receiving when he is conferring. He never speaks of himself except when compelled, never defends himself by a mere retort, he has no ears for slander or gossip, is scrupulous in imputing motives to those who interfere with him, and interprets everything for the best. He is never mean or little in his disputes, never takes unfair advantage, never mistakes personalities or sharp sayings for arguments, or insinuates evil which he dare not say out. From a long-sighted prudence, he observes the maxim of the ancient sage, that we should ever conduct ourselves towards our enemy as if he were one day to be our friend. He has too much good sense to be affronted at insults, he is too well employed to remember injuries, and too indolent to bear malice. He is patient, forbearing, and resigned, on philosophical principles; he submits to pain, because it is inevitable, to bereavement, because it is irreparable, and to death, because it is his destiny. If he engages in controversy of any kind, his disciplined intellect preserves him from the blundering discourtesy of better, though less educated minds; who, like blunt weapons, tear and hack instead of cutting clean, who mistake the point in argument, waste their strength on trifles, misconceive their adversary, and leave the question more involved than they find it. He may be right or wrong in his opinion, but he is too clear-headed to be unjust; he is as simple as he is forcible, and as brief as he is decisive. Nowhere shall we find greater candour, consideration, indulgence: he throws himself into the minds of his opponents, he accounts for their mistakes. He knows the weakness of human reason as well as its strength, its province and its limits. If he be an unbeliever, he will be too profound and large-minded to ridicule religion or to act against it; he is too wise to be a dogmatist or fanatic in his infidelity. He respects piety and devotion; he even supports institutions as venerable, beautiful, or useful, to which he does not assent; he honours the ministers of religion, and he is contented to decline its mysteries without assailing or denouncing them. He is a friend of religious toleration, and that, not only because his philosophy has taught him to look on all forms of faith with an impartial eye, but also from the gentleness and effeminacy of feeling, which is the attendant on civilisation.

Not that he may not hold a religion too, in his own way, even when he is not a Christian. In that case his religion is one of imagination and sentiment; it is the embodiment of those ideas of the sublime, majestic, and beautiful, without which there can be no large philosophy. Sometimes he acknowledges the being of God, sometimes he invests an unknown principle or quality with the attributes of perfection. And this deduction of his reason, or creation of his fancy, he makes the occasion of such excellent thoughts, and the starting-point of so varied and systematic a teaching, that he even seems like a disciple of Christianity itself. From the very accuracy and steadiness of his logical powers, he is able to see what sentiments are consistent in those who hold any religious doctrine at all, and he appears to others to feel and to hold a whole circle of theological truths which exist in his mind no otherwise than as a number of deductions.

Such are some of the lineaments of the ethical character, which the cultivated intellect will form, apart from religious principle. They are seen within the pale of the Church and without it, in holy men and in profligate; they form the *beau-idéal* of the world; they partly assist and partly distort the development of the Catholic. They may subserve the education of a St. Francis de Sales or a Cardinal Pole;

they may be the limits of the virtue of a Shaftesbury or a Gibbon.
Basil and Julian were fellow-students at the schools of Athens; and
one became the Saint and Doctor of the Church, the other her scoff-
ing and relentless foe.

Apologia Pro Vita Sua

❮ Newman's "apology for," or defense of, his life was written as a reply
to the Reverend Charles Kingsley, who had called Newman's intellectual
honesty into question in an article in *Macmillan's Magazine* for January
1864. "The original work consisted of seven Parts, which were published
in a series on consecutive Thursdays, between April 21 and June 2 [1864]."
Some of Newman's friends thought he had been unnecessarily hard on
Kingsley, and when the book publication appeared the following year, the
first two pamphlets ("Mr. Kingsley's Method of Disputation" and "The
True Mode of Meeting Mr. Kingsley") were omitted, "excepting certain passages subjoined to the Preface." The part here printed is the third part
of the serial publication and the first chapter of the revised edition (1865).
This chapter from the *Apologia*, together with *The Idea of a University*,
should perhaps be read in the light of Newman's statement, on receiving
the Cardinalate, that his life had been one long battle against Liberalism. ❯

History of My Religious Opinions to the Year 1833

IT may easily be conceived how great a trial it is to me to write the
following history of myself; but I must not shrink from the task. The
words "Secretum meum mihi," [1] keep ringing in my ears; but as men
draw towards their end, they care less for disclosures. Nor is it the
least part of my trial, to anticipate that my friends may, upon first
reading what I have written, consider much in it irrelevant to my purpose; yet I cannot help thinking that, viewed as a whole, it will effect
what I wish it to do.

I was brought up from a child to take great delight in reading the
Bible; but I had no formal religious convictions till I was fifteen. Of
course I had perfect knowledge of my Catechism.

After I was grown up, I put on paper such recollections as I had
of my thoughts and feelings on religious subjects, at the time that I
was a child and a boy. Out of these I select two, which are at once

1 "My secret unto me" — or, "My private life is my own affair."

the most definite among them, and also have a bearing on my later convictions.

In the paper to which I have referred, written either in the long
vacation of 1820, or in October 1823, the following notices of my
school days were sufficiently prominent in my memory for me to consider them worth recording: — "I used to wish the Arabian Tales
were true: my imagination ran on unknown influences, on magical
powers, and talismans. . . . I thought life might be a dream, or I an
Angel, and all this world a deception, my fellow-angels by a playful
device concealing themselves from me, and deceiving me with the
semblance of a material world."

Again, "Reading in the Spring of 1816 a sentence from [Dr. Watt's]
'Remnants of Time,' entitled 'the Saints unknown to the world,' to
the effect, that 'there is nothing in their figure or countenance to distinguish them,' etc., etc., I supposed he spoke of Angels who lived in
the world, as it were disguised."

The other remark is this: "I was very superstitious, and for some
time previous to my conversion" [when I was fifteen] "used constantly to cross myself on going into the dark."

Of course I must have got this practice from some external source
or other; but I can make no sort of conjecture whence; and certainly
no one had ever spoken to me on the subject of the Catholic religion,
which I only knew by name. The French master was an *émigré* priest,
but he was simply made a butt, as French masters too commonly were
in that day, and spoke English very imperfectly. There was a Catholic
family in the village, old maiden ladies we used to think; but I knew
nothing but their name. I have of late years heard that there were one
or two Catholic boys in the school; but either we were carefully kept
from knowing this, or the knowledge of it made simply no impression
on our minds. My brother will bear witness how free the school was
from Catholic ideas.

I had once been into Warwick Street Chapel, with my father, who,
I believe, wanted to hear some piece of music; all that I bore away
from it was the recollection of a pulpit and a preacher and a boy
swinging a censer.

When I was at Littlemore, I was looking over old copybooks of
my school days, and I found among them my first Latin verse-book;
and in the first page of it there was a device which almost took my
breath away with surprise. I have the book before me now, and have
just been showing it to others. I have written in the first page, in my
schoolboy hand, "John H. Newman, February 11th, 1811, Verse Book";
then follow my first verses. Between "Verse" and "Book" I have
drawn the figure of a solid cross upright, and next to it is, what may
indeed be meant for a necklace, but what I cannot make out to be
anything else than a set of beads suspended, with a little cross attached. At this time I was not quite ten years old. I suppose I got the

idea from some romance, Mrs. Radcliffe's or Miss Porter's;[2] or from some religious picture; but the strange thing is, how, among the thousand objects which meet a boy's eyes, these in particular should so have fixed themselves in my mind, that I made them thus practically my own. I am certain there was nothing in the churches I attended, or the prayer books I read, to suggest them. It must be recollected that churches and prayer books were not decorated in those days as I believe they are now.

When I was fourteen, I read Paine's tracts against the Old Testament, and found pleasure in thinking of the objections which were contained in them. Also, I read some of Hume's essays; and perhaps that on Miracles. So at least I gave my father to understand; but perhaps it was a brag. Also, I recollect copying out some French verses, perhaps Voltaire's, against the immortality of the soul, and saying to myself something like "How dreadful, but how plausible!"

When I was fifteen (in the autumn of 1816) a great change of thought took place in me. I fell under the influences of a definite creed, and received into my intellect impressions of dogma, which, through God's mercy, have never been effaced or obscured. Above and beyond the conversations and sermons of the excellent man, long dead, who was the human means of this beginning of divine faith in me, was the effect of the books which he put into my hands, all of the school of Calvin. One of the first books I read was a work of Romaine's;[3] I neither recollect the title nor the contents, except one doctrine, which of course I do not include among those which I believe to have come from a divine source, viz. the doctrine of final perseverance. I received it at once, and believed that the inward conversion of which I was conscious (and of which I still am more certain than that I have hands and feet) would last into the next life, and that I was elected to eternal glory. I have no consciousness that this belief had any tendency whatever to lead me to be careless about pleasing God. I retained it till the age of twenty-one, when it gradually faded away; but I believe that it had some influence on my opinions, in the direction of those childish imaginations which I have already mentioned, viz. in isolating me from the objects which surrounded me, in confirming me in my mistrust of the reality of material phenomena, and making me rest in the thought of two and two only supreme and luminously self-evident beings, myself and my Creator; — for while I considered myself predestined to salvation, I thought others simply passed over, not predestined to eternal death. I only thought of the mercy to myself.

The detestable doctrine last mentioned is simply denied and abjured, unless my memory strangely deceives me, by the writer who

2 Ann Radcliffe (1764–1823) and Jane Porter (1776–1850), authors of Gothic and other romances.
3 William Romaine (1714–1795), religious writer.

made a deeper impression on my mind than any other, and to whom
(humanly speaking) I almost owe my soul — Thomas Scott of Aston
Sandford.[4] I so admired and delighted in his writings, that, when I
was an undergraduate, I thought of making a visit to his parsonage,
in order to see a man whom I so deeply revered. I hardly think I
could have given up the idea of this expedition, even after I had taken
my degree; for the news of his death in 1821 came upon me as a disappointment as well as a sorrow. I hung upon the lips of Daniel Wilson,[5] afterwards Bishop of Calcutta, as in two sermons at St. John's
Chapel he gave the history of Scott's life and death. I had been possessed of his essays from a boy; his commentary I bought when I was
an undergraduate.

What, I suppose, will strike any reader of Scott's history and writings, is his bold unworldliness and vigorous independence of mind.
He followed truth wherever it led him, beginning with Unitarianism,
and ending in a zealous faith in the Holy Trinity. It was he who first
planted deep in my mind that fundamental truth of religion. With
the assistance of Scott's essays, and the admirable work of Jones
of Nayland,[6] I made a collection of Scripture texts in proof of the
doctrine, with remarks (I think) of my own upon them, before I was
sixteen; and a few months later I drew up a series of texts in support
of each verse of the Athanasian Creed. These papers I have still.

Besides his unworldliness, what I also admired in Scott was his resolute opposition to Antinomianism, and the minutely practical character of his writings. They show him to be a true Englishman, and I
deeply felt his influence; and for years I used almost as proverbs what
I considered to be the scope and issue of his doctrine, "Holiness before peace," and "Growth is the only evidence of life."

Calvinists make a sharp separation between the elect and the world;
there is much in this that is parallel or cognate to the Catholic doctrine; but they go on to say, as I understand them, very differently
from Catholicism, — that the converted and the unconverted can
be discriminated by man, that the justified are conscious of their
state of justification, and that the regenerate cannot fall away. Catholics on the other hand shade and soften the awful antagonism between
good and evil, which is one of their dogmas, by holding that there are
different degrees of justification, that there is a great difference in
point of gravity between sin and sin, that there is the possibility and
the danger of falling away, and that there is no certain knowledge
given to any one that he is simply in a state of grace, and much less
that he is to persevere to the end: — of the Calvinistic tenets the
only one which took root in my mind was the fact of heaven and

4 (1747–1821), author of a commentary on the Bible.
5 Daniel Wilson (1778–1858), Evangelical preacher.
6 William Jones, of Nayland, Suffolk (1726–1800), author of *The Catholic
Doctrine of the Trinity.*

hell, divine favour and divine wrath, of the justified and the unjustified. The notion that the regenerate and the justified were one and the same, and that the regenerate, as such, had the gift of perseverance, remained with me not many years, as I have said already.

This main Catholic doctrine of the warfare between the city of God and the powers of darkness was also deeply impressed upon my mind by a work of a very opposite character, Law's "Serious Call."

From this time I have given a full inward assent and belief to the doctrine of eternal punishment, as delivered by our Lord Himself, in as true a sense as I hold that of eternal happiness; though I have tried in various ways to make that truth less terrible to the reason.

Now I come to two other works, which produced a deep impression on me in the same autumn of 1816, when I was fifteen years old, each contrary to each, and planting in me the seeds of an intellectual inconsistency which disabled me for a long course of years. I read Joseph Milner's Church History,[7] and was nothing short of enamoured of the long extracts from St. Augustine and the other Fathers which I found there. I read them as being the religion of the primitive Christians: but simultaneously with Milner I read Newton on the Prophecies,[8] and in consequence became most firmly convinced that the Pope was the Antichrist predicted by Daniel, St. Paul, and St. John. My imagination was stained by the effects of this doctrine up to the year 1843; it had been obliterated from my reason and judgment at an earlier date; but the thought remained upon me as a sort of false conscience. Hence came that conflict of mind, which so many have felt besides myself; — leading some men to make a compromise between two ideas, so inconsistent with each other — driving others to beat out the one idea or the other from their minds — and ending in my own case, after many years of intellectual unrest, in the gradual decay and extinction of one of them — I do not say in its violent death, for why should I not have murdered it sooner, if I murdered it at all?

I am obliged to mention, though I do it with great reluctance, another deep imagination, which at this time, the autumn of 1816, took possession of me — there can be no mistake about the fact; — viz. that it was the will of God that I should lead a single life. This anticipation, which has held its ground almost continuously ever since — with the break of a month now and a month then, up to 1829, and, after that date, without any break at all — was more or less connected, in my mind, with the notion that my calling in life would require such a sacrifice as celibacy involved; as, for instance, missionary work among the heathen, to which I had a great drawing

7 (1744–1797), Evangelical divine, author of a *History of the Church of Christ.*
8 Thomas Newton (1704–1782), Bishop of Bristol, author of a *Dissertation on the Prophecies.*

for some years. It also strengthened my feeling of separation from the visible world, of which I have spoken above.

In 1822 I came under very different influences from those to which I had hitherto been subjected. At that time, Mr. Whately, as he was then, afterwards Archbishop of Dublin, for the few months he remained in Oxford, which he was leaving for good, showed great kindness to me. He renewed it in 1825, when he became Principal of Alban Hall, making me his vice-principal and tutor. Of Dr. Whately I will speak presently, for from 1822 to 1825 I saw most of the present Provost of Oriel, Dr. Hawkins, at that time Vicar of St. Mary's; and, when I took orders in 1824 and had a curacy at Oxford, then, during the long vacations, I was especially thrown into his company. I can say with a full heart that I love him, and have never ceased to love him; and I thus preface what otherwise might sound rude, that in the course of the many years in which we were together afterwards, he provoked me very much from time to time, though I am perfectly certain that I have provoked him a great deal more. Moreover, in me such provocation was unbecoming, both because he was the head of my college, and because in the first years that I knew him, he had been in many ways of great service to my mind.

He was the first who taught me to weigh my words, and to be cautious in my statements. He led me to that mode of limiting and clearing my sense in discussion and in controversy, and of distinguishing between cognate ideas, and of obviating mistakes by anticipation, which to my surprise has been since considered, even in quarters friendly to me, to savour of the polemics of Rome. He is a man of most exact mind himself, and he used to snub me severely, on reading, as he was kind enough to do, the first sermons that I wrote, and other compositions which I was engaged upon.

Then as to doctrine, he was the means of great additions to my belief. As I have noticed elsewhere, he gave me the "Treatise on Apostolical Preaching," by Sumner, afterwards Archbishop of Canterbury, from which I learned to give up my remaining Calvinism, and to receive the doctrine of Baptismal Regeneration. In many other ways too he was of use to me, on subjects semi-religious and semi-scholastic.

It was Dr. Hawkins too who taught me to anticipate that, before many years were over, there would be an attack made upon the books and the canon of Scripture. I was brought to the same belief by the conversation of Mr. Blanco White,[9] who also led me to have freer views on the subject of inspiration than were usual in the Church of England at the time.

There is one other principle, which I gained from Dr. Hawkins,

9 Joseph Blanco White (1775–1841), theological writer.

more directly bearing upon Catholicism, than any that I [...]
tioned; and that is the doctrine of Tradition. When I [...]
dergraduate, I heard him preach in the University pul[...]
brated sermon on the subject, and recollect how long [...]
to me, though he was at that time a very striking preacher; but, when
I read it and studied it as his gift, it made a most serious impression
upon me. He does not go one step, I think, beyond the high Anglican doctrine, nay he does not reach it; but he does his work
thoroughly, and his view was original with him, and his subject was
a novel one at the time. He lays down a proposition, self-evident as
soon as stated, to those who have at all examined the structure of
Scripture, viz. that the sacred text was never intended to teach
doctrine, but only to prove it, and that, if we would learn doctrine,
we must have recourse to the formularies of the Church; for instance to the Catechism, and to the Creeds. He considers, that,
after learning from them the doctrines of Christianity, the inquirer
must verify them by Scripture. This view, most true in its outline,
most fruitful in its consequences, opened upon me a large field of
thought. Dr. Whately held it too. One of its effects was to strike at
the root of the principle on which the Bible Society was set up. I
belonged to its Oxford Association; it became a matter of time when
I should withdraw my name from its subscription-list, though I did
not do so at once.

It is with pleasure that I pay here a tribute to the memory of the
Rev. William James, then Fellow of Oriel; who, about the year
1823, taught me the doctrine of Apostolical Succession, in the course
of a walk, I think, round Christ Church meadow: I recollect being
somewhat impatient on the subject at the time.

It was at about this date, I suppose, that I read Bishop Butler's
Analogy; the study of which has been to so many, as it was to me,
an era in their religious opinions. Its inculcation of a visible church,
the oracle of truth and a pattern of sanctity, of the duties of external
religion, and of the historical character of revelation, are characteristics of this great work which strike the reader at once; for myself,
if I may attempt to determine what I most gained from it, it lay
in two points, which I shall have an opportunity of dwelling on in
the sequel; they are the underlying principles of a great portion of
my teaching. First, the very idea of an analogy between the separate
works of God leads to the conclusion that the system which is of
less importance is economically or sacramentally connected with
the more momentous system, and of this conclusion the theory, to
which I was inclined as a boy, viz. the unreality of material phenomena, is an ultimate resolution. At this time I did not make the
distinction between matter itself and its phenomena, which is so
necessary and so obvious in discussing the subject. Secondly, Butler's doctrine that probability is the guide of life, led me, at least

under the teaching to which a few years later I was introduced, to the question of the logical cogency of faith, on which I have written so much. Thus to Butler I trace those two principles of my teaching, which have led to a charge against me both of fancifulness and of scepticism.

And now as to Dr. Whately. I owe him a great deal. He was a man of generous and warm heart. He was particularly loyal to his friends, and to use the common phrase, "all his geese were swans." While I was still awkward and timid in 1822, he took me by the hand, and acted the part to me of a gentle and encouraging instructor. He, emphatically, opened my mind, and taught me to think and to use my reason. After being first noticed by him in 1822, I became very intimate with him in 1825, when I was his vice-principal at Alban Hall. I gave up that office in 1826, when I became tutor of my college, and his hold upon me gradually relaxed. He had done his work towards me or nearly so, when he had taught me to see with my own eyes and to walk with my own feet. Not that I had not a good deal to learn from others still, but I influenced them as well as they me, and co-operated rather than merely concurred with them. As to Dr. Whately, his mind was too different from mine for us to remain long on one line. I recollect how dissatified he was with an article of mine in the *London Review*,[10] which Blanco White, good-humouredly, only called platonic. When I was diverging from him (which he did not like), I thought of dedicating my first book to him, in words to the effect that he had not only taught me to think, but to think for myself. He left Oxford in 1831; after that, as far as I can recollect, I never saw him but twice — when he visited the University; once in the street, once in a room. From the time that he left, I have always felt a real affection for what I must call his memory; for thenceforward he made himself dead to me. My reason told me that it was impossible that we could have got on together longer; yet I loved him too much to bid him farewell without pain. After a few years had passed, I began to believe that his influence on me in a higher respect than intellectual advance (I will not say through his fault) had not been satisfactory. I believe that he has inserted sharp things in his later works about me. They have never come in my way, and I have not thought it necessary to seek out what would pain me so much in the reading.

What he did for me in point of religious opinion, was first to teach me the existence of the Church, as a substantive body or corporation; next to fix in me those anti-Erastian views of Church polity, which were one of the most prominent features of the Tractarian Movement. On this point, and, as far as I know, on this point alone, he and Hurrell Froude [11] intimately sympathised, though Froude's de-

10 The article was "Poetry, with Reference to Aristotle's *Poetics*."
11 Richard Hurrell Froude (1803–1836), brother of James Anthony Froude.

velopment of opinion here was of a later date. In the year 1826, in
the course of a walk he said much to me about a work then just
published, called "Letters on the Church by an Episcopalian." He
said that it would make my blood boil. It was certainly a most powerful composition. One of our common friends told me, that, after
reading it, he could not keep still, but went on walking up and down
his room. It was ascribed at once to Whately; I gave eager expression to the contrary opinion; but I found the belief of Oxford in the
affirmative to be too strong for me; rightly or wrongly I yielded to
the general voice; and I have never heard, then or since, of any dis-
claimer of authorship on the part of Dr. Whately.

The main positions of this able essay are these; first that Church
and State should be independent of each other: — he speaks of the
duty of protesting "against the profanation of Christ's kingdom, by
that *double usurpation,* the interference of the Church in temporals,
of the State in spirituals" (p. 191); and, secondly, that the Church
may justly and by right retain its property, though separated from
the State. "The clergy," he says, p. 133, "though they ought not
to be the hired servants of the Civil Magistrate, may justly retain
their revenues; and the State, though it has no right of interference in spiritual concerns, not only is justly entitled to support from
the ministers of religion, and from all other Christians, but would,
under the system I am recommending, obtain it much more effectually." The author of this work, whoever he may be, argues out both
these points with great force and ingenuity, and with a thorough-going
vehemence, which perhaps we may refer to the circumstance, that he
wrote, not *in propriâ personâ,* but in the professed character of a
Scotch Episcopalian. His work had a gradual, but a deep effect on
my mind.

I am not aware of any other religious opinion which I owe to Dr.
Whately. For his special theological tenets I had no sympathy. In
the next year, 1827, he told me he considered that I was Arianising.
The case was this: though at that time I had not read Bishop Bull's
Defensio nor the Fathers,[12] I was just then very strong for that ante-
Nicene view of the Trinitarian doctrine, which some writers, both
Catholic and non-Catholic, have accused of wearing a sort of Arian
exterior. This is the meaning of a passage in Froude's Remains, in
which he seems to accuse me of speaking against the Athanasian
Creed. I had contrasted the two aspects of the Trinitarian doctrine,
which are respectively presented by the Athanasian Creed and the
Nicene. My criticisms were to the effect that some of the verses of
the former Creed were unnecessarily scientific. This is a specimen of
a certain disdain for antiquity which had been growing on me now
for several years. It showed itself in some flippant language against

12 George Bull (1634–1710), Anglican theologican, author of *Defensio Fidei
Nicænae.*

the Fathers in the Encyclopædia Metropolitana, about whom I knew little at the time, except what I had learnt as a boy from Joseph Milner. In writing on the Scripture Miracles in 1825–6, I had read Middleton [13] on the Miracles of the early Church, and had imbibed a portion of his spirit.

The truth is, I was beginning to prefer intellectual excellence to moral; I was drifting in the direction of liberalism. I was rudely awakened from my dream at the end of 1827 by two great blows — illness and bereavement.

In the beginning of 1829, came the formal break between Dr. Whately and me; Mr. Peel's attempted re-election was the occasion of it. I think in 1828 or 1827 I had voted in the minority, when the petition to Parliament against the Catholic claims was brought into Convocation. I did so mainly on the views suggested to me by the theory of the Letters of an Episcopalian. Also I disliked the bigoted "two bottle orthodox," as they were invidiously called. I took part against Mr. Peel, on a simple academical, not at all an ecclesiastical or a political ground; and this I professed at the time. I considered that Mr. Peel had taken the University by surprise, that he had no right to call upon us to turn round on a sudden, and to expose ourselves to the imputation of time-serving, and that a great university ought not to be bullied even by a great Duke of Wellington. Also by this time I was under the influence of Keble and Froude; who, in addition to the reasons I have given, disliked the duke's change of policy as dictated by liberalism.

Whately was considerably annoyed at me, and he took a humorous revenge, of which he had given me due notice beforehand. As head of a house, he had duties of hospitality to men of all parties; he asked a set of the least intellectual men in Oxford to dinner, and men most fond of port; he made me one of the party; placed me between Provost this, and Principal that, and then asked me if I was proud of my friends. However, he had a serious meaning in his act; he saw, more clearly than I could do, that I was separating from his own friends for good and all.

Dr. Whately attributed my leaving his *clientela* to a wish on my part to be the head of a party myself. I do not think that it was deserved. My habitual feeling then and since has been, that it was not I who sought friends, but friends who sought me. Never man had kinder or more indulgent friends than I have had, but I expressed my own feeling as to the mode in which I gained them, in this very year 1829, in the course of a copy of verses. Speaking of my blessings, I said, "Blessings of friends, which to my door, *unasked, unhoped*, have come." They have come, they have gone; they came to my great joy, they went to my great grief. He who gave, took away. Dr. Whately's impression about me, however, admits of this explanation: —

13 Conyers Middleton (1683–1750), author of a liberal treatise on *Miracles*.

During the first years of my residence at Oriel, though proud of my college, I was not at home there. I was very much alone, and I used often to take my daily walk by myself. I recollect once meeting Dr. Copleston,[14] then provost, with one of the fellows. He turned round, and with the kind courteousness which sat so well on him, made me a bow and said "Nunquam minus solus, quàm cùm solus." At that time indeed (from 1823) I had the intimacy of my dear and true friend Dr. Pusey, and could not fail to admire and revere a soul so devoted to the cause of religion, so full of good works, so faithful in his affections; but he left residence when I was getting to know him well. As to Dr. Whately himself, he was too much my superior to allow of my being at my ease with him; and to no one in Oxford at this time did I open my heart fully and familiarly. But things changed in 1826. At that time I became one of the tutors of my college, and this gave me position; besides, I had written one or two essays which had been well received. I began to be known. I preached my first University sermon. Next year I was one of the public examiners for the B.A. degree. It was to me like the feeling of spring weather after winter; and, if I may so speak, I came out of my shell; I remained out of it till 1841.

The two persons who knew me best at that time are still alive, beneficed clergymen, no longer my friends. They could tell better than any one else what I was in those years. From this time my tongue was, as it were, loosened, and I spoke spontaneously and without effort. A shrewd man, who knew me at this time, said, "Here is a man who, when he is silent, will never begin to speak; and when he once begins to speak, will never stop." It was at this time that I began to have influence, which steadily increased for a course of years. I gained upon my pupils, and was in particular intimate and affectionate with two of our probationer fellows, Robert I. Wilberforce [15] (afterwards archdeacon) and Richard Hurrell Froude. Whately then, an acute man, perhaps saw around me the signs of an incipient party of which I was not conscious myself. And thus we discern the first elements of that movement afterwards called Tractarian.

The true and primary author of it, however, as is usual with great motive-powers, was out of sight. Having carried off as a mere boy the highest honours of the university, he had turned from the admiration which haunted his steps, and sought for a better and holier satisfaction in pastoral work in the country. Need I say that I am speaking of John Keble? The first time that I was in a room with him was on occasion of my election to a fellowship at Oriel, when I was sent for into the tower, to shake hands with the provost and

14 Edward Copleston (1776–1849), Provost of Oriel College, Bishop of Llandaff, and Dean of St. Paul's.

15 Robert Isaacs Wilberforce (1802–1857), son of a leading Evangelical, joined the Roman Catholic Church.

fellows. How is that hour fixed in my memory after the changes of
forty-two years, forty-two this very day on which I write! I have
lately had a letter in my hands, which I sent at the time to my
great friend, John Bowden,[16] with whom I passed almost exclusively
my undergraduate years. "I had to hasten to the tower," I say to
him, "to receive the congratulations of all the fellows. I bore it till
Keble took my hand, and then felt so abashed and unworthy of the
honour done me, that I seemed desirous of quite sinking into the
ground." His had been the first name which I had heard spoken
of, with reverence rather than admiration, when I came up to Oxford.
When one day I was walking in High Street with my dear earliest
friend just mentioned, with what eagerness did he cry out, "There's
Keble!" and with what awe did I look at him! Then at another time
I heard a master of arts of my college give an account how he had
just then had occasion to introduce himself on some business to
Keble, and how gentle, courteous, and unaffected Keble had been,
so as almost to put him out of countenance. Then too it was reported,
truly or falsely, how a rising man of brilliant reputation, the present
Dean of St. Paul's, Dr. Milman, admired and loved him, adding,
that somehow he was unlike any one else. However, at the time
when I was elected Fellow of Oriel he was not in residence, and he
was shy of me for years in consequence of the marks which I bore
upon me of the evangelical and liberal schools. At least so I have
ever thought. Hurrell Froude brought us together about 1828: it
is one of the sayings preserved in his "Remains," — "Do you know
the story of the murderer who had done one good thing in his life?
Well; if I was ever asked what good deed I had ever done, I should
say that I had brought Keble and Newman to understand each other."

The Christian Year made its appearance in 1827. It is not necessary, and scarcely becoming, to praise a book which has already become one of the classics of the language. When the general tone of
religious literature was so nerveless and impotent, as it was at that
time, Keble struck an original note and woke up in the hearts of
thousands a new music, the music of a school, long unknown in England. Nor can I pretend to analyse, in my own instance, the effect
of religious teaching so deep, so pure, so beautiful. I have never
till now tried to do so; yet I think I am not wrong in saying, that the
two main intellectual truths which it brought home to me, were the
same two, which I had learned from Butler, though recast in the
creative mind of my new master. The first of these was what may
be called, in a large sense of the word, the sacramental system; that
is, the doctrine that material phenomena are both the types and the
instruments of real things unseen, — a doctrine, which embraces,
not only what Anglicans, as well as Catholics, believe about sacra-

16 John William Bowden (1798–1844), author of a *Life of Gregory VII.*

ments properly so called; but also the article of "the Communion of Saints" in its fullness; and likewise the mysteries of the faith. The connection of this philosophy of religion with what is sometimes called "Berkeleyism" has been mentioned above; I knew little of Berkeley at this time except by name; nor have I ever studied him.

On the second intellectual principle which I gained from Mr. Keble, I could say a great deal; if this were the place for it. It runs through very much that I have written, and has gained for me many hard names. Butler teaches us that probability is the guide of life. The danger of this doctrine, in the case of many minds, is, its tendency to destroy in them absolute certainty, leading them to consider every conclusion as doubtful, and resolving truth into an opinion, which it is safe to obey or to profess, but not possible to embrace with full internal assent. If this were to be allowed, then the celebrated saying, "O God, if there be a God, save my soul, if I have a soul;" would be the highest measure of devotion: — but who can really pray to a being, about whose existence he is seriously in doubt?

I considered that Mr. Keble met this difficulty by ascribing the firmness of assent which we give to religious doctrine, not to the probabilities which introduced it, but to the living power of faith and love which accepted it. In matters of religion, he seemed to say, it is not merely probability which makes us intellectually certain, but probability as it is put to account by faith and love. It is faith and love which give to probability a force which it has not in itself. Faith and love are directed towards an object; in the vision of that object they live; it is that object, received in faith and love, which renders it reasonable to take probability as sufficient for internal conviction. Thus the argument about probability, in the matter of religion, became an argument from personality, which in fact is one form of the argument from authority.

In illustration, Mr. Keble used to quote the words of the psalm: "I will guide thee with mine *eye*. Be ye not like to horse and mule, which have no understanding; whose mouths must be held with bit and bridle, lest they fall upon thee." This is the very difference, he used to say, between slaves, and friends or children. Friends do not ask for literal commands; but, from their knowledge of the speaker, they understand his half-words, and from love of him they anticipate his wishes. Hence it is, that in his poem for St. Bartholomew's Day, he speaks of the "Eye of God's word"; and in the note quotes Mr. Miller, of Worcester College, who remarks, in his Bampton lectures, on the special power of Scripture, as having "this eye, like that of a portrait, uniformly fixed upon us, turn where we will." The view thus suggested by Mr. Keble, is brought forward in one of the earliest of the "Tracts for the Times." In No. 8 I say, "The Gospel is a Law

of Liberty. We are treated as sons, not as servants; not subjected
to a code of formal commandments, but addressed as those who love
God, and wish to please Him."

I did not at all dispute this view of the matter, for I made use of
it myself; but I was dissatisfied, because it did not go to the root
of the difficulty. It was beautiful and religious, but it did not even
profess to be logical; and accordingly I tried to complete it by considerations of my own, which are implied in my University sermons,
Essay on Ecclesiastical Miracles, and Essay on Development of Doctrine. My argument is in outline as follows: that that absolute certitude which we were able to possess, whether as to the truths of
natural theology, or as to the fact of a revelation, was the result of an
assemblage of concurring and converging probabilities, and that, both
according to the constitution of the human mind and the will of its
Maker; that certitude was a habit of mind, that certainty was a quality
of propositions; that probabilities which did not reach to logical certainty, might create a mental certitude; that the certitude thus created
might equal in measure and strength the certitude which was created
by the strictest scientific demonstration; and that to have such certitude might in given cases and to given individuals be a plain duty,
though not to others in other circumstances: —

Moreover, that as there were probabilities which sufficed to create
certitude, so there were other probabilities which were legitimately
adapted to create opinion; that it might be quite as much a matter
of duty in given cases and to given persons to have about a fact an
opinion of a definite strength and consistency, as in the case of
greater or of more numerous probabilities it was a duty to have a
certitude; that accordingly we were bound to be more or less sure,
on a sort of (as it were) graduated scale of assent, viz. according as
the probabilities attaching to a professed fact were brought home
to us, and, as the case might be, to entertain about it a pious belief,
or a pious opinion, or a religious conjecture, or at least, a tolerance
of such belief, or opinion, or conjecture in others; that on the other
hand, as it was a duty to have a belief, of more or less strong texture,
in given cases, so in other cases it was a duty not to believe, not to
opine, not to conjecture, not even to tolerate the notion that a professed fact was true, inasmuch as it would be credulity or superstition,
or some other moral fault, to do so. This was the region of private
judgment in religion; that is, of a private judgment, not formed
arbitrarily and according to one's fancy or liking, but conscientiously,
and under a sense of duty.

Considerations such as these throw a new light on the subject of
Miracles, and they seem to have led me to reconsider the view which
I took of them in my essay in 1825-6. I do not know what was the
date of this change in me, nor of the train of ideas on which it was

founded. That there had been already great miracles, as those of
Scripture, as the Resurrection, was a fact establishing the principle
that the laws of nature had sometimes been suspended by their
Divine Author; and since what had happened once might happen
again, a certain probability, at least no kind of improbability, was
attached to the idea, taken in itself, of miraculous intervention in
later times, and miraculous accounts were to be regarded in connection with the verisimilitude, scope, instrument, character, testimony,
and circumstances, with which they presented themselves to us; and,
according to the final result of those various considerations, it was
our duty to be sure, or to believe, or to opine, or to surmise, or to
tolerate, or to reject, or to denounce. The main difference between
my essay on Miracles in 1826 and my essay in 1842 is this: that in
1826 I considered that miracles were sharply divided into two classes,
those which were to be received, and those which were to be rejected;
whereas in 1842 I saw that they were to be regarded according to
their greater or less probability, which was in some cases sufficient
to create certitude about them, in other cases only belief or opinion.

Moreover, the argument from analogy, on which this view of the
question was founded, suggested to me something besides, in recommendation of the ecclesiastical miracles. It fastened itself upon the
theory of church history which I had learned as a boy from Joseph
Milner. It is Milner's doctrine, that upon the visible Church come
down from above, from time to time, large and temporary *Effusions*
of divine grace. This is the leading idea of his work. He begins by
speaking of the Day of Pentecost, as marking "the first of those *Effusions* of the Spirit of God, which from age to age have visited the
earth since the coming of Christ" (vol. i. p. 3). In a note he adds
that "in the term 'Effusion' there is not here included the idea of the
miraculous or extraordinary operations of the Spirit of God"; but
still it was natural for me, admitting Milner's general theory, and
applying to it the principle of analogy, not to stop short at his abrupt
ipse dixit,[17] but boldly to pass forward to the conclusion, on other
grounds plausible, that, as miracles accompanied the first effusion of
grace, so they might accompany the later. It is surely a natural and on
the whole, a true anticipation (though of course there are exceptions
in particular cases), that gifts and graces go together; now, according to the ancient Catholic doctrine, the gift of miracles was viewed as
the attendant and shadow of transcendent sanctity: and moreover, as
such sanctity was not of every day's occurrence, nay further, as one
period of church history differed widely from another, and, as Joseph
Milner would say, there had been generations or centuries of degeneracy or disorder, and times of revival, and as one region might be in
the mid-day of religious fervour, and another in twilight or gloom,
there was no force in the popular argument, that, because we did

17 "he himself has said it."

not see miracles with our own eyes, miracles had not happened in former times, or were not now at this very time taking place in distant places: — but I must not dwell longer on a subject, to which in a few words it is impossible to do justice.

Hurrell Froude was a pupil of Keble's, formed by him, and in turn reacting upon him. I knew him first in 1826, and was in the closest and most affectionate friendship with him from about 1829 till his death in 1836. He was a man of the highest gifts — so truly many-sided, that it would be presumptuous in me to attempt to describe him, except under those aspects, in which he came before me. Nor have I here to speak of the gentleness and tenderness of nature, the playfulness, the free elastic force and graceful versatility of mind, and the patient winning considerateness in discussion, which endeared him to those to whom he opened his heart; for I am all along engaged upon matters of belief and opinion, and am introducing others into my narrative, not for their own sake, or because I love and have loved them, so much as because, and so far as, they have influenced my theological views. In this respect then, I speak of Hurrell Froude — in his intellectual aspect — as a man of high genius, brimful and overflowing with ideas and views, in him original, which were too many and strong even for his bodily strength, and which crowded and jostled against each other in their effort after distinct shape and expression. And he had an intellect as critical and logical as it was speculative and bold. Dying prematurely, as he did, and in the conflict and transition-state of opinion, his religious views never reached their ultimate conclusion, by the very reason of their multitude and their depth. His opinions arrested and influenced me, even when they did not gain my assent. He professed openly his admiration of the Church of Rome, and his hatred of the reformers. He delighted in the notion of an hierarchical system, of sacerdotal power and of full ecclesiastical liberty. He felt scorn of the maxim, "The Bible and the Bible only is the religion of Protestants"; and he gloried in accepting tradition as a main instrument of religious teaching. He had a high severe idea of the intrinsic excellence of virginity; and he considered the Blessed Virgin its great pattern. He delighted in thinking of the saints; he had a keen appreciation of the idea of sanctity, its possibility and its heights; and he was more than inclined to believe a large amount of miraculous interference as occurring in the early and middle ages. He embraced the principle of penance and mortification. He had a deep devotion to the Real Presence, in which he had a firm faith. He was powerfully drawn to the medieval church, but not to the primitive.

He had a keen insight into abstract truth; but he was an Englishman to the backbone in his severe adherence to the real and the concrete. He had a most classical taste, and a genius for philosophy and art; and he was fond of historical inquiry, and the politics of religion. He had no turn for theology as such. He had no appreciation of the writings of the Fathers, of the detail or development of doctrine, of the definite traditions of the Church viewed in their matter, of the teaching of the ecumenical councils, or of the controversies out of which they arose. He took an eager, courageous view of things on the whole. ı should say that his power of entering into the minds of others did not equal his other gifts; he could not believe, for instance, that I really held the Roman Church to be Antichristian. On many points he would not believe but that I agreed with him, when I did not. He seemed not to understand my difficulties. His were of a different kind, the contrariety between theory and fact. He was a high Tory of the cavalier stamp, and was disgusted with the Toryism of the opponents of the Reform Bill. He was smitten with the love of the theocratic church; he went abroad and was shocked by the degeneracy which he thought he saw in the Catholics of Italy.

It is difficult to enumerate the precise additions to my theological creed which I derived from a friend to whom I owe so much. He made me look with admiration towards the Church of Rome, and in the same degree to dislike the Reformation. He fixed deep in me the idea of devotion to the Blessed Virgin, and he led me gradually to believe in the Real Presence.

There is one remaining source of my opinions to be mentioned, and that far from the least important. In proportion as I moved out of the shadow of liberalism which had hung over my course, my early devotion towards the fathers returned; and in the long vacation of 1828 I set about to read them chronologically, beginning with St. Ignatius and St. Justin. About 1830 a proposal was made to me by Mr. Hugh Rose, who with Mr. Lyall [18] (afterwards Dean of Canterbury) was providing writers for a theological library, to furnish them with a history of the principal councils. I accepted it, and at once set to work on the Council of Nicæa. It was launching myself on an ocean with currents innumerable; and I was drifted back first to the ante-Nicene history, and then to the Church of Alexandria. The work at last appeared under the title of "The Arians of the Fourth Century"; and of its 422 pages, the first 117 consisted of introductory matter, and the Council of Nicæa did not appear till the 254th, and then occupied at most twenty pages.

I do not know when I first learnt to consider that antiquity was the true exponent of the doctrines of Christianity and the basis of the Church of England; but I take it for granted that Bishop Bull, whose works at this time I read, was my chief introduction to this principle.

18 Hugh James Rose (1795–1838) and William Rowe Lyall (1788–1857), the former a theologian connected with the beginnings of Tractarianism, the latter editor of the *Theological Library*.

The course of reading which I pursued in the composition of my work was directly adapted to develop it in my mind. What principally attracted me in the ante-Nicene period was the great Church of Alexandria, the historical centre of teaching in those times. Of Rome for some centuries comparatively little is known. The battle of Arianism was first fought in Alexandria; Athanasius, the champion of the truth, was Bishop of Alexandria; and in his writings he refers to the great religious names of an earlier date, to Origen, Dionysius, and others who were the glory of its see, or of its school. The broad philosophy of Clement and Origen carried me away; the philosophy, not the theological doctrine; and I have drawn out some features of it in my volume, with the zeal and freshness, but with the partiality of a neophyte. Some portions of their teaching, magnificent in themselves, came like music to my inward ear, as if the response to ideas, which, with little external to encourage them, I had cherished so long. These were based on the mystical or sacramental principle, and spoke of the various economies or dispensations of the eternal. I understood them to mean that the exterior world, physical and historical, was but the outward manifestation of realities greater than itself. Nature was a parable: Scripture was an allegory: pagan literature, philosophy, and mythology, properly understood, were but a preparation for the Gospel. The Greek poets and sages were in a certain sense prophets; for "thoughts beyond their thought to those high bards were given." There had been a divine dispensation granted to the Jews; there had been in some sense a dispensation carried on in favour of the Gentiles. He who had taken the seed of Jacob for His elect people, had not therefore cast the rest of mankind out of His sight. In the fullness of time both Judaism and Paganism had come to nought; the outward framework, which concealed yet suggested the living truth, had never been intended to last, and it was dissolving under the beams of the sun of justice behind it and through it. The process of change had been slow; it had been done not rashly, but by rule, and measure, "at sundry times and in divers manners," first one disclosure and then another, till the whole was brought into full manifestation. And thus room was made for the anticipation of further and deeper disclosures, of truths still under the veil of the letter, and in their season to be revealed. The visible world still remains without its divine interpretation; Holy Church in her sacraments and her hierarchical appointments, will remain even to the end of the world, only a symbol of those heavenly facts which fill eternity. Her mysteries are but the expressions in human language of truths to which the human mind is unequal. It is evident how much there was in all this in correspondence with the thoughts which had attracted me when I was young, and with the doctrine which I have already connected with the Analogy and the Christian Year.

I suppose it was to the Alexandrian school and to the early church that I owe in particular what I definitely held about the angels. I viewed them, not only as the ministers employed by the Creator in the Jewish and Christian dispensations, as we find on the face of Scripture, but as carrying on, as Scripture also implies, the economy of the visible world. I considered them as the real causes of motion, light, and life, and of those elementary principles of the physical universe, which, when offered in their developments to our senses, suggest to us the notion of cause and effect, and of what are called the laws of nature. I have drawn out this doctrine in my sermon for Michaelmas day, written not later than 1834. I say of the angels, "Every breath of air and ray of light and heat, every beautiful prospect is, as it were, the skirts of their garments, the waving of the robes of those whose faces see God." Again, I ask what would be the thoughts of a man who, "when examining a flower, or a herb, or a pebble, or a ray of light, which he treats as something so beneath him in the scale of existence, suddenly discovered that he was in the presence of some powerful being who was hidden behind the visible things he was inspecting, who, though concealing his wise hand, was giving them their beauty, grace, and perfection, as being God's instrument for the purpose, nay, whose robe and ornaments those objects were, which he was so eager to analyse?" and I therefore remark that "we may say with grateful and simple hearts with the Three Holy Children, 'O all ye works of the Lord, etc., etc., bless ye the Lord, praise Him, and magnify Him for ever.'"

Also, besides the hosts of evil spirits, I considered there was a middle race, δαιμόνια, neither in heaven, nor in hell; partially fallen, capricious, wayward; noble or crafty, benevolent or malicious, as the case might be. They gave a sort of inspiration or intelligence to races, nations, and classes of men. Hence the action of bodies politic and associations, which is so different often from that of the individuals who compose them. Hence the character and the instinct of states and governments, of religious communities and communions. I thought they were inhabited by unseen intelligences. My preference of the personal to the abstract would naturally lead me to this view. I thought it countenanced by the mention of "the Prince of Persia" in the Prophet Daniel, and I think I considered that it was of such intermediate beings that the Apocalypse spoke, when it introduced "the Angels of the Seven Churches."

In 1837 I made a further development of this doctrine. I said to my great friend, Samuel Francis Wood, in a letter which came into my hands on his death, "I have an idea. The mass of the Fathers (Justin, Athenagoras,[19] Irenæus,[20] Clement, Tertullian, Origen, Lactantius,[21]

[19] Athenagoras was a second-century Christian apologist.
[20] Irenæus was a Greek Father of the Church.
[21] Lactantius Firmianus was a theological writer and preacher of the 3rd and 4th centuries.

Sulpicius,[22] Ambrose, Nazianzen [23]), hold that, though Satan fell from the beginning, the Angels fell before the deluge, falling in love with the daughters of men. This has lately come across me as a remarkable solution of a notion which I cannot help holding. Daniel speaks as if each nation had its guardian Angel. I cannot but think that there are beings with a great deal of good in them, yet with great defects, who are the animating principles of certain institutions, etc., etc. . . . Take England, with many high virtues, and yet a low Catholicism. It seems to me that John Bull is a spirit neither of heaven nor hell. . . . Has not the Christian Church, in its parts, surrendered itself to one or other of these simulations of the truth? . . . How are we to avoid Scylla and Charybdis and go straight on to the very image of Christ?" etc., etc.

I am aware that what I have been saying will, with many men, be doing credit to my imagination at the expense of my judgment — "Hippoclides doesn't care;" [24] I am not setting myself up as a pattern of good sense or of anything else: I am but vindicating myself from the charge of dishonesty. — There is indeed another view of the economy brought out, in the course of the same dissertation on the subject, in my History of the Arians, which has afforded matter for the latter imputation; but I reserve it for the concluding portion of my reply.

While I was engaged in writing my work upon the Arians, great events were happening at home and abroad, which brought out into form and passionate expression the various beliefs which had so gradually been winning their way into my mind. Shortly before, there had been a revolution in France; the Bourbons had been dismissed: and I believed that it was unchristian for nations to cast off their governors, and, much more, sovereigns who had the divine right of inheritance. Again, the great Reform agitation was going on around me as I wrote. The Whigs had come into power; Lord Grey had told the bishops to set their house in order, and some of the prelates had been insulted and threatened in the streets of London. The vital question was how were we to keep the Church from being liberalised? there was such apathy on the subject in some quarters, such imbecile alarm in others; the true principles of churchmanship seemed so radically decayed, and there was such distraction in the councils of the clergy. The Bishop of London of the day, an active and openhearted man, had been for years engaged in diluting the high orthodoxy of the Church by the introduction of the Evangelical body into places of influence and trust. He had deeply offended men who

22 Sulpicius Severus was an ecclesiastical writer of the 4th and 5th centuries.
23 St. Gregory of Nazianzus, fourth-century Father of the Eastern Church, was a vigorous opponent of Arianism.
24 According to Herodotus, this is what Hippoclides said when his would-be father-in-law told him that his foolishness had lost him his bride.

agreed with myself, by an off-hand saying (as it was reported) to the effect that belief in the Apostolical succession had gone out with the non-jurors.[25] "We can count you," he said to some of the gravest and most venerated persons of the old school. And the Evangelical party itself seemed, with their late successes, to have lost that simplicity and unworldliness which I admired so much in Milner and Scott. It was not that I did not venerate such men as the then Bishop of Lichfield, and others of similar sentiments, who were not yet promoted out of the ranks of the clergy, but I thought little of them as a class. I thought they played into the hands of the Liberals. With the establishment thus divided and threatened, thus ignorant of its true strength, I compared that fresh vigorous power of which I was reading in the first centuries. In her triumphant zeal on behalf of that primeval mystery, to which I had had so great a devotion from my youth, I recognised the movement of my Spiritual Mother. "Incessu patuit Dea." [26] The self-conquest of her ascetics, the patience of her martyrs, the irresistible determination of her bishops, the joyous swing of her advance, both exalted and abashed me. I said to myself, "Look on this picture and on that;" I felt affection for my own Church, but not tenderness; I felt dismay at her prospects, anger and scorn at her do-nothing perplexity. I thought that if Liberalism once got a footing within her, it was sure of the victory in the event. I saw that Reformation principles were powerless to rescue her. As to leaving her, the thought never crossed my imagination; still I ever kept before me that there was something greater than the Established Church, and that that was the Church Catholic and Apostolic, set up from the beginning, of which she was but the local presence and organ. She was nothing, unless she was this. She must be dealt with strongly, or she would be lost. There was need of a second Reformation.

At this time I was disengaged from college duties, and my health had suffered from the labour involved in the composition of my volume. It was ready for the press in July 1832, though not published till the end of 1833. I was easily persuaded to join Hurrell Froude and his father, who were going to the south of Europe for the health of the former.

We set out in December 1832. It was during this expedition that my verses which are in the Lyra Apostolica were written; — a few indeed before it, but not more than one or two of them after it. Exchanging, as I was, definite tutorial labours, and the literary quiet and pleasant friendships of the last six years, for foreign countries and an unknown future, I naturally was led to think that some inward changes, as well as some larger course of action, was coming

25 English and Scottish clergymen with benefices who refused to take the oath of allegiance to William and Mary and their successors.
26 "The goddess stood revealed by her walk."

upon me. At Whitchurch, while waiting for the down mail to
Falmouth, I wrote the verses about my Guardian Angel, which begin
with these words: "Are these the tracks of some unearthly Friend?"
and go on to speak of "the vision" which haunted me: — that vision
is more or less brought out in the whole series of these compositions.

I went to various coasts of the Mediterranean, parted with my
friends at Rome; went down for the second time to Sicily, at the end
of April, and got back to England by Palermo in the early part of
July. The strangeness of foreign life threw me back into myself;
I found pleasure in historical sites and beautiful scenes, not in men
and manners. We kept clear of Catholics throughout our tour. I
had a conversation with the Dean of Malta, a most pleasant man,
lately dead; but it was about the fathers, and the library of the great
church. I knew the Abbate Santini, at Rome, who did no more than
copy for me the Gregorian tones. Froude and I made two calls
upon Monsignore (now Cardinal) Wiseman at the Collegio Inglese,
shortly before we left Rome. I do not recollect being in a room with
any other ecclesiastics, except a priest at Castro-Giovanni in Sicily,
who called on me when I was ill, and with whom I wished to hold
a controversy. As to church services, we attended the Tenebræ, at
the Sestine, for the sake of the Miserere; and that was all. My general feeling was, "All, save the spirit of man, is divine." I saw
nothing but what was external; of the hidden life of Catholics I knew
nothing. I was still more driven back into myself, and felt my isolation. England was in my thoughts solely, and the news from England came rarely and imperfectly. The Bill for the Suppression of
the Irish Sees was in progress, and filled my mind. I had fierce
thoughts against the Liberals.

It was the success of the Liberal cause which fretted me inwardly.
I became fierce against its instruments and its manifestations. A
French vessel was at Algiers; I would not even look at the tricolour.
On my return, though forced to stop a day in Paris, I kept indoors
the whole time, and all that I saw of that beautiful city, was what
I saw from the diligence. The Bishop of London had already sounded
me as to my filling one of the Whitehall preacherships, which he had
just then put on a new footing; but I was indignant at the line which
he was taking, and from my steamer I had sent home a letter declining the appointment by anticipation, should it be offered to me.
At this time I was specially annoyed with Dr. Arnold,[27] though it did
not last into later years. Some one, I think, asked in conversation at
Rome, whether a certain interpretation of Scripture was Christian?
it was answered that Dr. Arnold took it; I interposed, "But is *he* a
Christian?" The subject went out of my head at once; when afterwards I was taxed with it I could say no more in explanation, than

27 Thomas Arnold of Rugby (1795–1842), father of Matthew Arnold, an
educational and religious reformer with liberal views.

that I thought I must have been alluding to some free views of Dr. Arnold about the Old Testament: — I thought I must have meant, "But who is to answer for Arnold?" It was at Rome too that we began the Lyra Apostolica which appeared monthly in the *British Magazine*. The motto shows the feeling of both Froude and myself at the time: we borrowed from M. Bunsen [28] a Homer, and Froude chose the words in which Achilles, on returning to the battle, says, "You shall know the difference, now that I am back again."

Especially when I was left by myself, the thought came upon me that deliverance is wrought, not by the many but by the few, not by bodies but by persons. Now it was, I think, that I repeated to myself the words, which had ever been dear to me from my school days, "Exoriare aliquis!" [29] — now too, that Southey's beautiful poem of Thalaba, for which I had an immense liking, came forcibly to my mind. I began to think that I had a mission. There are sentences of my letters to my friends to this effect, if they are not destroyed. When we took leave of Monsignore Wiseman, he had courteously expressed a wish that we might make a second visit to Rome; I said with great gravity, "We have a work to do in England." I went down at once to Sicily, and the presentiment grew stronger. I struck into the middle of the island, and fell ill of a fever at Leonforte. My servant thought that I was dying, and begged for my last directions. I gave them, as he wished; but I said, "I shall not die." I repeated, "I shall not die, for I have not sinned against light, I have not sinned against light." I never have been able to make out at all what I meant.

I got to Castro-Giovanni, and was laid up there for nearly three weeks. Towards the end of May I set off for Palermo, taking three days for the journey. Before starting from my inn in the morning of May 26th or 27th, I sat down on my bed, and began to sob bitterly. My servant, who had acted as my nurse, asked what ailed me. I could only answer, "I have a work to do in England."

I was aching to get home; yet for want of a vessel I was kept at Palermo for three weeks. I began to visit the churches, and they calmed my impatience, though I did not attend any services. I knew nothing of the presence of the Blessed Sacrament there. At last I got off in an orange boat, bound for Marseilles. We were becalmed a whole week in the Straits of Bonifacio. Then it was that I wrote the lines, "Lead, kindly light," which have since become well known. I was writing verses the whole time of my passage. At length I got to Marseilles, and set off for England. The fatigue of travelling was too much for me, and I was laid up for several days at Lyons. At last I got off again, and did not stop night or day till I reached

28 Christian Charles Josias, Baron von Bunsen (1791–1860), Prussian diplomat and scholar, envoy to the Papal court.
29 "May someone arise!"

England, and my mother's house. My brother had arrived from
Persia only a few hours before. This was on the Tuesday. The following Sunday, July 14th, Mr. Keble preached the assize sermon in
the University pulpit. It was published under the title of "National
Apostasy." I have ever considered and kept the day as the start of
the religious movement of 1833.

John Stuart Mill

JOHN STUART MILL

CHRONOLOGY

1806   Born May 20 in London.

1809–1820   Educated by his father, James Mill.

1820–1821   Spent six months in southern France with the family of the brother of Jeremy Bentham.

1823   Became a clerk with the East India Company.

1824   Became a chief contributor to the *Westminster Review,* organ of the "philosophical radicals."

1825   Founded the "Speculative Society."

1826   Experienced a mental crisis.

1830–1831   Visited Paris after the Revolution of July 1830; met Mrs. Taylor in London.

1835   Became editor of the *London Review.*

1836–1840   Editor of the *London and Westminster Review.*

1838–1840   Published significant essays on Bentham and Coleridge.

1843   Published the *System of Logic.*

1848   Published *Principles of Political Economy.*

1851   Married Mrs. Taylor.

1857   Retired from the East India Company, at its dissolution, with a pension of £1,500 a year.

1859   Published *On Liberty* and *Thoughts on Parliamentary Reform.*

1861   Published *Representative Government.*

1863   Published *Utilitarianism.*

1865   Entered Parliament for Westminster.

1869   Published *The Subjection of Women.*

1873   Died May 8.

Posthumously published: *Autobiography,* 1873; *Three Essays on Religion,* 1874; *Chapters on Socialism,* in the *Fortnightly Review,* 1879.

On Liberty

⟪ *On Liberty* consists of five chapters: I. "Introductory"; II. "Of the Liberty of Thought and Discussion"; III. "Of Individuality, As One of the Elements of Well-Being"; IV. "Of the Limits to the Authority of Society over the Individual"; V. "Applications." The second and third chapters, the finest part of the book, are here printed. In the first chapter Mill stated that his object in *On Liberty* was "to assert one very simple principle, as entitled to govern absolutely the dealings of society with the individual in the way of compulsion and control, whether the means used be physical force in the form of legal penalties, or the moral coercion of public opinion. That principle is, that the sole end for which mankind are warranted, individually or collectively, in interfering with the liberty of action of any of their number, is self-protection. That the only purpose for which power can be rightfully exercised over any member of a civilized community, against his will, is to prevent harm to others." *On Liberty* is a major document in the long Victorian discussion of the relation of the individual to the group and a fine illustration of the "enlightenment" of Mill's utilitarianism. ⟫

CHAPTER II

Of the Liberty of Thought and Discussion

THE time, it is to be hoped, is gone by, when any defence would be necessary of the "liberty of the press" as one of the securities against corrupt or tyrannical government. No argument, we may suppose, can now be needed, against permitting a legislature or an executive, not identified in interest with the people, to prescribe opinions to them, and determine what doctrines or what arguments they shall be allowed to hear. This aspect of the question, besides, has been so often and so triumphantly enforced by preceding writers, that it needs not be specially insisted on in this place. Though the law of England, on the subject of the press, is as servile to this day as it was in the time of the Tudors, there is little danger of its being actually put in force against political discussion, except during some temporary panic, when fear of insurrection drives ministers and judges from their propriety; [1] and, speaking generally, it is not, in

---

[1] These words had scarcely been written, when, as if to give them an emphatic contradiction, occurred the Government Press Prosecutions of 1858. That ill-judged interference with the liberty of public discussion has not, however, induced me to alter a single word in the text, nor has it at all weakened my conviction that, moments of panic excepted, the era of pains and penalties for political discussion has, in our own country, passed away. For, in the first place, the prosecutions were not persisted in; and, in the second, they were never, properly speaking, political prosecutions. The offence charged was not that of

251

constitutional countries, to be apprehended, that the government, whether completely responsible to the people or not, will often attempt to control the expression of opinion, except when in doing so it makes itself the organ of the general intolerance of the public. Let us suppose, therefore, that the government is entirely at one with the people, and never thinks of exerting any power of coercion unless in agreement with what it conceives to be their voice. But I deny the right of the people to exercise such coercion, either by themselves or by their government. The power itself is illegitimate. The best government has no more title to it than the worst. It is as noxious, or more noxious, when exerted in accordance with public opinion, than when in opposition to it. If all mankind minus one, were of one opinion, and only one person were of the contrary opinion, mankind would be no more justified in silencing that one person, than he, if he had the power, would be justified in silencing mankind. Were an opinion a personal possession of no value except to the owner; if to be obstructed in the enjoyment of it were simply a private injury, it would make some difference whether the injury was inflicted only on a few persons or on many. But the peculiar evil of silencing the expression of an opinion is, that it is robbing the human race; posterity as well as the existing generation; those who dissent from the opinion, still more than those who hold it. If the opinion is right, they are deprived of the opportunity of exchanging error for truth; if wrong, they lose, what is almost as great a benefit, the clearer perception and livelier impression of truth, produced by its collision with error.

It is necessary to consider separately these two hypotheses, each of which has a distinct branch of the argument corresponding to it. We can never be sure that the opinion we are endeavouring to stifle is a false opinion; and if we were sure, stifling it would be an evil still.

---

criticizing institutions, or the acts or persons of rulers, but of circulating what was deemed an immoral doctrine, the lawfulness of Tyrannicide.

If the arguments of the present chapter are of any validity, there ought to exist the fullest liberty of professing and discussing, as a matter of ethical conviction, any doctrine, however immoral it may be considered. It would, therefore, be irrelevant and out of place to examine here, whether the doctrine of Tyrannicide deserves that title. I shall content myself with saying that the subject has been at all times one of the open questions of morals; that the act of a private citizen in striking down a criminal, who, by raising himself above the law, has placed himself beyond the reach of legal punishment or control, has been accounted by whole nations, and by some of the best and wisest of men, not a crime, but an act of exalted virtue; and that, right or wrong, it is not of the nature of assassination, but of civil war. As such, I hold that the instigation to it, in a specific case, may be a proper subject of punishment, but only if an overt act has followed, and at least a probable connexion can be established between the act and the instigation. Even then, it is not a foreign government, but the very government assailed, which alone, in the exercise of self-defence, can legitimately punish attacks directed against its own existence. [Mill's note.]

First: the opinion which it is attempted to suppress by authority may possibly be true. Those who desire to suppress it, of course deny its truth; but they are not infallible. They have no authority to decide the question for all mankind, and exclude every other person from the means of judging. To refuse a hearing to an opinion, because they are sure that it is false, is to assume that *their* certainty is the same thing as *absolute* certainty. All silencing of discussion is an assumption of infallibility. Its condemnation may be allowed to rest on this common argument, not the worse for being common.

Unfortunately for the good sense of mankind, the fact of their fallibility is far from carrying the weight in their practical judgement, which is always allowed to it in theory; for while every one well knows himself to be fallible, few think it necessary to take any precautions against their own fallibility, or admit the supposition that any opinion, of which they feel very certain, may be one of the examples of the error to which they acknowledge themselves to be liable. Absolute princes, or others who are accustomed to unlimited deference, usually feel this complete confidence in their own opinions on nearly all subjects. People more happily situated, who sometimes hear their opinions disputed, and are not wholly unused to be set right when they are wrong, place the same unbounded reliance only on such of their opinions as are shared by all who surround them, or to whom they habitually defer: for in proportion to a man's want of confidence in his own solitary judgement, does he usually repose, with implicit trust, on the infallibility of "the world" in general. And the world, to each individual, means the part of it with which he comes in contact; his party, his sect, his church, his class of society: the man may be called, by comparison, almost liberal and large-minded to whom it means anything so comprehensive as his own country or his own age. Nor is his faith in this collective authority at all shaken by his being aware that other ages, countries, sects, churches, classes, and parties have thought, and even now think, the exact reverse. He devolves upon his own world the responsibility of being in the right against the dissentient worlds of other people; and it never troubles him that mere accident has decided which of these numerous worlds is the object of his reliance, and that the same causes which make him a Churchman in London, would have made him a Buddhist or a Confucian in Pekin. Yet it is as evident in itself, as any amount of argument can make it, that ages are no more infallible than individuals; every age having held many opinions which subsequent ages have deemed not only false but absurd; and it is as certain that many opinions, now general, will be rejected by future ages, as it is that many, once general, are rejected by the present.

The objection likely to be made to this argument would probably take some such form as the following. There is no greater assumption of infallibility in forbidding the propagation of error, than in any other thing which is done by public authority on its own judgement and responsibility. Judgement is given to men that they may use it. Because it may be used erroneously, are men to be told that they ought not to use it at all? To prohibit what they think pernicious, is not claiming exemption from error, but fulfilling the duty incumbent on them, although fallible, of acting on their conscientious conviction. If we were never to act on our opinions, because those opinions may be wrong, we should leave all our interests uncared for, and all our duties unperformed. An objection which applies to all conduct, can be no valid objection to any conduct in particular. It is the duty of governments, and of individuals, to form the truest opinions they can; to form them carefully, and never impose them upon others unless they are quite sure of being right. But when they are sure (such reasoners may say), it is not conscientiousness but cowardice to shrink from acting on their opinions, and allow doctrines which they honestly think dangerous to the welfare of mankind, either in this life or in another, to be scattered abroad without restraint, because other people, in less enlightened times, have persecuted opinions now believed to be true. Let us take care, it may be said, not to make the same mistake: but governments and nations have made mistakes in other things, which are not denied to be fit subjects for the exercise of authority: they have laid on bad taxes, made unjust wars. Ought we therefore to lay on no taxes, and, under whatever provocation, make no wars? Men, and governments, must act to the best of their ability. There is no such thing as absolute certainty, but there is assurance sufficient for the purposes of human life. We may, and must, assume our opinion to be true for the guidance of our own conduct: and it is assuming no more when we forbid bad men to pervert society by the propagation of opinions which we regard as false and pernicious.

I answer, that it is assuming very much more. There is the greatest difference between presuming an opinion to be true, because, with every opportunity for contesting it, it has not been refuted, and assuming its truth for the purpose of not permitting its refutation. Complete liberty of contradicting and disproving our opinion, is the very condition which justifies us in assuming its truth for purposes of action; and on no other terms can a being with human faculties have any rational assurance of being right.

When we consider either the history of opinion, or the ordinary conduct of human life, to what is it to be ascribed that the one and the other are no worse than they are? Not certainly to the inherent force of the human understanding; for, on any matter not self-evident, there are ninety-nine persons totally incapable of judging of it, for one who is capable; and the capacity of the hundredth person is only comparative; for the majority of the eminent men of every past generation held many opinions now known to be erroneous, and did or approved numerous things which no one will now justify. Why is it, then, that there is on the whole a preponderance among mankind of rational opinions and rational conduct? If there really is this preponderance — which there must be unless human affairs are, and have always been, in an almost desperate state — it is owing to a quality of the human mind, the source of everything respectable in man either as an intellectual or as a moral being, namely, that his errors are corrigible. He is capable of rectifying his mistakes, by discussion and experience. Not by experience alone. There must be discussion, to show how experience is to be interpreted. Wrong opinions and practices gradually yield to fact and argument: but facts and arguments, to produce any effect on the mind, must be brought before it. Very few facts are able to tell their own story, without comments to bring out their meaning. The whole strength and value, then, of human judgement, depending on the one property, that it can be set right when it is wrong, reliance can be placed on it only when the means of setting it right are kept constantly at hand. In the case of any person whose judgement is really deserving of confidence, how has it become so? Because he has kept his mind open to criticism of his opinions and conduct. Because it has been his practice to listen to all that could be said against him; to profit by as much of it as was just, and expound to himself, and upon occasion to others, the fallacy of what was fallacious. Because he has felt, that the only way in which a human being can make some approach to knowing the whole of a subject, is by hearing what can be said about it by persons of every variety of opinion, and studying all modes in which it can be looked at by every character of mind. No wise man ever acquired his wisdom in any mode but this; nor is it in the nature of human intellect to become wise in any other manner. The steady habit of correcting and completing his own opinion by collating it with those of others, so far from causing doubt and hesitation in carrying it into practice, is the only stable foundation for a just reliance on it: for, being cognisant of all that can, at least obviously, be said against him, and having taken up his position against all gainsayers — knowing that he has sought for objections and difficulties, instead of avoiding them, and has shut out no light which can be thrown upon the subject from any quarter — he has a right to think his judgement better than that of any person, or any multitude, who have not gone through a similar process.

It is not too much to require that what the wisest of mankind, those who are best entitled to trust their own judgement, find necessary to warrant their relying on it, should be submitted to by that miscellaneous collection of a few wise and many foolish individuals, called the public. The most intolerant of churches, the Roman Catholic Church, even at the canonization of a saint, admits, and listens patiently to, a "devil's advocate." The holiest of men, it appears, cannot be admitted to posthumous honours, until all that the devil could say against him is known and weighed. If even the Newtonian philosophy were not permitted to be questioned, mankind could not feel as complete assurance of its truth as they now do. The beliefs which we have most warrant for, have no safeguard to rest on, but a standing invitation to the whole world to prove them unfounded. If the challenge is not accepted, or is accepted and the attempt fails, we are far enough from certainty still; but we have done the best that the existing state of human reason admits of; we have neglected nothing that could give the truth a chance of reaching us: if the lists are kept open, we may hope that if there be a better truth, it will be found when the human mind is capable of receiving it; and in the meantime we may rely on having attained such approach to truth, as is possible in our own day. This is the amount of certainty attainable by a fallible being, and this the sole way of attaining it.

Strange it is, that men should admit the validity of the arguments for free discussion, but object to their being "pushed to an extreme"; not seeing that unless the reasons are good for an extreme case, they are not good for any case. Strange that they should imagine that they are not assuming infallibility, when they acknowledge that there should be free discussion on all subjects which can possibly be *doubtful,* but think that some particular principle or doctrine should be forbidden to be questioned because it is so *certain,* that is, because *they are certain* that it is certain. To call any proposition certain, while there is any one who would deny its certainty if permitted, but who is not permitted, is to assume that we ourselves, and those who agree with us, are the judges of certainty, and judges without hearing the other side.

In the present age — which has been described as "destitute of faith, but terrified at scepticism" — in which people feel sure, not so much that their opinions are true, as that they should not know what to do without them — the claims of an opinion to be protected from public attack are rested not so much on its truth, as on its importance to society. There are, it is alleged, certain beliefs, so useful, not to say indispensable to well-being, that it is as much the duty of governments to uphold those beliefs, as to protect any other of the interests of society. In a case of such necessity, and so directly in the line of their duty, something less than infallibility may, it is maintained, warrant, and even bind, governments, to act on their own opinion, confirmed by the general opinion of mankind. It is also often argued, and still oftener thought, that none but bad men would desire to weaken these salutary beliefs; and there can be nothing wrong, it is thought, in restraining bad men, and prohibiting what only such men would wish to practise. This mode of thinking makes the justification of restraints on discussion not a question of the truth of doctrines, but of their usefulness; and flatters itself by that means to escape the responsibility of claiming to be an infallible judge of opinions. But those who thus satisfy themselves, do not perceive that the assumption of infallibility is merely shifted from one point to another. The usefulness of an opinion is itself matter of opinion: as disputable, as open to discussion, and requiring discussion as much, as the opinion itself. There is the same need of an infallible judge of opinions to decide an opinion to be noxious, as to decide it to be false, unless the opinion condemned has full opportunity of defending itself. And it will not do to say that the heretic may be allowed to maintain the utility or harmlessness of his opinion, though forbidden to maintain its truth. The truth of an opinion is part of its utility. If we would know whether or not it is desirable that a proposition should be believed, is it possible to exclude the consideration of whether or not it is true? In the opinion, not of bad men, but of the best men, no belief which is contrary to truth can be really useful: and can you prevent such men from urging that plea, when they are charged with culpability for denying some doctrine which they are told is useful, but which they believe to be false? Those who are on the side of received opinions, never fail to take all possible advantage of this plea; you do not find *them* handling the question of utility as if it could be completely abstracted from that of truth: on the contrary, it is, above all, because their doctrine is the "truth," that the knowledge or the belief of it is held to be so indispensable. There can be no fair discussion of the question of usefulness, when an argument so vital may be employed on one side, but not on the other. And in point of fact, when law or public feeling do not permit the truth of an opinion to be disputed, they are just as little tolerant of a denial of its usefulness. The utmost they allow is an extenuation of its absolute necessity, or of the positive guilt of rejecting it. . . .

To pass from this to the only other instance of judicial iniquity,[2] the mention of which, after the condemnation of Socrates, would not be an anti-climax: the event which took place on Calvary rather more than eighteen hundred years ago. The man who left on the memory of those who witnessed his life and conversation, such an impression of his moral grandeur, that eighteen subsequent centuries have done homage to him as the Almighty in person, was ignominiously put to death, as what? As a blasphemer. Men did not merely mistake their benefactor; they mistook him for the exact contrary of what he was, and treated him as that prodigy of impiety, which they themselves are now held to be, for their treatment of him. The feelings with which mankind now regard these lamentable transactions, especially the later of the two, render them extremely unjust in their judgement of the unhappy actors. These were, to all appearance, not bad men —

2 In the portion here omitted, Mill had discussed the execution of Socrates as another example of judicial iniquity.

not worse than men commonly are, but rather the contrary; men who possessed in a full, or somewhat more than a full measure, the religious, moral and patriotic feelings of their time and people: the very kind of men who, in all times, our own included, have every chance of passing through life blameless and respected. The high-priest who rent his garments when the words were pronounced, which, according to all the ideas of his country, constituted the blackest guilt, was in all probability quite as sincere in his horror and indignation, as the generality of respectable and pious men now are in the religious and moral sentiments they profess; and most of those who now shudder at his conduct, if they had lived in his time, and been born Jews, would have acted precisely as he did. Orthodox Christians who are tempted to think that those who stoned to death the first martyrs must have been worse men than they themselves are, ought to remember that one of those persecutors was Saint Paul.

Let us add one more example, the most striking of all, if the impressiveness of an error is measured by the wisdom and virtue of him who falls into it. If ever any one, possessed of power, had grounds for thinking himself the best and most enlightened among his contemporaries, it was the Emperor Marcus Aurelius. Absolute monarch of the whole civilized world, he preserved through life not only the most unblemished justice, but what was less to be expected from his Stoical breeding, the tenderest heart. The few failings which are attributed to him, were all on the side of indulgence: while his writings, the highest ethical product of the ancient mind, differ scarcely perceptibly, if they differ at all, from the most characteristic teachings of Christ. This man, a better Christian in all but the dogmatic sense of the word, than almost any of the ostensibly Christian sovereigns who have since reigned, persecuted Christianity. Placed at the summit of all the previous attainments of humanity, with an open, unfettered intellect, and a character which led him of himself to embody in his moral writings the Christian ideal, he yet failed to see that Christianity was to be a good and not an evil to the world, with his duties to which he was so deeply penetrated. Existing society he knew to be in a deplorable state. But such as it was, he saw, or thought he saw, that it was held together, and prevented from being worse, by belief and reverence of the received divinities. As a ruler of mankind, he deemed it his duty not to suffer society to fall in pieces; and saw not how, if its existing ties were removed, any others could be formed which could again knit it together. The new religion openly aimed at dissolving these ties: unless, therefore, it was his duty to adopt that religion, it seemed to be his duty to put it down. Inasmuch then as the theology of Christianity did not appear to him true or of divine origin; inasmuch as this strange history of a crucified God was not credible to him, and a system which purported to rest entirely upon a foundation to him so wholly unbelievable, could not be foreseen by him to be that renovating agency which, after all abatements, it has in fact proved to be; the gentlest and most amiable of philosophers and rulers, under a solemn sense of duty, authorized the persecution of Christianity. To my mind this is one of the most tragical facts in all history. It is a bitter thought, how different a thing the Christianity of the world might have been, if the Christian faith had been adopted as the religion of the empire under the auspices of Marcus Aurelius instead of those of Constantine. But it would be equally unjust to him and false to truth, to deny, that no one plea which can be urged for punishing anti-Christian teaching, was wanting to Marcus Aurelius for punishing, as he did, the propagation of Christianity. No Christian more firmly believes that Atheism is false, and tends to the dissolution of society, than Marcus Aurelius believed the same things of Christianity; he who, of all men then living, might have been thought the most capable of appreciating it. Unless any one who approves of punishment for the promulgation of opinions, flatters himself that he is a wiser and better man than Marcus Aurelius — more deeply versed in the wisdom of his time, more elevated in his intellect above it — more earnest in his search for truth, or more single-minded in his devotion to it when found; — let him abstain from that assumption of the joint infallibility of himself and the multitude, which the great Antoninus made with so unfortunate a result. . . .[3]

Let us now pass to the second division of the argument, and dismissing the supposition that any of the received opinions may be false, let us assume them to be true, and examine into the worth of the manner in which they are likely to be held, when their truth is not freely and openly canvassed. However unwillingly a person who has a strong opinion may admit the possibility that his opinion may be false, he ought to be moved by the consideration that however true it may be, if it is not fully, frequently, and fearlessly discussed, it will be held as a dead dogma, not a living truth.

There is a class of persons (happily not quite so numerous as formerly) who think it enough if a person assents undoubtingly to what they think true, though he has no knowledge whatever of the grounds of the opinion, and could not make a tenable defence of it against the most superficial objections. Such persons, if they can once get their creed taught from authority, naturally think that no good, and some harm, comes of its being allowed to be questioned. Where their influence prevails, they make it nearly impossible for the received opinion to be rejected wisely and considerately, though it may still be rejected rashly and ignorantly; for to shut out discussion entirely is seldom possible, and when it once gets in, beliefs not grounded on conviction are apt to give way before the slightest sem-

---

3 In the portion here omitted, Mill attacks the notion that "persecution is an ordeal through which truth ought to pass."

blance of an argument. Waiving, however, this possibility — assuming that the true opinion abides in the mind, but abides as a prejudice, a belief independent of, and proof against, argument — this is not the way in which truth ought to be held by a rational being. This is not knowing the truth. Truth, thus held, is but one superstition the more, accidentally clinging to the words which enunciate a truth.

If the intellect and judgement of mankind ought to be cultivated, a thing which Protestants at least do not deny, on what can these faculties be more appropriately exercised by any one, than on the things which concern him so much that it is considered necessary for him to hold opinions on them? If the cultivation of the understanding consists in one thing more than in another, it is surely in learning the grounds of one's own opinions. Whatever people believe, on subjects on which it is of the first importance to believe rightly, they ought to be able to defend against at least the common objections. But, some one may say, "Let them be *taught* the grounds of their opinions. It does not follow that opinions must be merely parroted because they are never heard controverted. Persons who learn geometry do not simply commit the theorems to memory, but understand and learn likewise the demonstrations; and it would be absurd to say that they remain ignorant of the grounds of geometrical truths, because they never hear any one deny, and attempt to disprove them." Undoubtedly: and such teaching suffices on a subject like mathematics, where there is nothing at all to be said on the wrong side of the question. The peculiarity of the evidence of mathematical truths is, that all the argument is on one side. There are no objections, and no answers to objections. But on every subject on which difference of opinion is possible, the truth depends on a balance to be struck between two sets of conflicting reasons. Even in natural philosophy, there is always some other explanation possible of the same facts; some geocentric theory instead of heliocentric, some phlogiston instead of oxygen; and it has to be shown why that other theory cannot be the true one: and until this is shown, and until we know how it is shown, we do not understand the grounds of our opinion. But when we turn to subjects infinitely more complicated, to morals, religion, politics, social relations, and the business of life, three-fourths of the arguments for every disputed opinion consist in dispelling the appearances which favour some opinion different from it. The greatest orator, save one, of antiquity, has left it on record that he always studied his adversary's case with as great, if not with still greater, intensity than even his own. What Cicero practised as the means of forensic success, requires to be imitated by all who study any subject in order to arrive at the truth. He who knows only his own side of the case, knows little of that. His reasons may be good, and no one may have been able to refute them. But if he is equally unable to refute the reasons on the opposite side; if he does not so much as know what they are, he has no ground for preferring either opinion. The rational position for him would be suspension of judgement, and unless he contents himself with that, he is either led by authority, or adopts, like the generality of the world, the side to which he feels most inclination. Nor is it enough that he should hear the arguments of adversaries from his own teachers, presented as they state them, and accompanied by what they offer as refutations. That is not the way to do justice to the arguments, or bring them into real contact with his own mind. He must be able to hear them from persons who actually believe them; who defend them in earnest, and do their very utmost for them. He must know them in their most plausible and persuasive form; he must feel the whole force of the difficulty which the true view of the subject has to encounter and dispose of; else he will never really possess himself of the portion of truth which meets and removes that difficulty. Ninety-nine in a hundred of what are called educated men are in this condition; even of those who can argue fluently for their opinions. Their conclusion may be true, but it might be false for anything they know: they have never thrown themselves into the mental position of those who think differently from them, and considered what such persons may have to say; and consequently they do not, in any proper sense of the word, know the doctrine which they themselves profess. They do not know those parts of it which explain and justify the remainder; the considerations which show that a fact which seemingly conflicts with another is reconcilable with it, or that, of two apparently strong reasons, one and not the other ought to be preferred. All that part of the truth which turns the scale, and decides the judgement of a completely informed mind, they are strangers to; nor is it ever really known, but to those who have attended equally and impartially to both sides, and endeavoured to see the reasons of both in the strongest light. So essential is this discipline to a real understanding of moral and human subjects, that if opponents of all important truths do not exist, it is indispensable to imagine them, and supply them with the strongest arguments which the most skilful devil's advocate can conjure up.

To abate the force of these considerations, an enemy of free discussion may be supposed to say, that there is no necessity for mankind in general to know and understand all that can be said against or for their opinions by philosophers and theologians. That it is not needful for common men to be able to expose all the misstatements or fallacies of an ingenious opponent. That it is enough if there is always somebody capable of answering them, so that nothing likely to mislead uninstructed persons remains unrefuted. That simple minds, having been taught the obvious grounds of the truths inculcated on them, may trust to authority for the rest, and being aware that they have neither knowledge nor talent to resolve every difficulty which can be raised, may repose in the assurance that all those which have been

raised have been or can be answered, by those who are specially
trained to the task.

Conceding to this view of the subject the utmost that can be
claimed for it by those most easily satisfied with the amount of understanding of truth which ought to accompany the belief of it; even so,
the argument for free discussion is no way weakened. For even this
doctrine acknowledges that mankind ought to have a rational assurance
that all objections have been satisfactorily answered; and how are
they to be answered if that which requires to be answered is not
spoken? or how can the answer be known to be satisfactory, if the
objectors have no opportunity of showing that it is unsatisfactory?
If not the public, at least the philosophers and theologians who are
to resolve the difficulties, must make themselves familiar with those
difficulties in their most puzzling form; and this cannot be accomplished unless they are freely stated, and placed in the most advantageous light which they admit of. The Catholic Church has its own
way of dealing with this embarrassing problem. It makes a broad
separation between those who can be permitted to receive its doctrines on conviction, and those who must accept them on trust.
Neither, indeed, are allowed any choice as to what they will accept;
but the clergy, such at least as can be fully confided in, may admissibly
and meritoriously make themselves acquainted with the arguments
of opponents, in order to answer them, and may, therefore, read
heretical books; the laity, not unless by special permission, hard to
be obtained. This discipline recognizes a knowledge of the enemy's
case as beneficial to the teachers, but finds means, consistent with
this, of denying it to the rest of the world: thus giving to the élite
more mental culture, though not more mental freedom, than it allows
to the mass. By this device it succeeds in obtaining the kind of mental
superiority which its purposes require; for though culture without
freedom never made a large and liberal mind, it can make a clever
nisi prius advocate of a cause. But in countries professing Protestantism, this resource is denied; since Protestants hold, at least in theory,
that the responsibility for the choice of a religion must be borne by
each for himself, and cannot be thrown off upon teachers. Besides,
in the present state of the world, it is practically impossible that
writings which are read by the instructed can be kept from the uninstructed. If the teachers of mankind are to be cognizant of all
that they ought to know, everything must be free to be written and
published without restraint.

If, however, the mischievous operation of the absence of free discussion, when the received opinions are true, were confined to leaving
men ignorant of the grounds of those opinions, it might be thought
that this, if an intellectual, is no moral evil, and does not affect the
worth of the opinions, regarded in their influence on the character.
The fact, however, is, that not only the grounds of the opinion are

forgotten in the absence of discussion, but too often the meaning of the opinion itself. The words which convey it cease to suggest ideas, or suggest only a small portion of those they were originally employed to communicate. Instead of a vivid conception and a living belief, there remain only a few phrases retained by rote; or, if any part, the shell and husk only of the meaning is retained, the finer essence being lost. The great chapter in human history which this fact occupies and fills, cannot be too earnestly studied and meditated on.

It is illustrated in the experience of almost all ethical doctrines and religious creeds. They are all full of meaning and vitality to those who originate them, and to the direct disciples of the originators. Their meaning continues to be felt in undiminished strength, and is perhaps brought out into even fuller consciousness, so long as the struggle lasts to give the doctrine or creed an ascendancy over other creeds. At last it either prevails, and becomes the general opinion, or its progress stops; it keeps possession of the ground it has gained, but ceases to spread further. When either of these results has become apparent, controversy on the subject flags, and gradually dies away. The doctrine has taken its place, if not as a received opinion, as one of the admitted sects or divisions of opinion: those who hold it have generally inherited, not adopted it; and conversion from one of these doctrines to another, being now an exceptional fact, occupies little place in the thoughts of their professors. Instead of being, as at first, constantly on the alert either to defend themselves against the world, or to bring the world over to them, they have subsided into acquiescence, and neither listen, when they can help it, to arguments against their creed, nor trouble dissentients (if there be such) with arguments in its favour. From this time may usually be dated the decline in the living power of the doctrine. We often hear the teachers of all creeds lamenting the difficulty of keeping up in the minds of believers a lively apprehension of the truth which they nominally recognize, so that it may penetrate the feelings, and acquire a real mastery over the conduct. No such difficulty is complained of while the creed is still fighting for its existence: even the weaker combatants then know and feel what they are fighting for, and the difference between it and other doctrines; and in that period of every creed's existence, not a few persons may be found, who have realized its fundamental principles in all the forms of thought, have weighed and considered them in all their important bearings, and have experienced the full effect on the character, which belief in that creed ought to produce in a mind thoroughly imbued with it. But when it has come to be an hereditary creed, and to be received passively, not actively — when the mind is no longer compelled, in the same degree as at first, to exercise its vital powers on the questions which its belief presents to it, there is a progressive tendency to forget all of the belief except the formularies, or to give it a dull and torpid assent, as if accepting it on trust dispensed with the necessity of realizing it in consciousness, or testing it by personal experience; until it almost ceases to connect itself at all with the inner life of the human being. Then are seen the cases, so frequent in this age of the world as almost to form the majority, in which the creed remains as it were outside the mind, encrusting and petrifying it against all other influences addressed to the higher parts of our nature; manifesting its power by not suffering any fresh and living conviction to get in, but itself doing nothing for the mind or heart, except standing sentinel over them to keep them vacant.

To what an extent doctrines intrinsically fitted to make the deepest impression upon the mind may remain in it as dead beliefs, without being ever realized in the imagination, the feelings, or the understanding, is exemplified by the manner in which the majority of believers hold the doctrines of Christianity. By Christianity I here mean what is accounted such by all churches and sects — the maxims and precepts contained in the New Testament. These are considered sacred, and accepted as laws, by all professing Christians. Yet it is scarcely too much to say that not one Christian in a thousand guides or tests his individual conduct by reference to those laws. The standard to which he does refer it, is the custom of his nation, his class, or his religious profession. He has thus, on the one hand, a collection of ethical maxims, which he believes to have been vouchsafed to him by infallible wisdom as rules for his government; and on the other, a set of everyday judgements and practices, which go a certain length with some of those maxims, not so great a length with others, stand in direct opposition to some, and are, on the whole, a compromise between the Christian creed and the interests and suggestions of worldly life. To the first of these standards he gives his homage; to the other his real allegiance. All Christians believe that the blessed are the poor and humble, and those who are ill-used by the world; that it is easier for a camel to pass through the eye of a needle than for a rich man to enter the kingdom of heaven; that they should judge not, lest they be judged; that they should swear not at all; that they should love their neighbour as themselves; that if one take their cloak, they should give him their coat also; that they should take no thought for the morrow; that if they would be perfect, they should sell all that they have and give it to the poor. They are not insincere when they say that they believe these things. They do believe them, as people believe what they have always heard lauded and never discussed. But in the sense of that living belief which regulates conduct, they believe these doctrines just up to the point to which it is usual to act upon them. The doctrines in their integrity are serviceable to pelt adversaries with; and it is understood that they are to be put forward (when possible) as the reasons for whatever people do that they think laudable. But any one who reminded them that the maxims require an infinity of things which they never even think of doing, would gain nothing but to be classed among those very unpopular characters who affect to be better than other people. The doctrines have no hold on ordinary believers — are not a power in their minds. They have an habitual respect for the sound of them, but no feeling which spreads from the words to the things signified, and forces the mind to take *them* in, and make them conform to the formula. Whenever conduct is concerned, they look round for Mr. A and B to direct them how far to go in obeying Christ. . . .

It still remains to speak of one of the principal causes which make diversity of opinion advantageous, and will continue to do so until mankind shall have entered a stage of intellectual advancement which at present seems at an incalculable distance. We have hitherto considered only two possibilities: that the received opinion may be false, and some other opinion, consequently, true; or that, the received opinion being true, a conflict with the opposite error is essential to a clear apprehension and deep feeling of its truth. But there is a commoner case than either of these; when the conflicting doctrines, instead of being one true and the other false, share the truth between them; and the nonconforming opinion is needed to supply the remainder of the truth, of which the received doctrine embodies only a part. Popular opinions, on subjects not palpable to sense, are often true, but seldom or never the whole truth. They are a part of the truth; sometimes a greater, sometimes a smaller part, but exaggerated, distorted, and disjoined from the truths by which they ought to be accompanied and limited. Heretical opinions, on the other hand, are generally some of these suppressed and neglected truths, bursting the bonds which kept them down, and either seeking reconciliation with the truth contained in the common opinion, or fronting it as enemies, and setting themselves up, with similar exclusiveness, as the whole truth. The latter case is hitherto the most frequent, as, in the human mind, one-sidedness has always been the rule, and many-sidedness the exception. Hence, even in revolutions of opinion, one part of the truth usually sets while another rises. Even progress, which ought to superadd, for the most part only substitutes, one partial and incomplete truth for another; improvement consisting chiefly in this, that the new fragment of truth is more wanted, more adapted to the needs of the time, than that which it displaces. Such being the partial character of prevailing opinions, even when resting on a true foundation, every opinion which embodies somewhat of the portion of truth which the common opinion omits, ought to be considered precious, with whatever amount of error and confusion that truth may be blended. No sober judge of human affairs will feel bound to be indignant because those who force on our notice truths which we should otherwise have overlooked, overlook some of those which we see. Rather, he will think that so long as popular truth is one-sided, it is more desirable than otherwise that unpopular truth should have one-sided asserters too; such being usually the most energetic, and the most likely to compel reluctant attention to the fragment of wisdom which they proclaim as if it were the whole.

Thus, in the eighteenth century, when nearly all the instructed, and all those of the uninstructed who were led by them, were lost in admiration of what is called civilization, and of the marvels of modern science, literature, and philosophy, and while greatly overrating the amount of unlikeness between the men of modern and those of ancient times, indulged the belief that the whole of the difference was in their own favour; with what a salutary shock did the paradoxes of Rousseau explode like bombshells in the midst, dislocating the compact mass of one-sided opinion, and forcing its elements to recombine in a better form and with additional ingredients. Not that the current opinions were on the whole farther from the truth than Rousseau's were; on the contrary, they were nearer to it; they contained more of positive truth, and very much less of error. Nevertheless there lay in Rousseau's doctrine, and has floated down the stream of opinion along with it, a considerable amount of exactly those truths which the popular opinion wanted; and these are the deposit which was left behind when the flood subsided. The superior worth of simplicity of life, the enervating and demoralizing effect of the trammels and hypocrisies of artificial society, are ideas which have never been entirely absent from cultivated minds since Rousseau wrote; and they will in time produce their due effect, though at present needing to be asserted as much as ever, and to be asserted by deeds, for words, on this subject, have nearly exhausted their power.

In politics, again, it is almost a commonplace, that a party of order or stability, and a party of progress or reform, are both necessary elements of a healthy state of political life; until the one or the other shall have so enlarged its mental grasp as to be a party equally of order and of progress, knowing and distinguishing what is fit to be preserved from what ought to be swept away. Each of these modes of thinking derives its utility from the deficiencies of the other; but it is in a great measure the opposition of the other that keeps each within the limits of reason and sanity. Unless opinions favourable to democracy and to aristocracy, to property and to equality, to co-operation and to competition, to luxury and to abstinence, to sociality and individuality, to liberty and discipline, and all the other standing antagonisms of practical life, are expressed with equal freedom, and enforced and defended with equal talent and energy, there is no chance of both elements obtaining their due; one scale is sure to go up, and the other down. Truth, in the great practical concerns of life, is so much a question of the reconciling and combining of opposites, that very few have minds sufficiently capacious and impartial to make the adjustment with an approach to correctness, and it has to be made by the rough process of a struggle between combatants fighting under hostile banners. On any of the great open questions just enumerated, if either of the two opinions has a better claim than the other, not merely to be tolerated, but to be encouraged and countenanced, it is the one which happens at the particular time and place to be in a minority. That is the opinion which, for the time being, represents the neglected interests, the side of human well-being which is in danger of obtaining less than its share. I am aware that there is not, in this country, any intolerance of differences of opinion on most of these topics. They are adduced to show, by admitted and multiplied examples, the universality of the fact, that only through diversity of opinion is there, in the existing state of human intellect, a chance of fair play to all sides of the truth. When there are persons to be found, who form an exception to the apparent unanimity of the world on any subject, even if the world is in the right, it is always probable that dissentients have something worth hearing to say for themselves, and that truth would lose something by their silence.

It may be objected, "But *some* received principles, especially on the highest and most vital subjects, are more than half-truths. The Christian morality, for instance, is the whole truth on that subject, and if any one teaches a morality which varies from it, he is wholly in error." As this is of all cases the most important in practice, none can be fitter to test the general maxim. But before pronouncing what Christian morality is or is not, it would be desirable to decide what is meant by Christian morality. If it means the morality of the New Testament, I wonder that any one who derives his knowledge of this from the book itself, can suppose that it was announced, or intended, as a complete doctrine of morals. The Gospel always refers to a pre-existing morality, and confines its precepts to the particulars in which that morality was to be corrected, or superseded by a wider and higher; expressing itself, moreover, in terms most general, often impossible to be interpreted literally, and possessing rather the impressiveness of poetry or eloquence than the precision of legislation. To extract from it a body of ethical doctrine, has never been possible without eking it out from the Old Testament, that is, from a system elaborate indeed, but in many respects barbarous, and intended only for a barbarous people. St. Paul, a declared enemy to this Judaical mode of interpreting the doctrine and filling up the scheme of his Master, equally assumes a pre-existing morality, namely that of the Greeks and Romans; and his advice to Christians is in a great measure a system of accommodation to that; even to the extent of giving an apparent sanction to slavery. What is called Christian, but should rather be termed theological, morality, was not the work of Christ or the Apostles, but is of much later origin, having been gradually built up by the Catholic church of the first five centuries, and though not implicitly adopted by moderns and Protestants, has been much less modified by them than might have been expected. For the most part, indeed, they have contented themselves with cutting off the additions which had been made to it in the middle ages, each sect supplying the place by fresh additions, adapted to its own character and tendencies. That mankind owe a great debt to this morality, and to its early teachers, I should be the last person to deny; but I do not scruple to say of it, that it is, in many important points, incomplete and one-sided, and that unless ideas and feelings, not sanctioned by it, had contributed to the formation of European life and character, human affairs would have been in a worse condition than they now are. Christian morality (so called) has all the characters of a reaction; it is, in great part, a protest against Paganism. Its ideal is negative rather than positive; passive rather than active; Innocence rather than Nobleness; Abstinence from Evil, rather than energetic Pursuit of Good: in its precepts (as has been well said) "thou shalt not" predominates unduly over "thou shalt." In its horror of sensuality, it made an idol of asceticism, which has been gradually compromised away into one of legality. It holds out the hope of heaven and the threat of hell, as the appointed and appropriate motives to a virtuous life: in this falling far below the best of the ancients, and doing what lies in it to give to human morality an essentially selfish character, by disconnecting each man's feelings of duty from the interests of his fellow-creatures, except so far as a self-interested inducement is offered to him for consulting them. It is essentially a doctrine of passive obedience; it inculcates submission to all authorities found established; who indeed are not to be actively obeyed when they command what religion forbids, but who are not to be resisted, far less rebelled against, for any amount of wrong to ourselves. And while, in the morality of the best Pagan nations, duty to the State holds even a disproportionate place, infringing on the just liberty of the individual; in purely Christian ethics, that grand department of duty is scarcely noticed or acknowledged. It is in the Koran, not the New Testament, that we read the maxim — "A ruler who appoints any man to an office, when there is in his dominions another man better qualified for it, sins against God and against the State." What little recognition the idea of obligation to the public obtains in modern morality, is derived from Greek and Roman sources, not from Christian; as, even in the morality of private life, whatever exists of magnanimity, high-mindedness, personal dignity, even the sense of honour, is derived from the purely human, not the religious part of our education, and never could have grown out of a standard of ethics in which the only worth, professedly recognized, is that of obedience.

I am as far as any one from pretending that these defects are necessarily inherent in the Christian ethics, in every manner in which it can be conceived, or that the many requisites of a complete moral doctrine which it does not contain, do not admit of being reconciled with it. Far less would I insinuate this of the doctrines and precepts of Christ himself. I believe that the sayings of Christ are all, that I can see any evidence of their having been intended to be; that they are irreconcilable with nothing which a comprehensive morality requires; that everything which is excellent in ethics may be brought within them, with no greater violence to their language than has been done to it by all who have attempted to deduce from them any practical system of conduct whatever. But it is quite consistent with this, to believe that they contain, and were meant to contain, only a part of the truth; that many essential elements of the highest morality are among the things which are not provided for, nor intended to be provided for, in the recorded deliverances of the Founder of Christianity, and which have been entirely thrown aside in the system of ethics erected on the basis of those deliverances by the Christian Church. And this being so, I think it a great error to persist in attempting to find in the Christian doctrine that complete rule for our guidance, which its author intended it to sanction and enforce, but only partially to provide. I believe, too, that this narrow theory is becoming a grave practical evil, detracting greatly from the value of the moral training and instruction, which so many well-meaning persons are now at length exerting themselves to promote. I much fear that by attempting to form the mind and feelings on an exclusively religious type, and discarding those secular standards (as for want of a better name they may be called) which heretofore co-existed with and supplemented the Christian ethics, receiving some of its spirit, and infusing into it some of theirs, there will result, and is even now resulting, a low, abject, servile type of character, which, submit itself as it may to what it deems the Supreme Will, is incapable of rising to or sympathizing in the conception of Supreme Goodness. I believe that other ethics than any which can be evolved from exclusively Christian sources, must exist side by side with Christian ethics to produce the moral regeneration of mankind; and that the Christian system is no exception to the rule, that in an imperfect state of the human mind, the interests of truth require a diversity of opinions. It is not necessary that in ceasing to ignore the moral truths not contained in Christianity, men should ignore any of those which it does contain. Such prejudice, or oversight, when it occurs, is altogether an evil; but it is one from which we cannot hope to be always exempt, and must be regarded as the price paid for an inestimable good. The exclusive pretension made by a part of the truth to be the whole, must and ought to be protested against; and if a reactionary impulse should make the protestors unjust in their turn, this one-sidedness, like the other, may be lamented, but must be tolerated. If Christians would teach infidels to be just to Christianity, they should themselves be just to infidelity. It can do truth no service to blink the fact, known to all who have

the most ordinary acquaintance with literary history, that a large portion of the noblest and most valuable moral teaching has been the
work, not only of men who did not know, but of men who knew and
rejected, the Christian faith.

I do not pretend that the most unlimited use of the freedom of
enunciating all possible opinions would put an end to the evils of
religious or philosophical sectarianism. Every truth which men of
narrow capacity are in earnest about, is sure to be asserted, inculcated, and in many ways even acted on, as if no other truth existed
in the world, or at all events none that could limit or qualify the first.
I acknowledge that the tendency of all opinions to become sectarian
is not cured by the freest discussion, but is often heightened and
exacerbated thereby; the truth which ought to have been, but was
not, seen, being rejected all the more violently because proclaimed by
persons regarded as opponents. But it is not on the impassioned partisan, it is on the calmer and more disinterested bystander, that this
collision of opinions works its salutary effect. Not the violent conflict
between parts of the truth, but the quiet suppression of half of it,
is the formidable evil; there is always hope when people are forced
to listen to both sides; it is when they attend only to one that errors
harden into prejudices, and truth itself ceases to have the effect of
truth, by being exaggerated into falsehood. And since there are few
mental attributes more rare than that judicial faculty which can sit
in intelligent judgement between two sides of a question, of which
only one is represented by an advocate before it, truth has no chance
but in proportion as every side of it, every opinion which embodies
any fraction of the truth, not only finds advocates, but is so advocated
as to be listened to.

We have now recognized the necessity to the mental well-being of
mankind (on which all their other well-being depends) of freedom
of opinion, and freedom of the expression of opinion, on four distinct
grounds; which we will now briefly recapitulate.

First, if any opinion is compelled to silence, that opinion may,
for aught we can certainly know, be true. To deny this is to assume
our own infallibility.

Secondly, though the silenced opinion be an error, it may, and
very commonly does, contain a portion of truth; and since the general
or prevailing opinion on any subject is rarely or never the whole
truth, it is only by the collision of adverse opinions that the remainder
of the truth has any chance of being supplied.

Thirdly, even if the received opinion be not only true, but the
whole truth; unless it is suffered to be, and actually is, vigorously
and earnestly contested, it will, by most of those who receive it, be
held in the manner of a prejudice, with little comprehension or
feeling of its rational grounds. And not only this, but, fourthly, the
meaning of the doctrine itself will be in danger of being lost, or

enfeebled, and deprived of its vital effect on the character and conduct: the dogma becoming a mere formal profession, inefficacious for good, but cumbering the ground, and preventing the growth of any real and heartfelt conviction, from reason or personal experience.

Before quitting the subject of freedom of opinion, it is fit to take some notice of those who say, that the free expression of all opinions should be permitted, on condition that the manner be temperate, and do not pass the bounds of fair discussion. Much might be said on the impossibility of fixing where these supposed bounds are to be placed; for if the test be offence to those whose opinion is attacked, I think experience testifies that this offence is given whenever the attack is telling and powerful, and that every opponent who pushes them hard, and whom they find it difficult to answer, appears to them, if he shows any strong feeling on the subject, an intemperate opponent. But this, though an important consideration in a practical point of view, merges in a more fundamental objection. Undoubtedly the manner of asserting an opinion, even though it be a true one, may be very objectionable, and may justly incur severe censure. But the principal offences of the kind are such as it is mostly impossible, unless by accidental self-betrayal, to bring home to conviction. The gravest of them is, to argue sophistically, to suppress facts or arguments, to misstate the elements of the case, or misrepresent the opposite opinion. But all this, even to the most aggravated degree, is so continually done in perfect good faith, by persons who are not considered, and in many other respects may not deserve to be considered, ignorant or incompetent, that it is rarely possible on adequate grounds conscientiously to stamp the misrepresentation as morally culpable; and still less could law presume to interfere with this kind of controversial misconduct. With regard to what is commonly meant by intemperate discussion, namely invective, sarcasm, personality, and the like, the denunciation of these weapons would deserve more sympathy if it were ever proposed to interdict them equally to both sides; but it is only desired to restrain the employment of them against the prevailing opinion: against the unprevailing they may not only be used without general disapproval, but will be likely to obtain for him who uses them the praise of honest zeal and righteous indignation. Yet whatever mischief arises from their use, is greatest when they are employed against the comparatively defenceless; and whatever unfair advantage can be derived by any opinion from this mode of asserting it, accrues almost exclusively to received opinions. The worst offence of this kind which can be committed by a polemic, is to stigmatize those who hold the contrary opinion as bad and immoral men. To calumny of this sort, those who hold any unpopular opinion are peculiarly exposed, because they are in general few and uninfluential, and nobody but themselves feels much interested in seeing justice done them; but this weapon is, from the nature of the case, denied to those who attack a prevailing opinion: they can neither use it with safety to themselves, nor, if they could, would it do anything but recoil on their own cause. In general, opinions contrary to those commonly received can only obtain a hearing by studied moderation of language, and the most cautious avoidance of unnecessary offence, from which they hardly ever deviate even in a slight degree without losing ground: while unmeasured vituperation employed on the side of the prevailing opinion, really does deter people from professing contrary opinions, and from listening to those who profess them. For the interest, therefore, of truth and justice, it is far more important to restrain this employment of vituperative language than the other; and, for example, if it were necessary to choose, there would be much more need to discourage offensive attacks on infidelity, than on religion. It is, however, obvious that law and authority have no business with restraining either, while opinion ought, in every instance, to determine its verdict by the circumstances of the individual case; condemning every one, on whichever side of the argument he places himself, in whose mode of advocacy either want of candour, or malignity, bigotry, or intolerance of feeling manifest themselves; but not inferring these vices from the side which a person takes, though it be the contrary side of the question to our own: and giving merited honour to every one, whatever opinion he may hold, who has calmness to see and honesty to state what his opponents and their opinions really are, exaggerating nothing to their discredit, keeping nothing back which tells, or can be supposed to tell, in their favour. This is the real morality of public discussion: and if often violated, I am happy to think that there are many controversialists who to a great extent observe it, and a still greater number who conscientiously strive towards it.

Chapter III

Of Individuality, As One of the Elements of Well-Being

SUCH being the reasons which make it imperative that human beings should be free to form opinions, and to express their opinions without reserve; and such the baneful consequences to the intellectual, and through that to the moral nature of man, unless this liberty is either conceded, or asserted in spite of prohibition; let us next examine whether the same reasons do not require that men should be free to act upon their opinions — to carry these out in their lives, without hindrance, either physical or moral, from their fellow men, so long as it is at their own risk and peril. This last proviso is of course indispensable. No one pretends that actions should be as free as opinions. On the contrary, even opinions lose their immunity, when the circumstances in which they are expressed are such as to constitute their

expression a positive instigation to some mischievous act. A
that corn-dealers are starvers of the poor, or that private p
robbery, ought to be unmolested when simply circulated th
press, but may justly incur punishment when delivered orally to an
excited mob assembled before the house of a corn-dealer, or when
handed about among the same mob in the form of a placard. Acts, of
whatever kind, which, without justifiable cause, do harm to others,
may be, and in the more important cases absolutely require to be,
controlled by the unfavourable sentiments, and, when needful, by the
active interference of mankind. The liberty of the individual must
be thus far limited; he must not make himself a nuisance to other
people. But if he refrains from molesting others in what concerns
them, and merely acts according to his own inclination and judgement
in things which concern himself, the same reasons which show that
opinion should be free, prove also that he should be allowed, without molestation, to carry his opinions into practice at his own cost.
That mankind are not infallible; that their truths, for the most part,
are only half-truths; that unity of opinion, unless resulting from the
fullest and freest comparison of opposite opinions, is not desirable,
and diversity not an evil, but a good, until mankind are much more
capable than at present of recognizing all sides of the truth, are
principles applicable to men's modes of action, not less than to their
opinions. As it is useful that while mankind are imperfect there should
be different opinions, so is it that there should be different experiments
of living; that free scope should be given to varieties of character,
short of injury to others; and that the worth of different modes of life
should be proved practically, when any one thinks fit to try them.
It is desirable, in short, that in things which do not primarily concern
others, individuality should assert itself. Where, not the person's own
character, but the traditions or customs of other people are the rule
of conduct, there is wanting one of the principal ingredients of human
happiness, and quite the chief ingredient of individual and social
progress.

In maintaining this principle, the greatest difficulty to be encountered does not lie in the appreciation of means towards an acknowledged end, but in the indifference of persons in general to the
end itself. If it were felt that the free development of individuality
is one of the leading essentials of well-being; that it is not only a co-
ordinate element with all that is designated by the terms civilization,
instruction, education, culture, but is itself a necessary part and condition of all those things; there would be no danger that liberty
should be undervalued, and the adjustment of the boundaries between
it and social control would present no extraordinary difficulty. But
the evil is, that individual spontaneity is hardly recognized by the
common modes of thinking, as having any intrinsic worth, or deserving
any regard on its own account. The majority, being satisfied with

the ways of mankind as they now are (for it is they who make them what they are), cannot comprehend why those ways should not be good enough for everybody; and what is more, spontaneity forms no part of the ideal of the majority of moral and social reformers, but is rather looked on with jealousy, as a troublesome and perhaps rebellious obstruction to the general acceptance of what these reformers, in their own judgement, think would be best for mankind. Few persons, out of Germany, even comprehend the meaning of the doctrine which Wilhelm von Humboldt, so eminent both as a savant and as a politician, made the text of a treatise — that "the end of man, or that which is prescribed by the eternal or immutable dictates of reason, and not suggested by vague and transient desires, is the highest and most harmonious development of his powers to a complete and consistent whole;" that, therefore, the object "towards which every human being must ceaselessly direct his efforts, and on which especially those who design to influence their fellow men must ever keep their eyes, is the individuality of power and development;" that for this there are two requisities, "freedom, and variety of situations;" and that from the union of these arise "individual vigour and manifold diversity," which combine themselves in "originality." [1]

Little, however, as people are accustomed to a doctrine like that of Von Humboldt, and surprising as it may be to them to find so high a value attached to individuality, the question, one must nevertheless think, can only be one of degree. No one's idea of excellence in conduct is that people should do absolutely nothing but copy one another. No one would assert that people ought not to put into their mode of life, and into the conduct of their concerns, any impress whatever of their own judgement, or of their own individual character. On the other hand, it would be absurd to pretend that people ought to live as if nothing whatever had been known in the world before they came into it; as if experience had as yet done nothing towards showing that one mode of existence, or of conduct, is preferable to another. Nobody denies that people should be so taught and trained in youth, as to know and benefit by the ascertained results of human experience. But it is the privilege and proper condition of a human being, arrived at the maturity of his faculties, to use and interpret experience in his own way. It is for him to find out what part of recorded experience is properly applicable to his own circumstances and character. The traditions and customs of other people are, to a certain extent, evidence of what their experience has taught *them;* presumptive evidence, and as such, have a claim to his deference: but, in the first place, their experience may be too narrow; or they may not have interpreted it rightly. Secondly, their interpretation of experience may be correct, but unsuitable to him.

1 *The Sphere and Duties of Government,* from the German of Baron Wilhelm von Humboldt, pp. 11–13. [Mill's note.]

Customs are made for customary circumstances, and customary characters; and his circumstances or his character may be uncustomary. Thirdly, though the customs be both good as customs, and suitable to him, yet to conform to custom, merely *as* custom, does not educate or develop in him any of the qualities which are the distinctive endowment of a human being. The human faculties of perception, judgement, discriminative feeling, mental activity, and even moral preference, are exercised only in making a choice. He who does anything because it is the custom makes no choice. He gains no practice either in discerning or in desiring what is best. The mental and moral, like the muscular powers, are improved only by being used. The faculties are called into no exercise by doing a thing merely because others do it, no more than by believing a thing only because others believe it. If the grounds of an opinion are not conclusive to the person's own reason, his reason cannot be strengthened, but is likely to be weakened, by his adopting it: and if the inducements to an act are not such as are consentaneous to his own feelings and character (where affection, or the rights of others, are not concerned) it is so much done towards rendering his feelings and character inert and torpid, instead of active and energetic.

He who lets the world, or his own portion of it, choose his plan of life for him, has no need of any other faculty than the ape-like one of imitation. He who chooses his plan for himself, employs all his faculties. He must use observation to see, reasoning and judgement to foresee, activity to gather materials for decision, discrimination to decide, and when he has decided, firmness and self-control to hold to his deliberate decision. And these qualities he requires and exercises exactly in proportion as the part of his conduct which he determines according to his own judgement and feelings is a large one. It is possible that he might be guided in some good path, and kept out of harm's way, without any of these things. But what will be his comparative worth as a human being? It really is of importance, not only what men do, but also what manner of men they are that do it. Among the works of man, which human life is rightly employed in perfecting and beautifying, the first in importance surely is man himself. Supposing it were possible to get houses built, corn grown, battles fought, causes tried, and even churches erected and prayers said, by machinery — by automatons in human form — it would be a considerable loss to exchange for these automatons even the men and women who at present inhabit the more civilized parts of the world, and who assuredly are but starved specimens of what nature can and will produce. Human nature is not a machine to be built after a model, and set to do exactly the work prescribed for it, but a tree, which requires to grow and develop itself on all sides, according to the tendency of the inward forces which make it a living thing.

It will probably be conceded that it is desirable people should exercise their understandings, and that an intelligent following of custom, or even occasionally an intelligent deviation from custom, is better than a blind and simply mechanical adhesion to it. To a certain extent it is admitted, that our understanding should be our own: but there is not the same willingness to admit that our desires and impulses should be our own likewise; or that to possess impulses of our own, and of any strength, is anything but a peril and a snare. Yet desires and impulses are as much a part of a perfect human being, as beliefs and restraints: and strong impulses are only perilous when not properly balanced; when one set of aims and inclinations is developed into strength, while others, which ought to co-exist with them, remain weak and inactive. It is not because men's desires are strong that they act ill; it is because their consciences are weak. There is no natural connexion between strong impulses and a weak conscience. The natural connexion is the other way. To say that one person's desires and feelings are stronger and more various than those of another, is merely to say that he has more of the raw material of human nature, and is therefore capable, perhaps of more evil, but certainly of more good. Strong impulses are but another name for energy. Energy may be turned to bad uses; but more good may always be made of an energetic nature, than of an indolent and impassive one. Those who have most natural feeling, are always those whose cultivated feelings may be made the strongest. The same strong susceptibilities which make the personal impulses vivid and powerful, are also the source from whence are generated the most passionate love of virtue, and the sternest self-control. It is through the cultivation of these, that society both does its duty and protects its interests: not by rejecting the stuff of which heroes are made, because it knows not how to make them. A person whose desires and impulses are his own — are the expression of his own nature, as it has been developed and modified by his own culture — is said to have a character. One whose desires and impulses are not his own, has no character, no more than a steam-engine has a character. If, in addition to being his own, his impulses are strong, and are under the government of a strong will, he has an energetic character. Whoever thinks that individuality of desires and impulses should not be encouraged to unfold itself, must maintain that society has no need of strong natures — is not the better for containing many persons who have much character — and that a high general average of energy is not desirable.

In some early states of society, these forces might be, and were, too much ahead of the power which society then possessed of disciplining and controlling them. There has been a time when the element of spontaneity and individuality was in excess, and the social principle had a hard struggle with it. The difficulty then was, to induce men of strong bodies or minds to pay obedience to any rules which required them to control their impulses. To overcome this difficulty, law and discipline, like the Popes struggling against the Emperors, asserted a power over the whole man, claiming to control all his life in order to control his character — which society had not found any other sufficient means of binding. But society has now fairly got the better of individuality; and the danger which threatens human nature is not the excess, but the deficiency, of personal impulses and preferences. Things are vastly changed, since the passions of those who were strong by station or by personal endowment were in a state of habitual rebellion against laws and ordinances, and required to be rigorously chained up to enable the persons within their reach to enjoy any particle of security. In our times, from the highest class of society down to the lowest, every one lives as under the eye of a hostile and dreaded censorship. Not only in what concerns others, but in what concerns only themselves, the individual or the family do not ask themselves — what do I prefer? or, what would suit my character and disposition? or, what would allow the best and highest in me to have fair play, and enable it to grow and thrive? They ask themselves, what is suitable to my position? what is usually done by persons of my station and pecuniary circumstances? or (worse still) what is usually done by persons of a station and circumstances superior to mine? I do not mean that they choose what is customary, in preference to what suits their own inclination. It does not occur to them to have any inclination, except for what is customary. Thus the mind itself is bowed to the yoke: even in what people do for pleasure, conformity is the first thing thought of; they like in crowds; they exercise choice only among things commonly done: peculiarity of taste, eccentricity of conduct, are shunned equally with crimes: until by dint of not following their own nature, they have no nature to follow: their human capacities are withered and starved: they become incapable of any strong wishes or native pleasures, and are generally without either opinions or feelings of home growth, or properly their own. Now is this, or is it not, the desirable condition of human nature?

It is so, on the Calvinistic theory. According to that, the one great offence of man is self-will. All the good of which humanity is capable is comprised in obedience. You have no choice; thus you must do, and no otherwise: "whatever is not a duty, is a sin." Human nature being radically corrupt, there is no redemption for any one until human nature is killed within him. To one holding this theory of life, crushing out any of the human faculties, capacities, and susceptibilities, is no evil: man needs no capacity, but that of surrendering himself to the will of God: and if he uses any of his faculties for any other purpose but to do that supposed will more effectually, he is better without them. This is the theory of Calvinism; and it is held, in a mitigated form, by many who do not consider themselves Calvinists; the mitigation consisting in giving a less ascetic interpretation to the alleged will of God; asserting it to be his will that mankind should gratify some of their inclinations; of course not in the manner they themselves prefer, but in the way of obedience, that is, in a way prescribed to them by authority; and, therefore, by the necessary conditions of the case, the same for all.

In some such insidious form there is at present a strong tendency to this narrow theory of life, and to the pinched and hidebound type of human character which it patronises. Many persons, no doubt, sincerely think that human beings thus cramped and dwarfed, are as their Maker designed them to be; just as many have thought that trees are a much finer thing when clipped into pollards, or cut out into figures of animals, than as nature made them. But if it be any part of religion to believe that man was made by a good Being, it is more consistent with that faith to believe, that this Being gave all human faculties that they might be cultivated and unfolded, not rooted out and consumed, and that he takes delight in every nearer approach made by his creatures to the ideal conception embodied in them, every increase in any of their capabilities of comprehension, of action, or of enjoyment. There is a different type of human excellence from the Calvinistic; a conception of humanity as having its nature bestowed on it for other purposes than merely to be abnegated. "Pagan self-assertion" is one of the elements of human worth, as well as "Christian self-denial." [2] There is a Greek ideal of self-development, which the Platonic and Christian ideal of self-government blends with, but does not supersede. It may be better to be a John Knox than an Alcibiades, but it is better to be a Pericles than either; nor would a Pericles, if we had one in these days, be without anything good which belonged to John Knox.

It is not by wearing down into uniformity all that is individual in themselves, but by cultivating it and calling it forth, within the limits imposed by the rights and interests of others, that human beings become a noble and beautiful object of contemplation; and as the works partake the character of those who do them, by the same process human life also becomes rich, diversified, and animating, furnishing more abundant aliment to high thoughts and elevating feelings, and strengthening the tie which binds every individual to the race, by making the race infinitely better worth belonging to. In proportion to the development of his individuality, each person becomes more valuable to himself, and is therefore capable of being more valuable to others. There is a greater fullness of life about his own existence, and when there is more life in the units there is more in the mass which is composed of them. As much compression as is necessary to prevent the stronger specimens of human nature from encroaching on the rights of others, cannot be dispensed with; but for this there is ample compensation even in the point of view of human development. The means of development which the individual loses by being pre-

2 Sterling's *Essays*. [Mill's note.]

vented from gratifying his inclinations to the injury of others, are chiefly obtained at the expense of the development of other people. And even to himself there is a full equivalent in the better development of the social part of his nature, rendered possible by the restraint put upon the selfish part. To be held to rigid rules of justice for the sake of others, develops the feelings and capacities which have the good of others for their object. But to be restrained in things not affecting their good, by their mere displeasure, develops nothing valuable, except such force of character as may unfold itself in resisting the restraint. If acquiesced in, it dulls and blunts the whole nature. To give any fair play to the nature of each, it is essential that different persons should be allowed to lead different lives. In proportion as this latitude has been exercised in any age, has that age been noteworthy to posterity. Even despotism does not produce its worst effects, so long as individuality exists under it; and whatever crushes individuality is despotism, by whatever name it may be called, and whether it professes to be enforcing the will of God or the injunctions of men.

Having said that Individuality is the same thing with development, and that it is only the cultivation of individuality which produces, or can produce, well-developed human beings, I might here close the argument: for what more or better can be said of any condition of human affairs, than that it brings human beings themselves nearer to the best thing they can be? or what worse can be said of any obstruction to good, than that it prevents this? Doubtless, however, these considerations will not suffice to convince those who most need convincing; and it is necessary further to show, that these developed human beings are of some use to the undeveloped — to point out to those who do not desire liberty, and would not avail themselves of it, that they may be in some intelligible manner rewarded for allowing other people to make use of it without hindrance.

In the first place, then, I would suggest that they might possibly learn something from them. It will not be denied by anybody, that originality is a valuable element in human affairs. There is always need of persons not only to discover new truths, and point out when what were once truths are true no longer, but also to commence new practices, and set the example of more enlightened conduct, and better taste and sense in human life. This cannot well be gainsaid by anybody who does not believe that the world has already attained perfection in all its ways and practices. It is true that this benefit is not capable of being rendered by everybody alike: there are but few persons, in comparison with the whole of mankind, whose experiments, if adopted by others, would be likely to be any improvement on established practice. But these few are the salt of the earth; without them, human life would become a stagnant pool. Not only is it they who introduce good things which did not before exist; it is they who keep the life in those which already existed. If there were nothing new to be done, would human intellect cease to be necessary? Would it be a reason why those who do the old things should forget why they are done, and do them like cattle, not like human beings? There is only too great a tendency in the best beliefs and practices to degenerate into the mechanical; and unless there were a succession of persons whose ever-recurring originality prevents the grounds of those beliefs and practices from becoming merely traditional, such dead matter would not resist the smallest shock from anything really alive, and there would be no reason why civilisation should not die out, as in the Byzantine Empire. Persons of genius, it is true, are, and are always likely to be, a small minority; but in order to have them, it is necessary to preserve the soil in which they grow. Genius can only breathe freely in an *atmosphere* of freedom. Persons of genius are, *ex vi termini, more* individual than any other people — less capable, consequently, of fitting themselves, without hurtful compression, into any of the small number of moulds which society provides in order to save its members the trouble of forming their own character. If from timidity they consent to be forced into one of these moulds, and to let all that part of themselves which cannot expand under the pressure remain unexpanded, society will be little the better for their genius. If they are of a strong character, and break their fetters, they become a mark for the society which has not succeeded in reducing them to commonplace, to point at with solemn warning as "wild," "erratic," and the like; much as if one should complain of the Niagara river for not flowing smoothly between its banks like a Dutch canal.

I insist thus emphatically on the importance of genius, and the necessity of allowing it to unfold itself freely both in thought and in practice, being well aware that no one will deny the position in theory, but knowing also that almost every one, in reality, is totally indifferent to it. People think genius a fine thing if it enables a man to write an exciting poem, or paint a picture. But in its true sense, that of originality in thought and action, though no one says that it is not a thing to be admired, nearly all, at heart, think that they can do very well without it. Unhappily this is too natural to be wondered at. Originality is the one thing which unoriginal minds cannot feel the use of. They cannot see what it is to do for them: how should they? If they could see what it would do for them, it would not be originality. The first service which originality has to render them, is that of opening their eyes: which being once fully done, they would have a chance of being themselves original. Meanwhile, recollecting that nothing was ever yet done which some one was not the first to do, and that all good things which exist are the fruits of originality, let them be modest enough to believe that there is something still left for it to accomplish, and assure themselves that they are more in need of originality, the less they are conscious of the want.

In sober truth, whatever homage may be professed, or even paid, to real or supposed mental superiority, the general tendency of things throughout the world is to render mediocrity the ascendant power among mankind. In ancient history, in the middle ages, and in a diminishing degree through the long transition from feudality to the present time, the individual was a power in himself; and if he had either great talents or a high social position, he was a considerable power. At present individuals are lost in the crowd. In politics it is almost a triviality to say that public opinion now rules the world. The only power deserving the name is that of masses, and of governments while they make themselves the organ of the tendencies and instincts of masses. This is as true in the moral and social relations of private life as in public transactions. Those whose opinions go by the name of public opinion are not always the same sort of public: in America they are the whole white population; in England, chiefly the middle class. But they are always a mass, that is to say, collective mediocrity. And what is a still greater novelty, the mass do not now take their opinions from dignitaries in Church or State, from ostensible leaders, or from books. Their thinking is done for them by men much like themselves, addressing them or speaking in their name, on the spur of the moment, through the newspapers. I am not complaining of all this. I do not assert that anything better is compatible, as a general rule, with the present low state of the human mind. But that does not hinder the government of mediocrity from being mediocre government. No government by a democracy or a numerous aristocracy, either in its political acts or in the opinions, qualities, and tone of mind which it fosters, ever did or could rise above mediocrity, except in so far as the sovereign Many have let themselves be guided (which in their best times they always have done) by the counsels and influence of a more highly gifted and instructed One or Few. The initiation of all wise or noble things comes and must come from individuals; generally at first from some one individual. The honour and glory of the average man is that he is capable of following that initiative; that he can respond internally to wise and noble things, and be led to them with his eyes open. I am not countenancing the sort of "hero-worship" which applauds the strong man of genius for forcibly seiz- ing on the government of the world and making it do his bidding in spite of itself. All he can claim is, freedom to point out the way. The power of compelling others into it, is not only inconsistent with the freedom and development of all the rest, but corrupting to the strong man himself. It does seem, however, that when the opinions of masses of merely average men are everywhere become or becoming the dominant power, the counterpoise and corrective to that tendency would be, the more and more pronounced individuality of those who stand on the higher eminences of thought. It is in these circumstances most especially, that exceptional individuals, instead of being deterred, should be encouraged in acting differently from the mass. In other times there was no advantage in their doing so, unless they acted not only differently, but better. In this age, the mere example of non-conformity, the mere refusal to bend the knee to custom, is itself a service. Precisely because the tyranny of opinion is such as to make eccentricity a reproach, it is desirable, in order to break through that tyranny, that people should be eccentric. Eccentricity has always abounded when and where strength of character has abounded; and the amount of eccentricity in a society has generally been proportional to the amount of genius, mental vigour, and moral courage it contained. That so few now dare to be eccentric marks the chief danger of the time.

I have said that it is important to give the freest scope possible to uncustomary things, in order that it may in time appear which of these are fit to be converted into customs. But independence of action, and disregard of custom, are not solely deserving of encouragement for the chance they afford that better modes of action, and customs more worthy of general adoption, may be struck out; nor is it only persons of decided mental superiority who have a just claim to carry on their lives in their own way. There is no reason that all human existence should be constructed on some one or some small number of patterns. If a person possesses any tolerable amount of common sense and experience, his own mode of laying out his existence is the best, not because it is the best in itself, but because it is his own mode. Human beings are not like sheep; and even sheep are not undistinguishably alike. A man cannot get a coat or a pair of boots to fit him, unless they are either made to his measure, or he has a whole warehouseful to choose from: and is it easier to fit him with a life than with a coat, or are human beings more like one another in their whole physical and spiritual conformation than in the shape of their feet? If it were only that people have diversities of taste, that is reason enough for not attempting to shape them all after one model. But different persons also require different conditions for their spiritual development; and can no more exist healthily in the same moral, than all the variety of plants can in the same physical, atmosphere and climate. The same things which are helps to one person towards the cultivation of his higher nature, are hindrances to another. The same mode of life is a healthy excitement to one, keeping all his faculties of action and enjoyment in their best order, while to another it is a distracting burthen, which suspends or crushes all internal life. Such are the differences among human beings in their sources of pleasure, their susceptibilities of pain, and the operation on them of different physical and moral agencies, that unless there is a corresponding diversity in their modes of life, they neither obtain their fair share of happiness, nor grow up to the mental, moral, and aesthetic stature of which their nature is capable. Why then should tolerance, as far as the public sentiment is concerned, extend only to tastes and modes of life which extort acquiescence by the multitude of their adherents? Nowhere (except in some monastic institutions) is diversity of taste entirely unrecognized; a person may, without blame, either like or dislike rowing, or smoking, or music, or athletic exercises, or chess, or cards, or study, because both those who like each of these things, and those who dislike them, are too numerous to be put down. But the man, and still more the woman, who can be accused either of doing "what nobody does," or of not doing "what everybody does," is the subject of as much depreciatory remark as if he or she had committed some grave moral delinquency. Persons require to possess a title, or some other badge of rank, or of the consideration of people of rank, to be able to indulge somewhat in the luxury of doing as they like without detriment to their estimation. To indulge somewhat, I repeat: for whoever allow themselves much of that indulgence, incur the risk of something worse than disparaging speeches — they are in peril of a commission *de lunatico,* and of having their property taken from them and given to their relations.[3]

There is one characteristic of the present direction of public opinion, peculiarly calculated to make it intolerant of any marked demonstration of individuality. The general average of mankind are not only moderate in intellect, but also moderate in inclinations: they have no tastes or wishes strong enough to incline them to do anything unusual, and they consequently do not understand those who have, and class all such with the wild and intemperate whom they are accustomed to look down upon. Now, in addition to this fact which is general, we have only to suppose that a strong movement has set

[3] There is something both contemptible and frightful in the sort of evidence on which, of late years, any person can be judicially declared unfit for the management of his affairs; and after his death, his disposal of his property can be set aside, if there is enough of it to pay the expenses of litigation — which are charged on the property itself. All the minute details of his daily life are pried into, and whatever is found which, seen through the medium of the perceiving and describing faculties of the lowest of the low, bears an appearance unlike absolute commonplace, is laid before the jury as evidence of insanity, and often with success; the jurors being little, if at all, less vulgar and ignorant than the witnesses; while the judges, with that extraordinary want of knowledge of human nature and life which continually astonishes us in English lawyers, often help to mislead them. These trials speak volumes as to the state of feeling and opinion among the vulgar with regard to human liberty. So far from setting any value on individuality — so far from respecting the right of each individual to act in things indifferent, as seems good to his own judgment and inclinations, judges and juries cannot even conceive that a person in a state of sanity can desire such freedom. In former days, when it was proposed to burn atheists, charitable people used to suggest putting them in a mad-house instead: it would be nothing surprising now-a-days were we to see this done, and the doers applauding themselves, because, instead of persecuting for religion, they had adopted so humane and Christian a mode of treating these unfortunates, not without a silent satisfaction at their having thereby obtained their deserts. [Mill's note.]

in towards the improvement of morals, and it is evident what we
have to expect. In these days such a movement has set in; much
has actually been effected in the way of increased regularity of conduct, and discouragement of excesses; and there is a philanthropic
spirit abroad, for the exercise of which there is no more inviting
field than the moral and prudential improvement of our fellow creatures. These tendencies of the times cause the public to be more disposed than at most former periods to prescribe general rules of conduct, and endeavour to make every one conform to the approved
standard. And that standard, express or tacit, is to desire nothing
strongly. Its ideal of character is to be without any marked character; to maim by compression, like a Chinese lady's foot, every part
of human nature which stands out prominently, and tends to make
the person markedly dissimilar in outline to commonplace humanity.

As is usually the case with ideals which exclude one-half of what
is desirable, the present standard of approbation produces only an
inferior imitation of the other half. Instead of great energies guided
by vigorous reason, and strong feelings strongly controlled by a conscientious will, its result is weak feelings and weak energies, which
therefore can be kept in outward conformity to rule without any
strength either of will or of reason. Already energetic characters
on any large scale are becoming merely traditional. There is now
scarcely any outlet for energy in this country except business. The
energy expended in this may still be regarded as considerable. What
little is left from that employment, is expended on some hobby;
which may be a useful, even a philanthropic hobby, but is always
some one thing, and generally a thing of small dimensions. The greatness of England is now all collective: individually small, we only appear capable of anything great by our habit of combining; and with
this our moral and religious philanthropists are perfectly contented.
But it was men of another stamp than this that made England what
it has been; and men of another stamp will be needed to prevent its
decline.

The despotism of custom is everywhere the standing hindrance to
human advancement, being in unceasing antagonism to that disposition to aim at something better than customary, which is called, according to circumstances, the spirit of liberty, or that of progress or
improvement. The spirit of improvement is not always a spirit of
liberty, for it may aim at forcing improvements on an unwilling
people; and the spirit of liberty, in so far as it resists such attempts,
may ally itself locally and temporarily with the opponents of improvement; but the only unfailing and permanent source of improvement is liberty, since by it there are as many possible independent
centres of improvement as there are individuals. The progressive
principle, however, in either shape, whether as the love of liberty
or of improvement, is antagonistic to the sway of Custom, involving at

least emancipation from that yoke; and the contest between the two constitutes the chief interest of the history of mankind. The greater part of the world has, properly speaking, no history, because the despotism of Custom is complete. This is the case over the whole East. Custom is there, in all things, the final appeal; justice and right mean conformity to custom; the argument of custom no one, unless some tyrant intoxicated with power, thinks of resisting. And we see the result. Those nations must once have had originality; they did not start out of the ground populous, lettered, and versed in many of the arts of life; they made themselves all this, and were then the greatest and most powerful nations of the world. What are they now? The subjects or dependents of tribes whose forefathers wandered in the forests when theirs had magnificent palaces and gorgeous temples, but over whom custom exercised only a divided rule with liberty and progress. A people, it appears, may be progressive for a certain length of time, and then stop: when does it stop? When it ceases to possess individuality. If a similar change should befall the nations of Europe, it will not be in exactly the same shape: the despotism of custom with which these nations are threatened is not precisely stationariness. It proscribes singularity, but it does not preclude change, provided all change together. We have discarded the fixed costumes of our forefathers; every one must still dress like other people, but the fashion may change once or twice a year. We thus take care that when there is change it shall be for change's sake, and not from any idea of beauty or convenience; for the same idea of beauty or convenience would not strike all the world at the same moment, and be simultaneously thrown aside by all at another moment. But we are progressive as well as changeable: we continually make new inventions in mechanical things, and keep them until they are again superseded by better; we are eager for improvement in politics, in education, even in morals, though in this last our idea of improvement chiefly consists in persuading or forcing other people to be as good as ourselves. It is not progress that we object to; on the contrary, we flatter ourselves that we are the most progressive people who ever lived. It is individuality that we war against: we should think we had done wonders if we had made ourselves all alike; forgetting that the unlikeness of one person to another is generally the first thing which draws the attention of either to the imperfection of his own type, and the superiority of another, or the possibility, by combining the advantages of both, of producing something better than either. We have a warning example in China — a nation of much talent, and, in some respects, even wisdom, owing to the rare good fortune of having been provided at an early period with a particularly good set of customs, the work, in some measure, of men to whom even the most enlightened European must accord, under certain limitations, the title of sages and philosophers. They are remarkable, too, in the

excellence of their apparatus for impressing, as far as possible, the
best wisdom they possess upon every mind in the community, and
securing that those who have appropriated most of it shall occupy
the posts of honour and power. Surely the people who did this
have discovered the secret of human progressiveness, and must have
kept themselves steadily at the head of the movement of the world.
On the contrary, they have become stationary — have remained so
for thousands of years; and if they are ever to be farther improved,
it must be by foreigners. They have succeeded beyond all hope in
what English philanthropists are so industriously working at — in
making a people all alike, all governing their thoughts and conduct by
the same maxims and rules; and these are the fruits. The modern
régime of public opinion is, in an unorganized form, what the Chinese educational and political systems are in an organized; and unless
individuality shall be able successfully to assert itself against this
yoke, Europe, notwithstanding its noble antecedents and its professed
Christianity, will tend to become another China.

What is it that has hitherto preserved Europe from this lot? What
has made the European family of nations an improving, instead of a
stationary portion of mankind? Not any superior excellence in them,
which, when it exists, exists as the effect, not as the cause; but their
remarkable diversity of character and culture. Individuals, classes,
nations, have been extremely unlike one another: they have struck
out a great variety of paths, each leading to something valuable; and
although at every period those who travelled in different paths have
been intolerant of one another, and each would have thought it an
excellent thing if all the rest could have been compelled to travel his
road, their attempts to thwart each other's development have rarely
had any permanent success, and each has in time endured to receive
the good which the others have offered. Europe is, in my judgement,
wholly indebted to this plurality of paths for its progressive and many-
sided development. But it already begins to possess this benefit in
a considerably less degree. It is decidedly advancing towards the
Chinese ideal of making all people alike. M. de Tocqueville, in his
last important work, remarks how much more the Frenchmen of the
present day resemble one another, than did those even of the last
generation. The same remark might be made of Englishmen in a
far greater degree. In a passage already quoted from Wilhelm von
Humboldt, he points out two things as necessary conditions of human
development, because necessary to render people unlike one another;
namely, freedom, and variety of situations. The second of these two
conditions is in this country every day diminishing. The circumstances
which surround different classes and individuals, and shape their characters, are daily becoming more assimilated. Formerly, different
ranks, different neighbourhoods, different trades and professions,
lived in what might be called different worlds; at present, to a great

degree in the same. Comparatively speaking, they now read the same things, listen to the same things, see the same things, go to the same places, have their hopes and fears directed to the same objects, have the same rights and liberties, and the same means of asserting them. Great as are the differences of position which remain, they are nothing to those which have ceased. And the assimilation is still proceeding. All the political changes of the age promote it, since they all tend to raise the low and to lower the high. Every extension of education promotes it, because education brings people under common influences, and gives them access to the general stock of facts and sentiments. Improvements in the means of communication promote it, by bringing the inhabitants of distant places into personal contact, and keeping up a rapid flow of changes of residence between one place and another. The increase of commerce and manufactures promotes it, by diffusing more widely the advantages of easy circumstances, and opening all objects of ambition, even the highest, to general competition, whereby the desire of rising becomes no longer the character of a particular class, but of all classes. A more powerful agency than even all these, in bringing about a general similarity among mankind, is the complete establishment, in this and other free countries, of the ascendancy of public opinion in the State. As the various social eminences which enabled persons entrenched on them to disregard the opinion of the multitude gradually become levelled; as the very idea of resisting the will of the public, when it is positively known that they have a will, disappears more and more from the minds of practical politicians; there ceases to be any social support for nonconformity — any substantive power in society, which, itself opposed to the ascendancy of numbers, is interested in taking under its protection opinions and tendencies at variance with those of the public.

The combination of all these causes forms so great a mass of influences hostile to Individuality, that it is not easy to see how it can stand its ground. It will do so with increasing difficulty, unless the intelligent part of the public can be made to feel its value — to see that it is good there should be differences, even though not for the better, even though, as it may appear to them, some should be for the worse. If the claims of Individuality are ever to be asserted, the time is now, while much is still wanting to complete the enforced assimilation. It is only in the earlier stages that any stand can be successfully made against the encroachment. The demand that all other people shall resemble ourselves grows by what it feeds on. If resistance waits till life is reduced *nearly* to one uniform type, all deviations from that type will come to be considered impious, immoral, even monstrous and contrary to nature. Mankind speedily become unable to conceive diversity, when they have been for some time unaccustomed to see it.

Autobiography

❡ Written over a long period of time (partly before 1861, partly after 1871), Mill's *Autobiography* was published shortly after his death (1873). The book consists of seven chapters: I. "Childhood and Early Education"; II. "Moral Influences in Early Youth. My Father's Character and Opinions"; III. "Last Stage of Education and First of Self-education"; IV. "Youthful Propagandism. The Westminster Review"; V. "A Crisis in My Mental History. One Stage Onward"; VI. "Commencement of the Most Valuable Friendship of My Life. My Father's Death. Writings and Other Proceedings up to 1840"; VII. "General View of the Remainder of My Life." The experiences described in Chapter V, printed here, are universally recognized as of key importance in the making of John Stuart Mill and in the intellectual history of the nineteenth century. Here we can see most explicitly to what extent Mill departed from the strict Benthamite tradition. It is useful to contrast Mill's crisis and his account of it with Carlyle's, as described in *Sartor Resartus.* ❡❘

CHAPTER V

A Crisis in My Mental History. One Stage Onward

FOR some years after this time [1] I wrote very little, and nothing regularly, for publication: and great were the advantages which I derived from the intermission. It was of no common importance to me, at this period, to be able to digest and mature my thoughts for my own mind only, without any immediate call for giving them out in print. Had I gone on writing, it would have much disturbed the important transformation in my opinions and character, which took place during those years. The origin of this transformation, or at least the process by which I was prepared for it, can only be explained by turning some distance back.

From the winter of 1821, when I first read Bentham,[2] and especially from the commencement of the Westminster Review, I had what might truly be called an object in life; to be a reformer of the world. My conception of my own happiness was entirely identified with this object. The personal sympathies I wished for were those of fellow labourers in this enterprise. I endeavoured to pick up as many flowers as I could by the way; but as a serious and permanent personal satisfaction to rest upon, my whole reliance was placed on this; and I was accustomed to felicitate myself on the certainty of a

1 1828, when Mill ceased to write for the *Westminster Review.*
2 Jeremy Bentham (1748–1832), chief formulator of English Utilitarianism (sometimes called Benthamism).

happy life which I enjoyed, through placing my happiness in something durable and distant, in which some progress might be always making, while it could never be exhausted by complete attainment. This did very well for several years, during which the general improvement going on in the world and the idea of myself as engaged with others in struggling to promote it, seemed enough to fill up an interesting and animated existence. But the time came when I awakened from this as from a dream. It was in the autumn of 1826. I was in a dull state of nerves, such as everybody is occasionally liable to; unsusceptible to enjoyment or pleasurable excitement; one of those moods when what is pleasure at other times, becomes insipid or indifferent; the state, I should think, in which converts to Methodism usually are, when smitten by their first "conviction of sin." In this frame of mind it occurred to me to put the question directly to myself: "Suppose that all your objects in life were realized; that all the changes in institutions and opinions which you are looking forward to, could be completely effected at this very instant: would this be a great joy and happiness to you?" And an irrepressible self-consciousness distinctly answered, "No!" At this my heart sank within me: the whole foundation on which my life was constructed fell down. All my happiness was to have been found in the continual pursuit of this end. The end had ceased to charm, and how could there ever again be any interest in the means? I seemed to have nothing left to live for.

At first I hoped that the cloud would pass away of itself; but it did not. A night's sleep, the sovereign remedy for the smaller vexations of life, had no effect on it. I awoke to a renewed consciousness of the woful fact. I carried it with me into all companies, into all occupations. Hardly anything had power to cause me even a few minutes' oblivion of it. For some months the cloud seemed to grow thicker and thicker. The lines in Coleridge's "Dejection" — I was not then acquainted with them — exactly describe my case:

> A grief without a pang, void, dark and drear,
> A drowsy, stifled, unimpassioned grief,
> Which finds no natural outlet or relief
> In word, or sigh, or tear.

In vain I sought relief from my favourite books; those memorials of past nobleness and greatness from which I had always hitherto drawn strength and animation. I read them now without feeling, or with the accustomed feeling *minus* all its charm; and I became persuaded, that my love of mankind, and of excellence for its own sake, had worn itself out. I sought no comfort by speaking to others of what I felt. If I had loved any one sufficiently to make confiding my griefs a necessity, I should not have been in the condition I was. I felt, too, that mine was not an interesting, or in any way respectable

distress. There was nothing in it to attract sympathy. Advice, if I
had known where to seek it, would have been most precious. The
words of Macbeth to the physician often occurred to my thoughts.
But there was no one on whom I could build the faintest hope of
such assistance. My father, to whom it would have been natural to me
to have recourse in any practical difficulties, was the last person to
whom, in such a case as this, I looked for help. Everything convinced
me that he had no knowledge of any such mental state as I was suffering from, and that even if he could be made to understand it, he
was not the physician who could heal it. My education, which was
wholly his work, had been conducted without any regard to the possibility of its ending in this result; and I saw no use in giving him the
pain of thinking that his plans had failed, when the failure was probably irremediable, and, at all events, beyond the power of *his* remedies. Of other friends, I had at that time none to whom I had any
hope of making my condition intelligible. It was however abundantly
intelligible to myself; and the more I dwelt upon it, the more hopeless it appeared.

My course of study had led me to believe, that all mental and moral
feelings and qualities, whether of a good or of a bad kind, were the
results of association; that we love one thing, and hate another, take
pleasure in one sort of action or contemplation, and pain in another
sort, through the clinging of pleasurable or painful ideas to those
things, from the effect of education or of experience. As a corollary
from this, I had always heard it maintained by my father, and was
myself convinced, that the object of education should be to form the
strongest possible associations of the salutary class; associations of
pleasure with all things beneficial to the great whole, and of pain
with all things hurtful to it. This doctrine appeared inexpugnable;
but it now seemed to me, on retrospect, that my teachers had occupied
themselves but superficially with the means of forming and keeping up
these salutary associations. They seemed to have trusted altogether to
the old familiar instruments, praise and blame, reward and punishment. Now, I did not doubt that by these means, begun early, and
applied unremittingly, intense associations of pain and pleasure, especially of pain, might be created, and might produce desires and
aversions capable of lasting undiminished to the end of life. But there
must always be something artificial and casual in associations thus
produced. The pains and pleasures thus forcibly associated with
things, are not connected with them by any natural tie; and it is therefore, I thought, essential to the durability of these associations, that
they should have become so intense and inveterate as to be practically
indissoluble, before the habitual exercise of the power of analysis
had commenced. For I now saw, or thought I saw, what I had always
before received with incredulity — that the habit of analysis has a
tendency to wear away the feelings: as indeed it has, when no other

mental habit is cultivated, and the analysing spirit remains without its natural complements and correctives. The very excellence of analysis (I argued) is that it tends to weaken and undermine whatever is the result of prejudice; that it enables us mentally to separate ideas which have only casually clung together: and no associations whatever could ultimately resist this dissolving force, were it not that we owe to analysis our clearest knowledge of the permanent sequences in nature; the real connexions between Things, not dependent on our will and feelings; natural laws, by virtue of which, in many cases, one thing is inseparable from another in fact; which laws, in proportion as they are clearly perceived and imaginatively realized, cause our ideas of things which are always joined together in Nature, to cohere more and more closely in our thoughts. Analytic habits may thus even strengthen the associations between causes and effects, means and ends, but tend altogether to weaken those which are, to speak familiarly, a *mere* matter of feeling. They are therefore (I thought) favourable to prudence and clear-sightedness, but a perpetual worm at the root both of the passions and of the virtues; and, above all, fearfully undermine all desires, and all pleasures, which are the effects of association, that is, according to the theory I held, all except the purely physical and organic; of the entire insufficiency of which to make life desirable, no one had a stronger conviction than I had. These were the laws of human nature, by which, as it seemed to me, I had been brought to my present state. All those to whom I looked up, were of opinion that the pleasure of sympathy with human beings, and the feelings which made the good of others, and especially of mankind on a large scale, the object of existence, were the greatest and surest sources of happiness. Of the truth of this I was convinced, but to know that a feeling would make me happy if I had it, did not give me the feeling. My education, I thought, had failed to create these feelings in sufficient strength to resist the dissolving influence of analysis, while the whole course of my intellectual cultivation had made precocious and premature analysis the inveterate habit of my mind. I was thus, as I said to myself, left stranded at the commencement of my voyage, with a well-equipped ship and a rudder, but no sail; without any real desire for the ends which I had been so carefully fitted out to work for: no delight in virtue, or the general good, but also just as little in anything else. The fountains of vanity and ambition seemed to have dried up within me, as completely as those of benevolence. I had had (as I reflected) some gratification of vanity at too early an age: I had obtained some distinction, and felt myself of some importance, before the desire of distinction and of importance had grown into a passion: and little as it was which I had attained, yet having been attained too early, like all pleasures enjoyed too soon, it had made me *blasé* and indifferent to the pursuit. Thus neither selfish nor unselfish pleasures were pleasures to me. And there seemed no power in nature sufficient to begin the formation of my character anew, and create in a mind now irretrievably analytic, fresh associations of pleasure with any of the objects of human desire.

These were the thoughts which mingled with the dry heavy dejection of the melancholy winter of 1826–7. During this time I was not incapable of my usual occupations. I went on with them mechanically, by the mere force of habit. I had been so drilled in a certain sort of mental exercise, that I could still carry it on when all the spirit had gone out of it. I even composed and spoke several speeches at the debating society, how, or with what degree of success, I know not. Of four years continual speaking at that society, this is the only year of which I remember next to nothing. Two lines of Coleridge, in whom alone of all writers I have found a true description of what I felt, were often in my thoughts, not at this time (for I had never read them), but in a later period of the same mental malady:

> Work without hope draws nectar in a sieve,
> And hope without an object cannot live.

In all probability my case was by no means so peculiar as I fancied it, and I doubt not that many others have passed through a similar state; but the idiosyncrasies of my education had given to the general phenomenon a special character, which made it seem the natural effect of causes that it was hardly possible for time to remove. I frequently asked myself, if I could, or if I was bound to go on living, when life must be passed in this manner. I generally answered to myself, that I did not think I could possibly bear it beyond a year. When, however, not more than half that duration of time had elapsed, a small ray of light broke in upon my gloom. I was reading, accidentally, Marmontel's "Memoires," and came to the passage which relates his father's death, the distressed position of the family, and the sudden inspiration by which he, then a mere boy, felt and made them feel that he would be everything to them — would supply the place of all that they had lost. A vivid conception of that scene and its feelings came over me, and I was moved to tears. From this moment my burden grew lighter. The oppression of the thought that all feeling was dead within me, was gone. I was no longer hopeless: I was not a stock or a stone. I had still, it seemed, some of the material out of which all worth of character, and all capacity for happiness, are made. Relieved from my ever present sense of irremediable wretchedness, I gradually found that the ordinary incidents of life could again give me some pleasure; that I could again find enjoyment, not intense, but sufficient for cheerfulness, in sunshine and sky, in books, in conversation, in public affairs; and that there was, once more, excitement, though of a moderate kind, in exerting myself for my opinions, and for the public good. Thus the cloud gradually drew off, and I again enjoyed life: and though I had several relapses, some of which lasted many months, I never again was as miserable as I had been.

The experiences of this period had two very marked effects on my opinions and character. In the first place, they led me to adopt a theory of life, very unlike that on which I had before acted, and having much in common with what at that time I certainly had never heard of, the anti-self-consciousness theory of Carlyle. I never, indeed, wavered in the conviction that happiness is the test of all rules of conduct, and the end of life. But I now thought that this end was only to be attained by not making it the direct end. Those only are happy (I thought) who have their minds fixed on some object other than their own happiness; on the happiness of others, on the improvement of mankind, even on some art or pursuit, followed not as a means, but as itself an ideal end. Aiming thus at something else, they find happiness by the way. The enjoyments of life (such was now my theory) are sufficient to make it a pleasant thing, when they are taken *en passant*, without being made a principal object. Once make them so, and they are immediately felt to be insufficient. They will not bear a scrutinizing examination. Ask yourself whether you are happy, and you cease to be so. The only chance is to treat, not happiness, but some end external to it, as the purpose of life. Let your self-consciousness, your scrutiny, your self-interrogation, exhaust themselves on that; and if otherwise fortunately circumstanced you will inhale happiness with the air you breathe, without dwelling on it or thinking about it, without either forestalling it in imagination, or putting it to flight by fatal questioning. This theory now became the basis of my philosophy of life. And I still hold to it as the best theory for all those who have but a moderate degree of sensibility and of capacity for enjoyment, that is, for the great majority of mankind.

The other important change which my opinions at this time underwent, was that I, for the first time, gave its proper place, among the prime necessities of human well-being, to the internal culture of the individual. I ceased to attach almost exclusive importance to the ordering of outward circumstances, and the training of the human being for speculation and for action.

I had now learnt by experience that the passive susceptibilities needed to be cultivated as well as the active capacities, and required to be nourished and enriched as well as guided. I did not, for an instant, lose sight of, or undervalue, that part of the truth which I had seen before; I never turned recreant to intellectual culture, or ceased to consider the power and practice of analysis as an essential condition both of individual and of social improvement. But I thought that it had consequences which required to be corrected, by joining other kinds of cultivation with it. The maintenance of a due balance among the faculties, now seemed to me of primary importance. The cultivation of the feelings became one of the cardinal points in my ethical and philosophical creed. And my thoughts and inclinations turned in an increasing degree towards whatever seemed capable of being instrumental to that object.

I now began to find meaning in the things which I had read or heard about the importance of poetry and art as instruments of human culture. But it was some time longer before I began to know this by personal experience. The only one of the imaginative arts in which I had from childhood taken great pleasure, was music; the best effect of which (and in this it surpasses perhaps every other art) consists in exciting enthusiasm; in winding up to a high pitch those feelings of an elevated kind which are already in the character, but to which this excitement gives a glow and a fervour, which, though transitory at its utmost height, is precious for sustaining them at other times. This effect of music I had often experienced; but like all my pleasurable susceptibilities it was suspended during the gloomy period. I had sought relief again and again from this quarter, but found none. After the tide had turned, and I was in process of recovery, I had been helped forward by music, but in a much less elevated manner. I at this time first became acquainted with Weber's Oberon, and the extreme pleasure which I drew from its delicious melodies did me good, by showing me a source of pleasure to which I was as susceptible as ever. The good, however, was much impaired by the thought, that the pleasure of music (as is quite true of such pleasure as this was, that of mere tune) fades with familiarity, and requires either to be revived by intermittence, or fed by continual novelty. And it is very characteristic both of my then state, and of the general tone of my mind at this period of my life, that I was seriously tormented by the thought of the exhaustibility of musical combinations. The octave consists only of five tones and two semitones, which can be put together in only a limited number of ways, of which but a small proportion are beautiful: most of these, it seemed to me, must have been already discovered, and there could not be room for a long succession of Mozarts and Webers, to strike out, as these had done, entirely new and surpassingly rich veins of musical beauty. This source of anxiety may, perhaps, be thought to resemble that of the philosophers of Laputa, who feared lest the sun should be burnt out. It was, however, connected with the best feature in my character, and the only good point to be found in my very unromantic and in no way honourable distress. For though my dejection, honestly looked at, could not be called other than egotistical, produced by the ruin, as I thought, of my fabric of happiness, yet the destiny of mankind in general was ever in my thoughts, and could not be separated from my own. I felt that the flaw in my life, must be a flaw in life itself; that the question was, whether, if the reformers of society and government could succeed in their objects, and every person in the community were free and in a state of physical comfort, the pleasures of life, being no longer kept up by struggle and privation, would cease to be pleasures. And I felt that unless I could see my way to some better hope than this for human happiness in general, my dejection must continue; but that if I could see such an outlet, I should then look on the world with pleasure; content as far as I was myself concerned, with any fair share of the general lot.

This state of my thoughts and feelings made the fact of my reading Wordsworth for the first time (in the autumn of 1828), an important event in my life. I took up the collection of his poems from curiosity, with no expectation of mental relief from it, though I had before resorted to poetry with that hope. In the worst period of my depression, I had read through the whole of Byron (then new to me), to try whether a poet, whose peculiar department was supposed to be that of the intenser feelings, could rouse any feeling in me. As might be expected, I got no good from this reading, but the reverse. The poet's state of mind was too like my own. His was the lament of a man who had worn out all pleasures, and who seemed to think that life, to all who possess the good things of it, must necessarily be the vapid, uninteresting thing which I found it. His Harold and Manfred had the same burden on them which I had; and I was not in a frame of mind to desire any comfort from the vehement sensual passion of his Giaours, or the sullenness of his Laras. But while Byron was exactly what did not suit my condition, Wordsworth was exactly what did. I had looked into the Excursion two or three years before, and found little in it; and I should probably have found as little, had I read it at this time. But the miscellaneous poems, in the two-volume edition of 1815 (to which little of value was added in the latter part of the author's life), proved to be the precise thing for my mental wants at that particular juncture.

In the first place, these poems addressed themselves powerfully to one of the strongest of my pleasurable susceptibilities, the love of rural objects and natural scenery; to which I had been indebted not only for much of the pleasure of my life, but quite recently for relief from one of my longest relapses into depression. In this power of rural beauty over me, there was a foundation laid for taking pleasure in Wordsworth's poetry; the more so, as his scenery lies mostly among mountains, which, owing to my early Pyrenean excursion, were my ideal of natural beauty. But Wordsworth would never have had any great effect on me, if he had merely placed before me beautiful pictures of natural scenery. Scott does this still better than Wordsworth, and a very second-rate landscape does it more effectually than any poet. What made Wordsworth's poems a medicine for my state of mind, was that they expressed, not mere outward beauty, but states of feeling, and of thought coloured by feeling, under the excitement of beauty. They seemed to be the very culture of the feelings, which I was in quest of. In them I seemed to draw from a source of inward joy, of sympathetic and imaginative pleasure, which could be shared

in by all human beings; which had no connexion with struggle or imperfection, but would be made richer by every improvement in the
physical or social condition of mankind. From them I seemed to learn
what would be the perennial sources of happiness, when all the greater
evils of life shall have been removed. And I felt myself at once better
and happier as I came under their influence. There have certainly
been, even in our own age, greater poets than Wordsworth; but poetry
of deeper and loftier feeling could not have done for me at that time
what his did. I needed to be made to feel that there was real, permanent happiness in tranquil contemplation. Wordsworth taught me
this, not only without turning away from, but with a greatly increased
interest in the common feelings and common destiny of human beings.
And the delight which these poems gave me, proved that with culture
of this sort, there was nothing to dread from the most confirmed
habit of analysis. At the conclusion of the Poems came the famous
Ode, falsely called Platonic, "Intimations of Immortality": in which,
along with more than his usual sweetness of melody and rhythm, and
along with the two passages of grand imagery but bad philosophy so
often quoted, I found that he too had had similar experience to mine:
that he also had felt that the first freshness of youthful enjoyment of
life was not lasting; but that he had sought for compensation, and
found it, in the way in which he was now teaching me to find it. The
result was that I gradually, but completely, emerged from my habitual
depression, and was never again subject to it. I long continued to
value Wordsworth less according to his intrinsic merits, than by the
measure of what he had done for me. Compared with the greatest
poets, he may be said to be the poet of unpoetical natures, possessed
of quiet and contemplative tastes. But unpoetical natures are precisely
those which require poetic cultivation. This cultivation Wordsworth is
much more fitted to give, than poets who are intrinsically far more
poets than he.

It so fell out that the merits of Wordsworth were the occasion of
my first public declaration of my new way of thinking, and separation
from those of my habitual companions who had not undergone a similar
change. The person with whom at that time I was most in the habit
of comparing notes on such subjects was Roebuck,[3] and I induced
him to read Wordsworth, in whom he also at first seemed to find
much to admire: but I, like most Wordsworthians, threw myself into
strong antagonism to Byron, both as a poet and as to his influence on
the character. Roebuck, all whose instincts were those of action
and struggle, had, on the contrary, a strong relish and great admiration of Byron, whose writings he regarded as the poetry of human
life, while Wordsworth's, according to him, was that of flowers and
butterflies. We agreed to have the fight out at our Debating Society,
where we accordingly discussed for two evenings the comparative

3 John Arthur Roebuck (1801–1879), politician and social reformer.

merits of Byron and Wordsworth, propounding and illustrating by long recitations our respective theories of poetry: Sterling [4] also, in a brilliant speech, putting forward his particular theory. This was the first debate on any weighty subject in which Roebuck and I had been on opposite sides. The schism between us widened from this time more and more, though we continued for some years longer to be companions. In the beginning, our chief divergence related to the cultivation of the feelings. Roebuck was in many respects very different from the vulgar notion of a Benthamite or Utilitarian. He was a lover of poetry and of most of the fine arts. He took great pleasure in music, in dramatic performances, especially in painting, and himself drew and designed landscapes with great facility and beauty. But he never could be made to see that these things have any value as aids in the formation of character. Personally, instead of being, as Benthamites are supposed to be, void of feeling, he had very quick and strong sensibilities. But, like most Englishmen who have feelings, he found his feelings stand very much in his way. He was much more susceptible to the painful sympathies than to the pleasurable, and looking for his happiness elsewhere, he wished that his feelings should be deadened rather than quickened. And, in truth, the English character, and English social circumstances, make it so seldom possible to derive happiness from the exercise of the sympathies, that it is not wonderful if they count for little in an Englishman's scheme of life. In most other countries the paramount importance of the sympathies as a constituent of individual happiness is an axiom, taken for granted rather than needing any formal statement; but most English thinkers almost seem to regard them as necessary evils, required for keeping men's actions benevolent and compassionate. Roebuck was, or appeared to be, this kind of Englishman. He saw little good in any cultivation of the feelings, and none at all in cultivating them through the imagination, which he thought was only cultivating illusions. It was in vain I urged on him that the imaginative emotion which an idea, when vividly conceived, excites in us, is not an illusion but a fact, as real as any of the other qualities of objects; and far from implying anything erroneous and delusive in our mental apprehension of the object, is quite consistent with the most accurate knowledge and most perfect practical recognition of all its physical and intellectual laws and relations. The intensest feeling of the beauty of a cloud lighted by the setting sun, is no hindrance to my knowing that the cloud is vapour of water, subject to all the laws of vapours in a state of suspension; and I am just as likely to allow for, and act on, these physical laws whenever there is occasion to do so, as if I had been incapable of perceiving any distinction between beauty and ugliness.

4 John Sterling (1806–1844), center of a literary group including Carlyle, Tennyson, Mill, and others.

While my intimacy with Roebuck diminished, I fell more and more into friendly intercourse with our Coleridgian adversaries in the Society, Frederick Maurice [5] and John Sterling, both subsequently so well known, the former by his writings, the latter through the biographies by Hare [6] and Carlyle. Of these two friends, Maurice was the thinker, Sterling the orator, and impassioned expositor of thoughts which, at this period, were almost entirely formed for him by Maurice.

With Maurice I had for some time been acquainted through Eyton Tooke,[7] who had known him at Cambridge, and although my discussions with him were almost always disputes, I had carried away from them much that helped to build up my new fabric of thought, in the same way as I was deriving much from Coleridge, and from the writings of Goethe and other German authors which I read during these years. I have so deep a respect for Maurice's character and purposes, as well as for his great mental gifts, that it is with some unwillingness I say anything which may seem to place him on a less high eminence than I would gladly be able to accord him. But I have always thought that there was more intellectual power wasted in Maurice than in any other of my contemporaries. Few of them certainly have had so much to waste. Great powers of generalization, rare ingenuity and subtlety, and a wide perception of important and unobvious truths, served him not for putting something better into the place of the worthless heap of received opinions on the great subjects of thought, but for proving to his own mind that the Church of England had known everything from the first, and that all the truths on the ground of which the Church and orthodoxy have been attacked (many of which he saw as clearly as any one) are not only consistent with the Thirty-nine Articles, but are better understood and expressed in those Articles than by any one who rejects them. I have never been able to find any other explanation of this, than by attributing it to that timidity of conscience, combined with original sensitiveness of temperament, which has so often driven highly gifted men into Romanism from the need of a firmer support than they can find in the independent conclusions of their own judgment. Any more vulgar kind of timidity no one who knew Maurice would ever think of imputing to him, even if he had not given public proof of his freedom from it, by his ultimate collision with some of the opinions commonly regarded as orthodox, and by his noble origination of the Christian Socialist movement. The nearest parallel to him, in a moral point of view, is Coleridge, to whom, in merely intellectual power, apart from poetical genius, I think him decidedly superior. At this time, however, he might be described as a disciple of Coleridge, and Sterling as a disciple of Cole-

---

5 Frederick Denison Maurice (1805–1872), popular theological writer and Christian socialist.
6 Julius Charles Hare (1795–1855), religious philosopher and translator.
7 Son of Thomas Tooke (1774–1858), an economist.

ridge and of him. The modifications which were taking place in my old opinions gave me some points of contact with them; and both Maurice and Sterling were of considerable use to my development. With Sterling I soon became very intimate, and was more attached to him than I have ever been to any other man. He was indeed one of the most loveable of men. His frank, cordial, affectionate, and expansive character; a love of truth alike conspicuous in the highest things and the humblest; a generous and ardent nature which threw itself with impetuosity into the opinions it adopted, but was as eager to do justice to the doctrines and the men it was opposed to, as to make war on what it thought their errors; and an equal devotion to the two cardinal points of Liberty and Duty, formed a combination of qualities as attractive to me, as to all others who knew him as well as I did. With his open mind and heart, he found no difficulty in joining hands with me across the gulf which as yet divided our opinions. He told me how he and others had looked upon me (from hearsay information), as a "made" or manufactured man, having had a certain impress of opinion stamped on me which I could only reproduce; and what a change took place in his feelings when he found, in the discussion on Wordsworth and Byron, that Wordsworth, and all which that name implies, "belonged" to me as much as to him and his friends. The failure of his health soon scattered all his plans of life, and compelled him to live at a distance from London, so that after the first year or two of our acquaintance, we only saw each other at distant intervals. But (as he said himself in one of his letters to Carlyle) when we did meet it was like brothers. Though he was never, in the full sense of the word, a profound thinker, his openness of mind, and the moral courage in which he greatly surpassed Maurice, made him outgrow the dominion which Maurice and Coleridge had once exercised over his intellect; though he retained to the last a great but discriminating admiration of both, and towards Maurice a warm affection. Except in that short and transitory phasis of his life, during which he made the mistake of becoming a clergyman, his mind was ever progressive: and the advance he always seemed to have made when I saw him after an interval, made me apply to him what Goethe said of Schiller, "er hatte eine furchtliche Fortschreitung." [8] He and I started from intellectual points almost as wide apart as the poles, but the distance between us was always diminishing: if I made steps towards some of his opinions, he, during his short life, was constantly approximating more and more to several of mine: and if he had lived, and had health and vigour to prosecute his ever assiduous self-culture, there is no knowing how much further this spontaneous assimilation might have proceeded.

After 1829 I withdrew from attendance on the Debating Society. I had had enough of speech-making, and was glad to carry on my

[8] "he had a terrible development."

private studies and meditations without any immediate call for outward assertion of their results. I found the fabric of my old and taught opinions giving way in many fresh places, and I never allowed it to fall to pieces, but was incessantly occupied in weaving it anew. I never, in the course of my transition, was content to remain, for ever so short a time, confused and unsettled. When I had taken in any new idea, I could not rest till I had adjusted its relation to my old opinions, and ascertained exactly how far its effect ought to extend in modifying or superseding them.

The conflicts which I had so often had to sustain in defending the theory of government laid down in Bentham's and my father's writings, and the acquaintance I had obtained with other schools of political thinking, made me aware of many things which that doctrine, professing to be a theory of government in general, ought to have made room for and did not. But these things, as yet, remained with me rather as corrections to be made in applying the theory to practice, than as defects in the theory. I felt that politics could not be a science of specific experience; and that the accusations against the Benthamic theory of *being* a theory, of proceeding *à priori* by way of general reasoning, instead of Baconian experiment, showed complete ignorance of Bacon's principles, and of the necessary conditions of experimental investigation. At this juncture appeared in the Edinburgh Review, Macaulay's famous attack on my father's Essay on Government. This gave me much to think about. I saw that Macaulay's conception of the logic of politics was erroneous; that he stood up for the empirical mode of treating political phenomena, against the philosophical; that even in physical science his notions of philosophizing might have recognised Kepler, but would have excluded Newton and Laplace. But I could not help feeling, that though the tone was unbecoming (an error for which the writer, at a later period, made the most ample and honourable amends), there was truth in several of his strictures on my father's treatment of the subject; that my father's premises were really too narrow, and included but a small number of the general truths, on which, in politics, the important consequences depend. Identity of interest between the governing body and the community at large, is not, in any practical sense which can be attached to it, the only thing on which good government depends; neither can this identity of interest be secured by the mere conditions of election. I was not at all satisfied with the mode in which my father met the criticisms of Macaulay. He did not, as I thought he ought to have done, justify himself by saying, "I was not writing a scientific treatise on politics, I was writing an argument for parliamentary reform." He treated Macaulay's argument as simply irrational; an attack upon the reasoning faculty; an example of the saying of Hobbes, that when reason is against a man, a man will be against reason. This made me think that there was really something more fundamentally erroneous in my father's conception of philosophical method, as applicable to politics, than I had hitherto supposed there was. But I did not at first see clearly what the error might be. At last it flashed upon me all at once in the course of other studies. In the early part of 1830 I had begun to put on paper the ideas on Logic (chiefly on the distinctions among Terms, and the import of Propositions) which had been suggested and in part worked out in the morning conversations already spoken of. Having secured these thoughts from being lost, I pushed on into the other parts of the subject, to try whether I could do anything further towards clearing up the theory of logic generally. I grappled at once with the problem of Induction, postponing that of Reasoning, on the ground that it is necessary to obtain premises before we can reason from them. Now, Induction is mainly a process for finding the causes of effects: and in attempting to fathom the mode of tracing causes and effects in physical science, I soon saw that in the more perfect of the sciences, we ascend, by generalization from particulars, to the tendencies of causes considered singly, and then reason downward from those separate tendencies, to the effect of the same causes when combined. I then asked myself, what is the ultimate analysis of this deductive process; the common theory of the syllogism evidently throwing no light upon it. My practice (learnt from Hobbes and my father) being to study abstract principles by means of the best concrete instances I could find, the Composition of Forces, in dynamics, occurred to me as the most complete example of the logical process I was investigating. On examining, accordingly, what the mind does when it applies the principle of the Composition of Forces, I found that it performs a simple act of addition. It adds the separate effect of the one force to the separate effect of the other, and puts down the sum of these separate effects as the joint effect. But is this a legitimate process? In dynamics, and in all the mathematical branches of physics, it is; but in some other cases, as in chemistry, it is not; and I then recollected that something not unlike this was pointed out as one of the distinctions between chemical and mechanical phenomena, in the introduction to that favourite of my boyhood, Thomson's System of Chemistry. This distinction at once made my mind clear as to what was perplexing me in respect to the philosophy of politics. I now saw, that a science is either deductive or experimental, according as, in the province it deals with, the effects of causes when conjoined, are or are not the sums of the effects which the same causes produce when separate. It followed that politics must be a deductive science. It thus appeared, that both Macaulay and my father were wrong; the one in assimilating the method of philosophizing in politics to the purely experimental method of chemistry; while the other, though right in adopting a deductive method, had made a wrong selection of one, having taken as the type of deduction, not the appropriate process, that of the deductive branches of natural philosophy, but the

inappropriate one of pure geometry, which, not being a science of
causation at all, does not require or admit of any summing-up of effects. A foundation was thus laid in my thoughts for the principal
chapters of what I afterwards published on the Logic of the Moral
Sciences; and my new position in respect to my old political creed,
now became perfectly definite.

If I am asked, what system of political philosophy I substituted
for that which, as a philosophy, I had abandoned, I answer, No
system: only a conviction that the true system was something much
more complex and many-sided than I had previously had any idea of,
and that its office was to supply, not a set of model institutions, but
principles from which the institutions suitable to any given circumstances might be deduced. The influences of European, that is to say,
Continental, thought, and especially those of the reaction of the nineteenth century against the eighteenth, were now streaming in upon
me. They came from various quarters: from the writings of Coleridge,
which I had begun to read with interest even before the change in my
opinions; from the Coleridgians with whom I was in personal intercourse; from what I had read of Goethe; from Carlyle's early
articles in the Edinburgh and Foreign Reviews, though for a long
time I saw nothing in these (as my father saw nothing in them to the
last) but insane rhapsody. From these sources, and from the acquaintance I kept up with the French literature of the time, I derived,
among other ideas which the general turning upside down of the
opinions of European thinkers had brought uppermost, these in
particular: That the human mind has a certain order of possible
progress, in which some things must precede others, an order which
governments and public instructors can modify to some, but not to
an unlimited extent: that all questions of political institutions are
relative, not absolute, and that different stages of human progress
not only *will* have, but *ought* to have, different institutions: that government is always either in the hands, or passing into the hands, of
whatever is the strongest power in society, and that what this power
is, does not depend on institutions, but institutions on it: that any
general theory or philosophy of politics supposes a previous theory of
human progress, and that this is the same thing with a philosophy
of history. These opinions, true in the main, were held in an exaggerated and violent manner by the thinkers with whom I was now
most accustomed to compare notes, and who, as usual with a reaction, ignored that half of the truth which the thinkers of the eighteenth century
saw. But though, at one period of my progress, I for some time undervalued that great century, I never joined in the reaction against it,
but kept as firm hold of one side of the truth as I took of the other.
The fight between the nineteenth century and the eighteenth always
reminded me of the battle about the shield, one side of which was
white and the other black. I marvelled at the blind rage with which

the combatants rushed against one another. I applied to
Coleridge himself, many of Coleridge's sayings about
and Goethe's device, "many-sidedness," was one which
willingly, at this period, have taken for mine.

The writers by whom, more than by any others, a
political thinking was brought home to me, were those of the St.
Simonian school in France. In 1829 and 1830 I became acquainted
with some of their writings. They were then only in the earlier stages
of their speculations. They had not yet dressed out their philosophy
as a religion, nor had they organized their scheme of Socialism. They
were just beginning to question the principle of hereditary property.
I was by no means prepared to go with them even this length; but
I was greatly struck with the connected view which they for the
first time presented to me, of the natural order of human progress; and
especially with their division of all history into organic periods and
critical periods. During the organic periods (they said) mankind accept
with firm conviction some positive creed, claiming jurisdiction over all
their actions, and containing more or less of truth and adaptation to the
needs of humanity. Under its influence they make all the progress compatible with the creed, and finally outgrow it; when a period follows of
criticism and negation, in which mankind lose their old convictions without acquiring any new ones, of a general or authoritative character, except the conviction that the old are false. The period of Greek and Roman polytheism, so long as really believed in by instructed Greeks and
Romans, was an organic period, succeeded by the critical or sceptical
period of the Greek philosophers. Another organic period came in
with Christianity. The corresponding critical period began with the
Reformation, has lasted ever since, still lasts, and cannot altogether
cease until a new organic period has been inaugurated by the triumph
of a yet more advanced creed. These ideas, I knew, were not peculiar
to the St. Simonians; on the contrary, they were the general property
of Europe, or at least of Germany and France, but they had never,
to my knowledge, been so completely systematized as by these writers,
nor the distinguishing characteristics of a critical period so powerfully
set forth; for I was not then acquainted with Fichte's Lectures on
"The Characteristics of the Present Age." In Carlyle, indeed, I
found bitter denunciations of an "age of unbelief," and of the present
age as such, which I, like most people at that time, supposed to be
passionate protests in favour of the old modes of belief. But all that
was true in these denunciations, I thought that I found more calmly
and philosophically stated by the St. Simonians. Among their publications, too, there was one which seemed to me far superior to the
rest; in which the general idea was matured into something much more
definite and instructive. This was an early work of Auguste Comte,
who then called himself, and even announced himself in the title-page

as, a pupil of Saint Simon. In this tract M. Comte first put forth the doctrine, which he afterwards so copiously illustrated, of the natural succession of three stages in every department of human knowledge: first, the theological, next the metaphysical, and lastly, the positive stage; and contended, that social science must be subject to the same law; that the feudal and Catholic system was the concluding phasis of the theological state of the social science, Protestantism the commencement, and the doctrines of the French Revolution the consummation, of the metaphysical; and that its positive state was yet to come. This doctrine harmonized well with my existing notions, to which it seemed to give a scientific shape. I already regarded the methods of physical science as the proper models for political. But the chief benefit which I derived at this time from the trains of thought suggested by the St. Simonians and by Comte, was, that I obtained a clearer conception than ever before of the peculiarities of an era of transition in opinion, and ceased to mistake the moral and intellectual characteristics of such an era, for the normal attributes of humanity. I looked forward, through the present age of loud disputes but generally weak convictions, to a future which shall unite the best qualities of the critical with the best qualities of the organic periods; unchecked liberty of thought, unbounded freedom of individual action in all modes not hurtful to others; but also, convictions as to what is right and wrong, useful and pernicious, deeply engraven on the feelings by early education and general unanimity of sentiment, and so firmly grounded in reason and in the true exigencies of life, that they shall not, like all former and present creeds, religious, ethical, and political, require to be periodically thrown off and replaced by others.

M. Comte soon left the St. Simonians, and I lost sight of him and his writings for a number of years. But the St. Simonians I continued to cultivate. I was kept *au courant* of their progress by one of their most enthusiastic disciples, M. Gustave d'Eichthal, who about that time passed a considerable interval in England. I was introduced to their chiefs, Bazard and Enfantin, in 1830; and as long as their public teachings and proselytism continued, I read nearly everything they wrote. Their criticisms on the common doctrines of Liberalism seemed to me full of important truth; and it was partly by their writings that my eyes were opened to the very limited and temporary value of the old political economy, which assumes private property and inheritance as indefeasible facts, and freedom of production and exchange as the *dernier mot* of social improvement. The scheme gradually unfolded by the St. Simonians, under which the labour and capital of society would be managed for the general account of the community, every individual being required to take a share of labour, either as thinker, teacher, artist, or producer, all being classed according to their capacity, and remunerated according to their work,

appeared to me a far superior description of Socialism to Owen's.[9]
Their aim seemed to me desirable and rational, however their means
might be inefficacious; and though I neither believed in the practica-
bility, nor in the beneficial operation of their social machinery, I felt
that the proclamation of such an ideal of human society could not but
tend to give a beneficial direction to the efforts of others to bring society, as at present constituted, nearer to some ideal standard. I
honoured them most of all for what they have been most cried down
for — the boldness and freedom from prejudice with which they
treated the subject of family, the most important of any, and needing
more fundamental alterations than remain to be made in any other
great social institution, but on which scarcely any reformer has the
courage to touch. In proclaiming the perfect equality of men and
women, and an entirely new order of things in regard to their relations
with one another, the St. Simonians, in common with Owen and
Fourier, have entitled themselves to the grateful remembrance of
future generations.

In giving an account of this period of my life, I have only specified
such of my new impressions as appeared to me, both at the time and
since, to be a kind of turning points, marking a definite progress in
my mode of thought. But these few selected points give a very insufficient idea of the quantity of thinking which I carried on respecting
a host of subjects during these years of transition. Much of this, it is
true, consisted in rediscovering things known to all the world, which
I had previously disbelieved, or disregarded. But the rediscovery was
to me a discovery, giving me plenary possession of the truths, not
as traditional platitudes, but fresh from their source: and it seldom
failed to place them in some new light, by which they were reconciled
with, and seemed to confirm while they modified, the truths less generally known which lay in my early opinions, and in no essential part
of which I at any time wavered. All my new thinking only laid the
foundation of these more deeply and strongly, while it often removed
misapprehension and confusion of ideas which had perverted their
effect. For example, during the later returns of my dejection, the
doctrine of what is called Philosophical Necessity weighed on my
existence like an incubus. I felt as if I was scientifically proved to
be the helpless slave of antecedent circumstances; as if my character
and that of all others had been formed for us by agencies beyond
our control, and was wholly out of our own power. I often said to
myself, what a relief it would be if I could disbelieve the doctrine
of the formation of character by circumstances; and remembering the
wish of Fox respecting the doctrine of resistance to governments,
that it might never be forgotten by kings, nor remembered by subjects, I said that it would be a blessing if the doctrine of necessity

could be believed by all *quoad* the characters of others, and disbelieved in regard to their own. I pondered painfully on the subject, till gradually I saw light through it. I perceived, that the word Necessity, as a name for the doctrine of Cause and Effect applied to human action, carried with it a misleading association; and that this association was the operative force in the depressing and paralysing influence which I had experienced: I saw that though our character is formed by circumstances, our own desires can do much to shape those circumstances; and that what is really inspiriting and ennobling in the doctrine of freewill, is the conviction that we have real power over the formation of our own character; that our will, by influencing some of our circumstances, can modify our future habits or capabilities of willing. All this was entirely consistent with the doctrine of circumstances, or rather, was that doctrine itself, properly understood. From that time I drew in my own mind, a clear distinction between the doctrine of circumstances, and Fatalism; discarding altogether the misleading word Necessity. The theory, which I now for the first time rightly apprehended, ceased altogether to be discouraging, and besides the relief to my spirits, I no longer suffered under the burden, so heavy to one who aims at being a reformer in opinions, of thinking one doctrine true, and the contrary doctrine morally beneficial. The train of thought which had extricated me from this dilemma, seemed to me, in after years, fitted to render a similar service to others; and it now forms the chapter on Liberty and Necessity in the concluding Book of my system of Logic.

Again, in politics, though I no longer accepted the doctrine of the Essay on Government as a scientific theory; though I ceased to consider representative democracy as an absolute principle, and regarded it as a question of time, place, and circumstance; though I now looked upon the choice of political institutions as a moral and educational question more than one of material interests, thinking that it ought to be decided mainly by the consideration, what great improvement in life and culture stands next in order for the people concerned, as the condition of their further progress, and what institutions are most likely to promote that; nevertheless, this change in the premises of my political philosophy did not alter my practical political creed as to the requirements of my own time and country. I was as much as ever a Radical and Democrat for Europe, and especially for England. I thought the predominance of the aristocratic classes, the noble and the rich, in the English constitution, an evil worth any struggle to get rid of; not on account of taxes, or any such comparatively small inconvenience, but as the great demoralizing agency in the country. Demoralizing, first, because it made the conduct of the Government an example of gross public immorality, through the predominance of private over public interests in the State, and the abuse of the powers of legislation for the advantage of classes. Secondly, and in a still greater degree, because the respect of the multitude always attaching itself principally to that which, in the existing state of society, is the chief passport to power; and under English institutions, riches, hereditary or acquired, being the almost exclusive source of political importance; riches, and the signs of riches, were almost the only things really respected, and the life of the people was mainly devoted to the pursuit of them. I thought, that while the higher and richer classes held the power of government, the instruction and improvement of the mass of the people were contrary to the self-interest of those classes, because tending to render the people more powerful for throwing off the yoke: but if the democracy obtained a large, and perhaps the principal share, in the governing power, it would become the interest of the opulent classes to promote their education, in order to ward off really mischievous errors, and especially those which would lead to unjust violations of property. On these grounds I was not only as ardent as ever for democratic institutions, but earnestly hoped that Owenite, St. Simonian, and all other anti-property doctrines might spread widely among the poorer classes; not that I thought those doctrines true, or desired that they should be acted on, but in order that the higher classes might be made to see that they had more to fear from the poor when uneducated, than when educated.

In this frame of mind the French Revolution of July found me. It roused my utmost enthusiasm, and gave me, as it were, a new existence. I went at once to Paris, was introduced to Lafayette, and laid the groundwork of the intercourse I afterwards kept up with several of the active chiefs of the extreme popular party. After my return I entered warmly, as a writer, into the political discussions of the time; which soon became still more exciting, by the coming in of Lord Grey's Ministry, and the proposing of the Reform Bill. For the next few years I wrote copiously in newspapers. It was about this time that Fonblanque,[10] who had for some time written the political articles in the Examiner, became the proprietor and editor of the paper. It is not forgotten with what verve and talent, as well as fine wit, he carried it on, during the whole period of Lord Grey's Ministry, and what importance it assumed as the principal representative, in the newspaper press, of Radical opinions. The distinguishing character of the paper was given to it entirely by his own articles, which formed at least three-fourths of all the original writing contained in it: but of the remaining fourth I contributed during those years a much larger share than any one else. I wrote nearly all the articles on French subjects, including a weekly summary of French politics, often extending to considerable length; together with many leading articles on general politics, commercial and financial legislation, and any miscellaneous subjects in which I felt interested, and which were

10 Albany Fonblanque (1793–1872), radical journalist, editor of the *Examiner*.

suitable to the paper, including occasional reviews of books. Mere newspaper articles on the occurrences or questions of the moment, gave no opportunity for the development of any general mode of thought; but I attempted, in the beginning of 1831, to embody in a series of articles, headed "The Spirit of the Age," some of my new opinions, and especially to point out in the character of the present age, the anomalies and evils characteristic of the transition from a system of opinions which had worn out, to another only in process of being formed. These articles were, I fancy, lumbering in style, and not lively or striking enough to be, at any time, acceptable to newspaper readers; but had they been far more attractive, still, at that particular moment, when great political changes were impending, and engrossing all minds, these discussions were ill-timed, and missed fire altogether. The only effect which I know to have been produced by them, was that Carlyle, then living in a secluded part of Scotland, read them in his solitude, and saying to himself (as he afterwards told me) "Here is a new Mystic," inquired on coming to London that autumn respecting their authorship; an inquiry which was the immediate cause of our becoming personally acquainted.

I have already mentioned Carlyle's earlier writings as one of the channels through which I received the influences which enlarged my early narrow creed; but I do not think that those writings, by themselves, would ever have had any effect on my opinions. What truths they contained, though of the very kind which I was already receiving from other quarters, were presented in a form and vesture less suited than any other to give them access to a mind trained as mine had been. They seemed a haze of poetry and German metaphysics, in which almost the only clear thing was a strong animosity to most of the opinions which were the basis of my mode of thought; religious scepticism, utilitarianism, the doctrine of circumstances, and the attaching any importance to democracy, logic, or political economy. Instead of my having been taught anything, in the first instance, by Carlyle, it was only in proportion as I came to see the same truths through media more suited to my mental constitution, that I recognised them in his writings. Then, indeed, the wonderful power with which he put them forth made a deep impression upon me, and I was during a long period one of his most fervent admirers; but the good his writings did me, was not as philosophy to instruct, but as poetry to animate. Even at the time when our acquaintance commenced, I was not sufficiently advanced in my new modes of thought, to appreciate him fully; a proof of which is, that on his showing me the manuscript of Sartor Resartus, his best and greatest work, which he had just then finished, I made little of it; though when it came out about two years afterwards in Fraser's Magazine I read it with enthusiastic admiration and the keenest delight. I did not seek and cultivate Carlyle less on account of the fundamental differences in our philosophy. He soon found out that I was not "another mystic," and when for the sake of my own integrity I wrote to him a distinct profession of all those of my opinions which I knew he most disliked, he replied that the chief difference between us was that I "was as yet consciously nothing of a mystic." I do not know at what period he gave up the expectation that I was destined to become one; but though both his and my opinions underwent in subsequent years considerable changes, we never approached much nearer to each other's modes of thought than we were in the first years of our acquaintance. I did not, however, deem myself a competent judge of Carlyle. I felt that he was a poet, and that I was not; that he was a man of intuition, which I was not; and that as such, he not only saw many things long before me, which I could, only when they were pointed out to me, hobble after and prove, but that it was highly probable he could see many things which were not visible to me even after they were pointed out. I knew that I could not see round him, and could never be certain that I saw over him; and I never presumed to judge him with any definiteness, until he was interpreted to me by one greatly the superior of us both — who was more a poet than he, and more a thinker than I — whose own mind and nature included his, and infinitely more.

Among the persons of intellect whom I had known of old, the one with whom I had now most points of agreement was the elder Austin. I have mentioned that he always set himself in opposition to our early sectarianism; and latterly he had, like myself, come under new influences. Having been appointed Professor of Jurisprudence in the London University (now University College), he had lived for some time at Bonn to study for his Lectures; and the influences of German literature and of the German character and state of society had made a very perceptible change in his views of life. His personal disposition was much softened; he was less militant and polemic; his tastes had begun to turn themselves towards the poetic and contemplative. He attached much less importance than formerly to outward changes; unless accompanied by a better cultivation of the inward nature. He had a strong distaste for the general meanness of English life, the absence of enlarged thoughts and unselfish desires, the low objects on which the faculties of all classes of the English are intent. Even the kind of public interests which Englishmen care for, he held in very little esteem. He thought that there was more practical good government, and (which is true enough) infintely more care for the education and mental improvement of all ranks of the people, under the Prussian monarchy, than under the English representative government: and he held, with the French *Economistes,* that the real security for good government is "un peuple éclairé," which is not always the fruit of popular institutions, and which if it could be had without them, would do their work better than they. Though he approved of the Reform Bill, he predicted, what in fact occurred, that it would not produce the great immediate improvements in government, which many expected from it. The men, he said, who could do these great things, did not exist in the country. There were many points of sympathy between him and me, both in the new opinions he had adopted and in the old ones which he retained. Like me, he never ceased to be an utilitarian, and with all his love of the Germans, and enjoyment of their literature, never became in the smallest degree reconciled to the innate-principle metaphysics. He cultivated more and more a kind of German religion, a religion of poetry and feeling with little, if anything, of positive dogma; while, in politics (and here it was that I most differed with him) he acquired an indifference, bordering on contempt, for the progress of popular institutions: though he rejoiced in that of Socialism, as the most effectual means of compelling the powerful classes to educate the people, and to impress on them the only real means of permanently improving their material condition, a limitation of their numbers. Neither was he, at this time, fundamentally opposed to Socialism in itself as an ultimate result of improvement. He professed great disrespect for what he called "the universal principles of human nature of the political economists," and insisted on the evidence which history and daily experience afford of the "extraordinary pliability of human nature" (a phrase which I have somewhere borrowed from him); nor did he think it possible to set any positive bounds to the moral capabilities which might unfold themselves in mankind, under an enlightened direction of social and educational influences. Whether he retained all these opinions to the end of life I know not. Certainly the modes of thinking of his later years, and especially of his last publication, were much more Tory in their general character than those which he held at this time.

✗   My father's tone of thought and feeling, I now felt myself at a great distance from: greater, indeed, than a full and calm explanation and reconsideration on both sides, might have shown to exist in reality. But my father was not one with whom calm and full explanations on fundamental points of doctrine could be expected, at least with one whom he might consider as, in some sort, a deserter from his standard. Fortunately we were almost always in strong agreement on the political questions of the day, which engrossed a large part of his interest and of his conversation. On those matters of opinion on which we differed, we talked little. He knew that the habit of thinking for myself, which his mode of education had fostered, sometimes led me to opinions different from his, and he perceived from time to time that I did not always tell him *how* different. I expected no good, but only pain to both of us, from discussing our differences: and I never expressed them but when he gave utterance to some opinion or feeling repugnant to mine, in a manner which would have made it disingenuousness on my part to remain silent.

It remains to speak of what I wrote during these years, which, independently of my contributions to newspapers, was considerable. In 1830 and 1831 I wrote the five Essays since published under the title of "Essays on some Unsettled Questions of Political Economy," almost as they now stand, except that in 1833 I partially rewrote the fifth Essay. They were written with no immediate purpose of publication; and when, some years later, I offered them to a publisher, he declined them. They were only printed in 1844, after the success of the "System of Logic." I also resumed my speculations on this last subject, and puzzled myself, like others before me, with the great paradox of the discovery of new truths by general reasoning. As to the fact, there could be no doubt. As little could it be doubted, that all reasoning is resolvable into syllogisms, and that in every syllogism the conclusion is actually contained and implied in the premises. How, being so contained and implied, it could be new truth, and how the theorems of geometry, so different in appearance from the definitions and axioms, could be all contained in these, was a difficulty which no one, I thought, had sufficiently felt, and which, at all events, no one had succeeded in clearing up. The explanations offered by Whately and others, though they might give a temporary satisfaction, always, in my mind, left a mist still hanging over the subject. At last, when reading a second or third time the chapters on Reasoning in the second volume of Dugald Stewart, interrogating myself on every point, and following out, as far as I knew how, every topic of thought which the book suggested, I came upon an idea of his respecting the use of axioms in ratiocination, which I did not remember to have before noticed, but which now, in meditating on it, seemed to me not only true of axioms, but of all general propositions whatever, and to be the key of the whole perplexity. From this germ grew the theory of the Syllogism propounded in the Second Book of the Logic; which I immediately fixed by writing it out. And now, with greatly increased hope of being able to produce a work on Logic, of some originality and value, I proceeded to write the First Book, from the rough and imperfect draft I had already made. What I now wrote became the basis of that part of the subsequent Treatise; except that it did not contain the Theory of Kinds, which was a later addition, suggested by otherwise inextricable difficulties which met me in my first attempt to work out the subject of some of the concluding chapters of the Third Book. At the point which I had now reached I made a halt, which lasted five years. I had come to the end of my tether; I could make nothing satisfactory of Induction, at this time. I continued to read any book which seemed to promise light on the subject, and appropriated, as well as I could, the results;

but for a long time I found nothing which seemed to open to me
any very important vein of meditation.

In 1832 I wrote several papers for the first series of Tait's Magazine, and one for a quarterly periodical called the Jurist, which had
been founded, and for a short time carried on, by a set of friends,
all lawyers and law reformers, with several of whom I was acquainted.
The paper in question is the one on the rights and duties of the
States respecting Corporation and Church Property, now standing
first among the collected "Dissertations and Discussions"; where one
of my articles in "Tait," "The Currency Juggle," also appears. In the
whole mass of what I wrote previous to these, there is nothing of
sufficient permanent value to justify reprinting. The paper in the
Jurist, which I still think a very complete discussion of the rights of
the State over Foundations, showed both sides of my opinions,
asserting as firmly as I should have done at any time, the doctrine
that all endowments are national property, which the government
may and ought to control; but not, as I should once have done, condemning endowments in themselves, and proposing that they should
be taken to pay off the national debt. On the contrary, I urged strenuously the importance of having a provision for education, not dependent on the mere demand of the market, that is, on the knowledge
and discernment of average parents, but calculated to establish and
keep up a higher standard of instruction than is likely to be spontaneously demanded by the buyers of the article. All these opinions
have been confirmed and strengthened by the whole course of my
subsequent reflections.

Three Essays on Religion

(*Three Essays on Religion* ("Nature," "Utility of Religion," "Theism")
was published posthumously, in 1874. The essays on "Nature" and "Utility
of Religion," however, were written, according to Helen Taylor, Mill's step-
daughter, between 1850 and 1855 — that is, sometime between the publication of *In Memoriam* and *Origin of Species*. The essay represents, therefore,
a thoughtful man's observations on nature *after* the recession of romantic
spiritualization but *before* Darwin had more fully documented the evolution-
ary attitude toward nature.)

Nature

NATURE, natural, and the group of words derived from them, or
allied to them in etymology, have at all times filled a great place in

the thoughts and taken a strong hold on the feelings of mankind. That they should have done so is not surprising, when we consider what the words, in their primitive and most obvious signification, represent; but it is unfortunate that a set of terms which play so great a part in moral and metaphysical speculation, should have acquired many meanings different from the primary one, yet sufficiently allied to it to admit of confusion. The words have thus become entangled in so many foreign associations, mostly of a very powerful and tenacious character, that they have come to excite, and to be the symbols of, feelings which their original meaning will by no means justify; and which have made them one of the most copious sources of false taste, false philosophy, false morality, and even bad law.

The most important application of the Socratic Elenchus, as exhibited and improved by Plato, consists in dissecting large abstractions of this description; fixing down to a precise definition the meaning which as properly used they merely shadow forth, and questioning and testing the common maxims and opinions in which they bear a part. It is to be regretted that among the instructive specimens of this kind of investigation which Plato has left, and to which subsequent times have been so much indebted for whatever intellectual clearness they have attained, he has not enriched posterity with a dialogue περὶ φύσεως.[1] If the idea denoted by the word had been subjected to his searching analysis, and the popular commonplaces in which it figures had been submitted to the ordeal of his powerful dialectics, his successors probably would not have rushed, as they speedily did, into modes of thinking and reasoning of which the fallacious use of that word formed the corner stone; a kind of fallacy from which he was himself singularly free.

According to the Platonic method which is still the best type of such investigations, the first thing to be done with so vague a term is to ascertain precisely what it means. It is also a rule of the same method, that the meaning of an abstraction is best sought for in the concrete — of an universal in the particular. Adopting this course with the word Nature, the first question must be, what is meant by the "nature" of a particular object? as of fire, of water, or of some individual plant or animal? Evidently the *ensemble* or aggregate of its powers or properties: the modes in which it acts on other things (counting among those things the senses of the observer) and the modes in which other things act upon it; to which, in the case of a sentient being, must be added, its own capacities of feeling, or being conscious. The Nature of the thing means all this; means its entire capacity of exhibiting phenomena. And since the phenomena which a thing exhibits, however much they vary in different circumstances, are always the same in the same circumstances, they admit of being

[1] "On Nature."

described in general forms of words, which are called the *laws* of the thing's nature. Thus it is a law of the nature of water that under the mean pressure of the atmosphere at the level of the sea, it boils at 212° Fahrenheit.

As the nature of any given thing is the aggregate of its powers and properties, so Nature in the abstract is the aggregate of the powers and properties of all things. Nature means the sum of all phenomena, together with the causes which produce them; including not only all that happens, but all that is capable of happening; the unused capabilities of causes being as much a part of the idea of Nature, as those which take effect. Since all phenomena which have been sufficiently examined are found to take place with regularity, each having certain fixed conditions, positive and negative, on the occurrence of which it invariably happens; mankind have been able to ascertain, either by direct observation or by reasoning processes grounded on it, the conditions of the occurrence of many phenomena; and the progress of science mainly consists in ascertaining those conditions. When discovered they can be expressed in general propositions, which are called laws of the particular phenomenon, and also, more generally, Laws of Nature. Thus, the truth that all material objects tend towards one another with a force directly as their masses and inversely as the square of their distance, is a law of Nature. The proposition that air and food are necessary to animal life, if it be as we have good reason to believe, true without exception, is also a law of nature, though the phenomenon of which it is the law is special, and not, like gravitation, universal.

Nature, then, in this its simplest acceptations, is a collective name for all facts, actual and possible: or (to speak more accurately) a name for the mode, partly known to us and partly unknown, in which all things take place. For the word suggests, not so much the multitudinous detail of the phenomena, as the conception which might be formed of their manner of existence as a mental whole, by a mind possessing a complete knowledge of them: to which conception it is the aim of science to raise itself, by successive steps of generalization from experience.

Such, then, is a correct definition of the word Nature. But this definition corresponds only to one of the senses of that ambiguous term. It is evidently inapplicable to some of the modes in which the word is familiarly employed. For example, it entirely conflicts with the common form of speech by which Nature is opposed to Art, and natural to artificial. For in the sense of the word Nature which has just been defined, and which is the true scientific sense, Art is as much Nature as anything else; and everything which is artificial is natural — Art has no independent powers of its own: Art is but the employment of the powers of Nature for an end. Phenomena produced by human agency, no less than those which as far as we are concerned are spontaneous, depend on the properties of the elementary forces, or of the elementary substances and their compounds. The united powers of the whole human race could not create a new property of matter in general, or of any one of its species. We can only take advantage for our purposes of the properties which we find. A ship floats by the same laws of specific gravity and equilibrium, as a tree uprooted by the wind and thrown into the water. The corn which men raise for food, grows and produces its grain by the same laws of vegetation by which the wild rose and the mountain strawberry bring forth their flowers and fruit. A house stands and holds together by the natural properties, the weight and cohesion of the materials which compose it: a steam engine works by the natural expansive force of steam, exerting a pressure upon one part of a system of arrangements, which pressure, by the mechanical properties of the lever, is transferred from that to another part where it raises the weight or removes the obstacle brought into connexion with it. In these and all other artificial operations the office of man is, as has often been remarked, a very limited one; it consists in moving things into certain places. We move objects, and by doing this, bring some things into contact which were separate, or separate others which were in contact: and by this simple change of place, natural forces previously dormant are called into action, and produce the desired effect. Even the volition which designs, the intelligence which contrives, and the muscular force which executes these movements, are themselves powers of Nature.

It thus appears that we must recognize at least two principal meanings in the word Nature. In one sense, it means all the powers existing in either the outer or the inner world and everything which takes place by means of those powers. In another sense, it means, not everything which happens, but only what takes place without the agency, or without the voluntary and intentional agency, of man. This distinction is far from exhausting the ambiguities of the word; but it is the key to most of those on which important consequences depend.

Such, then, being the two principal senses of the word Nature; in which of these is it taken, or is it taken in either, when the word and its derivatives are used to convey ideas of commendation, approval, and even moral obligation?

It has conveyed such ideas in all ages. *Naturam sequi* [2] was the fundamental principle of morals in many of the most admired schools of philosophy. Among the ancients, especially in the declining period of ancient intellect and thought, it was the test to which all ethical doctrines were brought. The Stoics and the Epicureans, however irreconcilable in the rest of their systems, agreed in holding themselves bound to prove that their respective maxims of conduct were

2 "To follow Nature."

the dictates of nature. Under their influence the Roman jurists, when attempting to systematize jurisprudence, placed in the front of their exposition a certain *Jus Naturale,* "quod natura," as Justinian declares in the Institutes, "omnia animalia docuit": [3] and as the modern systematic writers not only on law but on moral philosophy, have generally taken the Roman jurists for their models, treatises on the so-called Law of Nature have abounded; and references to this Law as a supreme rule and ultimate standard have pervaded literature. The writers on International Law have done more than any others to give currency to this style of ethical speculation; inasmuch as having no positive law to write about, and yet being anxious to invest the most approved opinions respecting international morality with as much as they could of the authority of law, they endeavoured to find such an authority in Nature's imaginary code. The Christian theology during the period of its greatest ascendency, opposed some, though not a complete, hindrance to the modes of thought which erected Nature into the criterion of morals, inasmuch as, according to the creed of most denominations of Christians (though assuredly not of Christ) man is by nature wicked. But this very doctrine, by the reaction which it provoked, has made the deistical moralists almost unanimous in proclaiming the divinity of Nature, and setting up its fancied dictates as an authoritative rule of action. A reference to that supposed standard is the predominant ingredient in the vein of thought and feeling which was opened by Rousseau, and which has infiltrated itself most widely into the modern mind, not excepting that portion of it which calls itself Christian. The doctrines of Christianity have in every age been largely accommodated to the philosophy which happened to be prevalent, and the Christianity of our day has borrowed a considerable part of its colour and flavour from sentimental deism. At the present time it cannot be said that Nature, or any other standard, is applied as it was wont to be, to deduce rules of action with juridical precision, and with an attempt to make its application coextensive with all human agency. The people of this generation do not commonly apply principles with any such studious exactness, nor own such binding allegiance to any standard, but live in a kind of confusion of many standards; a condition not propitious to the formation of steady moral convictions, but convenient enough to those whose moral opinions sit lightly on them, since it gives them a much wider range of arguments for defending the doctrine of the moment. But though perhaps no one could now be found who like the institutional writers of former times, adopts the so-called Law of Nature as the foundation of ethics, and endeavours consistently to reason from it, the word and its cognates must still be counted among those which carry great weight in moral argumentation. That any mode of thinking, feeling, or acting, is "according to nature" is usually accepted as

3 "Natural Law": "because nature has taught all living beings."

a strong argument for its goodness. If it can be said with any plausibility that "nature enjoins" anything, the propriety of obeying the injunction is by most people considered to be made out: and conversely, the imputation of being contrary to nature, is thought to bar the door against any pretension on the part of the thing so designated, to be tolerated or excused; and the word unnatural has not ceased to be one of the most vituperative epithets in the language. Those who deal in these expressions, may avoid making themselves responsible for any fundamental theorem respecting the standard of moral obligation, but they do not the less imply such a theorem, and one which must be the same in substance with that on which the more logical thinkers of a more laborious age grounded their systematic treatises on Natural Law.

Is it necessary to recognize in these forms of speech, another distinct meaning of the word Nature? Or can they be connected, by any rational bond of union, with either of the two meanings already treated of? At first it may seem that we have no option but to admit another ambiguity in the term. All inquiries are either into what is, or into what ought to be: science and history belonging to the first division, art, morals and politics to the second. But the two senses of the word Nature first pointed out, agree in referring only to what is. In the first meaning, Nature is a collective name for everything which is. In the second, it is a name for everything which is of itself, without voluntary human intervention. But the employment of the word Nature as a term of ethics seems to disclose a third meaning, in which Nature does not stand for what is, but for what ought to be; or for the rule or standard of what ought to be. A little consideration, however, will show that this is not a case of ambiguity; there is not here a third sense of the word. Those who set up Nature as a standard of action do not intend a merely verbal proposition; they do not mean that the standard, whatever it be, should be *called* Nature; they think they are giving some information as to what the standard of action really is. Those who say that we ought to act according to Nature do not mean the mere identical proposition that we ought to do what we ought to do. They think that the word Nature affords some external criterion of what we should do; and if they lay down as a rule for what ought to be, a word which in its proper signification denotes what is, they do so because they have a notion, either clearly or confusedly, that what is, constitutes the rule and standard of what ought to be.

The examination of this notion, is the object of the present Essay. It is proposed to inquire into the truth of the doctrines which make Nature a test of right and wrong, good and evil, or which in any mode or degree attach merit or approval to following, imitating, or obeying Nature. To this inquiry the foregoing discussion respecting the meaning of terms, was an indispensable introduction. Language is as it were the atmosphere of philosophical investigation, which must be made transparent before anything can be seen through it in the true figure and position. In the present case it is necessary to guard against a further ambiguity, which though abundantly obvious, has sometimes misled even sagacious minds, and of which it is well to take distinct note before proceeding further. No word is more commonly associated with the word Nature, than Law; and this last word has distinctly two meanings, in one of which it denotes some definite portion of what is, in the other, of what ought to be. We speak of the law of gravitation, the three laws of motion, the law of definite proportions in chemical combination, the vital laws of organized beings. All these are portions of what is. We also speak of the criminal law, the civil law, the law of honour, the law of veracity, the law of justice; all of which are portions of what ought to be, or of somebody's suppositions, feelings, or commands respecting what ought to be. The first kind of laws, such as the laws of motion, and of gravitation, are neither more nor less than the observed uniformities in the occurrence of phenomena: partly uniformities of antecedence and sequence, partly of concomitance. These are what, in science, and even in ordinary parlance, are meant by laws of Nature. Laws in the other sense are the laws of the land, the law of nations, or moral laws; among which, as already noticed, is dragged in, by jurists and publicists, something which they think proper to call the Law of Nature. Of the liability of these two meanings of the word to be confounded there can be no better example than the first chapter of Montesquieu; where he remarks, that the material world has its laws, the inferior animals have their laws, and man has his laws; and calls attention to the much greater strictness with which the first two sets of laws are observed, than the last; as if it were an inconsistency, and a paradox, that things always are what they are, but men not always what they ought to be. A similar confusion of ideas pervades the writings of Mr. George Combe,[4] from whence it has overflowed into a large region of popular literature, and we are now continually reading injunctions to obey the physical laws of the universe, as being obligatory in the same sense and manner as the moral. The conception which the ethical use of the word Nature implies, of a close relation if not absolute identity between what is and what ought to be, certainly derives part of its hold on the mind from the custom of designating what is, by the expression "laws of nature," while the same word Law is also used, and even more familiarly and emphatically, to express what ought to be.

When it is asserted, or implied, that Nature, or the laws of Nature, should be conformed to, is the Nature which is meant, Nature in the first sense of the term, meaning all which is — the powers and properties of all things? But in this signification, there is no need of a

[4] George Combe (1788–1858), a phrenologist.

recommendation to act according to nature, since it is what nobody can possibly help doing, and equally whether he acts well or ill. There is no mode of acting which is not conformable to Nature in this sense of the term, and all modes of acting are so in exactly the same degree. Every action is the exertion of some natural power, and its effects of all sorts are so many phenomena of nature, produced by the powers and properties of some of the objects of nature, in exact obedience to some law or laws of nature. When I voluntarily use my organs to take in food, the act, and its consequences, take place according to laws of nature: if instead of food I swallow poison, the case is exactly the same. To bid people conform to the laws of nature when they have no power but what the laws of nature give them — when it is a physical impossibility for them to do the smallest thing otherwise than through some law of nature, is an absurdity. The thing they need to be told is, what particular law of nature they should make use of in a particular case. When, for example, a person is crossing a river by a narrow bridge to which there is no parapet, he will do well to regulate his proceedings by the laws of equilibrium in moving bodies, instead of conforming only to the law of gravitation, and falling into the river.

Yet, idle as it is to exhort people to do what they cannot avoid doing, and absurd as it is to prescribe as a rule of right conduct what agrees exactly as well with wrong; nevertheless a rational rule of conduct *may* be constructed out of the relation which it ought to bear to the laws of nature in this widest acceptation of the term. Man necessarily obeys the laws of nature, or in other words the properties of things, but he does not necessarily *guide* himself by them. Though all conduct is in conformity to laws of nature, all conduct is not grounded on knowledge of them, and intelligently directed to the attainment of purposes by means of them. Though we cannot emancipate ourselves from the laws of nature as a whole, we can escape from any particular law of nature, if we are able to withdraw ourselves from the circumstances in which it acts. Though we can do nothing except through laws of nature, we can use one law to counteract another. According to Bacon's maxim, we can obey nature in such a manner as to command it. Every alteration of circumstances alters more or less the laws of nature under which we act; and by every choice which we make either of ends or of means, we place ourselves to a greater or less extent under one set of laws of nature instead of another. If, therefore, the useless precept to follow nature were changed into a precept to study nature; to know and take heed of the properties of the things we have to deal with, so far as these properties are capable of forwarding or obstructing any given purpose; we should have arrived at the first principle of all intelligent action, or rather at the definition of intelligent action itself. And a confused notion of this true principle, is, I doubt not, in the minds of many of those who set up the unmeaning doctrine which superficially resembles it. They perceive that the essential difference between wise and foolish conduct consists in attending, or not attending, to the particular laws of nature on which some important result depends. And they think, that a person who attends to a law of nature in order to shape his conduct by it, may be said to obey it, while a person who practically disregards it, and acts as if no such law existed, may be said to disobey it: the circumstance being overlooked, that what is thus called disobedience to a law of nature is obedience to some other or perhaps to the very law itself. For example, a person who goes into a powder magazine either not knowing, or carelessly omitting to think of, the explosive force of gunpowder, is likely to do some act which will cause him to be blown to atoms in obedience to the very law which he has disregarded.

But however much of its authority the "Naturam sequi" doctrine may owe to its being confounded with the rational precept "Naturam observare," its favourers and promoters unquestionably intend much more by it than that precept. To acquire knowledge of the properties of things, and make use of the knowledge for guidance, is a rule of prudence, for the adaptation of means to ends; for giving effect to our wishes and intentions whatever they may be. But the maxim of obedience to Nature, or conformity to Nature, is held up not as a simply prudential but as an ethical maxim; and by those who talk of *jus naturae*, even as a law, fit to be administered by tribunals and enforced by sanctions. Right action, must mean something more and other than merely intelligent action: yet no precept beyond this last, can be connected with the word Nature in the wider and more philosophical of its acceptations. We must try it therefore in the other sense, that in which Nature stands distinguished from Art, and denotes, not the whole course of the phenomena which come under our observation, but only their spontaneous course.

Let us then consider whether we can attach any meaning to the supposed practical maxim of following Nature, in this second sense of the word, in which Nature stands for that which takes place without human intervention. In Nature as thus understood, is the spontaneous course of things when left to themselves, the rule to be followed in endeavouring to adapt things to our use? But it is evident at once that the maxim, taken in this sense, is not merely, as it is in the other sense, superfluous and unmeaning, but palpably absurd and self-contradictory. For while human action cannot help conforming to Nature in the one meaning of the term, the very aim and object of action is to alter and improve Nature in the other meaning. If the natural course of things were perfectly right and satisfactory, to act at all would be a gratuitous meddling, which as it could not make things better, must make them worse. Or if action at all could be justified, it would only be when in direct obedience to instincts, since these might perhaps be accounted part of the spontaneous order of Nature; but to do anything with forethought and purpose, would be a violation of that perfect order. If the artificial is not better than the natural, to what end are all the arts of life? To dig, to plough, to build, to wear clothes, are direct infringements of the injunction to follow nature.

Accordingly it would be said by every one, even of those most under the influence of the feelings which prompt the injunction, that to apply it to such cases as those just spoken of, would be to push it too far. Everybody professes to approve and admire many great triumphs of Art over Nature: the junction by bridges of shores which Nature had made separate, the draining of Nature's marshes, the excavation of her wells, the dragging to light of what she has buried at immense depths in the earth; the turning away of her thunderbolts by lightning rods, of her inundations by embankments, of her ocean by breakwaters. But to commend these and similar feats, is to acknowledge that the ways of Nature are to be conquered, not obeyed: that her powers are often towards man in the position of enemies, from whom he must wrest, by force and ingenuity, what little he can for his own use, and deserves to be applauded when that little is rather more than might be expected from his physical weakness in comparison to those gigantic powers. All praise of Civilization, or Art, or Contrivance, is so much dispraise of Nature; an admission of imperfection, which it is man's business, and merit, to be always endeavouring to correct or mitigate.

The consciousness that whatever man does to improve his condition is in so much a censure and a thwarting of the spontaneous order of Nature, has in all ages caused new and unprecedented attempts at improvement to be generally at first under a shade of religious suspicion; as being in any case uncomplimentary, and very probably offensive to the powerful beings (or, when polytheism gave place to monotheism, to the all-powerful Being) supposed to govern the various phenomena of the universe, and of whose will the course of nature was conceived to be the expression. Any attempt to mould natural phenomena to the convenience of mankind might easily appear an interference with the government of those superior beings: and though life could not have been maintained, much less made pleasant, without perpetual interferences of the kind, each new one was doubtless made with fear and trembling, until experience had shown that it could be ventured on without drawing down the vengeance of the Gods. The sagacity of priests showed them a way to reconcile the impunity of particular infringements with the maintenance of the general dread of encroaching on the divine administration. This was effected by representing each of the principal human inventions as the gift and favour of some God. The old religions also afforded many resources for consulting the Gods, and obtaining their express permission for what would otherwise have appeared a breach of their prerogative. When oracles had ceased, any religion which recognized a revelation afforded expedients for the same purpose. The Catholic religion had the resource of an infallible Church, authorized to declare what exertions of human spontaneity were permitted or forbidden; and in default of this, the case was always open to argument from the Bible whether any particular practice had expressly or by implication been sanctioned. The notion remained that this liberty to control Nature was conceded to man only by special indulgence, and as far as required by his necessities; and there was always a tendency, though a diminishing one, to regard any attempt to exercise power over nature, beyond a certain degree, and a certain admitted range, as an impious effort to usurp divine power, and dare more than was permitted to man. The lines of Horace in which the familiar arts of shipbuilding and navigation are reprobated as *vetitum nefas*,[5] indicate even in that sceptical age a still unexhausted vein of the old sentiment. The intensity of the corresponding feeling in the middle ages is not a precise parallel, on account of the superstition about dealing with evil spirits with which it was complicated: but the imputation of prying into the secrets of the Almighty long remained a powerful weapon of attack against unpopular inquiries into nature: and the charge of presumptuously attempting to defeat the designs of Providence, still retains enough of its original force to be thrown in as a make-weight along with other objections when there is a desire to find fault with any new exertion of human forethought and contrivance. No one, indeed, asserts it to be the intention of the Creator that the spontaneous order of the creation should not be altered in any new way. But there still exists a vague notion that though it is very proper to control this or the other natural phenomenon, the general scheme of nature is a model for us to imitate: that with more or less liberty in details, we should on the whole be guided by the spirit and general conception of nature's own ways: that they are God's work, and as such perfect; that man cannot rival their unapproachable excellence, and can best show his skill and piety by attempting, in however imperfect a way, to reproduce their likeness; and that if not the whole, yet some particular parts of the spontaneous order of nature, selected according to the speaker's predilections, are in a peculiar sense, manifestations of the Creator's will; a sort of finger posts pointing out the direction which things in general, and therefore our voluntary actions, are intended to take. Feelings of this sort, though repressed on ordinary occasions by the contrary current of life, are ready to break out whenever custom is silent, and the native promptings of the mind have nothing opposed to them but reason: and appeals are continually made to them by rhetoricians, with the effect, if not of convincing opponents, at least of making

5 "contrary to what is forbidden."

those who already hold the opinion which the rhetorician desires to recommend, better satisfied with it. For in the present day it probably seldom happens that any one is persuaded to approve any course of action because it appears to him to bear an analogy to the divine government of the world, though the argument tells on him with great force, and is felt by him to be a great support, in behalf of anything which he is already inclined to approve.

If this notion of imitating the ways of Providence as manifested in Nature, is seldom expressed plainly and downrightly as a maxim of general application, it also is seldom directly contradicted. Those who find it on their path, prefer to turn the obstacle rather than to attack it, being often themselves not free from the feeling, and in any case afraid of incurring the charge of impiety by saying anything which might be held to disparage the works of the Creator's power. They therefore, for the most part, rather endeavour to show, that they have as much right to the religious argument as their opponents, and that if the course they recommend seems to conflict with some part of the ways of Providence, there is some other part with which it agrees better than what is contended for on the other side. In this mode of dealing with the great *à priori* fallacies, the progress of improvement clears away particular errors while the causes of errors are still left standing, and very little weakened by each conflict: yet by a long series of such partial victories precedents are accumulated, to which an appeal may be made against these powerful prepossessions, and which afford a growing hope that the misplaced feeling, after having so often learnt to recede, may some day be compelled to an unconditional surrender. For however offensive the proposition may appear to many religious persons, they should be willing to look in the face the undeniable fact, that the order of nature, in so far as unmodified by man, is such as no being, whose attributes are justice and benevolence, would have made, with the intention that his rational creatures should follow it as an example. If made wholly by such a Being, and not partly by beings of very different qualities, it could only be as a designedly imperfect work, which man, in his limited sphere, is to exercise justice and benevolence in amending. The best persons have always held it to be the essence of religion, that the paramount duty of man upon earth is to amend himself: but all except monkish quietists have annexed to this in their inmost minds (though seldom willing to enunciate the obligation with the same clearness) the additional religious duty of amending the world, and not solely the human part of it but the material; the order of physical nature.

In considering this subject it is necessary to divest ourselves of certain preconceptions which may justly be called natural prejudices, being grounded on feelings which, in themselves natural and inevitable, intrude into matters with which they ought to have no concern. One of these feelings is the astonishment, rising into awe, which is inspired (even independently of all religious sentiment) by any of the greater natural phenomena. A hurricane; a mountain precipice; the desert; the ocean, either agitated or at rest; the solar system, and the great cosmic forces which hold it together; the boundless firmament, and to an educated mind any single star; excite feelings which make all human enterprises and powers appear so insignificant, that to a mind thus occupied it seems insufferable presumption in so puny a creature as man to look critically on things so far above him, or dare to measure himself against the grandeur of the universe. But a little interrogation of our own consciousness will suffice to convince us, that what makes these phenomena so impressive is simply their vastness. The enormous extension in space and time, or the enormous power they exemplify, constitutes their sublimity; a feeling in all cases, more allied to terror than to any moral emotion. And though the vast scale of these phenomena may well excite wonder, and sets at defiance all idea of rivalry, the feeling it inspires is of a totally different character from admiration of excellence. Those in whom awe produces admiration may be aesthetically developed, but they are morally uncultivated. It is one of the endowments of the imaginative part of our mental nature that conceptions of greatness and power, vividly realized, produce a feeling which though in its higher degrees closely bordering on pain, we prefer to most of what are accounted pleasures. But we are quite equally capable of experiencing this feeling towards maleficent power; and we never experience it so strongly towards most of the powers of the universe, as when we have most present to our consciousness a vivid sense of their capacity of inflicting evil. Because these natural powers have what we cannot imitate, enormous might, and overawe us by that one attribute, it would be a great error to infer that their other attributes are such as we ought to emulate, or that we should be justified in using our small powers after the example which Nature sets us with her vast forces.

For how stands the fact? That next to the greatness of these cosmic forces, the quality which most forcibly strikes every one who does not avert his eyes from it, is their perfect and absolute recklessness. They go straight to their end, without regarding what or whom they crush on the road. Optimists, in their attempts to prove that "whatever is, is right," are obliged to maintain, not that Nature ever turns one step from her path to avoid trampling us into destruction, but that it would be very unreasonable in us to expect that she should. Pope's "Shall gravitation cease when you go by?" may be a just rebuke to any one who should be so silly as to expect common human morality from nature. But if the question were between two men, instead of between a man and a natural phenomenon, that triumphant apostrophe would be thought a rare piece of impudence. A man who should persist in hurling stones or firing cannon when another man "goes by," and having killed him should urge a similar plea in exculpation, would very deservedly be found guilty of murder.

In sober truth, nearly all the things which men are hanged or imprisoned for doing to one another, are nature's every day performances. Killing, the most criminal act recognized by human laws, Nature does once to every being that lives; and in a large proportion of cases, after protracted tortures such as only the greatest monsters whom we read of ever purposely inflicted on their living fellow-creatures. If, by an arbitrary reservation, we refuse to account anything murder but what abridges a certain term supposed to be allotted to human life, nature also does this to all but a small percentage of lives, and does it in all the modes, violent or insidious, in which the worst human beings take the lives of one another. Nature impales men, breaks them as if on the wheel, casts them to be devoured by wild beasts, burns them to death, crushes them with stones like the first christian martyr, starves them with hunger, freezes them with cold, poisons them by the quick or slow venom of her exhalations, and has hundreds of other hideous deaths in reserve, such as the ingenious cruelty of a Nabis [6] or a Domitian never surpassed. All this, Nature does with the most supercilious disregard both of mercy and of justice, emptying her shafts upon the best and noblest indifferently with the meanest and worst; upon those who are engaged in the highest and worthiest enterprises, and often as the direct consequence of the noblest acts; and it might almost be imagined as a punishment for them. She mows down those on whose existence hangs the well-being of a whole people, perhaps the prospects of the human race for generations to come, with as little compunction as those whose death is a relief to themselves, or a blessing to those under their noxious influence. Such are Nature's dealings with life. Even when she does not intend to kill, she inflicts the same tortures in apparent wantonness. In the clumsy provision which she has made for that perpetual renewal of animal life, rendered necessary by the prompt termination she puts to it in every individual instance, no human being ever comes into the world but another human being is literally stretched on the rack for hours or days, not unfrequently issuing in death. Next to taking life (equal to it according to a high authority) is taking the means by which we live; and Nature does this too on the largest scale and with the most callous indifference. A single hurricane destroys the hopes of a season; a flight of locusts, or an inundation, desolates a district; a trifling chemical change in an edible root, starves a million of people. The waves of the sea like banditti seize and appropriate the wealth of the rich and the little all of the poor with the same accompaniments of stripping, wounding, and killing as their human antitypes. Everything in short, which the worst men commit either against life or property is perpetrated on a larger scale by natural agents. Nature

6 Nabis was a notoriously cruel tyrant of Lacedaemon.

has Noyades more fatal than those of Carrier; [7] her explosions of fire damp are as destructive as human artillery; her plague and cholera far surpass the poison cups of the Borgias. Even the love of "order" which is thought to be a following of the ways of Nature, is in fact a contradiction of them. All which people are accustomed to deprecate as "disorder" and its consequences, is precisely a counterpart of Nature's ways. Anarchy and the Reign of Terror are overmatched in injustice, ruin, and death, by a hurricane and a pestilence.

But, it is said, all these things are for wise and good ends. On this I must first remark that whether they are so or not, is altogether beside the point. Supposing it true that contrary to appearances these horrors when perpetrated by Nature, promote good ends, still as no one believes that good ends would be promoted by our following the example, the course of Nature cannot be a proper model for us to imitate. Either it is right that we should kill because nature kills; torture because nature tortures; ruin and devastate because nature does the like; or we ought not to consider at all what nature does, but what it is good to do. If there is such a thing as a *reductio ad absurdum*, this surely amounts to one. If it is a sufficient reason for doing one thing, that nature does it, why not another thing? If not all things, why anything? The physical government of the world being full of the things which when done by men are deemed the greatest enormities, it cannot be religious or moral in us to guide our actions by the analogy of the course of nature. This proposition remains true, whatever occult quality of producing good may reside in those facts of nature which to our perceptions are most noxious, and which no one considers it other than a crime to produce artificially.

But, in reality, no one consistently believes in any such occult quality. The phrases which ascribe perfection to the course of nature can only be considered as the exaggerations of poetic or devotional feeling, not intended to stand the test of a sober examination. No one, either religious or irreligious, believes that the hurtful agencies of nature, considered as a whole, promote good purposes, in any other way than by inciting human rational creatures to rise up and struggle against them. If we believed that those agencies were appointed by a benevolent Providence as the means of accomplishing wise purposes which could not be compassed if they did not exist, then everything done by mankind which tends to chain up these natural agencies or to restrict their mischievous operation, from draining a pestilential marsh down to curing the toothache, or putting up an umbrella, ought to be accounted impious; which assuredly nobody does account them, notwithstanding an undercurrent of sentiment setting in that direction which is occasionally perceptible. On the con-

[7] Jean Baptiste Carrier (1756–1794), French revolutionist notorious for mass-executions, especially by drowning.

trary, the improvements on which the civilized part of mankind most pride themselves, consist in more successfully warding off those natural calamities which if we really believed what most people profess to believe, we should cherish as medicines provided for our earthly state by infinite wisdom. Inasmuch too as each generation greatly surpasses its predecessors in the amount of natural evil which it succeeds in averting, our condition, if the theory were true, ought by this time to have become a terrible manifestation of some tremendous calamity, against which the physical evils we have learnt to overmaster, had previously operated as a preservative. Any one, however, who acted as if he supposed this to be the case, would be more likely, I think, to be confined as a lunatic, than reverenced as a saint.

It is undoubtedly a very common fact that good comes out of evil, and when it does occur, it is far too agreeable not to find people eager to dilate on it. But in the first place, it is quite as often true of human crimes, as of natural calamities. The fire of London, which is believed to have had so salutary an effect on the healthiness of the city, would have produced that effect just as much if it had been really the work of the "furor papisticus" [8] so long commemorated on the Monument.[9] The deaths of those whom tyrants or persecutors have made martyrs in any noble cause, have done a service to mankind which would not have been obtained if they had died by accident or disease. Yet whatever incidental and unexpected benefits may result from crimes, they are crimes nevertheless. In the second place, if good frequently comes out of evil, the converse fact, evil coming out of good, is equally common. Every event public or private, which, regretted on its occurrence, was declared providential at a later period on account of some unforeseen good consequence, might be matched by some other event, deemed fortunate at the time, but which proved calamitous or fatal to those whom it appeared to benefit. Such conflicts between the beginning and the end, or between the event and the expectation, are not only as frequent, but as often held up to notice, in the painful cases as in the agreeable; but there is not the same inclination to generalize on them; or at all events they are not regarded by the moderns (though they were by the ancients) as similarly an indication of the divine purposes: men satisfy themselves with moralizing on the imperfect nature of our foresight, the uncertainty of events, and the vanity of human expectations. The simple fact is, human interests are so complicated, and the effects of any incident whatever so multitudinous, that if it touches mankind at all, its influence on them is, in the great majority of cases, both good and bad. If the greater number of personal misfortunes have their good side, hardly any good fortune ever befell any one which did not

---

[8] "papist hatred."
[9] Column erected by Sir Christopher Wren, originally attributing the Fire of London to the Roman Catholics.

give either to the same or to some other person, something to regret:
and unhappily there are many misfortunes so overwhelming that their
favourable side, if it exist, is entirely overshadowed and made insignificant; while the corresponding statement can seldom be made concerning blessings. The effects too of every cause depend so much
on the circumstances which accidentally accompany it, that many
cases are sure to occur in which even the total result is markedly
opposed to the predominant tendency: and thus not only evil has its
good and good its evil side, but good often produces an overbalance
of evil and evil an overbalance of good. This, however, is by no
means the general tendency of either phenomenon. On the contrary, both good and evil naturally tend to fructify, each in its own
kind, good producing good, and evil, evil. It is one of Nature's general rules, and part of her habitual injustice, that "to him that hath
shall be given, but from him that hath not, shall be taken even that
which he hath." The ordinary and predominant tendency of good is
towards more good. Health, strength, wealth, knowledge, virtue, are
not only good in themselves but facilitate and promote the acquisition
of good, both of the same and of other kinds. The person who can
learn easily, is he who already knows much: it is the strong and not
the sickly person who can do everything which most conduces to
health; those who find it easy to gain money are not the poor but
the rich; while health, strength, knowledge, talents, are all means
of acquiring riches, and riches are often an indispensable means of
acquiring these. Again, *e converso*, whatever may be said of evil
turning into good, the general tendency of evil is towards further
evil. Bodily illness renders the body more susceptible of disease; it
produces incapacity of exertion, sometimes debility of mind, and
often the loss of means of subsistence. All severe pain, either bodily
or mental, tends to increase the susceptibilities of pain for ever
after. Poverty is the parent of a thousand mental and moral evils.
What is still worse, to be injured or oppressed, when habitual, lowers
the whole tone of the character. One bad action leads to others, both
in the agent himself, in the bystanders, and in the sufferers. All bad
qualities are strengthened by habit, and all vices and follies tend to
spread. Intellectual defects generate moral, and moral, intellectual;
and every intellectual or moral defect generates others, and so on
without end.

That much applauded class of authors, the writers on natural theology, have, I venture to think, entirely lost their way, and missed the
sole line of argument which could have made their speculations acceptable to any one who can perceive when two propositions contradict one another. They have exhausted the resources of sophistry to
make it appear that all the suffering in the world exists to prevent
greater — that misery exists, for fear lest there should be misery: a
thesis which if ever so well maintained, could only avail to explain

and justify the works of limited beings, compelled to labour under conditions independent of their own will; but can have no application to a Creator assumed to be omnipotent, who, if he bends to a supposed necessity, himself makes the necessity which he bends to. If the maker of the world *can* all that he will, he wills misery, and there is no escape from the conclusion. The more consistent of those who have deemed themselves qualified to "vindicate the ways of God to man" have endeavoured to avoid the alternative by hardening their hearts, and denying that misery is an evil. The goodness of God, they say, does not consist in willing the happiness of his creatures, but their virtue; and the universe, if not a happy, is a just, universe. But waiving the objections to this scheme of ethics, it does not at all get rid of the difficulty. If the Creator of mankind willed that they should all be virtuous, his designs are as completely baffled as if he had willed that they should all be happy: and the order of nature is constructed with even less regard to the requirements of justice than to those of benevolence. If the law of all creation were justice and the Creator omnipotent, then in whatever amount suffering and happiness might be dispensed to the world, each person's share of them would be exactly proportioned to that person's good or evil deeds; no human being would have a worse lot than another, without worse deserts; accident or favouritism would have no part in such a world, but every human life would be the playing out of a drama constructed like a perfect moral tale. No one is able to blind himself to the fact that the world we live in is totally different from this; insomuch that the necessity of redressing the balance has been deemed one of the strongest arguments for another life after death, which amounts to an admission that the order of things in this life is often an example of injustice, not justice. If it be said that God does not take sufficient account of pleasure and pain to make them the reward or punishment of the good or the wicked, but that virtue is itself the greatest good and vice the greatest evil, then these at least ought to be dispensed to all according to what they have done to deserve them; instead of which, every kind of moral depravity is entailed upon multitudes by the fatality of their birth; through the fault of their parents, of society, or of uncontrollable circumstances, certainly through no fault of their own. Not even on the most distorted and contracted theory of good which ever was framed by religious or philosophical fanaticism, can the government of Nature be made to resemble the work of a being at once good and omnipotent.

The only admissible moral theory of Creation is that the Principle of Good *cannot* at once and altogether subdue the powers of evil, either physical or moral; could not place mankind in a world free from the necessity of an incessant struggle with the maleficent powers, or make them always victorious in that struggle, but could and did make them capable of carrying on the fight with vigour and with progressively increasing success. Of all the religious explanations of the order of nature, this alone is neither contradictory to itself, nor to the facts for which it attempts to account. According to it, man's duty would consist, not in simply taking care of his own interests by obeying irresistible power, but in standing forward a not ineffectual auxiliary to a Being of perfect beneficence; a faith which seems much better adapted for nerving him to exertion than a vague and inconsistent reliance on an Author of Good who is supposed to be also the author of evil. And I venture to assert that such has really been, though often unconsciously, the faith of all who have drawn strength and support of any worthy kind from trust in a superintending Providence. There is no subject on which men's practical belief is more incorrectly indicated by the words they use to express it, than religion. Many have derived a base confidence from imagining themselves to be favourites of an omnipotent but capricious and despotic Deity. But those who have been strengthened in goodness by relying on the sympathizing support of a powerful and good Governor of the world, have, I am satisfied, never really believed that Governor to be, in the strict sense of the term, omnipotent. They have always saved his goodness at the expense of his power. They have believed, perhaps, that he could, if he willed, remove all the thorns from their individual path, but not without causing greater harm to some one else, or frustrating some purpose of greater importance to the general well-being. They have believed that he could do any one thing, but not any combination of things: that his government, like human government, was a system of adjustments and compromises; that the world is inevitably imperfect, contrary to his intention. And since the exertion of all his power to make it as little imperfect as possible, leaves it no better than it is, they cannot but regard that power, though vastly beyond human estimate, yet as in itself not merely finite, but extremely limited. They are bound, for example, to suppose that the best he could do for his human creatures was to make an immense majority of all who have yet existed, be born (without any fault of their own) Patagonians, or Esquimaux, or something nearly as brutal and degraded, but to give them capacities which by being cultivated for very many centuries in toil and suffering, and after many of the best specimens of the race have sacrificed their lives for the purpose, have at last enabled some chosen portions of the species to grow into something better, capable of being improved in centuries more into something really good, of which hitherto there are only to be found individual instances. It may be possible to believe with Plato that perfect goodness, limited and thwarted in every direction by the intractableness of the material, has done this because it could do no better. But that the same perfectly wise and good Being had absolute power over the material, and made it, by voluntary choice, what it is; to admit this might have been supposed impossible to any one who has the simplest notions of moral good and evil. Nor can any such person, whatever kind of religious phrases he may use, fail to believe, that if Nature and Man are both the works of a Being of perfect goodness, that Being intended Nature as a scheme to be amended, not imitated, by Man.

But even though unable to believe that Nature, as a whole, is a realization of the designs of perfect wisdom and benevolence, men do not willingly renounce the idea that some part of Nature, at least, must be intended as an exemplar, or type; that on some portion or other of the Creator's works, the image of the moral qualities which they are accustomed to ascribe to him, must be impressed; that if not all which is, yet something which is, must not only be a faultless model of what ought to be, but must be intended to be our guide and standard in rectifying the rest. It does not suffice them to believe, that what tends to good is to be imitated and perfected, and what tends to evil is to be corrected: they are anxious for some more definite indication of the Creator's designs; and being persuaded that this must somewhere be met with in his works, undertake the dangerous responsibility of picking and choosing among them in quest of it. A choice which except so far as directed by the general maxim that he intends all the good and none of the evil, must of necessity be perfectly arbitrary; and if it leads to any conclusions other than such as can be deduced from that maxim, must be, exactly in that proportion, pernicious.

It has never been settled by any accredited doctrine, what particular departments of the order of nature shall be reputed to be designed for our moral instruction and guidance; and accordingly each person's individual predilections, or momentary convenience, have decided to what parts of the divine government the practical conclusions that he was desirous of establishing, should be recommended to approval as being analogous. One such recommendation must be as fallacious as another, for it is impossible to decide that certain of the Creator's works are more truly expressions of his character than the rest; and the only selection which does not lead to immoral results, is the selection of those which most conduce to the general good, in other words, of those which point to an end which if the entire scheme is the expression of a single omnipotent and consistent will, is evidently not the end intended by it.

There is however one particular element in the construction of the world, which to minds on the look-out for special indication of the Creator's will, has appeared, not without plausibility, peculiarly fitted to afford them; viz. the active impulses of human and other animated beings. One can imagine such persons arguing that when the Author of Nature only made circumstances, he may not have meant to indicate the manner in which his rational creatures were to adjust themselves to those circumstances; but that when he implanted positive stimuli in the creatures themselves, stirring them up to a particular kind of action, it is impossible to doubt that he intended that sort of action to be practised by them. This reasoning, followed out consistently, would lead to the conclusion that the Deity intended, and approves, whatever human beings do; since all that they do being the consequence of some of the impulses with which their Creator must have endowed them, all must equally be considered as done in obedience to his will. As this practical conclusion was shrunk from, it was necessary to draw a distinction, and to pronounce that not the whole, but only parts of the active nature of mankind point to a special intention of the Creator in respect to their conduct. These parts it seemed natural to suppose, must be those in which the Creator's hand is manifested rather than the man's own: and hence the frequent antithesis between man as God made him, and man as he has made himself. Since what is done with deliberation seems more the man's own act, and he is held more completely responsible for it than for what he does from sudden impulse, the considerate part of human conduct is apt to be set down as man's share in the business, and the inconsiderate as God's. The result is the vein of sentiment so common in the modern world (though unknown to the philosophic ancients) which exalts instinct at the expense of reason; an aberration rendered still more mischievous by the opinion commonly held in conjunction with it, that every, or almost every, feeling or impulse which acts promptly without waiting to ask questions, is an instinct. Thus almost every variety of unreflecting and uncalculating impulse receives a kind of consecration, except those which, though unreflecting at the moment, owe their origin to previous habits of reflection: these, being evidently not instinctive, do not meet with the favour accorded to the rest; so that all unreflecting impulses are invested with authority over reason, except the only ones which are most probably right. I do not mean, of course, that this mode of judgment is even pretended to be consistently carried out: life could not go on if it were not admitted that impulses must be controlled, and that reason ought to govern our actions. The pretension is not to drive Reason from the helm but rather to bind her by articles to steer only in a particular way. Instinct is not to govern, but reason is to practise some vague and unassignable amount of deference to Instinct. Though the impression in favour of instinct as being a peculiar manifestation of the divine purposes, has not been cast into the form of a consistent general theory, it remains a standing prejudice, capable of being stirred up into hostility to reason in any case in which the dictate of the rational faculty has not acquired the authority of prescription.

I shall not here enter into the difficult psychological question, what are, or are not instincts: the subject would require a volume to itself.

Without touching upon any disputed theoretical points, it is possible to judge how little worthy is the instinctive part of human nature to be held up as its chief excellence — as the part in which the hand of infinite goodness and wisdom is peculiarly visible. Allowing everything to be an instinct which anybody has ever asserted to be one, it remains true that nearly every respectable attribute of humanity is the result not of instinct, but of a victory over instinct; and that there is hardly anything valuable in the natural man except capacities — a whole world of possibilities, all of them dependent upon eminently artificial discipline for being realized.

It is only in a highly artificialized condition of human nature that the notion grew up, or, I believe, ever could have grown up, that goodness was natural: because only after a long course of artificial education did good sentiments become so habitual, and so predominant over bad, as to arise unprompted when occasion called for them. In the times when mankind were nearer to their natural state, cultivated observers regarded the natural man as a sort of wild animal, distinguished chiefly by being craftier than the other beasts of the field; and all worth of character was deemed the result of a sort of taming; a phrase often applied by the ancient philosophers to the appropriate discipline of human beings. The truth is that there is hardly a single point of excellence belonging to human character, which is not decidedly repugnant to the untutored feelings of human nature.

If there be a virtue which more than any other we expect to find, and really do find, in an uncivilized state, it is the virtue of courage. Yet this is from first to last a victory achieved over one of the most powerful emotions of human nature. If there is any one feeling or attribute more natural than all others to human beings, it is fear; and no greater proof can be given of the power of artificial discipline than the conquest which it has at all times and places shown itself capable of achieving over so mighty and so universal a sentiment. The widest difference no doubt exists between one human being and another in the facility or difficulty with which they acquire this virtue. There is hardly any department of human excellence in which difference of original temperament goes so far. But it may fairly be questioned if any human being is naturally courageous. Many are naturally pugnacious, or irascible, or enthusiastic, and these passions when strongly excited may render them insensible to fear. But take away the conflicting emotion, and fear reasserts its dominion: consistent courage is always the effect of cultivation. The courage which is occasionally though by no means generally found among tribes of savages, is as much the result of education as that of the Spartans or Romans. In all such tribes there is a most emphatic direction of the public sentiment into every channel of expression through which honour can be paid to courage and cowardice held up to contempt and derision. It will perhaps be said, that as the expression of a sentiment implies the sentiment itself, the training of the young to courage presupposes an originally courageous people. It presupposes only what all good customs presuppose — that there must have been individuals better than the rest, who set the customs going. Some individuals, who like other people had fears to conquer, must have had strength of mind and will to conquer them for themselves. These would obtain the influence belonging to heroes, for that which is at once astonishing and obviously useful never fails to be admired: and partly through this admiration, partly through the fear they themselves excite, they would obtain the power of legislators, and could establish whatever customs they pleased.

Let us next consider a quality which forms the most visible, and one of the most radical of the moral distinctions between human beings and most of the lower animals; that of which the absence, more than of anything else, renders men bestial; the quality of cleanliness. Can anything be more entirely artificial? Children, and the lower classes of most countries, seem to be actually fond of dirt: the vast majority of the human race are indifferent to it: whole nations of otherwise civilized and cultivated human beings tolerate it in some of its worst forms, and only a very small minority are consistently offended by it. Indeed the universal law of the subject appears to be, that uncleanliness offends only those to whom it is unfamiliar, so that those who have lived in so artificial a state as to be unused to it in any form, are the sole persons whom it disgusts in all forms. Of all virtues this is the most evidently not instinctive, but a triumph over instinct. Assuredly neither cleanliness nor the love of cleanliness is natural to man, but only the capacity of acquiring a love of cleanliness.

Our examples have thus far been taken from the personal, or as they are called by Bentham, the self regarding virtues, because these, if any, might be supposed to be congenial even to the uncultivated mind. Of the social virtues it is almost superfluous to speak; so completely is it the verdict of all experience that selfishness is natural. By this I do not in any wise mean to deny that sympathy is natural also; I believe on the contrary that on that important fact rests the possibility of any cultivation of goodness and nobleness, and the hope of their ultimate entire ascendancy. But sympathetic characters, left uncultivated, and given up to their sympathetic instincts, are as selfish as others. The difference is in the *kind* of selfishness: theirs is not solitary but sympathetic selfishness; *l'egoïsme à deux, à trois,* or *à quatre;* and they may be very amiable and delightful to those with whom they sympathize, and grossly unjust and unfeeling to the rest of the world. Indeed the finer nervous organizations which are most capable of and most require sympathy, have, from their fineness, so much stronger impulses of all sorts, that they often furnish the most striking examples of selfishness, though of a less repulsive kind than that of colder natures. Whether there ever was a person in whom, apart from all teaching of instructors, friends or books, and from all intentional self-modelling according to an ideal, natural benevolence was a more powerful attribute than selfishness in any of its forms, may remain undecided. That such cases are extremely rare, every one must admit, and this is enough for the argument.

But (to speak no further of self-control for the benefit of others) the commonest self-control for one's own benefit — that power of sacrificing a present desire to a distant object or a general purpose which is indispensable for making the actions of the individual accord with his own notions of his individual good; even this is most unnatural to the undisciplined human being: as may be seen by the long apprenticeship which children serve to it; the very imperfect manner in which it is acquired by persons born to power, whose will is seldom resisted, and by all who have been early and much indulged; and the marked absence of the quality in savages, in soldiers and sailors, and in a somewhat less degree in nearly the whole of the poorer classes in this and many other countries. The principal difference, on the point under consideration, between this virtue and others, is that although, like them, it requires a course of teaching, it is more susceptible than most of them of being self-taught. The axiom is trite that self-control is only learnt by experience: and this endowment is only thus much nearer to being natural than the others we have spoken of, inasmuch as personal experience, without external inculcation, has a certain tendency to engender it. Nature does not of herself bestow this, any more than other virtues; but nature often administers the rewards and punishments which cultivate it, and which in other cases have to be created artificially for the express purpose.

Veracity might seem, of all virtues, to have the most plausible claim to being natural, since in the absence of motives to the contrary, speech usually conforms to, or at least does not intentionally deviate from, fact. Accordingly this is the virtue with which writers like Rousseau delight in decorating savage life, and setting it in advantageous contrast with the treachery and trickery of civilization. Unfortunately this is a mere fancy picture, contradicted by all the realities of savage life. Savages are always liars. They have not the faintest notion of truth as a virtue. They have a notion of not betraying to their hurt, as of not hurting in any other way, persons to whom they are bound by some special tie of obligation; their chief, their guest, perhaps, or their friend: these feelings of obligation being the taught morality of the savage state, growing out of its characteristic circumstances. But of any point of honour respecting truth for truth's sake, they have not the remotest idea; no more than the whole East, and the greater part of Europe: and in the few countries which are sufficiently improved to have such a point of honour, it is confined to a small minority, who alone, under any circumstances of real temptation practise it.

From the general use of the expression "natural justice," it must be presumed that justice is a virtue generally thought to be directly implanted by nature. I believe, however, that the sentiment of justice is entirely of artificial origin; the idea of natural justice not preceding but following that of conventional justice. The farther we look back into the early modes of thinking of the human race, whether we consider ancient times (including those of the Old Testament) or the portions of mankind who are still in no more advanced a condition than that of ancient times, the more completely do we find men's notions of justice defined and bounded by the express appointment of law. A man's just rights, meant the rights which the law gave him: a just man, was he who never infringed, nor sought to infringe, the legal property or other legal rights of others. The notion of a higher justice, to which laws themselves are amenable, and by which the conscience is bound without a positive prescription of law, is a later extension of the idea, suggested by, and following the analogy of, legal justice, to which it maintains a parallel direction through all the shares and varieties of the sentiment, and from which it borrows nearly the whole of its phraseology. The very words *justus* and *justitia* are derived from *jus*, law. Courts of justice, administration of justice, always mean the tribunals.

If it be said, that there must be the germs of all these virtues in human nature, otherwise mankind would be incapable of acquiring them, I am ready, with a certain amount of explanation, to admit the fact. But the weeds that dispute the ground with these beneficent germs, are themselves not germs but rankly luxuriant growths, and would, in all but some one case in a thousand, entirely stifle and destroy the former, were it not so strongly the interest of mankind to cherish the good germs in one another, that they always do so, in as far as their degree of intelligence (in this as in other respects still very imperfect) allows. It is through such fostering, commenced early, and not counteracted by unfavourable influences, that, in some happily circumstanced specimens of the human race, the most elevated sentiments of which humanity is capable become a second nature, stronger than the first, and not so much subduing the original nature as merging it into itself. Even those gifted organizations which have attained the like excellence by self-culture, owe it essentially to the same cause; for what self-culture would be possible without aid from the general sentiment of mankind delivered through books, and from the contemplation of exalted characters real or ideal? This artificially created or at least artificially perfected nature of the best and noblest human beings, is the only nature which it is ever commendable to follow. It is almost superfluous to say that even this cannot be erected into a standard of conduct, since it is itself the fruit of a training and culture the choice of which, if rational and not accidental, must have been determined by a standard already chosen.

This brief survey is amply sufficient to prove that the duty of man is the same in respect to his own nature as in respect to the nature of all other things, namely not to follow but to amend it. Some people however who do not attempt to deny that instinct ought to be subordinate to reason, pay deference to nature so far as to maintain that every natural inclination must have some sphere of action granted to it, some opening left for its gratification. All natural wishes, they say, must have been implanted for a purpose: and this argument is carried so far, that we often hear it maintained that every wish, which it is supposed to be natural to entertain, must have a corresponding provision in the order of the universe for its gratification: insomuch (for instance) that the desire of an indefinite prolongation of existence, is believed by many to be in itself a sufficient proof of the reality of a future life.

I conceive that there is a radical absurdity in all these attempts to discover, in detail, what are the designs of Providence, in order when they are discovered to help Providence in bringing them about. Those who argue, from particular indications, that Providence intends this or that, either believe that the Creator can do all that he will or that he cannot. If the first supposition is adopted — if Providence is omnipotent, Providence intends whatever happens, and the fact of its happening proves that Providence intended it. If so, everything which a human being can do, is predestined by Providence and is a fulfilment of its designs. But if as is the more religious theory, Providence intends not all which happens, but only what is good, then indeed man has it in his power, by his voluntary actions, to aid the intentions of Providence; but he can only learn those intentions by considering what tends to promote the general good, and not what man has a natural inclination to; for, limited as, on this showing, the divine power must be, by inscrutable but insurmountable obstacles, who knows that man *could* have been created without desires which never are to be, and even which never ought to be, fulfilled? The inclinations with which man has been endowed, as well as any of the other contrivances which we observe in Nature, may be the expression not of the divine will, but of the fetters which impede its free action; and to take hints from these for the guidance of our own conduct may be falling into a trap laid by the enemy. The assumption that everything which infinite goodness can desire, actually comes to pass in this universe, or at least that we must never say or suppose that it does not, is worthy only of those whose slavish fears make them offer the homage of lies to a Being who, they profess to think, is incapable of being deceived and holds all falsehood in abomination.

With regard to this particular hypothesis, that all natural impulses, all propensities sufficiently universal and sufficiently spontaneous to be capable of passing for instincts, must exist for good ends and ought to be only regulated, not repressed; this is of course true of the majority of them, for the species could not have continued to exist unless most of its inclinations had been directed to things needful or useful for its preservation. But unless the instincts can be reduced to a very small number indeed, it must be allowed that we have also bad instincts which it should be the aim of education not simply to regulate but to extirpate, or rather (what can be done even to an instinct) to starve them by disuse. Those who are inclined to multiply the number of instincts, usually include among them one which they call destructiveness: an instinct to destroy for destruction's sake. I can conceive no good reason for preserving this, no more than another propensity which if not an instinct is very like one, what has been called the instinct of domination; a delight in exercising despotism, in holding other beings in subjection to our will. The man who takes pleasure in the mere exertion of authority, apart from the purpose for which it is to be employed, is the last person in whose hands one would willingly entrust it. Again, there are persons who are cruel by character, or, as the phrase is, naturally cruel: who have a real pleasure in inflicting, or seeing the infliction of pain. This kind of cruelty is not mere hardheartedness, absence of pity or remorse; it is a positive thing; a particular kind of voluptuous excitement. The East, and Southern Europe, have afforded, and probably still afford, abundant examples of this hateful propensity. I suppose it will be granted that this is not one of the natural inclinations which it would be wrong to suppress. The only question would be whether it is not a duty to suppress the man himself along with it.

But even if it were true that every one of the elementary impulses of human nature has its good side, and may by a sufficient amount of artificial training be made more useful than hurtful; how little would this amount to, when it must in any case be admitted that without such training all of them, even those which are necessary to our preservation, would fill the world with misery, making human life an exaggerated likeness of the odious scene of violence and tyranny which is exhibited by the rest of the animal kingdom, except in so far as tamed and disciplined by man. There, indeed, those who flatter themselves with the notion of reading the purposes of the Creator in his works, ought in consistency to have seen grounds for inferences from which they have shrunk. If there are any marks at all of special design in creation, one of the things most evidently designed is that a large proportion of all animals should pass their existence in tormenting and devouring other animals. They have been lavishly fitted out with the instruments necessary for that purpose; their strongest instincts impel them to it, and many of them seem to have been constructed incapable of supporting themselves by any other food. If a tenth part of the pains which have been expended in finding benevolent adaptations in all nature, had been employed in collecting evidence to blacken the character of the Creator, what scope for comment would not have been found in the entire existence of the lower animals, divided, with scarcely an exception, into devourers and devoured, and a prey to a thousand ills from which they are denied the faculties necessary for protecting themselves! If we are not obliged to believe the animal creation to be the work of a demon, it is because we need not suppose it to have been made by a Being of infinite power. But if imitation of the Creator's will as revealed in nature, were applied as a rule of action in this case, the most atrocious enormities of the worst men would be more than justified by the apparent intention of Providence that throughout all animated nature the strong should prey upon the weak.

The preceding observations are far from having exhausted the almost infinite variety of modes and occasions in which the idea of conformity to nature is introduced as an element into the ethical appreciation of actions and dispositions. The same favourable prejudgment follows the word nature through the numerous acceptations, in which it is employed as a distinctive term for certain parts of the constitution of humanity as contrasted with other parts. We have hitherto confined ourselves to one of these acceptations, in which it stands as a general designation for those parts of our mental and moral constitution which are supposed to be innate, in contradistinction to those which are acquired; as when nature is contrasted with education; or when a savage state, without laws, arts, or knowledge, is called a state of nature; or when the question is asked whether benevolence, or the moral sentiment, is natural or acquired; or whether some persons are poets or orators by nature and others not. But in another and a more lax sense, any manifestations by human beings are often termed natural, when it is merely intended to say that they are not studied or designedly assumed in the particular case; as when a person is said to move or speak with natural grace; or when it is said that a person's natural manner or character is so and so; meaning that it is so when he does not attempt to control or disguise it. In a still looser acceptation, a person is said to be naturally, that which he was until some special cause had acted upon him, or which it is supposed he would be if some such cause were withdrawn. Thus a person is said to be naturally dull, but to have made himself intelligent by study and perseverance; to be naturally cheerful, but soured by misfortune; naturally ambitious, but kept down by want of opportunity. Finally, the word natural, applied to feelings or conduct, often seems to mean no more than that they are such as are ordinarily found in human beings; as when it is said that a person acted, on some particular occasion, as it was natural to do; or that to be affected in a particular way by some sight, or sound, or thought, or incident in life, is perfectly natural.

In all these senses of the term, the quality called natural is very often confessedly a worse quality than the one contrasted with it; but whenever its being so is not too obvious to be questioned, the idea seems to be entertained that by describing it as natural, something has been said amounting to a considerable presumption in its favour. For my part I can perceive only one sense in which nature, or naturalness, in a human being, are really terms of praise; and then the praise is only negative: namely when used to denote the absence of affectation. Affectation may be defined, the effort to appear what one is not, when the motive or the occasion is not such as either to excuse the attempt, or to stamp it with the more odious name of hypocrisy. It must be added that the deception is often attempted to be practised on the deceiver himself as well as on others; he imitates the external signs of qualities which he would like to have, in hopes to persuade himself that he has them. Whether in the form of deception or of self-deception, or of something hovering between the two, affectation is very rightly accounted a reproach, and naturalness, understood as the reverse of affectation, a merit. But a more proper term by which to express this estimable quality would be sincerity; a term which has fallen from its original elevated meaning, and popularly denotes only a subordinate branch of the cardinal virtue it once designated as a whole.

Sometimes also, in cases where the term affectation would be inappropriate, since the conduct or demeanour spoken of is really praiseworthy, people say in disparagement of the person concerned, that such conduct or demeanour is not natural to him; and make uncomplimentary comparisons between him and some other person, to whom it is natural: meaning that what in the one seemed excellent was the effect of temporary excitement, or of a great victory over himself, while in the other it is the result to be expected from the habitual character. This mode of speech is not open to censure, since nature is here simply a term for the person's ordinary disposition, and if he is praised it is not for being natural, but for being naturally good.

Conformity to nature, has no connection whatever with right and wrong. The idea can never be fitly introduced into ethical discussions at all, except, occasionally and partially, into the question of degrees of culpability. To illustrate this point, let us consider the phrase by which the greatest intensity of condemnatory feeling is conveyed in connection with the idea of nature — the word unnatural. That a thing is unnatural, in any precise meaning which can be attached to the word, is no argument for its being blamable; since the most criminal actions are to a being like man, not more unnatural than most of the virtues. The acquisition of virtue has in all ages been accounted a work of labour and difficulty, while the *descensus Averni* [10] on the

10 Non-literally, "descent into Hell."

contrary is of proverbial facility: and it assuredly requires in most persons a greater conquest over a greater number of natural inclinations to become eminently virtuous than transcendently vicious. But if an action, or an inclination, has been decided on other grounds to be blamable, it may be a circumstance in aggravation that it is unnatural, that is, repugnant to some strong feeling usually found in human beings; since the bad propensity, whatever it be, has afforded evidence of being both strong and deeply rooted, by having overcome that repugnance. This presumption of course fails if the individual never had the repugnance: and the argument, therefore, is not fit to be urged unless the feeling which is violated by the act, is not only justifiable and reasonable, but is one which it is blamable to be without.

The corresponding plea in extenuation of a culpable act because it was natural, or because it was prompted by a natural feeling, never, I think, ought to be admitted. There is hardly a bad action ever perpetrated which is not perfectly natural, and the motives to which are not perfectly natural feelings. In the eye of reason, therefore, this is no excuse, but it is quite "natural" that it should be so in the eyes of the multitude; because the meaning of the expression is, that they have a fellow feeling with the offender. When they say that something which they cannot help admitting to be blamable, is nevertheless natural, they mean that they can imagine the possibility of their being themselves tempted to commit it. Most people have a considerable amount of indulgence towards all acts of which they feel a possible source within themselves, reserving their rigour for those which, though perhaps really less bad, they cannot in any way understand how it is possible to commit. If an action convinces them (which it often does on very inadequate grounds) that the person who does it must be a being totally unlike themselves, they are seldom particular in examining the precise degree of blame due to it, or even if blame is properly due to it at all. They measure the degree of guilt by the strength of their antipathy; and hence differences of opinion, and even differences of taste, have been objects of as intense moral abhorrence as the most atrocious crimes.

It will be useful to sum up in a few words the leading conclusions of this Essay.

The word Nature has two principal meanings: it either denotes the entire system of things, with the aggregate of all their properties, or it denotes things as they would be, apart from human intervention.

In the first of these senses, the doctrine that man ought to follow nature is unmeaning; since man has no power to do anything else than follow nature; all his actions are done through, and in obedience to, some one or many of nature's physical or mental laws.

In the other sense of the term, the doctrine that man ought to follow nature, or in other words, ought to make the spontaneous course of things the model of his voluntary actions, is equally irrational and immoral.

Irrational, because all human action whatever, consists in altering, and all useful action in improving, the spontaneous course of nature:

Immoral, because the course of natural phenomena being replete with everything which when committed by human beings is most worthy of abhorrence, any one who endeavoured in his actions to imitate the natural course of things would be universally seen and acknowledged to be the wickedest of men.

The scheme of Nature regarded in its whole extent, cannot have had, for its sole or even principal object, the good of human or other sentient beings. What good it brings to them, is mostly the result of their own exertions. Whatsoever, in nature, gives indication of beneficent design, proves this beneficence to be armed only with limited power; and the duty of man is to co-operate with the beneficent powers, not by imitating but by perpetually striving to amend the course of nature — and bringing that part of it over which we can exercise control, more nearly into conformity with a high standard of justice and goodness.

John Ruskin

JOHN RUSKIN

CHRONOLOGY

1819   Born February 8 in London.

1819–1833   Privately educated by parents and tutors.

1833   Traveled with parents to France, Switzerland, and Italy.

1837   Entered Christ Church College, Oxford.

1839   Received Newdigate Poetry Prize.

1843   Published *Modern Painters*, Vol. I.

1846   Published *Modern Painters*, Vol. II.

1848   Married Euphemia Chalmers Gray.

1849   Published *The Seven Lamps of Architecture*.

1851   Published *Stones of Venice*, Vol. I, and *Pre-Raphaelitism* (letters to the *Times*).

1853   Published *Stones of Venice*, Vols. II–III.

1854   Marriage annulled.

1856   Published *Modern Painters*, Vols. III–IV.

1860   Published *Modern Painters*, Vol. V.

1862   Published, in book form, *Unto This Last*.

1865   Published *Sesame and Lilies*.

1866   Published *Ethics of the Dust* and *The Crown of Wild Olive*.

1867   Published *Time and Tide*; received LL. D. at Cambridge.

1869   Published *The Queen of the Air*.

1870–1878   Slade Professor of Fine Arts, Oxford.

1871–1884   Published, at intervals, *Fors Clavigera*.

1872   Published, in book form, *Munera Pulveris*.

1878   Began to experience attacks of mania.

1880   Published *Fiction, Fair and Foul*.

1883–1885   Re-elected Professor at Oxford.

1885–1889   Wrote *Praeterita* ("at irregular intervals").

1900   Died January 21.

Modern Painters

⟨ *Modern Painters* began with Ruskin's decision, in 1842, to write a paper defending Turner (1775–1851), the English landscape painter, against his critics. However, he found, he tells us, "that *demonstration* in matters of art was no such easy matter, and the pamphlet turned into a volume. Before the volume was half way dealt with it hydraized into three heads, and each head became a volume. Finding that nothing could be done except on such an enormous scale, I determined to take the hydra by the horns, and produce a complete treatise on landscape art." *Modern Painters,* in fact, grew to five substantial volumes. Ruskin was the chief formal expositor of the moral aesthetic, maintaining that there is an absolutely necessary connection between the morality of the artist and the nobility of his ideas, on the one hand, and the greatness of his art, on the other. ⟩

VOLUME III — PART IV.
OF MANY THINGS

CHAPTER III

Of the Real Nature of Greatness of Style

1. I DOUBT not that the reader was ill-satisfied with the conclusion arrived at in the last chaper.[1] That "great art" is art which represents what is beautiful and good, may not seem a very profound discovery; and the main question may be thought to have been all the time lost sight of, namely, "What is beautiful, and what is good?" No; those are not the main, at least not the first questions; on the contrary, our subject becomes at once opened and simplified as soon as we have left those the *only* questions. For observe, our present task, according to our old plan, is merely to investigate the relative degrees of the *beautiful* in the art of different masters; and it is an encouragement to be convinced, first of all, that what is lovely will also be great and what is pleasing, noble. Nor is the conclusion so much a matter of course as it at first appears, for, surprising as the statement may seem, all the confusion into which Reynolds has plunged both himself and his readers, in the essay we have been examining,[2] results primarily from a doubt in his own mind *as to the existence of beauty at all.* In the next paper I alluded to, No. 82 (which needs not, how-

1 "Of Realization," in which Ruskin had concluded that "true criticism of art never can consist in the mere application of rules; it can be just only when it is founded on quick sympathy with the innumerable instincts and changeful efforts of human nature, chastened and guided by unchanging love of all things that God has created to be beautiful, and pronounced to be good."

2 From *The Idler.*

ever, to be examined at so great length), he calmly attributes the
whole influence of beauty to custom, saying, that "he has no doubt,
if we were more used to deformity than to beauty, deformity would
then lose the idea now annexed to it, and take that of beauty; as if
the whole world shall agree that Yes and No should change their
meanings. Yes would then deny, and No would affirm!"

2. The world does, indeed, succeed — oftener than is, perhaps,
altogether well for the world — in making Yes mean No, and No
mean Yes. But the world has never succeeded, nor ever will, in
making itself delight in black clouds more than in blue sky, or love
the dark earth better than the rose that grows from it. Happily
for mankind, beauty and ugliness are as positive in their nature as
physical pain and pleasure, as light and darkness, or as life and death;
and, though they may be denied or misunderstood in many fantastic
ways, the most subtle reasoner will at last find that colour and sweetness are still attractive to him, and that no logic will enable him to
think the rainbow sombre, or the violet scentless. But the theory
that beauty was merely a result of custom was very common in Johnson's time. Goldsmith has, I think, expressed it with more force and
wit than any other writer, in various passages of the *Citizen of the
World.* And it was indeed, a curious retribution of the folly of the
world of art, which for some three centuries had given itself recklessly
to the pursuit of beauty, that at last it should be led to deny the
very existence of what it had so morbidly and passionately sought. It
was as if a child should leave its home to pursue the rainbow, and
then, breathless and hopeless, declare that it did not exist. Nor is
the lesson less useful which may be gained in observing the adoption
of such a theory by Reynolds himself. It shows how completely an
artist may be unconscious of the principles of his own work, and
how he may be led by instinct to *do* all that is right, while he is
misled by false logic to *say* all that is wrong. For nearly every word
that Reynolds wrote was contrary to his own practice; he seems to
have been born to teach all error by his precept, and all excellence by
his example; he enforced with his lips generalization and idealism,
while with his pencil he was tracing the patterns of the dresses of
the belles of his day; he exhorted his pupils to attend only to the
invariable, while he himself was occupied in distinguishing every
variation of womanly temper; and he denied the existence of the
beautiful, at the same instant that he arrested it as it passed, and per-
petuated it for ever.

3. But we must not quit the subject here. However inconsistently
or dimly expressed, there is, indeed, some truth in that commonly
accepted distinction between high and low art. That a thing should
be beautiful is not enough; there is, as we said in the outset, a higher
and lower range of beauty, and some ground for separating into
various and unequal ranks painters who have, nevertheless, each in

his several way, represented something that was beautiful or good.

Nor, if we would, can we get rid of this conviction. We have at all times some instinctive sense that the function of one painter is greater than that of another, even supposing each equally successful in his own way; and we feel that, if it were possible to conquer prejudice, and do away with the iniquities of personal feeling, and the insufficiencies of limited knowledge, we should all agree in this estimate, and be able to place each painter in his right rank, measuring them by a true scale of nobleness. We feel that the men in the higher classes of the scale would be, in the full sense of the word, Great, — men whom one would give much to see the faces of but for an instant; and that those in the lower classes of the scale (though none were admitted but who had true merit of some kind) would be very small men, not greatly exciting either reverence or curiosity. And with this fixed instinct in our minds, we permit our teachers daily to exhort their pupils to the cultivation of "great art" — neither they nor we having any very clear notion as to what the greatness consists in: but sometimes inclining to think it must depend on the space of the canvas, and that art on a scale of 6 feet by 10 is something spiritually separated from that on a scale of 3 feet by 5; — sometimes holding it to consist in painting the nude body, rather than the body decently clothed; — sometimes being convinced that it is connected with the study of past history, and that the art is only great which represents what the painter never saw, and about which he knows nothing; — and sometimes being firmly persuaded that it consists in generally finding fault with, and endeavouring to mend, whatsoever the Divine Wisdom has made. All which various errors, having yet some motes and atoms of truth in the make of each of them, deserve some attentive analysis, for they come under that general law, — that "the corruption of the best is the worst." There are not *worse* errors going than these four; and yet the truth they contain, and the instinct which urges many to preach them, are at the root of all healthy growth in art. We ruin one young painter after another by telling him to follow great art, without knowing, ourselves, what greatness is; and yet the feeling that it verily *is* something, and that there are depths and breadths, shallows and narrows, in the matter, is all that we have to look to, if we would ever make our art serviceable to ourselves or others. To follow art for the sake of being a great man, and therefore to cast about continually for some means of achieving position or attracting admiration, is the surest way of ending in total extinction. And yet it is only by honest reverence for art itself, and by great self-respect in the practice of it, that it can be rescued from dilettantism, raised to approved honourableness, and brought to the proper work it has to accomplish in the service of man.

4. Let us therefore look into the facts of the thing, not with any metaphysical, or otherwise vain and troublesome effort at acuteness,

but in a plain way; for the facts themselves are plain enough, and
may be plainly stated, only the difficulty is that out of these facts,
right and left, the different forms of misapprehension branch into
grievous complexity, and branch so far and wide, that if once we try
to follow them, they will lead us quite from our mark into other
separate, though not less interesting discussions. The best way will
be, therefore, I think, to sketch out at once in this chapter, the different characters which really constitute "greatness" of style, and to
indicate the principal directions of the outbranching misapprehen-
sions of them; then, in the succeeding chapters, to take up in succession those which need more talk about them, and follow out at leisure
whatever inquiries they may suggest.

5. I. CHOICE OF NOBLE SUBJECT. — Greatness of style consists,
then: first, in the habitual choice of subjects of thought which involve
wide interests and profound passions, as opposed to those which involve narrow interests and slight passions. The style is greater or less
in exact proportion to the nobleness of the interests and passions involved in the subject. The habitual choice of sacred subjects, such
as the Nativity, Transfiguration, Crucifixion (if the choice be sincere),
implies that the painter has a natural disposition to dwell on the highest thoughts of which humanity is capable; it constitutes him so far
forth a painter of the highest order, as, for instance, Leonardo, in his
painting of the Last Supper: he who delights in representing the acts
or meditations of great men, as, for instance, Raphael painting the
School of Athens, is, so far forth, a painter of the second order: he
who represents the passions and events of ordinary life, of the third.
And in this ordinary life, he who represents deep thoughts and sorrows, as, for instance, Hunt, in his Claudio and Isabella, and such
other works, is of the highest rank in his sphere: and he who represents the slight malignities and passions of the drawing-room, as, for
instance, Leslie,[3] of the second rank; he who represents the sports
of boys, or simplicities of clowns, as Webster [4] or Teniers, of the third
rank; and he who represents brutalities and vices (for delight in them,
and not for rebuke of them), of no rank at all, or rather of a negative rank, holding a certain order in the abyss.

6. The reader will, I hope, understand how much importance is to
be attached to the sentence in the first parenthesis, "if the choice be
sincere"; for choice of subject is, of course, only available as a criterion
of the rank of the painter, when it is made from the heart. Indeed,
in the lower orders of painting, the choice is always made from such
heart as the painter has; for his selection of the brawls of peasants or
sports of children can, of course, proceed only from the fact that he
has more sympathy with such brawls or pastimes than with nobler

3 Charles Robert Leslie (1794–1859), fashionable painter and professor of
painting at the Royal Academy (1848–1852).
4 Thomas Webster (1800–1886), member of the Royal Academy.

subjects. But the choice of the higher kind of subjects is often insincere; and may, therefore, afford no real criterion of the painter's rank. The greater number of men who have lately painted religious or heroic subjects have done so in mere ambition, because they had been taught that it was a good thing to be a "high-art" painter; and the fact is that, in nine cases out of ten, the so-called historical or "high-art" painter is a person infinitely inferior to the painter of flowers or still life. He is, in modern times, nearly always a man who has great vanity without pictorial capacity, and differs from the landscape or fruit painter merely in misunderstanding and overestimating his own powers. He mistakes his vanity for inspiration, his ambition for greatness of soul, and takes pleasure in what he calls "the ideal," merely because he has neither humility nor capacity enough to comprehend the real.

7. But also observe, it is not enough even that the choice be sincere. It must also be wise. It happens very often that a man of weak intellect, sincerely desiring to do what is good and useful, will devote himself to high art subjects because he thinks them the only ones on which time and toil can be usefully spent, or, sometimes, because they are really the only ones he has pleasure in contemplating. But not having intellect enough to enter into the minds of truly great men, or to imagine great events as they really happened, he cannot become a great painter; he degrades the subjects he intended to honour, and his work is more utterly thrown away, and his rank as an artist in reality lower, than if he had devoted himself to the imitation of the simplest objects of natural history. The works of Overbeck [5] are a most notable instance of this form of error.

8. It must also be remembered, that in nearly all the great periods of art the choice of subject has not been left to the painter. His employer, — abbot, baron, or monarch, — determined for him whether he should earn his bread by making cloisters bright with choirs of saints, painting coats of arms on leaves of romances, or decorating presence-chambers with complimentary mythology; and his own personal feelings are ascertainable only by watching, in the themes assigned to him, what are the points in which he seems to take most pleasure. Thus, in the prolonged ranges of varied subjects with which Benozzo Gozzoli [6] decorated the cloisters of Pisa, it is easy to see that love of simple domestic incident, sweet landscape, and glittering ornament, prevails slightly over the solemn elements of religious feeling, which, nevertheless, the spirit of the age instilled into him in such measure as to form a very lovely and noble mind, though still one of the second order. In the work of Orcagna, an intense solemnity and energy in the sublimest groups of his figures,

5 Johann Friedrich Overbeck (1789–1869), German painter and leader of the German "Pre-Raphaelites."

6 Benozzo Gozzoli (1420–1497)

fading away as he touches inferior subjects, indicates that his home
was among the archangels, and his rank among the first of the sons
of men: while Correggio, in the sidelong grace, artificial smiles, and
purple languors of his saints, indicates the inferior instinct which
would have guided his choice in quite other directions, had it not
been for the fashion of the age, and the need of the day.

9. It will follow, of course, from the above considerations, that
the choice which characterizes the school of high art is seen as much
in the treatment of a subject as in its selection, and that the expression of the thoughts of the persons represented will always be the
first thing considered by the painter who worthily enters that highest
school. For the artist who sincerely chooses the noblest subject will
also choose chiefly to represent what makes that subject noble, namely,
the various heroism or other noble emotions of the persons represented.
If, instead of this, the artist seeks only to make his picture agreeable
by the composition of its masses and colours, or by any other merely
pictorial merit, as fine drawing of limbs, it is evident, not only that
any other subject would have answered his purpose as well, but that
he is unfit to approach the subject he has chosen, because he cannot
enter into its deepest meaning, and therefore cannot in reality have
chosen it for that meaning. Nevertheless, while the expression is
always to be the first thing considered, all other merits must be
added to the utmost of the painter's power; for until he can both
colour and draw beautifully he has no business to consider himself
a painter at all, far less to attempt the noblest subjects of painting;
and, when he has once possessed himself of these powers, he will
naturally and fitly employ them to deepen and perfect the impression made by the sentiment of his subject.

The perfect unison of expression, as the painter's main purpose, with
the full and natural exertion of his pictorial power in the details of
the work, is found only in the old Pre-Raphaelite periods, and in
the modern Pre-Raphaelite school. In the works of Giotto, Angelico,
Orcagna, John Bellini, and one or two more, these two conditions of
high art are entirely fulfilled, so far as the knowledge of those days
enable them to be fulfilled; and in the modern Pre-Raphaelite school
they are fulfilled nearly to the uttermost. Hunt's Light of the World
is, I believe, the most perfect instance of expressional purpose with
technical power, which the world has yet produced.

10. Now in the Post-Raphaelite period of ancient art, and in the
spurious high art of modern times, two broad forms of error divide
the schools; the one consisting in (A) the superseding of expression
by technical excellence, and the other in (B) the superseding of
technical excellence by expression.

(A). Superseding expression by technical excellence. — This takes
place most frankly, and therefore most innocently, in the work of the
Venetians. They very nearly ignore expression altogether, directing

their aim exclusively to the rendering of external truths of colour and form. Paul Veronese will make the Magdalene wash the feet of Christ with a countenance as absolutely unmoved as that of any ordinary servant bringing a ewer to her master, and will introduce the supper at Emmaus as a background to the portraits of two children playing with a dog. Of the wrongness or rightness of such a proceeding we shall reason in another place; at present we have to note it merely as displacing the Venetian work from the highest or expressional rank of art. But the error is generally made in a more subtle and dangerous way. The artist deceives himself into the idea that he is doing all he can to elevate his subject by treating it under rules of art, introducing into it accurate science, and collecting for it the beauties of (so-called) ideal form; whereas he may, in reality, be all the while sacrificing his subject to his own vanity or pleasure, and losing truth, nobleness, and impressiveness for the sake of delightful lines or credit able pedantries.

11. (B). Superseding technical excellence by expression. — This is usually done under the influence of another kind of vanity. The artist desires that men should think he has an elevated soul, affects to despite the ordinary excellence of art, contemplates with separated egotism the course of his own imaginations or sensations, and refuses to look at the real facts round about him, in order that he may adore at leisure the shadow of himself. He lives in an element of what he calls tender emotions and loftly aspirations; which are, in fact, nothing more than very ordinary weaknesses or instincts, contemplated through a mist of pride. A large range of modern German art comes under this head.

A more interesting and respectable form of this error is fallen into by some truly earnest men, who, finding their powers not adequate to the attainment of great artistical excellence, but adequate to rendering, up to a certain point, the expression of the human countenance, devote themselves to that object alone, abandoning effort in other directions, and executing the accessories of their pictures feebly or carelessly. With these are associated another group of philosophical painters, who suppose the artistical merits of other parts *adverse* to the expression, as drawing the spectator's attention away from it, and who paint in grey colour, and imperfect light and shade, by way of enforcing the purity of their conceptions. Both these classes of conscientious but narrow-minded artists labour under the same grievous mistake of imagining that wilful fallacy can ever be either pardonable or helpful. They forget that colour, if used at all, must be either true or false, and that what *they* call chastity, dignity, and reserve, is, to the eye of any person accustomed to nature, pure, bold, and impertinent falsehood. It does not, in the eyes of any soundly minded man, exalt the expression of a female face that the cheeks should be painted of the colour of clay, nor does it in the least enhance his reverence for a saint to find the scenery around him deprived, by his presence, of sunshine. It is an important consolation, however, to reflect that no artist ever fell into any of these last three errors (under head B.) who had really the capacity of becoming a great painter. No man ever despised colour who could produce it; and the error of these sentimentalists and philosophers is not so much in the choice of their manner of painting, as in supposing themselves capable of painting at all. Some of them might have made efficient sculptors, but the greater number had their mission in some other sphere than that of art, and would have found, in works of practical charity, better employment for their gentleness and sentimentalism, than in denying to human beauty its colour, and to natural scenery its light; in depriving heaven of its blue, and modesty of its blush.

12. II. Love of Beauty. — The second characteristic of the great school of art is, that it introduces in the conception of its subject as much beauty as is possible, consistently with truth.[7]

[7] As here, for the first time, I am obliged to use the terms Truth and Beauty in a kind of opposition, I must therefore stop for a moment to state clearly the relation of these two qualities of art; and to protest against the vulgar and foolish habit of confusing truth and beauty with each other. People with shallow powers of thought, desiring to flatter themselves with the sensation of having attained profundity, are continually doing the most serious mischief by introducing confusion into plain matters, and then valuing themselves on being confounded. Nothing is more common than to hear people who desire to be thought philosophical, declare that "beauty is truth," and "truth is beauty." I would most earnestly beg every sensible person who hears such an assertion made to nip the germinating philosopher in his ambiguous bud, and beg him, if he really believes his own assertion, never thenceforward to use two words for the same thing. The fact is, truth and beauty are entirely distinct, though often related, things. One is a property of statements, the other of objects. The statement that "two and two make four" is true, but it is neither beautiful nor ugly, for it is invisible; a rose is lovely, but it is neither true nor false, for it is silent. That which shows nothing cannot be fair, and that which asserts nothing cannot be false. Even the ordinary use of the words false and true as applied to artificial and real things, is inaccurate. An artificial rose is not a "false" rose, it is not a rose at all. The falseness is in the person who states, or induces the belief, that it *is* a rose.

Now, therefore, in things concerning art, the words true and false are only to be rightly used while the picture is considered as a statement of facts. The painter asserts that this which he has painted is the form of a dog, a man, or a tree. If it be *not* the form of a dog, a man, or a tree, the painter's statement is false; and therefore we justly speak of a false line, or false colour; not that any line or colour can in themselves be false, but they become so when they convey a statement that they resemble something which they do *not* resemble. But the beauty of the lines or colours is wholly independent of any such statement. They may be beautiful lines, though quite inaccurate, and ugly lines, though quite faithful. A picture may be frightfully ugly, which represents with fidelity some base circumstance of daily life; and a painted window may be exquisitely beautiful, which represents men with eagles' faces, and dogs with blue heads and crimson tails (though, by the way, this is not in the strict sense *false* art, as we shall see hereafter, inasmuch as it means no assertion that men ever *had* eagles' faces). If this were not so, it would be impossible to sacrifice truth to beauty; for to attain the one would always be to attain the other. But, unfortunately, this sacrifice is exceedingly possible, and it is chiefly this which characterises the false schools of high art, so far as high art consists in the pursuit of beauty. For although truth and beauty are independent of each other, it does not follow that

For instance, in any subject consisting of a number of figures, it will make as many of those figures beautiful as the faithful representation of humanity will admit. It will not deny the facts of ugliness or decrepitude, or relative inferiority and superiority of feature as necessarily manifested in a crowd, but it will, so far as it is in its power, seek for and dwell upon the fairest forms, and in all things insist on the beauty that is in them, not on the ugliness. In this respect, schools of art become higher in exact proportion to the degree in which they apprehend and love the beautiful. Thus, Angelico, intensely loving all spiritual beauty, will be of the highest rank; and Paul Veronese and Correggio, intensely loving physical and corporeal beauty, of the second rank; and Albert Dürer, Rubens, and in general the Northern artists, apparently insensible to beauty, and caring only for truth, whether shapely or not, of the third rank; and Teniers and Salvator, Caravaggio, and other such worshippers of the depraved, of no rank, or, as we said before, of a certain order in the abyss.

13. The corruptions of the schools of high art, so far as this particular quality is concerned, consists in the sacrifice of truth to beauty. Great art dwells on all that is beautiful; but false art omits or changes all that is ugly. Great art accepts Nature as she is, but directs the eyes and thoughts to what is most perfect in her; false art saves itself the trouble of direction by removing or altering whatever it thinks objectionable. The evil results of which proceeding are twofold.

14. First. That beauty deprived of its proper foils and adjuncts ceases to be enjoyed as beauty, just as light deprived of all shadow ceases to be enjoyed as light. A white canvas cannot produce an effect of sunshine; the painter must darken it in some places before he can make it look luminous in others; nor can an uninterrupted succession of beauty produce the true effect of beauty; it must be foiled by inferiority before its own power can be developed. Nature has for the most part mingled her inferior and nobler elements as she mingles sunshine with shade, giving due use and influence to both, and the painter who chooses to remove the shadow, perishes in the burning desert he has created. The truly high and beautiful art of Angelico is continually refreshed and strengthened by his frank portraiture of the most ordinary features of his brother monks, and of the recorded peculiarities of ungainly sanctity; but the modern German and Raphaelesque schools lose all honour and nobleness in barber-like admiration of handsome faces, and have, in fact, no real faith except in straight noses and curled hair. Paul Veronese opposes the dwarf to the soldier, and the negress to the queen; Shakspeare places Caliban beside Miranda, and Autolycus beside Perdita; but the vulgar idealist

we are at liberty to pursue whichever we please. They are indeed separable, but it is wrong to separate them: they are to be sought together in the order of their worthiness; that is to say, truth first, and beauty afterwards. High art differs from low art in possessing an excess of beauty in addition to its truth, not in possessing an excess of beauty inconsistent with truth. [Ruskin's note.]

withdraws his beauty to the safety of the saloon, and his innocence to the seclusion of the cloister; he pretends that he does this in delicacy of choice and purity of sentiment, while in truth he has neither courage to front the monster, nor wit enough to furnish the knave.

15. It is only by the habit of representing faithfully all things, that we can truly learn what is beautiful, and what is not. The ugliest objects contain some element of beauty; and in all, it is an element peculiar to themselves, which cannot be separated from their ugliness, but must either be enjoyed together with it, or not at all. The more a painter accepts nature as he finds it, the more unexpected beauty he discovers in what he at first despised; but once let him arrogate the right of rejection, and he will gradually contract his circle of enjoyment, until what he supposed to be nobleness of selection ends in narrowness of perception. Dwelling perpetually upon one class of ideas, his art becomes at once monstrous and morbid; until at last he cannot faithfully represent even what he chooses to retain; his discrimination contracts into darkness, and his fastidiousness fades into fatuity.

High art, therefore, consists neither in altering, nor in improving nature; but in seeking throughout nature for "whatsoever things are lovely, and whatsoever things are pure"; in loving these, in displaying to the utmost of the painter's power such loveliness as is in them, and directing the thoughts of others to them by winning art, or gentle emphasis. Of the degree in which this can be done, and in which it may be permitted to gather together, without falsifying, the finest forms or thoughts, so as to create a sort of perfect vision, we shall have to speak hereafter: at present, it is enough to remember that art (*cæteris paribus*) [8] is great in exact proportion to the love of beauty shown by the painter, provided that love of beauty forfeit no atom of truth.

16. III. SINCERITY. — The next [9] characteristic of great art is that it includes the largest possible quantity of Truth in the most perfect possible harmony. If it were possible for art to give all the truths of nature, it ought to do it. But this is not possible. Choice must always be made of some facts which *can* be represented, from among others which must be passed by in silence, or even, in some respects, misrepresented. The inferior artist chooses unimportant and scattered truths; the great artist chooses the most necessary first, and afterwards the most consistent with these, so as to obtain the greatest possible and most harmonious *sum*. For instance, Rembrandt always chooses to represent the exact force with which the light on the most illuminated part of an object is opposed to its obscurer portions. In order to obtain this, in most cases, not very important truth, he sac-

8 "other things being equal."
9 I name them in order of *in*creasing, not decreasing, importance. [Ruskin's note.]

rifices the light and colour of five sixths of his picture; and the expression of every character of objects which depends on tenderness of shape or tint. But he obtains his single truth, and what picturesque and forcible expression is dependent upon it, with magnificent skill and subtlety. Veronese, on the contrary, chooses to represent the great relations of visible things to each other, to the heaven above, and to the earth beneath them. He holds it more important to show how a figure stands relieved from delicate air, or marble wall; how as a red, or purple, or white figure, it separates itself, in clear discernibility, from things not red, nor purple, nor white; how infinite daylight shines round it; how innumerable veils of faint shadow invest it; how its blackness and darkness are, in the excess of their nature, just as limited and local as its intensity of light: all this, I say, he feels to be more important than showing merely the exact *measure* of the spark of sunshine that gleams on a dagger-hilt, or glows on a jewel. All this, moreover, he feels to be harmonious, — capable of being joined in one great system of spacious truth. And with inevitable watchfulness, inestimable subtlety, he unites all this in tenderest balance, noting in each hair's-breadth of colour, not merely what its rightness or wrongness is in itself, but what its relation is to every other on his canvas; restraining, for truth's sake, his exhaustless energy; reining back, for truth's sake, his fiery strength; veiling, before truth, the vanity of brightness; penetrating, for truth, the discouragement of gloom; ruling his restless invention with a rod of iron; pardoning no error, no thoughtlessness, no forgetfulness; and subduing all his powers, impulses, and imaginations, to the arbitrement of a merciless justice, and the obedience of an incorruptible verity.

I give this instance with respect to colour and shade; but, in the whole field of art, the difference between the great and inferior artists is of the same kind, and may be determined at once by the question, which of them conveys the largest sum of truth?

17. It follows from this principle, that in general all *great* drawing is *distinct* drawing; for truths which are rendered indistinctly might, for the most part, as well not be rendered at all. There are, indeed, certain facts of mystery, and facts of indistinctness, in all objects, which must have their proper place in the general harmony, and the reader will presently find me, when we come to that part of our investigation, telling him that all good drawing must in some sort be *indistinct*. We may, however, understand this apparent contradiction by reflecting that the highest knowledge always involves a more advanced perception of the fields of the unknown; and, therefore, it may most truly be said, that to know anything well involves a profound sensation of ignorance, while yet it is equally true that good and noble knowledge is distinguished from vain and useless knowledge chiefly by its clearness and distinctness, and by the vigorous consciousness of what is known and what is not.

So in art. The best drawing involves a wonderful perception and expression of indistinctness; and yet all noble drawing is separated from the ignoble by its distinctness, by its fine expression and firm assertion of *Something*; whereas the bad drawing, without either firmness or fineness, expresses and asserts *Nothing*. The first thing, therefore, to be looked for as a sign of noble art, is a clear consciousness of what is drawn and what is not; the bold statement, and frank confession — *"This* I know," *"that* I know not"; and, generally speaking, all haste, slurring, obscurity, indecision, are signs of low art, and all calmness, distinctness, luminousness, and positiveness, of high art.

18. It follows, secondly, from this principle, that as the great painter is always attending to the sum and harmony of his truths rather than to one or the other of any group, a quality of Grasp is visible in his work, like the power of a great reasoner over his subject, or a great poet over his conception, manifesting itself very often in missing out certain details or less truths (which, though good in themselves, he finds are in the way of others), and in a sweeping manner of getting the beginnings and ends of things shown at once, and the squares and depths rather than the surfaces: hence, on the whole, a habit of looking at large masses rather than small ones; and even a physical largeness of handling, and love of working, if possible, on a large scale; and various other qualities, more or less imperfectly expressed by such technical terms as breadth, massing, unity, boldness, &c., all of which are, indeed, great qualities when they mean breadth of truth, weight of truth, unity of truth, and courageous assertion of truth; but which have all their correlative errors and mockeries, almost universally mistaken for them, — the breadth which has no contents, the weight which has no value, the unity which plots deception, and the boldness which faces out fallacy.

19. And it is to be noted especially respecting largeness of scale, that though for the most part it is characteristic of the more powerful masters, they having both more invention wherewith to fill space (as Ghirlandajo wished that he might paint all the walls of Florence), and, often, an impetuosity of mind which makes them like free play for hand and arm (besides that they usually desire to paint everything in the foreground of their picture of the natural size), yet, as this largeness of scale involves the placing of the picture at a considerable distance from the eye, and this distance involves the loss of many delicate details, and especially of the subtle lines of expression in features, it follows that the masters of refined detail and human expression are apt to prefer a small scale to work upon; so that the chief masterpieces of expression which the world possesses are small pictures by Angelico, in which the figures are rarely more than six or seven inches high; in the best works of Raphael and Leonardo the figures are almost always less than life; and the best works of Turner do not exceed the sizes of 18 inches by 12.

20. As its greatness depends on the sum of truth, and this sum of truth can always be increased by delicacy of handling, it follows that all great art must have this delicacy to the utmost possible degree. This rule is infallible and inflexible. All coarse work is the sign of low art. Only, it is to be remembered, that coarseness must be estimated by the distance from the eye; it being necessary to consult this distance, when great, by laying on touches which appear coarse when seen near; but which, so far from being coarse, are, in reality, more delicate in a master's work than the finest close handling, for they involve a calculation of result, and are laid on with a subtlety of sense precisely correspondent to that with which a good archer draws his bow; the spectator seeing in the action nothing but the strain of the strong arm, while there is, in reality, in the finger and eye, an ineffably delicate estimate of distance, and touch on the arrow plume. And, indeed, this delicacy is generally quite perceptible to those who know what the truth is, for strokes by Tintoret or Paul Veronese, which were done in an instant, and look to an ignorant spectator merely like a violent dash of loaded colour (and are, as such, imitated by blundering artists), are, in fact, modulated by the brush and finger to that degree of delicacy that no single grain of the colour could be taken from the touch without injury; and little golden particles of it, not the size of a gnat's head, have important share and function in the balances of light in a picture perhaps fifty feet long. Nearly *every* other rule applicable to art has some exception but this. This has absolutely none. All great art is delicate art, and all coarse art is bad art. Nay, even to a certain extent, all *bold* art is bad art; for boldness is not the proper word to apply to the courage and swiftness of a great master, based on knowledge, and coupled with fear and love. There is as much difference between the boldness of the true and the false masters, as there is between the courage of a pure woman and the shamelessness of a lost one.

21. IV. Invention. — The last characteristic of great art is that it must be inventive, that is, be produced by the imagination. In this respect, it must precisely fulfil the definition already given of poetry; and not only present grounds for noble emotion, but furnish these grounds by *imaginative power*. Hence there is at once a great bar fixed between the two schools of Lower and Higher Art. The lower merely copies what is set before it, whether in portrait, landscape, or still-life; the higher either entirely imagines its subject, or arranges the materials presented to it, so as to manifest the imaginative power in all the three phases which have been already explained in the second volume.

And this was the truth which was confusedly present in Reynolds's mind when he spoke, as above quoted, of the difference between Historical and Poetical painting. *Every relation of the plain facts which the painter saw* is proper *historical* painting. If those facts are unimportant (as that he saw a gambler quarrel with another gambler, or a sot enjoying himself with another sot), then the history is trivial; if the facts are important (as that he saw such and such a great man look thus, or act thus, at such a time), then the history is noble: in each case perfect truth of narrative being supposed, otherwise the whole thing is worthless, being neither history nor poetry, but plain falsehood. And farther, as greater or less elegance and precision are manifested in the relation or painting of the incidents, the merit of the work varies; so that, what with difference of subject, and what with difference of treatment, historical painting falls or rises in changeful eminence, from Dutch trivialities to a Velasquez portrait, just as historical talking or writing varies in eminence, from an old woman's story-telling up to Herodotus. Besides which, certain operations of the imagination come into play inevitably, here and there, so as to touch the history with some light of poetry, that is, with some light shot forth of the narrator's mind, or brought out by the way he has put the accidents together: and wherever the imagination has thus had anything to do with the matter at all (and it must be somewhat cold work where it has not), then, the confines of the lower and higher schools touching each other, the work is coloured by both; but there is no reason why, therefore, we should in the least confuse the historical and poetical characters, any more than that we should confuse blue with crimson, because they may overlap each other, and produce purple.

22. Now, historical or simply narrative art is very precious in its proper place and way, but it is never *great* art until the poetical or imaginative power touches it; and in proportion to the stronger manifestation of this power, it becomes greater and greater, while the highest art is purely imaginative, all its materials being wrought into their form by invention. . . .

23. Farther, imaginative art always *includes* historical art; so that, strictly speaking, according to the analogy above used, we meet with the pure blue, and with the crimson ruling the blue and changing it into kingly purple, but not with the pure crimson: for all imagination must deal with the knowledge it has before accumulated; it never produces anything but by combination or contemplation. Creation, in the full sense, is impossible to it. And the mode in which the historical faculties are included by it is often quite simple, and easily seen. Thus, in Hunt's great poetical picture of the Light of the World, the whole thought and arrangement of the picture being imaginative, the several details of it are wrought out with simple portraiture; the ivy, the jewels, the creeping plants, and the moonlight being calmly studied or remembered from the things themselves. But of all these special ways in which the invention works with plain facts, we shall have to treat farther afterwards.

24. And now, finally, since this poetical power includes the histor-

ical, if we glance back to the other qualities required in great art, and put all together, we find that the sum of them is simply the sum of all the powers of man. For as (1) the choice of the high subject involves all conditions of right moral choice, and as (2) the love of beauty involves all conditions of right admiration, and as (3) the grasp of truth involves all strength of sense, evenness of judgment, and honesty of purpose, and as (4) the poetical power involves all swiftness of invention, and accuracy of historical memory, the sum of all these powers is the sum of the human soul. Hence we see why the word "Great" is used of this art. It is literally great. It compasses and calls forth the entire human spirit, whereas any other kind of art, being more or less small or narrow, compasses and calls forth only *part* of the human spirit. Hence the idea of its magnitude is a literal and just one, the art being simply less or greater in proportion to the number of faculties it exercises and addresses. And this is the ultimate meaning of the definition I gave of it long ago, as containing the "greatest number of the greatest ideas."

25. Such, then, being the characters required in order to constitute high art, if the reader will think over them a little, and over the various ways in which they may be falsely assumed, he will easily perceive how spacious and dangerous a field of discussion they open to the ambitious critic, and of error to the ambitious artist; he will see how difficult it must be, either to distinguish what is truly great art from the mockeries of it, or to rank the real artists in anything like a progressive system of greater and less. For it will have been observed that the various qualities which form greatness are partly inconsistent with each other (as some virtues are, docility and firmness for instance), and partly independent of each other; and the fact is, that artists differ not more by mere capacity, than by the component *elements* of their capacity, each possessing in very different proportions the several attributes of greatness; so that, classed by one kind of merit, as, for instance, purity of expression, Angelico will stand highest; classed by another, sincerity of manner, Veronese will stand highest; classed by another, love of beauty, Leonardo will stand highest; and so on: hence arise continual disputes and misunderstandings among those who think that high art must always be one and the same, and that great artists ought to unite all great attributes in an equal degree.

26. In one of the exquisitely finished tales of Marmontel, a company of critics are received at dinner by the hero of the story, an old gentleman, somewhat vain of his *acquired* taste, and his niece, by whose incorrigible *natural* taste he is seriously disturbed and tormented. During the entertainment, "On parcourut tous les genres de littérature, et pour donner plus d'essor à l'érudition et à la critique, on mit sur le tapis cette question toute neuve, sçavoir, lequel méritoit la préférence de Corneille ou de Racine. L'on disoit même là-dessus les plus belles choses du monde, lorsque la petite nièce, qui n'avoit pas dit un mot,

s'avisa de demander naïvement lequel des deux fruits, de l'orange ou de la pêche, avoit le goût le plus exquis et méritoit le plus d'éloges. Son oncle rougit de sa simplicité, et les convives baissèrent tous les yeux sans daigner répondre à cette bêtise. Ma nièce, dit Fintac, à votre âge, il faut sçavoir écouter, et se tair." [10]

I cannot close this chapter with shorter or better advice to the reader, than merely, whenever he hears discussions about the relative merits of great masters, to remember the young lady's question. It is, indeed, true that there *is* a relative merit, that a peach is nobler than a hawthorn berry, and still more a hawthorn berry than a bead of the nightshade; but in each rank of fruits, as in each rank of masters, one is endowed with one virtue, and another with another; their glory is their dissimilarity, and they who propose to themselves in the training of an artist that he should unite the colouring of Tintoret, the finish of Albert Durer, and the tenderness of Correggio, are no wiser than a horticulturist would be, who made it the object of his labour to produce a fruit which should unite in itself the lusciousness of the grape, the crispness of the nut, and the fragrance of the pine.

27. And from these considerations one most important practical corollary is to be deduced, with the good help of Mademoiselle Agathe's simile, namely, that the greatness or smallness of a man is, in the most conclusive sense, determined for him at his birth, as strictly as it is determined for a fruit whether it is to be a currant or an apricot. Education, favourable circumstances, resolution, and industry can do much; in a certain sense they do *everything*; that is to say, they determine whether the poor apricot shall fall in the form of a green bead, blighted by the east wind, and be trodden under foot, or whether it shall expand into tender pride, and sweet brightness of golden velvet. But apricot out of currant, — great man out of small, — did never yet art or effort make; and, in a general way, men have their excellence nearly fixed for them when they are born; a little cramped and frost-bitten on one side, a little sun-burnt and fortune-spotted on the other, they reach, between good and evil chances, such size and taste as generally belong to the men of their calibre, and, the small in their serviceable bunches, the great in their golden isolation, have, these no cause for regret, nor those for disdain.

28. Therefore it is, that every system of teaching is false which holds forth "great art" as in any wise to be taught to students, or even to be aimed at by them. Great art is precisely that which never

10 "They ran through all kinds of literature; and in order to give more scope to erudition and criticism, they brought on the carpet this entirely new question, viz. 'Which merited the preference, Corneille or Racine?' They said also on the subject the finest things in the world, when the little niece, who had not spoken a word, took it into her head to ask simply which of the two fruits, the orange or the peach, had the most exquisite taste, and merited the most commendation? Her uncle blushed at her simplicity, and the guests all looked down without deigning to reply to this idle foolery. 'Niece,' said Fintac, 'at your age one should hear and hold one's tongue.' "

was, nor will be taught, it is preeminently and finally the expression of the spirits of great men; so that the only wholesome teaching is that which simply endeavours to fix those characters of nobleness in the pupil's mind, of which it seems easily susceptible; and without holding out to him, as a possible or even probable result, that he should ever paint like Titian, or carve like Michael Angelo, enforces upon him the manifest possibility, and assured duty, of endeavouring to draw in a manner at least honest and intelligible; and cultivates in him those general charities of heart, sincerities of thought, and graces of habit which are likely to lead him, throughout life, to prefer openness to affectation, realities to shadows, and beauty to corruption.

The Stones of Venice

❮ Ruskin wrote *The Stones of Venice*, he tells us in *The Crown of Wild Olive,* "to show that certain right states of temper and moral feeling were the magic powers by which all good architecture, without exception, had been produced. *The Stones of Venice* had, from beginning to end, no other aim than to show that the Gothic architecture of Venice had risen out of, and indicated in all its features, a state of pure national faith, and of domestic virtue; and that its Renaissance architecture had arisen out of, and in all its features indicated, a state of concealed national infidelity, and of domestic corruption." The chapter on "The Nature of Gothic," which Ruskin himself named "precisely and accurately the most important in the whole book," reveals Ruskin turning from criticism of art to criticism of society. ❯

VOLUME II

CHAPTER VI

The Nature of Gothic

1. IF the reader will look back to the division of our subject which was made in the first chapter of the first volume, he will find that we are now about to enter upon the examination of that school of Venetian architecture which forms an intermediate step between the Byzantine and Gothic forms; but which I find may be conveniently considered in its connection with the latter style. In order that we may discern the tendency of each step of this change, it will be wise in the outset to endeavour to form some general idea of its final result. We know already what the Byzantine architecture is from which the transition was made, but we ought to know something of the

Gothic architecture into which it led. I shall endeavour therefore to give the reader in this chapter an idea, at once broad and definite, of the true nature of *Gothic* architecture, properly so called; not of that of Venice only, but of universal Gothic: for it will be one of the most interesting parts of our subsequent inquiry, to find out how far Venetian architecture reached the universal or perfect type of Gothic, and how far it either fell short of it, or assumed foreign and independent forms.

2. The principal difficulty in doing this arises from the fact that every building of the Gothic period differs in some important respect from every other; and many include features which, if they occurred in other buildings, would not be considered Gothic at all; so that all we have to reason upon is merely, if I may be allowed so to express it, a greater or less degree of Gothicness in each building we examine. And it is this Gothicness, — the character which, according as it is found more or less in a building, makes it more or less Gothic, — of which I want to define the nature; and I feel the same kind of difficulty in doing so which would be encountered by any one who undertook to explain, for instance, the nature of Redness, without any actually red thing to point to, but only orange and purple things. Suppose he had only a piece of heather and a dead oak-leaf to do it with. He might say, the colour which is mixed with the yellow in this oak-leaf, and with the blue in this heather, would be red, if you had it separate; but it would be difficult, nevertheless, to make the abstraction perfectly intelligible: and it is so in a far greater degree to make the abstraction of the Gothic character intelligible, because that character itself is made up of many mingled ideas, and can consist only in their union. That is to say, pointed arches do not constitute Gothic, nor vaulted roofs, nor flying buttresses, nor grotesque sculptures; but all or some of these things, and many other things with them, when they come together so as to have life.

3. Observe also, that, in the definition proposed, I shall only endeavour to analyse the idea which I suppose already to exist in the reader's mind. We all have some notion, most of us a very determined one, of the meaning of the term Gothic; but I know that many persons have this idea in their minds without being able to define it: that is to say, understanding generally that Westminster Abbey is Gothic, and St. Paul's is not, that Strasburg Cathedral is Gothic, and St. Peter's is not, they have, nevertheless, no clear notion of what it is that they recognise in the one or miss in the other, such as would enable them to say how far the work at Westminster or Strasburg is good and pure of its kind; still less to say of any nondescript building, like St. James's Palace or Windsor Castle, how much right Gothic element there is in it, and how much wanting. And I believe this inquiry to be a pleasant and profitable one; and that there will be found something more than usually interesting in tracing out this grey,

shadowy, many-pinnacled image of the Gothic spirit within us; and discerning what fellowship there is between it and our Northern hearts. And if, at any point of the inquiry, I should interfere with any of the reader's previously formed conceptions, and use the term Gothic in any sense which he would not willingly attach to it, I do not ask him to accept, but only to examine and understand, my interpretation, as necessary to the intelligibility of what follows in the rest of the work.

4. We have, then, the Gothic character submitted to our analysis, just as the rough mineral is submitted to that of the chemist, entangled with many other foreign substances, itself perhaps in no place pure, or ever to be obtained or seen in purity for more than an instant; but nevertheless a thing of definite and separate nature, however inextricable or confused in appearance. Now observe: the chemist defines his mineral by two separate kinds of character; one external, its crystalline form, hardness, lustre, &c.; the other internal, the proportions and nature of its constituent atoms. Exactly in the same manner, we shall find that Gothic architecture has external forms, and internal elements. Its elements are certain mental tendencies of the builders, legibly expressed in it; as fancifulness, love of variety, love of richness, and such others. Its external forms are pointed arches, vaulted roofs, &c. And unless both the elements and the forms are there, we have no right to call the style Gothic. It is not enough that it has the Form, if it have not also the power and life. It is not enough that it has the Power, if it have not the form. We must therefore inquire into each of these characters successively; and determine first, what is the Mental Expression, and secondly, what the Material Form, of Gothic architecture, properly so called.

1st. Mental Power of Expression. What characters, we have to discover, did the Gothic builders love, or instinctively express in their work, as distinguished from all other builders?

5. Let us go back for a moment to our chemistry, and note that, in defining a mineral by its constituent parts, it is not one nor another of them, that can make up the mineral, but the union of all: for instance, it is neither in charcoal, nor in oxygen, nor in lime, that there is the making of chalk, but in the combination of all three in certain measures; they are all found in very different things from chalk, and there is nothing like chalk either in charcoal or in oxygen, but they are nevertheless necessary to its existence.

So in the various mental characters which make up the soul of Gothic. It is not one nor another that produces it; but their union of certain measures. Each one of them is found in many other architectures besides Gothic; but Gothic cannot exist where they are not found, or, at least, where their place is not in some way supplied. Only there is this great difference between the composition of the mineral, and of the architectural style, that if we withdraw one of its elements

from the stone, its form is utterly changed, and its existence as such
and such a mineral is destroyed; but if we withdraw one of its mental
elements from the Gothic style, it is only a little less Gothic than it was
before, and the union of two or three of its elements is enough already to
bestow a certain Gothicness of character, which gains in intensity as
we add the others, and loses as we again withdraw them.

6. I believe, then, that the characteristic or moral elements of
Gothic are the following, placed in the order of their importance:

1. Savageness.	4. Grotesqueness.
2. Changefulness.	5. Rigidity.
3. Naturalism.	6. Redundance.

These characters are here expressed as belonging to the building; as
belonging to the builder, they would be expressed thus: — 1. Savageness, or Rudeness. 2. Love of Change. 3. Love of Nature. 4. Disturbed
Imagination. 5. Obstinacy. 6. Generosity. And I repeat, that the with-
drawal of any one, or any two, will not at once destroy the Gothic
character of a building, but the removal of a majority of them will.
I shall proceed to examine them in their order.

7. SAVAGENESS. I am not sure when the word "Gothic" was
first generically applied to the architecture of the North; but I presume that, whatever the date of its original usage, it was intended to
imply reproach, and express the barbaric character of the nations
among whom that architecture arose. It never implied that they were
literally of Gothic lineage, far less that their architecture had been
originally invented by the Goths themselves; but it did imply that they
and their buildings together exhibited a degree of sternness and rudeness, which, in contradistinction to the character of Southern and
Eastern nations, appeared like a perpetual reflection of the contrast
between the Goth and the Roman in their first encounter. And when
that fallen Roman, in the utmost impotence of his luxury, and inso-
lence of his guilt, became the model for the imitation of civilised
Europe, at the close of the so-called Dark ages, the word Gothic became a term of unmitigated contempt, not unmixed with aversion.
From that contempt, by the exertion of the antiquaries and architects
of this century, Gothic architecture has been sufficiently vindicated;
and perhaps some among us, in our admiration of the magnificent
science of its structure, and sacredness of its expression, might desire
that the term of ancient reproach should be withdrawn, and some other,
of more apparent honourableness, adopted in its place. There is no
chance, as there is no need, of such a substitution. As far as the
epithet was used scornfully, it was used falsely; but there is no reproach
in the word, rightly understood; on the contrary, there is a profound
truth, which the instinct of mankind almost unconsciously recognises.
It is true, greatly and deeply true, that the architecture of the North
is rude and wild; but it is not true, that, for this reason, we are to

condemn it, or despise. Far otherwise: I believe it is in this very character that it deserves our profoundest reverence.

8. The charts of the world which have been drawn up by modern science have thrown into a narrow space the expression of a vast amount of knowledge, but I have never yet seen any one pictorial enough to enable the spectator to imagine the kind of contrast in physical character which exists between Northern and Southern countries. We know the differences in detail, but we have not that broad glance and grasp which would enable us to feel them in their fulness. We know that gentians grow on the Alps, and olives on the Apennines; but we do not enough conceive for ourselves that variegated mosaic of the world's surface which a bird sees in its migration, that difference between the district of the gentian and of the olive which the stork and the swallow see far off, as they lean upon the sirocco wind. Let us, for a moment, try to raise ourselves even above the level of their flight, and imagine the Mediterranean lying beneath us like an irregular lake, and all its ancient promontories sleeping in the sun: here and there an angry spot of thunder, a grey stain of storm, moving upon the burning field; and here and there a fixed wreath of white volcano smoke, surrounded by its circle of ashes; but for the most part a great peacefulness of light, Syria and Greece, Italy and Spain, laid like pieces of a golden pavement into the sea-blue, chased, as we stoop nearer to them, with bossy beaten work of mountain chains, and glowing softly with terraced gardens, and flowers heavy with frankincense, mixed among masses of laurel, and orange, and plumy palm, that abate with their grey-green shadows the burning of the marble rocks, and of the ledges of porphyry sloping under lucent sand. Then let us pass farther towards the north, until we see the orient colours change gradually into a vast belt of rainy green, where the pastures of Switzerland, and poplar valleys of France, and dark forests of the Danube and Carpathians stretch from the mouths of the Loire to those of the Volga, seen through clefts in grey swirls of rain-cloud and flaky veils of the mist of the brooks, spreading low along the pasture lands: and then, farther north still, to see the earth heave into mighty masses of leaden rock and heathy moor, bordering with a broad waste of gloomy purple that belt of field and wood, and splintering into irregular and grisly islands amidst the northern seas, beaten by storm, and chilled by ice-drift, and tormented by furious pulses of contending tide, until the roots of the last forests fail from among the hill ravines, and the hunger of the north wind bites their peaks into barrenness; and, at last, the wall of ice, durable like iron, sets, deathlike, its white teeth against us out of the polar twilight. And, having once traversed in thought this gradation of the zoned iris of the earth in all its material vastness, let us go down nearer to it, and watch the parallel change in the belt of animal life: the multitudes of swift and brilliant creatures that glance in the air and sea, or tread the sands of the

southern zone; striped zebras and spotted leopards, glistening serpents, and birds arrayed in purple and scarlet. Let us contrast their delicacy and brilliancy of colour, and swiftness of motion, with the frost-cramped strength, and shaggy covering, and dusky plumage of the northern tribes; contrast the Arabian horse with the Shetland, the tiger and leopard with the wolf and bear, the antelope with the elk, the bird of paradise with the osprey: and then, submissively acknowledging the great laws by which the earth and all that it bears are ruled throughout their being, let us not condemn, but rejoice in the expression by man of his own rest in the statutes of the lands that gave him birth. Let us watch him with reverence as he sets side by side the burning gems, and smooths with soft sculpture the jasper pillars, that are to reflect a ceaseless sunshine, and rise into a cloudless sky: but not with less reverence let us stand by him, when, with rough strength and hurried stroke, he smites an uncouth animation out of the rocks which he has torn from among the moss of the moorland, and heaves into the darkened air the pile of iron buttress and rugged wall, instinct with work of an imagination as wild and wayward as the northern sea; creations of ungainly shape and rigid limb, but full of wolfish life; fierce as the winds that beat, and changeful as the clouds that shade them.

There is, I repeat, no degradation, no reproach in this, but all dignity and honourableness: and we should err grievously in refusing either to recognise as an essential character of the existing architecture of the North, or to admit as a desirable character in that which it yet may be, this wildness of thought, and roughness of work; this look of mountain brotherhood between the cathedral and the Alp; this magnificence of sturdy power, put forth only the more energetically because the fine finger-touch was chilled away by the frosty wind, and the eye dimmed by the moor-mist, or blinded by the hail; this outspeaking of the strong spirit of men who may not gather redundant fruitage from the earth, nor bask in dreamy benignity of sunshine, but must break the rock for bread, and cleave the forest for fire, and show, even in what they did for their delight, some of the hard habits of the arm and heart that grew on them as they swung the axe or pressed the plough.

9. If, however, the savageness of Gothic architecture, merely as an expression of its origin among Northern nations, may be considered, in some sort, a noble character, it possesses a higher nobility still, when considered as an index, not of climate, but of religious principle.

In the 13th and 14th paragraphs of Chapter XXI. of the first volume of this work, it was noticed that the systems of architectural ornament, properly so called, might be divided into three: — 1. Servile ornament, in which the execution or power of the inferior workman is entirely subjected to the intellect of the higher; — 2. Constitutional ornament, in which the executive inferior power is, to a certain point, emancipated and independent, having a will of its own, yet confessing its inferiority and rendering obedience to higher powers; — and 3. Revolutionary ornament, in which no executive inferiority is admitted at all. I must here explain the nature of these divisions at somewhat greater length.

Of Servile ornament, the principal schools are the Greek, Ninevite, and Egyptian; but their servility is of different kinds. The Greek master-workman was far advanced in knowledge and power above the Assyrian or Egyptian. Neither he nor those for whom he worked could endure the appearance of imperfection in anything; and, therefore, what ornament he appointed to be done by those beneath him was composed of mere geometrical forms, — balls, ridges, and perfectly symmetrical foliage, — which could be executed with absolute precision by line and rule, and were as perfect in their way, when completed, as his own figure sculpture. The Assyrian and Egyptian, on the contrary, less cognisant of accurate form in anything, were content to allow their figure sculpture to be executed by inferior workmen, but lowered the method of its treatment to a standard which every workman could reach, and then trained him by discipline so rigid, that there was no chance of his falling beneath the standard appointed. The Greek gave to the lower workman no subject which he could not perfectly execute. The Assyrian gave him subjects which he could only execute imperfectly, but fixed a legal standard for his imperfection. The workman was, in both systems, a slave.[1]

10. But in the mediæval, or especially Christian, system of ornament, this slavery is done away with altogether; Christianity having recognised, in small things as well as great, the individual value of every soul. But it not only recognises its value; it confesses its imperfection, in only bestowing dignity upon the acknowledgment of unworthiness. That admission of lost power and fallen nature, which the Greek or Ninevite felt to be intensely painful, and, as far as might be, altogether refused, the Christian makes daily and hourly, contemplating the fact of it without fear, as tending, in the end, to God's greater glory. Therefore, to every spirit which Christianity summons to her service, her exhortation is: Do what you can, and confess frankly what you are unable to do; neither let your effort be shortened for fear of failure, nor your confession silenced for fear of shame. And it is, perhaps, the principal admirableness of the Gothic schools of architecture, that they thus receive the results of the labour of

[1] The third kind of ornament, the Renaissance, is that in which the inferior detail becomes principal, the executor of every minor portion being required to exhibit skill and possess knowledge as great as that which is possessed by the master of the design; and in the endeavour to endow him with this skill and knowledge, his own original power is overwhelmed, and the whole building becomes a wearisome exhibition of well-educated imbecility. We must fully inquire into the nature of this form of error, when we arrive at the examination of the Renaissance schools. [Ruskin's note.]

inferior minds; and out of fragments full of imperfection, and betraying that imperfection in every touch, indulgently raise up a stately and unaccusable whole.

11. But the modern English mind has this much in common with that of the Greek, that it intensely desires, in all things, the utmost completion or perfection compatible with their nature. This is a noble character in the abstract, but becomes ignoble when it causes us to forget the relative dignities of that nature itself, and to prefer the perfectness of the lower nature to the imperfection of the higher; not considering that as, judged by such a rule, all the brute animals would be preferable to man, because more perfect in their functions and kind, and yet are always held inferior to him, so also in the works of man, those which are more perfect in their kind are always inferior to those which are, in their nature, liable to more faults and shortcomings. For the finer the nature, the more flaws it will show through the clearness of it; and it is a law of this universe, that the best things shall be seldomest seen in their best form. The wild grass grows well and strongly, one year with another; but the wheat is, according to the greater nobleness of its nature, liable to the bitterer blight. And therefore, while in all things that we see, or do, we are to desire perfection, and strive for it, we are nevertheless not to set the meaner thing, in its narrow accomplishment, above the nobler thing, in its mighty progress; not to esteem smooth minuteness above shattered majesty; not to prefer mean victory to honourable defeat; not to lower the level of our aim, that we may the more surely enjoy the complacency of success. But above all, in our dealings with the souls of other men, we are to take care how we check, by severe requirement or narrow caution, efforts which might otherwise lead to a noble issue; and, still more, how we withhold our admiration from great excellencies, because they are mingled with rough faults. Now, in the make and nature of every man, however rude or simple, whom we employ in manual labour, there are some powers for better things: some tardy imagination, torpid capacity of emotion, tottering steps of thought, there are, even at the worst; and in most cases it is all our own fault that they *are* tardy or torpid. But they cannot be strengthened, unless we are content to take them in their feebleness, and unless we prize and honour them in their imperfection above the best and most perfect manual skill. And this is what we have to do with all our labourers; to look for the *thoughtful* part of them, and get that out of them, whatever we lose for it, whatever faults and errors we are obliged to take with it. For the best that is in them cannot manifest itself, but in company with much error. Understand this clearly: You can teach a man to draw a straight line, and to cut one; to strike a curved line, and to carve it; and to copy and carve any number of given lines or forms, with admirable speed and perfect precision; and you find his work perfect of its kind: but if you ask

him to think about any of those forms, to consider if he cannot find any better in his own head, he stops; his execution becomes hesitating; he thinks, and ten to one he thinks wrong; ten to one he makes a mistake in the first touch he gives to his work as a thinking being. But you have made a man of him for all that. He was only a machine before, an animated tool.

12. And observe, you are put to stern choice in this matter. You must either make a tool of the creature, or a man of him. You cannot make both. Men were not intended to work with the accuracy of tools, to be precise and perfect in all their actions. If you will have that precision out of them, and make their fingers measure degrees like cog-wheels, and their arms strike curves like compasses, you must unhumanise them. All the energy of their spirits must be given to make cogs and compasses of themselves. All their attention and strength must go to the accomplishment of the mean act. The eye of the soul must be bent upon the finger-point, and the soul's force must fill all the invisible nerves that guide it, ten hours a day, that it may not err from its steely precision, and so soul and sight be worn away, and the whole human being be lost at last — a heap of sawdust, so far as its intellectual work in this world is concerned; saved only by its Heart, which cannot go into the form of cogs and compasses, but expands, after the ten hours are over, into fireside humanity. On the other hand, if you will make a man of the working creature, you cannot make a tool. Let him but begin to imagine, to think, to try to do anything worth doing; and the engine-turned precision is lost at once. Out come all his roughness, all his dulness, all his incapability; shame upon shame, failure upon failure, pause after pause: but out comes the whole majesty of him also; and we know the height of it only, when we see the clouds settling upon him. And, whether the clouds be bright or dark, there will be transfiguration behind and within them.

13. And now, reader, look round this English room of yours, about which you have been proud so often, because the work of it was so good and strong, and the ornaments of it so finished. Examine again all those accurate mouldings, and perfect polishings, and unerring adjustments of the seasoned wood and tempered steel. Many a time you have exulted over them, and thought how great England was, because her slightest work was done so thoroughly. Alas! if read rightly, these perfectnesses are signs of a slavery in our England a thousand times more bitter and more degrading than that of the scourged African, or helot Greek. Men may be beaten, chained, tormented, yoked like cattle, slaughtered like summer flies, and yet remain in one sense, and the best sense, free. But to smother their souls within them, to blight and hew into rotting pollards the suckling branches of their human intelligence, to make the flesh and skin which, after the worm's work on it, is to see God, into leathern thongs to yoke ma-

chinery with, — this is to be slave-masters indeed; and there might be more freedom in England, though her feudal lords' lightest words were worth men's lives, and though the blood of the vexed husband-man dropped in the furrows of her fields, than there is while the animation of her multitudes is sent like fuel to feed the factory smoke, and the strength of them is given daily to be wasted into the fineness of a web, or racked into the exactness of a line.

14. And, on the other hand, go forth again to gaze upon the old cathedral front, where you have smiled so often at the fantastic ig-norance of the old sculptors: examine once more those ugly goblins, and formless monsters, and stern statues, anatomiless and rigid; but do not mock at them, for they are signs of the life and liberty of every workman who struck the stone; a freedom of thought, and rank in scale of being, such as no laws, no charters, no charities can secure; but which it must be the first aim of all Europe at this day to regain for her children.

15. Let me not be thought to speak wildly or extravagantly. It is verily this degradation of the operative into a machine, which, more than any other evil of the times, is leading the mass of the nations everywhere into vain, incoherent, destructive struggling for a freedom of which they cannot explain the nature to themselves. Their universal outcry against wealth, and against nobility, is not forced from them either by the pressure of famine, or the sting of mortified pride. These do much, and have done much in all ages; but the foundations of society were never yet shaken as they are at this day. It is not that men are ill fed, but that they have no pleasure in the work by which they make their bread, and therefore look to wealth as the only means of pleasure. It is not that men are pained by the scorn of the upper classes, but they cannot endure their own; for they feel that the kind of labour to which they are condemned is verily a degrading one, and makes them less than men. Never had the upper classes so much sympathy with the lower, or charity for them, as they have at this day, and yet never were they so much hated by them: for, of old, the separation between the noble and the poor was merely a wall built by law; now it is a veritable difference in level of standing, a preci-pice between upper and lower grounds in the field of humanity, and there is pestilential air at the bottom of it. I know not if a day is ever to come when the nature of right freedom will be understood, and when men will see that to obey another man, to labour for him, yield reverence to him or to his place, is not slavery. It is often the best kind of liberty, — liberty from care. The man who says to one, Go, and he goeth, and to another, Come, and he cometh, has, in most cases, more sense of restraint and difficulty than the man who obeys him. The movements of the one are hindered by the burden on his shoulder; of the other, by the bridle on his lips: there is no way by which the burden may be lightened; but we need not suffer from the

bridle if we do not champ at it. To yield reverence to another, to hold ourselves and our lives at his disposal, is not slavery; often, it is the noblest state in which a man can live in this world. There is, indeed, a reverence which is servile, that is to say irrational or selfish: but there is also noble reverence, that is to say, reasonable and loving; and a man is never so noble as when he is reverent in this kind; nay, even if the feeling pass the bounds of mere reason, so that it be loving, a man is raised by it. Which had, in reality, most of the serf nature in him, — the Irish peasant who was lying in wait yesterday for his landlord, with his musket muzzle thrust through the ragged hedge; or that old mountain servant, who, 200 years ago, at Inverkeithing, gave up his own life and the lives of his seven sons for his chief? — as each fell, calling forth his brother to the death, "Another for Hector!" And therefore, in all ages and all countries, reverence has been paid and sacrifice made by men to each other, not only without complaint, but rejoicingly; and famine, and peril, and sword, and all evil, and all shame, have been borne willingly in the causes of masters and kings; for all these gifts of the heart ennobled the men who gave, not less than the men who received them, and nature prompted, and God rewarded the sacrifice. But to feel their souls withering within them, unthanked, to find their whole being sunk into an unrecognised abyss, to be counted off into a heap of mechanism, numbered with its wheels, and weighed with its hammer strokes; — this nature bade not, — this God blesses not, — this humanity for no long time is able to endure.

16. We have much studied and much perfected, of late, the great civilised invention of the division of labour; only we give it a false name. It is not, truly speaking, the labour that is divided; but the men: — Divided into mere segments of men — broken into small fragments and crumbs of life; so that all the little piece of intelligence that is left in a man is not enough to make a pin, or a nail, but exhausts itself in making the point of a pin, or the head of a nail. Now it is a good and desirable thing, truly, to make many pins in a day; but if we could only see with what crystal sand their points were polished, — sand of human soul, much to be magnified before it can be discerned for what it is, — we should think there might be some loss in it also. And the great cry that rises from all our manufacturing cities, louder than their furnace blast, is all in very deed for this, — that we manufacture everything there except men; we blanch cotton, and strengthen steel, and refine sugar, and shape pottery; but to brighten, to strengthen, to refine, or to form a single living spirit, never enters into our estimate of advantages. And all the evil to which that cry is urging our myriads can be met only in one way: not by teaching nor preaching, for to teach them is but to show them their misery, and to preach to them, if we do nothing more than preach, is to mock at it. It can be met only by a right understanding,

on the part of all classes, of what kinds of labour are good for men, raising them, and making them happy; by a determined sacrifice of such convenience, or beauty, or cheapness as is to be got only by the degradation of the workman; and by equally determined demand for the products and results of healthy and ennobling labour.

17. And how, it will be asked, are these products to be recognised, and this demand to be regulated? Easily: by the observance of three broad and simple rules:

1. Never encourage the manufacture of any article not absolutely necessary, in the production of which *Invention* has no share.

2. Never demand an exact finish for its own sake, but only for some practical or noble end.

3. Never encourage imitation or copying of any kind, except for the sake of preserving record of great works.

The second of these principles is the only one which directly rises out of the consideration of our immediate subject; but I shall briefly explain the meaning and extent of the first also, reserving the enforcement of the third for another place.

1. Never encourage the manufacture of anything not necessary, in the production of which invention has no share.

For instance. Glass beads are utterly unnecessary, and there is no design or thought employed in their manufacture. They are formed by first drawing out the glass into rods; these rods are chopped up into fragments of the size of beads by the human hand, and the fragments are then rounded in the furnace. The men who chop up the rods sit at their work all day, their hands vibrating with a perpetual and exquisitely timed palsy, and the beads dropping beneath their vibration like hail. Neither they, nor the men who draw out the rods or fuse the fragments, have the smallest occasion for the use of any single human faculty; and every young lady, therefore, who buys glass beads is engaged in the slave-trade, and in a much more cruel one than that which we have so long been endeavouring to put down.

But glass cups and vessels may become the subjects of exquisite invention; and if in buying these we pay for the invention, that is to say for the beautiful form, or colour, or engraving, and not for mere finish of execution, we are doing good to humanity.

18. So, again, the cutting of precious stones, in all ordinary cases, requires little exertion of any mental faculty; some tact and judgment in avoiding flaws, and so on, but nothing to bring out the whole mind. Every person who wears cut jewels merely for the sake of their value is, therefore, a slave-driver.

But the working of the goldsmith, and the various designing of grouped jewellery and enamel-work, may become the subject of the most noble human intelligence. Therefore, money spent in the purchase of well-designed plate, of precious engraved vases, cameos, or enamels, does good to humanity; and, in work of this kind, jewels may be employed to heighten its splendour; and their cutting is then a price paid for the attainment of a noble end, and thus perfectly allowable.

19. I shall perhaps press this law farther elsewhere, but our immediate concern is chiefly with the second, namely, never to demand an exact finish, when it does not lead to a noble end. For observe, I have only dwelt upon the rudeness of Gothic, or any other kind of imperfectness, as admirable, where it was impossible to get design or thought without it. If you are to have the thought of a rough and untaught man, you must have it in a rough and untaught way; but from an educated man, who can without effort express his thoughts in an educated way, take the graceful expression, and be thankful. Only *get* the thought, and do not silence the peasant because he cannot speak good grammar, or until you have taught him his grammar. Grammar and refinement are good things, both, only be sure of the better thing first. And thus in art, delicate finish is desirable from the greatest masters, and is always given by them. In some places Michael Angelo, Leonardo, Phidias, Perugino, Turner, all finished with the most exquisite care; and the finish they give always leads to the fuller accomplishment of their noble purposes. But lower men than these cannot finish, for it requires consummate knowledge to finish consummately, and then we must take their thoughts as they are able to give them. So the rule is simple: Always look for invention first, and after that, for such execution as will help the invention, and as the inventor is capable of without painful effort, and *no more*. Above all, demand no refinement of execution where there is no thought, for that is slaves' work, unredeemed. Rather choose rough work than smooth work, so only that the practical purpose be answered, and never imagine there is reason to be proud of anything that may be accomplished by patience and sand-paper.

20. I shall only give one example, which however will show the reader what I mean, from the manufacture already alluded to, that of glass. Our modern glass is exquisitely clear in its substance, true in its form, accurate in its cutting. We are proud of this. We ought to be ashamed of it. The old Venice glass was muddy, inaccurate in all its forms, and clumsily cut, if at all. And the old Venetian was justly proud of it. For there is this difference between the English and Venetian workman, that the former thinks only of accurately matching his patterns, and getting his curves perfectly true and his edges perfectly sharp, and becomes a mere machine for rounding curves and sharpening edges, while the old Venetian cared not a whit whether his edges were sharp or not, but he invented a new design for every glass that he made, and never moulded a handle or a lip without a new fancy in it. And therefore, though some Venetian glass is ugly and clumsy enough, when made by clumsy and uninventive workmen, other Venetian glass is so lovely in its forms that no price is too

great for it; and we never see the same form in it twice. Now you cannot have the finish and the varied form too. If the workman is thinking about his edges, he cannot be thinking of his design; if of his design, he cannot think of his edges. Choose whether you will pay for the lovely form or the perfect finish, and choose at the same moment whether you will make the worker a man or a grindstone.

21. Nay, but the reader interrupts me, — "If the workman can design beautifully, I would not have him kept at the furnace. Let him be taken away and made a gentleman, and have a studio, and design his glass there, and I will have it blown and cut for him by common workmen, and so I will have my design and my finish too."

All ideas of this kind are founded upon two mistaken suppositions: the first, that one man's thoughts can be, or ought to be, executed by another man's hands; the second, that manual labour is a degradation, when it is governed by intellect.

On a large scale, and in work determinable by line and rule, it is indeed both possible and necessary that the thoughts of one man should be carried out by the labour of others; in this sense I have already defined the best architecture to be the expression of the mind of manhood by the hands of childhood. But on a smaller scale, and in a design which cannot be mathematically defined, one man's thoughts can never be expressed by another: and the difference between the spirit of touch of the man who is inventing, and of the man who is obeying directions, is often all the difference between a great and a common work of art. How wide the separation is between original and second-hand execution, I shall endeavour to show elsewhere; it is not so much to our purpose here as to mark the other and more fatal error of despising manual labour when governed by intellect; for it is no less fatal an error to despise it when thus regulated by intellect, than to value it for its own sake. We are always in these days endeavouring to separate the two; we want one man to be always thinking, and another to be always working, and we call one a gentleman, and the other an operative; whereas the workman ought often to be thinking, and the thinker often to be working, and both should be gentlemen, in the best sense. As it is, we make both ungentle, the one envying, the other despising, his brother; and the mass of society is made up of morbid thinkers, and miserable workers. Now it is only by labour that thought can be made healthy, and only by thought that labour can be made happy, and the two cannot be separated with impunity. It would be well if all of us were good handicraftsmen in some kind, and the dishonour of manual labour done away with altogether; so that though there should still be a trenchant distinction of race between nobles and commoners, there should not, among the latter, be a trenchant distinction of employment, as between idle and working men, or between men of liberal and illiberal professions. All professions should be liberal, and there should be less pride felt in peculiarity of employment, and more in excellence of achievement. And yet more, in each several profession, no master should be too proud to do its hardest work. The painter should grind his own colours; the architect work in the mason's yard with his men; the master-manufacturer be himself a more skilful operative than any man in his mills; and the distinction between one man and another be only in experience and skill, and the authority and wealth which these must naturally and justly obtain.

22. I should be led far from the matter in hand, if I were to pursue this interesting subject. Enough, I trust, has been said to show the reader that the rudeness or imperfection which at first rendered the term "Gothic" one of reproach is indeed, when rightly understood, one of the most noble characters of Christian architecture, and not only a noble but an *essential* one. It seems a fantastic paradox, but it is nevertheless a most important truth, that no architecture can be truly noble which is *not* imperfect. And this is easily demonstrable. For since the architect, whom we will suppose capable of doing all in perfection, cannot execute the whole with his own hands, he must either make slaves of his workmen in the old Greek, and present English fashion, and level his work to a slave's capacities, which is to degrade it; or else he must take his workmen as he finds them, and let them show their weaknesses together with their strength, which will involve the Gothic imperfection, but render the whole work as noble as the intellect of the age can make it.

23. But the principle may be stated more broadly still. I have confined the illustration of it to architecture, but I must not leave it as if true of architecture only. Hitherto I have used the words imperfect and perfect merely to distinguish between work grossly unskilful, and work executed with average precision and science; and I have been pleading that any degree of unskilfulness should be admitted, so only that the labourer's mind had room for expression. But, accurately speaking, no good work whatever can be perfect, and *the demand for perfection is always a sign of a misunderstanding of the ends of art.*

24. This for two reasons, both based on everlasting laws. The first, that no great man ever stops working till he has reached his point of failure; that is to say, his mind is always far in advance of his powers of execution, and the latter will now and then give way in trying to follow it; besides that he will always give to the inferior portions of his work only such inferior attention as they require; and according to his greatness he becomes so accustomed to the feeling of dissatisfaction with the best he can do, that in moments of lassitude or anger with himself he will not care though the beholder be dissatisfied also. I believe there has only been one man who would not acknowledge this necessity, and strove always to reach perfection, Leonardo; the end of his vain effort being merely that he would

take ten years to a picture, and leave it unfinished. And therefore, if we are to have great men working at all, or less men doing their best, the work will be imperfect, however beautiful. Of human work none but what is bad can be perfect, in its own bad way.[2]

25. The second reason is, that imperfection is in some sort essential to all that we know of life. It is the sign of life in a mortal body, that is to say, of a state of progress and change. Nothing that lives is, or can be, rigidly perfect; part of it is decaying, part nascent. The foxglove blossom, — a third part bud, a third part past, a third part in full bloom, — is a type of the life of this world. And in all things that live there are certain irregularities and deficiencies which are not only signs of life, but sources of beauty. No human face is exactly the same in its lines on each side, no leaf perfect in its lobes, no branch in its symmetry. All admit irregularity as they imply change; and to banish imperfection is to destroy expression, to check exertion, to paralyse vitality. All things are literally better, lovelier, and more beloved for the imperfections which have been divinely appointed, that the law of human life may be Effort, and the law of human judgment, Mercy.

Accept this then for a universal law, that neither architecture nor any other noble work of man can be good unless it be imperfect; and let us be prepared for the otherwise strange fact, which we shall discern clearly as we approach the period of the Renaissance, that the first cause of the fall of the arts of Europe was a relentless requirement of perfection, incapable alike either of being silenced by veneration for greatness, or softened into forgiveness of simplicity.

Thus far then of the Rudeness or Savageness, which is the first mental element of Gothic architecture. It is an element in many other healthy architectures also, as in Byzantine and Romanesque; but true Gothic cannot exist without it.

26. The second mental element above named was CHANGEFULNESS, or Variety.

I have already enforced the allowing independent operation to the inferior workman, simply as a duty *to him,* and as ennobling the architecture by rendering it more Christian. We have now to consider what reward we obtain for the performance of this duty, namely, the perpetual variety of every feature of the building.

Wherever the workman is utterly enslaved, the parts of the building must of course be absolutely like each other; for the perfection of his execution can only be reached by exercising him in doing one thing, and giving him nothing else to do. The degree in which the workman is degraded may be thus known at a glance, by observing

2 The Elgin marbles are supposed by many persons to be "perfect." In the most important portions they indeed approach perfection, but only there. The draperies are unfinished, the hair and wool of the animals are unfinished, and the entire bas-reliefs of the frieze are roughly cut. [Ruskin's note.]

whether the several parts of the building are similar or not; and if, as in Greek work, all the capitals are alike, and all the mouldings unvaried, then the degradation is complete; if, as in Egyptian or Ninevite work, though the manner of executing certain figures is always the same, the order of design is perpetually varied, the degradation is less total; if, as in Gothic work, there is perpetual change both in design and execution, the workman must have been altogether set free.

27. How much the beholder gains from the liberty of the labourer may perhaps be questioned in England, where one of the strongest instincts in nearly every mind is that Love of Order which makes us desire that our house windows should pair like our carriage horses, and allows us to yield our faith unhesitatingly to architectural theories which fix a form for everything, and forbid variation from it. I would not impeach love of order: it is one of the most useful elements of the English mind; it helps us in our commerce and in all purely practical matters; and it is in many cases one of the foundation stones of morality. Only do not let us suppose that love of order is love of art. It is true that order, in its highest sense, is one of the necessities of art, just as time is a necessity of music; but love of order has no more to do with our right enjoyment of architecture or painting, than love of punctuality with the appreciation of an opera. Experience, I fear, teaches us that accurate and methodical habits in daily life are seldom characteristic of those who either quickly perceive, or richly possess, the creative powers of art; there is, however, nothing inconsistent between the two instincts, and nothing to hinder us from retaining our business habits, and yet fully allowing and enjoying the noblest gifts of Invention. We already do so, in every other branch of art except architecture, and we only do *not* so there because we have been taught that it would be wrong. Our architects gravely inform us that, as there are four rules of arithmetic, there are five orders of architecture; we, in our simplicity, think that this sounds consistent, and believe them. They inform us also that there is one proper form for Corinthian capitals, another for Doric, and another for Ionic. We, considering that there is also a proper form for the letters A, B, and C, think that this also sounds consistent, and accept the proposition. Understanding, therefore, that one form of the said capitals is proper, and no other, and having a conscientious horror of all impropriety, we allow the architect to provide us with the said capitals, of the proper form, in such and such a quantity, and in all other points to take care that the legal forms are observed; which having done, we rest in forced confidence that we are well housed.

28. But our higher instincts are not deceived. We take no pleasure in the building provided for us, resembling that which we take in a new book or a new picture. We may be proud of its size, complacent in its correctness, and happy in its convenience. We may take the

same pleasure in its symmetry and workmanship as in a well-ordered room, or a skilful piece of manufacture. And this we suppose to be all the pleasure that architecture was ever intended to give us. The idea of reading a building as we would read Milton or Dante, and getting the same kind of delight out of the stones as out of the stanzas, never enters our minds for a moment. And for good reason: — There is indeed rhythm in the verses, quite as strict as the symmetries or rhythm of the architecture, and a thousand times more beautiful, but there is something else than rhythm. The verses were neither made to order, nor to match, as the capitals were; and we have therefore a kind of pleasure in them other than a sense of propriety. But it requires a strong effort of common sense to shake ourselves quit of all that we have been taught for the last two centuries, and wake to the perception of a truth just as simple and certain as it is new: that great art whether expressing itself in words, colours, or stones, does *not* say the same thing over and over again; that the merit of architectural, as of every other art, consists in its saying new and different things; that to repeat itself is no more a characteristic of genius in marble than it is of genius in print; and that we may, without offending any laws of good taste, require of an architect, as we do of a novelist, that he should be not only correct, but entertaining.

Yet all this is true, and self-evident; only hidden from us, as many other self-evident things are, by false teaching. Nothing is a great work of art, for the production of which either rules or models can be given. Exactly so far as architecture works on known rules, and from given models, it is not an art, but a manufacture; and it is, of the two procedures, rather less rational (because more easy) to copy capitals or mouldings from Phidias, and call ourselves architects, than to copy heads and hands from Titian, and call ourselves painters.

29. Let us then understand at once, that change or variety is as much a necessity to the human heart and brain in buildings as in books; that there is no merit, though there is some occasional use, in monotony; and that we must no more expect to derive either pleasure or profit from an architecture whose ornaments are of one pattern, and whose pillars are of one proportion, than we should out of a universe in which the clouds were all of one shape, and the trees all of one size.

30. And this we confess in deeds, though not in words. All the pleasure which the people of the nineteenth century take in art, is in pictures, sculpture, minor objects of virtù, or mediæval architecture, which we enjoy under the term picturesque: no pleasure is taken anywhere in modern buildings, and we find all men of true feeling delighting to escape out of modern cities into natural scenery: hence, as I shall hereafter show, that peculiar love of landscape which is characteristic of the age. It would be well, if, in all other matters,

we were as ready to put up with what we dislike, for the sake of compliance with established law, as we are in architecture.

31. How so debased a law ever came to be established, we shall see when we come to describe the Renaissance schools: here we have only to note, as the second most essential element of the Gothic spirit, that it broke through that law wherever it found it in existence; it not only dared, but delighted in, the infringement of every servile principle; and invented a series of forms of which the merit was, not merely that they were new, but that they were *capable of perpetual novelty*. The pointed arch was not merely a bold variation from the round, but it admitted of millions of variations in itself; for the proportions of a pointed arch are changeable to infinity, while a circular arch is always the same. The grouped shaft was not merely a bold variation from the single one, but it admitted of millions of variations in its grouping, and in the proportions resultant from its grouping. The introduction of tracery was not only a startling change in the treatment of window lights, but admitted endless changes in the interlacement of the tracery bars themselves. So that, while in all living Christian architecture the love of variety exists, the Gothic schools exhibited that love in culminating energy; and their influence, wherever it extended itself, may be sooner and farther traced by this character than by any other; the tendency to the adoption of Gothic types being always first shown by greater irregularity and richer variation in the forms of the architecture it is about to supersede, long before the appearance of the pointed arch or of any other recognisable *outward* sign of the Gothic mind.

32. We must, however, herein note carefully what distinction there is between a healthy and a diseased love of change; for as it was in healthy love of change that the Gothic architecture rose, it was partly in consequence of diseased love of change that it was destroyed. In order to understand this clearly, it will be necessary to consider the different ways in which change and monotony are presented to us in nature; both having their use, like darkness and light, and the one incapable of being enjoyed without the other: change being most delightful after some prolongation of monotony, as light appears most brilliant after the eyes have been for some time closed.

33. I believe that the true relations of monotony and change may be most simply understood by observing them in music. We may therein notice, first, that there is a sublimity and majesty in monotony which there is not in rapid or frequent variation. This is true throughout all nature. The greater part of the sublimity of the sea depends on its monotony; so also that of desolate moor and mountain scenery; and especially the sublimity of motion, as in the quiet, unchanged fall and rise of an engine beam. So also there is sublimity in darkness which there is not in light.

34. Again, monotony after a certain time, or beyond a certain de-

gree, becomes either uninteresting or intolerable, and the musician is obliged to break it in one or two ways: either while the air or passage is perpetually repeated, its notes are variously enriched and harmonised; or else, after a certain number of repeated passages, an entirely new passage is introduced, which is more or less delightful according to the length of the previous monotony. Nature, of course, uses both these kinds of variation perpetually. The sea-waves, resembling each other in general mass, but none like its brother in minor divisions and curves, are a monotony of the first kind; the great plain, broken by an emergent rock or clump of trees, is a monotony of the second.

35. Farther: in order to the enjoyment of the change in either case, a certain degree of patience is required from the hearer or observer. In the first case, he must be satisfied to endure with patience the recurrence of the great masses of sound or form, and to seek for entertainment in a careful watchfulness of the minor details. In the second case, he must bear patiently the infliction of the monotony for some moments, in order to feel the full refreshment of the change. This is true even of the shortest musical passage in which the element of monotony is employed. In cases of more majestic monotony, the patience required is so considerable that it becomes a kind of pain, — a price paid for the future pleasure.

36. Again: the talent of the composer is not in the monotony, but in the changes: he may show feeling and taste by his use of monotony in certain places or degrees; that is to say, by his *various* employment of it; but it is always in the new arrangement or invention that his intellect is shown, and not in the monotony which relieves it.

Lastly: if the pleasure of change be too often repeated, it ceases to be delightful, for then change itself becomes monotonous, and we are driven to seek delight in extreme and fantastic degrees of it. This is the diseased love of change of which we have above spoken.

37. From these facts we may gather generally that monotony is, and ought to be, in itself painful to us, just as darkness is; that an architecture which is altogether monotonous is a dark or dead architecture; and, of those who love it, it may be truly said, "they love darkness rather than light." But monotony in certain measure, used in order to give value to change, and, above all, that *transparent* monotony which, like the shadows of a great painter, suffers all manner of dimly suggested form to be seen through the body of it, is an essential in architectural as in all other composition; and the endurance of monotony has about the same place in a healthy mind that the endurance of darkness has: that is to say, as a strong intellect will have pleasure in the solemnities of storm and twilight, and in the broken and mysterious lights that gleam among them, rather than in mere brilliancy and glare, while a frivolous mind will dread the shadow and the storm; and as a great man will be ready to endure much darkness of fortune in order to reach greater eminence of power or felicity, while

an inferior man will not pay the price; exactly in like manner a great mind will accept, or even delight in, monotony which would be wearisome to an inferior intellect, because it has more patience and power of expectation, and is ready to pay the full price for the great future pleasure of change. But in all cases it is not that the noble nature loves monotony, any more than it loves darkness or pain. But it can bear with it, and receives a high pleasure in the endurance or patience, a pleasure necessary to the well-being of this world; while those who will not submit to the temporary sameness, but rush from one change to another, gradually dull the edge of change itself, and bring a shadow and weariness over the whole world from which there is no more escape.

38. From these general uses of variety in the economy of the world, we may at once understand its use and abuse in architecture. The variety of the Gothic schools is the more healthy and beautiful, because in many cases it is entirely unstudied, and results, not from the mere love of change, but from practical necessities. For in one point of view Gothic is not only the best, but the *only rational* architecture, as being that which can fit itself most easily to all services, vulgar or noble. Undefined in its slope of roof, height of shaft, breadth of arch, or disposition of ground plan, it can shrink into a turret, expand into a hall, coil into a staircase, or spring into a spire, with undegraded grace and unexhausted energy; and whenever it finds occasion for change in its form or purpose, it submits to it without the slightest sense of loss either to its unity or majesty, — subtle and flexible like a fiery serpent, but ever attentive to the voice of the charmer. And it is one of the chief virtues of the Gothic builders, that they never suffered ideas of outside symmetries and consistencies to interfere with the real use and value of what they did. If they wanted a window, they opened one; a room, they added one; a buttress, they built one; utterly regardless of any established conventionalities of external appearance, knowing (as indeed it always happened) that such daring interruptions of the formal plan would rather give additional interest to its symmetry than injure it. So that, in the best times of Gothic, a useless window would rather have been opened in an unexpected place for the sake of the surprise, than a useful one forbidden for the sake of symmetry. Every successive architect, employed upon a great work, built the pieces he added in his own way, utterly regardless of the style adopted by his predecessors; and if two towers were raised in nominal correspondence at the sides of a cathedral front, one was nearly sure to be different from the other, and in each the style at the top to be different from the style at the bottom.

39. These marked variations were, however, only permitted as part of the great system of perpetual change which ran through every member of Gothic design, and rendered it as endless a field for the beholder's inquiry, as for the builder's imagination: change, which in

the best schools is subtle and delicate, and rendered more delightful by intermingling of a noble monotony; in the more barbaric schools is somewhat fantastic and redundant; but, in all, a necessary and constant condition of the life of the school. Sometimes the variety is in one feature, sometimes in another; it may be in the capitals or crockets, in the niches or the traceries, or in all together, but in some one or other of the features it will be found always. If the mouldings are constant, the surface sculpture will change; if the capitals are of a fixed design, the traceries will change; if the traceries are monotonous, the capitals will change; and if even, as in some fine schools, the early English for example, there is the slightest approximation to an unvarying type of mouldings, capitals, and floral decoration, the variety is found in the disposition of the masses, and in the figure sculpture.

40. I must now refer for a moment, before we quit the consideration of this, the second mental element of Gothic, to the opening of the third chapter of the "Seven Lamps of Architecture," in which the distinction was drawn (§2) between man gathering and man governing; between his acceptance of the sources of delight from nature, and his development of authoritative or imaginative power in their arrangement: for the two mental elements, not only of Gothic, but of all good architecture, which we have just been examining, belong to it, and are admirable in it, chiefly as it is, more than any other subject of art, the work of man, and the expression of the average power of man. A picture or poem is often little more than a feeble utterance of man's admiration of something out of himself; but architecture approaches more to a creation of his own, born of his necessities, and expressive of his nature. It is also, in some sort, the work of the whole race, while the picture or statue is the work of one only, in most cases more highly gifted than his fellows. And therefore we may expect that the first two elements of good architecture should be expressive of some great truths commonly belonging to the whole race, and necessary to be understood or felt by them in all their work that they do under the sun. And observe what they are: the confession of Imperfection, and the confession of Desire of Change. The building of the bird and the bee needs not express anything like this. It is perfect and unchanging. But just because we are something better than birds or bees, our building must confess that we have not reached the perfection we can imagine, and cannot rest in the condition we have attained. If we pretend to have reached either perfection or satisfaction, we have degraded ourselves and our work. God's work only may express that; but ours may never have that sentence written upon it, —"And behold, it was very good." And, observe again, it is not merely as it renders the edifice a book of various knowledge, or a mine of precious thought, that variety is essential to its nobleness. The vital principle is not the love of *Knowledge*, but the love of *Change*. It is that strange *disquietude* of the Gothic spirit that is its

greatness; that restlessness of the dreaming mind, that wanders hither and thither among the niches, and flickers feverishly around the pinnacles, and frets and fades in labyrinthine knots and shadows along wall and roof, and yet is not satisfied, nor shall be satisfied. The Greek could stay in his triglyph furrow, and be at peace; but the work of the Gothic heart is fretwork still, and it can neither rest in, nor from, its labour, but must pass on, sleeplessly, until its love of change shall be pacified for ever in the change that must come alike on them that wake and them that sleep.

41. The third constituent element of the Gothic mind was stated to be NATURALISM; that is to say, the love of natural objects for their own sake, and the effort to represent them frankly, unconstrained by artistical laws.

This characteristic of the style partly follows in necessary connection with those named above. For, so soon as the workman is left free to represent what subjects he chooses, he must look to the nature that is round him for material, and will endeavour to represent it as he sees it, with more or less accuracy according to the skill he possesses, and with much play of fancy, but with small respect for law. There is, however, a marked distinction between the imaginations of the Western and Eastern races, even when both are left free; the Western, or Gothic, delighting most in the representation of facts, and the Eastern (Arabian, Persian, and Chinese) in the harmony of colours and forms. Each of these intellectual dispositions has its particular forms of error and abuse, which, though I have often before stated, I must here again briefly explain; and this the rather, because the word Naturalism is, in one of its senses, justly used as a term of reproach, and the questions respecting the real relations of art and nature are so many and so confused throughout all the schools of Europe at this day, that I cannot clearly enunciate any single truth without appearing to admit, in fellowship with it, some kind of error, unless the reader will bear with me in entering into such an analysis of the subject as will serve us for general guidance.

42. We are to remember, in the first place, that the arrangement of colours and lines is an art analogous to the composition [3] of music, and entirely independent of the representation of facts. Good colour-

[3] I am always afraid to use this word "Composition"; it is so utterly misused in the general parlance respecting art. Nothing is more common than to hear divisions of art into "form, composition, and colour," or "light and shade and composition," or "sentiment and composition," or it matters not what else and composition; the speakers in each case attaching a perfectly different meaning to the word, generally an indistinct one, and always a wrong one. Composition is, in plain English, "putting together," and it means the putting together of lines, of forms, of colours, of shades, or of ideas. Painters compose in colour, compose in thought, compose in form, and compose in effect; the word being of use merely in order to express a scientific, disciplined, and inventive arrangement of any of these, instead of a merely natural or accidental one. [Ruskin's note.]

ing does not necessarily convey the image of anything but itself. It consists in certain proportions and arrangements of rays of light, but not in likenesses to anything. A few touches of certain greys and purples laid by a master's hand on white paper, will be good colouring; as more touches are added beside them, we may find out that they were intended to represent a dove's neck, and we may praise, as the drawing advances, the perfect imitation of the dove's neck. But the good colouring does not consist in that imitation, but in the abstract qualities and relations of the grey and purple.

In like manner, as soon as a great sculptor begins to shape his work out of the block, we shall see that its lines are nobly arranged, and of noble character. We may not have the slightest idea for what the forms are intended, whether they are of man or beast, of vegetation or drapery. Their likeness to anything does not affect their nobleness. They are magnificent forms, and that is all we need care to know of them, in order to say whether the workman is a good or bad sculptor.

43. Now the noblest art is an exact unison of the abstract value, with the imitative power, of forms and colours. It is the noblest composition, used to express the noblest facts. But the human mind cannot in general unite the two perfections: it either pursues the fact to the neglect of the composition, or pursues the composition to the neglect of the fact.

44. And it is intended by the Deity that it *should* do this; the best art is not always wanted. Facts are often wanted without art, as in a geological diagram; and art often without facts, as in a Turkey carpet. And most men have been made capable of giving either one or the other, but not both; only one or two, the very highest, can give both.

Observe then. Men are universally divided, as respects their artistical qualifications, into three great classes; a right, a left, and a centre. On the right side are the men of facts, on the left the men of design,[4] in the centre the men of both.

The three classes of course pass into each other by imperceptible gradations. The men of facts are hardly ever altogether without powers of design; the men of design are always in some measure cognisant of facts; and as each class possesses more or less of the powers of the opposite one, it approaches to the character of the central class. Few men, even in that central rank, are so exactly thronged on the summit of the crest that they cannot be perceived to incline in the least one way or the other, embracing both horizons with their glance. Now each of these classes has, as I above said, a healthy function in the world, and correlative diseases or unhealthy functions; and, when the work of either of them is seen in its morbid condition, we are apt to find fault with the class of workmen, instead

4 Design is used in this place as expressive of the power to arrange lines and colours nobly. By facts, I mean facts perceived by the eye and mind, not facts accumulated by knowledge. . . . [Ruskin's note.]

of finding fault only with the particular abuse which has perverted their action. . . .

What, then, are the diseased operations to which the three classes of workmen are liable?

46. Primarily, two; affecting the two inferior classes:

1st, When either of those two classes Despises the other;

2nd, When either of the two classes Envies the other; producing, therefore, four forms of dangerous error.

First, when the men of facts despise design. This is the error of the common Dutch painters, of merely imitative painters of still life, flowers, &c., and other men who, having either the gift of accurate imitation or strong sympathies with nature, suppose that all is done when the imitation is perfected or sympathy expressed. A large body of English landscapists come into this class, including most clever sketches from nature, who fancy that to get a sky of true tone, and a gleam of sunshine or sweep of shower faithfully expressed, is all that can be required of art. These men are generally themselves answerable for much of their deadness of feeling to the higher qualities of composition. They probably have not originally the high gifts of design, but they lose such powers as they originally possessed by despising, and refusing to study, the results of great power of design in others. Their knowledge, as far as it goes, being accurate, they are usually presumptuous and self-conceited, and gradually become incapable of admiring anything but what is like their own works. They see nothing in the works of great designers but the faults, and do harm almost incalculable in the European society of the present day by sneering at the compositions of the greatest men of the earlier ages, because they do not absolutely tally with their own ideas of "Nature."

47. The second form of error is when the men of design despise facts. All noble design must deal with facts to a certain extent, for there is no food for it but in nature. The best colourist invents best by taking hints from natural colours; from birds, skies, or groups of figures. And if, in the delight of inventing fantastic colour and form, the truths of nature are wilfully neglected, the intellect becomes comparatively decrepit, and that state of art results which we find among the Chinese. The Greek designers delighted in the facts of the human form, and became great in consequence; but the facts of lower nature were disregarded by them, and their inferior ornament became, therefore, dead and valueless.

48. The third form of error is when the men of facts envy design: that is to say, when, having only imitative powers, they refuse to employ those powers upon the visible world around them; but, having been taught that composition is the end of art, strive to obtain the inventive powers which nature has denied them, study nothing but the works of reputed designers, and perish in a fungous growth of plagiarism and laws of art.

Here was the great error of the beginning of this century; it is the error of the meanest kind of men that employ themselves in painting, and it is the most fatal of all, rendering those who fall into it utterly useless, incapable of helping the world with either truth or fancy, while, in all probability, they deceive it by base resemblances of both, until it hardly recognises truth or fancy when they really exist.

49. The fourth form of error is when the men of design envy facts; that is to say, when the temptation of closely imitating nature leads them to forget their own proper ornamental function, and when they lose the power of the composition for the sake of graphic truth; as, for instance, in the hawthorn moulding so often spoken of round the porch of Bourges Cathedral, which, though very lovely, might perhaps, as we saw above, have been better, if the old builder, in his excessive desire to make it look like hawthorn, had not painted it green.

50. It is, however, carefully to be noted, that the two morbid conditions to which the men of facts are liable are much more dangerous and harmful than those to which the men of design are liable. The morbid state of men of design injures themselves only; that of the men of facts injures the whole world. The Chinese porcelain-painter is, indeed, not so great a man as he might be, but he does not want to break everything that is not porcelain: but the modern English fact-hunter, despising design, wants to destroy everything that does not agree with his own notions of truth, and becomes the most dangerous and despicable of iconoclasts, excited by egotism instead of religion. Again: the Bourges sculptor, painting his hawthorns green, did indeed somewhat hurt the effect of his own beautiful design, but did not prevent any one from loving hawthorn: but Sir George Beaumont,[5] trying to make Constable paint grass brown *instead* of green, was setting himself between Constable and nature, blinding the painter, and blaspheming the work of God. . . .

68. There is, however, one direction in which the Naturalism of the Gothic workmen is peculiarly manifested; and this direction is even more characteristic of the school than the Naturalism itself; I mean their peculiar fondness for the forms of Vegetation. In rendering the various circumstances of daily life, Egyptian and Ninevite sculpture is as frank and as diffuse as the Gothic. From the highest pomps of state or triumphs of battle, to the most trivial domestic arts and amusements, all is taken advantage of to fill the field of granite with the perpetual interest of a crowded drama; and the early Lombardic and Romanesque sculpture is equally copious in its description of the familiar circumstances of war and the chase. But in all the scenes portrayed by the workmen of these nations, vegetation occurs only as an explanatory accessary; the reed is introduced to mark the course of the river, or the tree to mark the covert of the

5 Sir George Howland Beaumont (1753–1827), landscape painter and patron of art.

wild beast, or the ambush of the enemy, but there is no especial interest in the forms of the vegetation strong enough to induce them to make it a subject of separate and accurate study. Again, among the nations who followed the arts of design exclusively, the forms of foliage introduced were meagre and general, and their real intricacy and life were neither admired nor expressed. But to the Gothic workman the living foliage became a subject of intense affection, and he struggled to render all its characters with as much accuracy as was compatible with the laws of his design and the nature of his material, not unfrequently tempted in his enthusiasm to transgress the one and disguise the other.

69. There is a peculiar significance in this, indicative both of higher civilisation and gentler temperament, than had before been manifested in architecture. Rudeness, and the love of change, which we have insisted upon as the first elements of Gothic, are also elements common to all healthy schools. But here is a softer element mingled with them, peculiar to the Gothic itself. The rudeness or ignorance which would have been painfully exposed in the treatment of the human form, are still not so great as to prevent the successful rendering of the wayside herbage; and the love of change, which becomes morbid and feverish in following the haste of the hunter, and the rage of the combatant, is at once soothed and satisfied as it watches the wandering of the tendril, and the budding of the flower. Nor is this all: the new direction of mental interest marks an infinite change in the means and the habits of life. The nations whose chief support was in the chase, whose chief interest was in the battle, whose chief pleasure was in the banquet, would take small care respecting the shapes of leaves and flowers; and notice little in the forms of the forest trees which sheltered them, except the signs indicative of the wood which would make the toughest lance, the closest roof, or the clearest fire. The affectionate observation of the grace and outward character of vegetation is the sure sign of a more tranquil and gentle existence, sustained by the gifts, and gladdened by the splendour, of the earth. In that careful distinction of species, and richness of delicate and undisturbed organisation, which characterise the Gothic design, there is the history of rural and thoughtful life, influenced by habitual tenderness, and devoted to subtle inquiry; and every discriminating and delicate touch of the chisel, as it rounds the petal or guides the branch, is a prophecy of the development of the entire body of the natural sciences, beginning with that of medicine, of the recovery of literature, and the establishment of the most necessary principles of domestic wisdom and national peace.

70. I have before alluded to the strange and vain supposition, that the original conception of Gothic architecture had been derived from vegetation, — from the symmetry of avenues, and the interlacing of branches. It is a supposition which never could have existed for

a moment in the mind of any person acquainted with early Gothic; but, however idle as a theory, it is most valuable as a testimony to the character of the perfected style. It is precisely because the reverse of this theory is the fact, because the Gothic did not arise out of, but developed itself into, a resemblance to vegetation, that this resemblance is so instructive as an indication of the temper of the builders. It was no chance suggestion of the form of an arch from the bending of a bough, but a gradual and continual discovery of a beauty in natural forms which could be more and more perfectly transferred into those of stone, that influenced at once the heart of the people, and the form of the edifice. The Gothic architecture arose in massy and mountainous strength, axe-hewn, and iron-bound, block heaved upon block by the monk's enthusiasm and the soldier's force; and cramped and stanchioned into such weight of grisly wall, as might bury the anchoret in darkness, and beat back the utmost storm of battle, suffering but by the same narrow crosslet the passing of the sunbeam, or of the arrow. Gradually, as that monkish enthusiasm became more thoughtful, and as the sound of war became more and more intermittent beyond the gates of the convent or the keep, the stony pillar grew slender and the vaulted roof grew light, till they had wreathed themselves into the semblance of the summer woods at their fairest, and of the dead field-flowers, long trodden down in blood, sweet monumental statues were set to bloom for ever, beneath the porch of the temple, or the canopy of the tomb.

71. Nor is it only as a sign of greater gentleness or refinement of mind, but as a proof of the best possible direction of this refinement, that the tendency of the Gothic to the expression of vegetative life is to be admired. That sentence of Genesis, "I have given thee every green herb for meat," like all the rest of the book, has a profound symbolical as well as a literal meaning. It is not merely the nourishment of the body, but the food of the soul, that is intended. The green herb is, of all nature, that which is most essential to the healthy spiritual life of man. Most of us do not need fine scenery; the precipice and the mountain peak are not intended to be seen by all men, — perhaps their power is greatest over those who are unaccustomed to them. But trees, and fields, and flowers were made for all, and are necessary for all. God has connected the labour which is essential to the bodily sustenance, with the pleasures which are healthiest for the heart; and while He made the ground stubborn, He made its herbage fragrant, and its blossoms fair. The proudest architecture that man can build has no higher honour than to bear the image and recall the memory of that grass of the field which is, at once, the type and the support of his existence; the goodly building is then most glorious when it is sculptured into the likeness of the leaves of Paradise; and the great Gothic spirit, as we showed it to be noble in its disquietude, is also noble in its hold of nature; it is, indeed, like the dove of Noah,

in that she found no rest upon the face of the waters, — but like her in this also, "Lo, IN HER MOUTH WAS AN OLIVE BRANCH, PLUCKED OFF."

72. The fourth essential element of the Gothic mind was above stated to be the sense of the GROTESQUE; but I shall defer the endeavour to define this most curious and subtle character until we have occasion to examine one of the divisions of the Renaissance schools, which was morbidly influenced by it (Vol.III Chap.III.). It is the less necessary to insist upon it here, because every reader familiar with Gothic architecture must understand what I mean, and will, I believe, have no hesitation in admitting that the tendency to delight in fantastic and ludicrous, as well as in sublime, images, is a universal instinct of the Gothic imagination.

73. The fifth element above named was RIGIDITY; and this character I must endeavour carefully to define, for neither the word I have used, nor any other that I can think of, will express it accurately. For I mean, not merely stable, but *active* rigidity; the peculiar energy which gives tension to movement, and stiffness to resistance, which makes the fiercest lightning forked rather than curved, and the stoutest oak-branch angular rather than bending, and is as much seen in the quivering of the lance as in the glittering of the icicle.

74. I have before had occasion (Vol.I Chap.XIII. § VII.) to note some manifestations of this energy or fixedness; but it must be still more attentively considered here, as it shows itself throughout the whole structure and decoration of Gothic work. Egyptian and Greek buildings stand, for the most part, by their own weight and mass, one stone passively incumbent on another: but in the Gothic vaults and traceries there is a stiffness analogous to that of the bones of a limb, or fibres of a tree; an elastic tension and communication of force from part to part, and also a studious expression of this throughout every visible line of the building. And, in like manner, the Greek and Egyptian ornament is either mere surface engraving, as if the face of the wall had been stamped with a seal, or its lines are flowing, lithe, and luxuriant; in either case, there is no expression of energy in the framework of the ornament itself. But the Gothic ornament stands out in prickly independence, and frosty fortitude, jutting into crockets, and freezing into pinnacles; here starting up into a monster, there germinating into a blossom; anon knitting itself into a branch, alternately thorny, bossy, and bristly, or writhed into every form of nervous entanglement; but, even when most graceful, never for an instant languid, always quickset; erring, if at all, ever on the side of brusquerie. . . .

78. Last, because the least essential, of the constituent elements of this noble school, was placed that of REDUNDANCE, — the uncalculating bestowal of the wealth of its labour. There is, indeed, much Gothic, and that of the best period, in which this element is hardly traceable, and which depends for its effect almost exclusively on love-

liness of simple design and grace of uninvolved proportion: still, in
the most characteristic buildings, a certain portion of their effect depends upon accumulation of ornament; and many of those which have
most influence on the minds of men, have attained it by means of
this attribute alone. And although, by careful study of the school, it
is possible to arrive at a condition of taste which shall be better contented by a few perfect lines than by a whole façade covered with
fretwork, the building which only satisfies such a taste is not to be
considered the best. For the very first requirement of Gothic architecture being, as we saw above, that it shall both admit the aid, and
appeal to the admiration, of the rudest as well as the most refined
minds, the richness of the work is, paradoxical as the statement may
appear, a part of its humility. No architecture is so haughty as that
which is simple; which refuses to address the eye, except in a few
clear and forceful lines; which implies, in offering so little to our regards, that all it has offered is perfect; and disdains, either by the
complexity or the attractiveness of its features, to embarrass our investigation, or betray us into delight. That humility, which is the
very life of the Gothic school, is shown not only in the imperfection,
but in the accumulation, of ornament. The inferior rank of the workman is often shown as much in the richness, as the roughness, of his
work; and if the co-operation of every hand, and the sympathy of
every heart, are to be received, we must be content to allow the redundance which disguises the failure of the feeble, and wins the regard of the inattentive. There are, however, far nobler interests
mingling, in the Gothic heart, with the rude love of decorative accumulation: a magnificent enthusiasm, which feels as if it never
could do enough to reach the fulness of its ideal; and unselfishness of
sacrifice, which would rather cast fruitless labour before the altar
than stand idle in the market; and, finally, a profound sympathy with
the fulness and wealth of the material universe, rising out of that
Naturalism whose operation we have already endeavoured to define.
The sculptor who sought for his models among the forest leaves, could
not but quickly and deeply feel that complexity need not involve the
loss of grace, nor richness that of repose; and every hour which he
spent in the study of the minute and various work of Nature, made
him feel more forcibly the barrenness of what was best in that of
man: nor is it to be wondered at, that, seeing her perfect and exquisite creations poured forth in a profusion which conception could
not grasp nor calculation sum, he should think that it ill became him
to be niggardly of his own rude craftsmanship; and where he saw
throughout the universe a faultless beauty lavished on measureless
spaces of broidered field and blooming mountain, to grudge his poor
and imperfect labour to the few stones that he had raised one upon
another, for habitation or memorial. The years of his life passed away
before his task was accomplished; but generation succeeded generation
with unwearied enthusiasm, and the cathedral front was at last lost

in the tapestry of its traceries, like a rock among the thickets and herbage of spring. . . .

106. We have now, I believe, obtained a sufficiently accurate knowledge both of the spirit and form of Gothic architecture; but it may, perhaps, be useful to the general reader, if, in conclusion, I set down a few plain and practical rules for determining, in every instance, whether a given building be good Gothic or not, and, if not Gothic, whether its architecture is of a kind which will probably reward the pains of careful examination.

107. First. Look if the roof rises in a steep gable, high above the walls. If it does not do this, there is something wrong; the building is not quite pure Gothic, or has been altered.

108. Secondly. Look if the principal windows and doors have pointed arches with gables over them. If not pointed arches, the building is not Gothic; if they have not any gables over them, it is either not pure, or not first-rate.

If, however, it has the steep roof, the pointed arch, and gable all united, it is nearly certain to be a Gothic building of a very fine time.

109. Thirdly. Look if the arches are cusped, or apertures foliated. If the building has met the first two conditions, it is sure to be foliated somewhere; but, if not everywhere, the parts which are unfoliated are imperfect, unless they are large bearing arches, or small and sharp arches in groups, forming a kind of foliation by their own multiplicity, and relieved by sculpture and rich mouldings. The upper windows, for instance, in the east end of Westminster Abbey are imperfect for want of foliation. If there be no foliation anywhere, the building is assuredly imperfect Gothic.

110. Fourthly. If the building meets all the first three conditions, look if its arches in general, whether of windows and doors, or of minor ornamentation, are carried on *true shafts with bases and capitals*. If they are, then the building is assuredly of the finest Gothic style. It may still, perhaps, be an imitation, a feeble copy, or a bad example, of a noble style; but the manner of it, having met all these four conditions, is assuredly first-rate.

If its apertures have not shafts and capitals, look if they are plain openings in the walls, studiously simple, and unmoulded at the sides. . . . If so, the building may still be of the finest Gothic, adapted to some domestic or military service. But if the sides of the window be moulded, and yet there are no capitals at the spring of the arch, it is assuredly of an inferior school.

This is all that is necessary to determine whether the building be of a fine Gothic style. The next tests to be applied are in order to discover whether it be good architecture or not: for it may be very impure Gothic, and yet very noble architecture; or it may be very pure Gothic, and yet, if a copy, or originally raised by an ungifted builder, very bad architecture.

If it belong to any of the great schools of colour, its criticism becomes as complicated, and needs as much care, as that of a piece of music, and no general rules for it can be given; but if not —

111. First. See if it looks as if it had been built by strong men; if it has the sort of roughness, and largeness, and nonchalance, mixed in places with the exquisite tenderness which seems always to be the sign-manual of the broad vision, and massy power of men who can see *past* the work they are doing, and betray here and there something like disdain for it. If the building has this character, it is much already in its favour; it will go hard but it proves a noble one. If it has not this, but is altogether accurate, minute, and scrupulous in its workmanship, it must belong to either the very best or the very worst of schools: the very best, in which exquisite design is wrought out with untiring and conscientious care, as in the Giottesque Gothic; or the very worst, in which mechanism has taken the place of design. It is more likely, in general, that it should belong to the worst than the best: so that, on the whole, very accurate workmanship is to be esteemed a bad sign; and if there is nothing remarkable about the building but its precision, it may be passed at once with contempt.

112. Secondly. Observe if it be irregular, its different parts fitting themselves to different purposes, no one caring what becomes of them, so that they do their work. If one part always answers accurately to another part, it is sure to be a bad building; and the greater and more conspicuous the irregularities, the greater the chances are that it is a good one. . . .

113. Thirdly. Observe if all the traceries, capitals, and other ornaments are of perpetually varied design. If not, the work is assuredly bad.

114. Lastly. *Read* the sculpture. Preparatory to reading it, you will have to discover whether it is legible (and, if legible, it is nearly certain to be worth reading). On a good building, the sculpture is *always* so set, and on such a scale, that at the ordinary distance from which the edifice is seen, the sculpture shall be thoroughly intelligible and interesting. In order to accomplish this, the uppermost statues will be ten or twelve feet high, and the upper ornamentation will be colossal, increasing in fineness as it descends, till on the foundation it will often be wrought as if for a precious cabinet in a king's chamber; but the spectator will not notice that the upper sculptures are colossal. He will merely feel that he can see them plainly, and make them all out at his ease.

And having ascertained this, let him set himself to read them. Thenceforward the criticism of the building is to be conducted precisely on the same principles as that of a book; and it must depend on the knowledge, feeling, and not a little on the industry and perseverance of the reader, whether, even in the case of the best works, he either perceive them to be great, or feel them to be entertaining.

Unto This Last

❪ *Unto This Last* ("Four Essays on the First Principles of Political Economy") appeared in the *Cornhill Magazine* from August to November 1860 and raised a storm of indignant protest from subscribers. "The Roots of Honour" was the first essay. Here we have the explicit statement of Ruskin's grounds for disagreement with the dominant *laissez-faire* economists and an important landmark in the ideological background of what, in our century, resulted in the British Labour Party. It should be remembered that Mill's *On Liberty*, the great popular statement of a humanized utilitarianism, had appeared in 1859. ❫

ESSAY I

The Roots of Honour

1. AMONG the delusions which at different periods have possessed themselves of the minds of large masses of the human race, perhaps the most curious — certainly the least creditable — is the modern *soi-disant* science of political economy, based on the idea that an advantageous code of social action may be determined irrespectively of the influence of social affection.

Of course, as in the instances of alchemy, astrology, witchcraft, and other such popular creeds, political economy has a plausible idea at the root of it. "The social affections," says the economist, "are accidental and disturbing elements in human nature; but avarice and the desire of progress are constant elements. Let us eliminate the inconstants, and, considering the human being merely as a covetous machine, examine by what laws of labour, purchase, and sale, the greatest accumulative result in wealth is obtainable. Those laws once determined, it will be for each individual afterwards to introduce as much of the disturbing affectionate element as he chooses, and to determine for himself the result on the new conditions supposed."

2. This would be a perfectly logical and successful method of analysis, if the accidentals afterwards to be introduced were of the same nature as the powers first examined. Supposing a body in motion to be influenced by constant and inconstant forces, it is usually the simplest way of examining its course to trace it first under the persistent conditions, and afterwards introduce the causes of variation. But the disturbing elements in the social problem are not of the same nature as the constant ones; they alter the essence of the creature under examination the moment they are added; they operate, not

mathematically, but chemically, introducing conditions which render all our previous knowledge unavailable. We made learned experiments upon pure nitrogen, and have convinced ourselves that it is a very manageable gas: but, behold! the thing which we have practically to deal with is its chloride; and this, the moment we touch it on our established principles, sends us and our apparatus through the ceiling.

3. Observe, I neither impugn nor doubt the conclusion of the science, if its terms are accepted. I am simply uninterested in them, as I should be in those of a science of gymnastics which assumed that men had no skeletons. It might be shown, on that supposition, that it would be advantageous to roll the students up into pellets, flatten them into cakes, or stretch them into cables; and that when these results were effected, the re-insertion of the skeleton would be attended with various inconveniences to their constitution. The reasoning might be admirable, the conclusions true, and the science deficient only in applicability. Modern political economy stands on a precisely similar basis. Assuming, not that the human being has no skeleton, but that it is all skeleton, it founds an ossifiant theory of progress on this negation of a soul; and having shown the utmost that may be made of bones, and constructed a number of interesting geometrical figures with death's-head and humeri, successfully proves the inconvenience of the reappearance of a soul among these corpuscular structures. I do not deny the truth of this theory: I simply deny its applicability to the present phase of the world.

4. The inapplicability has been curiously manifested during the embarrassment caused by the late strikes of our workmen. Here occurs one of the simplest cases, in a pertinent and positive form, of the first vital problem which political economy has to deal with (the relation between employer and employed); and, at a severe crisis, when lives in multitudes and wealth in masses are at stake, the political economists are helpless — practically mute: no demonstrable solution of the difficulty can be given by them, such as may convince or calm the opposing parties. Obstinately the masters take one view of the matter; obstinately the operatives another; and no political science can set them at one.

5. It would be strange if it could, it being not by "science" of any kind that men were ever intended to be set at one. Disputant after disputant vainly strives to show that the interests of the masters are, or are not, antagonistic to those of the men: none of the pleaders ever seeming to remember that it does not absolutely or always follow that the persons must be antagonistic because their interests are. If there is only a crust of bread in the house, and mother and children are starving, their interests are not the same. If the mother eats it, the children want it; if the children eat it, the mother must go hungry to her work. Yet it does not necessarily follow that there will be "antago-

nism" between them, that they will fight for the crust, and that the mother, being strongest, will get it, and eat it. Neither, in any other case, whatever the relations of the persons may be, can it be assumed for certain that, because their interests are diverse, they must necessarily regard each other with hostility, and use violence or cunning to obtain the advantage.

6. Even if this were so, and it were as just as it is convenient to consider men as actuated by no other moral influences than those which affect rats or swine, the logical conditions of the question are still indeterminable. It can never be shown generally either that the interests of master and labourer are alike, or that they are opposed; for, according to circumstances, they may be either. It is, indeed, always the interest of both that the work should be rightly done, and a just price obtained for it; but, in the division of profits, the gain of one may or may not be the loss of the other. It is not the master's interest to pay wages so low as to leave the men sickly and depressed, nor the workman's interest to be paid high wages if the smallness of the master's profits hinders him from enlarging his business, or conducting it in a safe and liberal way. A stoker ought not to desire high pay if the company is too poor to keep the engine-wheels in repair.

7. And the varieties of circumstance which influence these reciprocal interests are so endless, that all endeavour to deduce rules of action from balance of expediency is in vain. And it is meant to be in vain. For no human actions ever were intended by the Maker of men to be guided by balances of expediency, but by balances of justice. He has therefore rendered all endeavours to determine expediency futile for evermore. No man ever knew, or can know, what will be the ultimate result to himself, or to others, of any given line of conduct. But every man may know, and most of us do know, what is a just and unjust act. And all of us may know also, that the consequences of justice will be ultimately the best possible, both to others and ourselves, though we can neither say what *is* best, nor how it is likely to come to pass.

I have said balances of justice, meaning, in the term justice, to include affection, — such affection as one man *owes* to another. All right relations between master and operative, and all their best interests, ultimately depend on these.

8. We shall find the best and simplest illustration of the relations of master and operative in the position of domestic servants.

We will suppose that the master of a household desires only to get as much work out of his servants as he can, at the rate of wages he gives. He never allows them to be idle; feeds them as poorly and lodges them as ill as they will endure, and in all things pushes his requirements to the exact point beyond which he cannot go without forcing the servant to leave him. In doing this, there is no violation on his part of what is commonly called "justice." He agrees with the domestic for his whole time and service, and takes them; — the limits of hardship in treatment being fixed by the practice of other masters in his neighbourhood; that is to say, by the current rate of wages for domestic labour. If the servant can get a better place, he is free to take one, and the master can only tell what is the real market value of his labour, by requiring as much as he will give.

This is the politico-economical view of the case, according to the doctors of that science; who assert that by this procedure the greatest average of work will be obtained from the servant, and therefore the greatest benefit to the community, and through the community, by reversion, to the servant himself.

That, however, is not so. It would be so if the servant were an engine of which the motive power was steam, magnetism, gravitation, or any other agent or calculable force. But he being, on the contrary, an engine whose motive power is a Soul, the force of this very peculiar agent, as an unknown quantity, enters into all the political economist's equations, without his knowledge, and falsifies every one of their results. The largest quantity of work will not be done by this curious engine for pay, or under pressure, or by help of any kind of fuel which may be applied by the chaldron. It will be done only when the motive force, that is to say, the will or spirit of the creature, is brought to its greatest strength by its own proper fuel: namely, by the affections.

9. It may indeed happen, and does happen often, that if the master is a man of sense and energy, a large quantity of material work may be done under mechanical pressure, enforced by strong will and guided by wise method; also it may happen, and does happen often, that if the master is indolent and weak (however good-natured), a very small quantity of work, and that bad, may be produced by the servant's undirected strength, and contemptuous gratitude. But the universal law of the matter is that, assuming any given quantity of energy and sense in master and servant, the greatest material result obtainable by them will be, not through antagonism to each other, but through affection for each other; and that if the master, instead of endeavouring to get as much work as possible from the servant, seeks rather to render his appointed and necessary work beneficial to him, and to forward his interests in all just and wholesome ways, the real amount of work ultimately done, or of good rendered, by the person so cared for, will indeed be the greatest possible.

Observe, I say, "of good rendered," for a servant's work is not necessarily or always the best thing he can give his master. But good of all kinds, whether in material service, in protective watchfulness of his master's interest and credit, or in joyful readiness to seize unexpected and irregular occasions of help.

Nor is this one whit less generally true because indulgence will be frequently abused, and kindness met with ingratitude. For the servant who, gently treated, is ungrateful, treated ungently, will be revengeful; and the man who is dishonest to a liberal master, will be injurious to an unjust one.

10. In any case, and with any person, this unselfish treatment will produce the most effective return. Observe, I am here considering the affections wholly as a motive power; not at all as things in themselves desirable or noble, or in any other way abstractedly good. I look at them simply as an anomalous force, rendering every one of the ordinary political economist's calculations nugatory; while, even if he desired to introduce this new element into his estimates, he has no power of dealing with it; for the affections only become a true motive power when they ignore every other motive and condition of political economy. Treat the servant kindly, with the idea of turning his gratitude to account, and you will get, as you deserve, no gratitude, nor any value for your kindness; but treat him kindly without any economical purpose, and all economical purposes will be answered; in this, as in all other matters, whosoever will save his life shall lose it, and whoso loses it shall find it.[1]

11. The next clearest and simplest example of relation between master and operative is that which exists between the commander of a regiment and his men.

Supposing the officer only desires to apply the rules of discipline so as, with least trouble to himself, to make the regiment most effective, he will not be able, by any rules, or administration of rules, on this selfish principle, to develop the full strength of his subordinates. If a man of sense and firmness, he may, as in the former instance, pro-

---

1 The difference between the two modes of treatment, and between their effective material results, may be seen very accurately by a comparison of the relations of Esther and Charlie in *Bleak House*, with those of Miss Brass and the Marchioness in *Master Humphrey's Clock*.

The essential value and truth of Dickens's writings have been unwisely lost sight of by many thoughtful persons merely because he presents his truth with some colour of caricature. Unwisely, because Dickens's caricature, though often gross, is never mistaken. Allowing for his manner of telling them, the things he tells us are always true. I wish that he could think it right to limit his brilliant exaggeration to works written only for public amusement; and when he takes up a subject of high national importance, such as that which he handled in *Hard Times*, that he would use severer and more accurate analysis. The usefulness of that work (to my mind, in several respects, the greatest he has written) is with many persons seriously diminished because Mr. Bounderby is a dramatic monster, instead of a characteristic example of a worldly master; and Stephen Blackpool a dramatic perfection, instead of a characteristic example of an honest workman. But let us not lose the use of Dickens's wit and insight, because he chooses to speak in a circle of stage fire. He is entirely right in his main drift and purpose in every book he has written; and all of them, but especially *Hard Times*, should be studied with close and earnest care by persons interested in social questions. They will find much that is partial, and, because partial, apparently unjust; but if they examine all the evidence on the other side, which Dickens seems to overlook, it will appear, after all their trouble, that his view was the finally right one, grossly and sharply told. [Ruskin's note.]

duce a better result than would be obtained by the irregular kindness
of a weak officer; but let the sense and firmness be the same in both
cases, and assuredly the officer who has the most direct personal relations with his men, the most care for their interests, and the most
value for their lives, will develop their effective strength, through
their affection for his own person, and trust in his character, to a degree wholly unattainable by other means. The law applies still more
stringently as the numbers concerned are larger: a charge may often
be successful, though the men dislike their officers; a battle has rarely
been won, unless they loved their general.

12. Passing from these simple examples to the more complicated
relations existing between a manufacturer and his workmen, we are
met first by certain curious difficulties, resulting, apparently, from a
harder and colder state of moral elements. It is easy to imagine an
enthusiastic affection existing among soldiers for the colonel. Not so
easy to imagine an enthusiastic affection among cotton-spinners for
the proprietor of the mill. A body of men associated for the purposes
of robbery (as a Highland clan in ancient times) shall be animated
by perfect affection, and every member of it be ready to lay down his
life for the life of his chief. But a band of men associated for purposes
of legal production and accumulation is usually animated, it appears,
by no such emotions, and none of them are in anywise willing to give
his life for the life of his chief. Not only are we met by this apparent
anomaly, in moral matters, but by others connected with it, in administration of system. For a servant or a soldier is engaged at a definite rate of wages, for a definite period; but a workman at a rate of
wages variable according to the demand for labour, and with the risk of
being at any time thrown out of his situation by chances of trade. Now,
as, under these contingencies, no action of the affections can take place,
but only an explosive action of *dis*affections, two points offer themselves for consideration in the matter.

The first — How far the rate of wages may be so regulated as not
to vary with the demand for labour.

The second — How far it is possible that bodies of workmen may be
engaged and maintained at such fixed rate of wages (whatever the
state of trade may be), without enlarging or diminishing their number, so as to give them permanent interest in the establishment with
which they are connected, like that of the domestic servants in an old
family, or an esprit de corps, like that of the soldiers in a crack regiment.

13. The first question is, I say, how far it may be possible to fix
the rate of wages, irrespectively of the demand for labour.

Perhaps one of the most curious facts in the history of human
error is the denial by the common political economist of the possibility
of thus regulating wages; while, for all the important, and much of

the unimportant, labour on the earth, wages are already regulated.

We do not sell our prime-ministership by Dutch auction;[2] nor, on the decease of a bishop, whatever may be the general advantages of simony, do we (yet) offer his diocese to the clergyman who will take the episcopacy at the lowest contract. We (with exquisite sagacity of political economy!) do indeed sell commissions; but not openly, generalships: sick, we do not inquire for a physician who takes less than a guinea; litigious, we never think of reducing six-and-eight-pence to four-and-sixpence; caught in a shower, we do not canvass the cabmen, to find one who values his driving at less than sixpence a mile.

It is true that in all these cases there is, and in every conceivable case there must be, ultimate reference to the presumed difficulty of the work, or number of candidates for the office. If it were thought that the labour necessary to make a good physician would be gone through by a sufficient number of students with the prospect of only half-guinea fees, public consent would soon withdraw the unnecessary half-guinea. In this ultimate sense, the price of labour is indeed always regulated by the demand for it; but so far as the practical and immediate administration of the matter is regarded, the best labour always has been, and is, as *all* labour ought to be, paid by an invariable standard.

14. "What!" the reader, perhaps, answers amazedly: "pay good and bad workmen alike?"

Certainly. The difference between one prelate's sermons and his successor's, — or between one physician's opinion and another's — is far greater, as respects the qualities of mind involved, and far more important in result to you personally, than the difference between good and bad laying of bricks (though that is greater than most people suppose). Yet you pay with equal fee, contentedly, the good and bad workmen upon your soul, and the good and bad workmen upon your body; much more may you pay, contentedly, with equal fees, the good and bad workmen upon your house.

"Nay, but I choose my physician and (?) my clergyman, thus indicating my sense of the quality of their work." By all means, also, choose your bricklayer; that is the proper reward of the good workman, to be "chosen." The natural and right system respecting all labour is, that it should be paid at a fixed rate, but the good workman employed, and the bad workman unemployed. The false, unnatural, and destructive system is when the bad workman is allowed to offer his work at half-price, and either take the place of the good, or force him by his competition to work for an inadequate sum.

15. This equality of wages, then, being the first object towards which we have to discover the directest available road, the second is,

2 An auction which moves from a higher price to a lower.

as above stated, that of maintaining constant numbers of workmen in employment, whatever may be the accidental demand for the article they produce.

I believe the sudden and extensive inequalities of demand, which necessarily arise in the mercantile operations of an active nation, constitute the only essential difficulty which has to be overcome in a just organization of labour.

The subject opens into too many branches to admit of being investigated in a paper of this kind; but the following general facts bearing on it may be noted.

The wages which enable any workman to live are necessarily higher, if his work is liable to intermission, than if it is assured and continuous; and however severe the struggle for work may become, the general law will always hold, that men must get more daily pay if, on the average, they can only calculate on work three days a week than they would require if they were sure of work six days a week. Supposing that a man cannot live on less than a shilling a day, his seven shillings he must get, either for three days' violent work, or six days' deliberate work. The tendency of all modern mercantile operations is to throw both wages and trade into the form of a lottery, and to make the workman's pay depend on intermittent exertion, and the principal's profit on dexterously used chance.

16. In what partial degree, I repeat, this may be necessary, in consequence of the activities of modern trade, I do not here investigate; contenting myself with the fact, that in its fatalest aspects it is assuredly unnecessary, and results merely from love of gambling on the part of the masters, and from ignorance and sensuality in the men. The masters cannot bear to let any opportunity of gain escape them, and frantically rush at every gap and breach in the walls of Fortune, raging to be rich, and affronting, with impatient covetousness, every risk of ruin, while the men prefer three days of violent labour, and three days of drunkenness, to six days of moderate work and wise rest. There is no way in which a principal, who really desires to help his workmen, may do it more effectually than by checking these disorderly habits both in himself and them; keeping his own business operations on a scale which will enable him to pursue them securely, not yielding to temptations of precarious gain; and, at the same time, leading his workmen into regular habits of labour and life, either by inducing them rather to take low wages, in the form of a fixed salary, than high wages, subject to the chance of their being thrown out of work; or if this be impossible, by discouraging the system of violent exertion for nominally high day wages, and leading the men to take lower pay for more regular labour.

In effecting any radical changes of this kind, doubtless there would be great inconvenience and loss incurred by all the originators of the movement. That which can be done with perfect convenience and without loss, is not always the thing that most needs to be done, or which we are most imperatively required to do.

17. I have already alluded to the difference hitherto existing between regiments of men associated for purposes of violence, and for purposes of manufacture; in that the former appear capable of self-sacrifice — the latter, not; which singular fact is the real reason of the general lowness of estimate in which the profession of commerce is held, as compared with that of arms. Philosophically, it does not, at first sight, appear reasonable (many writers have endeavoured to prove it unreasonable) that a peaceable and rational person, whose trade is buying and selling, should be held in less honour than an unpeaceable and often irrational person, whose trade is slaying. Nevertheless, the consent of mankind has always, in spite of the philosophers, given precedence to the soldier.

And this is right.

For the soldier's trade, verily and essentially, is not slaying, but being slain. This, without well knowing its own meaning, the world honours it for. A bravo's trade is slaying; but the world has never respected bravos more than merchants: the reason it honours the soldier is, because he holds his life at the service of the State. Reckless he may be — fond of pleasure or of adventure — all kinds of bye-motives and mean impulses may have determined the choice of his profession, and may affect (to all appearance exclusively) his daily conduct in it; but our estimate of him is based on this ultimate fact — of which we are well assured — that, put him in a fortress breach, with all the pleasures of the world behind him, and only death and his duty in front of him, he will keep his face to the front; and he knows that this choice may be put to him at any moment — and has beforehand taken his part — virtually takes such part continually — does, in reality, die daily.

18. Not less is the respect we pay to the lawyer and physician, founded ultimately on their self-sacrifice. Whatever the learning or acuteness of a great lawyer, our chief respect for him depends on our belief that, set in a judge's seat, he will strive to judge justly, come of it what may. Could we suppose that he would take bribes, and use his acuteness and legal knowledge to give plausibility to iniquitous decisions, no degree of intellect would win for him our respect. Nothing will win it, short of our tacit conviction, that in all important acts of his life justice is first with him; his own interest, second.

In the case of a physician, the ground of the honour we render him is clearer still. Whatever his science, we should shrink from him in horror if we found him regard his patients merely as subjects to experiment upon; much more, if we found that, receiving bribes from persons interested in their deaths, he was using his best skill to give poison in the mask of medicine.

Finally, the principle holds with utmost clearness, as it respects clergymen. No goodness of disposition will excuse want of science in a physician or of shrewdness in an advocate; but a clergyman, even though his power of intellect be small, is respected on the presumed ground of his unselfishness and serviceableness.

19. Now, there can be no question but that the tact, foresight, decision, and other mental powers, required for the successful management of a large mercantile concern, if not such as could be compared with those of a great lawyer, general, or divine, would at least match the general conditions of mind required in the subordinate officers of a ship, or of a regiment, or in the curate of a country parish. If, therefore, all the efficient members of the so-called liberal professions are still, somehow, in public estimate of honour, preferred before the head of a commercial firm, the reasons must lie deeper than in the measurement of their several powers of mind.

And the essential reason for such preference will be found to lie in the fact that the merchant is presumed to act always selfishly. His work may be very necessary to the community; but the motive of it is understood to be wholly personal. The merchant's first object in all his dealings must be (the public believe) to get as much for himself, and leave as little to his neighbour (or customer) as possible. Enforcing this upon him, by political statute, as the necessary principle of his action; recommending it to him on all occasions, and themselves reciprocally adopting it, proclaiming vociferously, for law of the universe, that a buyer's function is to cheapen, and a seller's to cheat, — the public, nevertheless, involuntarily condemn the man of commerce for his compliance with their own statement, and stamp him forever as belonging to an inferior grade of human personality.

20. This they will find, eventually, they must give up doing. They must not cease to condemn selfishness; but they will have to discover a kind of commerce which is not exclusively selfish. Or, rather, they will have to discover that there never was, or can be, any other kind of commerce; that this which they have called commerce was not commerce at all, but cozening; and that a true merchant differs as much from a merchant according to laws of modern political economy, as the hero of the *Excursion* from Autolycus.[3] They will find that commerce is an occupation which gentlemen will every day see more need to engage in, rather than in the businesses of talking to men, or slaying them; that, in true commerce, as in true preaching, or true fighting, it is necessary to admit the idea of occasional voluntary loss; — that sixpences have to be lost, as well as lives, under a sense of duty; that the market may have its martyrdoms as well as the pulpit; and trade its heroisms, as well as war.

May have — in the final issue, must have — and only has not had yet, because men of heroic temper have always been misguided in

3 In Wordsworth's poem, the Wanderer is a peddler and a philosopher; Autolycus, in *The Winter's Tale*, is a peddler and a rogue.

their youth into other fields; not recognizing what is in our days, perhaps, the most important of all fields; so that, while many a zealous person loses his life in trying to teach the form of a gospel, very few will lose a hundred pounds in showing the practice of one.

21. The fact is, that people never have had clearly explained to them the true functions of a merchant with respect to other people. I should like the reader to be very clear about this.

Five great intellectual professions, relating to daily necessities of life, have hitherto existed — three exist necessarily, in every civilized nation: —

The Soldier's profession is to *defend* it.

The Pastor's to *teach* it.

The Physician's to *keep it in health*.

The Lawyer's to *enforce justice* in it.

The Merchant's to *provide* for it.

And the duty of all these men is, on due occasion, to *die* for it.

"On due occasion," namely: —

The Soldier, rather than leave his post in battle.

The Physician, rather than leave his post in plague.

The Pastor, rather than teach Falsehood.

The Lawyer, rather than countenance Injustice.

The Merchant — What is *his* "due occasion" of death?

22. It is the main question for the merchant, as for all of us. For, truly, the man who does not know when to die, does not know how to live.

Observe, the merchant's function (or manufacturer's, for in the broad sense in which it is here used the word must be understood to include both) is to provide for the nation. It is no more his function to get profit for himself out of that provision than it is a clergyman's function to get his stipend. The stipend is a due and necessary adjunct, but not the object, of his life, if he be a true clergyman, any more than his fee (or honorarium) is the object of life to a true physician. Neither is his fee the object of life to a true merchant. All three, if true men, have a work to be done irrespective of fee — to be done even at any cost, or for quite the contrary of fee; the pastor's function being to teach, the physician's to heal, and the merchant's, as I have said, to provide. That is to say, he has to understand to their very root the qualities of the thing he deals in, and the means of obtaining or producing it; and he has to apply all his sagacity and energy to the producing or obtaining it in perfect state, and distributing it at the cheapest possible price where it is most needed.

And because the production or obtaining of any commodity involves necessarily the agency of many lives and hands, the merchant becomes in the course of his business the master and governor of large masses of men in a more direct, though less confessed way, than a military officer or pastor; so that on him falls, in great part, the re-

sponsibility for the kind of life they lead; and it becomes his duty, not
only to be always considering how to produce what he sells, in the
purest and cheapest forms, but how to make the various employments
involved in the production, or transference of it, most beneficial to
the men employed.

23. And as into these two functions, requiring for their right exercise the highest intelligence, as well as patience, kindness, and tact,
the merchant is bound to put all his energy, so for their just discharge
he is bound, as soldier or physician is bound, to give up, if need be, his
life, in such way as it may be demanded of him. Two main points
he has in his providing function to maintain: first, his engagements
(faithfulness to engagements being the real root of all possibilities, in
commerce); and, secondly, the perfectness and purity of the thing
provided; so that, rather than fail in any engagement, or consent to any
deterioration, adulteration, or unjust and exorbitant price of that which
he provides, he is bound to meet fearlessly any form of distress,
poverty, or labour, which may, through maintenance of these points,
come upon him.

24. Again: in his office as governor of the men employed by him,
the merchant or manufacturer is invested with a distinctly paternal
authority and responsibility. In most cases, a youth entering a commercial establishment is withdrawn altogether from home influence;
his master must become his father, else he has, for practical and constant help, no father at hand: in all cases the master's authority, together with the general tone and atmosphere of his business, and the
character of the men with whom the youth is compelled in the course
of it to associate, have more immediate and pressing weight than the
home influence, and will usually neutralize it either for good or evil; so
that the only means which the master has of doing justice to the men
employed by him is to ask himself sternly whether he is dealing with
such subordinate as he would with his own son, if compelled by circumstances to take such a position.

Supposing the captain of a frigate saw it right, or were by any
chance obliged, to place his own son in the position of a common sailor;
as he would then treat his son, he is bound always to treat every one
of the men under him. So, also, supposing the master of a manufac-
tory saw it right, or were by any chance obliged, to place his own son
in the position of an ordinary workman; as he would then treat his
son, he is bound always to treat every one of his men. This is the
only effective, true, or practical RULE which can be given on this point
of political economy.

And as the captain of a ship is bound to be the last man to leave
his ship in case of wreck, and to share his last crust with the sailors
in case of famine, so the manufacturer, in any commercial crisis or
distress, is bound to take the suffering of it with his men, and even
to take more of it for himself than he allows his men to feel; as a

father would in a famine, shipwreck, or battle, sacrifice himself for his son.

25. All which sounds very strange: the only real strangeness in the matter being, nevertheless, that it should so sound. For all this is true, and that not partially nor theoretically, but everlastingly and practically: all other doctrine than this respecting matters political being false in premises, absurd in deduction, and impossible in practice, consistently with any progressive state of national life; all the life which we now possess as a nation showing itself in the resolute denial and scorn, by a few strong minds and faithful hearts, of the economic principles taught to our multitudes, which principles, so far as accepted, lead straight to national destruction. . . .

Matthew Arnold

MATTHEW ARNOLD

CHRONOLOGY

1822   Born December 24 at Laleham, Middlesex.

1836–1841   Attended Winchester School and Rugby.

1841   Entered Balliol College, Oxford.

1843   Received Newdigate Poetry Prize.

1844   Graduated from Oxford with second class honors in *Litterae Humaniores*.

1845   Became Fellow of Oriel College, Oxford.

1847   Became private secretary to Lord Lansdowne.

1849   Published *The Strayed Reveller and Other Poems,* by A.

1851   Married; appointed an inspector of schools.

1852   Published *Empedocles on Etna, and Other Poems,* by A.

1853   Published *Poems.*

1855   Published *Poems, Second Series.*

1857–1867   Professor of Poetry at Oxford.

1858   Published *Merope.*

1859   Published *England and the Italian Question,* a pamphlet.

1861   Published *On Translating Homer* and *Popular Education in France.*

1864   Published *A French Eton; or, Middle-Class Education and the State.*

1865   Published *Essays in Criticism.*

1867   Published *On the Study of Celtic Literature* and *New Poems.*

1868   Published *Schools and Universities on the Continent.*

1869   Published *Culture and Anarchy,* in book form.

1870   Published *St. Paul and Protestantism;* received D.C.L. degree at Oxford.

1871   Published *Friendship's Garland.*

1873   Published *Literature and Dogma.*

1875   Published *God and the Bible.*

1877   Published *Last Essays on Church and Religion.*

1879   Published *Mixed Essays.*

1882   Published *Irish Essays, and Others.*

1883   Received a government pension of £250 a year.

1883–1884   Made a lecture tour in America.

1885   Published *Discourses in America.*

1886   Resigned as inspector of schools; visited America a second time.

1888   Died April 15; *Essays in Criticism, Second Series* published posthumously.

Preface to Poems, 1853

❨ This Preface, the most important single essay in literary criticism Arnold ever wrote, was prefixed to the first edition of his *Poems*. He reprinted it, together with the brief Preface to the second edition of the *Poems* (1854), in *Irish Essays and Others* (1882). George Saintsbury has called this Preface "the most important critical document issued in England for something like a generation, and which, as prefixed by a poet to his poetry, admits no competitors in English, except some work of Dryden's and some of Wordsworth's." And another critic has labeled this Preface and Volume III of Ruskin's *Modern Painters* the two most important critical documents of the whole Victorian period. It is important for the student to determine to what extent Arnold is being prescriptive, on the one hand, and merely descriptive, on the other. ❩

In two small volumes of Poems, published anonymously, one in 1849, the other in 1852,[1] many of the Poems which compose the present volume have already appeared. The rest are now published for the first time.

I have, in the present collection, omitted the poem from which the volume published in 1852 took its title. I have done so, not because the subject of it was a Sicilian Greek born between two and three thousand years ago, although many persons would think this a sufficient reason. Neither have I done so because I had, in my own opinion, failed in the delineation which I intended to effect. I intended to delineate the feelings of one of the last of the Greek religious philosophers, one of the family of Orpheus and Musæus, having survived his fellows, living on into a time when the habits of Greek thought and feeling had begun fast to change, character to dwindle, the influence of the Sophists to prevail. Into the feelings of a man so situated there entered much that we are accustomed to consider as exclusively modern; how much the fragments of Empedocles himself which remain to us are sufficient at least to indicate. What those who are familiar only with the great monuments of early Greek genius suppose to be its exclusive characteristics, have disappeared; the calm, the cheerfulness, the disinterested objectivity have disappeared; the dialogue of the mind with itself has commenced; modern problems have presented themselves; we hear already the doubts, we witness the discouragement, of Hamlet and of Faust.

The representation of such a man's feelings must be interesting if consistently drawn. We all naturally take pleasure, says Aristotle, in

[1] *The Strayed Reveller, and Other Poems* (1849) and *Empedocles on Etna, and Other Poems* (1852).

409

any imitation or representation whatever; this is the basis of our love of poetry; and we take pleasure in them, he adds, because all knowledge is naturally agreeable to us; not to the philosopher only, but to mankind at large. Every representation, therefore, which is consistently drawn may be supposed to be interesting, inasmuch as it gratifies this natural interest in knowledge of all kinds. What is *not* interesting is that which does not add to our knowledge of any kind; that which is vaguely conceived and loosely drawn; a representation which is general, indeterminate, and faint, instead of being particular, precise, and firm.

Any accurate representation may therefore be expected to be interesting; but, if the representation be a poetical one, more than this is demanded. It is demanded not only that it shall interest, but also that it shall inspirit and rejoice the reader; that it shall convey a charm, and infuse delight. For the Muses, as Hesiod says, were born that they might be "a forgetfulness of evils, and a truce from cares": and it is not enough that the poet should add to the knowledge of men, it is required of him also that he should add to their happiness. "All art," says Schiller, "is dedicated to joy, and there is no higher and no more serious problem than how to make men happy. The right art is that alone which creates the highest enjoyment."

A poetical work, therefore, is not yet justified when it has been shown to be an accurate and therefore interesting representation; it has to be shown also that it is a representation from which men can derive enjoyment. In presence of the most tragic circumstances, represented in a work of art, the feeling of enjoyment, as is well known, may still subsist: the representation of the most utter calamity, of the liveliest anguish, is not sufficient to destroy it; the more tragic the situation, the deeper becomes the enjoyment; and the situation is more tragic in proportion as it becomes more terrible.

What then are the situations, from the representation of which, though accurate, no poetical enjoyment can be derived? They are those in which the suffering finds no vent in action; in which a continuous state of mental distress is prolonged, unrelieved by incident, hope, or resistance; in which there is everything to be endured, nothing to be done. In such situations there is inevitably something morbid, in the description of them something monotonous. When they occur in actual life, they are painful, not tragic; the representation of them in poetry is painful also.

To this class of situations, poetically faulty as it appears to me, that of Empedocles, as I have endeavoured to represent him, belongs; and I have therefore excluded the poem from the present collection.

And why, it may be asked, have I entered into this explanation respecting a matter so unimportant as the admission or exclusion of the poem in question? I have done so, because I was anxious to avow that the sole reason for its exclusion was that which has been stated

above; and that it has not been excluded in deference to the opinion
which many critics of the present day appear to entertain against subjects chosen from distant times and countries: against the choice, in
short, of any subjects but modern ones.

"The poet," it is said, and by an intelligent critic, " the poet who
would really fix the public attention must leave the exhausted past
and draw his subjects from matters of present import, and *therefore*
both of interest and novelty."

Now this view I believe to be completely false. It is worth examining, inasmuch as it is a fair sample of a class of critical dicta everywhere current at the present day, having a philosophical form and
air, but no real basis in fact; and which are calculated to vitiate the
judgment of readers of poetry, while they exert, so far as they are
adopted, a misleading influence on the practice of those who make it.

What are the eternal objects of poetry, among all nations and at all
times? They are actions; human actions; possessing an inherent interest in themselves, and which are to be communicated in an interesting manner by the art of the poet. Vainly will the latter imagine that
he has everything in his own power; that he can make an intrinsically
inferior action equally delightful with a more excellent one by his
treatment of it. He may indeed compel us to admire his skill, but his
work will possess, within itself, an incurable defect.

The poet, then, has in the first place to select an excellent action;
and what actions are the most excellent? Those, certainly, which most
powerfully appeal to the great primary human affections: to those
elementary feelings which subsist permanently in the race, and which
are independent of time. These feelings are permanent and the same;
that which interests them is permanent and the same also. The mod-
ernness or antiquity of an action, therefore, has nothing to do with
its fitness for poetical representation; this depends upon its inherent
qualities. To the elementary part of our nature, to our passions, that
which is great and passionate is eternally interesting; and interesting
solely in proportion to its greatness and to its passion. A great human
action of a thousand years ago is more interesting to it than a smaller
human action of to-day, even though upon the representation of this
last the most consummate skill may have been expended, and though
it has the advantage of appealing by its modern language, familiar
manners, and contemporary allusions, to all our transient feelings and
interests. These, however, have no right to demand of a poetical work
that it shall satisfy them; their claims are to be directed elsewhere.
Poetical works belong to the domain of our permanent passions; let
them interest these, and the voice of all subordinate claims upon them
is at once silenced.

Achilles, Prometheus, Clytemnestra, Dido, — what modern poem
presents personages as interesting, even to us moderns, as these personages of an "exhausted past"? We have the domestic epic dealing

with the details of modern life which pass daily under our eyes; we have poems representing modern personages in contact with the problems of modern life, moral, intellectual, and social; these works have been produced by poets the most distinguished of their nation and time; yet I fearlessly assert that *Hermann and Dorothea, Childe Harold, Jocelyn,* the *Excursion,*[2] leave the reader cold in comparison with the effect produced upon him by the latter books of the *Iliad,* by the *Oresteia,* or by the episode of Dido. And why is this? Simply because in the three last-named cases the action is greater, the personages nobler, the situations more intense: and this is the true basis of the interest in a poetical work, and this alone.

It may be urged, however, that past actions may be interesting in themselves, but that they are not to be adopted by the modern poet, because it is impossible for him to have them clearly present to his own mind, and he cannot therefore feel them deeply, nor represent them forcibly. But this is not necessarily the case. The externals of a past action, indeed, he cannot know with the precision of a contemporary; but his business is with its essentials. The outward man of Œdipus or of Macbeth, the houses in which they lived, the ceremonies of their courts, he cannot accurately figure to himself; but neither do they essentially concern him. His business is with their inward man; with their feelings and behaviour in certain tragic situations, which engage their passions as men; these have in them nothing local and casual; they are as accessible to the modern poet as to a contemporary.

The date of an action, then, signifies nothing; the action itself, its selection and construction, this is what is all-important. This the Greeks understood far more clearly than we do. The racial difference between their poetical theory and ours consists, as it appears to me, in this: that, with them, the poetical character of the action in itself, and the conduct of it, was the first consideration; with us, attention is fixed mainly on the value of the separate thoughts and images which occur in the treatment of an action. They regarded the whole; we regard the parts. With them the action predominated over the expression of it; with us the expression predominates over the action. Not that they failed in expression, or were inattentive to it; on the contrary, they are the highest models of expression, the unapproached masters of the *grand style.* But their expression is so excellent because it is so admirably kept in its right degree of prominence; because it is so simple and so well subordinated; because it draws its force directly from the pregnancy of the matter which it conveys. For what reason was the Greek tragic poet confined to so limited a range of subjects? Because there are so few actions which unite in themselves, in the

2 Long narrative poems by Goethe, Byron, Lamartine, and Wordsworth, respectively.

highest degree, the conditions of excellence: and it was not thought that on any but an excellent subject could an excellent poem be con structed. A few actions, therefore, eminently adapted for tragedy, maintained almost exclusive possession of the Greek tragic stage. Their significance appeared inexhaustible; they were as permanent problems, perpetually offered to the genius of every fresh poet. This, too, is the reason of what appears to us moderns a certain baldness of expression in Greek tragedy; of the triviality with which we often reproach the remarks of the chorus, where it takes part in the dialogue: that the action itself, the situation of Orestes, or Merope, or Alcmæon,[3] was to stand the central point of interest, unforgotten, absorbing, principal; that no accessories were for a moment to distract the spectator's attention from this; that the tone of the parts was to be perpetually kept down, in order not to impair the grandiose effect of the whole. The terrible old mythic story on which the drama was founded stood, before he entered the theatre, traced in its bare outlines upon the spectator's mind; it stood in his memory as a group of statuary, faintly seen, at the end of a long and dark vista: then came the poet, embodying outlines, developing situations, not a word wasted, not a sentiment capriciously thrown in; stroke upon stroke, the drama proceeded; the light deepened upon the group; more and more it revealed itself to the riveted gaze of the spectator, until at last, when the final words were spoken, it stood before him in broad sunlight, a model of immortal beauty.

This was what a Greek critic demanded; this was what a Greek poet endeavoured to effect. It signified nothing to what time an action belonged. We do not find that the *Persæ* occupied a particularly high rank among the dramas of Æschylus because it represented a matter of contemporary interest; this was not what a cultivated Athenian required. He required that the permanent elements of his nature should be moved; and dramas of which the action, though taken from a long-distant mythic time, yet was calculated to accomplish this in a higher degree than that of the *Persæ*, stood higher in his estimation accordingly. The Greeks felt, no doubt, with their exquisite sagacity of taste, that an action of present times was too near them, too much mixed up with what was accidental and passing, to form a sufficiently grand, detached, and self-subsistent object for a tragic poem. Such objects belonged to the domain of the comic poet, and of the lighter kinds of poetry. For the more serious kinds, for *pragmatic* poetry, to use an excellent expression of Polybius, they were more difficult and severe in the range of subjects which they permitted. Their theory and practice alike, the admirable treatise of Aristotle, and the unrivalled works of their poets, exclaim with a

3 Orestes and Alcmæon avenged the murder of their fathers, Merope of her husband.

thousand tongues — "All depends upon the subject; choose a fitting action, penetrate yourself with the feeling of its situations; this done, everything else will follow."

But for all kinds of poetry alike there was one point on which they were rigidly exacting: the adaptability of the subject to the kind of poetry selected, and the careful construction of the poem.

How different a way of thinking from this is ours! We can hardly at the present day understand what Menander meant, when he told a man who inquired as to the progress of his comedy that he had finished it, not having yet written a single line, because he had constructed the action of it in his mind. A modern critic would have assured him that the merit of his piece depended on the brilliant things which arose under his pen as he went along. We have poems which seem to exist merely for the sake of single lines and passages; not for the sake of producing any total impression. We have critics who seem to direct their attention merely to detached expressions, to the language about the action, not to the action itself. I verily think that the majority of them do not in their hearts believe that there is such a thing as a total-impression to be derived from a poem at all, or to be demanded from a poet; they think the term a commonplace of metaphysical criticism. They will permit the poet to select any action he pleases, and to suffer that action to go as it will, provided he gratifies them with occasional bursts of fine writing, and with a shower of isolated thoughts and images. That is, they permit him to leave their poetical sense ungratified, provided that he gratifies their rhetorical sense and their curiosity. Of his neglecting to gratify these, there is little danger. He needs rather to be warned against the danger of attempting to gratify these alone; he needs rather to be perpetually reminded to prefer his action to everything else; so to treat this, as to permit its inherent excellences to develop themselves, without interruption from the intrusion of his personal peculiarities; most fortunate when he most entirely succeeds in effacing himself, and in enabling a noble action to subsist as it did in nature.

But the modern critic not only permits a false practice; he absolutely prescribes false aims. "A true allegory of the state of one's own mind in a representative history," me poet is told, "is perhaps the highest thing that one can attempt in the way of poetry." And accordingly he attempts it. An allegory of the state of one's own mind, the highest problem of an art which imitates actions! No, assuredly, it is not, it never can be so: no great poetical work has ever been produced with such an aim. Faust itself, in which something of the kind is attempted, wonderful passages as it contains, and in spite of the unsurpassed beauty of the scenes which relate to Margaret, Faust itself, judged as a whole, and judged strictly as a poetical work, is defective: its illustrious author, the greatest poet of modern times, the greatest critic of all times, would have been the first to acknowledge it; he only defended his work, indeed, by asserting it to be "something incommensurable."

The confusion of the present times is great, the multitude of voices counselling different things bewildering, the number of existing works capable of attracting a young writer's attention and of becoming his models, immense. What he wants is a hand to guide him through the confusion, a voice to prescribe to him the aim which he should keep in view, and to explain to him that the value of the literary works which offer themselves to his attention is relative to their power of helping him forward on his road towards this aim. Such a guide the English writer at the present day will nowhere find. Failing this, all that can be looked for, all indeed that can be desired, is, that his attention should be fixed on excellent models; that he may reproduce, at any rate, something of their excellence, by penetrating himself with their works and by catching their spirit, if he cannot be taught to produce what is excellent independently.

Foremost among these models for the English writer stands Shakspeare: a name the greatest perhaps of all poetical names; a name never to be mentioned without reverence. I will venture, however, to express a doubt whether the influence of his works, excellent and fruitful for the readers of poetry, for the great majority, has been an unmixed advantage to the writers of it. Shakspeare indeed chose excellent subjects — the world could afford no better than *Macbeth,* or *Romeo and Juliet,* or *Othello;* he had no theory respecting the necessity of choosing subjects of present import, or the paramount interest attaching to allegories of the state of one's own mind; like all great poets, he knew well what constituted a poetical action; like them, wherever he found such an action, he took it; like them, too, he found his best in past times. But to these general characteristics of all great poets he added a special one of his own; a gift, namely, of happy, abundant, and ingenious expression, eminent and unrivalled: so eminent as irresistibly to strike the attention first in him, and even to throw into comparative shade his other excellences as a poet. Here has been the mischief. These other excellences were his fundamental excellences *as a poet*; what distinguishes the artist from a mere amateur, says Goethe, is *Architectonicè* in the highest sense; that power of execution which creates, forms, and constitutes: not the profoundness of single thoughts, nor the richness of imagery, not the abundance of illustration. But these attractive accessories of a poetical work being more easily seized than the spirit of the whole, and these accessories being possessed by Shakspeare in an unequalled degree, a young writer having recourse to Shakspeare as his model runs great risk of being vanquished and absorbed by them, and, in consequence, of reproducing, according to the measure of his power, these, and these alone. Of this preponding quality of Shakspeare's genius, accordingly, almost the whole of modern English poetry has it appears to me, felt the influence. To the exclusive attention on the part of his imitators to this it is in a great degree owing, that of the majority of modern poetical works the details alone are valuable, the composition worthless. In reading them one is perpetually reminded of that terrible sentence on a modern French poet, — *il dit tout ce qu'il veut, mais malheureusement il n'a rien à dire.*[4]

Let me give an instance of what I mean. I will take it from the works of the very chief among those who seem to have been formed in the school of Shakspeare; of one whose exquisite genius and pathetic death render him forever interesting. I will take the poem of *Isabella, or the Pot of Basil,* by Keats. I choose this rather than the *Endymion,* because the latter work (which a modern critic has classed with the *Faery Queen!*), although undoubtedly there blows through it the breath of genius, is yet as a whole so utterly incoherent, as not strictly to merit the name of a poem at all. The poem of *Isabella,* then, is a perfect treasure-house of graceful and felicitous words and images: almost in every stanza there occurs one of those vivid and picturesque turns of expression, by which the object is made to flash upon the eye of the mind, and which thrill the reader with a sudden delight. This one short poem contains, perhaps, a greater number of happy single expressions which one could quote than all the extant tragedies of Sophocles. But the action, the story? The action in itself is an excellent one; but so feebly is it conceived by the poet, so loosely constructed, that the effect produced by it, in and for itself, is absolutely null. Let the reader, after he has finished the poem of Keats, turn to the same story in the *Decameron*: he will then feel how pregnant and interesting the same action has become in the hands of a great artist, who above all things delineates his object; who subordinates expression to that which it is designed to express.

I have said that the imitators of Shakspeare, fixing their attention on his wonderful gift of expression, have directed their imitation to this, neglecting his other excellences. These excellences, the fundamental excellences of poetical art, Shakspeare no doubt possessed them, — possessed many of them in a splendid degree; but it may perhaps be doubted whether even he himself did not sometimes give scope to his faculty of expression to the prejudice of a higher poetical duty. For we must never forget that Shakspeare is the great poet he is from his skill in discerning and firmly conceiving an excellent action, from his power of intensely feeling a situation, of intimately associating himself with a character; not from his gift of expression, which rather even leads him astray, degenerating sometimes into a fondness for curiosity of expression, into an irritability of fancy, which seems to make it impossible for him to say a thing plainly, even when the press of the action demands the very directest language, or its level character the very simplest. Mr. Hallam, than whom it is im-

4 "he says all that he wishes to say, but unfortunately he has nothing to say."

possible to find a saner and more judicious critic, has had the courage
(for at the present day it needs courage) to remark, how extremely
and faultily difficult Shakspeare's language often is. It is so: you may
find main scenes in some of his greatest tragedies, *King Lear,* for
instance, where the language is so artificial, so curiously tortured, and
so difficult, that every speech has to be read two or three times before its meaning can be comprehended. This over-curiousness of expression is indeed but the excessive employment of a wonderful gift, —
of the power of saying a thing in a happier way than any other man;
nevertheless, it is carried so far that one understands what M. Guizot
meant when he said that Shakspeare appears in his language to have
tried all styles except that of simplicity. He has not the severe and
scrupulous self-restraint of the ancients, partly, no doubt, because he
has a far less cultivated and exacting audience. He has indeed a
far wider range than they had, a far richer fertility of thought; in this
respect he rises above them. In his strong conception of his subject,
in the genuine way in which he is penetrated with it, he resembles
them, and is unlike the moderns. But in the accurate limitation of it,
the conscientious rejection of superfluities, the simple and rigorous
development of it from the first line of his work to the last, he falls
below them, and comes nearer to the moderns. In his chief works,
besides what he has of his own, he has the elementary soundness of
the ancients; he has their important action and their large and broad
manner; but he has not their purity of method. He is therefore a less
safe model; for what he has of his own is personal, and inseparable
from his own rich nature; it may be imitated and exaggerated, it cannot be learned or applied as an art. He is above all suggestive; more
valuable, therefore, to young writers as men than as artists. But clearness of arrangement, rigour of development, simplicity of style, —
these may to a certain extent be learned; and these may, I am convinced, be learned best from the ancients, who, although infinitely
less suggestive than Shakspeare, are thus, to the artist, more instructive.

What then, it will be asked, are the ancients to be our sole models?
the ancients with their comparatively narrow range of experience, and
their widely different circumstances? Not, certainly, that which is
narrow in the ancients, nor that in which we can no longer sympathize.
An action like the action of the *Antigone* of Sophocles, which turns
upon the conflict between the heroine's duty to her brother's corpse
and that to the laws of her country, is no longer one in which it is
possible that we should feel a deep interest. I am speaking too, it will
be remembered, not of the best sources of intellectual stimulus for
the general reader, but of the best models of instruction for the individual writer. This last may certainly learn of the ancients, better than
anywhere else, three things which it is vitally important for him to
know — the all-importance of the choice of a subject; the necessity

of accurate construction; and the subordinate charac..r of expression. He will learn from them how unspeakably superior is the effect of the one moral impression left by a great action treated as a whole, to the effect produced by the most striking single thought or by the happiest image. As he penetrates into the spirit of the great classical works, as he becomes gradually aware of their intense significance, their noble simplicity, and their calm pathos, he will be convinced that it is this effect, unity and profoundness of moral impression, at which the ancient poets aimed; that it is this which constitutes the grandeur of their works, and which makes them immortal. He will desire to direct his own efforts towards producing the same effect. Above all, he will deliver himself from the jargon of modern criticism, and escape the danger of producing poetical works conceived in the spirit of the passing time, and which partake of its transitoriness.

The present age makes great claims upon us; we owe it service, it will not be satisfied without our admiration. I know not how it is, but their commerce with the ancients appears to me to produce, in those who constantly practise it, a steadying and composing effect upon their judgment, not of literary works only, but of men and events in general. They are like persons who have had a very weighty and impressive experience; they are more truly than others under the em- pire of facts, and more independent of the language current among those with whom they live. They wish neither to applaud nor to re- vile their age; they wish to know what it is, what it can give them, and whether this is what they want. What they want, they know very well; they want to educe and cultivate what is best and noblest in themselves; they know, too, that this is no easy task — χαλεπόν, as Pitticus said, χαλεπὸν ἐσθλὸν ἔμμεναι[5] — and they ask themselves sin- cerely whether their age and its literature can assist them in the attempt. If they are endeavouring to practise any art, they remember the plain and simple proceedings of the old artists, who attained their grand results by penetrating themselves with some noble and sig- nificant action, not by inflating themselves with a belief in the pre- eminent importance and greatness of their own times. They do not talk of their mission, nor of interpreting their age, nor of the coming poet; all this, they know, is the mere delirium of vanity; their business is not to praise their age, but to afford to the men who live in it the highest pleasure which they are capable of feeling. If asked to afford this by means of subjects drawn from the age itself, they ask what special fitness the present age has for supplying them. They are told that it is an era of progress, an age commissioned to carry out the great ideas of industrial development and social amelioration. They reply that with all this they can do nothing; that the elements they need for the exercise of their art are great actions, calculated powerfully and delightfully to affect what is permanent in the human

5 "it is hard to be excellent." Pittacus was one of the Seven Sages of Greece.

soul; that so far as the present age can supply such actions, they will gladly make use of them; but that an age wanting in moral grandeur can with difficulty supply such, and an age of spiritual discomfort with difficulty be powerfully and delightfully affected by them.

A host of voices will indignantly rejoin that the present age is inferior to the past neither in moral grandeur nor in spiritual health. He who possesses the discipline I speak of will content himself with remembering the judgments passed upon the present age, in this respect, by the men of strongest head and widest culture whom it has produced; by Goethe and by Niebuhr. It will be sufficient for him that he knows the opinions held by these two great men respecting the present age and its literature; and that he feels assured in his own mind that their aims and demands upon life were such as he would wish, at any rate, his own to be; and their judgment as to what is impeding and disabling such as he may safely follow. He will not, however, maintain a hostile attitude towards the false pretensions of his age: he will content himself with not being overwhelmed by them. He will esteem himself fortunate if he can succeed in banishing from his mind all feelings of contradiction, and irritation, and impatience; in order to delight himself with the contemplation of some noble action of a heroic time, and to enable others, through his representation of it, to delight in it also.

I am far indeed from making any claim, for myself, that I possess this discipline; or for the following poems, that they breathe its spirit. But I say, that in the sincere endeavour to learn and practise, amid the bewildering confusion of our times, what is sound and true in poetical art, I seemed to myself to find the only sure guidance, the only solid footing, among the ancients. They, at any rate, knew what they wanted in art, and we do not. It is this uncertainty which is disheartening, and not hostile criticism. How often have I felt this when reading words of disparagement or of cavil: that it is the uncertainty as to what is really to be aimed at which makes our difficulty, not the dissatisfaction of the critic, who himself suffers from the same uncertainty. *Non me tua fervida terrent Dicta; . . . Dii me terrent, et Jupiter hostis.*[6]

Two kinds of *dilettanti*, says Goethe, there are in poetry: he who neglects the indispensable mechanical part, and thinks he has done enough if he shows spirituality and feeling; and he who seeks to arrive at poetry merely by mechanism, in which he can acquire an artisan's readiness, and is without soul and matter. And he adds, that the first does most harm to art, and the last to himself. If we must be *dilettanti*: if it is impossible for us, under the circumstances amidst which we live, to think clearly, to feel nobly, and to delineate firmly: if we cannot attain to the mastery of the great artists; — let us, at

6 "Your hot words do not frighten me; . . . The gods frighten me, and Jupiter as an enemy."

least, have so much respect for our art as to prefer it to ourselves.
Let us not bewilder our successors; let us transmit to them the practice of poetry, with its boundaries and wholesome regulative laws,
under which excellent works may again, perhaps, at some future
time, be produced, not yet fallen into oblivion through our neglect,
not yet condemned and cancelled by the influence of their eternal
enemy, caprice.

Essays in Criticism

❨ *Essays in Criticism* (1865) contained the following essays, all previously
printed in periodicals: "The Function of Criticism at the Present Time";
"The Literary Influence of Academies"; "Maurice de Guérin"; Eugénie de
Guérin"; "Heinrich Heine"; "Pagan and Mediæval Religious Sentiment";
"Joubert"; "Spinoza"; "Marcus Aurelius." The two essays printed first in the
volume, and reprinted here, were actually written last; they show the principles toward which Arnold had been somewhat inductively working. They
contain, moreover, a sign of the many directions, other than the purely literary, in which Arnold's critical thinking was to lead him: social conditions,
science, philosophy, religion. The first six paragraphs of "The Literary Influence of Academies" have been omitted. ❩

The Function of Criticism at the Present Time

MANY objections have been made to a proposition which, in some
remarks of mine on translating Homer, I ventured to put forth; a
proposition about criticism, and its importance at the present day. I
said: "Of the literature of France and Germany, as of the intellect of
Europe in general, the main effort, for now many years, has been a
critical effort; the endeavour, in all branches of knowledge, theology,
philosophy, history, art, science, to see the object as in itself it really
is." I added, that owing to the operation in English literature of certain causes, "almost the last thing for which one would come to
English literature is just that very thing which now Europe most desires, — criticism"; and that the power and value of English literature was thereby impaired. More than one rejoinder declared that
the importance I here assigned to criticism was excessive, and asserted
the inherent superiority of the creative effort of the human spirit over
its critical effort. And the other day, having been led by a Mr.
Shairp's [1] excellent notice of Wordsworth [2] to turn again to his biog-

---

[1] John Campbell Shairp (1819–1885), critic and professor of poetry at Oxford, 1877–1884.
[2] I cannot help thinking that a practice, common in England during the last

raphy, I found, in the words of this great man, whom I, for one, must always listen to with the profoundest respect, a sentence passed on the critic's business, which seems to justify every possible disparagement of it. Wordsworth says in one of his letters: —

"The writers in these publications" (the Reviews), "while they prosecute their inglorious employment, cannot be supposed to be in a state of mind very favourable for being affected by the finer influences of a thing so pure as genuine poetry."

And a trustworthy reporter of his conversation quotes a more elaborate judgment to the same effect: —

"Wordsworth holds the critical power very low, infinitely lower than the inventive; and he said to-day that if the quantity of time consumed in writing critiques on the works of others were given to original composition, of whatever kind it might be, it would be much better employed; it would make a man find out sooner his own level, and it would do infinitely less mischief. A false or malicious criticism may do much injury to the minds of others; a stupid invention, either in prose or verse, is quite harmless."

It is almost too much to expect of poor human nature, that a man capable of producing some effect in one line of literature, should, for the greater good of society, voluntarily doom himself to impotence and obscurity in another. Still less is this to be expected from men addicted to the composition of the "false or malicious criticism" of which Wordsworth speaks. However, everybody would admit that a false or malicious criticism had better never have been written. Everybody, too, would be willing to admit, as a general proposition, that the critical faculty is lower than the inventive. But is it true that criticism is really, in itself, a baneful and injurious employment; is it true that all time given to writing critiques on the works of others would be much better employed if it were given to original composition, of whatever kind this may be? Is it true that Johnson had better have gone on producing more *Irenes* instead of writing his *Lives of the Poets*; nay, is it certain that Wordsworth himself was better employed in making his Ecclesiastical Sonnets than when he made his celebrated Preface,[3] so full of criticism, and criticism of the works of others? Wordsworth was himself a great critic, and it is to be sincerely regretted that he has not left us more criticism; Goethe was

century, and still followed in France, of printing a notice of this kind, — a notice by á competent critic, — to serve as an introduction to an eminent author's works, might be revived among us with advantage. To introduce all succeeding editions of Wordsworth, Mr. Shairp's notice might, it seems to me, excellently serve; it is written from the point of view of an admirer, nay, of a disciple, and that is right; but then the disciple must be also, as in this case he is, a critic, a man of letters, not, as too often happens, some relation or friend with no qualification for his task except affection for his author. [Arnold's note.] Shairp's notice — "Wordsworth: The Man and the Poet" — had appeared in the *North British Review* for August 1864.

3 Preface to the second edition (1800) of *Lyrical Ballads*.

one of the greatest of critics, and we may sincerely congratulate ourselves that he has left us so much criticism. Without wasting time over the exaggeration which Wordsworth's judgment on criticism clearly contains, or over an attempt to trace the causes, — not difficult, I think, to be traced, — which may have led Wordsworth to this exaggeration, a critic may with advantage seize an occasion for trying his own conscience, and for asking himself of what real service, at any given moment, the practice of criticism either is or may be made to his own mind and spirit, and to the minds and spirits of others.

The critical power is of lower rank than the creative. True; but in assenting to this proposition, one or two things are to be kept in mind. It is undeniable that the exercise of a creative power, that a free creative activity, is the highest function of man; it is proved to be so by man's finding in it his true happiness. But it is undeniable, also, that men may have the sense of exercising this free creative activity in other ways than in producing great works of literature or art; if it were not so, all but a very few men would be shut out from the true happiness of all men. They may have it in well-doing, they may have it in learning, they may have it even in criticising. This is one thing to be kept in mind. Another is, that the exercise of the creative power in the production of great works of literature or art, however high this exercise of it may rank, is not at all epochs and under all conditions possible; and that therefore labour may be vainly spent in attempting it, which might with more fruit be used in preparing for it, in rendering it possible. This creative power works with elements, with materials; what if it has not those materials, those elements, ready for its use? In that case it must surely wait till they are ready. Now, in literature, — I will limit myself to literature, for it is about literature that the question arises, — the elements with which the creative power works are ideas; the best ideas on every matter which literature touches, current at the time. At any rate we may lay it down as certain that in modern literature no manifestation of the creative power not working with these can be very important or fruitful. And I say *current* at the time, not merely accessible at the time; for creative literary genius does not principally show itself in discovering new ideas, that is rather the business of the philosopher. The grand work of literary genius is a work of synthesis and exposition, not of analysis and discovery; its gift lies in the faculty of being happily inspired by a certain intellectual and spiritual atmosphere, by a certain order of ideas, when it finds itself in them; of dealing divinely with these ideas, presenting them in the most effective and attractive combinations, — making beautiful works with them, in short. But it must have the atmosphere, it must find itself amidst the order of ideas, in order to work freely; and these it is not so easy to command. This is why great creative epochs in literature are so rare, this is why there is so much that is unsatisfactory in the productions of many men of real genius; because, for the creation of a master-work of literature two powers must concur, the power of the man and the power of the moment, and the man is not enough without the moment; the creative power has, for its happy exercise, appointed elements, and those elements are not in its own control.

Nay, they are more within the control of the critical power. It is the business of the critical power, as I said in the words already quoted, "in all branches of knowledge, theology, philosophy, history, art, science, to see the object as in itself it really is." Thus it tends, at last, to make an intellectual situation of which the creative power can profitably avail itself. It tends to establish an order of ideas, if not absolutely true, yet true by comparison with that which it displaces; to make the best ideas prevail. Presently these new ideas reach society, the touch of truth is the touch of life, and there is a stir and growth everywhere; out of this stir and growth come the creative epochs of literature.

Or, to narrow our range, and quit these considerations of the general march of genius and of society, — considerations which are apt to become too abstract and impalpable, — every one can see that a poet, for instance, ought to know life and the world before dealing with them in poetry; and life and the world being in modern times very complex things, the creation of a modern poet, to be worth much, implies a great critical effort behind it; else it must be a comparatively poor, barren, and short-lived affair. This is why Byron's poetry had so little endurance in it, and Goethe's so much; both Byron and Goethe had a great productive power, but Goethe's was nourished by a great critical effort providing the true materials for it, and Byron's was not; Goethe knew life and the world, the poet's necessary subjects, much more comprehensively and thoroughly than Byron. He knew a great deal more of them, and he knew them much more as they really are.

It has long seemed to me that the burst of creative activity in our literature, through the first quarter of this century, had about it in fact something premature; and that from this cause its productions are doomed, most of them, in spite of the sanguine hopes which accompanied and do still accompany them, to prove hardly more lasting than the productions of far less splendid epochs. And this prematureness comes from its having proceeded without having its proper data, without sufficient materials to work with. In other words, the English poetry of the first quarter of this century, with plenty of energy, plenty of creative force, did not know enough. This makes Byron so empty of matter, Shelley so incoherent, Wordsworth even, profound as he is, yet so wanting in completeness and variety. Wordsworth cared little for books, and disparaged Goethe. I admire Wordsworth, as he is, so much that I cannot wish him different; and it is vain, no doubt, to imagine such a man different from what he is, to suppose that he *could* have been different. But surely the one thing wanting to make Wordsworth an even greater poet than he is, — his thought richer, and his influence of wider application, — was that he should have read more books, among them, no doubt, those of that Goethe whom he disparaged without reading him.

But to speak of books and reading may easily lead to a misunderstanding here. It was not really books and reading that lacked to our poetry at this epoch: Shelley had plenty of reading, Coleridge had immense reading. Pindar and Sophocles, — as we all say so glibly, and often with so little discernment of the real import of what we are saying, — had not many books; Shakspeare was no deep reader. True; but in the Greece of Pindar and Sophocles, in the England of Shakspeare, the poet lived in a current of ideas in the highest degree animating and nourishing to the creative power; society was, in the fullest measure, permeated by fresh thought, intelligent and alive. And this state of things is the true basis for the creative power's exercise, in this it finds its data, its materials, truly ready for its hand; all the books and reading in the world are only valuable as they are helps to this. Even when this does not actually exist, books and reading may enable a man to construct a kind of semblance of it in his own mind, a world of knowledge and intelligence in which he may live and work. This is by no means an equivalent to the artist for the nationally diffused life and thought of the epochs of Sophocles or Shakspeare; but, besides that it may be a means of preparation for such epochs, it does really constitute, if many share in it, a quickening and sustaining atmosphere of great value. Such an atmosphere the many-sided learning and the long and widely combined critical effort of Germany formed for Goethe, when he lived and worked. There was no national glow of life and thought there as in the Athens of Pericles or the England of Elizabeth. That was the poet's weakness. But there was a sort of equivalent for it in the complete culture and unfettered thinking of a large body of Germans. That was his strength. In the England of the first quarter of this century there was neither a national glow of life and thought, such as we had in the age of Elizabeth, nor yet a culture and a force of learning and criticism such as were to be found in Germany. Therefore the creative power of poetry wanted, for success in the highest sense, materials and a basis; a thorough interpretation of the world was necessarily denied to it.

At first sight it seems strange that out of the immense stir of the French Revolution and its age should not have come a crop of works of genius equal to that which came out of the stir of the great productive time of Greece, or out of that of the Renascence, with its powerful episode the Reformation. But the truth is that the stir of the French Revolution took a character which essentially distinguished

it from such movements as these. These were, in the main, dis-
interestedly intellectual and spiritual movements; movements in which
the human spirit looked for its satisfaction in itself and in the increased play of its own activity. The French Revolution took a political, practical character. The movement, which went on in France
under the old *régime,* from 1700 to 1789, was far more really akin
than that of the Revolution itself to the movement of the Renascence;
the France of Voltaire and Rousseau told far more powerfully upon
the mind of Europe than the France of the Revolution. Goethe reproached this last expressly with having "thrown quiet culture back."
Nay, and the true key to how much in our Byron, even in our Wordsworth, is this! — that they had their source in a great movement of
feeling, not in a great movement of mind. The French Revolution,
however, — that object of so much blind love and so much blind
hatred, — found undoubtedly its motive-power in the intelligence of
men, and not in their practical sense; this is what distinguishes it
from the English Revolution of Charles the First's time. This is what
makes it a more spiritual event than our Revolution, an event of much
more powerful and world-wide interest, though practically less successful; it appeals to an order of ideas which are universal, certain,
permanent. 1789 asked of a thing, Is it rational? 1642 asked of a
thing, Is it legal? or, when it went furthest, Is it according to conscience? This is the English fashion, a fashion to be treated, within
its own sphere, with the highest respect; for its success, within its
own sphere, has been prodigious. But what is law in one place is
not law in another; what is law here today is not law even here to-
morrow; and as for conscience, what is binding on one man's conscience is not binding on another's. The old woman who threw her
stool at the head of the surpliced minister in St. Giles's Church at
Edinburgh obeyed an impulse to which millions of the human race
may be permitted to remain strangers. But the prescriptions of
reason are absolute, unchanging, of universal validity; *to count by
tens is the easiest way of counting* — that is a proposition of which
every one, from here to the Antipodes, feels the force; at least I
should say so if we did not live in a country where it is not impossible
that any morning we may find a letter in the *Times* declaring that a
decimal coinage is an absurdity. That a whole nation should have
been penetrated with an enthusiasm for pure reason, and with an
ardent zeal for making its prescriptions triumph, is a very remarkable
thing, when we consider how little of mind, or anything so worthy
and quickening as mind, comes into the motives which alone, in
general, impel great masses of men. In spite of the extravagant direction given to this enthusiasm, in spite of the crimes and follies in which
it lost itself, the French Revolution derives from the force, truth,
and universality of the ideas which it took for its law, and from the
passion with which it could inspire a multitude for these ideas, a

unique and still living power; it is, — it will probably long remain, — the greatest, the most animating event in history. And as no sincere passion for the things of the mind, even though it turn out in many respects an unfortunate passion, is ever quite thrown away and quite barren of good, France has reaped from hers one fruit — the natural and legitimate fruit though not precisely the grand fruit she expected: she is the country in Europe where *the people* is most alive.

But the mania for giving an immediate political and practical application to all these fine ideas of the reason was fatal. Here an Englishman is in his element: on this theme we can all go on for hours. And all we are in the habit of saying on it has undoubtedly a great deal of truth. Ideas cannot be too much prized in and for themselves, cannot be too much lived with; but to transport them abruptly into the world of politics and practice, violently to revolutionise this world to their bidding, — that is quite another thing. There is the world of ideas and there is the world of practice; the French are often for suppressing the one and the English the other; but neither is to be suppressed. A member of the House of Commons said to me the other day: "That a thing is an anomaly, I consider to be no objection to it whatever." I venture to think he was wrong; that a thing is an anomaly *is* an objection to it, but absolutely and in the sphere of ideas: it is not necessarily, under such and such circumstances, or at such and such a moment, an objection to it in the sphere of politics and practice. Joubert has said beautifully: "C'est la force et le droit qui règlent toutes choses dans le monde; la force en attendant le droit." (Force and right are the governors of this world; force till right is ready.) *Force till right is ready;* and till right is ready, force, the existing order of things, is justified, is the legitimate ruler. But right is something moral, and implies inward recognition, free assent of the will; we are not ready for right, — *right*, so far as we are concerned, *is not ready,* — until we have attained this sense of seeing it and willing it. The way in which for us it may change and transform force, the existing order of things, and become, in its turn, the legitimate ruler of the world, should depend on the way in which, when our time comes, we see it and will it. Therefore for other people enamoured of their own newly discerned right, to attempt to impose it upon us as ours, and violently to substitute their right for our force, is an act of tyranny, and to be resisted. It sets at nought the second great half of our maxim, *force till right is ready.* This was the grand error of the French Revolution; and its movement of ideas, by quitting the intellectual sphere and rushing furiously into the political sphere, ran, indeed, a prodigious and memorable course, but produced no such intellectual fruit as the movement of ideas of the Renascence, and created, in opposition to itself, what I may call an *epoch of concentration.* The great force of that epoch of concentration was England; and the great voice of that epoch of concentration was Burke. It is

the fashion to treat Burke's writings on the French Revolution as superannuated and conquered by the event; as the eloquent but unphilo-
sophical tirades of bigotry and prejudice. I will not deny that they
are often disfigured by the violence and passion of the moment, and
that in some directions Burke's view was bounded, and his observation
therefore at fault. But on the whole, and for those who can make
the needful corrections, what distinguishes these writings is their
profound, permanent, fruitful, philosophical truth. They contain the
true philosophy of an epoch of concentration, dissipate the heavy atmosphere which its own nature is apt to engender round it, and make
its resistance rational instead of mechanical.

But Burke is so great because, almost alone in England, he brings
thought to bear upon politics, he saturates politics with thought. It is
his accident that his ideas were at the service of an epoch of concentration, not of an epoch of expansion; it is his characteristic that
he so lived by ideas, and had such a source of them welling up
within him, that he could float even an epoch of concentration and
English Tory politics with them. It does not hurt him that Dr. Price [4]
and the Liberals were enraged with him; it does not even hurt him
that George the Third and the Tories were enchanted with him. His
greatness is that he lived in a world which neither English Liberalism
nor English Toryism is apt to enter; — the world of ideas, not the
world of catchwords and party habits. So far is it from being really
true of him that he "to party gave up what was meant for mankind,"
that at the very end of his fierce struggle with the French Revolution,
after all his invectives against its false pretensions, hollowness, and
madness, with his sincere convictions of its mischievousness, he can
close a memorandum on the best means of combating it, some of the
last pages he ever wrote, — the *Thoughts on French Affairs*, in December 1791, — with these striking words: —

"The evil is stated, in my opinion, as it exists. The remedy must be
where power, wisdom, and information, I hope, are more united with
good intentions than they can be with me. I have done with this
subject, I believe, for ever. It has given me many anxious moments
for the last two years. *If a great change is to be made in human
affairs, the minds of men will be fitted to it; the general opinions and
feelings will draw that way. Every fear, every hope will forward it;
and then they who persist in opposing this mighty current in human
affairs, will appear rather to resist the decrees of Providence itself,
than the mere designs of men. They will not be resolute and firm,
but perverse and obstinate.*"

That return of Burke upon himself has always seemed to me one
of the finest things in English literature, or indeed in any literature.
That is what I call living by ideas: when one side of a question

4 Richard Price, D.D. (1723–1791), Nonconformist minister and liberal commentator on morals, politics, and economics.

has long had your earnest support, when all your feelings are engaged, when you hear all round you no language but one, when your party talks this language like a steam-engine and can imagine no other, — still to be able to think, still to be irresistibly carried, if so it be, by the current of thought to the opposite side of the question, and, like Balaam, to be unable to speak anything *but what the Lord has put in your mouth.* I know nothing more striking, and I must add that I know nothing more un-English.

For the Englishman in general is like my friend the Member of Parliament, and believes, point-blank, that for a thing to be an anomaly is absolutely no objection to it whatever. He is like the Lord Auckland [5] of Burke's day, who, in a memorandum on the French Revolution, talks of certain "miscreants, assuming the name of philosophers, who have presumed themselves capable of establishing a new system of society." The Englishman has been called a political animal, and he values what is political and practical so much that ideas easily become objects of dislike in his eyes, and thinkers, "miscreants," because ideas and thinkers have rashly meddled with politics and practice. This would be all very well if the dislike and neglect confined themselves to ideas transported out of their own sphere, and meddling rashly with practice; but they are inevitably extended to ideas as such, and to ᵗhe whole life of intelligence; practice is everything, a free play of the mind is nothing. The notion of the free play of the mind upon all subjects being a pleasure in itself, being an object of desire, being an essential provider of elements without which a nation's spirit, whatever compensations it may have for them, must, in the long run, die of inanition, hardly enters into an Englishman's thoughts. It is noticeable that the word *curiosity,* which in other languages is used in a good sense, to mean, as a high and fine quality of man's nature, just this disinterested love of a free play of the mind on all subjects, for its own sake, — it is noticeable, I say, that this word has in our language no sense of the kind, no sense but a rather bad and disparaging one. But criticism, real criticism, is essentially the exercise of this very quality. It obeys an instinct prompting it to try to know the best that is known and thought in the world, irrespectively of practice, politics, and everything of the kind; and to value knowledge and thought as they approach this best, without the intrusion of any other considerations whatever. This is an instinct for which there is, I think, little original sympathy in the practical English nature, and what there was of it has undergone a long benumbing period of blight and suppression in the epoch of concentration which followed the French Revolution.

But epochs of concentration cannot well endure for ever; epochs of expansion, in the due course of things, follow them. Such an epoch of expansion seems to be opening in this country. In the first place

5 William Eden, 1st Baron Auckland (1744–1814), author and diplomat.

all danger of a hostile forcible pressure of foreign ideas upon our practice has long disappeared; like the traveller in the fable, therefore, we begin to wear our cloak a little more loosely. Then, with a long peace, the ideas of Europe steal gradually and amicably in, and mingle, though in infinitesimally small quantities at a time, with our own notions. Then, too, in spite of all that is said about the absorbing and brutalising influence of our passionate material progress, it seems to me indisputable that this progress is likely, though not certain, to lead in the end to an apparition of intellectual life; and that man, after he has made himself perfectly comfortable and has now to determine what to do with himself next, may begin to remember that he has a mind, and that the mind may be made the source of great pleasure. I grant it is mainly the privilege of faith, at present, to discern this end to our railways, our business, and our fortune-making; but we shall see if, here as elsewhere, faith is not in the end the true prophet. Our ease, our travelling, and our unbounded liberty to hold just as hard and securely as we please to the practice to which our notions have given birth, all tend to beget an inclination to deal a little more freely with these notions themselves, to canvass them a little, to penetrate a little into their real nature. Flutterings of curiosity, in the foreign sense of the word, appear amongst us, and it is in these that criticism must look to find its account. Criticism first; a time of true creative activity, perhaps, — which, as I have said, must inevitably be preceded amongst us by a time of criticism, — hereafter, when criticism has done its work.

It is of the last importance that English criticism should clearly discern what rule for its course, in order to avail itself of the field now opening to it, and to produce fruit for the future, it ought to take. The rule may be summed up in one word, — *disinterestedness*. And how is criticism to show disinterestedness? By keeping aloof from what is called "the practical view of things"; by resolutely following the law of its own nature, which is to be a free play of the mind on all subjects which it touches. By steadily refusing to lend itself to any of those ulterior, political, practical considerations about ideas, which plenty of people will be sure to attach to them, which perhaps ought often to be attached to them, which in this country at any rate are certain to be attached to them quite sufficiently, but which criticism has really nothing to do with. Its business is, as I have said, simply to know the best that is known and thought in the world, and by in its turn making this known, to create a current of true and fresh ideas. Its business is to do this with inflexible honesty, with due ability; but its business is to do no more, and to leave alone all questions of practical consequences and applications, questions which will never fail to have due prominence given to them. Else criticism, besides being really false to its own nature, merely continues in the old rut which it has hitherto followed in this country, and will certainly miss the chance now given to it. For what is at present the bane of criticism in this country? It is that practical considerations cling to it and stifle it. It subserves interests not its own. Our organs of criticism are organs of men and parties having practical ends to serve, and with them those practical ends are the first thing and the play of mind the second; so much play of mind as is compatible with the prosecution of those practical ends is all that is wanted. An organ like the *Revue des Deux Mondes,* having for its main function to understand and utter the best that is known and thought in the world, existing, it may be said, as just an organ for a free play of the mind, we have not. But we have the *Edinburgh Review,* existing as an organ of the old Whigs, and for as much play of mind as may suit its being that; we have the *Quarterly Review,* existing as an organ of the Tories, and for as much play of mind as may suit its being that; we have the *British Quarterly Review,* existing as an organ of the political Dissenters, and for as much play of mind as may suit its being that; we have the *Times,* existing as an organ of the common, satisfied, well-to-do Englishman, and for as much play of mind as may suit its being that. And so on through all the various fractions, political and religious, of our society; every fraction has, as such, its organ of criticism, but the notion of combining all fractions in the common pleasure of a free disinterested play of mind meets with no favour. Directly this play of mind wants to have more scope, and to forget the pressure of practical considerations a little, it is checked, it is made to feel the chain. We saw this the other day in the extinction, so much to be regretted, of the *Home and Foreign Review.* Perhaps in no organ of criticism in this country was there so much knowledge, so much play of mind; but these could not save it. The *Dublin Review* subordinates play of mind to the practical business of English and Irish Catholicism, and lives. It must needs be that men should act in sects and parties, that each of these sects and parties should have its organ, and should make this organ subserve the interests of its action; but it would be well, too, that there should be a criticism, not the minister of these interests, not their enemy, but absolutely and entirely independent of them. No other criticism will ever attain any real authority or make any real way towards its end, — the creating a current of true and fresh ideas.

It is because criticism has so little kept in the pure intellectual sphere, has so little detached itself from practice, has been so directly polemical and controversial, that it has so ill accomplished, in this country, its best spiritual work; which is to keep man from a self-satisfaction which is retarding and vulgarising, to lead him towards perfection, by making his mind dwell upon what is excellent in itself, and the absolute beauty and fitness of things. A polemical practical criticism makes men blind even to the ideal imperfection of their practice, makes them willingly assert its ideal perfection, in order the better to secure it against attack; and clearly this is narrowing and baneful for them. If they were reassured on the practical side, speculative considerations of ideal perfection they might be brought to entertain, and their spiritual horizon would thus gradually widen. Sir Charles Adderley [6] says to the Warwickshire farmers: —

"Talk of the improvement of breed! Why, the race we ourselves represent, the men and women, the old Anglo-Saxon race, are the best breed in the whole world. . . . The absence of a too enervating climate, too unclouded skies, and a too luxurious nature, has produced so vigorous a race of people, and has rendered us so superior to all the world."

Mr. Roebuck [7] says to the Sheffield cutlers: —

"I look around me and ask what is the state of England? Is not property safe? Is not every man able to say what he likes? Can you not walk from one end of England to the other in perfect security? I ask you whether, the world over or in past history, there is anything like it? Nothing. I pray that our unrivalled happiness may last."

Now obviously there is a peril for poor human nature in words and thoughts of such exuberant self-satisfaction, until we find ourselves safe in the streets of the Celestial City.

> "Das wenige verschwindet leicht dem Blicke,
> Der vorwärts sieht, wie viel noch übrig bleibt — "

says Goethe; "the little that is done seems nothing when we look forward and see how much we have yet to do." Clearly this is a better line of reflection for weak humanity, so long as it remains on this earthly field of labour and trial.

But neither Sir Charles Adderley nor Mr. Roebuck is by nature inaccessible to considerations of this sort. They only lose sight of them owing to the controversial life we all lead, and the practical form which all speculation takes with us. They have in view opponents whose aim is not ideal, but practical; and in their zeal to uphold their own practice against these innovators, they go so far as even to attribute to this practice an ideal perfection. Somebody has been wanting to introduce a six-pound franchise, or to abolish church-rates, or to collect agricultural statistics by force, or to diminish local self-government. How natural, in reply to such proposals, very likely improper or ill-timed, to go a little beyond the mark and to say stoutly, "Such a race of people as we stand, so superior to all the world! The old Anglo-Savon race, the best breed in the whole world! I pray that our unrivalled happiness may last! I ask you whether, the world over or in past history, there is anything like it?" And so long as

---

[6] Charles Bowyer Adderley, 1st Baron Norton (1814–1905), Conservative politician.

[7] John Arthur Roebuck (1801–1879), prominent radical reformer.

criticism answers this dithyramb by insisting that the old Anglo-Saxon race would be still more superior to all others if it had no church-rates, or that our unrivalled happiness would last yet longer with a six-pound franchise, so long will the strain, "The best breed in the whole world!" swell louder and louder, everything ideal and refining will be lost out of sight, and both the assailed and their critics will remain in a sphere, to say the truth, perfectly unvital, a sphere in which spiritual progression is impossible. But let criticism leave church-rates and the franchise alone, and in the most candid spirit, without a single lurking thought of practical innovation, confront with our dithyramb this paragraph on which I stumbled in a newspaper immediately after reading Mr. Roebuck: —

"A shocking child murder has just been committed at Nottingham. A girl named Wragg left the workhouse there on Saturday morning with her young illegitimate child. The child was soon afterwards found dead on Mapperly Hills, having been strangled. Wragg is in custody."

Nothing but that; but, in juxtaposition with the absolute eulogies of Sir Charles Adderley and Mr. Roebuck, how eloquent, how suggestive are those few lines! "Our old Anglo-Saxon breed, the best in the whole world!" — how much that is harsh and ill-favoured there is in this best! Wragg! If we are to talk of ideal perfection, of "the best in the whole world," has any one reflected what a touch of grossness in our race, what an original shortcoming in the more delicate spiritual perceptions, is shown by the natural growth amongst us of such hideous names, — Higginbottom, Stiggins, Bugg! In Ionia and Attica they were luckier in this respect than "the best race in the world"; by the Ilissus there was no Wragg, poor thing! And "our unrivalled happiness"; — what an element of grimness, bareness, and hideousness mixes with it and blurs it; the workhouse, the dismal Mapperly Hills, — how dismal those who have seen them will remember; — the gloom, the smoke, the cold, the strangled illegitimate child! "I ask you whether, the world over or in past history, there is anything like it?" Perhaps not, one is inclined to answer; but at any rate, in that case, the world is very much to be pitied. And the final touch, — short, bleak and inhuman: Wragg is in custody. The sex lost in the confusion of our unrivalled happiness; or (shall I say?) the superfluous Christian name lopped off by the straightforward vigour of our old Anglo-Saxon breed! There is profit for the spirit in such contrasts as this; criticism serves the cause of perfection by establishing them. By eluding sterile conflict, by refusing to remain in the sphere where alone narrow and relative conceptions have any worth and validity, criticism may diminish its momentary importance, but only in this way has it a chance of gaining admittance for those wider and more perfect conceptions to which all its duty is really owed. Mr. Roebuck will have a poor opinion of an adversary who replies to his defiant songs of triumph only by murmuring under his breath, *Wragg is in custody;* but in no other way will these songs of triumph be induced gradually to moderate themselves, to get rid of what in them is excessive and offensive, and to fall into a softer and truer key.

It will be said that it is a very subtle and indirect action which I am thus prescribing for criticism, and that, by embracing in this manner the Indian virtue of detachment and abandoning the sphere of practical life, it condemns itself to a slow and obscure work. Slow and obscure it may be, but it is the only proper work of criticism. The mass of mankind will never have any ardent zeal for seeing things as they are; very inadequate ideas will always satisfy them. On these inadequate ideas reposes, and must repose, the general practice of the world. That is as much as saying that whoever sets himself to see things as they are will find himself one of a very small circle; but it is only by this small circle resolutely doing its own work that adequate ideas will ever get current at all. The rush and roar of practical life will always have a dizzying and attracting effect upon the most collected spectator, and tend to draw him into its vortex; most of all will this be the case where that life is so powerful as it is in England. But it is only by remaining collected, and refusing to lend himself to the point of view of the practical man, that the critic can do the practical man any service; and it is only by the greatest sincerity in pursuing his own course, and by at last convincing even the practical man of his sincerity, that he can escape misunderstandings which perpetually threaten him.

For the practical man is not apt for fine distinctions, and yet in these distinctions truth and the highest culture greatly find their account. But it is not easy to lead a practical man, — unless you reassure him as to your practical intentions, you have no chance of leading him, — to see that a thing which he has always been used to look at from one side only, which he greatly values, and which, looked at from that side, quite deserves, perhaps, all the prizing and admiring which he bestows upon it, — that this thing, looked at from another side, may appear much less beneficent and beautiful, and yet retain all its claims to our practical allegiance. Where shall we find language innocent enough, how shall we make the spotless purity of our intentions evident enough, to enable us to say to the political Englishman that the British Constitution itself, which, seen from the practical side, looks such a magnificent organ of progress and virtue, seen from the speculative side, — with its compromises, its love of facts, its horror of theory, its studied avoidance of clear thoughts, — that, seen from this side, our august Constitution sometimes looks, — forgive me, shade of Lord Somers! [8] — a colossal machine for the

8 John Somers, Baron Somers (1651–1716), one of the great champions of the English Constitution.

manufacture of Philistines? How is Cobbett to say this and not be misunderstood, blackened as he is with the smoke of a lifelong conflict in the field of political practice? how is Mr. Carlyle to say it and not be misunderstood, after his furious raid into this field with his *Latter-day Pamphlets?* how is Mr. Ruskin, after his pugnacious political economy? I say, the critic must keep out of the region of immediate practice in the political, social, humanitarian sphere if he wants to make a beginning for that more free speculative treatment of things, which may perhaps one day make its benefits felt even in this sphere, but in a natural and thence irresistible manner.

Do what he will, however, the critic will still remain exposed to frequent misunderstandings, and nowhere so much as in this country. For here people are particularly indisposed even to comprehend that without this free disinterested treatment of things, truth and the highest culture are out of he question. So immersed are they in practical life, so accustomed to take all their notions from this life and its processes, that they are apt to think that truth and culture themselves can be reached by the processes of this life, and that it is an impertinent singularity to think of reaching them in any other. "We are all *terræ filii*," [9] cries their eloquent advocate; "all Philistines together. Away with the notion of proceeding by any other course than the course dear to the Philistines; let us have a social movement, let us organise and combine a party to pursue truth and new thought, let us call it *the liberal party*, and let us all stick to each other, and back each other up. Let us have no nonsense about independent criticism, and intellectual delicacy, and the few and the many. Don't let us trouble ourselves about foreign thought; we shall invent the whole thing for ourselves as we go along. If one of us speaks well, applaud him; if one of us speaks ill, applaud him too; we are all in the same movement, we are all liberals, we are all in pursuit of truth." In this way the pursuit of truth becomes really a social, practical, pleasurable affair, almost requiring a chairman, a secretary, and advertisements; with the excitement of an occasional scandal, with a little resistance to give the happy sense of difficulty overcome; but, in general, plenty of bustle and very little thought. To act is so easy, as Goethe says; to think is so hard! It is true that the critic has many temptations to go with the stream, to make one of the party movement, one of these *terræ filii;* it seems ungracious to refuse to be a *terræ filius* when so many excellent people are; but the critic's duty is to refuse, or, if resistance is vain, at least to cry with Obermann: *Périssons en résistant.*[10]

How serious a matter it is to try and resist, I had ample opportunity of experiencing when I ventured some time ago to criticise the cel-

[9] "sons of the earth."
[10] "Let us die resisting." E. P. de Senancour, author of *Obermann,* was a major influence on Arnold.

ebrated first volume of Bishop Colenso.[11] The echoes of the storm
which was then raised I still, from time to time, hear grumbling round
me. That storm arose out of a misunderstanding almost inevitable.
It is a result of no little culture to attain to a clear perception that science and religion are two wholly different things. The multitude will
for ever confuse them; but happily that is of no great real importance,
for while the multitude imagines itself to live by its false science, it
does really live by its true religion. Dr. Colenso, however, in his first
volume did all he could to strengthen the confusion, and to make it
dangerous. He did this with the best intentions, I freely admit, and
with the most candid ignorance that this was the natural effect of
what he was doing; but, says Joubert, "Ignorance, which in matters of
morals extenuates the crime, is itself, in intellectual matters, a crime
of the first order." [12] I criticised Bishop Colenso's speculative confusion. Immediately there was a cry raised: "What is this? here is a
liberal attacking a liberal. Do not you belong to the movement? are
you not a friend of truth? Is not Bishop Colenso in pursuit of truth?
then speak with proper respect of his book. Dr. Stanley is another
friend of truth, and you speak with proper respect of his book; why
make these invidious differences? both books are excellent, admirable,
liberal; Bishop Colenso's perhaps the most so, because it is the boldest,
and will have the best practical consequences for the liberal cause.
Do you want to encourage to the attack of a brother liberal his, and
your, and our implacable enemies, the *Church and State Review* or the
Record, — the High Church rhinoceros and the Evangelical hyaena?
Be silent, therefore; or rather speak, speak as loud as ever you can!
and go into ecstasies over the eighty and odd pigeons."

But criticism cannot follow this coarse and indiscriminate method.
It is unfortunately possible for a man in pursuit of truth to write a
book which reposes upon a false conception. Even the practical consequences of a book are to genuine criticism no recommendation of it,
if the book is, in the highest sense, blundering. I see that a lady who
herself, too, is in pursuit of truth, and who writes with great ability,

11 So sincere is my dislike to all personal attack and controversy, that I
abstain from reprinting, at this distance of time from the occasion which called
them forth, the essays in which I criticised Dr. Colenso's book; I feel bound,
however, after all that has passed, to make here a final declaration, of my sincere impenitence for having published them. Nay, I cannot forbear repeating
yet once more, for his benefit and that of his readers, this sentence from my
original remarks upon him. *There is truth of science and truth of religion;
truth of science does not become truth of religion till it is made religious.* Let
us have all the science there is from the men of science; from the men of
religion let us have religion. [Arnold's note.] John William Colenso (1814–
1883), Bishop of Natal, had published in 1862 *The Pentateuch and Book of
Joshua Critically Examined*, a work in historical criticism of the Bible which
caused much religious furor.

12 It has been said that I make it "a crime against literary criticism and the
higher culture to attempt to inform the ignorant." Need I point out that the
ignorant are not informed by being confirmed in a confusion? [Arnold's note.]

but a little too much, perhaps, under the influence of the practical
spirit of the English liberal movement, classes Bishop Colenso's book
and M. Renan's together, in her survey of the religious state of Europe, as facts of the same order, works, both of them, of "great importance"; "great ability, power, and skill"; Bishop Colenso's, perhaps,
the most powerful; at least, Miss Cobbe gives special expression to
her gratitude that to Bishop Colenso "has been given the strength to
grasp, and the courage to teach, truths of such deep import." In the
same way, more than one popular writer has compared him to Luther.
Now it is just this kind of false estimate which the critical spirit is,
it seems to me, bound to resist. It is really the strongest possible
proof of the low ebb at which, in England, the critical spirit is, that
while the critical hit in the religious literature of Germany is Dr.
Strauss's book, in that of France M. Renan's book, the book of
Bishop Colenso is the critical hit in the religious literature of England. Bishop Colenso's book reposes on a total misconception of the
essential elements of the religious problem, as that problem is now
presented for solution. To criticism, therefore, which seeks to have
the best that is known and thought on this problem, it is, however
well meant, of no importance whatever. M. Renan's book attempts a
new synthesis of the elements furnished to us by the Four Gospels.
It attempts, in my opinion, a synthesis, perhaps premature, perhaps
impossible, certainly not successful. Up to the present time, at any
rate, we must acquiesce in Fleury's sentence on such recastings of
the Gospel story: *Quiconque s'imagine la pouvoir mieux écrire, ne
l'entend pas.*[13] M. Renan had himself passed by anticipation a like
sentence on his own work, when he said: "If a new presentation of
the character of Jesus were offered to me, I would not have it; its
very clearness would be, in my opinion, the best proof of its insufficiency." His friends may with perfect justice rejoin that at the
sight of the Holy Land, and of the actual scene of the Gospel-story,
all the current of M. Renan's thoughts may have naturally changed,
and a new casting of that story irresistibly suggested itself to him;
and that this is just a case for applying Cicero's maxim: Change of
mind is not inconsistency — *nemo doctus unquam mutationem consilii
inconstantiam dixit esse.*[14] Nevertheless, for criticism, M. Renan's
first thought must still be the truer one, as long as his new casting
so fails more fully to commend itself, more fully (to use Coleridge's
happy phrase about the Bible) to *find* us. Still M. Renan's attempt is,
for criticism, of the most real interest and importance, since, with all
its difficulty, a fresh synthesis of the New Testament *data* — not a
making war on them, in Voltaire's fashion, not a leaving them out
of mind, in the world's fashion, but the putting a new construction
upon them, the taking them from under the old, traditional, conven-

13 "Whoever thinks he can write it better does not understand it."
14 "no learned person has ever said that change of mind is inconsistency."

tional point of view and placing them under a new one, — is the very essence of the religious problem, as now presented; and only by efforts in this direction can it receive a solution.

Again, in the same spirit in which she judges Bishop Colenso, Miss Cobbe, like so many earnest liberals of our practical race, both here and in America, herself sets vigorously about a positive reconstruction of religion, about making a religion of the future out of hand, or at least setting about making it. We must not rest, she and they are always thinking and saying, in negative criticism, we must be creative and constructive; hence we have such works as her recent *Religious Duty*, and works still more considerable, perhaps, by others, which will be in every one's mind. These works often have much ability; they often spring out of sincere convictions, and a sincere wish to do good; and they sometimes, perhaps, do good. Their fault is (if I may be permitted to say so) one which they have in common with the British College of Health, in the New Road. Every one knows the British College of Health; it is that building with the lion and the statue of the Goddess Hygeia before it; at least I am sure about the lion, though I am not absolutely certain about the Goddess Hygeia. This building does credit, perhaps, to the resources of Dr. Morrison [15] and his disciples; but it falls a good deal short of one's idea of what a British College of Health ought to be. In England, where we hate public interference and love individual enterprise, we have a whole crop of places like the British College of Health; the grand name without the grand thing. Unluckily, creditable to individual enterprise as they are, they tend to impair our taste by making us forget what more grandiose, noble, or beautiful character properly belongs to a public institution. The same may be said of the religions of the future of Miss Cobbe and others. Creditable, like the British College of Health, to the resources of their authors, they yet tend to make us forget what more grandiose, noble, or beautiful character properly belongs to religious constructions. The historic religions, with all their faults, have had this; it certainly belongs to the religious sentiment, when it truly flowers, to have this; and we impoverish our spirit if we allow a religion of the future without it. What then is the duty of criticism here? To take the practical point of view, to applaud the liberal movement and all its works, — its New Road religions of the future into the bargain, — for their general utility's sake? By no means; but to be perpetually dissatisfied with these works, while they perpetually fall short of a high and perfect ideal.

For criticism, these are elementary laws; but they never can be popular, and in this country they have been very little followed, and one meets with immense obstacles in following them. That is a reason for asserting them again and again. Criticism must maintain its inde-

---

15 James Morrison (1770–1840), seller of Morrison's Pills as universal cure-alls.

pendence of the practical spirit and its aims. Even with well-meant
efforts of the practical spirit it must express dissatisfaction, if in the
sphere of the ideal they seem impoverishing and limiting. It must
not hurry on to the goal because of its practical importance. It must
be patient, and know how to wait; and flexible, and know how to attach itself to things and how to withdraw from them. It must be apt
to study and praise elements that for the fulness of spiritual perfection
are wanted, even though they belong to a power which in the practical sphere may be maleficent. It must be apt to discern the spiritual
shortcomings or illusions of powers that in the practical sphere may be
beneficent. And this without any notion of favouring or injuring, in
the practical sphere, one power or the other; without any notion of
playing off, in this sphere, one power against the other. When one
looks, for instance, at the English Divorce Court, — an institution
which perhaps has its practical conveniences, but which in the ideal
sphere is so hideous; an institution which neither makes divorce impossible nor makes it decent, which allows a man to get rid of his wife,
or a wife of her husband, but makes them drag one another first, for
the public edification, through a mire of unutterable infamy, — when
one looks at this charming institution, I say, with its crowded trials,
its newspaper reports, and its money compensations, this institution
in which the gross unregenerate British Philistine has indeed stamped
an image of himself, — one may be permitted to find the marriage
theory of Catholicism refreshing and elevating. Or when Protestantism,
in virtue of its supposed rational and intellectual origin, gives the
law to criticism too magisterially, criticism may and must remind it
that its pretensions, in this respect, are illusive and do it harm; that
the Reformation was a moral rather than an intellectual event; that
Luther's theory of grace no more exactly reflects the mind of the
spirit than Bossuet's philosophy of history reflects it; and that there is
no more antecedent probability of the Bishop of Durham's stock of
ideas being agreeable to perfect reason than of Pope Pius the Ninth's.
But criticism will not on that account forget the achievements of
Protestantism in the practical and moral sphere; nor that, even in
the intellectual sphere, Protestantism, though in a blind and stumbling
manner, carried forward the Renascence, while Catholicism threw
itself violently across its path.

I lately heard a man of thought and energy contrasting the want of
ardour and movement which he now found amongst young men in
this country with what he remembered in his own youth, twenty years
ago. "What reformers we were then!" he exclaimed; "What a zeal
we had! how we canvassed every institution in Church and State, and
were prepared to remodel them all on first principles!" He was inclined to regret, as a spiritual flagging, the lull which he saw. I am
disposed rather to regard it as a pause in which the turn to a new
mode of spiritual progress is being accomplished. Everything was long

seen, by the young and ardent amongst us, in inseparable connection
with politics and practical life. We have pretty well exhausted the
benefits of seeing things in this connection, we have got all that can be
got by so seeing them. Let us try a more disinterested mode of seeing
them; let us betake ourselves more to the serener life of the mind and
spirit. This life, too, may have its excesses and dangers; but they are
not for us at present. Let us think of quietly enlarging our stock of
true and fresh ideas, and not, as soon as we get an idea or half an idea,
be running out with it into the street, and trying to make it rule there.
Our ideas will, in the end, shape the world all the better for maturing
a little. Perhaps in fifty years' time it will in the English House of
Commons be an objection to an institution that it is an anomaly, and
my friend the Member of Parliament will shudder in his grave. But
let us in the meanwhile rather endeavour that in twenty years' time
it may, in English literature, be an objection to a proposition that it is
absurd. That will be a change so vast, that the imagination almost
fails to grasp it. *Ab integro sæclorum nascitur ordo.*[16]

If I have insisted so much on the course which criticism must take
where politics and religion are concerned, it is because, where these
burning matters are in question, it is more likely to go astray. I have
wished, above all, to insist on the attitude which criticism should adopt
towards things in general; on its right tone and temper of mind. But
then comes another question as to the subject-matter which literary
criticisms should most seek. Here, in general, its course is determined
for it by the idea which is the law of its being; the idea of a disinterested endeavour to learn and propagate the best that is known and
thought in the world, and thus to establish a current of fresh and true
ideas. By the very nature of things, as England is not all the world,
much of the best that is known and thought in the world cannot be of
English growth, must be foreign; by the nature of things, again, it is
just this that we are least likely to know, while English thought is
streaming in upon us from all sides, and takes excellent care that we
shall not be ignorant of its existence. The English critic of literature,
therefore, must dwell much on foreign thought, and with particular
heed on any part of it, which, while significant and fruitful in itself,
is for any reason specially likely to escape him. Again, judging is often
spoken of as the critic's one business, and so in some sense it is; but
the judgment which almost insensibly forms itself in a fair and clear
mind, along with fresh knowledge, is the valuable one; and thus knowledge, and ever fresh knowledge, must be the critic's great concern for
himself. And it is by communicating fresh knowledge, and letting his
own judgment pass along with it, — but insensibly, and in the second
place, not the first, as a sort of companion and clue, not as an abstract
lawgiver, — that the critic will generally do most good to his readers.
Sometimes, no doubt, for the sake of establishing an author's place

16 "Order is born from the renewal of the ages."

in literature, and his relation to a central standard (and if this is not done, how are we to get at our *best in the world*?), criticism may have to deal with a subject-matter so familiar that fresh knowledge is out of the question, and then it must be all judgment; an enunciation and detailed application of principles. Here the great safeguard is never to let oneself become abstract, always to retain an intimate and lively consciousness of the truth of what one is saying, and, the moment this fails us, to be sure that something is wrong. Still under all circumstances, this mere judgment and application of principles is, in itself, not the most satisfactory work to the critic; like mathematics, it is tautological, and cannot well give us, like fresh learning, the sense of creative activity.

But stop, some one will say; all this talk is of no practical use to us whatever; this criticism of yours is not what we have in our minds when we speak of criticism; when we speak of critics and criticism, we mean critics and criticism of the current English literature of the day; when you offer to tell criticism its function, it is to this criticism that we expect you to address yourself. I am sorry for it, for I am afraid I must disappoint these expectations. I am bound by my own definition of criticism: *a disinterested endeavour to learn and propagate the best that is known and thought in the world*. How much of current English literature comes into this "best that is known and thought in the world"? Not very much, I fear; certainly less, at this moment, than of the current literature of France or Germany. Well, then, am I to alter my definition of criticism, in order to meet the requirements of a number of practising English critics, who, after all, are free in their choice of a business? That would be making criticism lend itself just to one of those alien practical considerations, which, I have said, are so fatal to it. One may say, indeed, to those who have to deal with the mass — so much better disregarded — of current English literature, that they may at all events endeavour, in dealing with this, to try it, so far as they can, by the standard of the best that is known and thought in the world; one may say, that to get anywhere near this standard, every critic should try and possess one great literature, at least, besides his own; and the more unlike his own, the better. But, after all, the criticism I am really concerned with, — the criticism which alone can much help us for the future, the criticism which, throughout Europe, is at the present day meant, when so much stress is laid on the importance of criticism and the critical spirit, — is a criticism which regards Europe as being, for intellectual and spiritual purposes, one great confederation, bound to a joint action and working to a common result; and whose members have, for their proper outfit, a knowledge of Greek, Roman, and Eastern antiquity, and of one another. Special, local, and temporary advantages being put out of account, that modern nation will in the intellectual and spiritual sphere make most progress, which most thoroughly carries out this program. And what is that but saying that we too, all of us, as individuals, the more thoroughly we carry it out, shall make the more progress?

There is so much inviting us! — what are we to take? what will nourish us in growth towards perfection? That is the question which, with the immense field of life and of literature lying before him, the critic has to answer; for himself first, and afterwards for others. In this idea of the critic's business the essays brought together in the following pages have had their origin; in this idea, widely different as are their subjects, they have, perhaps, their unity.

I conclude with what I said at the beginning: to have the sense of creative activity is the great happiness and the great proof of being alive, and it is not denied to criticism to have it; but then criticism must be sincere, simple, flexible, ardent, ever widening its knowledge. Then it may have, in no contemptible measure, a joyful sense of creative activity; a sense which a man of insight and conscience will prefer to what he might derive from a poor, starved, fragmentary, inadequate creation. And at some epochs no other creation is possible.

Still, in full measure, the sense of creative activity belongs only to genuine creation; in literature we must never forget that. But what true man of letters ever can forget it? It is no such common matter for a gifted nature to come into possession of a current of true and living ideas, and to produce amidst the inspiration of them, that we are likely to underrate it. The epochs of Æschylus and Shakspeare make us feel their pre-eminence. In an epoch like those is, no doubt, the true life of literature; there is the promised land, towards which criticism can only beckon. That promised land it will not be ours to enter, and we shall die in the wilderness: but to have desired to enter it, to have saluted it from afar, is already, perhaps, the best distinction among contemporaries; it will certainly be the best title to esteem with posterity.

The Literary Influence of Academies

. . . What are the essential characteristics of the spirit of our nation? Not, certainly, an open and clear mind, not a quick and flexible intelligence. Our greatest admirers would not claim for us that we have these in a pre-eminent degree; they might say that we had more of them than our detractors gave us credit for; but they would not assert them to be our essential characteristics. They would rather allege, as our chief spiritual characteristics, energy and honesty; and, if we are judged favourably and positively, not invidiously and negatively, our chief characteristics are no doubt, these: — energy and honesty, not an open and clear mind, not a quick and flexible intelligence. Openness of mind and flexibility of intelligence were very signal character-

istics of the Athenian people in ancient times; everybody will feel
that. Openness of mind and flexibility of intelligence are remarkable
characteristics of the French people in modern times; at any rate, they
strikingly characterise them as compared with us; I think everybody,
or almost everybody, will feel that. I will not now ask what more the
Athenian or the French spirit has than this, nor what shortcomings
either of them may have as a set-off against this; all I want now to
point out is that they have this, and that we have it in a much lesser
degree. Let me remark, however, that not only in the moral sphere,
but also in the intellectual and spiritual sphere, energy and honesty
are most important and fruitful qualities; that, for instance, of what
we call genius energy is the most essential part. So, by assigning to
a nation energy and honesty as its chief spiritual characteristics, — by
refusing to it, as at all eminent characteristics, openness of mind and
flexibility of intelligence, — we do not by any means, as some people
might at first suppose, relegate its importance and its power of manifesting itself with effect from the intellectual to the moral sphere. We
only indicate its probable special line of successful activity in the intellectual sphere, and, it is true, certain imperfections and failings
to which, in this sphere, it will always be subject. Genius is mainly
an affair of energy, and poetry is mainly an affair of genius; therefore
a nation whose spirit is characterised by energy may well be eminent
in poetry; — and we have Shakspeare. Again, the highest reach of
science is, one may say, an inventive power, a faculty of divination,
akin to the highest power exercised in poetry; therefore, a nation
whose spirit is characterised by energy may well be eminent in
science; — and we have Newton. Shakspeare and Newton: in the
intellectual sphere there can be no higher names. And what that
energy, which is the life of genius, above everything demands and insists upon, is freedom; entire independence of all authority, prescription,
and routine, — the fullest room to expand as it will. Therefore, a
nation whose chief spiritual characteristic is energy, will not be very
apt to set up, in intellectual matters, a fixed standard, an authority,
like an academy. By this it certainly escapes certain real inconveniences and dangers, and it can, at the same time, as we have seen,
reach undeniably splendid heights in poetry and science. On the other
hand, some of the requisites of intellectual work are specially the affair
of quickness of mind and flexibility of intelligence. The form, the
method of evolution, the precision, the proportions, the relations of
the parts to the whole, in an intellectual work, depend mainly upon
them. And these are the elements of an intellectual work which are
really most communicable from it, which can most be learned and
adopted from it, which have, therefore, the greatest effect upon the
intellectual performance of others. Even in poetry, these requisites
are very important; and the poetry of a nation, not eminent for the
gifts on which they depend, will, more or less, suffer by this short-

coming. In poetry, however, they are, after all, secondary, and energy is the first thing; but in prose they are of first-rate importance. In its prose literature, therefore, and in the routine of intellectual work generally, a nation with no particular gifts for these will not be so successful. These are what, as I have said, can to a certain degree be learned and appropriated, while the free activity of genius cannot. Academies consecrate and maintain them, and, therefore, a nation with an eminent turn for them naturally establishes academies. So far as routine and authority tend to embarrass energy and inventive genius, academies may be said to be obstructive to energy and inventive genius, and, to this extent, to the human spirit's general advance. But then this evil is so much compensated by the propagation, on a large scale, of the mental aptitudes and demands which an open mind and a flexible intelligence naturally engender, genius itself, in the long run, so greatly finds its account in this propagation, and bodies like the French Academy have such power for promoting it, that the general advance of the human spirit is perhaps, on the whole, rather furthered than impeded by their existence.

How much greater is our nation in poetry than prose! how much better, in general, do the productions of its spirit show in the qualities of genius than in the qualities of intelligence! One may constantly remark this in the work of individuals; how much more striking, in general, does any Englishman, — of some vigour of mind, but by no no means a poet, — seem in his verse than in his prose! His verse partly suffers from his not being really a poet, partly, no doubt, from the very same defects which impair his prose, and he cannot express himself with thorough success in it. But how much more powerful a personage does he appear in it, by dint of feeling, and of originality and movement of ideas, than when he is writing prose! With a Frenchman of like stamp, it is just the reverse: set him to write poetry, he is limited, artificial, and impotent; set him to write prose, he is free, natural, and effective. The power of French literature is in its prose-writers, the power of English literature is in its poets. Nay, many of the celebrated French poets depend wholly for their fame upon the qualities of intelligence which they exhibit, — qualities which are the distinctive support of prose; many of the celebrated English prose-writers depend wholly for their fame upon the qualities of genius and imagination which they exhibit, — qualities which are the distinctive support of poetry. But, as I have said, the qualities of genius are less transferable than the qualities of intelligence; less can be immediately learned and appropriated from their product; they are less direct and stringent intellectual agencies, though they may be more beautiful and divine. Shakspeare and our great Elizabethan group were certainly more gifted writers than Corneille and his group; but what was the sequel to this great literature, this literature of genius, as we may call it, stretching from Marlowe to Milton? What

did it lead up to in English literature? To our provincial and second-
rate literature of the eighteenth century. What, on the other hand,
was the sequel to the literature of the French "great century," to this
literature of intelligence, as, by comparison with our Elizabethan
literature, we may call it; what did it lead up to? To the French
literature of the eighteenth century, one of the most powerful and
pervasive intellectual agencies that have ever existed, — the greatest
European force of the eighteenth century. In science, again, we had
Newton, a genius of the very highest order, a type of genius in
science, if ever there was one. On the continent, as a sort of counterpart to Newton, there was Leibnitz; a man, it seems to me (though
on these matters I speak under correction), of much less creative
energy of genius, much less power of divination than Newton, but
rather a man of admirable intelligence, a type of intelligence in
science, if ever there was one. Well, and what did they each directly
lead up to in science? What was the intellectual generation that
sprang from each of them? I only repeat what the men of science
have themselves pointed out. The man of genius was continued by
the English analysts of the eighteenth century, comparatively powerless and obscure followers of the renowned master; the man of intelligence was continued by successors like Bernouilli, Euler, Lagrange,
and Laplace,[1] the greatest names in modern mathematics.

What I want the reader to see is, that the question as to the utility
of academies to the intellectual life of a nation is not settled when
we say, for instance: "Oh, we have never had an academy, and yet
we have, confessedly, a very great literature." It still remains to be
asked: "What sort of a great literature? a literature great in the special
qualities of genius, or great in the special qualities of intelligence?" If
in the former, it is by no means sure that either our literature, or the
general intellectual life of our nation, has got already, without academies, all that academies can give. Both the one and the other may
very well be somewhat wanting in those qualities of intelligence, out of
a lively sense for which a body like the French Academy, as I have
said, springs, and which such a body does a great deal to spread and
confirm. Our literature, in spite of the genius manifested in it, may
fall short in form, method, precision, proportions, arrangement, — all
of them, I have said, things where intelligence proper comes in. It
may be comparatively weak in prose, that branch of literature where
intelligence proper is, so to speak, all in all. In this branch it may show
many grave faults to which the want of a quick, flexible intelligence,
and of the strict standard which such an intelligence tends to impose,
makes it liable; it may be full of haphazard, crudeness, provincialism,

---

1 Daniel Bernouilli (1700–1782) and Leonhard Euler (1707–1783) were
Swiss mathematicians; Joseph Louis, Comte Lagrange (1736–1813) and Pierre
Simon, Marquis de Laplace (1749–1827) were French mathematicians, the
latter also an astronomer.

eccentricity, violence, blundering. It may be a less stringent and effective intellectual agency, both upon our own nation and upon the world at large, than other literatures which show less genius, perhaps, but more intelligence.

The right conclusion certainly is that we should try, so far as we can, to make up our shortcomings; and that to this end, instead of always fixing our thoughts upon the points in which our literature, and our intellectual life generally, are strong, we should, from time to time, fix them upon those in which they are weak, and so learn to perceive clearly what we have to amend. What is our second great spiritual characteristic, — our honesty, — good for, if it is not good for this? But it will, — I am sure it will, — more and more, as time goes on, be found good for this.

Well, then, an institution like the French Academy, — an institution owing its existence to a national bent towards the things of the mind, towards culture, towards clearness, correctness and propriety in thinking and speaking, and, in its turn, promoting this bent, — sets standards in a number of directions, and creates, in all these directions, a force of educated opinion, checking and rebuking those who fall below these standards, or who set them at nought. Educated opinion exists here as in France; but in France the Academy serves as a sort of centre and rallying-point to it, and gives it a force which it has not got here. Why is all the *journeyman-work* of literature, as I may call it, so much worse done here than it is in France? I do not wish to hurt anyone's feelings; but surely this is so. Think of the difference between our books of reference and those of the French, between our biographical dictionaries (to take a striking instance) and theirs; think of the difference between the translations of the classics turned out for Mr. Bohn's library and those turned out for M. Nisard's collection! [2] As a general rule, hardly any one amongst us, who knows French and German well, would use an English book of reference when he could get a French or German one; or would look at an English prose translation of an ancient author when he could get a French or German one. It is not that there do not exist in England, as in France, a number of people perfectly well able to discern what is good, in these things, from what is bad, and preferring what is good; but they are isolated, they form no powerful body of opinion, they are not strong enough to set a standard, up to which even the journeyman-work of literature must be brought, if it is to be vendible. Ignorance and charlatanism in work of this kind are always trying to pass off their wares as excellent, and to cry down criticism as the voice of an insignificant, over-fastidious minority; they easily persuade the multitude that this is so when the minority is scattered about as it is here,

2 Henry George Bohn (1796–1884), publisher of a famous "Classical Library"; Désiré Nisard (1806–1888), collaborator in the publication of an extensive set of translations of Latin authors.

not so easily when it is banded together as in the French Academy. So, again, with freaks in dealing with language; certainly all such freaks tend to impair the power and beauty of language; and how far more common they are with us than with the French! To take a very familiar instance. Every one has noticed the way in which the *Times* chooses to spell the word "diocese"; it always spells it "dioce*ss*," deriving it, I suppose, from *Zeus* and *census*. The *Journal des Débats* might just as well write "diocess" instead of "diocèse," but imagine the *Journal des Débats* doing so! Imagine an educated Frenchman indulging himself in an orthographical antic of this sort, in face of the grave respect with which the Academy and its dictionary invest the French language! Some people will say these are little things; they are not; they are of bad example. They tend to spread the baneful notion that there is no such thing as a high correct standard in intellectual matters; that every one may as well take his own way; they are at variance with the severe discipline necessary for all real culture; they confirm us in habits of wilfulness and eccentricity, which hurt our minds, and damage our credit with serious people. The late Mr. Donaldson [3] was certainly a man of great ability, and I, who am not an Orientalist, do not pretend to judge his *Jashar*: but let the reader observe the form which a foreign Orientalist's judgment of it naturally takes. M. Renan calls it a *tentative malheureuse*,[4] a failure, in short; this it may be, or it may not be; I am no judge. But he goes on: "It is astonishing that a recent article" (in a French periodical, he means) "should have brought forward as the last word of German exegesis a work like this, composed by a doctor of the University of Cambridge, and universally condemned by German critics." You see what he means to imply: an extravagance of this sort could never have come from Germany, where there is a great force of critical opinion controlling a learned man's vagaries, and keeping him straight; it comes from the native home of intellectual eccentricity of all kinds,[5] — from England — from a doctor of the University of Cambridge: — and I daresay he would not expect much better things from a doctor of the University of Oxford. Again, after speaking of what Germany and France have done for the history of Mahomet: "America and England," M. Renan goes on, "have also occupied themselves with Mahomet." He mentions Washington Irving's *Life of Mahomet*, which does not, he says, evince much of an historical sense, a *sentiment historique fort élevé*; "but," he proceeds, "this book shows a real progress, when one thinks that in 1829 Mr. Charles Forster published two thick volumes,[6]

3 John William Donaldson (1811–1861), philologist.
4 "an unhappy attempt."
5 A critic declares that I am wrong in saying that M. Renan's language implies this. I still think that there is a shade, a *nuance* of expression, in M. Renan's language, which does imply this; but I confess, the only person who can really settle such a question is M. Renan himself. [Arnold's note.]
6 *Mahometanism Unveiled! an Inquiry.*

which enchanted the English *révérends,* to make out that Mahomet was the little horn of the he-goat that figures in the eighth chapter of Daniel, and that the Pope was the great horn. Mr. Forster founded on this ingenious parallel a whole philosophy of history, according to which the Pope represented the Western corruption of Christianity, and Mahomet the Eastern; thence the striking resemblances between Mahometanism and Popery." And in a note M. Renan adds: "This is the same Mr. Charles Forster who is the author of a mystification about the Sinaitic inscriptions, in which he declares he finds the primitive language." As much as to say: "It is an Englishman, be surprised at no extravagance." If these innuendoes had no ground, and were made in hatred and malice, they would not be worth a moment's attention; but they come from a grave Orientalist, on his own subject, and they point to a real fact; — the absence, in this country, of any force of educated literary and scientific opinion, making aberrations like those of the author of *The One Primeval Language* out of the question. Not only the author of such aberrations, often a very clever man, suffers by the want of check, by the not being kept straight, and spends force in vain on a false road, which, under better discipline, he might have used with profit on a true one; but all his adherents, both "reverends" and others, suffer too, and the general rate of information and judgment is in this way kept low.

In a production which we have all been reading lately, a production stamped throughout with a literary quality very rare in this country, and of which I shall have a word to say presently — *urbanity;* in this production, the work of a man never to be named by any son of Oxford without sympathy, a man who alone in Oxford of his generation, alone of many generations, conveyed to us in his genius that same charm, that same ineffable sentiment which this exquisite place itself conveys, — I mean Dr. Newman, — an expression is frequently used which is more common in theological than in literary language, but which seems to me fitted to be of general service; the *note* of so and so, the note of catholicity, the note of antiquity, the note of sanctity, and so on. Adopting this expressive word, I say that in the bulk of the intellectual work of a nation which has no centre, no intellectual metropolis like an academy, like M. Sainte-Beuve's "sovereign organ of opinion," like M. Renan's "recognised authority in matters of tone and taste," — there is observable a *note of provinciality.* Now to get rid of provinciality is a certain stage of culture; a stage the positive result of which we must not make of too much importance, but which is, nevertheless, indispensable; for it brings us on to the platform where alone the best and highest intellectual work can be said fairly to begin. Work done after men have reached this platform is *classical;* and that is the only work which, in the long run, can stand. All the *scoriæ* in the work of men of great genius who have not lived on this platform are due to their not having lived on it. Genius raises them to it by moments, and the portions of their work which are immortal are done at these moments; but more of it would have been immortal if they had not reached this platform at moments only, if they had had the culture which makes men live there.

The less a literature has felt the influence of a supposed centre of correct information, correct judgment, correct taste, the more we shall find in it this note of provinciality. I have shown the note of provinciality as caused by remoteness from a centre of correct information. Of course the note of provinciality from the want of a centre of correct taste is still more visible, and it is also still more common. For here great — even the greatest — powers of mind most fail a man. Great powers of mind will make him inform himself thoroughly, great powers of mind will make him think profoundly, even with ignorance and platitude all round him; but not even great powers of mind will keep his taste and style perfectly sound and sure, if he is left too much to himself, with no "sovereign organ of opinion" in these matters near him. Even men like Jeremy Taylor and Burke suffer here. Take this passage from Taylor's funeral sermon on Lady Carbery: —

"So have I seen a river, deep and smooth, passing with a still foot and a sober face, and paying to the *fiscus*, the great exchequer of the sea, a tribute large and full; and hard by it a little brook, skipping and making a noise upon its unequal and neighbour bottom; and after all its talking and bragged motion, it paid to its common audit no more than the revenues of a little cloud or a contemptible vessel: so have I sometimes compared the issues of her religion to the solemnities and famed outsides of another's piety."

That passage has been much admired, and, indeed, the genius in it is undeniable. I should say, for my part, that genius, the ruling divinity of poetry, had been too busy in it, and intelligence, the ruling divinity of prose, not busy enough. But can any one, with the best models of style in his head, help feeling the note of provinciality there, the want of simplicity, the want of measure, the want of just the qualities that make prose classical? If he does not feel what I mean, let him place beside the passage of Taylor this passage from the Panegyric of St. Paul, by Taylor's contemporary, Bossuet: —

"Il ira, cet ignorant dans l'art de bien dire, avec cette locution rude, avec cette phrase qui sent l'étranger il ira en cette Grèce polie, la mère des philosophes et des orateurs; et malgré la résistance du monde, il y établira plus d'Eglises que Platon n'y a gagné de disciples par cette éloquence qu'on a crue divine." [7]

---

[7] "He will go, this man ignorant of the art of fine speech, with his crude discourse, with that phrase smacking of the foreigner, he will go into this cultured Greece, the mother of philosophers and orators; and in spite of the opposition of the world, he will establish there more churches than Plato gained disciples by that eloquence which was believed divine."

There we have prose without the note of provinciality — classical prose, prose of the centre.

Or take Burke, our greatest English prose-writer, as I think; take expressions like this: —

"Blindfold themselves, like bulls that shut their eyes when they push, they drive, by the point of their bayonets, their slaves, blindfolded, indeed, no worse than their lords, to take their fictions for currencies, and to swallow down paper pills by thirty-four millions sterling at a dose."

Or this: —

"They used it" (the royal name) "as a sort of navel-string, to nourish their unnatural offspring from the bowels of royalty itself. Now that the monster can purvey for its own subsistence, it will only carry the mark about it, as a token of its having torn the womb it came from."

Or this: —

"Without one natural pang, he" (Rousseau) "casts away, as a sort of offal and excrement, the spawn of his disgustful amours, and sends his children to the hospital of foundlings."

Or this: —

"I confess I never liked this continual talk of resistance and revolution, or the practice of making the extreme medicine of the constitution its daily bread. It renders the habit of society dangerously valetudinary; it is taking periodical doses of mercury sublimate, and swallowing down repeated provocatives of cantharides to our love of liberty."

I say that is extravagant prose; prose too much suffered to indulge its caprices; prose at too great a distance from the centre of good taste; prose, in short, with the note of provinciality. People may reply, it is rich and imaginative; yes, that is just it, it is *Asiatic* prose, as the ancient critics would have said; prose somewhat barbarously rich and over-loaded. But the true prose is Attic prose.

Well, but Addison's prose is Attic prose. Where, then, it may be asked, is the note of provinciality in Addison? I answer, in the commonplace of his ideas.[8] This is a matter worth remarking. Addison claims to take leading rank as a moralist. To do that, you must have

---

[8] A critic says this is paradoxical, and urges that many second-rate French academicians have uttered the most commonplace ideas possible. I agree that many second-rate French academicians have uttered the most commonplace ideas possible; but Addison is not a second-rate man. He is a man of the order, I will not say of Pascal, but at any rate of La Bruyère and Vauvenargues; why does he not equal them? I say because of the medium in which he finds himself, the atmosphere in which he lives and works; an atmosphere which tells unfavourably, or rather *tends* to tell unfavourably (for that is the truer way of putting it) either upon style or else upon ideas; tends to make even a man of great ability either a Mr. Carlyle or else a Lord Macaulay.

It is to be observed, however, that Lord Macaulay's style has in its turn suffered by his failure in ideas, and this cannot be said of Addison's. [Arnold's note.]

ideas of the first order on your subject — the best ideas, at any rate, attainable in your time — as well as be able to express them in a perfectly sound and sure style. Else you show your distance from the centre of ideas by your matter; you are provincial by your matter, though you may not be provincial by your style. It is comparatively a small matter to express oneself well, if one will be content with not expressing much, with expressing only trite ideas; the problem is to express new and profound ideas in a perfectly sound and classical style. He is the true classic, in every age, who does that. Now Addison has not, on his subject of morals, the force of ideas of the moralists of the first class — the classical moralists; he has not the best ideas attainable in or about his time, and which were, so to speak, in the air then, to be seized by the finest spirits; he is not to be compared for power, searchingness, or delicacy of thought to Pascal or La Bruyère or Vauvenargues;[9] he is rather on a level, in this respect, with a man like Marmontel; therefore, I say, he has the note of provinciality as a moralist; he is provincial by his matter, though not by his style.

To illustrate what I mean by an example. Addison, writing as a moralist on fixedness in religious faith, says: —

"Those who delight in reading books of controversy do very seldom arrive at a fixed and settled habit of faith. The doubt which was laid revives again, and shows itself in new difficulties; and that generally for this reason, — because the mind, which is perpetually tossed in controversies and disputes, is apt to forget the reasons which had once set it at rest, and to be disquieted with any former perplexity when it appears in a new shape, or is started by a different hand."

It may be said, that is classical English, perfect in lucidity, measure, and propriety. I make no objection; but, in my turn, I say that the idea expressed is perfectly trite and barren, and that it is a note of provinciality in Addison, in a man whom a nation puts forward as one of its great moralists, to have no profounder and more striking idea to produce on this great subject. Compare, on the same subject, these words of a moralist really of the first order, really at the centre by his ideas, — Joubert: —

"L'expérience de beaucoup d'opinions donne à l'esprit beaucoup de flexibilité et l'affermit dans celles qu'il croit les meilleures." [10]

With what a flash of light that touches the subject! how it sets us thinking! what a genuine contribution to moral science it is!

In short, where there is no centre like an academy, if you have genius and powerful ideas, you are apt not to have the best style going; if you have precision of style and not genius, you are apt not to have the best ideas going.

9 Luc de Clapiers de Vauvenargues (1715–1747), French philosopher.
10 "Knowledge of many opinions gives the spirit a great deal of flexibility and strengthens it in those opinions which it believes to be the best."

The provincial spirit, again, exaggerates the value of its ideas for want of a high standard at hand by which to try them. Or rather, for want of such a standard, it gives one idea too much prominence at the expense of others; it orders its ideas amiss; it is hurried away by fancies; it likes and dislikes too passionately, too exclusively. Its admiration weeps hysterical tears, and its disapprobation foams at the mouth. So we get the *eruptive* and the *aggressive* manner in literature; the former prevails most in our criticism, the latter in our newspapers. For, not having the lucidity of a large and centrally placed intelligence, the provincial spirit has not its graciousness; it does not persuade, it makes war; it has not urbanity, the tone of the city, of the centre, the tone which always aims at a spiritual and intellectual effect, and not excluding the use of banter, never disjoins banter itself from politeness, from felicity. But the provincial tone is more violent, and seems to aim rather at an effect upon the blood and senses than upon the spirit and intellect; it loves hard-hitting rather than persuading. The newspaper, with its party spirit, its thorough-goingness, its resolute avoidance of shades and distinctions, its short, highly-charged, heavy-shotted articles, its style so unlike that style *lenis minimèque pertinax* — easy and not too violently insisting, — which the ancients so much admired, is its true literature; the provincial spirit likes in the newspaper just what makes the newspaper such bad food for it, — just what made Goethe say, when he was pressed hard about the immorality of Byron's poems, that, after all, they were not so immoral as the newspapers. The French talk of the *brutalité des journaux anglais*.[11] What strikes them comes from the necessary inherent tendencies of newspaper-writing not being checked in England by any centre of intelligent and urbane spirit, but rather stimulated by coming in contact with a provincial spirit. Even a newspaper like the *Saturday Review*, that old friend of all of us, a newspaper expressly aiming at an immunity from the common newspaper-spirit, aiming at being a sort of organ of reason, — and, by thus aiming, it merits great gratitude and has done great good, — even the *Saturday Review*, replying to some foreign criticism on our precautions against invasion, falls into a strain of this kind: —

"To do this" (to take these precautions) "seems to us eminently worthy of a great nation, and to talk of it as unworthy of a great nation, seems to us eminently worthy of a great fool."

There is what the French mean when they talk of the *brutalité des journaux anglais;* there is a style certainly as far removed from urbanity as possible, — a style with what I call the note of provinciality. And the same note may not unfrequently be observed even in the ideas of this newspaper, full as it is of thought and cleverness: certain ideas allowed to become fixed ideas, to prevail too absolutely. I will not speak of the immediate present, but, to go a little while back, it had

11 "brutality of the English newspapers."

the critic who so disliked the Emperor of the French; it had the
critic who so disliked the subject of my present remarks — academies;
it had the critic who was so fond of the German element in our
nation, and, indeed, everywhere; who ground his teeth if one said
Charlemagne instead of *Charles the Great,* and, in short, saw all
things in Teutonism, as Malebranche saw all things in God. Certainly
any one may fairly find faults in the Emperor Napoleon or in academies, and merit in the German element; but it is a note of the
provincial spirit not to hold ideas of this kind a little more easily, to
be so devoured by them, to suffer them to become crotchets.

In England there needs a miracle of genius like Shakspeare's to
produce balance of mind, and a miracle of intellectual delicacy like
Dr. Newman's to produce urbanity of style. How prevalent all round
us is the want of balance of mind and urbanity of style! How much,
doubtless, it is to be found in ourselves, — in each of us! but, as
human nature is constituted, every one can see it clearest in his contemporaries. There, above all, we should consider it, because they
and we are exposed to the same influences; and it is in the best of
one's contemporaries that it is most worth considering, because one
then most feels the harm it does, when one sees what they would
be without it. Think of the difference between Mr. Ruskin exercising
his genius, and Mr. Ruskin exercising his intelligence; consider the
truth and beauty of this: —

"Go out, in the spring-time, among the meadows that slope from
the shores of the Swiss lakes to the roots of their lower mountains.
There, mingled with the taller gentians and the white narcissus, the
grass grows deep and free; and as you follow the winding mountain
paths, beneath arching boughs all veiled and dim with blossom, —
paths that for ever droop and rise over the green banks and mounds
sweeping down in scented undulation, steep to the blue water,
studded here and there with new-mown heaps, filling all the air with
fainter sweetness, — look up towards the higher hills, where the
waves of everlasting green roll silently into their long inlets among
the shadows of the pines. . . . . ."

There is what the genius, the feeling, the temperament in Mr.
Ruskin, the original and incommunicable part, has to do with; and
how exquisite it is! All the critic could possibly suggest, in the way
of objection, would be, perhaps, that Mr. Ruskin is there trying to
make prose do more than it can perfectly do; that what he is there
attempting he will never, except in poetry, be able to accomplish to
his own entire satisfaction: but he accomplishes so much that the
critic may well hesitate to suggest even this. Place beside this charming passage another, — a passage about Shakspeare's names, where
the intelligence and judgment of Mr. Ruskin, the acquired, trained,
communicable part in him, are brought into play, — and see the difference: —

"Of Shakspeare's names I will afterwards speak at more length; they are curiously — often barbarously — mixed out of various traditions and languages. Three of the clearest in meaning have been already noticed. Desdemona — 'δυσδαιμονία,' *miserable fortune* — is also plain enough. Othello is, I believe, 'the careful'; all the calamity of the tragedy arising from the single flaw and error in his magnificently collected strength. Ophelia, 'serviceableness,' the true, lost wife of Hamlet, is marked as having a Greek name by that of her brother, Laertes; and its signification is once exquisitely alluded to in that brother's last word of her, where her gentle preciousness is opposed to the uselessness of the churlish clergy: — 'A *ministering* angel shall my sister be, when thou liest howling.' Hamlet is, I believe, connected in some way with 'homely,' the entire event of the tragedy turning on betrayal of home duty. Hermione (ἕρμα), 'pillar-like' (ᾗεῖδος ἔχε χρυσῆς 'Αφροδίτης); Titania (τιτήνη), 'the queen'; Benedick and Beatrice, 'blessed and blessing'; Valentine and Proteus, 'enduring or strong' (*valens*), and 'changeful.' Iago and Iachimo have evidently the same root — probably the Spanish Iago, Jacob, 'the supplanter.' "

Now, really, what a piece of extravagance all that is! I will not say that the meaning of Shakspeare's names (I put aside the question as to the correctness of Mr. Ruskin's etymologies) has no effect at all, may be entirely lost sight of; but to give it that degree of prominence is to throw the reins to one's whim, to forget all moderation and proportion, to lose the balance of one's mind altogether. It is to show in one's criticism, to the highest excess, the note of provinciality.

Again, there is Mr. Palgrave, certainly endowed with a very fine critical tact: his *Golden Treasury* abundantly proves it. The plan of arrangement which he devised for that work, the mode in which he followed his plan out, nay, one might even say, merely the juxtaposition, in pursuance of it, of two such pieces as those of Wordsworth and Shelley which form the 285th and 286th in his collection, show a delicacy of feeling in these matters which is quite indisputable and very rare. And his notes are full of remarks which show it too. All the more striking, conjoined with so much justness of perception, are certain freaks and violences in Mr. Palgrave's criticism, mainly imputable, I think, to the critic's isolated position in this country, to his feeling himself too much left to take his own way, too much without any central authority representing high culture and sound judgment, by which he may be, on the one hand, confirmed as against the ignorant, on the other, held in respect when he himself is inclined to take liberties. I mean such things as this note on Milton's line, —

The great Emathian conqueror bade spare . . .

"When Thebes was destroyed, Alexander ordered the house of Pindar to be spared. *He was as incapable of appreciating the poet as Louis XIV. of appreciating Racine; but even the narrow and barbarian mind of Alexander could understand the advantage of a showy act of homage to poetry.*" A note like that I call a freak or a violence; if this disparaging view of Alexander and Louis XIV., so unlike the current view, is wrong, — if the current view is, after all, the truer one of them, — the note is a freak. But, even if its disparaging view is right, the note is a violence; for abandoning the true mode of intellectual action — persuasion, the instilment of conviction, — it simply astounds and irritates the hearer by contradicting without a word of proof or preparation, his fixed and familiar notions; and this is mere violence. In either case, the fitness, the measure, the centrality, which is the soul of all good criticism, is lost, and the note of provinciality shows itself.

Thus, in the famous *Handbook*,[12] marks of a fine power of perception are everywhere discernible, but so, too, are marks of the want of sure balance, of the check and support afforded by knowing one speaks before good and severe judges. When Mr. Palgrave dislikes a thing, he feels no pressure constraining him either to try his dislike closely or to express it moderately; he does not mince matters, he gives his dislike all its own way; both his judgment and his style would gain if he were under more restraint. "The style which has filled London with the dead monotony of Gower or Harley Streets, or the pale commonplace of Belgravia, Tyburnia, and Kensington; which has pierced Paris and Madrid with the feeble frivolities of the Rue Rivoli and the Strada de Toledo." He dislikes the architecture of the Rue Rivoli, and he puts it on a level with the architecture of Belgravia and Gower Street; he lumps them all together in one condemnation, he loses sight of the shade, the distinction, which is everything here; the distinction, namely, that the architecture of the Rue Rivoli expresses show, splendour, pleasure, — unworthy things, perhaps, to express alone and for their own sakes, but it expresses them; whereas the architecture of Gower Street and Belgravia merely expresses the impotence of the architect to express anything. Then, as to style: "sculpture which stands in a contrast with Woolner [13] hardly more shameful than diverting." . . . "passing from Davy or Faraday to the art of the mountebank or the science of the spirit-rapper." . . . "it is the old, old story with Marochetti, the frog trying to blow himself out to bull dimensions. He may puff and be puffed, but he will never do it." We all remember that shower of amenities on poor M. Marochetti.[14] Now, here Mr. Palgrave himself enables us to form a contrast which lets us see just what the presence of an academy does for

12 Palgrave's *Handbook to the Fine Art Collection in the International Exhibition of 1862.*
13 Thomas Woolner (1825–1892), sculptor.
14 Carlo Marochetti (1801–1868), Italian sculptor.

style; for he quotes a criticism by M. Gustave Planche [15] on this very
M. Marochetti. M. Gustave Planche was a critic of the very first
order, a man of strong opinions, which he expressed with severity;
he, too, condemns M. Marochetti's work, and Mr. Palgrave calls him
as a witness to back what he has himself said; certainly Mr. Palgrave's
translation will not exaggerate M. Planche's urbanity in dealing with
M. Marochetti, but, even in this translation, see the difference in
sobriety, in measure, between the critic writing in Paris and the
critic writing in London: —

"These conditions are so elementary, that I am at a perfect loss
to comprehend how M. Marochetti has neglected them. There are
soldiers here like the leaden playthings of the nursery: it is almost
impossible to guess whether there is a body beneath the dress. We
have here no question of style, not even of grammar; it is nothing
beyond mere matter of the alphabet of art. To break these conditions
is the same as to be ignorant of spelling."

That is really more formidable criticism than Mr. Palgrave's, and yet
in how perfectly temperate a style! M. Planche's advantage is, that he
feels himself to be speaking before competent judges, that there is
a force of cultivated opinion for him to appeal to. Therefore, he must
not be extravagant, and he need not storm; he must satisfy the reason
and taste, — that is his business. Mr. Palgrave, on the other hand,
feels himself to be speaking before a promiscuous multitude, with the
few good judges so scattered through it as to be powerless; therefore,
he has no calm confidence and no self-control; he relies on the strength
of his lungs; he knows that big words impose on the mob, and that,
even if he is outrageous, most of his audience are apt to be a great
deal more so.

Again, the first two volumes of Mr. Kinglake's *Invasion of the
Crimea* were certainly among the most successful and renowned English books of our time. Their style was one of the most renowned
things about them, and yet how conspicuous a fault in Mr. Kinglake's
style is this overcharge of which I have been speaking! Mr. James
Gordon Bennett, of the *New York Herald*, says, I believe, that the
highest achievement of the human intellect is what he calls "a good
editorial." This is not quite so; but, if it were so, on what a height
would these two volumes by Mr. Kinglake stand! I have already
spoken of the Attic and the Asiatic styles; besides these, there is the
Corinthian style. That is the style for "a good editorial," and Mr.
Kinglake has really reached perfection in it. It has not the warm glow,
blithe movement, and soft pliancy of life, as the Attic style has; it has
not the over-heavy richness and encumbered gait of the Asiatic style;
it has glitter without warmth, rapidity without ease, effectiveness
without charm. Its characteristic is, that it has no *soul;* all it exists
for, is to get its ends, to make its points, to damage its adversaries,

15 Gustave Planche (1808–1857), French critic.

to be admired, to triumph. A style so bent on effect at the expense
of soul, simplicity, and delicacy; a style so little studious of the charm
of the great models; so far from classic truth and grace, must surely
be said to have the note of provinciality. Yet Mr. Kinglake's talent
is a really eminent one, and so in harmony with our intellectual habits
and tendencies, that, to the great bulk of English people, the faults
of his style seem its merits; all the more needful that criticism should
not be dazzled by them.

We must not compare a man of Mr. Kinglake's literary talent with
French writers like M. de Bazancourt.[16] We must compare him with
M. Thiers. And what a superiority in style has M. Thiers from being
formed in a good school, with severe traditions, wholesome restraining influences! Even in this age of Mr. James Gordon Bennett, his
style has nothing Corinthian about it, its lightness and brightness
make it almost Attic. It is not quite Attic, however; it has not the infallible sureness of Attic taste. Sometimes his head gets a little hot
with the fumes of patriotism, and then he crosses the line, he loses
perfect measure, he declaims, he raises a momentary smile. France
condemned "à être l'effroi du monde *dont elle pourrait être l'amour*," [17]
— Cæsar, whose exquisite simplicity M. Thiers so much admires,
would not have written like that. There is, if I may be allowed to say
so, the slightest possible touch of fatuity in such language, — of that
failure in good sense which comes from too warm a self-satisfaction.
But compare this language with Mr. Kinglake's Marshal St. Arnaud —
"dismissed from the presence" of Lord Raglan or Lord Stratford,
"cowed and pressed down" under their "stern reproofs," or under "the
majesty of the great Elchi's Canning brow and tight, merciless lips!"
The failure in good sense and good taste there reaches far beyond
what the French mean by *fatuity;* they would call it by another word,
a word expressing blank defect of intelligence, a word for which we
have no exact equivalent in English, — *bête.* It is the difference between a venial, momentary, good-tempered excess, in a man of the
world, of an amiable and social weakness, — vanity; and a serious, settled, fierce, narrow, provincial misconception of the whole relative
value of one's own things and the things of others. So baneful to
the style of even the cleverest man may be the total want of checks.

In all I have said, I do not pretend that the examples given prove
my rule as to the influence of academies; they only illustrate it. Examples in plenty might very likely be found to set against them; the
truth of the rule depends, no doubt, on whether the balance of all the
examples is in its favour or not; but actually to strike this balance
is always out of the question. Here, as everywhere else, the rule, the
idea, if true, commends itself to the judicious, and then the examples
make it clearer still to them. This is the real use of examples, and
this alone is the purpose which I have meant mine to serve. There

16 César Lecat, Baron de Bazancourt (1810–1865), French historian.
17 "to be the terror of the world of which she could be the beloved."

is also another side to the whole question, — as to the limiting and prejudicial operation which academies may have; but this side of the question it rather behoves the French, not us, to study.

The reader will ask for some practical conclusion about the establishment of an Academy in this country, and perhaps I shall hardly give him the one he expects. But nations have their own modes of acting, and these modes are not easily changed; they are even consecrated, when great things have been done in them. When a literature has produced Shakspeare and Milton, when it has even produced Barrow and Burke, it cannot well abandon its traditions; it can hardly begin, at this late time of day, with an institution like the French Academy. I think academies with a limited, special, scientific scope, in the various lines of intellectual work, — academies like that of Berlin, for instance, — we with time may, and probably shall, establish. And no doubt they will do good; no doubt the presence of such influential centres of correct information will tend to raise the standard amongst us for what I have called the *journeyman-work* of literature, and to free us from the scandal of such biographical dictionaries as Chalmers's, or such translations as a recent one of Spinoza, or perhaps, such philological freaks as Mr. Forster's about the one primeval language. But an academy quite like the French Academy, a sovereign organ of the highest literary opinion, a recognised authority in matters of intellectual tone and taste, we shall hardly have, and perhaps we ought not to wish to have it. But then every one amongst us with any turn for literature will do well to remember to what shortcomings and excesses, which such an academy tends to correct, we are liable; and the more liable, of course, for not having it. He will do well constantly to try himself in respect of these, steadily to widen his culture, severely to check in himself the provincial spirit; and he will do this the better the more he keeps in mind that all mere glorification by ourselves of ourselves, or our literature, in the strain of what, at the beginning of these remarks, I quoted from Lord Macaulay,[18] is both vulgar, and, besides being vulgar, retarding.

Culture and Anarchy

❡ *Culture and Anarchy* first appeared as a series of articles in the *Cornhill Magazine* from July 1867 to August 1868. The first, entitled "Culture and Its Enemies," was Arnold's last lecture as Professor of Poetry at Oxford; it became, in part, Chapter I: "Sweetness and Light." The remaining articles

[18] "It may safely be said that the literature now extant in the English language is of far greater value than all the literature which three hundred years ago was extant in all the languages of the world together."

were entitled "Anarchy and Authority" and were to some extent controlled
in their argumentative method by criticisms of the position Arnold had
taken in "Culture and Its Enemies." (Arnold had, in fact, delayed the
"Anarchy and Authority" papers until he could make a judicious use of these
criticisms.) The sections of the volume were not given chapter headings
until 1875, when Arnold chose for them phrases from *Culture and Anarchy*
which had become famous: I. "Sweetness and Light"; II. "Doing as One
Likes"; III. "Barbarians, Philistines, Populace"; IV. "Hebraism and Hellenism"; V. "Porro Unum Est Necessarium"; VI. "Our Liberal Practitioners."
Culture and Anarchy is the most important example of Arnold's extension of
the function of criticism to the social condition and should be read against
the background of Newman's *Idea of a University*, Mill's *On Liberty*, and
the essays of Macaulay.]❩

Chapter I

Sweetness and Light

THE disparagers of culture make its motive curiosity; sometimes, indeed, they make its motive mere exclusiveness and vanity. The culture which is supposed to plume itself on a smattering of Greek and
Latin is a culture which is begotten by nothing so intellectual as
curiosity; it is valued either out of sheer vanity and ignorance or else
as an engine of social and class distinction, separating its holder, like
a badge or title, from other people who have not got it. No serious
man would call this *culture*, or attach any value to it, as culture, at all.
To find the real ground for the very different estimate which serious
people will set upon culture, we must find some motive for culture in
the terms of which may lie a real ambiguity; and such a motive the
word *curiosity* gives us.

I have before now pointed out that we English do not, like the
foreigners, use this word in a good sense as well as in a bad sense.
With us the word is always used in a somewhat disapproving sense.
A liberal and intelligent eagerness about the things of the mind may
be meant by a foreigner when he speaks of curiosity, but with us the
word always conveys a certain notion of frivolous and unedifying
activity. In the *Quarterly Review*, some little time ago, was an estimate of the celebrated French critic, M. Sainte-Beuve, and a very
inadequate estimate it in my judgment was. And its inadequacy consisted chiefly in this: that in our English way it left out of sight the
double sense really involved in the word *curiosity*, thinking enough
was said to stamp M. Sainte-Beuve with blame if it was said that he
was impelled in his operations as a critic by curiosity, and omitting
either to perceive that M. Sainte-Beuve himself, and many other
people with him, would consider that this was praiseworthy and not
blameworthy, or to point out why it ought really to be accounted

worthy of blame and not of praise. For as there is a curiosity about intellectual matters which is futile, and merely a disease, so there is certainly a curiosity, — a desire after the things of the mind simply for their own sakes and for the pleasure of seeing them as they are, — which is, in an intelligent being, natural and laudable. Nay, and the very desire to see things as they are implies a balance and regulation of mind which is not often attained without fruitful effort, and which is the very opposite of the blind and diseased impulse of mind which is what we mean to blame when we blame curiosity. Montesquieu says: "The first motive which ought to impel us to study is the desire to augment the excellence of our nature, and to render an intelligent being yet more intelligent." This is the true ground to assign for the genuine scientific passion, however manifested, and for culture, viewed simply as a fruit of this passion; and it is a worthy ground, even though we let the term *curiosity* stand to describe it.

But there is of culture another view, in which not solely the scientific passion, the sheer desire to see things as they are, natural and proper in an intelligent being, appears as the ground of it. There is a view in which all the love of our neighbour, the impulses towards action, help, and beneficence, the desire for removing human error, clearing human confusion, and diminishing human misery, the noble aspiration to leave the world better and happier than we found it, — motives eminently such as are called social, — come in as part of the grounds of culture, and the main and pre-eminent part. Culture is then properly described not as having its origin in curiosity, but as having its origin in the love of perfection; it is *a study of perfection.* It moves by the force, not merely or primarily of the scientific passion for pure knowledge, but also of the moral and social passion for doing good. As, in the first view of it, we took for its worthy motto Montesquieu's words: "To render an intelligent being yet more intelligent!" so, in the second view of it, there is no better motto which it can have than these words of Bishop Wilson:[1] "To make reason and the will of God prevail!"

Only, whereas the passion for doing good is apt to be overhasty in determining what reason and the will of God say, because its turn is for acting rather than thinking and it wants to be beginning to act; and whereas it is apt to take its own conceptions, which proceed from its own state of development and share in all the imperfections and immaturities of this, for a basis of action; what distinguishes culture is, that it is possessed by the scientific passion as well as by the passion of doing good; that it demands worthy notions of reason and the will of God, and does not readily suffer its own crude conceptions to substitute themselves for them. And knowing that no action or institution can be salutary and stable which is not based on reason

[1] Bishop Thomas Wilson, author of *Sacra Privata.*

and the will of God, it is not so bent on acting and instituting, even
with the great aim of diminishing human error and misery ever before its thoughts, but that it can remember that acting and instituting
are of little use, unless we know how and what we ought to act and
to institute.

This culture is more interesting and more far-reaching than that
other, which is founded solely on the scientific passion for knowing.
But it needs times of faith and ardour, times when the intellectual
horizon is opening and widening all round us, to flourish in. And is
not the close and bounded intellectual horizon within which we have
long lived and moved now lifting up, and are not new lights finding
free passage to shine in upon us? For a long time there was no passage for them to make their way in upon us, and then it was of no
use to think of adapting the world's action to them. Where was the
hope of making reason and the will of God prevail among people who
had a routine which they had christened reason and the will of God,
in which they were inextricably bound, and beyond which they had
no power of looking? But now the iron force of adhesion to the old
routine, — social, political, religious, — has wonderfully yielded; the
iron force of exclusion of all which is new has wonderfully yielded.
The danger now is, not that people should obstinately refuse to
allow anything but their old routine to pass for reason and the will
of God, but either that they should allow some novelty or other to
pass for these too easily, or else that they should underrate the importance of them altogether, and think it enough to follow action for
its own sake, without troubling themselves to make reason and the will
of God prevail therein. Now, then, is the moment for culture to be
of service, culture which believes in making reason and the will of
God prevail, believes in perfection, is the study and pursuit of perfection, and is no longer debarred, by a rigid invincible exclusion of
whatever is new, from getting acceptance for its ideas, simply because
they are new.

The moment this view of culture is seized, the moment it is regarded
not solely as the endeavour to see things as they are, to draw towards
a knowledge of the universal order which seems to be intended and
aimed at in the world, and which it is a man's happiness to go along
with or his misery to go counter to, — to learn, in short, the will of
God, — the moment, I say, culture is considered not merely as the
endeavour to *see* and *learn* this, but as the endeavour, also, to make
it *prevail*, the moral, social, and beneficent character of culture becomes manifest. The mere endeavour to see and learn the truth for
our own personal satisfaction is indeed a commencement for making
it prevail, a preparing the way for this, which always serves this, and
is wrongly, therefore, stamped with blame absolutely in itself and not
only in its caricature and degeneration. But perhaps it has got

stamped with blame, and disparaged with the dubious title of curiosity, because in comparison with this wider endeavour of such great and plain utility it looks selfish, petty, and unprofitable.

And religion, the greatest and most important of the efforts by which the human race has manifested its impulse to perfect itself, — religion, that voice of the deepest human experience, — does not only enjoin and sanction the aim which is the great aim of culture, the aim of setting ourselves to ascertain what perfection is and to make it prevail; but also, in determining generally in what human perfection consists, religion comes to a conclusion identical with that which culture, — culture seeking the determination of this question through *all* the voices of human experience which have been heard upon it, of art, science, poetry, philosophy, history, as well as of religion, in order to give a greater fulness and certainty to its solution, — likewise reaches. Religion says: *The kingdom of God is within you;* and culture, in like manner, places human perfection in an *internal* condition, in the growth and predominance of our humanity proper, as distinguished from our animality. It places it in the ever-increasing efficacy and in the general harmonious expansion of those gifts of thought and feeling, which make the peculiar dignity, wealth, and happiness of human nature. As I have said on a former occasion: "It is in making endless additions to itself, in the endless expansion of its powers, in endless growth in wisdom and beauty, that the spirit of the human race finds its ideal. To reach this ideal, culture is an indispensable aid, and that is the true value of culture." Not a having and a resting, but a growing and a becoming, is the character of perfection as culture conceives it; and here, too, it coincides with religion.

And because men are all members of one great whole, and the sympathy which is in human nature will not allow one member to be indifferent to the rest or to have a perfect welfare independent of the rest, the expansion of our humanity, to suit the idea of perfection which culture forms, must be a *general* expansion. Perfection, as culture conceives it, is not possible while the individual remains isolated. The individual is required, under pain of being stunted and enfeebled in his own development if he disobeys, to carry others along with him in his march towards perfection, to be continually doing all he can to enlarge and increase the volume of the human stream sweeping thitherward. And here, once more, culture lays on us the same obligation as religion which says, as Bishop Wilson has admirably put it, that "to promote the kingdom of God is to increase and hasten one's own happiness."

But, finally, perfection, — as culture from a thorough disinterested study of human nature and human experience learns to conceive it, — is a harmonious expansion of *all* the powers which make the beauty and worth of human nature, and is not consistent with the over-development of any one power at the expense of the rest. Here culture goes beyond religion, as religion is generally conceived by us.

If culture, then, is a study of perfection, and of harmonious perfection, general perfection, and perfection which consists in becoming something rather than in having something, in an inward condition of the mind and spirit, not in an outward set of circumstances, — it is clear that culture, instead of being the frivolous and useless thing which Mr. Bright, and Mr. Frederic Harrison, and many other Liberals are apt to call it, has a very important function to fulfil for mankind. And this function is particularly important in our modern world, of which the whole civilisation is, to a much greater degree than the civilisation of Greece and Rome, mechanical and external, and tends constantly to become more so. But above all in our own country has culture a weighty part to perform, because here that mechanical character, which civilisation tends to take everywhere, is shown in the most eminent degree. Indeed nearly all the characters of perfection, as culture teaches us to fix them, meet in this country with some powerful tendency which thwarts them and sets them at defiance. The idea of perfection as an *inward* condition of the mind and spirit is at variance with the mechanical and material civilisation in esteem with us, and nowhere, as I have said, so much in esteem as with us. The idea of perfection as a *general* expansion of the human family is at variance with our strong individualism, our hatred of all limits to the unrestrained swing of the individual's personality, our maxim of "every man for himself." Above all, the idea of perfection as a *harmonious* expansion of human nature is at variance with our want of flexibility, with our inaptitude for seeing more than one side of a thing, with our intense energetic absorption in the particular pursuit we happen to be following. So culture has a rough task to achieve in this country. Its preachers have, and are likely long to have, a hard time of it, and they will much oftener be regarded, for a great while to come, as elegant or spurious Jeremiahs than as friends and benefactors. That, however, will not prevent their doing in the end good service if they persevere. And, meanwhile, the mode of action they have to pursue, and the sort of habits they must fight against, ought to be made quite clear for every one to see, who may be willing to look at the matter attentively and dispassionately.

Faith in machinery, is, I said, our besetting danger; often in machinery most absurdly disproportioned to the end which this machinery, if it is to do any good at all, is to serve; but always in machinery, as if it had a value in and for itself. What is freedom but machinery? what is population but machinery? what is coal but machinery? what are railroads but machinery? what is wealth but machinery? what are, even, religious organisations but machinery? Now almost every voice in England is accustomed to speak of these things as if they were precious ends in themselves, and therefore had some of the characters of perfection indisputably joined to them. I have before now noticed Mr. Roebuck's [2] stock argument for proving the greatness and happiness of England as she is, and for quite stopping the mouths of all gainsayers. Mr. Roebuck is never weary of reiterating this argument of his, so I do not know why I should be weary of noticing it. "May not every man in England say what he likes?" — Mr. Roebuck perpetually asks; and that, he thinks, is quite sufficient, and when every man may say what he likes, our aspirations ought to be satisfied. But the aspirations of culture, which is the study of perfection, are not satisfied, unless what men say, when they may say what they like, is worth saying, — has good in it, and more good than bad. In the same way the *Times,* replying to some foreign strictures on the dress, looks, and behaviour of the English abroad, urges that the English ideal is that every one should be free to do and to look just as he likes. But culture indefatigably tries, not to make what each raw person may like the rule by which he fashions himself; but to draw ever nearer to a sense of what is indeed beautiful, graceful, and becoming, and to get the raw person to like that.

And in the same way with respect to railroads and coal. Every one must have observed the strange language current during the late discussions as to the possible failures of our supplies of coal. Our coal, thousands of people were saying, is the real basis of our national greatness; if our coal runs short, there is an end of the greatness of England. But what *is* greatness? — culture makes us ask. Greatness is a spiritual condition worthy to excite love, interest, and admiration; and the outward proof of possessing greatness is that we excite love, interest, and admiration. If England were swallowed up by the sea tomorrow, which of the two, a hundred years hence, would most excite the love, interest, and admiration of mankind, — would most, therefore, show the evidences of having possessed greatness, — the England of the last twenty years, or the England of Elizabeth, of a time of splendid spiritual effort, but when our coal, and our industrial operations depending on coal, were very little developed? Well, then, what an unsound habit of mind it must be which makes us talk of things like coal or iron as constituting the greatness of England, and how salutary a friend is culture, bent on seeing things as they are, and thus dissipating delusions of this kind and fixing standards of perfection that are real!

Wealth, again, that end to which our prodigious works for material advantage are directed, — the commonest of commonplaces tells us how men are always apt to regard wealth as a precious end in itself; and certainly they have never been so apt thus to regard it as they are in England at the present time. Never did people believe any-

2 John Arthur Roebuck (1801–1879).

thing more firmly than nine Englishmen out of ten at the present day believe that our greatness and welfare are proved by our being so very rich. Now, the use of culture is that it helps us, by means of its spiritual standard of perfection, to regard wealth as but machinery, and not only to say as a matter of words that we regard wealth as but machinery, but really to perceive and feel that it is so. If it were not for this purging effect wrought upon our minds by culture, the whole world, the future as well as the present, would inevitably belong to the Philistines. The people who believe most that our greatness and welfare are proved by our being very rich, and who most give their lives and thoughts to becoming rich, are just the very people whom we call Philistines. Culture says: "Consider these people, then, their way of life, their habits, their manners, the very tones of their voice; look at them attentively; observe the literature they read, the things which give them pleasure, the words which come forth out of their mouths, the thoughts which make the furniture of their minds; would any amount of wealth be worth having with the condition that one was to become just like these people by having it?" And thus culture begets a dissatisfaction which is of the highest possible value in stemming the common tide of men's thoughts in a wealthy and industrial community, and which saves the future, as one may hope, from being vulgarised, even if it cannot save the present.

Population, again, and bodily health and vigour, are things which are nowhere treated in such an unintelligent, misleading, exaggerated way as in England. Both are really machinery; yet how many people all around us do we see rest in them and fail to look beyond them! Why, one has heard people, fresh from reading certain articles of the *Times* on the Registrar-General's returns of marriages and births in this country, who would talk of our large English families in quite a solemn strain, as if they had something in itself beautiful, elevating, and meritorious in them; as if the British Philistine would have only to present himself before the Great Judge with his twelve children, in order to be received among the sheep as a matter of right!

But bodily health and vigour, it may be said, are not to be classed with wealth and population as mere machinery; they have a more real and essential value. True; but only as they are more intimately connected with a perfect spiritual condition than wealth or population are. The moment we disjoin them from the idea of a perfect spiritual condition, and pursue them, as we do pursue them, for their own sake and as ends in themselves, our worship of them becomes as mere worship of machinery, as our worship of wealth or population, and as unintelligent and vulgarising a worship as that is. Every one with anything like an adequate idea of human perfection has distinctly marked this subordination to higher and spiritual ends of the cultivation of bodily vigour and activity. "Bodily exercise profiteth little; but godliness is profitable unto all things," says the author of the Epistle to

Timothy. And the utilitarian Franklin says just as explicitly: —"Eat and drink such an exact quantity as suits the constitution of thy body, *in reference to the services of the mind.*" But the point of view of culture, keeping the mark of human perfection simply and broadly in view, and not assigning to this perfection, as religion or utilitarianism assigns to it, a special and limited character, this point of view, I say, of culture is best given by these words of Epictetus: — "It is a sign of ἀφυΐα," says he, — that is, of a nature not finely tempered, — "to give yourselves up to things which relate to the body; to make, for instance, a great fuss about exercise, a great fuss about eating, a great fuss about drinking, a great fuss about walking, a great fuss about riding. All these things ought to be done merely by the way: the formation of the spirit and character must be our real concern." This is admirable; and, indeed, the Greek word εὐφυΐα, a finely tempered nature, gives exactly the notion of perfection as culture brings us to conceive it: a harmonious perfection, a perfection in which the characters of beauty and intelligence are both present, which unites "the two noblest of things," — as Swift, who of one of the two, at any rate, had himself all too little, most happily calls them in his *Battle of the Books,* — "the two noblest of things, *sweetness and light.*" The εὐφυής is the man who tends towards sweetness and light; the ἀφυής, on the other hand, is our Philistine. The immense spiritual significance of the Greeks is due to their having been inspired with this central and happy idea of the essential character of human perfection; and Mr. Bright's [3] misconception of culture, as a smattering of Greek and Latin, comes itself, after all, from this wonderful significance of the Greeks having affected the very machinery of our education, and is in itself a kind of homage to it.

In thus making sweetness and light to be characters of perfection, culture is of like spirit with poetry, follows one law with poetry. Far more than on our freedom, our population, and our industrialism, many amongst us rely upon our religious organisations to save us. I have called religion a yet more important manifestation of human nature than poetry, because it has worked on a broader scale for perfection, and with greater masses of men. But the idea of beauty and of a human nature perfect on all its sides, which is the dominant idea of poetry, is a true and invaluable idea, though it has not yet had the success that the idea of conquering the obvious faults of our animality, and of a human nature perfect on the moral side, — which is the dominant idea of religion, — has been enabled to have; and it is destined, adding to itself the religious idea of a devout energy, to transform and govern the other.

The best art and poetry of the Greeks, in which religion and poetry are one, in which the idea of beauty and of a human nature perfect on all sides adds to itself a religious and devout energy, and

3 John Bright (1811–1889), Liberal politician.

works in the strength of that, is on this account of such surpassing interest and instructiveness for us, though it was, — as, having regard to the human race in general, and, indeed, having regard to the Greeks themselves, we must own, — a premature attempt, an attempt which for success needed the moral and religious fibre in humanity to be more braced and developed than it had yet been. But Greece did not err in having the idea of beauty, harmony, and complete human perfection, so present and paramount. It is impossible to have this idea too present and paramount; only, the moral fibre must be braced too. And we, because we have braced the moral fibre, are not on that account in the right way, if at the same time the idea of beauty, harmony, and complete human perfection, is wanting or misapprehended amongst us; and evidently it *is* wanting or misapprehended at present. And when we rely as we do on our religious organisations, which in themselves do not and cannot give us this idea, and think we have done enough if we make them spread and prevail, then, I say, we fall into our common fault of overvaluing machinery.

Nothing is more common than for people to confound the inward peace and satisfaction which follows the subduing of the obvious faults of our animality with what I may call absolute inward peace and satisfaction, — the peace and satisfaction which are reached as we draw near to complete spiritual perfection, and not merely to moral perfection, or rather to relative moral perfection. No people in the world have done more and struggled more to attain this relative moral perfection than our English race has. For no people in the world has the command to *resist the devil, to overcome the wicked one,* in the nearest and most obvious sense of those words, had such a pressing force and reality. And we have had our reward, not only in the great worldly prosperity which our obedience to this command has brought us, but also, and far more, in great inward peace and satisfaction. But to me few things are more pathetic than to see people, on the strength of the inward peace and satisfaction which their rudimentary efforts towards perfection have brought them, employ, concerning their incomplete perfection and the religious organisations within which they have found it, language which properly applies only to complete perfection, and is a far-off echo of the human soul's prophecy of it. Religion itself, I need hardly say, supplies them in abundance with this grand language. And very freely do they use it; yet it is really the severest possible criticism of such an incomplete perfection as alone we have yet reached through our religious organisations.

The impulse of the English race towards moral development and self-conquest has nowhere so powerfully manifested itself as in Puritanism. Nowhere has Puritanism found so adequate an expression as in the religious organisation of the Independents. The modern Independents have a newspaper, the *Noncomformist*, written with great sincerity and ability. The motto, the standard, the profession of faith which this organ of theirs carries aloft, is: "The Dissidence of Dissent and the Protestantism of the Protestant religion." There is sweetness and light, and an ideal of complete harmonious human perfection! One need not go to culture and poetry to find language to judge it. Religion, with its instinct for perfecion, supplies language to judge it, language, too, which is in our mouths every day. "Finally, be of one mind, united in feeling," says St. Peter. There is an ideal which judges the Puritan ideal: "The Dissidence of Dissent and the Protestantism of the Protestant religion!" And religious organisations like this are what people believe in, rest in, would give their lives for! Such, I say, is the wonderful virtue of even the beginnings of perfection, of having conquered even the plain faults of our animality, that the religious organisation which has helped us to, do it can seem to us something precious, salutary, and to be propagated, even when it wears such a brand of imperfection on its forehead as this. And men have got such a habit of giving to the language of religion a special application, of making it a mere jargon, that for the condemnation which religion itself passes on the shortcomings of their religious organisations they have no ear; they are sure to cheat themselves and to explain this condemnation away. They can only be reached by the criticism which culture, like poetry, speaking a language not to be sophisticated, and resolutely testing these organisations by the ideal of a human perfection complete on all sides, applies to them.

But men of culture and poetry, it will be said, are again and again failing, and failing conspicuously, in the necessary first stage to a harmonious perfection, in the subduing of the great obvious faults of our animality, which it is the glory of these religious organisations to have helped us to subdue. True, they do often so fail. They have often been without the virtues as well as the faults of the Puritan; it has been one of their dangers that they so felt the Puritan's faults that they too much neglected the practice of his virtues. I will not, however, exculpate them at the Puritan's expense. They have often failed in morality, and morality is indispensable. And they have been punished for their failure, as the Puritan has been rewarded for his performance. They have been punished wherein they erred; but their ideal of beauty, of sweetness and light, and a human nature complete on all its sides, remains the true ideal of perfection still; just as the Puritan's ideal of perfection remains narrow and inadequate, although for what he did well he has been richly rewarded. Notwithstanding the mighty results of the Pilgrim Fathers' voyage, they and their standard of perfection are rightly judged when we figure to ourselves Shakspeare or Virgil, — souls in whom sweetness and light, and all that in human nature is most humane, were eminent, — accompanying them on their voyage, and think what intolerable com-

pany Shakspeare and Virgil would have found them! In the same
way let us judge the religious organisations which we see all around
us. Do not let us deny the good and the happiness which they have
accomplished; but do not let us fail to see clearly that their idea of
human perfection is narrow and inadequate, and that the Dissidence
of Dissent and the Protestantism of the Protestant religion will never
bring humanity to its true goal. As I said with regard to wealth:
Let us look at the life of those who live in and for it, — so I say with
regard to the religious organisations. Look at the life imaged in
such a newspaper as the *Noncomformist,* — a life of jealousy of the
Establishment, disputes, tea-meetings, openings of chapels, sermons;
and then think of it as an ideal of a human life completing itself on
all sides, and aspiring with all its organs after sweetness, light, and
perfection!

Another newspaper, representing, like the *Noncomformist,* one of
the religious organisations of this country, was a short time ago giving an account of the crowd at Epsom on the Derby day, and of all
the vice and hideousness which was to be seen in that crowd; and
then the writer turned suddenly round upon Professor Huxley, and
asked him how he proposed to cure all this vice and hideousness without religion. I confess I felt disposed to ask the asker this question:
and how do you propose to cure it with such a religion as yours?
How is the ideal of a life so unlovely, so unattractive, so incomplete,
so narrow, so far removed from a true and satisfying ideal of human
perfection, as is the life of your religious organisation as you yourself
reflect it, to conquer and transform all this vice and hideousness? Indeed, the strongest plea for the study of perfection as pursued by culture, the clearest proof of the actual inadequacy of the idea of perfection held by the religious organisations, — expressing, as I have
said, the most widespread effort which the human race has yet made
after perfection, — is to be found in the state of our life and society
with these in possession of it, and having been in possession of it
I know not how many hundred years. We are all of us included in
some religious organisation or other; we all call ourselves, in the sublime and aspiring language of religion which I have before noticed,
children of God. Children of God; — it is an immense pretension!
— and how are we to justify it? By the works which we do, and the
words which we speak. And the work which we collective children of
God do, our grand centre of life, our *city* which we have builded
for us to dwell in, is London! London, with its unutterable external
hideousness, and with its internal canker of *publicè egestas privatim
opulentia,*[4] — to use the words which Sallust puts into Cato's mouth
about Rome, — unequalled in the world! The word, again, which we
children of God speak, the voice which most hits our collective thought,
the newspaper with the largest circulation in England, nay, with the

4 "publicly neediness, privately opulence."

largest circulation in the whole world, is the *Daily Telegraph!* I say that when our religious organisations, — which I admit to express the most considerable effort after perfection that our race has yet made, — land us in no better result than this, it is high time to examine carefully their idea of perfection, to see whether it does not leave out of account sides and forces of human nature which we might turn to great use; whether it would not be more operative if it were more complete. And I say that the English reliance on our religious organisations and on their ideas of human perfection just as they stand, is like our reliance on freedom, on muscular Christianity, on population, on coal, on wealth, — mere belief in machinery, and unfruitful; and that it is wholesomely counteracted by culture, bent on seeing things as they are, and on drawing the human race onwards to a more complete, a harmonious perfection.

Culture, however, shows its singleminded love of perfection, its desire simply to make reason and the will of God prevail, its freedom from fanaticism, by its attitude towards all this machinery, even while it insists that it *is* machinery. Fanatics, seeing the mischief men do themselves by their blind belief in some machinery or other, — whether it is wealth and industrialism, or whether it is the cultivation of bodily strength and activity, or whether it is a political organisation, — or whether it is a religious organisation, — oppose with might and main the tendency to this or that political and religious organisation, or to games and athletic exercises, or to wealth and industrialism, and try violently to stop it. But the flexibility which sweetness and light give, and which is one of the rewards of culture pursued in good faith, enables a man to see that a tendency may be necessary, and even, as a preparation for something in the future, salutary, and yet that the generations or individuals who obey this tendency are sacrificed to it, that they fall short of the hope of perfection by following it; and that its mischiefs are to be criticised, lest it should take too firm a hold and last after it has served its purpose.

Mr. Gladstone well pointed out, in a speech at Paris, — and others have pointed out the same thing, — how necessary is the present great movement towards wealth and industrialism, in order to lay broad foundations of material well-being for the society of the future. The worst of these justifications is, that they are generally addressed to the very people engaged, body and soul, in the movement in question; at all events, that they are always seized with the greatest avidity by these people, and taken by them as quite justifying their life; and thus they tend to harden them in their sins. Now, culture admits the necessity of the movement towards fortune-making and exaggerated industrialism, readily allows that the future may derive benefit from it; but insists, at the same time, that the passing generations of industrialists, — forming, for the most part, the stout main body of Philistinism, — are sacrificed to it. In the same way, the result of all the

games and sports which occupy the passing generation of boys and
young men may be the establishment of a better and sounder physical type for the future to work with. Culture does not set itself
against the games and sports; it congratulates the future, and hopes
it will make a good use of its improved physical basis; but it points
out that our passing generation of boys and young men is, meantime,
sacrificed. Puritanism was perhaps necessary to develop the moral
fibre of the English race, Noncomformity to break the yoke of ecclesiastical domination over men's minds and to prepare the way for
freedom of thought in the distant future; still, culture points out that
the harmonious perfection of generations of Puritans and Noncon-
formists has been, in consequence, sacrificed. Freedom of speech
may be necessary for the society of the future, but the young lions
of the *Daily Telegraph* in the meanwhile are sacrificed. A voice for
every man in his country's government may be necessary for the
society of the future, but meanwhile Mr. Beales [5] and Mr. Bradlaugh [6]
are sacrificed.

Oxford, the Oxford of the past, has many faults; and she has
heavily paid for them in defeat, in isolation, in want of hold upon
the modern world. Yet we in Oxford, brought up amidst the beauty
and sweetness of that beautiful place, have not failed to seize one
truth, — the truth that beauty and sweetness are essential characters
of a complete human perfection. When I insist on this, I am all in
the faith and tradition of Oxford. I say boldly that this our sentiment
for beauty and sweetness, our sentiment against hideousness and raw-
ness, has been at the bottom of our attachment to so many beaten
causes, of our opposition to so many triumphant movements. And the
sentiment is true, and has never been wholly defeated, and has shown
its power even in its defeat. We have not won our political battles,
we have not carried our main points, we have not stopped our adversaries' advance, we have not marched victoriously with the modern
world; but we have told silently upon the mind of the country, we have
prepared currents of feeling which sap our adversaries' position when
it seems gained, we have kept up our own communications with the
future. Look at the course of the great movement which shook Oxford
to its centre some thirty years ago! It was directed, as any one who
reads Dr. Newman's *Apology* may see, against what in one word may
be called "Liberalism." Liberalism prevailed; it was the appointed
force to do the work of the hour; it was necessary, it was inevitable
that it should prevail. The Oxford movement was broken, it failed;
our wrecks are scattered on every shore: —

Quæ regio in terris nostri non plena laboris? [7]

5 Edmond Beales (1803–1881), political agitator.
6 Charles Bradlaugh (1833–1891), political agitator and free-thinker.
7 "What region in the world is not full of our labor?"

But what was it, this liberalism, as Dr. Newman saw it, and as it really broke the Oxford movement? It was the great middle-class liberalism, which had for the cardinal points of its belief the Reform Bill of 1832, and local self-government, in politics; in the social sphere, free-trade, unrestricted competition, and the making of large industrial fortunes; in the religious sphere, the Dissidence of Dissent and the Protestantism of the Protestant religion. I do not say that other and more intelligent forces than this were not opposed to the Oxford movement: but this was the force which really beat it; this was the force which Dr. Newman felt himself fighting with; this was the force which till only the other day seemed to be the paramount force in this country, and to be in possession of the future; this was the force whose achievements fill Mr. Lowe [8] with such inexpressible admiration, and whose rule he was so horror-struck to see threatened. And where is this great force of Philistinism now? It is thrust into the second rank, it is become a power of yesterday, it has lost the future. A new power has suddenly appeared, a power which it is impossible yet to judge fully, but which is certainly a wholly different force from middle-class liberalism; different in its cardinal points of belief, different in its tendencies in every sphere. It loves and admires neither the legislation of middle-class Parliaments, nor the local self-government of middle-class vestries, nor the unrestricted competition of middle-class industrialists, nor the dissidence of middle-class Dissent and the Protestantism of middle-class Protestant religion. I am not now praising this new force, or saying that its own ideals are better; all I say is, that they are wholly different. And who will estimate how much the currents of feeling created by Dr. Newman's movements, the keen desire for beauty and sweetness which it nourished, the deep aversion it manifested to the hardness and vulgarity of middle-class liberalism, the strong light it turned on the hideous and grotesque illusions of middle-class Protestantism, — who will estimate how much all these contributed to swell the tide of secret dissatisfaction which has mined the ground under self-confident liberalism of the last thirty years, and has prepared the way for its sudden collapse and supersession? It is in this manner that the sentiment of Oxford for beauty and sweetness conquers, and in this manner long may it continue to conquer!

In this manner it works to the same end as culture, and there is plenty of work for it yet to do. I have said that the new and more democratic force which is now superseding our old middle-class liberalism cannot yet be rightly judged. It has its main tendencies still to form. We hear promises of its giving us administrative reform, law reform, reform of education, and I know not what; but those promises come rather from its advocates, wishing to make a good plea for it and to justify it for superseding middle-class liberalism, than from clear

8 Robert Lowe (Viscount Sherbrooke), member of Gladstone's Liberal cabinet.

tendencies which it has itself yet developed. But meanwhile it has plenty of well-intentioned friends against whom culture may with advantage continue to uphold steadily its ideal of human perfection; that this is *an inward spiritual activity, having for its characters increased sweetness, increased light, increased life, increased sympathy.* Mr. Bright, who has a foot in both worlds, the world of middle-class liberalism and the world of democracy, but who brings most of his ideas from the world of middle-class liberalism in which he was bred, always inclines to inculcate that faith in machinery to which, as we have seen, Englishmen are so prone, and which has been the bane of middle-class liberalism. He complains with a sorrowful indignation of people who "appear to have no proper estimate of the value of the franchise"; he leads his disciples to believe, — what the Englishman is always too ready to believe, — that the having a vote, like the having a large family, or a large business, or large muscles, has in itself some edifying and perfecting effect upon human nature. Or else he cries out to the democracy, — "the men," as he calls them, "upon whose shoulders the greatness of England rests," — he cries out to them: "See what you have done! I look over this country and see the cities you have built, the railroads you have made, the manufactures you have produced, the cargoes which freight the ships of the greatest mercantile navy the world has ever seen! I see that you have converted by your labours what was once a wilderness, these islands, into a fruitful garden; I know that you have created this wealth, and are a nation whose name is a word of power throughout all the world." Why, this is just the very style of laudation with which Mr. Roebuck or Mr. Lowe debauches the minds of the middle classes, and makes such Philistines of them. It is the same fashion of teaching a man to value himself not on what he *is,* not on his progress in sweetness and light, but on the number of the railroads he has constructed, or the bigness of the tabernacle he has built. Only the middle classes are told they have done it all with their energy, self-reliance, and capital, and the democracy are told they have done it all with their hands and sinews. But teaching the democracy to put its trust in achievements of this kind is merely training them to be Philistines to take the place of the Philistines whom they are superseding; and they too, like the middle class, will be encouraged to sit down at the banquet of the future without having on a wedding garment, and nothing excellent can then come from them. Those who know their besetting faults, those who have watched them and listened to them, or those who will read the instructive account recently given of them by one of themselves, the *Journeyman Engineer,*[9] will agree that the idea which culture sets before us of perfection, — an increased spiritual activity, having for its characters increased sweetness, increased light, increased life, in-

---

9 Pseudonym of Thomas Wright, author of *Some Habits and Customs of the Working Classes* (1867).

creased sympathy, — is an idea which the new democracy needs far more than the idea of the blessedness of the franchise, or the wonderfulness of its own industrial performances.

Other well-meaning friends of this new power are for leading it, not in the old ruts of middle-class Philistinism, but in ways which are naturally alluring to the feet of democracy, though in this country they are novel and untried ways. I may call them the ways of Jacobinism. Violent indignation with the past, abstract systems of renovation applied wholesale, a new doctrine drawn up in black and white for elaborating down to the very smallest details a rational society for the future, — these are the ways of Jacobinism. Mr. Frederic Harrison and other disciples of Comte, — one of them, Mr. Congreve,[10] is an old friend of mine, and I am glad to have an opportunity of publicly expressing my respect for his talents and character, — are among the friends of democracy who are for leading it in paths of this kind. Mr. Frederic Harrison is very hostile to culture, and from a natural enough motive; for culture is the eternal opponent of the two things which are the signal marks of Jacobinism, — its fierceness, and its addiction to an abstract system. Culture is always assigning to system-makers and systems a smaller share in the bent of human destiny than their friends like. A current in people's minds sets towards new ideas; people are dissatisfied with their old narrow stock of Philistine ideas, Anglo-Saxon ideas, or any other; and some man, some Bentham or Comte, who has the real merit of having early and strongly felt and helped the new current, but who brings plenty of narrowness and mistakes of his own into his feeling and help of it, is credited with being the author of the whole current, the fit person to be entrusted with its regulation and to guide the human race.

The excellent German historian of the mythology of Rome, Preller,[11] relating the introduction at Rome under the Tarquins of the worship of Apollo, the god of light, healing, and reconciliation, will have us observe that it was not so much the Tarquins who brought to Rome the new worship of Apollo, as a current in the mind of the Roman people which set powerfully at that time towards a new worship of this kind, and away from the old run of Latin and Sabine religious ideas. In a similar way, culture directs our attention to the natural current there is in human affairs, and to its continual working, and will not let us rivet our faith upon any one man and his doings. It makes us see not only his good side, but also how much in him was of necessity limited and transient; nay, it even feels a pleasure, a sense of an increased freedom and of an ampler future, in so doing.

I remember, when I was under the influence of a mind to which I feel the greatest obligations, the mind of a man who was the very

[10] Richard Congreve (1819–1899), one of Comte's principal followers in England.
[11] Ludwig Preller (1809–1861), German scholar.

incarnation of sanity and clear sense, a man the most considerable, it seems to me, whom America has yet produced, — Benjamin Franklin, — I remember the relief with which, after long feeling the sway of Franklin's imperturbable common-sense, I came upon a project of his for a new version of the Book of Job, to replace the old version, the style of which, says Franklin, has become obsolete, and thence less agreeable. "I give," he continues, "a few verses, which may serve as a sample of the kind of version I would recommend." We all recollect the famous verse in our translation: "Then Satan answered the Lord and said: 'Doth Job fear God for nought?' " Franklin makes this: "Does your Majesty imagine that Job's good conduct is the effect of mere personal attachment and affection?" I well remember how, when first I read that, I drew a deep breath of relief, and said to myself: "After all, there is a stretch of humanity beyond Franklin's victorious good sense!" So, after hearing Bentham cried loudly up as the renovator of modern society, and Bentham's mind and ideas proposed as the rulers of our future, I open the *Deontology*.[12] There I read: "While Xenophon was writing his history and Euclid teaching geometry, Socrates and Plato were talking nonsense under pretence of talking wisdom and morality. This morality of theirs consisted in words; this wisdom of theirs was the denial of matters known to every man's experience." From the moment of reading that, I am delivered from the bondage of Bentham! the fanaticism of his adherents can touch me no longer. I feel the inadequacy of his mind and ideas for supplying the rule of human society, for perfection.

Culture tends always thus to deal with the men of a system, of disciples, of a school; with men like Comte, or the late Mr. Buckle, or Mr. Mill. However much it may find to admire in these personages, or in some of them, it nevertheless remembers the text: "Be not ye called Rabbi!" and it soon passes on from any Rabbi. But Jacobinism loves a Rabbi; it does not want to pass on from its Rabbi in pursuit of a future and still unreached perfection; it wants its Rabbi and his ideas to stand for perfection, that they may with the more authority recast the world; and for Jacobinism, therefore, culture, — eternally passing onwards and seeking, — is an impertinence and an offence. But culture, just because it resists this tendency of Jacobinism to impose on us a man with limitations and errors of his own along with the true ideas of which he is the organ, really does the world and Jacobinism itself a service.

So, too, Jacobinism, in its fierce hatred of the past and of those whom it makes liable for the sins of the past, cannot away with the inexhaustible indulgence proper to culture, the consideration of circumstances, the severe judgment of actions joined to the merciful judgment of persons. "The man of culture is in politics," cries Mr.

12 *Deontology, or, The Science of Morality,* a posthumously published work of Jeremy Bentham's.

Frederic Harrison, "one of the poorest mortals alive!" Mr. Frederic Harrison wants to be doing business, and he complains that the man of culture stops him with a "turn for small fault-finding, love of selfish ease, and indecision in action." Of what use is culture, he asks, except for "a critic of new books or a professor of *belles-lettres*?" Why, it is of use because, in presence of the fierce exasperation which breathes, or rather, I may say, hisses through the whole production in which Mr. Frederic Harrison asks that question, it reminds us that the perfection of human nature is sweetness and light. It is of use because, like religion, — that other effort after perfection, — it testifies that, where bitter envying and strife are, there is confusion and every evil work.

The pursuit of perfection, then, is the pursuit of sweetness and light. He who works for sweetness and light, works to make reason and the will of God prevail. He who works for machinery, he who works for hatred, works only for confusion. Culture looks beyond machinery, culture hates hatred; culture has one great passion, the passion for sweetness and light. It has one even yet greater! — the passion for making them *prevail*. It is not satisfied till we *all* come to a perfect man; it knows that the sweetness and light of the few must be imperfect until the raw and unkindled masses of humanity are touched with sweetness and light. If I have not shrunk from saying that we must work for sweetness and light, so neither have I shrunk from saying that we must have a broad basis, must have sweetness and light for as many as possible. Again and again I have insisted how those are the happy moments of humanity, how those are the marking epochs of a people's life, how those are the flowering times for literature and art and all the creative power of genius, when there is a *national* glow of life and thought, when the whole of society is in the fullest measure permeated by thought, sensible to beauty, intelligent and alive. Only it must be *real* thought and *real* beauty; *real* sweetness and *real* light. Plenty of people will try to give the masses, as they call them, an intellectual food prepared and adapted in the way they think proper for the actual condition of the masses. The ordinary popular literature is an example of this way of working on the masses. Plenty of people will try to indoctrinate the masses with the set of ideas and judgments constituting the creed of their own profession or party. Our religious and political organizations give an example of this way of working on the masses. I condemn neither way; but culture works differently. It does not try to teach down to the level of inferior classes; it does not try to win them for this or that sect of its own, with ready-made judgments and watchwords. It seeks to do away with classes; to make the best that has been thought and known in the world current everywhere; to make all men live in an atmosphere of sweetness and light, where they may use ideas, as it uses them itself, freely, — nourished, and not bound by them.

This is the *social idea*; and the men of culture are the true apostles of equality. The great men of culture are those who have had a passion for diffusing, for making prevail, for carrying from one end of society to the other, the best knowledge, the best ideas of their time; who have laboured to divest knowledge of all that was harsh, uncouth, difficult, abstract, professional, exclusive; to humanise it, to make it efficient outside the clique of the cultivated and learned, yet still remaining the *best* knowledge and thought of the time, and a true source, therefore, of sweetness and light. Such a man was Abelard in the Middle Ages, in spite of all his imperfections; and thence the boundless emotion and enthusiasm which Abelard excited. Such were Lessing and Herder in Germany, at the end of the last century; and their services to Germany were in this way inestimably precious. Generations will pass, and literary monuments will accumulate, and works far more perfect than the works of Lessing and Herder will be produced in Germany; and yet the names of these two men will fill a German with a reverence and enthusiasm such as the names of the most gifted masters will hardly awaken. And why? Because they *humanised* knowledge; because they broadened the basis of life and intelligence; because they worked powerfully to diffuse sweetness and light, to make reason and the will of God prevail. With Saint Augustine they said: "Let us not leave thee alone to make in the secret of thy knowledge, as thou didst before the creation of the firmament, the division of light from darkness; let the children of thy spirit, placed in their firmament, make their light shine upon the earth, mark the division of night and day, and announce the revolution of the times; for the old order is passed, and the new arises; the night is spent, the day is come forth; and thou shalt crown the year with thy blessing, when thou shalt send forth labourers into thy harvest sown by other hands than theirs; when thou shalt send forth new labourers to new seed-times, whereof the harvest shall be not yet."

CHAPTER IV

Hebraism and Hellenism

THIS fundamental ground [1] is our preference of doing to thinking. Now this preference is a main element in our nature, and as we study it we find ourselves opening up a number of large questions on every side.

[1] Arnold had ended the preceding chapter, "Barbarians, Philistines, Populace," as follows: "We see how our habits and practice oppose themselves to such a recognition [of right reason], and the many inconveniences which we therefore suffer. But now let us try to go a little deeper, and to find, beneath our actual habits and practice, the very ground and cause out of which they spring."

Let me go back for a moment to Bishop Wilson, who says: "First, never go against the best light you have; secondly, take care that your light be not darkness." We show, as a nation, laudable energy and persistence in walking according to the best light we have, but are not quite careful enough, perhaps, to see that our light be not darkness. This is only another version of the old story that energy is our strong point and favourable characteristic, rather than intelligence. But we may give to this idea a more general form still, in which it will have a yet larger range of application. We may regard this energy driving at practice, this paramount sense of the obligation of duty, self-control, and work, this earnestness in going manfully with the best light we have, as one force. And we may regard the intelligence driving at those ideas which are, after all, the basis of right practice, the ardent sense for all the new and changing combinations of them which man's development brings with it, the indomitable impulse to know and adjust them perfectly, as another force. And these two forces we may regard as in some sense rivals, — rivals not by the necessity of their own nature, but as exhibited in man and his history, — and rivals dividing the empire of the world between them. And to give these forces names from the two races of men who have supplied the most signal and splendid manifestations of them, we may call them respectively the forces of Hebraism and Hellenism. Hebraism and Hellenism, — between these two points of influence moves our world. At one time it feels more powerfully the attraction of one of them, at another time of the other; and it ought to be, though it never is, evenly and happily balanced between them.

The final aim of both Hellenism and Hebraism, as of all great spiritual disciplines, is no doubt the same: man's perfection or salvation. The very language which they both of them use in schooling us to reach this aim is often identical. Even when their language indicates by variation, — sometimes a broad variation, often a but slight and subtle variation, — the different courses of thought which are uppermost in each discipline, even then the unity of the final end and aim is still apparent. To employ the actual words of that discipline with which we ourselves are all of us most familiar, and the words of which, therefore, come most home to us, that final end and aim is "that we might be partakers of the divine nature." These are the words of a Hebrew apostle, but of Hellenism and Hebraism alike this is, I say, the aim. When the two are confronted, as they very often are confronted, it is nearly always with what I may call a rhetorical purpose; the speaker's whole design is to exalt and enthrone one of the two, and he uses the other only as a foil and to enable him the better to give effect to his purpose. Obviously, with us, it is usually Hellenism which is thus reduced to minister to the triumph of Hebraism. There is a sermon on Greece and the Greek spirit by a man never to be men-

tioned without interest and respect, Frederick Robertson,[2] in which
this rhetorical use of Greece and the Greek spirit, and the inadequate
exhibition of them necessarily consequent upon this, is almost ludicrous, and would be censurable if it were not to be explained by the
exigencies of a sermon. On the other hand, Heinrich Heine, and other
writers of his sort, give us the spectacle of the tables completely
turned, and of Hebraism brought in just as a foil and contrast to
Hellenism, and to make the superiority of Hellenism more manifest. In
both these cases there is injustice and misrepresentation. The aim and
end of both Hebraism and Hellenism is, as I have said, one and the
same, and this aim and end is august and admirable.

Still, they pursue this aim by very different courses. The uppermost
idea with Hellenism is to see things as they really are; the uppermost
idea with Hebraism is conduct and obedience. Nothing can do away
with this ineffaceable difference. The Greek quarrel with the body
and its desires is, that they hinder right thinking; the Hebrew quarrel
with them is, that they hinder right acting. "He that keepeth the law,
happy is he"; "Blessed is the man that feareth the Eternal, that de-
lighteth greatly in his commandments"; — that is the Hebrew notion
of felicity; and, pursued with passion and tenacity, this notion would
not let the Hebrew rest till, as is well known, he had at last got out
of the law a network of prescriptions to enwrap his whole life, to
govern every moment of it, every impulse, every action. The Greek
notion of felicity, on the other hand, is perfectly conveyed in these
words of a great French moralist: *"C'est le bonheur des hommes,"* —
when? when they abhor that which is evil? — no; when they exercise
themselves in the law of the Lord day and night? — no; when they
die daily? — no; when they walk about the New Jerusalem with
palms in their hands? — no; but when they think aright, when their
thought hits: *"quand ils pensent juste."* [3] At the bottom of both the
Greek and the Hebrew notion is the desire, native in man, for reason
and the will of God, the feeling after the universal order, — in a word,
the love of God. But, while Hebraism seizes upon certain plain, capital intimations of the universal order, and rivets itself, one may say,
with unequalled grandeur of earnestness and intensity on the study
and observance of them, the bent of Hellenism is to follow, with
flexible activity, the whole play of the universal order, to be apprehensive of missing any part of it, of sacrificing one part to another, to
slip away from resting in this or that intimation of it, however capital.
An unclouded clearness of mind, an unimpeded play of thought, is
what this bent drives at. The governing idea of Hellenism is *spontaneity of consciousness;* that of Hebraism, *strictness of conscience.*

Christianity changed nothing in this essential bent of Hebraism to

2 Frederick William Robertson (1816–1853), clergyman, author, and famous
preacher.
3 "It is happiness for men when they think right."

set doing above knowing. Self-conquest, self-devotion, the following not our own individual will, but the will of God, *obedience,* is the fundamental idea of this form, also, of the discipline to which we have attached the general name of Hebraism. Only, as the old law and the network of prescriptions with which it enveloped human life were evidently a motive-power not driving and searching enough to produce the result aimed at, — patient continuance in well-doing, self-conquest, — Christianity substituted for them boundless devotion to that inspiring and affecting pattern of self-conquest offered by Jesus Christ; and by the new motive-power, of which the essence was this, though the love and admiration of Christian churches have for centuries been employed in varying, amplifying, and adoring the plain description of it, Christianity, as St. Paul truly says, "establishes the law," and in the strength of the ampler power which she has thus supplied to fulfil it, has accomplished the miracles, which we all see, of her history.

So long as we do not forget that both Hellenism and Hebraism are profound and admirable manifestations of man's life, tendencies, and powers, and that both of them aim at a like final result, we can hardly insist too strongly on the divergence of line and of operation with which they proceed. It is a divergence so great that it most truly, as the prophet Zechariah says, "has raised up thy sons, O Zion, against thy sons, O Greece!" The difference whether it is by doing or by knowing that we set most store, and the practical consequences which follow from this difference, leave their mark on all the history of our race and of its development. Language may be abundantly quoted from both Hellenism and Hebraism to make it seem that one follows the same current as the other towards the same goal. They are, truly, borne towards the same goal; but the currents which bear them are infinitely different. It is true, Solomon will praise knowing: "Understanding is a well-spring of life unto him that hath it." And in the New Testament, again, Jesus Christ is a "light," and "truth makes us free." It is true, Aristotle will undervalue knowing: "In what concerns virtue," says he, "three things are necessary — knowledge, deliberate will, and perseverance; but, whereas the two last are all-important, the first is a matter of little importance." It is true that with the same impatience with which St. James enjoins a man to be not a forgetful hearer, but a *doer of the work,* Epictetus exhorts us to *do* what we have demonstrated to ourselves we ought to do; or he taunts us with futility, for being armed at all points to prove that lying is wrong, yet all the time continuing to lie. It is true Plato, in words which are almost the words of the New Testament or the Imitation, calls life a learning to die. But underneath the superficial agreement the fundamental divergence still subsists. The understanding of Solomon is "the walking in the way of the commandments"; this is "the way of peace," and it is of this that blessedness comes. In the New Testament, the truth which gives us the peace of God and makes us free, is the

love of Christ constraining us to crucify, as he did, and with a like
purpose of moral regeneration, the flesh with its affections and lusts,
and thus establishing, as we have seen, the law. The moral virtues,
on the other hand, are with Aristotle but the porch and access to the
intellectual, and with these last is blessedness. That partaking of the
divine life, which both Hellenism and Hebraism, as we have said, fix
as their crowning aim, Plato expressly denies to the man of practical
virtue merely, of self-conquest with any other motive than that of perfect intellectual vision. He reserves it for the lover of pure knowledge, of seeing things as they really are, — the φιλομαθής.

Both Hellenism and Hebraism arise out of the wants of human nature, and address themselves to satisfying those wants. But their
methods are so different, they lay stress on such different points, and
call into being by their respective disciplines such different activities,
that the face which human nature presents when it passes from the
hands of one of them to those of the other, is no longer the same. To
get rid of one's ignorance, to see things as they are, and by seeing them
as they are to see them in their beauty, is the simple and attractive
ideal which Hellenism holds out before human nature; and from the
simplicity and charm of this ideal, Hellenism, and human life in the
hands of Hellenism, is invested with a kind of aërial ease, clearness,
and radiancy; they are full of what we call sweetness and light. Difficulties are kept out of view, and the beauty and rationalness of the
ideal have all our thoughts. "The best man is he who most tries to
perfect himself, and the happiest man is he who most feels that he *is*
perfecting himself," — this account of the matter by Socrates, the
true Socrates of the *Memorabilia,* has something so simple, spontaneous, and unsophisticated about it, that it seems to fill us with
clearness and hope when we hear it. But there is a saying which I
have heard attributed to Mr. Carlyle about Socrates, — a very happy
saying, whether it is really Mr. Carlyle's or not, — which excellently
marks the essential point in which Hebraism differs from Hellenism.
"Socrates," this saying goes, "is terribly *at ease in Zion.*" Hebraism, —
and here is the source of its wonderful strength, — has always been
severely preoccupied with an awful sense of the impossibility of being
at ease in Zion; of the difficulties which oppose themselves to man's
pursuit or attainment of that perfection of which Socrates talks so
hopefully, and, as from this point of view one might almost say, so
glibly. It is all very well to talk of getting rid of one's ignorance, of
seeing things in their reality, seeing them in their beauty; but how is
this to be done when there is something which thwarts and spoils all
our efforts?

This something is *sin*; and the space which sin fills in Hebraism, as
compared with Hellenism, is indeed prodigious. This obstacle to perfection fills the whole scene, and perfection appears remote and rising
away from earth, in the background. Under the name of sin, the diffi-

culties of knowing oneself and conquering oneself which impede man's passage to perfection, become, for Hebraism, a positive, active entity hostile to man, a mysterious power which I heard Dr. Pusey the other day, in one of his impressive sermons, compare to a hideous hunch-back seated on our shoulders, and which it is the main business of our lives to hate and oppose. The discipline of the Old Testament may be summed up as a discipline teaching us to abhor and flee from sin; the discipline of the New Testament, as a discipline teaching us to die to it. As Hellenism speaks of thinking clearly, seeing things in their essence and beauty, as a grand and precious feat for man to achieve, so Hebraism speaks of becoming conscious of sin, of wakening to a sense of sin, as a feat of this kind. It is obvious to what wide divergence these differing tendencies, actively followed, must lead. As one passes and repasses from Hellenism to Hebraism, from Plato to St. Paul, one feels inclined to rub one's eyes and ask oneself whether man is indeed a gentle and simple being, showing the traces of a noble and divine nature; or an unhappy chained captive, labouring with groanings that cannot be uttered to free himself from the body of this death.

Apparently it was the Hellenic conception of human nature which was unsound, for the world could not live by it. Absolutely to call it unsound, however, is to fall into the common error of its Hebraising enemies; but it was unsound at that particular moment of man's development, it was premature. The indispensable basis of conduct and self-control, the platform upon which alone the perfection aimed at by Greece can come into bloom, was not to be reached by our race so easily; centuries of probation and discipline were needed to bring us to it. Therefore the bright promise of Hellenism faded, and Hebraism ruled the world. Then was seen that astonishing spectacle, so well marked by the often-quoted words of the prophet Zechariah, when men of all languages and nations took hold of the skirt of him that was a Jew, saying: — "*We will go with you, for we have heard that God is with you.*" And the Hebraism which thus received and ruled a world all gone out of the way and altogether become unprofitable, was, and could not but be, the later, the more spiritual, the more attractive development of Hebraism. It was Christianity; that is to say, Hebraism aiming at self-conquest and rescue from the thrall of vile affections, not by obedience to the letter of a law, but by conformity to the image of a self-sacrificing example. To a world stricken with moral enervation Christianity offered its spectacle of an inspired self-sacrifice; to men who refused themselves nothing, it showed one who refused himself everything; — "*my Saviour banished joy!*" says George Herbert. When the *alma Venus*, the life-giving and joy-giving power of nature, so fondly cherished by the Pagan world, could not save her followers from self-dissatisfaction and ennui, the severe words of the apostle came bracingly and refreshingly: "Let no man deceive you with vain words, for because of these things cometh the wrath of God upon the

children of disobedience." Through age after age and generation after
generation, our race, or all that part of our race which was most living
and progressive, was *baptized into a death*; and endeavoured, by suffering in the flesh, to cease from sin. Of this endeavour, the animating labours and afflictions of early Christianity, the touching asceticism
of mediæval Christianity, are the great historical manifestations. Literary monuments of it, each in its own way incomparable, remain in
the Epistles of St. Paul, in St. Augustine's Confessions, and in the two
original and simplest books of the Imitation.[4]

Of two disciplines laying their main stress, the one, on clear intelligence, the other, on firm obedience; the one, on comprehensively
knowing the grounds of one's duty, the other, on diligently practising
it; the one, on taking all possible care (to use Bishop Wilson's words
again) that the light we have be not darkness, the other, that according to the best light we have we diligently walk, — the priority naturally belongs to that discipline which braces all man's moral powers,
and founds for him an indispensable basis of character. And, therefore, it is justly said of the Jewish people, who were charged with
setting powerfully forth that side of the divine order to which the
words *conscience* and *self-conquest* point, that they were "entrusted
with the oracles of God"; as it is justly said of Christianity, which followed Judaism and which set forth this side with a much deeper effectiveness and a much wider influence, that the wisdom of the old
Pagan world was foolishness compared to it. No words of devotion
and admiration can be too strong to render thanks to these beneficent
forces which have so borne forward humanity in its appointed work
of coming to the knowledge and possession of itself; above all, in
those great moments when their action was the wholesomest and the
most necessary.

But the evolution of these forces, separately and in themselves, is not
the whole evolution of humanity, — their single history is not the
whole history of man; whereas their admirers are always apt to make it
stand for the whole history. Hebraism and Hellenism are, neither of
them, the *law* of human development, as their admirers are prone to
make them; they are, each of them, *contributions* to human development, — august contributions, invaluable contributions; and each
showing itself to us more august, more invaluable, more preponderant
over the other, according to the moment in which we take them, and
the relation in which we stand to them. The nations of our modern
world, children of that immense and salutary movement which broke
up the Pagan world, inevitably stand to Hellenism in a relation which
dwarfs it, and to Hebraism in a relation which magnifies it. They are
inevitably prone to take Hebraism as the law of human development,
and not as simply a contribution to it, however precious. And yet the
lesson must perforce be learned, that the human spirit is wider than

4 The two first books. [Arnold's note.]

the most priceless of the forces which bear it onward, and that to the whole development of man Hebraism itself is, like Hellenism, but a contribution.

Perhaps we may help ourselves to see this clearer by an illustration drawn from the treatment of a single great idea which has profoundly engaged the human spirit, and has given it eminent opportunities for showing its nobleness and energy. It surely must be perceived that the idea of immortality, as this idea rises in its generality before the human spirit, is something grander, truer, and more satisfying, than it is in the particular forms by which St. Paul, in the famous fifteenth chapter of the Epistle to the Corinthians, and Plato, in the *Phædo*, endeavour to develop and establish it. Surely we cannot but feel, that the argumentation with which the Hebrew apostle goes about to expound this great idea is, after all, confused and inconclusive; and that the reasoning, drawn from analogies of likeness and equality, which is employed upon it by the Greek philosopher, is over-subtle and sterile. Above and beyond the inadequate solutions which Hebraism and Hellenism here attempt, extends the immense and august problem itself, and the human spirit which gave birth to it. And this single illustration may suggest to us how the same thing happens in other cases also.

But meanwhile, by alternations of Hebraism and Hellenism, of a man's intellectual and moral impulses, of the effort to see things as they really are, and the effort to win peace by self-conquest, the human spirit proceeds; and each of these two forces has its appointed hours of culmination and seasons of rule. As the great movement of Christianity was a triumph of Hebraism and man's moral impulses, so the great movement which goes by the name of the Renascence [5] was an uprising and reinstatement of man's intellectual impulses and of Hellenism. We in England, the devoted children of Protestantism, chiefly know the Renascence by its subordinate and secondary side of the Reformation. The Reformation has been often called a Hebraising revival, a return to the ardour and sincereness of primitive Christianity. No one, however, can study the development of Protestantism and of Protestant churches without feeling that into the Reformation too, — Hebraising child of the Renascence and offspring of its fervour, rather than its intelligence, as it undoubtedly was, — the subtle Hellenic leaven of the Renascence found its way, and that the exact respective parts, in the Reformation, of Hebraism and of Hellenism, are not easy to separate. But what we may with truth say is, that all which Protestantism was to itself clearly conscious of, all which it succeeded in clearly setting forth in words, had the characters of Hebraism rather than of Hellenism. The Reformation was strong, in that it was an earnest return to the Bible and to doing from the heart the will of

[5] I have ventured to give the foreign *Renaissance* — destined to become of more common use amongst us as the movement which its denotes comes, as it will come, increasingly to interest us — an English form. [Arnold's note.]

God as there written. It was weak, in that it never consciously
grasped or applied the central idea of the Renascence, — the Hellenic
idea of pursuing, in all lines of activity, the law and science, to use
Plato's words, of things as they really are. Whatever direct superiority,
therefore, Protestantism had over Catholicism was a moral superiority,
a superiority arising out of its greater sincerity and earnestness, — at
the moment of its apparition at any rate, — in dealing with the heart
and conscience. Its pretensions to an intellectual superiority are in
general quite illusory. For Hellenism, for the thinking side in man as
distinguished from the acting side, the attitude of mind of Protestantism towards the Bible in no respect differs from the attitude of mind
of Catholicism towards the Church. The mental habit of him who
imagines that Balaam's ass spoke, in no respect differs from the mental
habit of him who imagines that a Madonna of wood or stone winked;
and the one, who says that God's Church makes him believe what he
believes, and the other, who says that God's Word makes him believe
what he believes, are for the philosopher perfectly alike in not really
and truly knowing, when they say *God's Church* and *God's Word,*
what it is they say, or whereof they affirm.

In the sixteenth century, therefore, Hellenism re-entered the world,
and again stood in presence of Hebraism, — a Hebraism renewed and
purged. Now, it has not been enough observed, how, in the seventeenth
century, a fate befell Hellenism in some respects analogous to that
which befell it at the commencement of our era. The Renascence,
that great reawakening of Hellenism, that irresistible return of humanity to nature and to seeing things as they are, which in art, in literature,
and in physics, produced such splendid fruits, had, like the anterior
Hellenism of the Pagan world, a side of moral weakness and of relaxation or insensibility of the moral fibre, which in Italy showed itself
with the most startling plainness, but which in France, England, and
other countries was very apparent too. Again this loss of spiritual balance, this exclusive preponderance given to man's perceiving and
knowing side, this unnatural defect of his feeling and acting side,
provoked a reaction. Let us trace that reaction where it most nearly
concerns us.

Science has now made visible to everybody the great and pregnant
elements of difference which lie in race, and in how signal a manner
they make the genius and history of an Indo-European people vary
from those of a Semitic people. Hellenism is of Indo-European
growth, Hebraism is of Semitic growth; and we English, a nation of
Indo-European stock, seem to belong naturally to the movement of
Hellenism. But nothing more strongly marks the essential unity of
man, than the affinities we can perceive, in this point or that, between
members of one family of peoples and members of another. And no
affinity of this kind is more strongly marked than that likeness in the
strength and prominence of the moral fibre, which, notwithstanding

immense elements of difference, knits in some special sort the genius and history of us English, and our American descendants across the Atlantic, to the genius and history of the Hebrew people. Puritanism, which has been so great a power in the English nation, and in the strongest part of the English nation, was originally the reaction in the seventeenth century of the conscience and moral sense of our race, against the moral indifference and lax rule of conduct which in the sixteenth century came in with the Renascence. It was a reaction of Hebraism against Hellenism; and it powerfully manifested itself, as was natural, in a people with much of what we call a Hebraising turn, with a signal affinity for the bent which was the master-bent of Hebrew life. Eminently Indo-European by its *humour,* by the power it shows, through this gift, of imaginatively acknowledging the multiform aspects of the problem of life, and of thus getting itself unfixed from its own over-certainty, of smiling at its own over-tenacity, our race has yet (and a great part of its strength lies here), in matters of practical life and moral conduct, a strong share of the assuredness, the tenacity, the intensity of the Hebrews. This turn manifested itself in Puritanism, and has had a great part in shaping our history for the last two hundred years. Undoubtedly it checked and changed amongst us that movement of the Renascence which we see producing in the reign of Elizabeth such wonderful fruits. Undoubtedly it stopped the prominent rule and direct development of that order of ideas which we call by the name of Hellenism, and gave the first rank to a different order of ideas. Apparently, too, as we said of the former defeat of Hellenism, if Hellenism was defeated, this shows that Hellenism was imperfect, and that its ascendency at that moment would not have been for the world's good.

Yet there is a very important difference between the defeat inflicted on Hellenism by Christianity eighteen hundred years ago, and the check given to the Renascence by Puritanism. The greatness of the difference is well measured by the difference in force, beauty, significance, and usefulness, between primitive Christianity and Protestantism. Eighteen hundred years ago it was altogether the hour of Hebraism. Primitive Christianity was legitimately and truly the ascendent force in the world at that time, and the way of mankind's progress lay through its full development. Another hour in man's development began in the fifteenth century, and the main road of his progress then lay for a time through Hellenism. Puritanism was no longer the central current of the world's progress, it was a side stream crossing the central current and checking it. The cross and the check may have been necessary and salutary, but that does not do away with the essential difference between the main stream of man's advance and a cross or a side stream. For more than two hundred years the main stream of man's advance has moved towards knowing himself and the world, seeing things as they are, spontaneity of consciousness; the main impulse of a great part, and that the strongest part, of our nation has been towards strictness of conscience. They have made the secondary the principal at the wrong moment, and the principal they have at the wrong moment treated as secondary. This contravention of the natural order has produced, as such contravention always must produce, a certain confusion and false movement, of which we are now beginning to feel, in almost every direction, the inconvenience. In all directions our habitual courses of action seem to be losing efficaciousness, credit, and control, both with others and even with ourselves. Everywhere we see the beginnings of confusion, and we want a clue to some sound order and authority. This we can only get by going back upon the actual instincts and forces which rule our life, seeing them as they really are, connecting them with other instincts and forces, and enlarging our whole view and rule of life.

Discourses in America

❧ *Discourses in America* was composed of the three lectures which Arnold delivered on his lecture tour in America in 1883–1884: "Numbers; or, The Majority and the Remnant"; "Literature and Science"; "Emerson." "Literature and Science" had first been delivered as the Rede Lecture at Cambridge and published in the *Nineteenth Century* for August 1882; it was considerably revised, especially in the early part, for the American lecture tour. This essay may be instructively (if carefully) compared with Huxley's essay "Science and Culture," printed in this volume. ❧

Literature and Science

PRACTICAL people talk with a smile of Plato and of his absolute ideas; and it is impossible to deny that Plato's ideas do often seem unpractical and unpracticable, and especially when one views them in connexion with the life of a great work-a-day world like the United States. The necessary staple of the life of such a world Plato regards with disdain; handicraft and trade and the working professions he regards with disdain; but what becomes of the life of an industrial modern community if you take handicraft and trade and the working professions out of it? The base mechanic arts and handicrafts, says Plato, bring about a natural weakness in the principle of excellence in a man, so that he cannot govern the ignoble growths in him, but nurses them, and cannot understand fostering any other. Those who exercise such arts and trades, as they have their bodies, he says, marred by their vulgar businesses, so they have their souls, too, bowed and broken by them. And if one of these uncomely people has a mind to seek self-culture and philosophy, Plato compares him to a bald little tinker, who has scraped together money, and has got his release from service, and has had a bath, and bought a new coat, and is rigged out like a bridegroom about to marry the daughter of his master who has fallen into poor and helpless estate.

Nor do the working professions fare any better than trade at the hands of Plato. He draws for us an inimitable picture of the working lawyer, and of his life of bondage; he shows how this bondage from his youth up has stunted and warped him, and made him small and crooked of soul, encompassing him with difficulties which he is not man enough to rely on justice and truth as means to encounter, but has recourse, for help out of them, to falsehood and wrong. And so, says Plato, this poor creature is bent and broken, and grows up from boy to man without a particle of soundness in him, although exceedingly smart and clever in his own esteem.

One cannot refuse to admire the artist who draws these pictures. But we say to ourselves that his ideas show the influence of a primitive and obsolete order of things, when the warrior caste and the priestly caste were alone in honour, and the humble work of the world was done by slaves. We have now changed all that; the modern majesty consists in work, as Emerson declares; and in work, we may add, principally of such plain and dusty kind as the work of cultivators of the ground, handicraftsmen, men of trade and business, men of the working professions. Above all is this true in a great industrious community such as that of the United States.

Now education, many people go on to say, is still mainly governed by the ideas of men like Plato, who lived when the warrior caste and the priestly or philosophical class were alone in honour, and the really useful part of the community were slaves. It is an education fitted for persons of leisure in such a community. This education passed from Greece and Rome to the feudal communities of Europe, where also the warrior caste and the priestly caste were alone held in honour, and where the really useful and working part of the community, though not nominally slaves as in the pagan world, were practically not much better off than slaves, and not more seriously regarded. And how absurd it is, people end by saying, to inflict this education upon an industrious modern community, where very few indeed are persons of leisure, and the mass to be considered has not leisure, but is bound, for its own great good, and for the great good of the world at large, to plain labour and to industrial pursuits, and the education in question tends necessarily to make men dissatisfied with these pursuits and unfitted for them!

That is what is said. So far I must defend Plato, as to plead that his view of education and studies is in the general, as it seems to me, sound enough, and fitted for all sorts and conditions of men, whatever their pursuits may be. "An intelligent man," says Plato, "will prize those studies which result in his soul getting soberness, righteousness, and wisdom, and will less value the others." I cannot consider *that* a bad description of the aim of education, and of the motives which should govern us in the choice of studies, whether we are preparing ourselves for a hereditary seat in the English House of Lords or for the pork trade in Chicago.

Still I admit that Plato's world was not ours, that his scorn of trade and handicraft is fantastic, that he had no conception of a great industrial community such as that of the United States, and that such a community must and will shape its education to suit its own needs. If the usual education handed down to it from the past does not suit it, it will certainly before long drop this and try another. The usual education in the past has been mainly literary. The question is whether the studies which were long supposed to be the best for all of us are practically the best now; whether others are not better. The tyranny of the past, many think, weighs on us injuriously in the predominance given to letters in education. The question is raised whether, to meet the needs of our modern life, the predominance ought not now to pass from letters to science; and naturally the question is nowhere raised with more energy than here in the United States. The design of abasing what is called "mere literary instruction and education," and of exalting what is called "sound, extensive, and practical scientific knowledge," is, in this intensely modern world of the United States, even more perhaps than in Europe, a very popular design, and makes great and rapid progress.

I am going to ask whether the present movement for ousting letters from their old predominance in education, and for transferring the predominance in education to the natural sciences, whether this brisk and flourishing movement ought to prevail, and whether it is likely that in the end it really will prevail. An objection may be raised which I will anticipate. My own studies have been almost wholly in letters, and my visits to the field of the natural sciences have been very slight and inadequate, although those sciences have always strongly moved my curiosity. A man of letters, it will perhaps be said, is not competent to discuss the comparative merits of letters and natural science as means of education. To this objection I reply, first of all, that his incompetence, if he attempts the discussion but is really incompetent for it, will be abundantly visible; nobody will be taken in; he will have plenty of sharp observers and critics to save mankind from that danger. But the line I am going to follow is, as you will soon discover, so extremely simple, that perhaps it may be followed without failure even by one who for a more ambitious line of discussion would be quite incompetent.

Some of you may possibly remember a phrase of mine which has been the object of a good deal of comment; an observation to the effect that in our culture, the aim being *to know ourselves and the world*, we have, as the means to this end, *to know the best which has been thought and said in the world*. A man of science, who is also an excellent writer and the very prince of debaters, Professor Huxley, in a discourse at the opening of Sir Josiah Mason's college at Birmingham,[1] laying hold of this phrase, expanded it by quoting some more words of mine, which are these: "The civilised world is to be regarded as now being, for intellectual and spiritual purposes, one great confederation, bound to a joint action and working to a common result; and whose members have for their proper outfit a knowledge of Greek, Roman, and Eastern antiquity, and of one another. Special local and temporary advantages being put out of account, that modern nation will in the intellectual and spiritual sphere make most progress, which most thoroughly carries out this programme."

Now on my phrase, thus enlarged, Professor Huxley remarks that when I speak of the above-mentioned knowledge as enabling us to know ourselves and the world, I assert *literature* to contain the materials which suffice for thus making us know ourselves and the world. But it is not by any means clear, says he, that after having learnt all which ancient and modern literatures have to tell us, we have laid a sufficiently broad and deep foundation for that criticism of life, that knowledge of ourselves and the world, which constitutes culture. On the contrary, Professor Huxley declares that he finds himself "wholly unable to admit that either nations or individuals will really advance, if their outfit draws nothing from the stores of physical science. An army without weapons of precision, and with no particular base of operations, might more hopefully enter upon a campaign on the Rhine, than a man, devoid of a knowledge of what physical science has done in the last century, upon a criticism of life."

This shows how needful it is for those who are to discuss any matter together, to have a common understanding as to the sense of the terms they employ, — how needful, and how difficult. What Professor Huxley says, implies just the reproach which is so often brought against the study of *belles lettres*, as they are called: that the study is an elegant one, but slight and ineffectual; a smattering of Greek and Latin and other ornamental things, of little use for any one whose object is to get at truth, and to be a practical man. So, too, M. Renan talks of the "superficial humanism" of a school-course which treats us as if we were all going to be poets, writers, preachers, orators, and he opposes this humanism to positive science, or the critical search after truth. And there is always a tendency in those who are remonstrating against the predominance of letters in educa-

[1] Reprinted in this volume.

tion, to understand by letters *belles lettres,* and by *belles lettres* a superficial humanism, the opposite of science or true knowledge.

But when we talk of knowing Greek and Roman antiquity, for instance, which is the knowledge people have called the humanities, I for my part mean a knowledge which is something more than a superficial humanism, mainly decorative. "I call all teaching *scientific,*" says Wolf, the critic of Homer, "which is systematically laid out and followed up to its original sources. For example: a knowledge of classical antiquity is scientific when the remains of classical antiquity are correctly studied in the original languages." There can be no doubt that Wolf is perfectly right; that all learning is scientific which is systematically laid out and followed up to its original sources, and that a genuine humanism is scientific.

When I speak of knowing Greek and Roman antiquity, therefore, as a help to knowing ourselves and the world, I mean more than a knowledge of so much vocabulary, so much grammar, so many portions of authors in the Greek and Latin languages. I mean knowing the Greeks and Romans, and their life and genius, and what they were and did in the world; what we get from them, and what is its value. That, at least, is the ideal; and when we talk of endeavouring to know Greek and Roman antiquity, as a help to knowing ourselves and the world, we mean endeavouring so to know them as to satisfy this ideal, however much we may still fall short of it.

The same also as to knowing our own and other modern nations, with the like aim of getting to understand ourselves and the world. To know the best that has been thought and said by the modern nations, is to know, says Professor Huxley, "only what modern *literatures* have to tell us; it is the criticism of life contained in modern literature." And yet "the distinctive character of our times," he urges, "lies in the vast and constantly increasing part which is played by natural knowledge." And how, therefore, can a man, devoid of knowledge of what physical science has done in the last century, enter hopefully upon a criticism of modern life?

Let us, I say, be agreed about the meaning of the terms we are using. I talk of knowing the best which has been thought and uttered in the world; Professor Huxley says this means knowing *literature.* Literature is a large word; it may mean everything written with letters or printed in a book. Euclid's *Elements* and Newton's *Principia* are thus literature. All knowledge that reaches us through books is literature. But by literature Professor Huxley means *belles lettres.* He means to make me say, that knowing the best which has been thought and said by the modern nations is knowing their *belles lettres* and no more. And this is no sufficient equipment, he argues, for a criticism of modern life. But as I do not mean, by knowing ancient Rome, knowing merely more or less of Latin *belles lettres,* and taking no account of Rome's military, and political, and legal, and administrative work in the world; and as, by knowing ancient Greece, I understand knowing her as the giver of Greek art, and the guide to a free and right use of reason and to scientific method, and the founder of our mathematics and physics and astronomy and biology, — I understand knowing her as all this, and not merely knowing certain Greek poems, and histories, and treatises, and speeches, — so as to the knowledge of modern nations also. By knowing modern nations, I mean not merely knowing their *belles lettres,* but knowing also what has been done by such men as Copernicus, Galileo, Newton, Darwin. "Our ancestors learned," says Professor Huxley, "that the earth is the centre of the visible universe, and that man is the cynosure of things terrestrial; and more especially was it inculcated that the course of nature had no fixed order, but that it could be, and constantly was, altered." "But for us now," continues Professor Huxley, "the notions of the beginning and the end of the world entertained by our forefathers are no longer credible. It is very certain that the earth is not the chief body in the material universe, and that the world is not subordinated to man's use. It is even more certain that nature is the expression of a definite order, with which nothing interferes." "And yet," he cries, "the purely classical education advocated by the representatives of the humanists in our day gives no inkling of all this."

In due place and time I will just touch upon that vexed question of classical education; but at present the question is as to what is meant by knowing the best which modern nations have thought and said. It is not knowing their *belles lettres* merely which is meant. To know Italian *belles lettres* is not to know Italy, and to know English *belles lettres* is not to know England. Into knowing Italy and England there comes a great deal more, Galileo and Newton amongst it. The reproach of being a superficial humanism, a tincture of *belles lettres,* may attach rightly enough to some other disciplines; but to the particular discipline recommended when I proposed knowing the best that has been thought and said in the world, it does not apply. In that best I certainly include what in modern times has been thought and said by the great observers and knowers of nature.

There is, therefore, really no question between Professor Huxley and me as to whether knowing the great results of the modern scientific study of nature is not required as a part of our culture, as well as knowing the products of literature and art. But to follow the processes by which those results are reached, ought, say the friends of physical science, to be made the staple of education for the bulk of mankind. And here there does arise a question between those whom Professor Huxley calls with playful sarcasm "the Levites of culture," and those whom the poor humanist is sometimes apt to regard as its Nebuchadnezzars.

The great results of the scientific investigation of nature we are agreed upon knowing, but how much of our study are we bound to give to the processes by which those results are reached? The results have their visible bearing on human life. But all the processes, too, all the items of fact, by which those results are reached and established, are interesting. All knowledge is interesting to a wise man, and the knowledge of nature is interesting to all men. It is very interesting to know, that, from the albuminous white of the egg, the chick in the egg gets the materials for its flesh, bones, blood, and feathers; while, from the fatty yolk of the egg, it gets the heat and energy which enable it at length to break its shell and begin the world. It is less interesting, perhaps, but still it is interesting, to know that when a taper burns, the wax is converted into carbonic acid and water. Moreover, it is quite true that the habit of dealing with facts, which is given by the study of nature, is, as the friends of physical science praise it for being, an excellent discipline. The appeal, in the study of nature, is constantly to observation and experiment; not only is it said that the thing is so, but we can be made to see that it is so. Not only does a man tell us that when a taper burns the wax is converted into carbonic acid and water, as a man may tell us, if he likes, that Charon is punting his ferry-boat on the river Styx, or that Victor Hugo is a sublime poet, or Mr. Gladstone the most admirable of statesmen; but we are made to see that the conversion into carbonic acid and water does actually happen. This reality of natural knowledge it is, which makes the friends of physical science contrast it, as a knowledge of things, with the humanist's knowledge, which is, say they, a knowledge of words. And hence Professor Huxley is moved to lay it down that, "for the purpose of attaining real culture, an exclusively scientific education is at least as effectual as an exclusively literary education." And a certain President of the Section for Mechanical Science in the British Association is, in Scripture phrase, "very bold," and declares that if a man, in his mental training, "has substituted literature and history for natural science, he has chosen the less useful alternative." But whether we go these lengths or not, we must all admit that in natural science the habit gained of dealing with facts is a most valuable discipline, and that every one should have some experience of it.

More than this, however, is demanded by the reformers. It is proposed to make the training in natural science the main part of education, for the great majority of mankind at any rate. And here, I confess, I part company with the friends of physical science, with whom up to this point I have been agreeing. In differing from them, however, I wish to proceed with the utmost caution and diffidence. The smallness of my own acquaintance with the disciplines of natural science is ever before my mind, and I am fearful of doing these disciplines an injustice. The ability and pugnacity of the partisans of natural science make them formidable persons to contradict. The tone of tentative inquiry, which befits a being of dim faculties and bounded knowledge, is the tone I would wish to take and not to depart from. At present it seems to me, that those who are for giving to natural knowledge, as they call it, the chief place in the education of the majority of mankind, leave one important thing out of their account: the constitution of human nature. But I put this forward on the strength of some facts not at all recondite, very far from it; facts capable of being stated in the simplest possible fashion, and to which, if I so state them, the man of science will, I am sure, be willing to allow their due weight.

Deny the facts altogether, I think, he hardly can. He can hardly deny, that when we set ourselves to enumerate the powers which go to the building up of human life, and say that they are the power of conduct, the power of intellect and knowledge, the power of beauty, and the power of social life and manners, — he can hardly deny that this scheme, though drawn in rough and plain lines enough, and not pretending to scientific exactness, does yet give a fairly true representation of the matter. Human nature is built up by these powers; we have the need for them all. When we have rightly met and adjusted the claims of them all, we shall then be in a fair way for getting soberness and righteousness, with wisdom. This is evident enough, and the friends of physical science would admit it.

But perhaps they may not have sufficiently observed another thing: namely, that the several powers just mentioned are not isolated, but there is, in the generality of mankind, a perpetual tendency to relate them one to another in divers ways. With one such way of relating them I am particularly concerned now. Following our instinct for intellect and knowledge, we acquire pieces of knowledge; and presently, in the generality of men, there arises the desire to relate these pieces of knowledge to our sense for conduct, to our sense for beauty, — and there is weariness and dissatisfaction if the desire is baulked. Now in this desire lies, I think, the strength of that hold which letters have upon us.

All knowledge is, as I said just now, interesting; and even items of knowledge which from the nature of the case cannot well be related, but must stand isolated in our thoughts, have their interest. Even lists of exceptions have their interest. If we are studying Greek accents, it is interesting to know that *pais* and *pas,* and some other monosyllables of the same form of declension, do not take the circumflex upon the last syllable of the genitive plural, but vary, in this respect, from the common rule. If we are studying physiology, it is interesting to know that the pulmonary artery carries dark blood and the pulmonary vein carries bright blood, departing in this respect from the common rule for the division of labour between the veins and the arteries. But every one knows how we seek naturally to combine the pieces of our knowledge together, to bring them under general rules, to relate them to principles; and how unsatisfactory and tiresome it would be to go on for ever learning lists of exceptions, or accumulating items of fact which must stand isolated.

Well, that same need of relating our knowledge, which opérates here within the sphere of our knowledge itself, we shall find operating, also, outside that sphere. We experience, as we go on learning and knowing, — the vast majority of us experience, — the need of relating what we have learnt and known to the sense which we have in us for conduct, to the sense which we have in us for beauty.

A certain Greek prophetess of Mantineia in Arcadia, Diotima by name, once explained to the philosopher Socrates that love, and impulse, and bent of all kinds, is, in fact, nothing else but the desire in men that good should for ever be present to them. This desire for good, Diotima assured Socrates, is our fundamental desire, of which fundamental desire every impulse in us is only some one particular form. And therefore this fundamental desire it is, I suppose, — this desire in men that good should be for ever present to them, — which acts in us when we feel the impulse for relating our knowledge to our sense for conduct and to our sense for beauty. At any rate, with men in general the instinct exists. Such is human nature. And the instinct, it will be admitted, is innocent, and human nature is preserved by our following the lead of its innocent instincts. Therefore, in seeking to gratify this instinct in question, we are following the instinct of self-preservation in humanity.

But, no doubt, some kinds of knowledge cannot be made to directly serve the instinct in question, cannot be directly related to the sense for beauty, to the sense for conduct. These are instrument-knowledges; they lead on to other knowledges, which can. A man who passes his life in instrument knowledges is a specialist. They may be invaluable as instruments to something beyond, for those who have the gift thus to employ them; and they may be disciplines in themselves wherein it is useful for every one to have some schooling. But it is inconceivable that the generality of men should pass all their mental life with Greek accents or with formal logic. My friend Professor Sylvester,[2] who is one of the first mathematicians in the world, holds transcendental doctrines as to the virtue of mathematics, but those doctrines are not for common men. In the very Senate House and heart of our English Cambridge I once ventured, though not without an apology for my profaneness, to hazard the opinion that for the majority of mankind a little of mathematics, even, goes a long way. Of course this is quite consistent with their being of immense importance as an instrument to something else; but it is the few who have the aptitude for thus using them, not the bulk of mankind.

The natural sciences do not, however, stand on the same footing with these instrument-knowledges. Experience shows us that the general-

2 James Joseph Sylvester (1814–1897), English mathematician.

ity of men will find more interest in learning that, when a taper burns, the wax is converted into carbonic acid and water, or in learning the explanation of the phenomenon of dew, or in learning how the circulation of the blood is carried on, than they find in learning that the genitive plural of *pais* and *pas* does not take the circumflex on the termination. And one piece of natural knowledge is added to another, and others are added to that, and at last we come to propositions so interesting as Mr. Darwin's famous proposition that "our ancestor was a hairy quadruped furnished with a tail and pointed ears, probably arboreal in his habits." Or we come to propositions of such reach and magnitude as those which Professor Huxley delivers, when he says that the notions of our forefathers about the beginning and the end of the world were all wrong, and that nature is the expression of a definite order with which nothing interferes.

Interesting, indeed, these results of science are, important they are, and we should all of us be acquainted with them. But what I now wish you to mark is, that we are still, when they are propounded to us and we receive them, we are still in the sphere of intellect and knowledge. And for the generality of men there will be found, I say, to arise, when they have duly taken in the proposition that their ancestor was "a hairy quadruped furnished with a tail and pointed ears, probably arboreal in his habits," there will be found to arise an invincible desire to relate this proposition to the sense in us for conduct, and to the sense in us for beauty. But this the men of science will not do for us, and will hardly even profess to do. They will give us other pieces of knowledge, other facts, about other animals and their ancestors, or about plants, or about stones, or about stars; and they may finally bring us to those great "general conceptions of the universe, which are forced upon us all," says Professor Huxley, "by the progress of physical science." But still it will be *knowledge* only which they give us; knowledge not put for us into relation with our sense for conduct, our sense for beauty, and touched with emotion by being so put; not thus put for us, and therefore, to the majority of mankind, after a certain while, unsatisfying, wearying.

Not to the born naturalist, I admit. But what do we mean by a born naturalist? We mean a man in whom the zeal for observing nature is so uncommonly strong and eminent, that it marks him off from the bulk of mankind. Such a man will pass his life happily in collecting natural knowledge and reasoning upon it, and will ask for nothing, or hardly anything, more. I have heard it said that the sagacious and admirable naturalist whom we lost not very long ago, Mr. Darwin, once owned to a friend that for his part he did not experience the necessity for two things which most men find so necessary to them, — religion and poetry; science and the domestic affections, he thought, were enough. To a born naturalist, I can well understand that this should seem so. So absorbing is his occupation with nature, so strong his love for his occupation, that he goes on acquiring natural knowledge and reasoning upon it, and has little time or inclination for thinking about getting it related to the desire in man for conduct, the desire in man for beauty. He relates it to them for himself as he goes along, so far as he feels the need; and he draws from the domestic affections all the additional solace necessary. But then Darwins are extremely rare. Another great and admirable master of natural knowledge, Faraday, was a Sandemanian. That is to say, he related his knowledge to his instinct for conduct and to his instinct for beauty, by the aid of that respectable Scottish sectary, Robert Sandeman. And so strong, in general, is the demand of religion and poetry to have their share in a man, to associate themselves with his knowing, and to relieve and rejoice it, that, probably, for one man amongst us with the disposition to do as Darwin did in this respect, there are at least fifty with the disposition to do as Faraday.

Education lays hold upon us, in fact, by satisfying this demand. Professor Huxley holds up to scorn mediæval education, with its neglect of the knowledge of nature, its poverty even of literary studies, its formal logic devoted to "showing how and why that which the Church said was true and must be true." But the great mediæval Universities were not brought into being, we may be sure, by the zeal for giving a jejune and contemptible education. Kings have been their nursing fathers, and queens have been their nursing mothers, but not for this. The mediæval Universities came into being, because the supposed knowledge, delivered by Scripture and the Church, so deeply engaged men's hearts, by so simply, easily, and powerfully relating itself to their desire for conduct, their desire for beauty. All other knowledge was dominated by this supposed knowledge and was subordinated to it, because of the surpassing strength of the hold which it gained upon the affections of men, by allying itself profoundly with their sense for conduct, their sense for beauty.

But now, says Professor Huxley, conceptions of the universe fatal to the notions held by our forefathers have been forced upon us by physical science. Grant to him that they are thus fatal, that the new conceptions must and will soon become current everywhere, and that every one will finally perceive them to be fatal to the beliefs of our forefathers. The need of humane letters, as they are truly called, because they serve the paramount desire in men that good should be for ever present to them, — the need of humane letters, to establish a relation between the new conceptions, and our instinct for beauty, our instinct for conduct, is only the more visible. The Middle Age could do without humane letters, as it could do without the study of nature, because its supposed knowledge was made to engage its emotions so powerfully. Grant that the supposed knowledge disappears, its power of being made to engage the emotions will of course disappear along with it, — but the emotions themselves, and their claim to be engaged and satisfied, will remain. Now if we find by experience that humane letters have an undeniable power of engaging the emotions, the importance of humane letters in a man's training becomes not less, but greater, in proportion to the success of modern science in extirpating what it calls "mediæval thinking."

Have humane letters, then, have poetry and eloquence, the power here attributed to them of engaging the emotions, and do they exercise it? And if they have it and exercise it, *how* do they exercise it, so as to exert an influence upon man's sense for conduct, his sense for beauty? Finally, even if they both can and do exert an influence upon the senses in question, how are they to relate to them the results, — the modern results, — of natural science? All these questions may be asked. First, have poetry and eloquence the power of calling out the emotions? The appeal is to experience. Experience shows that for the vast majority of men, for mankind in general, they have the power. Next, do they exercise it? They do. But then, *how* do they exercise it so as to affect man's sense for conduct, his sense for beauty? And this is perhaps a case for applying the Preacher's words: "Though a man labour to seek it out, yet he shall not find it; yea, farther, though a wise man think to know it, yet shall he not be able to find it." Why should it be one thing, in its effect upon the emotions, to say, "Patience is a virtue," and quite another thing, in its effect upon the emotions, to say with Homer,

τλητὸν γὰρ Μοῖραι θυμὸν θέσαν ἀνθρώποισιν. —

"for an enduring heart have the destinies appointed to the children of men"? Why should it be one thing, in its effect upon the emotions, to say with the philosopher Spinoza, *Felicitas in eo consistit quod homo suum esse conservare potest* — "Man's happiness consists in his being able to preserve his own essence," and quite another thing, in its effect upon the emotions, to say with the Gospel, "What is a man advantaged, if he gain the whole world, and lose himself, forfeit himself?" How does this difference of effect arise? I cannot tell, and I am not much concerned to know; the important thing is that it does arise, and that we can profit by it. But how, finally, are poetry and eloquence to exercise the power of relating the modern results of natural science to man's instinct for conduct, his instinct for beauty? And here again I answer that I do not know *how* they will exercise it, but that they can and will exercise it I am sure. I do not mean that modern philosophical poets and modern philosophical moralists are to come and relate for us, in express terms, the results of modern scientific research to our instinct for conduct, our instinct for beauty. But I mean that we shall find, as a matter of experience, if we know the best that has been thought and uttered in the world, we shall find that the art and poetry and eloquence of men who lived, perhaps, long ago, who had the most limited natural knowledge, who had the

most erroneous conceptions about many important matters, we shall
find that this art, and poetry, and eloquence, have in fact not only
the power of refreshing and delighting us, they have also the power,
— such is the strength and worth, in essentials, of their authors'
criticism of life, — they have a fortifying, and elevating, and quickening, and suggestive power, capable of wonderfully helping us to relate
the results of modern science to our need for conduct, our need for
beauty. Homer's conceptions of the physical universe were, I imagine,
grotesque; but really, under the shock of hearing from modern science
that "the world is not subordinated to man's use, and that man is not
the cynosure of things terrestrial," I could, for my own part, desire
no better comfort than Homer's line which I quoted just now,

$$\tau\lambda\eta\tau\grave{o}\nu \ \gamma\grave{\alpha}\rho \ M o\hat{\imath}\rho\alpha\iota \ \theta\upsilon\mu\grave{o}\nu \ \theta\acute{\epsilon}\sigma\alpha\nu \ \grave{\alpha}\nu\theta\rho\acute{\omega}\pi o\iota\sigma\iota\nu. \ —$$

"for an enduring heart have the destinies appointed to the children of
men"!

And the more that men's minds are cleared, the more that the
results of science are frankly accepted, the more that poetry and
eloquence come to be received and studied as what in truth they really
are, — the criticism of life by gifted men, alive and active with extraordinary power at an unusual number of points; — so much the more
will the value of humane letters, and of art also, which is an utterance having a like kind of power with theirs, be felt and acknowledged,
and their place in education be secured.

Let us therefore, all of us, avoid indeed as much as possible any
invidious comparison between the merits of humane letters, as means
of education, and the merits of the natural sciences. But when some
President of a Section for Mechancial Science insists on making the
comparison, and tells us that "he who in his training has substituted
literature and history for natural science has chosen the less useful
alternative," let us make answer to him that the student of humane
letters only, will, at least, know also the great general conceptions
brought in by modern physical science; for science, as Professor Huxley says, forces them upon us all. But the student of the natural
sciences only, will, by our very hypothesis, know nothing of humane
letters; not to mention that in setting himself to be perpetually accumulating natural knowledge, he sets himself to do what only specialists have in general the gift for doing genially. And so he will probably
be unsatisfied, or at any rate incomplete, and even more incomplete
than the student of humane letters only.

I once mentioned in a school-report, how a young man in one of
our English training colleges having to paraphrase the passage in
Macbeth beginning,

"Can'st thou not minister to a mind diseased?"

turned this line into, "Can you not wait upon the lunatic?" And I remarked what a curious state of things it would be, if every pupil of our national schools knew, let us say, that the moon is two thousand one hundred and sixty miles in diameter, and thought at the same time that a good paraphrase for

"Can'st thou not minister to a mind diseased?"

was, "Can you not wait upon the lunatic?" If one is driven to choose, I think I would rather have a young person ignorant about the moon's diameter, but aware that "Can you not wait upon the lunatic?" is bad, than a young person whose education had been such as to manage things the other way.

Or to go higher than the pupils of our national schools. I have in my mind's eye a member of our British Parliament who comes to travel here in America, who afterwards relates his travels, and who shows a really masterly knowledge of the geology of this great country and of its mining capabilities, but who ends by gravely suggesting that the United States should borrow a prince from our Royal Family, and should make him their king, and should create a House of Lords of great landed proprietors after the pattern of ours; and then America, he thinks, would have her future happily and perfectly secured. Surely, in this case, the President of the Section for Mechanical Science would himself hardly say that our member of Parliament, by concentrating himself upon geology and mineralogy, and so on, and not attending to literature and history, had "chosen the more useful alternative."

If then there is to be separation and option between humane letters on the one hand, and the natural sciences on the other, the great majority of mankind, all who have not exceptional and overpowering aptitudes for the study of nature, would do well, I cannot but think, to choose to be educated in humane letters rather than in the natural sciences. Letters will call out their being at more points, will make them live more.

I said that before I ended I would just touch on the question of classical education, and I will keep my word. Even if literature is to retain a large place in our education, yet Latin and Greek, say the friends of progress, will certainly have to go. Greek is the grand offender in the eyes of these gentlemen. The attackers of the established course of study think that against Greek, at any rate, they have irresistible arguments. Literature may perhaps be needed in education, they say; but why on earth should it be Greek literature? Why not French or German? Nay, "has not an Englishman models in his own literature of every kind of excellence?" As before, it is not on any weak pleadings of my own that I rely for convincing the gainsayers; it is on the constitution of human nature itself, and on the instinct of self-preservation in humanity. The instinct for beauty is set in human nature, as surely as the instinct for knowledge is set

there, or the instinct for conduct. If the instinct for beauty is served
by Greek literature and art as it is served by no other literature and
art, we may trust to the instinct of self-preservation in humanity for
keeping Greek as part of our culture. We may trust to it for even
making the study of Greek more prevalent than it is now. Greek will
come, I hope, some day to be studied more rationally than at present;
but it will be increasingly studied as men increasingly feel the need
in them for beauty, and how powerfully Greek art and Greek literature can serve this need. Women will again study Greek, as Lady
Jane Grey did; I believe that in that chain of forts, with which the fair
host of the Amazons are now engirdling our English universities, I
find that here in America, in colleges like Smith College in Massa-
chusetts, and Vassar College in the State of New York, and in the
happy families of the mixed universities out West, they are studying it
already.

Defuit una mihi symmetria prisca, — "The antique symmetry was
the one thing wanting to me," said Leonardo da Vinci; and he was
an Italian. I will not presume to speak for the Americans, but I am
sure that, in the Englishman, the want of this admirable symmetry
of the Greeks is a thousand times more great and crying than in any
Italian. The results of the want show themselves most glaringly,
perhaps, in our architecture, but they show themselves, also, in all
our art. *Fit details strictly combined, in view of a large general result
nobly conceived;* that is just the beautiful *symmetria prisca* of the
Greeks, and it is just where we English fail, where all our art fails.
Striking ideas we have, and well-executed details we have; but that
high symmetry which, with satisfying and delightful effect, com-
bines them, we seldom or never have. The glorious beauty of the
Acropolis at Athens did not come from single fine things stuck about
on that hill, a statue here, a gateway there; — no, it arose from all
things being perfectly combined for a supreme total effect. What
must not an Englishman feel about our deficiencies in this respect,
as the sense for beauty, whereof this symmetry is an essential element,
awakens and strengthens within him! what will not one day be his
respect and desire for Greece and its *symmetria prisca,* when the scales
drop from his eyes as he walks the London streets, and he sees such
a lesson in meanness as the Strand, for instance, in its true deformity!
But here we are coming to our friend Mr. Ruskin's province, and I
will not intrude upon it, for he is its very sufficient guardian.

And so we at last find, it seems, we find flowing in favour of the
humanities the natural and necessary stream of things, which seemed
against them when we started. The "hairy quadruped furnished with
a tail and pointed ears, probably arboreal in his habits," this good fellow carried hidden in his nature, apparently, something destined to
develop into a necessity for humane letters. Nay, more; we seem

finally to be even led to the further conclusion that our hairy ancestor carried in his nature, also, a necessity for Greek.

And therefore, to say the truth, I cannot really think that humane letters are in much actual danger of being thrust out from their leading place in education, in spite of the array of authorities against them at this moment. So long as human nature is what it is, their attractions will remain irresistible. As with Greek, so with letters generally: they will some day come, we may hope, to be studied more rationally, but they will not lose their place. What will happen will rather be that there will be crowded into education other matters besides, far too many; there will be, perhaps, a period of unsettlement and confusion and false tendency; but letters will not in the end lose their leading place. If they lose it for a time, they will get it back again. We shall be brought back to them by our wants and aspirations. And a poor humanist may possess his soul in patience, neither strive nor cry, admit the energy and brilliancy of the partisans of physical science, and their present favour with the public, to be far greater than his own, and still have a happy faith that the nature of things works silently on behalf of the studies which he loves, and that, while we shall all have to acquaint ourselves with the great results reached by modern science, and to give ourselves as much training in its disciplines as we can conveniently carry, yet the majority of men will always require humane letters; and so much the more, as they have the more and the greater results of science to relate to the need in man for conduct, and to the need in him for beauty.

Essays in Criticism, Second Series

⟪ From his periodical essays, Arnold had chosen the contents of *Essays in Criticism, Second Series* before his death: "The Study of Poetry"; "Milton"; "Thomas Gray"; "John Keats"; "Wordsworth"; "Byron"; "Shelley"; "Count Leo Tolstoi"; "Amiel." "The Study of Poetry" itself had been written expressly as the general introduction to an extended anthology of *The English Poets* (ed. T. H. Ward), and the essay bears some mark of this purpose. Here only the first portion is printed, in which Arnold considers the value of poetry and one method of coming to a "real" estimate of it. ⟫

The Study of Poetry

"The future of poetry is immense, because in poetry, where it is worthy of its high destinies, our race, as time goes on, will find an ever surer and surer stay. There is not a creed which is not shaken, not an accredited dogma which is not shown to be questionable, not a received tradition which does not threaten to dissolve. Our religion has materialized itself in the fact, in the supposed fact; it has attached its emotion to the fact, and now the fact is failing it. But for poetry the idea is everything; the rest is a world of illusion, of divine illusion. Poetry attaches its emotion to the idea; the idea *is* the fact. The strongest part of our religion today is its unconscious poetry."

Let me be permitted to quote these words of my own, as uttering the thought which should, in my opinion, go with us and govern us in all our study of poetry. In the present work it is the course of one great contributory stream to the world-river of poetry that we are invited to follow. We are here invited to trace the stream of English poetry. But whether we set ourselves, as here, to follow only one of the several streams that make the mighty river of poetry, or whether we seek to know them all, our governing thought should be the same. We should conceive of poetry worthily, and more highly than it has been the custom to conceive of it. We should conceive of it as capable of higher uses, and called to higher destinies, than those which in general men have assigned to it hitherto. More and more mankind will discover that we have to turn to poetry to interpret life for us, to console us, to sustain us. Without poetry, our science will appear incomplete; and most of what now passes with us for religion and philosophy will be replaced by poetry. Science, I say, will appear incomplete without it. For finely and truly does Wordsworth call poetry "the impassioned expression which is in the countenance of all science"; and what is a countenance without its expression? Again, Wordsworth finely and truly calls poetry "the breath and finer spirit of all knowledge": our religion, parading evidences such as those on which the popular mind relies now; our philosophy, pluming itself on its reasonings about causation and finite and infinite being; what are they but the shadows and dreams and false shows of knowledge? The day will come when we shall wonder at ourselves for having trusted to them, for having taken them seriously; and the more we perceive their hollowness, the more we shall prize "the breath and finer spirit of knowledge" offered to us by poetry.

But if we conceive thus highly of the destinies of poetry, we must also set our standard for poetry high, since poetry, to be capable of fulfilling such high destinies, must be poetry of a high order of excellence. We must accustom ourselves to a high standard and to a strict judgment. Sainte-Beuve relates that Napoleon one day said, when somebody was spoken of in his presence as a charlatan: "Charlatan as much as you please; but where is there *not* charlatanism?" —"Yes," answers Sainte-Beuve, "in politics, in the art of governing mankind, that is perhaps true. But in the order of thought, in art, the glory, the eternal honour is that charlatanism shall find no entrance; herein lies the inviolableness of that noble portion of man's being." It is admirably said, and let us hold fast to it. In poetry, which is thought and art in one, it is the glory, the eternal honour, that charlatanism shall find no entrance; that this noble sphere be kept inviolate and inviolable. Charlatanism is for confusing or obliterating the distinctions between excellent and inferior, sound and unsound or only half-sound, true and untrue or only half-true. It is charlatanism, conscious or unconscious, whenever we confuse or obliterate these. And in poetry, more than anywhere else, it is unpermissible to confuse or obliterate them. For in poetry the distinction between excellent and inferior, sound and unsound or only half-sound, true and untrue or only half-true, is of paramount importance. It is of paramount importance because of the high destinies of poetry. In poetry, as a criticism of life under the conditions fixed for such a criticism by the laws of poetic truth and poetic beauty, the spirit of our race will find, we have said, as time goes on and as other helps fail, its consolation and stay. But the consolation and stay will be of power in proportion to the power of the criticism of life. And the criticism of life will be of power in proportion as the poetry conveying it is excellent rather than inferior, sound rather than unsound or half-sound, true rather than untrue or half-true.

The best poetry is what we want; the best poetry will be found to have a power of forming, sustaining, and delighting us, as nothing else can. A clearer, deeper sense of the best in poetry, and of the strength and joy to be drawn from it, is the most precious benefit which we can gather from a poetical collection such as the present. And yet in the very nature and conduct of such a collection there is inevitably something which tends to obscure in us the consciousness of what our benefit should be, and to distract us from the pursuit of it. We should therefore steadily set it before our minds at the outset, and should compel ourselves to revert constantly to the thought of it as we proceed.

Yes; constantly in reading poetry, a sense for the best, the really excellent, and of the strength and joy to be drawn from it, should be present in our minds and should govern our estimate of what we read. But this real estimate, the only true one, is liable to be superseded, if we are not watchful, by two other kinds of estimate, the historic estimate and the personal estimate, both of which are fallacious. A poet or a poem may count to us historically, they may count to us on grounds personal to ourselves, and they may count to us really. They may count to us historically. The course of development of a nation's language, thought, and poetry, is profoundly interesting; and by regarding a poet's work as a stage in this course of development we may easily bring ourselves to make it of more importance as poetry than in itself it really is, we may come to use a language of quite exaggerated praise in criticising it; in short, to

over-rate it. So arises in our poetic judgments the fallacy caused by
the estimate which we may call historic. Then, again, a poet or a poem
may count to us on grounds personal to ourselves. Our personal affinities, likings, and circumstances, have great power to sway our
estimate of this or that poet's work, and to make us attach more importance to it as poetry than in itself it really possesses, because to us
it is, or has been, of high importance. Here also we over-rate the object of our interest, and apply to it a language of praise which is quite
exaggerated. And thus we get the source of a second fallacy in our
poetic judgments — the fallacy caused by an estimate which we may
call personal.

Both fallacies are natural. It is evident how naturally the study of
the history and development of a poetry may incline a man to pause
over reputations and works once conspicuous but now obscure, and to
quarrel with a careless public for skipping, in obedience to mere
tradition and habit, from one famous name or work in its national
poetry to another, ignorant of what it misses, and of the reason for
keeping what it keeps, and of the whole process of growth in its poetry.
The French have become diligent students of their own early poetry,
which they long neglected; the study makes many of them dissatisfied with their so-called classical poetry, the court-tragedy of the
seventeenth century, a poetry which Pellisson [1] long ago reproached
with its want of the true poetic stamp, with its *politesse stérile et
rampante*,[2] but which nevertheless has reigned in France as absolutely
as if it had been the perfection of classical poetry indeed. The dissatisfaction is natural; yet a lively and accomplished critic, M. Charles
d'Héricault, the editor of Clément Marot, goes too far when he says
that "the cloud of glory playing round a classic is a mist as dangerous
to the future of a literature as it is intolerable for the purposes of
history." "It hinders," he goes on, "it hinders us from seeing more
than one single point, the culminating and exceptional point; the
summary, fictitious and arbitrary, of a thought and of a work. It substitutes a halo for a physiognomy, it puts a statue where there was
once a man, and hiding from us all trace of the labour, the attempts,
the weaknesses, the failures, it claims not study but veneration; it does
not show us how the thing is done, it imposes upon us a model.
Above all, for the historian this creation of classic personages is in-
admissible; for it withdraws the poet from his time, from his proper
life, it breaks historical relationships, it blinds criticism by conventional admiration, and renders the investigation of literary origins
unacceptable. It gives us a human personage no longer, but a God
seated immovable amidst His perfect work, like Jupiter on Olympus;
and hardly will it be possible for the young student, to whom such

1 Paul Pellisson (1624–1693), French author and critic.
2 "civility barren and bombastic."

work is exhibited at such a distance from him, to believe that it did not issue ready made from that divine head."

All this is brilliantly and tellingly said, but we must plead for a distinction. Everything depends on the reality of a poet's classic character. If he is a dubious classic, let us sift him; if he is a false classic, let us explode him. But if he is a real classic, if his work belongs to the class of the very best (for this is the true and right meaning of the word *classic, classical*), then the great thing for us is to feel and enjoy his work as deeply as ever we can, and to appreciate the wide difference between it and all work which has not the same high character. This is what is salutary, this is what is formative; this is the great benefit to be got from the study of poetry. Everything which interferes with it, which hinders it, is injurious. True, we must read our classic with open eyes, and not with eyes blinded with superstition; we must perceive when his work comes short, when it drops out of the class of the very best, and we must rate it, in such cases, at its proper value. But the use of this negative criticism is not in itself, it is entirely in its enabling us to have a clearer sense and a deeper enjoyment of what is truly excellent. To trace the labour, the attempts, the weaknesses, the failures of a genuine classic, to acquaint oneself with his time and his life and his historical relationships, is mere literary dilettantism unless it has that clear sense and deeper enjoyment for its end. It may be said that the more we know about a classic the better we shall enjoy him; and, if we lived as long as Methuselah and had all of us heads of perfect clearness and wills of perfect steadfastness, this might be true in fact as it is plausible in theory. But the case here is much the same as the case with the Greek and Latin studies of our schoolboys. The elaborate philological groundwork which we require them to lay is in theory an admirable preparation for appreciating the Greek and Latin authors worthily. The more thoroughly we lay the groundwork, the better we shall be able, it may be said, to enjoy the authors. True, if time were not so short, and schoolboys' wits not so soon tired and their power of attention exhausted; only, as it is, the elaborate philological preparation goes on, but the authors are little known and less enjoyed. So with the investigator of "historic origins" in poetry. He ought to enjoy the true classic all the better for his investigations; he often is distracted from the enjoyment of the best, and with the less good he overbusies himself, and is prone to over-rate it in proportion to the trouble which it has cost him.

The idea of tracing historic origins and historical relationships cannot be absent from a compilation like the present. And naturally the poets to be exhibited in it will be assigned to those persons for exhibition who are known to prize them highly, rather than to those who have no special inclination towards them. Moreover the very occupation with an author, and the business of exhibiting him, disposes us to affirm and amplify his importance. In the present work, therefore, we are sure of frequent temptation to adopt the historic estimate, or the personal estimate, and to forget the real esimate; which latter, nevertheless, we must employ if we are to make poetry yield us its full benefit. So high is that benefit, the benefit of clearly feeling and of deeply enjoying the really excellent, the truly classic in poetry, that we do well, I say, to set it fixedly before our minds as our object in studying poets and poetry, and to make the desire of attaining it the one principle to which, as the *Imitation* says, whatever we may read or come to know, we always return. *Cum multa legeris et cognoveris, ad unum semper oportet redire principium.*[3]

The historic estimate is likely in especial to affect our judgment and our language when we are dealing with ancient poets; the personal estimate when we are dealing with poets our contemporaries, or at any rate modern. The exaggerations due to the historic estimate are not in themselves, perhaps, of very much gravity. Their report hardly enters the general ear; probably they do not always impose even on the literary men who adopt them. But they lead to a dangerous abuse of language. So we hear Cædmon, amongst our own poets, compared to Milton. I have already noticed the enthusiasm of one accomplished French critic for "historic origins." Another eminent French critic, M. Vitet, comments upon that famous document of the early poetry of his nation, the *Chanson de Roland*. It is indeed a most interesting document. The *joculator* or *jongleur* Taillefer, who was with William the Conqueror's army at Hastings, marched before the Norman troops, so said the tradition, singing "of Charlemagne and of Roland and of Oliver, and of the vassals who died at Roncevaux"; and it is suggested that in the *Chanson de Roland* by one Turoldus or Théroulde, a poem preserved in a manuscript of the twelfth century in the Bodleian Library at Oxford, we have certainly the matter, perhaps even some of the words, of the chant which Taillefer sang. The poem has vigour and freshness; it is not without pathos. But M. Vitet is not satisfied with seeing in it a document of some poetic value, and of very high historic and linguistic value; he sees in it a grand and beautiful work, a monument of epic genius. In its general design he finds the grandiose conception, in its details he finds the constant union of simplicity with greatness, which are the marks, he truly says, of the genuine epic, and distinguish it from the artificial epic of literary ages. One thinks of Homer; this is the sort of praise which is given to Homer, and justly given. Higher praise there cannot well be, and it is the praise due to epic poetry of the highest order only, and to no other. Let us try, then, the *Chanson de Roland* at its best. Roland, mortally wounded, lays

---

[3] "When you have read and learned many things, you ought always to return to the one principle."

himself down under a pine-tree, with his face turned towards Spain
and the enemy —

> De plusurs choses a remembrer li prist,
> De tantes teres cume li bers cunquist,
> De dulce France, des humes de sun lign,
> De Carlemagne sun seignor ki l'nurrit.[4]

That is primitive work, I repeat, with an undeniable poetic quality
of its own. It deserves such praise, and such praise is sufficient for
it. But now turn to Homer —

> Ὣς φάτο τοὺς δ' ἤδη κάτεχεν φυσίζοος αἶα
> ἐν Λακεδαίμονι αὖθι, φίλη ἐν πατρίδι γαίῃ.[5]

We are here in another world, another order of poetry altogether;
here is rightly due such supreme praise as that which M. Vitet gives
to the *Chanson de Roland*. If our words are to have any meaning,
if our judgments are to have any solidity, we must not heap that supreme praise upon poetry of an order immeasurably inferior.

Indeed there can be no more useful help for discovering what poetry
belongs to the class of the truly excellent, and can therefore do us
most good, than to have always in one's mind lines and expressions
of the great masters, and to apply them as a touchstone to other
poetry. Of course we are not to require this other poetry to resemble
them; it may be very dissimilar. But if we have any tact we shall find
them, when we have lodged them well in our minds, an infallible
touchstone for detecting the presence or absence of high poetic quality, and also the degree of this quality, in all other poetry which we
may place beside them. Short passages, even single lines, will serve
our turn quite sufficiently. Take the two lines which I have just
quoted from Homer, the poet's comment on Helen's mention of her
brothers; — or take his

> Ἆ δειλώ, τί σφῶϊ δόμεν Πηλῆϊ ἄνακτι
> θνητῷ; ὑμεῖς δ' ἐστὸν ἀγήρω τ' ἀθανάτω τε
> ἦ ἵνα δυστήνοισι μετ' ἀνδράσιν ἄλγε' ἔχητον; [6]

the address of Zeus to the horses of Peleus; — or take finally his

> Καί σέ, γέρον, τὸ πρὶν μὲν ἀκούομεν ὄλβιον εἶναι· [7]

---

4 "Then began he to call many things to remembrance, — all the lands which
his valour conquered, and pleasant France, and the men of his lineage, and
Charlemagne his liege lord who nourished him." — *Chanson de Roland*, iii. 939–
942. [Arnold's note.]

5 "So said she; they long since in Earth's soft arms were reposing,
There, in their own dear land, their fatherland, Lacedaemon."
— *Iliad*, iii. 243, 244 (translated by Dr. Hawtrey). [Arnold's note.]

6 "Ah, unhappy pair, why gave we you to King Peleus, to a mortal? but ye
are without old age, and immortal. Was it that with men born to misery ye
might have sorrow?" — *Iliad*, xvii. 443–445. [Arnold's note.]

7 "Nay, and thou too, old man, in former days wast, as we hear, happy."
— *Iliad*, xxiv. 543. [Arnold's note.]

the words of Achilles to Priam, a suppliant before him. Take that
incomparable line and a half of Dante, Ugolino's tremendous words —

> Io no piangeva; sì dentro impietrai.
> Piangevan elli . . .[8]

take the lovely words of Beatrice to Virgil —

> Io son fatta da Dio, sua mercè, tale,
> Che la vostra miseria non mi tange,
> Nè fiamma d'esto incendio non m'assale . . .

take the simple, but perfect, single line —

> In la sua volontade e nostra pace.[10]

Take of Shakspeare a line or two of Henry the Fourth's expostulation
with sleep —

> Wilt thou upon the high and giddy mast
> Seal up the ship-boy's eyes, and rock his brains
> In cradle of the rude imperious surge . . .

and take, as well, Hamlet's dying request to Horatio —

> If thou didst ever hold me in thy heart,
> Absent thee from felicity awhile,
> And in this harsh world draw thy breath in pain
> To tell my story . . .

Take of Milton that Miltonic passage —

> Darken'd so, yet shone
> Above them all the archangel; but his face
> Deep scars of thunder had intrench'd, and care
> Sat on his faded cheek . . .

add two such lines as —

> And courage never to submit or yield
> And what is else not to be overcome . . .

and finish with exquisite close to the loss of Proserpine, the loss

> which cost Ceres all that pain
> To seek her through the world.

These few lines, if we have tact and can use them, are enough even
of themselves to keep clear and sound our judgments about poetry, to
save us from fallacious estimates of it, to conduct us to a real estimate.

---

8 "I wailed not, so of stone I grew within; — they wailed." — *Inferno*, xxxiii.
39, 40. [Arnold's note.]

9 "Of such sort hath God, thanked be His mercy, made me, that your misery
toucheth me not, neither doth the flame of this fire strike me." — *Inferno*, ii.
91–93. [Arnold's note.]

10 "In His will is our peace." — *Paradiso*, iii. 85. [Arnold's note.]

The specimens I have quoted differ widely from one another, but they have in common this: the possession of the very highest poetical quality. If we are thoroughly penetrated by their power, we shall find that we have acquired a sense enabling us, whatever poetry may be laid before us, to feel the degree in which a high poetical quality is present or wanting there. Critics give themselves great labour to draw out what in the abstract constitutes the characters of a high quality of poetry. It is much better simply to have recourse to concrete examples; — to take specimens of poetry of the high, the very highest quality, and to say: The characters of a high quality of poetry are what is expressed *there*. They are far better recognised by being felt in the verse of the master, than by being perused in the prose of the critic. Nevertheless if we are urgently pressed to give some critical account of them, we may safely, perhaps, venture on laying down, not indeed how and why the characters arise, but where and in what they arise. They are in the matter and substance of the poetry, and they are in its manner and style. Both of these, the substance and matter on the one hand, the style and manner on the other, have a mark, an accent, of high beauty, worth, and power. But if we are asked to define this mark and accent in the abstract, our answer must be: No, for we should thereby be darkening the question, not clearing it. The mark and accent are as given by the substance and matter of that poetry, by the style and manner of that poetry, and of all other poetry which is akin to it in quality.

Only one thing we may add as to the substance and matter of poetry, guiding ourselves by Aristotle's profound observation that the superiority of poetry over history consists in its possessing a higher truth and a higher seriousness (φιλοσοφώτερον καὶ σπουδαιότερον). Let us add, therefore, to what we have said, this: that the substance and matter of the best poetry acquire their special character from possessing, in an eminent degree, truth and seriousness. We may add yet further, what is in itself evident, that to the style and manner of the best poetry their special character, their accent, is given by their diction, and, even yet more, by their movement. And though we distinguish between the two characters, the two accents, of superiority, yet they are nevertheless vitally connected one with the other. The superior character of truth and seriousness, in the matter and substance of the best poetry, is inseparable from the superiority of diction and movement marking its style and manner. The two superiorities are closely related, and are in steadfast proportion one to the other. So far as high poetic truth and seriousness are wanting to a poet's matter and substance, so far also, we may be sure, will a high poetic stamp of diction and movement be wanting to his style and manner. In proportion as this high stamp of diction and movement, again, is absent from a poet's style and manner, we shall find, also, that high poetic truth and seriousness are absent from his substance and matter. . . .

Thomas Henry Huxley

THOMAS HENRY HUXLEY

CHRONOLOGY

1825   Born May 4 at Ealing, near London.

1825–1835   Childhood and early education at Ealing.

1835–1841   Unsystematic education at Coventry.

1841–1845   Studied medicine; received M. B., University of London.

1846–1850   Sailed as assistant surgeon on the Rattlesnake.

1851   Elected Fellow of the Royal Society.

1854   Became Lecturer in Natural History in the Royal School of Mines, London, and Naturalist to the Government Geological Survey.

1860   Made his famous reply to the Bishop of Oxford at a meeting of the British Association.

1863   Published *Man's Place in Nature*.

1866   Received LL. D. degree from Edinburgh University.

1870   Published *Lay Sermons, Addresses and Reviews*.

1872–1874   Lord Rector of Aberdeen University.

1876   Made a lecture tour in America.

1877   Published *American Addresses*.

1878   Published *Hume* in the English Men of Letters series; received LL. D. degree from Dublin University.

1879   Received LL. D. degree from Cambridge University.

1881   Published *Science and Culture and Other Essays*.

1883   Elected President of the Royal Society.

1885   Received D. C. L. degree from Oxford.

1891   Published *Social Diseases and Worse Remedies*.

1892   Published *Essays on Some Controverted Questions*.

1893–1894   Published his *Collected Essays*, in nine volumes.

1894   Received the Darwin Medal.

1895   Died June 29.

On the Physical Basis of Life

❲ This essay, originally delivered as a lecture, was first printed in the *Fortnightly Review* for 1 February 1869 and reprinted in the first edition of *Lay Sermons* and in *Methods and Results,* the first volume of the *Collected Essays.* Huxley said that the essay "was intended to contain a plain and untechnical statement of one of the great tendencies of modern biological thought, accompanied by a protest, from the philosophical side, against what is commonly called Materialism. The result of my well-meant efforts I find to be, that I am generally credited with having invented 'protoplasm' in the interests of 'materialism.' My unlucky 'Lay Sermon' has been attacked by microscopists, ignorant alike of Biology and Philosophy; by philosophers, not very learned in either Biology or Microscopy; by clergymen of several denominations; and by some few writers who have taken the trouble to understand the subject. I trust that these last will believe that I leave the essay unaltered from no want of respectful attention to all they have said." ❳

In order to make the title of this discourse generally intelligible, I have translated the term "Protoplasm," which is the scientific name of the substance of which I am about to speak, by the words "the physical basis of life." I suppose that, to many, the idea that there is such a thing as a physical basis, or matter, of life may be novel — so widely spread is the conception of life as a something which works through matter, but is independent of it; and even those who are aware that matter and life are inseparably connected, may not be prepared for the conclusion plainly suggested by the phrase, "*the* physical basis or matter of life," that there is some one kind of matter which is common to all living beings, and that their endless diversities are bound together by a physical, as well as an ideal, unity. In fact, when 'first apprehended, such a doctrine as this appears almost shocking to common sense.

What, truly, can seem to be more obviously different from one another, in faculty, in form, and in substance, than the various kinds of living beings? What community of faculty can there be between the bright-coloured lichen, which so nearly resembles a mere mineral incrustation of the bare rock on which it grows, and the painter, to whom it is instinct with beauty, or the botanist, whom it feeds with knowledge?

Again, think of the microscopic fungus — a mere infinitesimal ovoid particle, which finds space and duration enough to multiply into countless millions in the body of a living fly; and then of the wealth of foliage, the luxuriance of flower and fruit, which lies between this bald sketch of a plant and the giant pine of California, towering to the dimensions of a cathedral spire, or the Indian fig, which covers acres with its profound shadow, and endures while nations and empires come and go around its vast circumference. Or, turning to the other half of the world of life, picture to yourselves the great Finner whale, hugest of beasts that live, or have lived, disporting his eighty or ninety feet of bone, muscle and blubber, with easy roll, among waves in which the stoutest ship that ever left dockyard would flounder hopelessly; and contrast him with the invisible animalcules — mere gelatinous specks, multitudes of which could, in fact, dance upon the point of a needle with the same ease as the angels of the Schoolmen could, in imagination. With these images before your minds, you may well ask, what community of form, or structure, is there between the animalcule and the whale; or between the fungus and the fig-tree? And, *a fortiori,* between all four?

Finally, if we regard substance, or material composition, what hidden bond can connect the flower which a girl wears in her hair and the blood which courses through her youthful veins; or, what is there in common between the dense and resisting mass of the oak, or the strong fabric of the tortoise, and those broad disks of glassy jelly which may be seen pulsating through the waters of a calm sea, but which drain away to mere films in the hand which raises them out of their element?

Such objections as these must, I think, arise in the mind of every one who ponders, for the first time, upon the conception of a single physical basis of life underlying all the diversities of vital existence; but I propose to demonstrate to you that, notwithstanding these apparent difficulties, a threefold unity — namely, a unity of power or faculty, a unity of form, and a unity of substantial composition — does pervade the whole living world.

No very abstruse argumentation is needed, in the first place to prove that the powers, or faculties, of all kinds of living matter, diverse as they may be in degree, are substantially similar in kind.

Goethe has condensed a survey of all powers of mankind into the well-known epigram: —

"Warum treibt sich das Volk so und schreit? Es will sich ernähren
Kinder zeugen, und die nähren so gut es vermag.
. . . .
Weiter bringt es kein Mensch, stell' er sich wie er auch will." [1]

In physiological language this means, that all the multifarious and complicated activities of man are comprehensible under three categories. Either they are immediately directed towards the maintenance

[1] "Why do people shove one another so and shout? They want to support themselves, to beget children, and to support them as well as possible. . . . No man can advance further, let him put himself where he will."

and development of the body, or they effect transitory changes in the relative positions of parts of the body, or they tend towards the continuance of the species. Even those manifestations of intellect, of feeling, and of will, which we rightly name the higher faculties, are not excluded from this classification, inasmuch as to every one but the subject of them, they are known only as transitory changes in the relative positions of parts of the body. Speech, gesture, and every other form of human action are, in the long run, resolvable into muscular contraction, and muscular contraction is but a transitory change in the relative positions of the parts of a muscle. But the scheme which is large enough to embrace the activities of the highest form of life, covers all those of the lower creatures. The lowest plant, or animalcule, feeds, grows, and reproduces its kind. In addition, all animals manifest those transitory changes of form which we class under irritability and contractility; and, it is more than probable, that when the vegetable world is thoroughly explored, we shall find all plants in possession of the same powers, at one time or other of their existence.

I am not now alluding to such phænomena, at once rare and conspicuous, as those exhibited by the leaflets of the sensitive plants, or the stamens of the barberry, but to much more widely spread, and at the same time, more subtle and hidden, manifestations of vegetable contractility. You are doubtless aware that the common nettle owes its stinging property to the innumerable stiff and needle-like, though exquisitely delicate, hairs which cover its surface. Each stinging-needle tapers from a broad base to a slender summit, which, though rounded at the end, is of such microscopic fineness that it readily penetrates, and breaks off in, the skin. The whole hair consists of a very delicate outer case of wood, closely applied to the inner surface of which is a layer of semifluid matter, full of innumerable granules of extreme minuteness. This semi-fluid lining is protoplasm, which thus constitutes a kind of bag, full of a limpid liquid, and roughly corresponding in form with the interior of the hair which it fills. When viewed with a sufficiently high magnifying power, the protoplasmic layer of the nettle hair is seen to be in a condition of unceasing activity. Local contractions of the whole thickness of its substance pass slowly and gradually from point to point, and give rise to the appearance of progressive waves, just as the bending of successive stalks of corn by a breeze produces the apparent billows of a cornfield.

But, in addition to these movements, and independently of them, the granules are driven, in relatively rapid streams, through channels in the protoplasm which seem to have a considerable amount of persistence. Most commonly, the currents in adjacent parts of the protoplasm take similar directions; and, thus, there is a general stream up one side of the hair and down the other. But this does not prevent the existence of partial currents which take different routes; and sometimes trains of granules may be seen coursing swiftly in opposite directions within a twenty-thousandth of an inch of one another; while, occasionally, opposite streams come into direct collision, and, after a longer or shorter struggle, one predominates. The cause of these currents seems to lie in contractions of the protoplasm which bounds the channels in which they flow, but which are so minute that the best microscopes show only their effects, and not themselves.

The spectacle afforded by the wonderful energies prisoned within the compass of the microscopic hair of a plant, which we commonly regard as a merely passive organism, is not easily forgotten by one who has watched its display, continued hour after hour, without pause or sign of weakening. The possible complexity of many other organic forms, seemingly as simple as the protoplasm of the nettle, dawns upon one; and the comparison of such a protoplasm to a body with an internal circulation, which has been put forward by an eminent physiologist, loses much of its startling character. Currents similar to those of the hairs of the nettle have been observed in a great multitude of very different plants, and weighty authorities have suggested that they probably occur, in more or less perfection, in all young vegetable cells. If such be the case, the wonderful noonday silence of a tropical forest is, after all, due only to the dulness of our hearing; and could our ears catch the murmur of these tiny Maelstroms, as they whirl in the innumerable myriads of living cells which constitute each tree, we should be stunned, as with the roar of a great city.

Among the lower plants, it is the rule rather than the exception, that contractility should be still more openly manifested at some periods of their existence. The protoplasm of *Algæ* and *Fungi* becomes, under many circumstances, partially, or completely, freed from its woody case, and exhibits movements of its whole mass, or is propelled by the contractility of one, or more, hair-like prolongations of its body, which are called vibratile cilia. And, so far as the conditions of the manifestation of the phænomena of contractility have yet been studied, they are the same for the plant as for the animal. Heat and electric shocks influence both, and in the same way, though it may be in different degrees. It is by no means my intention to suggest that there is no difference in faculty between the lowest plant and the highest, or between plants and animals. But the difference between the powers of the lowest plant, or animal, and those of the highest, is one of degree, not of kind, and depends, as Milne-Edwards [2] long ago so well pointed out, upon the extent to which the principle of the division of labour is carried out in the living economy. In the lowest organism all parts are competent to perform all functions, and one and the same portion of protoplasm may successfully take on the function of feeding, moving, or reproducing apparatus. In the highest, on the contrary, a great number of parts combine to perform each function,

2 Henry Milne-Edwards (1800–1885), French zoologist.

each part doing its allotted share of the work with great accuracy and efficiency, but being useless for any other purpose.

On the other hand, notwithstanding all the fundamental resemblances which exist between the powers of the protoplasm in plants and in animals, they present a striking difference (to which I shall advert more at length presently), in the fact that plants can manufacture fresh protoplasm out of mineral compounds, whereas animals are obliged to procure it ready made, and hence, in the long run, depend upon plants. Upon what condition this difference in the powers of the two great divisions of the world of life depends, nothing is at present known.

With such qualifications as arise out of the last-mentioned fact, it may be truly said that the acts of all living things are fundamentally one. Is any such unity predicable of their forms? Let us seek in easily verified facts for a reply to this question. If a drop of blood be drawn by pricking one's finger, and viewed with proper precautions, and under a sufficiently high microscopic power, there will be seen, among the innumerable multitude of little, circular, discoidal bodies, or corpuscles, which float in it and give it its colour, a comparatively small number of colourless corpuscles, of somewhat larger size and very irregular shape. If the drop of blood be kept at the temperature of the body, these colourless corpuscles will be seen to exhibit a marvellous activity, changing their forms with great rapidity, drawing in and thrusting out prolongations of their substance, and creeping about as if they were independent organisms.

The substance which is thus active is a mass of protoplasm, and its activity differs in detail, rather than in principle, from that of the protoplasm of the nettle. Under sundry circumstances the corpuscle dies and becomes distended into a round mass, in the midst of which is seen a smaller spherical body, which existed, but was more or less hidden, in the living corpuscle, and is called a *nucleus*. Corpuscles of essentially similar structure are to be found in the skin, in the lining of the mouth, and scattered through the whole framework of the body. Nay, more; in the earliest condition of the human organism, in that state in which it has but just become distinguishable from the egg in which it arises, it is nothing but an aggregation of such corpuscles, and every organ of the body was, once, no more than such an aggregation.

Thus a nucleated mass of protoplasm turns out to be what may be termed the structural unit of the human body. As a matter of fact, the body, in its earliest state, is a mere multiple of such units; and in its perfect condition, it is a multiple of such units, variously modified.

But does the formula which expresses the essential structural character of the highest animal cover all the rest, as the statement of its powers and faculties covered that of all others? Very nearly. Beast and fowl, reptile and fish, mollusk, worm, and polype, are all composed of structural units of the same character, namely, masses of protoplasm with a nucleus. There are sundry very low animals, each of which, structurally, is a mere colourless blood-corpuscle, leading an independent life. But, at the very bottom of the animal scale, even this simplicity becomes simplified, and all the phænomena of life are manifested by a particle of protoplasm without a nucleus. Nor are such organisms insignificant by reason of their want of complexity. It is a fair question whether the protoplasm of those simplest forms of life, which people an immense extent of the bottom of the sea, would not outweigh that of all the higher living beings which inhabit the land put together. And in ancient times, no less than at the present day, such living beings as these have been the greatest of rock builders.

What has been said of the animal world is no less true of plants. Imbedded in the protoplasm at the broad, or attached, end of the nettle hair, there lies a spheroidal nucleus. Careful examination further proves that the whole substance of the nettle is made up of a repetition of such masses of nucleated protoplasm, each contained in a wooden case, which is modified in form, sometimes into a woody fibre, sometimes into a duct or spiral vessel, sometimes into a pollen grain, or an ovule. Traced back to its earliest state, the nettle arises as the man does, in a particle of nucleated protoplasm. And in the lowest plants, as in the lowest animals, a single mass of such protoplasm may constitute the whole plant, or the protoplasm may exist without a nucleus.

Under these circumstances it may well be asked, how is one mass of non-nucleated protoplasm to be distinguished from another? why call one "plant" and the other "animal"?

The only reply is that, so far as form is concerned, plants and animals are not separable, and that, in many cases, it is a mere matter of convention whether we call a given organism an animal or a plant. There is a living body called *Æthalium septicum,* which appears upon decaying vegetable substances, and, in one of its forms, is common upon the surfaces of tan-pits. In this condition it is, to all intents and purposes, a fungus, and formerly was always regarded as such; but the remarkable investigations of De Bary [3] have shown that, in another condition, the *Æthalium* is an actively locomotive creature, and takes in solid matters, upon which, apparently, it feeds, thus exhibiting the most characteristic feature of animality. Is this a plant; or is it an animal? Is it both; or is it neither? Some decide in favour of the last supposition, and establish an intermediate kingdom, a sort of biological No Man's Land for all these questionable forms. But, as it is admittedly impossible to draw any distinct boundary line between this no man's land and the vegetable world on the one hand, or the animal, on the other, it appears to me that this proceeding merely doubles the difficulty which, before, was single.

[3] Heinrich Anton De Bary (1831–1888), German botanist.

Protoplasm, simple or nucleated, is the formal basis of all life. It is the clay of the potter: which, bake it and paint it as he will, remains clay, separated by artifice, and not by nature, from the commonest brick or sun-dried clod.

Thus it becomes clear that all living powers are cognate, and that all living forms are fundamentally of one character. The researches of the chemist have revealed a no less striking uniformity of material composition in living matter.

In perfect strictness, it is true that chemical investigation can tell us little or nothing, directly, of the composition of living matter, inasmuch as such matter must needs die in the act of analysis, — and upon this very obvious ground, objections, which I confess seem to me to be somewhat frivolous, have been raised to the drawing of any conclusions whatever respecting the composition of actually living matter, from that of the dead matter of life, which alone is accessible to us. But objectors of this class do not seem to reflect that it is also, in strictness, true that we know nothing about the composition of any body whatever, as it is. The statement that a crystal of calc-spar consists of carbonate of lime, is quite true, if we only mean that, by appropriate processes, it may be resolved into carbonic acid and quicklime. If you pass the same carbonic acid over the very quicklime thus obtained, you will obtain carbonate of lime again; but it will not be calc-spar, nor anything like it. Can it, therefore, be said that chemical analysis teaches nothing about the chemical composition of calc-spar? Such a statement would be absurd; but it is hardly more so than the talk one occasionally hears about the uselessness of applying the results of chemical analysis to the living bodies which have yielded them.

One fact, at any rate, is out of reach of such refinements, and this is, that all the forms of protoplasm which have yet been examined contain the four elements, carbon, hydrogen, oxygen, and nitrogen, in very complex union, and that they behave similarly towards several reagents. To this complex combination, the nature of which has never been determined with exactness, the name of Protein has been applied. And if we use this term with such caution as may properly arise out of our comparative ignorance of the things for which it stands, it may be truly said, that all protoplasm is proteinaceous, or, as the white, or albumen, of an egg is one of the commonest examples of a nearly pure protein matter, we may say that all living matter is more or less albuminoid.

Perhaps it would not yet be safe to say that all forms of protoplasm are affected by the direct action of electric shocks; and yet the number of cases in which the contraction of protoplasm is shown to be affected by this agency increases every day.

Nor can it be affirmed with perfect confidence, that all forms of protoplasm are liable to undergo that peculiar coagulation at a temperature of 40° — 50° centigrade, which has been called "heat-stiffen-ing," though Kühne's [4] beautiful researches have proved this occur-rence to take place in so many and such diverse living beings, that it is hardly rash to expect that the law holds good for all.

Enough has, perhaps, been said to prove the existence of a general uniformity in the character of the protoplasm, or physical basis, of life, in whatever group of living beings it may be studied. But it will be understood that this general uniformity by no means excludes any amount of special modifications of the fundamental substance. The mineral, carbonate of lime, assumes an immense diversity of characters, though no one doubts that, under all these Protean changes, it is one and the same thing.

And now, what is the ultimate fate, and what the origin, of the matter of life?

Is it, as some of the older naturalists supposed, diffused throughout the universe in molecules, which are indestructible and unchangeable in themselves; but, in endless transmigration, unite in innumerable permutations, into the diversified forms of life we know? Or, is the matter of life composed of ordinary matter, differing from it only in the manner in which its atoms are aggregated? Is it built up of ordinary matter, and again resolved into ordinary matter when its work is done?

Modern science does not hesitate a moment between these alter-natives. Physiology writes over the portals of life —

"Debemur morti nos nostraque," [5]

with a profounder meaning than the Roman poet attached to that melancholy line.[5] Under whatever disguise it takes refuge, whether fungus or oak, worm or man, the living protoplasm not only ultimately dies and is resolved into its mineral and lifeless constituents, but is always dying, and, strange as the paradox may sound, could not live unless it died.

In the wonderful story of the "Peau de Chagrin," [6] the hero becomes possessed of a magical wild ass' skin, which yields him the means of gratifying all his wishes. But its surface represents the duration of the proprietor's life; and for every satisfied desire the skin shrinks in proportion to the intensity of fruition, until at length life and the last handbreadth of the *peau de chagrin,* disappear with the gratification of a last wish.

Balzac's studies had led him over a wide range of thought and speculation, and his shadowing forth of physiological truth in this strange story may have been intentional. At any rate, the matter of life is a veritable *peau de chagrin,* and for every vital act it is some-

---

4 Willy Kühne (1837–1900), German physiologist.
5 Horace: "We owe ourselves and all our possessions to death."
6 "Skin of a Wild Ass," title of a novel by Balzac.

what the smaller. All work implies waste, and the work of life results, directly or indirectly, in the waste of protoplasm.

Every word uttered by a speaker costs him some physical loss; and, in the strictest sense, he burns that others may have light — so much eloquence, so much of his body resolved into carbonic acid, water, and urea. It is clear that this process of expenditure cannot go on for ever. But, happily, the protoplasmic *peau de chagrin* differs from Balzac's in its capacity of being repaired, and brought back to its full size, after every exertion.

For example, this present lecture, whatever its intellectual worth to you, has a certain physical value to me, which is, conceivably, expressible by the number of grains of protoplasm and other bodily substance wasted in maintaining my vital processes during its delivery. My *peau de chagrin* will be distinctly smaller at the end of the discourse than it was at the beginning. By and by, I shall probably have recourse to the substance commonly called mutton, for the purpose of stretching it back to its original size. Now this mutton was once the living protoplasm, more or less modified, of another animal — a sheep. As I shall eat it, it is the same matter altered, not only by death, but by exposure to sundry artificial operations in the process of cooking.

But these changes, whatever be their extent, have not rendered it incompetent to resume its old functions as matter of life. A singular inward laboratory, which I possess, will dissolve a certain portion of the modified protoplasm; the solution so formed will pass into my veins; and the subtle influences to which it will then be subjected will convert the dead protoplasm into living protoplasm, and transubstantiate sheep into man.

Nor is this all. If digestion were a thing to be trifled with, I might sup upon lobster, and the matter of life of the crustacean would undergo the same wonderful metamorphosis into humanity. And were I to return to my own place by sea, and undergo shipwreck, the crustacean might, and probably would, return the compliment, and demonstrate our common nature by turning my protoplasm into living lobster. Or, if nothing better were to be had, I might supply my wants with mere bread, and I should find the protoplasm of the wheat-plant to be convertible into man, with no more trouble than that of the sheep, and with far less, I fancy, than that of the lobster.

Hence it appears to be a matter of no great moment what animal, or what plant, I lay under contribution for protoplasm, and the fact speaks volumes for the general identity of that substance in all living beings. I share this catholicity of assimilation with other animals, all of which, so far as we know, could thrive equally well on the protoplasm of any of their fellows, or of any plant; but here the assimilative powers of the animal world cease. A solution of smelling-salts in water, with an infinitesimal proportion of other saline matters, contains all the elementary bodies which enter into the composition of protoplasm; but, as I need hardly say, a hogshead of that fluid would not keep a hungry man from starving, nor would it save any animal whatever from a like fate. An animal cannot make protoplasm, but must take it ready-made from some other animal, or some plant — the animal's highest feat of constructive chemistry being to convert dead protoplasm into that living matter of life which is appropriate to itself.

Therefore, in seeking for the origin of protoplasm, we must eventually turn to the vegetable world. A fluid containing carbonic acid, water, and nitrogenous salts, which offers such a Barmecide feast to the animal, is a table richly spread to multitudes of plants; and, with a due supply of only such materials, many a plant will not only maintain itself in vigour, but grow and multiply until it has increased a million-fold, or a million million-fold, the quantity of protoplasm which it originally possessed; in this way building up the matter of life, to an indefinite extent, from the common matter of the universe.

Thus, the animal can only raise the complex substance of dead protoplasm to the higher power, as one may say, of living protoplasm; while the plant can raise the less complex substances — carbonic acid, water, and nitrogenous salts — to the same stage of living protoplasm, if not to the same level. But the plant also has its limitations. Some of the fungi, for example, appear to need higher compounds to start with; and no known plant can live upon the uncompounded elements of protoplasm. A plant supplied with pure carbon, hydrogen, oxygen, and nitrogen, phosphorus, sulphur, and the like, would as infallibly die as the animal in his bath of smelling-salts, though it would be surrounded by all the constituents of protoplasm. Nor, indeed, need the process of simplification of vegetable food be carried so far as this, in order to arrive at the limit of the plant's thaumaturgy. Let water, carbonic acid, and all the other needful constituents be supplied except nitrogenous salts, and an ordinary plant will still be unable to manufacture protoplasm.

Thus the matter of life, so far as we know it (and we have no right to speculate on any other), breaks up, in consequence of that continual death which is the condition of its manifesting vitality, into carbonic acid, water, and nitrogenous compounds, which certainly possess no properties but those of ordinary matter. And out of these same forms of ordinary matter, and from none which are simpler, the vegetable world builds up all the protoplasm which keeps the animal world a-going. Plants are the accumulators of the power which animals distribute and disperse.

But it will be observed, that the existence of the matter of life depends on the pre-existence of certain compounds; namely, carbonic acid, water, and certain nitrogenous bodies. Withdraw any one of these three from the world, and all vital phænomena come to an end. They are as necessary to the protoplasm of the plant, as the protoplasm of the plant is to that of the animal. Carbon, hydrogen, oxygen, and nitrogen are all lifeless bodies. Of these, carbon and oxygen unite in certain proportions and under certain conditions, to give rise to carbonic acid; hydrogen and oxygen produce water; nitrogen and other elements give rise to nitrogenous salts. These new compounds, like the elementary bodies of which they are composed, are lifeless. But when they are brought together, under certain conditions, they give rise to the still more complex body, protoplasm, and this protoplasm exhibits the phænomena of life.

I see no break in this series of steps in molecular complication, and I am unable to understand why the language which is applicable to any one term of the series may not be used to any of the others. We think fit to call different kinds of matter carbon, oxygen, hydrogen, and nitrogen, and to speak of the various powers and activities of these substances as the properties of the matter of which they are composed.

When hydrogen and oxygen are mixed in a certain proportion, and an electric spark is passed through them, they disappear, and a quantity of water, equal in weight to the sum of their weights, appears in their place. There is not the slightest parity between the passive and active powers of the water and those of the oxygen and hydrogen which have given rise to it. At 32° Fahrenheit, and far below that temperature, oxygen and hydrogen are elastic gaseous bodies, whose particles tend to rush away from one another with great force. Water, at the same temperature, is a strong though brittle solid whose particles tend to cohere into definite geometrical shapes, and sometimes build up frosty imitations of the most complex forms of vegetable foliage.

Nevertheless we call these, and many other strange phænomena, the properties of the water, and we do not hesitate to believe that, in some way or another, they result from the properties of the component elements of the water. We do not assume that a something called "aquosity" entered into and took possession of the oxidated hydrogen as soon as it was formed, and then guided the aqueous particles to their places in the facets of the crystal, or amongst the leaflets of the hoar-frost. On the contrary, we live in the hope and in the faith that, by the advance of molecular physics, we shall by and by be able to see our way as clearly from the constituents of water to the properties of water, as we are now able to deduce the operations of a watch from the form of its parts and the manner in which they are put together.

Is the case in any way changed when carbonic acid, water, and nitrogenous salts disappear, and in their place, under the influence of pre-existing living protoplasm, an equivalent weight of the matter of life makes its appearance?

It is true that there is no sort of parity between the properties of the components and the properties of the resultant, but neither was there in the case of the water. It is also true that what I have spoken of as the influence of pre-existing living matter is something quite unintelligible; but does anybody quite comprehend the *modus operandi* of an electric spark, which traverses a mixture of oxygen and hydrogen?

What justification is there, then, for the assumption of the existence in the living matter of a something which has no representative, or correlative, in the not living matter which gave rise to it? What better philosophical status has "vitality" than "aquosity"? And why should "vitality" hope for a better fate than the other "itys" which have disappeared since Martinus Scriblerus accounted for the operation of the meat-jack by its inherent "meat-roasting quality," and scorned the "materialism" of those who explained the turning of the spit by a certain mechanism worked by the draught of the chimney.

If scientific language is to possess a definite and constant signification wherever it is employed, it seems to me that we are logically bound to apply to the protoplasm, or physical basis of life, the same conceptions as those which are held to be legitimate elsewhere. If the phænomena exhibited by water are its properties, so are those presented by protoplasm, living or dead, its properties.

If the properties of water may be properly said to result from the nature and disposition of its component molecules, I can find no intelligible ground for refusing to say that the properties of protoplasm result from the nature and disposition of its molecules.

But I bid you beware that, in accepting these conclusions, you are placing your feet on the first rung of a ladder which, in most people's estimation, is the reverse of Jacob's, and leads to the antipodes of heaven. It may seem a small thing to admit that the dull vital actions of a fungus, or a foraminifer, are the properties of their protoplasm, and are the direct results of the nature of the matter of which they are composed. But if, as I have endeavoured to prove to you, their protoplasm is essentially identical with, and most readily converted into, that of any animal, I can discover no logical halting-place between the admission that such is the case, and the further concession that all vital action may, with equal propriety, be said to be the result of the molecular forces of the protoplasm which displays it. And if so, it must be true, in the same sense and to the same extent, that the thoughts to which I am now giving utterance, and your thoughts regarding them, are the expression of molecular changes in that matter of life which is the source of our other vital phænomena.

Past experience leads me to be tolerably certain that, when the propositions I have just placed before you are accessible to public comment and criticism, they will be condemned by many zealous persons, and perhaps by some few of the wise and thoughtful. I should not wonder if "gross and brutal materialism" were the mildest phrase applied to them in certain quarters. And, most undoubtedly, the terms of the propositions are distinctly materialistic Nevertheless two things are certain; the one, that I hold the statements to be substantially true; the other, that I, individually, am no materialist, but, on the contrary, believe materialism to involve grave philosophical error.

This union of materialistic terminology with the repudiation of materialistic philosophy, I share with some of the most thoughtful men with whom I am acquainted. . . .

Permit me to enforce this most wise advice.[7] Why trouble ourselves about matters of which, however important they may be, we do know nothing, and can know nothing? We live in a world which is full of misery and ignorance, and the plain duty of each and all of us is to try to make the little corner he can influence somewhat less miserable and somewhat less ignorant than it was before he entered it. To do this effectually it is necessary to be fully possessed of only two beliefs: the first, that the order of Nature is ascertainable by our faculties to an extent which is practically unlimited; the second, that our volition [8] counts for something as a condition of the course of events.

Each of these beliefs can be verified experimentally, as often as we like to try. Each, therefore, stands upon the strongest foundation upon which any belief can rest, and forms one of our highest truths. If we find that the ascertainment of the order of nature is facilitated by using one terminology, or one set of symbols, rather than another, it is our clear duty to use the former; and no harm can accrue, so long as we bear in mind, that we are dealing merely with terms and symbols.

In itself it is of little moment whether we express the phænomena of matter in terms of spirit; or the phænomena of spirit in terms of matter: matter may be regarded as a form of thought, thought may be regarded as a property of matter — each statement has a certain relative truth. But with a view to the progress of science, the materialistic terminology is in every way to be preferred. For it connects thought with the other phænomena of the universe, and suggests inquiry into the nature of those physical conditions, or concomitants of thought, which are more or less accessible to us, and a knowledge of which may, in future, help us to exercise the same kind of control over the world of thought, as we already possess in respect of the material world; whereas, the alternative, or spiritualistic, terminology is utterly barren, and leads to nothing but obscurity and confusion of ideas.

Thus there can be little doubt, that the further science advances, the more extensively and consistently will all the phænomena of Nature be represented by materialistic formulae and symbols.

But the man of science, who, forgetting the limits of philosophical

7 The advice, that is, of Hume: "If we take in hand any volume of Divinity, or school metaphysics, for instance, let us ask, *Does it contain any abstract reasoning concerning quantity or number?* No. *Does it contain any experimental reasoning concerning matter of fact and existence?* No. Commit it then to the flames; for it can contain nothing but sophistry and illusion."

8 Or, to speak more accurately, the physical state of which volition is the expression. [Huxley's note.]

inquiry, slides from these formulae and symbols into what is commonly understood by materialism, seems to me to place himself on a
level with the mathematician, who should mistake the x's and y's
with which he works his problems, for real entities — and with this
further disadvantage, as compared with the mathematician, that the
blunders of the latter are of no practical consequence, while the errors
of systematic materialism may paralyse the energies and destroy the
beauty of a life.

Science and Culture

⟨[This essay was delivered as a lecture at the opening of Sir Josiah Mason's
Science College at Birmingham on 1 October 1880. It was printed in
Science and Culture, and Other Essays (1881) and in the third volume of
Collected Essays (1893), entitled *Science and Education.*]⟩

. . . FROM the time that the first suggestion to introduce physical science
into ordinary education was timidly whispered, until now, the advocates of scientific education have met with opposition of two kinds.
On the one hand, they have been pooh-poohed by the men of business who pride themselves on being the representatives of practicality;
while, on the other hand, they have been excommunicated by the
classical scholars, in their capacity of Levites in charge of the ark of
culture and monopolists of liberal education.

The practical men believed that the idol whom they worship —
rule of thumb — has been the source of the past prosperity, and will
suffice for the future welfare of the arts and manufactures. They are
of opinion that science is speculative rubbish; that theory and practice have nothing to do with one another; and that the scientific habit
of mind is an impediment, rather than an aid, in the conduct of ordinary affairs.

I have used the past tense in speaking of the practical men — for
although they were very formidable thirty years ago, I am not sure
that the pure species has not been extirpated. In fact, so far as mere
argument goes, they have been subjected to such a *feu d'enfer* that
it is a miracle if any have escaped. But I have remarked that your
typical practical man has an unexpected resemblance to one of Milton's angels. His spiritual wounds, such as are inflicted by logical
weapons, may be as deep as a well and as wide as a church door,
but beyond shedding a few drops of ichor, celestial or otherwise, he
is no whit the worse. So, if any of these opponents be left, I will not
waste time in vain repetition of the demonstrative evidence of the

practical value of science; but knowing that a parable will sometimes penetrate where syllogisms fail to effect an entrance, I will offer a story for their consideration.

Once upon a time, a boy, with nothing to depend upon but his own vigorous nature, was thrown into the thick of the struggle for existence in the midst of a great manufacturing population. He seems to have had a hard fight, inasmuch as, by the time he was thirty years of age, his total disposable funds amounted to twenty pounds. Nevertheless, middle life found him giving proof of his comprehension of the practical problems he had been roughly called upon to solve, by a career of remarkable prosperity.

Finally, having reached old age with its well-earned surroundings of "honour, troops of friends," the hero of my story bethought himself of those who were making a like start in life, and how he could stretch out a helping hand to them.

After long and anxious reflection this successful practical man of business could devise nothing better than to provide them with the means of obtaining "sound, extensive, and practical scientific knowledge." And he devoted a large part of his wealth and five years of incessant work to this end.

I need not point the moral of a tale which, as the solid and spacious fabric of the Scientific College assures us, is no fable, nor can anything which I could say intensify the force of this practical answer to practical objections.

We may take it for granted then, that, in the opinion of those best qualified to judge, the diffusion of thorough scientific education is an absolutely essential condition of industrial progress; and that the College which has been opened today will confer an inestimable boon upon those whose livelihood is to be gained by the practise of the arts and manufactures of the district.

The only question worth discussion is, whether the conditions, under which the work of the College is to be carried out, are such as to give it the best possible chance of achieving permanent success.

Sir Josiah Mason, without doubt most wisely, has left very large freedom of action to the trustees, to whom he proposes ultimately to commit the administration of the College, so that they may be able to adjust its arrangements in accordance with the changing conditions of the future. But, with respect to three points, he has laid most explicit injunctions upon both administrators and teachers.

Party politics are forbidden to enter into the minds of either, so far as the work of the College is concerned; theology is as sternly banished from its precincts; and finally, it is especially declared that the College shall make no provision for "mere literary instruction and education."

It does not concern me at present to dwell upon the first two in-

junctions any longer than may be needful to express my full conviction of their wisdom. But the third prohibition brings us face to face
with those other opponents of scientific education, who are by no
means in the moribund condition of the practical man, but alive, alert,
and formidable.

It is not impossible that we shall hear this express exclusion of
"literary instruction and education" from a College which, nevertheless, professes to give a high and efficient education, sharply criticised.
Certainly the time was that the Levites of culture would have sounded
their trumpets against its walls as against an educational Jericho.

How often have we not been told that the study of physical science
is incompetent to confer culture; that it touches none of the higher
problems of life; and, what is worse, that the continual devotion to
scientific studies tends to generate a narrow and bigoted belief in the
applicability of scientific methods to the search after truth of all
kinds? How frequently one has reason to observe that no reply to
a troublesome argument tells so well as calling its author a "mere
scientific specialist." And, as I am afraid it is not permissible to speak
of this form of opposition to scientific education in the past tense; may
we not expect to be told that this, not only omission, but prohibition,
of "mere literary instruction and education" is a patent example of
scientific narrow-mindedness?

I am not acquainted with Sir Josiah Mason's reasons for the action
which he has taken; but if, as I apprehend is the case, he refers to
the ordinary classical course of our schools and universities by the
name of "mere literary instruction and education," I venture to offer
sundry reasons of my own in support of that action.

For I hold very strongly by two convictions: The first is, that neither
the discipline nor the subject-matter of classical education is of such
direct value to the student of physical science as to justify the expenditure of valuable time upon either; and the second is, that for
the purpose of attaining real culture, an exclusively scientific education is at least as effectual as an exclusively literary education.

I need hardly point out to you that these opinions, especially the
latter, are diametrically opposed to those of the great majority of
educated Englishmen, influenced as they are by school and university
traditions. In their belief, culture is obtainable only by a liberal education; and a liberal education is synonymous, not merely with education and instruction in literature, but in one particular form of literature, namely, that of Greek and Roman antiquity. They hold that the
man who has learned Latin and Greek, however little, is educated;
while he who is versed in other branches of knowledge, however
deeply, is a more or less respectable specialist, not admissible into
the cultured caste. The stamp of the educated man, the University
degree, is not for him.

I am too well acquainted with the generous catholicity of spirit, the true sympathy with scientific thought, which pervades the writings of our chief apostle of culture to identify him with these opinions; and yet one may cull from one and another of those epistles to the Philistines, which so much delight all who do not answer to that name, sentences which lend them some support.

Mr. Arnold tells us that the meaning of culture is "to know the best that has been thought and said in the world." It is the criticism of life contained in literature. That criticism regards "Europe as being, for intellectual and spiritual purposes, one great confederation, bound to a joint action and working to a common result; and whose members have, for their common outfit, a knowledge of Greek, Roman, and Eastern antiquity, and of one another. Special, local, and temporary advantages being put out of account, that modern nation will in the intellectual and spiritual sphere make most progress, which most thoroughly carries out this programme. And what is that but saying that we too, all of us, as individuals, the more thoroughly we carry it out, shall make the more progress?"

We have here to deal with two distinct propositions. The first, that a criticism of life is the essence of culture; the second, that literature contains the materials which suffice for the construction of such criticism.

I think that we must all assent to the first proposition. For culture certainly means something quite different from learning or technical skill. It implies the possession of an ideal, and the habit of critically estimating the value of things by comparison with a theoretic standard. Perfect culture should supply a complete theory of life, based upon a clear knowledge alike of its possibilities and of its limitations.

But we may agree to all this, and yet strongly dissent from the assumption that literature alone is competent to supply this knowledge. After having learnt all that Greek, Roman, and Eastern antiquity have thought and said, and all that modern literatures have to tell us, it is not self-evident that we have laid a sufficiently broad and deep foundation for that criticism of life, which constitutes culture.

Indeed, to any one acquainted with the scope of physical science, it is not at all evident. Considering progress only in the "intellectual and spiritual sphere," I find myself wholly unable to admit that either nations or individuals will really advance, if their common outfit draws nothing from the stores of physical science. I should say that an army, without weapons of precision and with no particular base of operations, might more hopefully enter upon a campaign on the Rhine, than a man, devoid of a knowledge of what physical science has done in the last century, upon a criticism of life.

When a biologist meets with an anomaly, he instinctively turn' the study of development to clear it up. The rationale of contradi' opinions may with equal confidence be sought in history.

Thomas Henry Huxley

It is, happily, no new thing that Englishmen should employ their wealth in building and endowing institutions for educational purposes. But, five or six hundred years ago, deeds of foundation expressed or implied conditions as nearly as possible contrary to those which have been thought expedient by Sir Josiah Mason. That is to say, physical science was practically ignored, while a certain literary training was enjoined as a means to the acquirement of knowledge which was essentially theological.

The reason of this singular contradiction between the actions of men alike animated by a strong and disinterested desire to promote the welfare of their fellows, is easily discovered.

At that time, in fact, if any one desired knowledge beyond such as could be obtained by his own observation, or by common conversation, his first necessity was to learn the Latin language, inasmuch as all the higher knowledge of the western world was contained in works written in that language. Hence, Latin grammar, with logic and rhetoric, studied through Latin, were the fundamentals of education. With respect to the substance of the knowledge imparted through this channel, the Jewish and Christian Scriptures, as interpreted and supplemented by the Romish Church, were held to contain a complete and infallibly true body of information.

Theological dicta were, to the thinkers of those days, that which the axioms and definitions of Euclid are to the geometers of these. The business of the philosophers of the middle ages was to deduce from the data furnished by the theologians, conclusions in accordance with ecclesiastical decrees. They were allowed the high privilege of showing, by logical process, how and why that which the Church said was true, must be true. And if their demonstrations fell short of or exceeded this limit, the Church was maternally ready to check their aberrations; if need were, by the help of the secular arm.

Between the two, our ancestors were furnished with a compact and complete criticism of life. They were told how the world began and how it would end; they learned that all material existence was but a base and insignificant blot upon the fair face of the spiritual world, and that nature was, to all intents and purposes, the playground of the devil; they learned that the earth is the centre of the visible universe, and that man is the cynosure of things terrestrial, and more especially was it inculcated that the course of nature had no fixed order, but that it could be, and constantly was, altered by the agency of innumerable spiritual beings, good and bad, according as they were moved by the deeds and prayers of men. The sum and substance of the whole doctrine was to produce the conviction that the only thing really worth knowing in this world was how to secure that place in a better which, under certain conditions, the Church promised.

Our ancestors had a living belief in this theory of life, and acted upon it in their dealings with education, as in all other matters. Culture meant saintliness — after the fashion of the saints of those days; the education that led to it was, of necessity, theological; and the way to theology lay through Latin.

That the study of nature — further than was requisite for the satisfaction of everyday wants — should have any bearing on human life was far from the thoughts of men thus trained. Indeed, as nature had been cursed for man's sake, it was an obvious conclusion that those who meddled with nature were likely to come into pretty close contact with Satan. And, if any born scientific investigator followed his instincts, he might safely reckon upon earning the reputation, and probably upon suffering the fate, of a sorcerer.

Had the western world been left to itself in Chinese isolation, there is no saying how long this state of things might have endured. But, happily, it was not left to itself. Even earlier than the thirteenth century, the development of Moorish civilisation in Spain and the great movement of the Crusades had introduced the leaven which, from that day to this, has never ceased to work. At first, through the intermediation of Arabic translations, afterwards by the study of the originals, the western nations of Europe became acquainted with the writings of the ancient philosophers and poets, and, in time, with the whole of the vast literature of antiquity.

Whatever there was of high intellectual aspiration or dominant capacity in Italy, France, Germany, and England, spent itself for centuries in taking possession of the rich inheritance left by the dead civilisations of Greece and Rome. Marvellously aided by the invention of printing, classical learning spread and flourished. Those who possessed it prided themselves on having attained the highest culture then within the reach of mankind.

And justly. For, saving Dante on his solitary pinnacle, there was no figure in modern literature at the time of the Renascence to compare with the men of antiquity; there was no art to compete with their sculpture; there was no physical science but that which Greece had created. Above all, there was no other example of perfect intellectual freedom — of the unhesitating acceptance of reason as the sole guide to truth and the supreme arbiter of conduct.

The new learning necessarily soon exerted a profound influence upon education. The language of the monks and schoolmen seemed little better than gibberish to scholars fresh from Virgil and Cicero, and the study of Latin was placed upon a new foundation. Moreover, Latin itself ceased to afford the sole key to knowledge. The student who sought the highest thought of antiquity, found only a second-hand reflection of it in Roman literature, and turned his face to the full light of the Greeks. And after a battle, not altogether dissimilar to that which is at present being fought over the teaching of physical science, the study of Greek was recognised as an essential element of all higher education.

Then the Humanists, as they were called, won the day; and the great reform which they effected was of incalculable service to mankind. But the Nemesis of all reformers is finality; and the reformers of education, like those of religion, fell into the profound, however common, error of mistaking the beginning for the end of the work of reformation.

The representatives of the Humanists, in the nineteenth century, take their stand upon classical education as the sole avenue to culture, as firmly as if we were still in the age of Renascence. Yet, surely, the present intellectual relations of the modern and the ancient worlds are profoundly different from those which obtained three centuries ago. Leaving aside the existence of a great and characteristically modern literature, of modern painting, and, especially, of modern music, there is one feature of the present state of the civilised world which separates it more widely from the Renascence, than the Renascence was separated from the middle ages.

This distinctive character of our own times lies in the vast and constantly increasing part which is played by natural knowledge. Not only is our daily life shaped by it; not only does the prosperity of millions of men depend upon it, but our whole theory of life has long been influenced, consciously or unconsciously, by the general conceptions of the universe, which have been forced upon us by physical science.

In fact, the most elementary acquaintance with the results of scientific investigation shows us that they offer a broad and striking contradiction to the opinion so implicitly credited and taught in the middle ages.

The notions of the beginning and the end of the world entertained by our forefathers are no longer credible. It is very certain that the earth is not the chief body in the material universe, and that the world is not subordinated to man's use. It is even more certain that nature is the expression of a definite order with which nothing interfeses, and that the chief business of mankind is to learn that order and govern themselves accordingly. Moreover this scientific "criticism of life" presents itself to us with different credentials from any other. It appeals not to authority, nor to what anybody may have thought or said, but to nature. It admits that all our interpretations of natural fact are more or less imperfect and symbolic, and bids the learner seek for truth not among words but among things. It warns us that the assertion which outstrips evidence is not only a blunder but a crime.

The purely classical education advocated by the representatives of the Humanists in our day, gives no inkling of all this. A man may be a better scholar than Erasmus, and know no more of the chief causes of the present intellectual fermentation than Erasmus did. Scholarly and pious persons, worthy of all respect, favour us with allocutions upon the sadness of the antagonism of science to their mediæval way of thinking, which betray an ignorance of the first principles of scientific investigation, an incapacity for understanding what a man of science means by veracity, and an unconsciousness of the weight of established scientific truths, which is almost comical.

There is no great force in the *tu quoque* argument, or else the advocates of scientific education might fairly enough retort upon the modern Humanists that they may be learned specialists, but that they possess no such sound foundation for a criticism of life as deserves the name of culture. And, indeed, if we were disposed to be cruel, we might urge that the Humanists have brought this reproach upon themselves, not because they are too full of the spirit of the ancient Greek, but because they lack it.

The period of the Renascence is commonly called that of the "Revival of Letters," as if the influences then brought to bear upon the mind of Western Europe had been wholly exhausted in the field of literature. I think it is very commonly forgotten that the revival of science, effected by the same agency, although less conspicuous, was not less momentous.

In fact, the few and scattered students of nature of that day picked up the clue to her secrets exactly as it fell from the hands of the Greeks a thousand years before. The foundations of mathematics were so well laid by them, that our children learn their geometry from a book written for the schools of Alexandria two thousand years ago. Modern astronomy is the natural continuation and development of the work of Hipparchus and of Ptolemy; modern physics of that of Democritus and of Archimedes; it was long before modern biological science outgrew the knowledge bequeathed to us by Aristotle, by Theophrastus, and by Galen.

We cannot know all the best thoughts and sayings of the Greeks unless we know what they thought about natural phenomena. We cannot fully apprehend their criticism of life unless we understand the extent to which that criticism was affected by scientific conceptions. We falsely pretend to be the inheritors of their culture, unless we are penetrated, as the best minds among them were, with an unhesitating faith that the free employment of reason, in accordance with scientific method, is the sole method of reaching truth.

Thus I venture to think that the pretensions of our modern Humanists to the possession of the monopoly of culture and to the exclusive inheritance of the spirit of antiquity must be abated, if not abandoned. But I should be very sorry that anything I have said should be taken to imply a desire on my part to depreciate the value of classical education, as it might be and as it sometimes is. The native capacities of mankind vary no less than their opportunities; and while culture is one, the road by which one man may best reach it is widely different from that which is most advantageous to another. Again, while scientific education is yet inchoate and tentative, classical education is thoroughly well organised upon the practical experience of generations of teachers. So that, given ample time for learning and estimation for ordinary life, or for a literary career, I do not think that a young Englishman in search of culture can do better than follow the course usually marked out for him, supplementing its deficiencies by his own efforts.

But for those who mean to make science their serious occupation; or who intend to follow the profession of medicine; or who have to enter early upon the business of life; for all these, in my opinion, classical education is a mistake; and it is for this reason that I am glad to see "mere literary education and instruction" shut out from the curriculum of Sir Josiah Mason's College, seeing that its inclusion would probably lead to the introduction of the ordinary smattering of Latin and Greek.

Nevertheless, I am the last person to question the importance of genuine literary education, or to suppose that intellectual culture can be complete without it. An exclusively scientific training will bring about a mental twist as surely as an exclusively literary training. The value of the cargo does not compensate for a ship's being out of trim; and I should be very sorry to think that the Scientific College would turn out none but lopsided men.

There is no need, however, that such a catastrophe should happen. Instruction in English, French, and German is provided, and thus the three greatest literatures of the modern world are made accessible to the student.

French and German, and especially the latter language, are absolutely indispensable to those who desire full knowledge in any department of science. But even supposing that the knowledge of these languages acquired is not more than sufficient for purely scientific purposes, every Englishman has, in his native tongue, an almost perfect instrument of literary expression; and, in his own literature, models of every kind of literary excellence. If an Englishman cannot get literary culture out of his Bible, his Shakespeare, his Milton, neither, in my belief, will the profoundest study of Homer and Sophocles, Virgil and Horace, give it to him.

Thus, since the constitution of the College makes sufficient provision for literary as well as for scientific education, and since artistic instruction is also contemplated, it seems to me that a fairly complete culture is offered to all who are willing to take advantage of it.

But I am not sure that at this point the "practical" man, scotched but not slain, may ask what all this talk about culture has to do with an Institution, the object of which is defined to be "to promote the prosperity of the manufactures and the industry of the country." He may suggest that what is wanted for this end is not culture, nor even a purely scientific discipline, but simply a knowledge of applied science.

I often wish that this phrase, "applied science," had never been invented. For it suggests that there is a sort of scientific knowledge of direct practical use, which can be studied apart from another sort of scientific knowledge, which is of no practical utility, and which is termed "pure science." But there is no more complete fallacy than this. What people call applied science is nothing but the application of pure science to particular classes of problems. It consists of deductions from those general principles, established by reasoning and observation, which constitute pure science. No one can safely make these deductions until he has a firm grasp of the principles; and he can obtain that grasp only by personal experience of the operations of observation and of reasoning on which they are founded.

Almost all the processes employed in the arts and manufactures fall within the range either of physics or of chemistry. In order to improve them, one must thoroughly understand them; and no one has a chance of really understanding them, unless he has obtained that mastery of principles and that habit of dealing with facts, which is given by long-continued and well-directed purely scientific training in the physical and the chemical laboratory. So that there really is no question as to the necessity of purely scientific discipline, even if the work of the College were limited by the narrowest interpretation of its stated aims.

And, as to the desirableness of a wider culture than that yielded by science alone, it is to be recollected that the improvement of manufacturing processes is only one of the conditions which contribute to the prosperity of industry. Industry is a means and not an end; and mankind work only to get something which they want. What that something is depends partly on their innate, and partly on their acquired, desires.

If the wealth resulting from prosperous industry is to be spent upon the gratification of unworthy desires, if the increasing perfection of manufacturing processes is to be accompanied by an increasing debasement of those who carry them on, I do not see the good of industry and prosperity.

Now it is perfectly true that men's views of what is desirable depend upon their characters; and that the innate proclivities to which we give that name are not touched by any amount of instruction. But it does not follow that even mere intellectual education may not, to an indefinite extent, modify the practical manifestation of the characters of men in their actions, by supplying them with motives unknown to the ignorant. A pleasure-loving character will have pleasure of some sort; but, if you give him the choice, he may prefer pleasures which do not degrade him to those which do. And this choice is offered to every man, who possesses in literary or artistic culture a never-failing source of pleasures, which are neither withered by age, nor staled by custom, nor embittered in the recollection by the pangs of self-reproach.

If the Institution opened today fulfils the intention of its founder, the picked intelligences among all classes of the population of this district will pass through it. No child born in Birmingham, henceforward, if he have the capacity to profit by the opportunities offered to him, first in the primary and other schools, and afterwards in the Scientific College, need fail to obtain, not merely the instruction, but the culture most appropriate to the conditions of his life.

Within these walls, the future employer and the future artisan may sojourn together for a while, and carry, through all their lives, the stamp of the influences then brought to bear upon them. Hence, it is not beside the mark to remind you, that the prosperity of industry depends not merely upon the improvement of manufacturing processes, not merely upon the ennobling of the individual character, but upon a third condition, namely, a clear understanding of the conditions of social life, on the part of both the capitalist and the operative, and their agreement upon common principles of social action. They must learn that social phenomena are as much the expression of natural laws as any others; that no social arrangements can be permanent unless they harmonise with the requirements of social statics and dynamics; and that, in the nature of things, there is an arbiter whose decisions execute themselves.

But this knowledge is only to be obtained by the application of the methods of investigation adopted in physical researches to the investigation of the phenomena of society. Hence, I confess, I should like to see one addition made to the excellent scheme of education propounded for the College, in the shape of provision for the teaching of Sociology. For though we are all agreed that party politics are to have no place in the instruction of the College; yet in this country, practically governed as it is now by universal suffrage, every man who does his duty must exercise political functions. And, if the evils which are inseparable from the good of political liberty are to be checked, if the perpetual oscillation of nations between anarchy and despotism is to be replaced by the steady march of self-restraining freedom; it will be because men will gradually bring themselves to deal with political, as they now deal with scientific questions; to be as ashamed of undue haste and partisan prejudice in the one case as in the other; and to believe that the machinery of society is at least as delicate as that of a spinning-jenny, and as little likely to be improved by the meddling of those who have not taken the trouble to master the principles of its action.

In conclusion, I am sure that I make myself the mouthpiece of all present in offering to the venerable founder of the Institution, which now commences its beneficent career, our congratulations on the completion of his work; and in expressing the conviction, that the remotest posterity will point to it as a crucial instance of the wisdom which natural piety leads all men to ascribe to their ancestors.

Agnosticism and Christianity

⟪ This essay was first printed in the *Nineteenth Century* as a reply to the charge that so-called "agnostics" were merely trying to evade being called by the exacter name "infidels." The essay was later reprinted in *Essays on Some Controverted Questions* (1892) and in the fifth volume of the *Collected Essays* (1894), entitled *Science and Christian Tradition.* ⟫

> NEMO ergo ex me scire quaerat, quod me nescire scio, nisi forte ut nescire discat. — Augustinus, *De Civ. Dei*, xii.7.[1]

The present discussion has arisen out of the use, which has become general in the last few years, of the terms "Agnostic" and "Agnosticism."

The people who call themselves "Agnostics" have been charged with doing so because they have not the courage to declare themselves "Infidels." It has been insinuated that they have adopted a new name in order to escape the unpleasantness which attaches to their proper denomination. To this wholly erroneous imputation, I have replied by showing that the term "Agnostic" did, as a matter of fact, arise in a manner which negatives it; and my statement has not been, and cannot be, refuted. Moreover, speaking for myself, and without impugning the right of any other person to use the term in another sense, I further say that Agnosticism is not properly described as a "negative" creed, nor indeed as a creed of any kind, except in so far as it expresses absolute faith in the validity of a principle, which is as much ethical as intellectual. This principle may be stated in various ways, but they all amount to this: that it is wrong for a man to say that he is certain of the objective truth of any proposition unless he can produce evidence which logically justifies that certainty. This is what Agnosticism asserts; and, in my opinion, it is all that

---

1 "No one, therefore, should seek to learn knowledge from me, for I know that I do not know — unless indeed he wishes to learn that he does not know." — Augustine, *City of God*, xii. 7.

is essential to Agnosticism. That which Agnostics deny and repudiate, as immoral, is the contrary doctrine, that there are propositions which men ought to believe, without logically satisfactory evidence; and that reprobation ought to attach to the profession of disbelief in such inadequately supported propositions. The justification of the Agnostic principle lies in the success which follows upon its application, whether in the field of natural, or in that of civil, history; and in the fact that, so far as these topics are concerned, no sane man thinks of denying its validity.

Still speaking for myself, I add, that though Agnosticism is not, and cannot be, a creed, except in so far as its general principle is concerned; yet that the application of that principle results in the denial of, or the suspension of judgment concerning, a number of propositions respecting which our contemporary ecclesiastical "gnostics" profess entire certainty. And, in so far as these ecclesiastical persons can be justified in their old-established custom (which many nowadays think more honoured in the breach than the observance) of using opprobrious names to those who differ from them, I fully admit their right to call me and those who think with me "Infidels"; all I have ventured to urge is that they must not expect us to speak of ourselves by that title.

The extent of the region of the uncertain, the number of the problems the investigation of which ends in a verdict of not proven, will vary according to the knowledge and the intellectual habits of the individual Agnostic. I do not very much care to speak of anything as "unknowable." What I am sure about is that there are many topics about which I know nothing; and which, so far as I can see, are out of reach of my faculties. But whether these things are knowable by any one else is exactly one of those matters which is beyond my knowledge, though I may have a tolerably strong opinion as to the probabilities of the case. Relatively to myself, I am quite sure that the region of uncertainty — the nebulous country in which words play the part of realities — is far more extensive than I could wish. Materialism and Idealism; Theism and Atheism; the doctrine of the soul and its mortality or immortality — appear in the history of philosophy like the shades of Scandinavian heroes, eternally slaying one another and eternally coming to life again in a metaphysical "Nifelheim." [2] It is getting on for twenty-five centuries, at least, since mankind began seriously to give their minds to these topics. Generation after generation, philosophy has been doomed to roll the stone uphill; and, just as all the world swore it was at the top, down it has rolled to the bottom again. All this is written in innumerable books; and he who will toil through them will discover that the stone is just where it was when the work began. Hume saw this; Kant saw it; since their time, more and more eyes have been cleansed of the

2 The cold, dark northern regions of Norse mythology.

films which prevented them from seeing it; until now the weight and number of those who refuse to be the prey of verbal mystifications has begun to tell in practical life.

It was inevitable that a conflict should arise between Agnosticism and Theology; or rather, I ought to say, between Agnosticism and Ecclesiasticism. For Theology, the science, is one thing; and Ecclesiasticism, the championship of a foregone conclusion [3] as to the truth of a particular form of Theology, is another. With scientific Theology, Agnosticism has no quarrel. On the contrary, the Agnostic, knowing too well the influence of prejudice and idiosyncrasy, even on those who desire most earnestly to be impartial, can wish for nothing more urgently than that the scientific theologian should not only be at perfect liberty to thresh out the matter in his own fashion; but that he should, if he can, find flaws in the Agnostic position; and, even if demonstration is not to be had, that he should put, in their full force, the grounds of the conclusions he thinks probable. The scientific theologian admits the Agnostic principle, however widely his results may differ from those reached by the majority of Agnostics.

But, as between Agnosticism and Ecclesiasticism, or, as our neighbours across the Channel call it, Clericalism, there can be neither peace nor truce. The Cleric asserts that it is morally wrong not to believe certain propositions, whatever the results of a strict scientific investigation of the evidence of these propositions. He tells us "that religious error is, in itself, of an immoral nature." [4] He declares that he has prejudged certain conclusions, and looks upon those who show cause for arrest of judgment as emissaries of Satan. It necessarily follows that, for him, the attainment of faith, not the ascertainment of truth, is the highest aim of mental life. And, on careful analysis of the nature of this faith, it will too often be found to be, not the mystic process of unity with the Divine, understood by the religious enthusiast; but that which the candid simplicity of a Sunday scholar once defined it to be. "Faith," said this unconscious plagiarist of Tertullian, "is the power of saying you believe things which are incredible."

Now I, and many other Agnostics, believe that faith, in this sense, is an abomination; and though we do not indulge in the luxury of self-righteousness so far as to call those who are not of our way of thinking hard names, we do feel that the disagreement between ourselves and those who hold this doctrine is even more moral than intellectual. It is desirable there should be an end of any mistakes on this topic. If our clerical opponents were clearly aware of the real state of the case, there would be an end of the curious delusion, which often appears between the lines of their writings, that those whom

3 "Let us maintain, before we have proved. This seeming paradox is the secret of happiness." (Dr. Newman: Tract 85, p. 85.) [Huxley's note.]
4 Dr. Newman, *Essay on Development*, p. 357. [Huxley's note.]

they are so fond of calling "Infidels" are people who not only ought
to be, but in their hearts are, ashamed of themselves. It would be
discourteous to do more than hint the antipodal opposition of this
pleasant dream of theirs to facts.

The clerics and their lay allies commonly tell us, that if we refuse
to admit that there is good ground for expressing definite convictions
about certain topics, the bonds of human society will dissolve and
mankind lapse into savagery. There are several answers to this assertion. One is that the bonds of human society were formed without
the aid of their theology; and, in the opinion of not a few competent
judges, have been weakened rather than strengthened by a good deal
of it. Greek science, Greek art, the ethics of old Israel, the social organisation of old Rome, contrived to come into being, without the
help of any one who believed in a single distinctive article of the
simplest of the Christian creeds. The science, the art, the jurisprudence, the chief political and social theories, of the modern world
have grown out of those of Greece and Rome — not by favour of,
but in the teeth of, the fundamental teachings of early Christianity,
to which science, art, and any serious occupation with the things of
this world, were alike despicable.

Again, all that is best in the ethics of the modern world, in so far
as it has not grown out of Greek thought, or Barbarian manhood, is
the direct development of the ethics of old Israel. There is no code
of legislation, ancient or modern, at once so just and so merciful, so
tender to the weak and poor, as the Jewish law; and, if the Gospels are
to be trusted, Jesus of Nazareth himself declared that he taught nothing but that which lay implicitly, or explicitly, in the religious and
ethical system of his people.

> "And the scribe said unto him, Of a truth, Teacher, thou hast well
> said that he is one; and there is none other but he and to love him with
> all the heart, and with all the understanding, and with all the strength,
> and to love his neighbour as himself, is much more than all whole burnt
> offerings and sacrifices." (Mark xii. 32,33.)

Here is the briefest of summaries of the teaching of the prophets of
Israel of the eighth century; does the Teacher, whose doctrine is thus
set forth in his presence, repudiate the exposition? Nay; we are told,
on the contrary, that Jesus saw that he "answered discreetly," and
replied, "Thou art not far from the kingdom of God."

So that I think that even if the creeds, from the so-called "Apostles'"
to the so-called "Athanasian," were swept into oblivion; and even if the
human race should arrive at the conclusion that, whether a bishop
washes a cup or leaves it unwashed, is not a matter of the least consequence, it will get on very well. The causes which have led to the
development of morality in mankind, which have guided or impelled
us all the way from the savage to the civilised state, will not cease

to operate because a number of ecclesiastical hypotheses turn out to be baseless. And, even if the absurd notion that morality is more the child of speculation than of practical necessity and inherited instinct, had any foundation; if all the world is going to thieve, murder, and otherwise misconduct itself as soon as it discovers that certain portions of ancient history are mythical; what is the relevance of such arguments to any one who holds by the Agnostic principle?

Surely, the attempt to cast out Beelzebub by the aid of Beelzebub is a hopeful procedure as compared to that of preserving morality by the aid of immorality. For I suppose it is admitted that an Agnostic may be perfectly sincere, may be competent, and may have studied the question at issue with as much care as his clerical opponents. But, if the Agnostic really believes what he says, the "dreadful consequence" argufier (consistently, I admit, with his own principles) virtually asks him to abstain from telling the truth, or to say what he believes to be untrue, because of the supposed injurious consequences to morality. "Beloved brethren, that we may be spotlessly moral, before all things let us lie," is the sum total of many an exhortation addressed to the "Infidel." Now, as I have already pointed out, we cannot oblige our exhorters. We leave the practical application of the convenient doctrines of "Reserve" and "Non-natural interpretation" to those who invented them.

I trust that I have now made amends for any ambiguity, or want of fulness, in my previous exposition of that which I hold to be the essence of the Agnostic doctrine. Henceforward, I might hope to hear no more of the assertion that we are necessarily Materialists, Idealists, Atheists, Theists, or any other ists, if experience had led me to think that the proved falsity of a statement was any guarantee against its repetition. And those who appreciate the nature of our position will see, at once, that when Ecclesiasticism declares that we ought to believe this, that, and the other, and are very wicked if we don't, it is impossible for us to give any answer but this: We have not the slightest objection to believe anything you like, if you will give us good grounds for belief; but, if you cannot, we must respectfully refuse, even if that refusal should wreck morality and insure our own damnation several times over. We are quite content to leave that to the decision of the future. The course of the past has impressed us with the firm conviction that no good ever comes of falsehood, and we feel warranted in refusing even to experiment in that direction. . . .

Walter Horatio Pater

WALTER HORATIO PATER

CHRONOLOGY

1839   Born August 4 at Shadwell, East London.

1853   Entered King's School, Canterbury.

1858   Entered Queen's College, Oxford.

1865   Became Classical Fellow at Brasenose College, Oxford.

1873   Published *Studies in the History of the Renaissance.*

1885   Published *Marius the Epicurean,* a spiritual romance.

1887   Published *Imaginary Portraits.*

1888   Published five chapters of *Gaston de Latour,* another romance.

1889   Published *Appreciations, With an Essay on Style.*

1893   Published *Plato and Platonism.*

1894   Received LL. D. degree from the University of Glasgow; died July 30.

Posthumously published: *Greek Studies,* 1895; *Miscellaneous Studies,* 1895; *Gaston de Latour,* 1896; *Essays from "The Guardian,"* 1901 (privately printed, 1897); *Uncollected Essays,* 1903; *Sketches and Reviews,* 1919.

The Renaissance

¶ *Studies in the History of the Renaissance* (1873) was, in later editions, retitled *The Renaissance: Studies in Art and Poetry*. Besides the famous Preface and Conclusion, the volume contained eight essays: "Two Early French Stories"; "Pico della Mirandola"; "Sandro Botticelli"; "Luca della Robbia"; "The Poetry of Michelangelo"; "Leonardo da Vinci"; "Joachim du Bellay"; "Winckelmann." Pater had an abiding interest in the Renaissance, "an age," he felt sure, "of which one may say, summarily, that it enjoyed itself, and found perhaps its chief enjoyment in the attitude of the scholar, in the enthusiastic acquisition of knowledge for its own sake." The Preface was written expressly for the book publication, but the Conclusion was written five years earlier, in 1868. This Conclusion was printed in the first edition, omitted from the second (1877), and restored in the third (1888) with this note by Pater: "This brief 'Conclusion' was omitted in the second edition of this book, as I conceived it might possibly mislead some of those young men into whose hands it might fall. On the whole, I have thought it best to reprint it here, with some slight changes which bring it closer to my original meaning. I have dealt more fully in *Marius the Epicurean* with the thoughts suggested by it." Actually, however, "those young men" would not free Pater of his unsought role as reluctant leader of the aesthetic movement which climaxed in Oscar Wilde. "La Gioconda" is an excerpt from the essay "Leonardo da Vinci"; it is a revealing example of subjective, impressionistic criticism (or appreciation) which gave rise, in part, to the extravagant critical theories and posings of Wilde. ▶

Preface

MANY attempts have been made by writers on art and poetry to define beauty in the abstract, to express it in the most general terms, to find some universal formula for it. The value of these attempts has most often been in the suggestive and penetrating things said by the way. Such discussions help us very little to enjoy what has been well done in art or poetry, to discriminate between what is more and what is less excellent in them, or to use words like beauty, excellence, art, poetry, with a more precise meaning than they would otherwise have. Beauty, like all other qualities presented to human experience, is relative; and the definition of it becomes unmeaning and useless in proportion to its abstractness. To define beauty, not in the most abstract but in the most concrete terms possible, to find not its universal formula, but the formula which expresses most adequately this or that special manifestation of it, is the aim of the true student of æsthetics.

"To see the object as in itself it really is," has been justly said to

be the aim of all true criticism whatever; and in æsthetic criticism
the first step towards seeing one's object as it really is, is to know
one's own impression as it really is, to discriminate it, to realise it
distinctly. The objects with which æsthetic criticism deals — music,
poetry, artistic and accomplished forms of human life — are indeed
receptacles of so many powers or forces: they possess, like the products of nature, so many virtues or qualities. What is this song or
picture, this engaging personality presented in life or in a book, to *me?*
What effect does it really produce on me? Does it give me pleasure?
and if so, what sort or degree of pleasure? How is my nature modified
by its presence, and under its influence? The answers to these questions are the original facts with which the æsthetic critic has to do;
and, as in the study of light, of morals, of number, one must realise
such primary data for one's self, or not at all. And he who experiences
these impressions strongly, and drives directly at the discrimination
and analysis of them, has no need to trouble himself with the abstract
question what beauty is in itself, or what its exact relation to truth or
experience — metaphysical questions, as unprofitable as metaphyical
questions elsewhere. He may pass them all by as being, answerable
or not, of no interest to him.

The æsthetic critic, then, regards all the objects with which he has
to do, all works of art, and the fairer forms of nature and human
life, as powers or forces producing pleasurable sensations, each of a
more or less peculiar or unique kind. This influence he feels, and
wishes to explain, by analysing and reducing it to its elements. To
him, the picture, the landscape, the engaging personality in life or in
a book, *La Gioconda,* the hills of Carrara, Pico of Mirandola, are
valuable for their virtues, as we say, in speaking of a herb, a wine,
a gem; for the property each has of affecting one with a special, a
unique, impression of pleasure. Our education becomes complete
in proportion as our susceptibility to these impressions increases in
depth and variety. And the function of the æsthetic critic is to distinguish, to analyse, and separate from its adjuncts, the virtue by
which a picture, a landscape, a fair personality in life or in a book,
produces this special impression of beauty or pleasure, to indicate
what the source of that impression is, and under what conditions it
is experienced. His end is reached when he has disengaged that
virtue, and noted it, as a chemist notes some natural element, for
himself and others; and the rule for those who would reach this end
is stated with great exactness in the words of a recent critic of Sainte-
Beauve: — *De se borner à connaître de près les belles choses, et à s'en
nourrir en exquis amateurs, en humanistes accomplis.*[1]

What is important, then, is not that the critic should possess a

---

[1] "To confine themselves to know at first hand beautiful things, and to develop themselves by these, as sensitive amateurs do, and accomplished humanists."

correct abstract definition of beauty for the intellect, but a certain kind of temperament, the power of being deeply moved by the presence of beautiful objects. He will remember always that beauty exists in many forms. To him all periods, types, schools of taste, are in themselves equal. In all ages there have been some excellent workmen, and some excellent work done. The question he asks is always: — In whom did the stir, the genius, the sentiment of the period find itself? where was the receptacle of its refinement, its elevation, its taste? "The ages are all equal," says William Blake, "but genius is always above its age."

Often it will require great nicety to disengage this virtue from the commoner elements with which it may be found in combination. Few artists, not Goethe or Byron even, work quite cleanly, casting off all *débris*, and leaving us only what the heat of their imagination has wholly fused and transformed. Take, for instance, the writings of Wordsworth. The heat of his genius, entering into the substance of his work, has crystallised a part, but only a part, of it; and in that great mass of verse there is much which might well be forgotten. But scattered up and down it, sometimes fusing and transforming entire compositions, like the Stanzas on *Resolution and Independence*, or the *Ode on the Recollections of Childhood*, sometimes, as if at random, depositing a fine crystal here or there, in a matter it does not wholly search through and transmute, we trace the action of his unique, incommunicable faculty, that strange, mystical sense of a life in natural things, and of man's life as a part of nature, drawing strength and colour and character from local influences, from the hills and streams, and from natural sights and sounds. Well! that is the *virtue*, the active principle in Wordsworth's poetry; and then the function of the critic of Wordsworth is to follow up that active principle, to disengage it, to mark the degree in which it penetrates his verse.

The subjects of the following studies are taken from the history of the *Renaissance*, and touch what I think the chief points in that complex, many-sided movement. I have explained in the first of them what I understand by the word, giving it a much wider scope than was intended by those who originally used it to denote that revival of classical antiquity in the fifteenth century which was only one of many results of a general excitement and enlightening of the human mind, but of which the great aim and achievements of what, as Christian art, is often falsely opposed to the Renaissance, were another result. This outbreak of the human spirit may be traced far into the middle age itself, with its motives already clearly pronounced, the care for physical beauty, the worship of the body, the breaking down of those limits which the religious system of the middle age imposed on the heart and the imagination. I have taken as an example of this movement, this earlier Renaissance within the middle age itself, and as an expression of its qualities, two little compositions in early French; not because they constitute the best possible expression of them, but because they help the unity of my series, inasmuch as the Renaissance ends also in France, in French poetry, in a phase of which the writings of Joachim du Bellay are in many ways the most perfect illustration. The Renaissance, in truth, put forth in France an aftermath, a wonderful later growth, the products of which have to the full that subtle and delicate sweetness which belongs to a refined and comely decadence, just as its earliest phases have the freshness which belongs to all periods of growth in art, the charm of *ascêsis*, of the austere and serious girding of the loins in youth.

But it is in Italy, in the fifteenth century, that the interest of the Renaissance mainly lies, — in that solemn fifteenth century which can hardly be studied too much, not merely for its positive results in the things of the intellect and the imagination, its concrete works of art, its special and prominent personalities, with their profound æsthetic charm, but for its general spirit and character, for the ethical qualities of which it is a consummate type.

The various forms of intellectual activity which together make up the culture of an age, move for the most part from different starting-points, and by unconnected roads. As products of the same generation they partake indeed of a common character, and unconsciously illustrate each other; but of the producers themselves, each group is solitary, gaining what advantage or disadvantage there may be in intellectual isolation. Art and poetry, philosophy and the religious life, and that other life of refined pleasure and action in the conspicuous places of the world, are each of them confined to its own circle of ideas, and those who prosecute either of them are generally little curious of the thoughts of others. There come, however, from time to time, eras of more favourable conditions, in which the thoughts of men draw nearer together than is their wont, and the many interests of the intellectual world combine in one complete type of general culture. The fifteenth century in Italy is one of these happier eras, and what is sometimes said of the age of Pericles is true of that of Lorenzo: — it is an age productive in personalities, many-sided, centralised, complete. Here, artists and philosophers and those whom the action of the world has elevated and made keen, do not live in isolation, but breathe a common air, and catch light and heat from each other's thoughts. There is a spirit of general elevation and enlightenment in which all alike communicate. The unity of this spirit gives unity to all the various products of the Renaissance; and it is to this intimate alliance with mind, this participation in the best thoughts which that age produced, that the art of Italy in the fifteenth century owes much of its grave dignity and influence.

I have added an essay on Winckelmann, as not incongruous with the studies which precede it, because Winckelmann, coming in the

eighteenth century, really belongs in spirit to an earlier age. By his
enthusiasm for the things of the intellect and the imagination for
their own sake, by his Hellenism, his life-long struggle to attain to
the Greek spirit, he is in sympathy with the humanists of a previous
century. He is the last fruit of the Renaissance, and explains in a
striking way its motive and tendencies.

Leonardo da Vinci
[*La Gioconda*]

. . . *La Gioconda* is, in the truest sense, Leonardo's masterpiece,
the revealing instance of his mode of thought and work. In sugges-
tiveness, only the *Melancholia* of Dürer is comparable to it; and no
crude symbolism disturbs the effect of its subdued and graceful mystery. We all know the face and hands of the figure, set in its marble
chair, in that circle of fantastic rocks, as in some faint light under
sea. Perhaps of all ancient pictures time has chilled it least.[1] As often
happens with works in which invention seems to reach its limit, there
is an element in it given to, not invented by, the master. In that inestimable folio of drawings, once in the possession of Vasari, were
certain designs by Verrocchio, faces of such impressive beauty that
Leonardo in his boyhood copied them many times. It is hard not to
connect with these designs of the elder, by-past master, as with its
germinal principle, the unfathomable smile, always with a touch of
something sinister in it, which plays over all Leonardo's work. Besides, the picture is a portrait. From childhood we see this image
defining itself on the fabric of his dreams, and but for express historical
testimony, we might fancy that this was but his ideal lady, embodied
and beheld at last. What was the relationship of a living Florentine
to this creature of his thought? By what strange affinities had the
dream and the person grown up thus apart, and yet so closely together? Present from the first incorporeally in Leonardo's brain,
dimly traced in the designs of Verrocchio, she is found present at
last in *Il Giocondo's* house. That there is much of mere portraiture
in the picture is attested by the legend that by artificial means, the
presence of mimes and fluteplayers, that subtle expression was protracted on the face. Again, was it in four years and by renewed labour
never really completed, or in four months and as by stroke of magic,
that the image was projected?

The presence that rose thus so strangely beside the waters, is expressive of what in the ways of a thousand years men had come to
desire. Hers is the head upon which all "the ends of the world are

---

[1] Yet for Vasari there was some further magic of crimson in the lips and cheeks,
lost for us. [Pater's note.]

come," and the eyelids are a little weary. It is a beauty wrought out from within upon the flesh, the deposit, little cell by cell, of strange thoughts and fantastic reveries and exquisite passions. Set it for a moment beside one of those white Greek goddesses or beautiful women of antiquity, and how would they be troubled by this beauty, into which the soul with all its maladies has passed! All the thoughts and experience of the world have etched and moulded there, in that which they have of power to refine and make expressive the outward form, the animalism of Greece, the lust of Rome, the mysticism of the middle age with its spiritual ambition and imaginative loves, the return of the Pagan world, the sins of the Borgias. She is older than the rocks among which she sits; like the vampire, she has been dead many times, and learned the secrets of the grave; and has been a diver in deep seas, and keeps their fallen day about her; and trafficked for strange webs with Eastern merchants, and, as Leda, was the mother of Helen of Troy, and, as Saint Anne, the mother of Mary; and all this has been to her but as the sound of lyres and flutes, and lives only in the delicacy with which it has moulded the changing lineaments, and tinged the eyelids and the hands. The fancy of a perpetual life, sweeping together ten thousand experiences, is an old one; and modern philosophy has conceived the idea of humanity as wrought upon by, and summing up in itself, all modes of thought and life. Certainly Lady Lisa might stand as the embodiment of the old fancy, the symbol of the modern idea. . . .

Conclusion

Λέγει που 'Ηράκλειτος ὅτι πάντα χωρεῖ καὶ οὐδὲν μένει [1]

To regard all things and principles of things as inconstant modes or fashions has more and more become the tendency of modern thought. Let us begin with that which is without — our physical life. Fix upon it in one of its more exquisite intervals, the moment, for instance, of delicious recoil from the flood of water in summer heat. What is the whole physical life in that moment but a combination of natural elements to which science gives their names? But those elements, phosphorus and lime and delicate fibres, are present not in the human body alone: we detect them in places most remote from it. Our physical life is a perpetual motion of them — the passage of the blood, the waste and repairing of the lenses of the eye, the modification of the tissues of the brain under every ray of light and sound — processes which science reduces to simpler and more elementary forces. Like the elements of which we are composed, the action of these

[1] "Heraclitus says, 'All things give way; nothing remaineth.'" [Pater's translation.]

forces extends beyond us: it rusts iron and ripens corn. Far out on every side of us those elements are broadcast, driven in many currents; and birth and gesture and death and the springing of violets from the grave are but a few out of ten thousand resultant combinations. That clear, perpetual outline of face and limb is but an image of ours, under which we group them — a design in a web, the actual threads of which pass out beyond it. This at least of flame-like our life has, that it is but the concurrence, renewed from moment to moment, of forces parting sooner or later on their ways.

Or, if we begin with the inward world of thought and feeling, the whirlpool is still more rapid, the flame more eager and devouring. There it is no longer the gradual darkening of the eye, the gradual fading of colour from the wall — movements of the shore-side, where the water flows down indeed, though in apparent rest — but the race of the mid-stream, a drift of momentary acts of sight and passion and thought. At first sight experience seems to bury us under a flood of external objects, pressing upon us with a sharp and importunate reality, calling us out of ourselves in a thousand forms of action. But when reflexion begins to play upon those objects they are dissipated under its influence; the cohesive force seems suspended like some trick of magic; each object is loosed into a group of impressions — colour, odour, texture — in the mind of the observer. And if we continue to dwell in thought on this world, not of objects in the solidity with which language invests them, but of impressions, unstable, flickering, inconsistent, which burn and are extinguished with our consciousness of them, it contracts still further: the whole scope of observation is dwarfed into the narrow chamber of the individual mind. Experience, already reduced to a group of impressions, is ringed round for each one of us by that thick wall of personality through which no real voice has ever pierced on its way to us, or from us to that which we can only conjecture to be without. Every one of those impressions is the impression of the individual in his isolation, each mind keeping as a solitary prisoner its own dream of a world. Analysis goes a step farther still, and assures us that those impressions of the individual mind to which, for each one of us, experience dwindles down, are in perpetual flight; that each of them is limited by time, and that as time is infinitely divisible, each of them is infinitely divisible also; all that is actual in it being a single moment, gone while we try to apprehend it, of which it may ever be more truly said that it has ceased to be than that it is. To such a tremulous wisp constantly reforming itself on the stream, to a single sharp impression, with a sense in it, a relic more or less fleeting, of such moments gone by, what is real in our life fines itself down. It is with this movement, with the passage and dissolution of impressions, images, sensations, that analysis leaves off — that continual vanishing away, that strange, perpetual weaving and unweaving of ourselves.

Philosophiren, says Novalis, *ist dephlegmatisiren, vivificiren.*[2] The service of philosophy, of speculative culture, towards the human spirit, is to rouse, to startle it to a life of constant and eager observation. Every moment some form grows perfect in hand or face; some tone on the hills or the sea is choicer than the rest; some mood of passion or insight or intellectual excitement is irresistibly real and attractive to us, — for that moment only. Not the fruit of experience, but experience itself, is the end. A counted number of pulses only is given to us of a variegated, dramatic life. How may we see in them all that is to be seen in them by the finest senses? How shall we pass most swiftly from point to point, and be present always at the focus where the greatest number of vital forces unite in their purest energy?

To burn always with this hard, gemlike flame, to maintain this ecstasy, is success in life. In a sense it might even be said that our failure is to form habits: for, after all, habit is relative to a stereotyped world, and meantime it is only the roughness of the eye that makes any two persons, things, situations, seem alike. While all melts under our feet, we may well grasp at any exquisite passion, or any contribution to knowledge that seems by a lifted horizon to set the spirit free for a moment, or any stirring of the senses, strange dyes, strange colours, and curious odours, or work of the artist's hands, or the face of one's friend. Not to discriminate every moment some passionate attitude in those about us, and in the very brilliancy of their gifts some tragic dividing of forces on their ways, is, on this short day of frost and sun, to sleep before evening. With this sense of the splendour of our experience and of its awful brevity, gathering all we are into one desperate effort to see and touch, we shall hardly have time to make theories about the things we see and touch. What we have to do is to be for ever curiously testing new opinions and courting new impressions, never acquiescing in a facile orthodoxy of Comte, or of Hegel, or of our own. Philosophical theories or ideas, as points of view, instruments of criticism, may help us to gather up what might otherwise pass unregarded by us. "Philosophy is the microscope of thought." The theory or idea or system which requires of us the sacrifice of any part of this experience, in consideration of some interest into which we cannot enter, or some abstract theory we have not identified with ourselves, or of what is only conventional, has no real claim upon us.

One of the most beautiful passages of Rousseau is that in the sixth book of the *Confessions,* where he describes the awakening in him of the literary sense. An undefinable taint of death had clung always about him, and now in early manhood he believed himself smitten by mortal disease. He asked himself how he might make as much as possible of the interval that remained; and he was not biased by anything in his previous life when he decided that it must be by intel-

[2] "To philosophize is to cast off inertia, to make oneself alive."

lectual excitement, which he found just then in the clear, fresh writings of Voltaire. Well! we are all *condamnés* as Victor Hugo says: we are all under sentence of death but with a sort of indefinite reprieve — *les hommes sont tous condamnés à mort avec des sursis indéfinis:* we have an interval, and then our place knows us no more. Some spend this interval in listlessness, some in high passions, the wisest, at least among "the children of this world," in art and song. For our one chance lies in expanding that interval, in getting as many pulsations as possible into the given time. Great passions may give us this quickened sense of life, ecstasy and sorrow of love, the various forms of enthusiastic activity, disinterested or otherwise, which come naturally to many of us. Only be sure it is passion — that it does yield you this fruit of a quickened, multiplied consciousness. Of such wisdom, the poetic passion, the desire of beauty, the love of art for its own sake, has most. For art comes to you proposing frankly to give nothing but the highest quality to your moments as they pass, and simply for those moments' sake.

Appreciations

❨ *Appreciations* (1889) contained, besides the essay on "Style" and a "Postscript" (previously published under the title "Romanticism"), Pater's largest collection of essays on English literature: "Wordsworth"; "Coleridge"; "Charles Lamb"; "Sir Thomas Browne"; " 'Love's Labour's Lost' "; " 'Measure for Measure' "; "Shakespeare's English Kings"; "Dante Gabriel Rossetti." "Style" is one of Pater's two or three most highly regarded essays. George Saintsbury, for example, though he thought Pater somewhat less than frank in drawing his distinction between "good art" and "great art," called the essay "on the whole, the most valuable thing yet written on that much-written-about subject." ❩

Style

SINCE all progress of mind consists for the most part in differentiation, in the resolution of an obscure and complex object into its component aspects, it is surely the stupidest of losses to confuse things which right reason has put asunder, to lose the sense of achieved distinctions, the distinction between poetry and prose, for instance, or, to speak more exactly, between the laws and characteristic excellences of verse and prose composition. On the other hand, those who have dwelt most emphatically on the distinction between prose and verse, prose and poetry, may sometimes have been tempted to limit the proper functions of prose too narrowly; and this again is at least false economy, as being, in effect, the renunciation of a certain means or faculty, in a world where after all we must needs make the most of things. Critical efforts to limit art *a priori*, by anticipations regarding the natural incapacity of the material with which this or that artist works, as the sculptor with solid form, or the prose-writer with the ordinary language of men, are always liable to be discredited by the facts of artistic production; and while prose is actually found to be a coloured thing with Bacon, picturesque with Livy and Carlyle, musical with Cicero and Newman, mystical and intimate with Plato and Michelet and Sir Thomas Browne, exalted or florid, it may be, with Milton and Taylor, it will be useless to protest that it can be nothing at all, except something very tamely and narrowly confined to mainly practical ends — a kind of "good round-hand"; as useless as the protest that poetry might not touch prosaic subjects as with Wordsworth, or an abstruse matter as with Browning, or treat contemporary life nobly as with Tennyson. In subordination to one essential beauty in all good literary style, in all literature as a fine art, as there are many beauties of poetry so the beauties of prose are many, and it is the business of criticism to estimate them as such; as it is good in the criticism of verse to look for those hard, logical, and quasi-prosaic excellences which that too has, or needs. To find in the poem, amid the flowers, the allusions, the mixed perspectives, of *Lycidas* for instance, the thought, the logical structure: — how wholesome! how delightful! as to identify in prose what we call the poetry, the imaginative power, not treating it as out of place and a kind of vagrant intruder, but by way of an estimate of its rights, that is, of its achieved powers, there.

Dryden, with the characteristic instinct of his age, loved to emphasise the distinction between poetry and prose, the protest against their confusion with each other, coming with somewhat diminished effect from one whose poetry was so prosaic. In truth, his sense of prosaic excellence affected his verse rather than his prose, which is not only fervid, richly figured, poetic, as we say, but vitiated, all unconsciously, by many a scanning line. Setting up correctness, that humble merit of prose, as the central literary excellence, he is really a less correct writer than he may seem, still with an imperfect mastery of the relative pronoun. It might have been foreseen that, in the rotations of mind, the province of poetry in prose would find its assertor; and, a century after Dryden, amid very different intellectual needs, and with the need therefore of great modifications in literary form, the range of the poetic force in literature was effectively enlarged by Wordsworth. The true distinction between prose and poetry he regarded as the almost technical or accidental one of the absence or presence of metrical beauty, or, say! metrical restraint; and for him the opposition came to be between verse and prose of course; but, as the essential dichotomy in this matter, between imaginative and unimaginative writing, parallel to De Quincey's distinction between "the literature of power and the literature of knowledge," in the former of which the composer gives us not fact, but his peculiar sense of fact, whether past or present.

Dismissing then, under sanction of Wordsworth, that harsher opposition of poetry to prose, as savouring in fact of the arbitrary psychology of the last century, and with it the prejudice that there can be but one only beauty of prose style, I propose here to point out certain qualities of all literature as a fine art, which, if they apply to the literature of fact, apply still more to the literature of the imaginative sense of fact, while they apply indifferently to verse and prose, so far as either is really imaginative — certain conditions of true art in both alike, which conditions may also contain in them the secret of the proper discrimination and guardianship of the peculiar excellences of either.

The line between fact and something quite different from external fact is, indeed, hard to draw. In Pascal, for instance, in the persuasive writers generally, how difficult to define the point where, from time to time, argument which, if it is to be worth anything at all, must consist of facts or groups of facts, becomes a pleading — a theorem no longer, but essentially an appeal to the reader to catch the writer's spirit, to think with him, if one can or will — an expression no longer of fact but of his sense of it, his peculiar intuition of a world, prospective, or discerned below the faulty conditions of the present, in either case changed somewhat from the actual world. In science, on the other hand, in history so far as it conforms to scientific rule, we have a literary domain where the imagination may be thought to be always an intruder. And as, in all science, the functions of literature reduce themselves eventually to the transcribing of fact, so all the excellences of literary form in regard to science are reducible to various kinds of painstaking; this good quality being involved in all "skilled work" whatever, in the drafting of an act of parliament, as in sewing. Yet here again, the writer's sense of fact, in history especially, and in all those complex subjects which do but lie on the borders of science, will still take the place of fact, in various degrees. Your historian, for instance, with absolutely truthful intention, amid the multitude of facts presented to him must needs select, and in selecting assert something of his own humour, something that comes not of the world without but of a vision within. So Gibbon moulds his unwieldy material to a preconceived view. Livy, Tacitus, Michelet, moving full of poignant sensibility amid the records of the past, each, after his own sense, modifies — who can tell where and to what degree? — and becomes something else than a transcriber; each, as he thus modifies, passing into the domain of art proper. For just in proportion as the writer's aim, consciously or unconsciously, comes to be the transcribing, not of the world, not of mere fact, but of his sense of it, he becomes an artist, his work *fine* art; and good art (as I hope ultimately to show) in proportion to the truth of his presentment of that sense; as in those humbler or plainer functions of literature also, truth — truth to bare fact, there — is the essence of such artistic quality as they may have. Truth! there can be no merit, no craft at all, without that. And further, all beauty is in the long run only *fineness* of truth, or what we call expression, the finer accommodation of speech to that vision within.

— The transcript of his sense of fact rather than the fact, as being preferable, pleasanter, more beautiful to the writer himself. In literature, as in every other product of human skill, in the moulding of a bell or a platter for instance, wherever this sense asserts itself, wherever the producer so modifies his work as, over and above its primary use or intention, to make it pleasing (to himself, of course, in the first instance) there, "fine" as opposed to merely serviceable art, exists. Literary art, that is, like all art which is in any way imitative or reproductive of fact — form, or colour, or incident — is the representation of such fact as connected with soul, of a specific personality, in its preferences, its volition and power.

Such is the matter of imaginative or artistic literature — this transcript, not of mere fact, but of fact in its infinite variety, as modified by human preference in all its infinitely varied forms. It will be good literary art not because it is brilliant or sober, or rich, or impulsive, or severe, but just in proportion as its representation of that sense, that soul-fact, is true, verse being only one department of such literature, and imaginative prose, it may be thought, being the special art of the modern world. That imaginative prose should be the special and opportune art of the modern world results from two important facts about the latter: first, the chaotic variety and complexity of its interests, making the intellectual issue, the really master currents of the present time incalculable — a condition of mind little susceptible of the restraint proper to verse form, so that the most characteristic verse of the nineteenth century has been lawless verse; and secondly, an all-pervading naturalism, a curiosity about everything whatever as it really is, involving a certain humility of attitude, cognate to what must, after all, be the less ambitious form of literature. And prose thus asserting itself as the special and privileged artistic faculty of the present day, will be, however critics may try to narrow its scope, as varied in its excellence as humanity itself reflecting on the facts of its latest experience — an instrument of many stops, meditative, observant, descriptive, eloquent, analytic, plaintive, fervid. Its beauties will be not exclusively "pedestrian": it will exert, in due measure, all the varied charms of poetry, down to the rhythm which, as in Cicero, or Michelet, or Newman, at their best, gives its musical value to every syllable.[1]

The literary artist is of necessity a scholar, and in what he proposes to do will have in mind, first of all, the scholar and the scholarly conscience — the male conscience in this matter, as we must think it, under a system of education which still to so large an extent limits real scholarship to men. In his self-criticism, he supposes always that sort of reader who will go (full of eyes) warily, considerately, though without consideration for him, over the ground which the female conscience traverses so lightly, so amiably. For the material in which he works is no more a creation of his own than the sculptor's marble. Product of a myriad various minds and contending tongues, compact of obscure and minute association, a language has its own abundant and often recondite laws, in the habitual and summary recognition of which scholarship consists. A writer, full of a matter he is before all things anxious to express, may think of those laws, the limitations of vocabulary, structure, and the like, as a restriction, but if a real artist will find in them an opportunity. His punctilious observance of the proprieties of his medium will diffuse through all he writes a general air of sensibility, of refined usage. *Exclusiones debitæ naturæ* — the exclusions, or rejections, which nature demands — we know how large a part these play, according to Bacon, in the science of nature. In a somewhat changed sense, we might say that the art of the scholar is summed up in the observance of those rejections demanded by the nature of his medium, the material he must use. Alive to the value of an atmosphere in which every term finds its utmost degree of expression, and with all the jealousy of a lover of words, he will resist a constant tendency on the part of the majority of those who use them to efface the distinctions of language, the facility of writers often reinforcing in this respect the work of the vulgar. He will feel the obligation not of the laws only, but of those affinities, avoidances, those mere preferences, of his language, which through the associations of literary history have become a part of its nature, prescribing the rejection of many a neology, many a license, many a gipsy phrase which might present itself as actually expressive. His appeal, again, is to the scholar, who has great experience in literature, and will show no favour to short-cuts, or hackneyed illustration, or an affectation of learning designed for the unlearned. Hence a contention, a sense of self-restraint and renunciation, having for the

---

1 Mr. Saintsbury, in his *Specimens of English Prose, from Malory to Macaulay*, has succeeded in tracing, through successive English prose-writers, the tradition of that severer beauty in them, of which this admirable scholar of our literature is known to be a lover. *English Prose, from Mandeville to Thackeray*, more recently "chosen and edited" by a younger scholar, Mr. Arthur Galton, of New College, Oxford, a lover of our literature at once enthusiastic and discreet, aims at a more various illustration of the eloquent powers of English prose, and is a delightful companion. [Pater's note.]

susceptible reader the effect of a challenge for minute consideration;
the attention of the writer, in every minutest detail, being a pledge
that it is worth the reader's while to be attentive too, that the writer
is dealing scrupulously with his instrument, and therefore, indirectly,
with the reader himself also, that he has the science of the instrument
he plays on, perhaps, after all, with a freedom which in such case will
be the freedom of a master.

For meanwhile, braced only by those restraints, he is really vindicating his liberty in the making of a vocabulary, an entire system of
composition, for himself, his own true manner; and when we speak
of the manner of a true master we mean what is essential in his art.
Pedantry being only the scholarship of *le cuistre* [2] (we have no
English equivalent) he is no pedant, and does but show his intelligence of the rules of language in his freedoms with it, addition or
expansion, which like the spontaneities of matter in a well-bred person
will still further illustrate good taste. — The right vocabulary! Translators have not invariably seen how all-important that is in the work
of translation, driving for the most part at idiom or construction;
whereas, if the original be first-rate, one's first care should be with
its elementary particles, Plato, for instance, being often reproducible
by an exact following, with no variation in structure, of word after
word, as the pencil follows a drawing under tracing-paper, so only
each word or syllable be not of false colour, to change my illustration
a little.

Well! that is because any writer worth translating at all has win-
nowed and searched through his vocabulary, is conscious of the words
he would select in systematic reading of a dictionary, and still more
of the words he would reject were the dictionary other than Johnson's; and doing this with his peculiar sense of the world ever in
view, in search of an instrument for the adequate expression of that,
he begets a vocabulary faithful to the colouring of his own spirit, and
in the strictest sense original. That living authority which language
needs lies, in truth, in its scholars, who recognising always that every
language possesses a genius, a very fastidious genius, of its own, expand at once and purify its very elements, which must needs change
along with the changing thoughts of living people. Ninety years ago,
for instance, great mental force, certainly, was needed by Wordsworth, to break through the consecrated poetic associations of a century, and speak the language that was his, that was to become in a
measure the language of the next generation. But he did it with
the tact of a scholar also. English, for a quarter of a century past,
has been assimilating the phraseology of pictorial art; for half a
century, the phraseology of the great German metaphysical movement of eighty years ago; in part also the language of mystical theology: and none but pedants will regret a great consequent increase of

2 A narrow-minded pedant.

its resources. For many years to come its enterprise may well lie in the naturalisation of the vocabulary of science, so only it be under the eye of a sensitive scholarship — in a liberal naturalisation of the ideas of science too, for after all the chief stimulus of good style is to possess a full, rich, complex matter to grapple with. The literary artist, therefore, will be well aware of physical science; science also attaining, in its turn, its true literary ideal. And then, as the scholar is nothing without the historic sense, he will be apt to restore not really obsolete or really worn-out words, but the finer edge of words still in use: *ascertain, communicate, discover* — words like these it has been part of our "business" to misuse. And still, as language was made for man, he will be no authority for correctnesses which, limiting freedom of utterance, were yet but accidents in their origin; as if one vowed not to say *"its,"* which ought to have been in Shakespeare; *"his"* and *"hers,"* for inanimate objects, being but a barbarous and really inexpressive survival. Yet we have known many things like this. Racy Saxon monosyllables, close to us as touch and sight, he will intermix readily with those long, savoursome, Latin words, rich in "second intention." In this late day certainly, no critical process can be conducted reasonably without eclecticism. Of such eclecticism we have a justifying example in one of the first poets of our time. How illustrative of monosyllabic effect, of sonorous Latin, of the phraseology of science, of metaphysic, of colloquialism even, are the writings of Tennyson; yet with what a fine, fastidious scholarship throughout!

A scholar writing for the scholarly, he will of course leave something to the willing intelligence of his reader. "To go preach to the first passer-by," says Montaigne, "to become tutor to the ignorance of the first I meet, is a thing I abhor"; a thing, in fact, naturally distressing to the scholar, who will therefore ever be shy of offering uncomplimentary assistance to the reader's wit. To really strenuous minds there is a pleasurable stimulus in the challenge for a continuous effort on their part, to be rewarded by securer and more intimate grasp of the author's sense. Self-restraint, a skilful economy of means, *ascêsis*, that too has a beauty of its own; and for the reader supposed there will be an æsthetic satisfaction in that frugal closeness of style which makes the most of a word, in the exaction from every sentence of a precise relief, in the just spacing out of word to thought, in the logically filled space connected always with the delightful sense of difficulty overcome.

Different classes of persons, at different times, make, of course, very various demands upon literature. Still, scholars, I suppose, and not only scholars, but all disinterested lovers of books, will always look to it, as to all other fine art, for a refuge, a sort of cloistral refuge, from a certain vulgarity in the actual world. A perfect poem like *Lycidas*, a perfect fiction like *Esmond*, the perfect handling of a

theory like Newman's *Idea of a University*, has for them something of
the uses of a religious "retreat." Here, then, with a view to the central
need of a select few, those "men of a finer thread" who have formed
and maintain the literary ideal, everything, every component element,
will have undergone exact trial, and, above all, there will be no uncharacteristic or tarnished or vulgar decoration, permissible ornament
being for the most part structural, or necessary. As the painter in his
picture, so the artist in his book, aims at the production by honourable artifice of a peculiar atmosphere. "The artist," says Schiller,
"may be known rather by what he *omits*"; and in literature, too, the
true artist may be best recognised by his tact of omission. For to the
grave reader words too are grave; and the ornamental word, the
figure, the accessory form or colour or reference, is rarely content to
die to thought precisely at the right moment, but will inevitably
linger awhile stirring a long "brain-wave" behind it of perhaps quite
alien associations.

Just there, it may be, is the detrimental tendency of the sort of
scholarly attentiveness of mind I am recommending. But the true
artist allows for it. He will remember that, as the very word ornament indicates what is in itself non-essential, so the "one beauty"
of all literary style is of its very essence, and independent, in prose
and verse alike, of all removable decoration; that it may exist in its
fullest lustre, as in Flaubert's *Madame Bovary*, for instance, or in
Stendhal's *Le Rouge et Le Noir*, in a composition utterly unadorned,
with hardly a single suggestion of visibly beautiful things. Parallel,
allusion, the allusive way generally, the flowers in the garden: — he
knows the narcotic force of these upon the negligent intelligence to
which any *diversion*, literally, is welcome, any vagrant intruder, because one can go wandering away with it from the immediate subject. Jealous, if he have a really quickening motive within, of all that
does not hold directly to that, of the facile, the otiose, he will never
depart from the strictly pedestrian process, unless he gains a ponder-
able something thereby. Even assured of its congruity, he will still
question its serviceableness. Is it worth while, can we afford, to
attend to just that, to just that figure or literary reference, just then?
— Surplusage! he will dread that, as the runner on his muscles. For
in truth all art does but consist in the removal of surplusage, from the
last finish of the gem-engraver blowing away the last particle of invisible dust, back to the earliest divination of the finished work to
be, lying somewhere, according to Michelangelo's fancy, in the rough-
hewn block of stone.

And what applies to figure or flower must be understood of all
other accidental or removable ornaments of writing whatever; and not
of specific ornament only, but of all that latent colour and imagery
which language as such carries in it. A lover of words for their own
sake, to whom nothing about them is unimportant, a minute and con-

stant observer of their physiognomy, he will be on the alert not only
for obviously mixed metaphors of course, but for the metaphor that
is mixed in all our speech, though a rapid use may involve no cog-
nition of it. Currently recognising the incident, the colour, the physical
elements of particles in words like *absorb, consider, extract,* to take
the first that occur, he will avail himself of them, as further adding
to the resources of expression. The elementary particles of language
will be realised as colour and light and shade through his scholarly
living in the full sense of them. Still opposing the constant degradation of language by those who use it carelessly, he will not treat
coloured glass as if it were clear; and while half the world is using
figure unconsciously, will be fully aware not only of all that latent
figurative texture in speech, but of the vague, lazy, half-formed personification — a rhetoric, depressing, and worse than nothing, because it has no really rhetorical motive — which plays so large a part
there, and, as in the case of more ostentatious ornament, scrupulously
exact of it, from syllable to syllable, its precise value.

So far I have been speaking of certain conditions of the literary art
arising out of the medium or material in or upon which it works, the
essential qualities of language and its aptitudes for contingent ornamentation, matters which define scholarship as science and good taste
respectively. They are both subservient to a more intimate quality of
good style: more intimate, as coming nearer to the artist himself. The
otiose, the facile, surplusage: why are these abhorrent to the true
literary artist, except because in literary as in all other art, structure is
all-important, felt, or painfully missed, everywhere? — that architectural conception of work, which foresees the end in the beginning
and never loses sight of it, and in every part is conscious of all the
rest, till the last sentence does but, with undiminished vigour, unfold
and justify the first — a condition of literary art, which, in contradistinction to another quality of the artist himself, to be spoken of later,
I shall call the necessity of *mind* in style.

An acute philosophical writer, the late Dean Mansel [3] (a writer
whose works illustrate the literary beauty there may be in closeness,
and with obvious repression or economy of a fine rhetorical gift)
wrote a book, of fascinating precision in a very obscure subject, to
show that all the technical laws of logic are but means of securing,
in each and all of its apprehensions, the unity, the strict identity with
itself, of the apprehending mind. All the laws of good writing aim
at a similar unity or identity of the mind in all the processes by which
the word is associated to its import. The term is right, and has its
essential beauty, when it becomes, in a manner, what it signifies, as
with the names of simple sensations. To give the phrase, the sentence,
the structural member, the entire composition, song, or essay, a sim-

[3] Henry L. Mansel (1820–1871), Dean of St. Paul's and author of *Prole-
gomena Logica.*

ilar unity with its subject and with itself: — style is in the right way
when it tends towards that. All depends upon the original unity, the
vital wholeness and identity, of the initiatory apprehension or view.
So much is true of all art, which therefore requires always its logic,
its comprehensive reason — insight, foresight, retrospect, in simultaneous action — true, most of all, of the literary art, as being of all
the arts most closely cognate to the abstract intelligence. Such logical
coherency may be evidenced not merely in the lines of composition
as a whole, but in the choice of a single word, while it by no means
interferes with, but may even prescribe, much variety, in the building
of the sentence for instance, or in the manner, argumentative, descriptive, discursive, of this or that part or member of the entire design.
The blithe, crisp sentence, decisive as a child's expression of its needs,
may alternate with the long-contending, victoriously intricate sentence;
the sentence, born with the integrity of a single word, relieving the
sort of sentence in which, if you look closely, you can see much contrivance, much adjustment, to bring a highly qualified matter into
compass at one view. For the literary architecture, if it is to be rich
and expressive, involves not only foresight of the end in the beginning, but also development or growth of design, in the process of
execution, with many irregularities, surprises, and afterthoughts; the
contingent as well as the necessary being subsumed under the unity
of the whole. As truly, to the lack of such architectural design, of a
single, almost visual, image, vigorously informing an entire, perhaps
very intricate, composition, which shall be austere, ornate, argumentative, fanciful, yet true from first to last to that vision within,
may be attributed those weaknesses of conscious or unconscious repetition of word, phrase, motive, or member of the whole matter,
indicating, as Flaubert was aware, an original structure in thought
not organically complete. With such foresight, the actual conclusion
will most often get itself written out of hand, before, in the more obvious sense, the work is finished. With some strong and leading sense
of the world, the tight hold of which secures true *composition* and
not mere loose accretion, the literary artist, I suppose, goes on considerately, setting joint to joint, sustained by yet restraining the productive ardour, retracing the negligences of his first sketch, repeating
his steps only that he may give the reader a sense of secure and restful
progress, readjusting mere assonances even, that they may soothe the
reader, or at least not interrupt him on his way; and then, somewhat
before the end comes, is burdened, inspired, with his conclusion, and
betimes delivered of it, leaving off, not in weariness and because he
finds *himself* at an end, but in all the freshness of volition. His work
now structurally complete, with all the accumulating effect of secondary shades of meaning, he finishes the whole up to the just proportion of that ante-penultimate conclusion, and all becomes expressive.
The house he has built is rather a body he has informed. And so it

happens, to its greater credit, that the better interest even of a narrative to be recounted, a story to be told, will often be in its second reading. And though there are instances of great writers who have been no artists, an unconscious tact sometimes directing work in which we may detect, very pleasurably, many of the effects of conscious art, yet one of the greatest pleasures of really good prose literature is in the critical tracing out of that conscious artistic structure, and the pervading sense of it as we read. Yet of poetic literature too; for, in truth, the kind of constructive intelligence here supposed is one of the forms of the imagination.

That is the special function of mind, in style. Mind and soul: — hard to ascertain philosophically, the distinction is real enough practically, for they often interfere, are sometimes in conflict, with each other. Blake, in the last century, is an instance of preponderating soul, embarrassed, at a loss, in an era of preponderating mind. As a quality of style, at all events, soul is a fact, in certain writers — the way they have of absorbing language, of attracting it into the peculiar spirit they are of, with a subtlety which makes the actual result seem like some inexplicable inspiration. By mind, the literary artist reaches us, through static and objective indications of design in his work, legible to all. By soul, he reaches us, somewhat capriciously perhaps, one and not another, through vagrant sympathy and a kind of immediate contact. Mind we cannot choose but approve where we recognise it; soul may repel us, not because we misunderstand it. The way in which theological interests sometimes avail themselves of language is perhaps the best illustration of the force I mean to indicate generally in literature, by the word *soul*. Ardent religious persuasion may exist, may make its way, without finding any equivalent heat in language: or, again, it may enkindle words to various degrees, and when it really takes hold of them doubles its force. Religious history presents many remarkable instances in which, through no mere phrase-worship, an unconscious literary tact has, for the sensitive, laid open a privileged pathway from one to another. "The altar-fire," people say, "has touched those lips!" The Vulgate, the English Bible, the English Prayer-Book, the writings of Swedenborg, the Tracts for the Times: — there, we have instances of widely different and largely diffused phases of religious feeling in operation as soul in style. But something of the same kind acts with similar power in certain writers of quite other than theological literature, on behalf of some wholly personal and peculiar sense of theirs. Most easily illustrated by theological literature, this quality lends to profane writers a kind of religious influence. At their best, these writers become, as we say sometimes, "prophets"; such character depending on the effect not merely of their matter, but of their matter as allied to, in "electric affinity" with, peculiar form, and working in all cases by an immediate sympathetic contact, on which account it is that it may be called soul, as opposed to mind, in style. And this too is a faculty of choosing and rejecting what is congruous or otherwise, with a drift towards unity — unity of atmosphere here, as there of design — soul securing colour (or perfume, might we say?) as mind secures form, the latter being essentially finite, the former vague or infinite, as the influence of a living person is practically infinite. There are some to whom nothing has any real interest, or real meaning, except as operative in a given person; and it is they who best appreciate the quality of soul in literary art. They seem to know a *person*, in a book, and make way by intuition: yet, although they thus enjoy the completeness of a personal information, it is still a characteristic of soul, in this sense of the word, that it does but suggest what can never be uttered, not as being different from, or more obscure than, what actually gets said, but as containing that plenary substance of which there is only one phase or facet in what is there expressed.

If all high things have their martyrs, Gustave Flaubert might perhaps rank as the martyr of literary style. In his printed correspondence, a curious series of letters, written in his twenty-fifth year, records what seems to have been his one other passion — a series of letters which, with its fine casuistries, its firmly repressed anguish, its tone of harmonious grey, and the sense of disillusion in which the whole matter ends, might have been, a few slight changes supposed, one of his own fictions. Writing to Madame X. certainly he does display, by "taking thought" mainly, by constant and delicate pondering, as in his love for literature, a heart really moved, but still more, and as the pledge of that emotion, a loyalty to his work. Madame X., too, is a literary artist, and the best gifts he can send her are precepts of perfection in art, counsels for the effectual pursuit of that better love. In his love-letters it is the pains and pleasures of art he insists on, its solaces: he comunicates secrets, reproves, encourages, with a view to that. Whether the lady was dissatisfied with such divided or indirect service, the reader is not enabled to see; but sees that, on Flaubert's part at least, a living person could be no rival of what was, from first to last, his leading passion, a somewhat solitary and exclusive one.

> "I must scold you," he writes, "for one thing, which shocks, scandalises me, the small concern, namely, you show for art just now. As regards glory be it so: there, I approve. But for art! — the one thing in life that is good and real — can you compare with it an earthly love? — prefer the adoration of a relative beauty to the *cultus* of the true beauty? Well! I tell you the truth. That is the one thing good in me: the one thing I have, to me estimable. For yourself, you blend with the beautiful a heap of alien things, the useful, the agreeable, what not? —
>
> "The only way not to be unhappy is to shut yourself up in art, and count everything else as nothing. Pride takes the place of all beside

when it is established on a large basis. Work! God wills it. That, it
seems to me, is clear. —

"I am reading over again the *Æneid,* certain verses of which I repeat
to myself to satiety. There are phrases there which stay in one's head,
by which I find myself beset, as with those musical airs which are for
ever returning, and cause you pain, you love them so much. I observe that I no longer laugh much, and am no longer depressed. I
am ripe. You talk of my serenity, and envy me. It may well surprise
you. Sick, irritated, the prey a thousand times a day of cruel pain, I
continue my labour like a true working-man, who, with sleeves turned
up, in the sweat of his brow, beats away at his anvil, never troubling
himself whether it rains or blows, for hail or thunder. I was not like
that formerly. The change has taken place naturally, though my will
has counted for something in the matter. —

"Those who write in good style are sometimes accused of a neglect
of ideas, and of the moral end, as if the end of the physician were
something else than healing, of the painter than painting — as if the
end of art were not, before all else, the beautiful."

What, then, did Flaubert understand by beauty, in the art he pursued with so much fervour, with so much self-command? Let us hear
a sympathetic commentator: — [4]

"Possessed of an absolute belief that there exists but one way of expressing one thing, one word to call it by, one adjective to qualify, one
verb to animate it, he gave himself to superhuman labour for the discovery, in every phrase, of that word, that verb, that epithet. In this
way, he believed in some mysterious harmony of expression, and when
a true word seemed to him to lack euphony still went on seeking another, with invincible patience, certain that he had not yet got hold
of the *unique* word. . . . A thousand preoccupations would beset him
at the same moment, always with this desperate certitude fixed in his
spirit: Among all the expressions in the world, all forms and turns of
expression, there is but *one* — one form, one mode — to express what
I want to say."

The one word for the one thing, the one thought, amid the multitude of words, terms, that might just do: the problem of style was
there! — the unique word, phrase, sentence, paragraph, essay, or song,
absolutely proper to the single mental presentation or vision within.
In that perfect justice, over and above the many contingent and removable beauties with which beautiful style may charm us, but which
it can exist without, independent of them yet dexterously availing
itself of them, omnipresent in good work, in function at every point,
from single epithets to the rhythm of a whole book, lay the specific,
indispensable, very intellectual, beauty of literature, the possibility of
which constitutes it a fine art.

One seems to detect the influence of a philosophic idea there, the
idea of a natural economy, of some pre-existent adaptation, between

[4] Guy de Maupassant.

a relative, somewhere in the world of thought, and its correlative, somewhere in the world of language — both alike, rather, somewhere in the mind of the artist, desiderative, expectant, inventive — meeting each other with the readiness of "soul and body reunited," in Blake's rapturous design; and, in fact, Flaubert was fond of giving his theory philosophical expression. —

> "There are no beautiful thoughts," he would say, "without beautiful forms, and conversely. As it is impossible to extract from a physical body the qualities which really constitute it — colour, extension, and the like — without reducing it to a hollow abstraction, in a word, without destroying it; just so it is impossible to detach the form from the idea, for the idea only exists by virtue of the form."

All the recognised flowers, the removable ornaments of literature (including harmony and ease in reading aloud, very carefully considered by him) counted certainly; for these too are part of the actual value of what one says. But still, after all, with Flaubert, the search, the unwearied research, was not for the smooth, or winsome, or forcible word, as such, as with false Ciceronians, but quite simply and honestly, for the word's adjustment to its meaning. The first condition of this must be, of course, to know yourself, to have ascertained your own sense exactly. Then, if we suppose an artist, he says to the reader, — I want you to see precisely what I see. Into the mind sensitive to "form," a flood of random sounds, colours, incidents, is ever penetrating from the world without, to become, by sympathetic selection, a part of its very structure, and, in turn, the visible vesture and expression of that other world it sees so steadily within, nay, already with a partial conformity thereto, to be refined, enlarged, corrected, at a hundred points; and it is just there, just at those doubtful points that the function of style, as tact or taste, intervenes. The unique term will come more quickly to one than another, at one time than another, according also to the kind of matter in question. Quickness and slowness, ease and closeness alike, have nothing to do with the artistic character of the true word found at last. As there is a charm of ease, so there is also a special charm in the signs of discovery, of effort and contention towards a due end, as so often with Flaubert himself — in the style which has been pliant, as only obstinate, durable metal can be, to the inherent perplexities and recusancy of a certain difficult thought. If Flaubert had not told us, perhaps we should never have guessed how tardy and painful his own procedure really was, and after reading his confession may think that his almost endless hesitation had much to do with diseased nerves. Often, perhaps, the felicity supposed will be the product of a happier, a more exuberant nature than Flaubert's. Aggravated, certainly, by a morbid physical condition, that anxiety in "seeking the phrase," which gathered all the other small *ennuis* of a really quiet existence into a kind of battle, was connected with his lifelong contention against facile poetry, facile art — art, facile and flimsy; and what constitutes the true artist is not the slowness or quickness of the process, but the absolute success of the result. As with those labourers in the parable, the prize is independent of the mere length of the actual day's work. "You talk," he writes, odd, trying lover, to Madame X. —

"You talk of the exclusiveness of my literary tastes. That might have enabled you to divine what kind of a person I am in the matter of love. I grow so hard to please as a literary artist, that I am driven to despair. I shall end by not writing another line."

"Happy," he cries, in a moment of discouragement at that patient labour, which for him, certainly, was the condition of a great success —

"Happy those who have no doubts of themselves! who lengthen out, as the pen runs on, all that flows forth from their brains. As for me, I hesitate, I disappoint myself, turn round upon myself in despite: my taste is augmented in proportion as my natural vigour decreases, and I afflict my soul over some dubious word out of all proportion to the pleasure I get from a whole page of good writing. One would have to live two centuries to attain a true idea of any matter whatever. What Buffon said is a big blasphemy: genius is not long-continued patience. Still, there is some truth in the statement, and more than people think, especially as regards our own day. Art! art! art! bitter deception! phantom that glows with light, only to lead one to destruction."

Again —

"I am growing so peevish about my writing. I am like a man whose ear is true but who plays falsely on the violin: his fingers refuse to reproduce precisely those sounds of which he has the inward sense. Then the tears come rolling down from the poor scraper's eyes and the bow falls from his hand."

Coming slowly or quickly, when it comes, as it came with so much labour of mind, but also with so much lustre, to Gustave Flaubert, this discovery of the word will be, like all artistic success and felicity, incapable of strict analysis: effect of an intuitive condition of mind, it must be recognised by like intuition on the part of the reader, and a sort of immediate sense. In every one of those masterly sentences of Flaubert there was, below all mere contrivance, shaping and afterthought, by some happy instantaneous concourse of the various faculties of the mind with each other, the exact apprehension of what was *needed* to carry the meaning. And that it fits with absolute justice will be a judgment of immediate sense in the appreciative reader. We

all feel this in what may be called inspired translation. Well! all
language involves translation from inward to outward. In literature,
as in all forms of art, there are the absolute and the merely relative or
accessory beauties; and precisely in that exact proportion of the term
to its purpose is the absolute beauty of style, prose or verse. All the
good qualities, the beauties, of verse also, are such, only as precise
expression.

In the highest as in the lowliest literature, then, the one indispensable
beauty is, after all, truth: — truth to bare fact in the latter, as to some
personal sense of fact, diverted somewhat from men's ordinary sense
of it, in the former; truth there as accuracy, truth here as expression,
that finest and most intimate form of truth, the *vraie vérité*. And what
an eclectic principle this really is! employing for its one sole purpose
— that absolute accordance of expression to idea — all other literary
beauties and excellences whatever: how many kinds of style it covers,
explains, justifies, and at the same time safeguards! Scott's facility,
Flaubert's deeply pondered evocation of "the phrase," are equally
good art. Say what you have to say, what you have a will to say, in
the simplest, the most direct and exact manner possible, with no surplusage: — there, is the justification of the sentence so fortunately
born, "entire, smooth, and round," that it needs no punctuation, and
also (that is the point!) of the most elaborate period, if it be right in its
elaboration. Here is the office of ornament: here also the purpose of
restraint in ornament. As the exponent of truth, that austerity (the
beauty, the function, of which in literature Flaubert understood so
well) becomes not the correctness or purism of the mere scholar, but a
security against the otiose, a jealous exclusion of what does not really
tell towards the pursuit of relief of life and vigour in the portraiture
of one's sense. License again, the making free with rule, if it be
indeed, as people fancy, a habit of genius, flinging aside or transforming all that opposes the liberty of beautiful production, will be but
faith to one's own meaning. The seeming baldness of *Le Rouge et Le
Noir* is nothing in itself; the wild ornament of *Les Misérables* is nothing in itself; and the restraint of Flaubert, amid a real natural opulence,
only redoubled beauty — the phrase so large and so precise at the
same time, hard as bronze, in service to the more perfect adaptation
of words to their matter. Afterthoughts, retouchings, finish, will be of
profit only so far as they too really serve to bring out the original,
initiative, generative, sense in them.

In this way, according to the well-known saying, "The style is the
man," complex or simple, in his individuality, his plenary sense of what
he really has to say, his sense of the world; all cautions regarding style
arising out of so many natural scruples as to the medium through which
alone he can expose that inward sense of things, the purity of this
medium, its laws or tricks of refraction: nothing is to be left there
which might give conveyance to any matter save that. Style in all its

varieties, reserved or opulent, terse, abundant, musical, stimulant, academic, so long as each is really characteristic or expressive, finds thus its justification, the sumptuous good taste of Cicero being as truly the man himself, and not another, justified, yet insured inalienably to him, thereby, as would have been his portrait by Raffaelle, in full consular splendour, on his ivory chair.

A relegation, you may say perhaps — a relegation of style to the subjectivity, the mere caprice, of the individual, which must soon transform it into mannerism. Not so! since there is, under the conditions supposed, for those elements of the man, for every lineament of the vision within, the one word, the one acceptable word, recognisable by the sensitive, by others "who have intelligence" in the matter, as absolutely as ever anything can be in the evanescent and delicate region of human language. The style, the manner, would be the man, not in his unreasoned and really uncharacteristic caprices, involuntary or affected, but in absolutely sincere apprehension of what is most real to him. But let us hear our French guide again. —

> "Styles," says Flaubert's commentator, "*Styles,* as so many peculiar moulds, each of which bears the mark of a particular writer, who is to pour into it the whole content of his ideas, were no part of his theory. What he believed in was *Style*: that is to say, a certain absolute and unique manner of expressing a thing, in all its intensity and colour. For him the *form* was the work itself. As in living creatures, the blood, nourishing the body, determines its very contour and external aspect, just so, to his mind, the *matter,* the basis, in a work of art, imposed, necessarily, the unique, the just expression, the measure, the rhythm — the *form* in all its characteristics." ˙

If the style be the man, in all the colour and intensity of a veritable apprehension, it will be in a real sense "impersonal."

I said, thinking of books like Victor Hugo's *Les Misérables,* that prose literature was the characteristic art of the nineteenth century, as others, thinking of its triumphs since the youth of Bach, have assigned that place to music. Music and prose literature are, in one sense, the opposite terms of art; the art of literature presenting to the imagination, through the intelligence, a range of interests, as free and various as those which music presents to it through sense. And certainly the tendency of what has been here said is to bring literature too under those conditions, by conformity to which music takes rank as the typically perfect art. If music be the ideal of all art whatever, precisely because in music it is impossible to distinguish the form from the substance or matter, the subject from the expression, then, literature, by finding its specific excellence in the absolute correspondence of the term to its import, will be but fulfilling the condition of all artistic quality in things everywhere, of all good art.

Good art, but not necessarily great art; the distinction between great art and good art depending immediately, as regards literature at all events, not on its form, but on the matter. Thackeray's *Esmond*, surely, is greater art than *Vanity Fair*, by the greater dignity of its interests. It is on the quality of the matter it informs or controls, its compass, its variety, its alliance to great ends, or the depth of the note of revolt, or the largeness of hope in it, that the greatness of literary art depends, as *The Divine Comedy, Paradise Lost, Les Misérables, The English Bible*, are great art. Given the conditions I have tried to explain as constituting good art; — then, if it be devoted further to the increase of men's happiness, to the redemption of the oppressed, or the enlargement of our sympathies with each other, or to such presentment of new or old truth about ourselves and our relation to the world as may ennoble and fortify us in our sojourn here, or immediately, as with Dante, to the glory of God, it will be also great art; if, over and above those qualities I summed up as mind and soul — that colour and mystic perfume, and that reasonable structure, it has something of the soul of humanity in it, and finds its logical, architectural place, in the great structure of human life.